D1558691

Stalin and Mao

Stalin and Mao

A Comparison of the Russian and Chinese Revolutions

By Lucien Bianco

Translated from the French Edition *La récidive: Révolution russe, révolution chinoise* by Krystyna Horko

THE CHINESE UNIVERSITY PRESS

Stalin and Mao: A Comparison of the Russian and Chinese Revolutions
  By Lucien Bianco
  Translated from French by Krystyna Horko

© The Chinese University of Hong Kong 2018
French edition © Editions GALLIMARD, Paris, 2014

ISBN: 978-988-237-065-4

Published by The Chinese University Press
        The Chinese University of Hong Kong
        Sha Tin, N.T., Hong Kong
        Fax: +852 2603 7355
        Email: cup@cuhk.edu.hk
        Website: www.chineseupress.com

Printed in Hong Kong

In memory of
Raymond Aron (1905–1983),
Claude Lefort (1924–2010),
and Kostas Papaïoannou (1925–1981).

"Hegel remarks somewhere that all great, world-historical facts and personages occur, as it were, twice. He has forgotten to add: the first time as tragedy, the second as farce."

—Karl Marx,
The Eighteenth Brumaire of Louis Bonaparte

For once Marx appears to stray too far from Hegel. While the Chinese revolution may, at times, has degenerated into farce, that did not prevent it from becoming as much a tragedy as the first revolution.

Contents

Foreword

Marie-Claire Bergère

This book presents a global comparison of the Russian and Chinese revolutions. Numerous studies compare—or more frequently oppose—a given aspect of the two revolutions, but Lucien Bianco's work stands out for providing an overall view and a synthesis. The author analyzes the nature of the two revolutions, their different origins and initial aims, the convergences in their trajectories, and their consequences. The question is not which of the two revolutions best applied (or most deformed and betrayed) ideological dogma, but rather to compare the reasons they were launched and the phases in their development, as well as to assess their consequences. More broadly, the aim is to consider the role of the two revolutions in the history of the twentieth century and their positive or negative contributions to the progress of human society. That historical and humanistic approach may surprise English-speaking readers, who are more used to monographic or theoretical studies. They may wonder if this is the result of some Gallic claim to universality, which, on occasion, can lead to superficial overviews. They may rest assured! No study is more solidly rooted in facts, or deals more closely with reality, than this one. It is an exploit that transports the reader from in-depth analyses to vast perspectives, made possible only by the author's excellence.

A former student at the École Normale Supérieure in Paris (a higher education establishment that has trained the intellectual elite of France for decades), Bianco received a solid classical education and hesitated for some time on whether to become an historian or a philosopher. He finally opted for history but never lost his love of philosophy, and he has succeeded in reconciling specific in-depth research with a truly philosophical approach to history.

Of course not every aspect of the exposition in this book derives from the author's own fundamental research. Nevertheless, the sixty years that Bianco has devoted to studying modern China have turned the indefatigable reader into an extremely well-informed one, with the ability to integrate knowledge drawn from the common fund of modern Sinology and to "acclimatize" it, as it were in his own argumentation. He has thus benefitted from the major advances in Chinese historiography, both in China and in the West, since the 1978 reforms partially opened up the archives, in addition to the proliferation of personal accounts.

Bianco is less familiar with Russia since he does not speak Russian, but he has devoted many years to reading translations of documents published in Moscow as well as studies of the Russian revolution by Western scholars. Paradoxically, since the historiographic documentation on the Russian revolution is far more prolific than that on the Chinese one, the author has more information on Russia than on China in some chapters (for instance the one on the gulag and *laogai* camps). When doing the spadework for what was, for him, a new historical field, Bianco acquired an expertise that has readily been recognized by Sovietologists. He was therefore able to dispense with requesting assistance from colleagues when dealing with the Russian aspect of his comparison, thereby avoiding the danger that so often occurs in collective works, of parallel developments being poorly or badly linked together. Having a common problematic structure throughout the entire work confers a unity on it and provides a dynamic. The quality of *Stalin and Mao* also lies in the author's own independent spirit, guided as he is by the results of his research, which opposes ideological fashions and political pressures with the "resistance of facts" (Lenin). We should bear in mind that Bianco was one of the first people to denounce the Maoist deception and the illusions of those who, in the 1960s and 1970s, had transferred their dashed hopes in the Soviet Union onto China. Based on the personal reflections of a highly cultivated historian with an impressive range of knowledge and sound judgment, the book invites the reader to challenge many accepted truths.

Stalin and Mao presents a vast panorama of two revolutions in different time periods: the triumph of Bolshevism and then Stalinism (1917–1953), which preceded that of Maoism (1949–1976) by some thirty years and paved the way for it. The book's principal argument is made clear by the epigraph, devoted to the repetition of a tragic event. Indeed, the author claims that the Chinese revolution was largely inspired by the Russian precedent, which implies the repetition of an offense or a crime. The author claims that, far from being original, the Chinese revolution was very largely inspired by the Russian precedent and succeeded in reproducing both its errors and its failures in economic modernization and social justice. Nine substantial chapters illustrate that thesis.

The brilliant opening chapter, titled "The Laggards," compares the original situations in both countries, characterized by economic backwardness and "otherness" in relation to the West (both being far more pronounced in China than in Russia) with nationalism prevailing in China, whereas in Russia there was far greater concern with social issues with dreams of a universal project and a new humanity. Last, there was the determining role of foreign wars in the successful obtainment of power (World War I in the case of Russia, and the 1937 Japanese invasion for China). This close comparison is carried out subject by subject in a penetrating and masterful synthesis.

After two chapters, one devoted to "Catching Up," mainly in economic terms, which was a priority for both regimes; and the other on "Politics," which reveals a ties to a "shared Leninist matrix" (chapter 3) we broach one of the highlights of the work and certainly the most original one, with chapters 4 ("The Peasants") and 5 ("Famines"). For Bianco, whose principal research for half a century has been devoted to rural issues, the peasantry in both revolutions proved to be a challenge that neither was able to meet, and that failure weighed heavily on their outcomes. For the Russian revolutionaries, the peasant issue was always a cursed one. The forced collectivization policy and dekulakization resulted in the Great Famine of 1932–1933, with the stagnation of agricultural production and the peasantry being sidelined, sacrificed on the altar of industrialization and urbanization.

Even though the Chinese leaders had closer ties with the rural world, their agrarian policy was as detrimental to the peasantry as that of their Soviet predecessors. After 1949 the Party confiscated and redistributed land belonging to the rich peasants, but two or three years later it launched into forced collectivization. In China, as in the Soviet Union, the priority went to industrial development financed by the agricultural surplus—to the detriment of the peasants who were transformed into veritable "slaves of primitive accumulation". Bianco goes on to demolish the myth that Mao's revolution was a peasant revolution. The Chinese peasants were mobilized in the context of the anti-imperialist movement and contributed to the Communists' rise to power, but they never played a leadership role or even an independent one in the revolutionary struggles. Nor was improving their lot a priority for the new regime once it was established. The 1958 Great Leap Forward was lauded by Maoist propaganda as a manifestation of the "Chinese way" and the achievement of a Communist utopia, but in reality it was nothing more than radicalized collectivization taken to its apogee, and was a direct cause of the famine that ensued.

The Russian famine of 1931–1933 left between six and seven million dead, while the one that accompanied and followed the Great Leap Forward resulted in between twenty and forty million victims. While Bianco does not neglect the importance of structural factors such as the vulnerability of agriculture in both countries to the vagaries of the weather, or the difficulty in managing the demographic transition, he makes clear that the agrarian policy implemented by the revolutionary governments in power was the primary cause of the famine in both cases. He also sheds light on Stalin's personal responsibility, since he used the war he waged against the peasantry to get rid of all forms of opposition, and also Mao's, carried away as he was by his utopic vision and his pride.

Chapter 6 demonstrates that bureaucracy and the "new class" that emerged in both regimes had very similar sociological foundations and behaviors. They exploited their privileges and practiced corruption. Only the dictators' attitudes to them differed: quiet acceptance in Stalin's case, for he appreciated the docility and social conservatism of those he had promoted, and in Mao's case the repeated attacks on the new bourgeoisie with criticisms of their "working style," although he rapidly handed power back to them after the turmoil of the Cultural Revolution.

In the cultural domain, broached in chapter 7, Soviet Russia and Maoist China were equally subject to the reign of socialist realism imposed by watchdogs, who were quick to censure and repress. Yet the Soviet intelligentsia reacted far more critically to that than their Chinese counterparts, whose response was more muted.

Lastly, chapter 8 provides a comparative study of the labor camps: the Soviet gulag and the Chinese *laogai*, the former serving as a model for the latter. In China the special emphasis on the prisoners' spiritual transformation and thought reform made the cruelty of *laogai* more insidious, but no less brutal, than that of the gulag.

The book concludes with a somewhat provocative comparison between the two "monsters," Stalin and Mao. Both were molded in the same system that turned them into dictators, but their personalities led to variations in the way they ruled. Stalin, the realist, coldly and methodically eradicated all his opponents, real or potential. Mao Zedong's cruelty was more detached. He was also less able, and doubtless less keen, to steer his country toward the economic development that had been the original objective of the revolution he had led.

This book is not only scholarly but extremely vivid. Readers familiar with Bianco's work will recognize his brisk, elegant, yet familiar style. Above all, they will find a deep sense of humanity. The many descriptions and anecdotes with which he illustrates the main body of the work succeed in bringing it to life. He shows a genuine interest in individual destinies and the fates of victims. He does not allow himself to get carried away by his emotions but feels—and makes us feel—the intensity of the personal dramas that are played out behind the cold statistics.

There is no doubt that this work will mark an epoch in twentieth-century historiography. Though Bianco refuses to let ideology become a hostage to history, he does not adhere to the fragmentary, pointillist approach so often present in contemporary historical research. He dares to return to the big picture and the major issues that faced the preceding generations, and returns to them with an open mind, armed only with his profound knowledge of the facts. That pragmatic approach cannot be qualified as scientistic. As a politically committed historian, Bianco feels free to make value judgments and his conclusions will not fail to ruffle a few feathers. No, he claims, the Chinese Way was not an original one—contrary to what is claimed by those partisans who made up for their disappointment in Communism by finding refuge in Maoism. The regime founded by Mao Zedong resembled the Soviet regime "like a brother," albeit not a twin. The Chinese revolution was merely a repeat offense, a repetition of the error and crime that was the Russian revolution. Neither revolution attained its proclaimed objective of social justice. As to economic modernization, Stalin achieved it only "conservatively," although it made greater advances in Russia than in China, but both countries continued to lag behind the West in full economic growth. Those negative judgments will shock a nostalgic few, but they will be left with little more than their faith in the Great Helmsman and the Little Red Book with which to counter it.

On a more serious note, some historians will be surprised by the author's extreme caution with regard to ideology and may wonder if he has not underestimated the role it played. Indeed, no chapter is devoted to the subject, which is a bit of a paradox given the role of ideology in the establishment and governance of both Communist regimes. That caution is probably most perceptible in the final chapter and Bianco's portrayal of Mao Zedong. True, the author admits that, unlike the Stalinist Great Terror, which was an enterprise of "social engineering" that exposed the motives of tyranny, the Maoist Cultural Revolution is debatable where ideas are concerned, and may have been the stuff of dreams for some. Unlike Stalin, Mao Zedong's sole objective was not just to preserve his power; he also wanted to preserve the revolution. Nevertheless the comparison as a whole and the enumeration of the many resemblances between the two "movements" tend to reduce the scope of the utopic Maoist vision. Mao Zedong mainly appears as a selfish, manipulating monster. Clearly Bianco does not share the indulgence of those who, while stating that Mao's utopic fervor is no excuse for his tyranny, nevertheless cloak it in a mantle of humanity and idealism.

Throughout *Stalin and Mao* Bianco denounces the illusion created by propaganda and refuses to substitute reality with dogmatism, or reason with belief. He even goes further and concludes from the failure of the two great twentieth-century revolutions, that there is an inevitable proximity between revolution and tyranny, stressing the unsuspected and almost insurmountable difficulties facing any revolution intent on curing humanity's ills. That skepticism should invigorate us rather than discourage us. In our "post-truth" society, in which the most outrageous lies are accepted in the name of pragmatism and efficiency rather than in the name of some radiant future, this book reminds us that "if we are not serious about facts and what's true and what's not, if we can't discriminate between serious arguments and propaganda, then we have problems" (Barack Obama). As difficult as truth may be to define and establish, truth alone will prevent us from returning to the totalitarianism of the past century.

Acknowledgments

I could not have found a kinder and more generous welcome than among the Russian specialists, starting with Amir Weiner at Stanford, who pointed out his choice of the most interesting among recent publications, including the review *Kritika*, every edition of which I went over. In Paris, Wladimir Berelowitch gave me a clear idea of what he thought about a good fifty titles that I suggested to him, before settling me into his office at CERCEC (the Center for Russian, Caucasian and Central European Studies, at the École des Hautes Études en Sciences Sociales). Valérie Mélikian in the next-door office guided me though the collection of *Cahiers du Monde Russe*. In rue de l'Amiral-Mouchez (Paris), Krystyna Frank and Dmitri Gouzevitch have been revealing the contents of the CERCEC library to me for years, and Alain Blum also welcomed me to his office whenever he feared that a meeting held in the library might hinder my research. In other words I felt as at home in the Russian Center as I do in the China Center, which I have been frequenting almost since it was established.

In the China Center at the Maison de l'Asie (Paris), Monique Abud and Wang Ju continued to move heaven and earth to satisfy or anticipate the slightest wish of an old regular.

Jean-Luc Domenach, author of a classic overview of Chinese labor camps, carefully read chapter 8 and, for good measure, chapter 9, and scattered them with remarks and suggestions that were as valuable as they were to the point.

Marie-Claire Bergère read each chapter, and improved every one of them, by her critical remarks as well as by her judicious suggestions.

The English edition has benefited from Stephen A. Smith's well-founded and constructive criticisms in *Cahiers du Monde Russe*, 55/3–4, July–December 2014, pp. 400–406, as well as from stimulating works published the same year as the French edition (Wemheuer 2014, Kinkley 2014, Filtzer 2014), or the following spring (Walder 2015). It also owes a great deal to Krystyna Horko's excellent translation.

Introduction

An epigraph that repeats Marx's famous quotation—and correction—of Hegel may seem provocative. The Chinese revolution, once inspired by the Soviet model, later turned against it, denouncing the "revisionist" degeneracy of a model it now disowned. A "Chinese way" was promoted in its place as the only possible revolutionary course and established in turn as a model.

The contrast between the two revolutionary enterprises and the disparity between the conditions in the two countries in which the projects were conceived matter more than the pretensions of the disciple—Mao in this instance. So the Czarist regime lagged behind and was obsolete? Yes, like Robert Musil's Kakania, but Russia was nevertheless part of Europe. The Russian revolutionaries, like Marx and Engels, were concerned about the fate of humanity as a whole. They sought a fair and fraternal world and, at the outset, did not imagine that such a grandiose project could be restricted to and spread within their own backward country. The fundamental motivation of the Chinese revolutionaries was not universal but specific. They were concerned with the Chinese nation rather than with humanity at large. In that respect their project resembled Hitler's more than that of Marx or of Lenin. I say that not to shock the reader (Paul Déroulède or Maurice Barrès would have been more innocuous), but to state their objectives from the outset. The Chinese revolutionaries were less concerned with reforming the world than with correcting its imbalance to benefit their ancient nation. The oppressor they fought against was not native capitalism but imperialism, and its economic appendage, the exogenous capitalism that it transplanted onto the Chinese "semi-colony." Lenin created a good argument (in *Imperialism, the Highest Stage of Capitalism*) for adopting those nationalists for his cause. For their part, once converted (not to Marxism, about which they knew hardly anything, but to the Leninist recipe for seizing power and transforming a backward country), they absorbed the "Marxist-Leninist" potion and internalized its social credo. They then made the well-being of the masses secondary to their principal aim, the grandeur of their nation.

Reducing the Chinese revolutionaries' objective from the universal to the particular is one thing, but I am doing them an injustice by comparing them to Déroulède and the like. The amputation of Alsace-Lorraine was merely a wound, at most a mutilation, compared to the effects of imperialist aggression on China. Whatever Europe's petty internal quarrels, Chinese intellectuals wanted to free themselves from Europe as a whole. They learned from Europe the better to resist it. The concerns and dreams of the nineteenth-century Russian intelligentsia were not for them; they sought to transplant the achievements of the Meiji Restoration onto their continent.

So here we have a discrepancy in the original conditions and aims, but a similarity in trajectories and results, so how is it possible to account for this distressing paradox? Add to that a contingent factor and above all a regret that, unlike Lenin, Mao hadn't died a few years after the revolution. Shakespeare could certainly have written a tragedy about the 1922–1923 episode, with the Lenin-Lear character exhausting his last resources in an attempt to prevent the power from falling into the hands of the worst candidate. It's clear that the revolution was condemned from the outset, Lear being first and foremost to blame, but less for having promoted that candidate to the post of secretary general just a few months earlier, than for having conceived of, imposed, and led that type of revolution. The contrast is no less striking with the repeat Chinese version, where there was no need of a devil to divert the heritage, or to fulfill the very worst of its potential—it was the founder himself who diverted the course of the revolution. After a few years and right until his death finally cleared the path, Mao was the problem. Mao led the revolution into a dead end and blocked the way out. He obstinately curbed and then repressed the timid but persistent attempts of his companions in arms to place the country and the revolution back on track. History is not a science, but it may be tempting to generalize from two experiences. Thus two different scenarios for two major twentieth-century revolutions: a catastrophic succession and a no less catastrophic absence of succession. But is that sufficient to incriminate the revolution itself?

Certainly not! To maintain a classic comparison, on balance the French Revolution is viewed more positively than the two major "socialist" revolutions of the past century, despite the September 1792 massacre and the Terror (less deliberate than that of 1937–1938 and less deadly than the 1967–1968 repression in China, not to mention the 1931–1933 and 1958–1962 state-inflicted famines). And this despite the immediate result of the French Revolution, Caesarism. In the long term its liberating effects benefitted many more countries than that in which the revolution erupted, even though for the past two centuries France has overindulged in claiming to be the depository of universal ideals.

To return to our two "socialist" giants, many other reasons than those accidental circumstances (a premature death and a belated one) can explain the failure of an enterprise that was condemned from the start. The remainder of the book explores those other reasons. It does not, therefore, deal with China's contemporary growth, the consequence of abandoning the revolutionary ideals and impossible to achieve so long as Mao took his time to join Marx. Since time was needed to rid the country of a poisonous heritage, this book deals with the first three decades (1949–1978) and compares them with the 1917–1953 period for the original. Nor does this book provide an exhaustive account of that first period. No chapter is devoted to the sacrosanct proletariat.[1] Not because the fate of the working class is unimportant, nor because it did not also suffer from the treatment of the very leaders who had placed it on a pedestal, but because the numbers were infinitesimal in 1917 and 1949, even though the proletariat grew massively in the early 1930s and again suddenly in 1958, before collapsing brutally in 1960 when the sorcerers' apprentices, who created a famine, decided to send twenty million newly urbanized people back to the countryside from whence they had come. The proletariat apart, my comparison of the two revolutions also relegates society and urban life in general largely to the shadows. Does that mean that I involuntarily rallied to the recurrent concern of the revolutionary leaders who considered that by far the greatest problem during that first period was the peasantry? In Marx's opinion, and then in Lenin's and Stalin's, that most populous class was the one most stubbornly resistant to revolutionary change, most unfamiliar with urban civilization and incarnated in a barbarity that made it quite impervious to civilization. Not in Mao's opinion however, even though his treatment of the peasants was hardly better, and we need to understand why that was the case.

Another major absence in the book is anything concerning the foreign relations of the young revolutionary states, and therefore the activities of the Third International, the Nazi invasion, the foundation of European people's democracies, and the problems posed by Tito (a budding Mao) and the second superpower, which would eventually prove not to be one, and so on. It seemed to me that the "Great Patriotic War," which was a terrible ordeal with major consequences for Soviet Communism, had no parallel in the development of the other Communism. Whatever Mao feared or claimed, imperialism spared his fragile offspring. When provoked in Korea, the American tiger confined itself to preventing Mainland China from uniting with Taiwan, which had already been separated from its motherland for half a century (1895–1945). One Soviet citizen out of seven died (in addition to natural deaths) between 1941 and 1945. China, which would have been a far more vulnerable prey, came near to that level of slaughter only between 1958 and 1962, in Xinyang prefecture, southern Henan province, the one that was the most impacted by a peacetime disaster it had provoked itself.[2] A more relevant comparison would be the effect of the two world wars on the former regimes. "Wars accelerate the fall of regimes that are incapable of winning them."[3] World War I accelerated the fall of Czarism while World War II provoked the fall of the Nationalist regime in China. Wars apart, the situation of the revolutionary pioneers who waited in vain for the revolution to occur in a more advanced country before being reduced to carrying out a "revolution in one country" was different to that of their younger brother who began by copying the model ("the Soviet Union of today is the China of tomorrow") before repudiating it. The "universal autarky" of the "world homeland of socialism" was no longer in the cards a generation later, or else it was the autarky of the entire socialist bloc, both a shield and a purveyor of modernity for a Chinese revolution then determined to "lean to one side" (Mao in 1949).[4] Similarly the "façade federalism" concealed behind the "union of sovereign nations equal in law" as stated in the Soviet Constitution of 1924 suited the Chinese Communists very well, but what would be the point in comparing the treatment of national minorities by the two revolutions, perceived as a secondary problem for the Chinese Communists (in 1949, they represented 6 percent of the Chinese population) but a major and recurrent issue in the Soviet Union?

Nor is there a chapter on ideology, even though it is omnipresent in chapter 3, devoted to policy, and pops up again here and there, especially in the last chapter. So what *are* the contents of the book? The first two chapters ("The Laggards" and then "Catching Up") are devoted to the preliminary path, which was always hovering in the background because, as Gramsci has stressed, October was a revolution "against Marx's *Capital*." That was even more the case in October 1949 after Gramsci's death. Next, as I have said, comes policy, where I attempt to dismantle Maoist claims to originality. Then (I criticize Marxism but remain influenced by Marxist doxa!) the social classes: peasants, the powerful and privileged (the bureaucracy), and finally the intellectuals.I nevertheless inserted a chapter 5 on famines (between the various social classes dealt with in chapters 4, 6, and 7), which follows on from chapter 4, devoted to the peasants who were its main victims. I could hardly place the famines anywhere else since the agrarian policies of the two regimes were the leading cause of the great famines. Then the ruling class (Milovan Djilas's new class) is the subject of chapter 6, while chapter 7 deals with culture in general, and writers, artists, and scholars in particular. Last, I compare the gulag with *laogai* in chapter 8, and Stalin with Mao in the ninth and final chapter.

1. The Laggards

This chapter will corroborate a recurrent thesis, namely that the backwardness of Tsarist Russia and Imperial China obliged the revolutionaries to devote themselves to the preliminary task of removing obstacles. It was necessary to halt backwardness and extreme poverty in order to concentrate on the only valid task—to achieve justice on earth. The expression used to summarize that ambition (lifting humanity out of prehistory) nevertheless suggests that Russian or Chinese backwardness was not the only explanation for later detours and derailments. In the eyes of Marx, Lenin, and Trotsky, prehistory prevailed not only in an incurable autocracy but over humanity as a whole, including the "advanced" Western European countries. And while they admired Western European technology and culture, they felt that these were nevertheless an incarnation of that same prehistory, albeit a capitalist one and, in its supreme form, an imperialistic one, from which it was urgent to liberate the exploited masses.

Backwardness was one of the very rare factors common to both Russia and China, along with their vast territorial expanses. Different as the nations were, a late and partial modernization led in both cases to a series of similar processes, practices, and problems. Above all, once the revolutions were unleashed they produced similar effects, despite their very different departure points.

Due in part to their country's geographical proximity to "more advanced" Europe, the Russians grew more aware of their country's backwardness (and much earlier), even though it was less flagrant than in

China. Remedying the backwardness had been a veritable obsession from Peter the Great onward, and the reasons, military ones at first, that incited Russia to modernize persisted into the next century. During the 1854–1855 operations of the Crimean War, the Russian army had been supplied by horses and carts, laboriously advancing on dirt tracks. Half a century later and on a different scale, the same slow progress and backwardness in transportation led to another humiliating defeat of the Russian army and navy (1904–1905), but this time not by the English or the French but by the Japanese (Japs crushing whites!). At least the lesson of the Crimean War had led Alexander II to undertake major reforms and encourage a first industrial project. That was not the case in China after the British obtained an easy victory with a small expeditionary force during the First Opium War (1839–1842). Half a century later (1895) China suffered a defeat as humiliating as the one that would later be inflicted on the Russian navy in Tsushima in 1905, at the hands of the same Japanese "dwarfs" whom the Chinese boasted of having civilized. That defeat finally made a minority of enlightened Chinese patriots aware of the extent of their country's backwardness and the urgent need to remedy the situation.

The Social Repercussions of Late Economic Development

The belated Chinese efforts and the concessions extracted by the victorious Japanese in 1895 (which were automatically extended to the other foreign powers) led to the beginnings of industrialization, restricted to a handful of open ports. A second stage followed, thanks to World War I, which removed foreign competition and gave national industries a boost that continued into the 1920s and, to a lesser extent, the 1930s. But although the industrial bases that the Chinese revolutionaries inherited in 1949 were, by then, far from insignificant, they were nevertheless very modest in comparison with the remarkable progress made by Russian industry between 1861 and 1914, and especially after 1890.

In half a century (1860–1910) Russia's industrial production increased more than tenfold, four times the rate of Victorian England and slightly above that of Japan—a more relevant comparison since the two countries were at a similar stage of early development when serfdom was abolished in the one (1861) and the Meiji Restoration began in the other (1868). Russia's rapid growth led to profound social upheavals that destabilized the old agrarian empire but failed to close the divide that separated it from the "advanced" nations. In 1913, Russia was still producing ten times less coal than the United States. Its per capita gross national product (GNP) advanced more slowly over the half century, and was equivalent to 40 percent of US per capita GNP in 1860, but only 24 percent in 1913.[1]

Although Russia's industrialization was far more impressive than China's later industrialization (between 1895 and 1937), the two companions in misfortune nevertheless shared a number of "late starter" characteristics: geographic concentration, with the lion's share in Saint Petersburg and Shanghai, resistance from the crafts and workshops, which were as dispersed as modern industry was concentrated, outdated industrial equipment that was largely imported (from Germany in Russia's case, with serious consequences during World War I), and a shortage of capital, which Russia was obliged to borrow from abroad (mainly from France), while Chinese enterprises were unable to compete with foreign ones on an equal footing. Last but not least, industrial growth was hindered by weak domestic demand due to the extreme poverty of the peasants, who, on the eve of the revolution, accounted for more than 80 percent of the population in both Russia and China.

Agriculture was stagnating in both these agrarian countries, but still took up most of the workforce. Primitive equipment, archaic agricultural techniques, and a very limited use of fertilizer produced only mediocre yields, far below those of European agriculture in the same period. Such low yields were obtained from tiny plots in China, due to long-standing demographic pressure. To quote an ancient Chinese proverb, *ren duo, tian shao* ("too many people, too little land"). While undoubtedly having more space, the Russians had to contend with harsh winters and a shorter agricultural season. However, they soon grew cramped in the Central Chernozem Region, where the population density was akin to that of the French countryside, which produced twice the yields. Between 1863 and 1897, the rural population in European Russia rose from fifty-five to eighty-two million, and exceeded a hundred million in 1914.

Although the rural exodus grew from year to year, it took up only a small portion of the annual rural population growth, and the *mujiks'* (peasants) hunger for land made them impatient to proceed with the so-called "Black Repartition" (*tcherny peredel*) of the landlords' land. The slogan popularized by Sun Yat-sen ("land belongs to those who work it") was whispered to him by his Soviet advisors and resonated with the profound conviction of the Russian peasants. There was not the same class hatred in China as in central Russia in 1917, but that did not prevent the Chinese Communist Party (CCP) from claiming its existence and, above all, stirring up hatred and attributing to the rural Chinese "masses" revolutionary aspirations that were, in fact, quite alien to them.

It never occurred to Chinese peasants to covet the land of the rich, for theirs was a card that "fate" had dealt them since time immemorial—or at least since their ancestors, or they themselves in a previous life, had proved to be less deserving than the privileged few. Nevertheless, as a rule, like their Russian counterparts, they felt alienated from the state, from "outsiders," the parasite city, and any privileged people whose intrusion into the villages was always perceived as a threat or potential spoliation. In China, as in Russia, the peasant majority was a world apart, cut off from the rest of society. Under the Tsarist autocracy and the Imperial Chinese regime alike, the countryside was undergoverned (although this became less true in the last decades of the "Republican interlude" between 1928 and 1949). This enabled Chinese villages and Russian *mir*[2] alike to enjoy relative autonomy. However, autonomy was in no way synonymous with democracy, for a restricted clique of "ancients" managed everything related to the *mir* or the *xiang* (village in China). They comprised heads of households—male, it goes without saying—who were better off than the average villager, and fairly uniformly conservative as well as being creatures of habit. Within the family—*jia* south of the Great Wall, *dvor* from Belarus to the Ural Mountains and beyond—a patriarchal system reigned over joint family property, although married sons were consulted.

The father's power reflected that of the tsar or the emperor, the Orthodox Church or popular Daoism. Different though these religions were, neither ever challenged the prevailing dogma, inherited values, or established order. With the exception of the scholars and the nobility, society was fairly uniform. People stuck together (a precarious existence demands solidarity), hardly ever leaving their home regions but developing a great nostalgia for them if they were "exiled" to the city. From the outside, this type of society appeared to be simple and static, but it was not. It simply evolved so slowly that it appeared to be ossified in relation to modern society. Holistic values characteristic of traditional societies predominated and subordinated individuals to the all-encompassing whole; individuals were relegated to the role of an element, a part of that whole, a pawn.[3]

However, that society was in the process of falling apart, especially in Russia, where modernization came faster. Little by little the monetary economy penetrated the countryside, farmers began to use new techniques, and the railways, roads, and post and telegraph services opened up the villages to the world. Above all, education made headway—at a snail's pace in China but fairly rapidly in Russia, where one person in five (21 percent) was literate in 1897, and two in five by 1913. The number of primary schools increased sixfold (from 25,000 to 150,000) between 1878 and 1914, when just over half of peasant school-age children went to school.[4] The better-educated young people began to shed patriarchal authority, and some set off to try their luck in the cities. Families were split, and the number of family members in a household fell from an average of nine in 1860 to five in 1900.

While China was more "backward" than Russia and its peasants far poorer,[5] the parallels between the belated efforts of both to modernize their respective empires are no less striking. In the last decade of China's imperial regime, officials launched an ambitious reform program that included the establishment of a modern army, support for industrial development, the dispatching of thousands of students to Japan, and, last but not least, the abolition of the imperial examination system. This reform was almost as bold as that launched decades later by Deng Xiaoping. The century started as it ended, with a decisive break with stagnation and the stultifying burden of a rigid ideology.

Alas, this conversion to modernity came too late, much like the contemporary reforms carried out by Pyotr Stolypin, who asked for twenty years to bring them to fruition. His request was not granted, both because he was assassinated in 1911 but also, and more crucially, because war obstructed the implementation of the reforms and revolution terminated them. The comparison does not end there. The court granted Stolypin a free hand (and then not always) only after the country had experienced the disasters of the Russo-Japanese War and the 1905 Revolution, and when a more docile Duma was elected in 1907. Similarly in China, the Qing (Manchu) court initiated a reform program only after it was defeated by the international force that came to the rescue of the foreign legations under siege (the Empress Dowager having rashly taken sides with the Boxers and declared an unwinnable war on the foreign powers on 21 June 1900). The reforms to which the Qing court grudgingly agreed were much like those it had suspended three years earlier by triggering a coup against the reforming emperor. Similarly, the unfortunate Hundred Days' Reform episode (June–September 1898) and the prior support for industrial development by Li Hongzhang and other enlightened conservatives resembled Sergei Witte's reforms before the fiascos suffered by both courts in 1900–1901 and 1904–1905, except that Witte's were more ambitious and more fruitful.

Rapid industrial growth in the 1890s, which continued between 1908 and 1914, brought about the formation of a proletariat that was every bit as concentrated as the industry it served. Those budding workers, fresh from the countryside, had yet to break ties with their villages, to which they frequently returned, if only to help with the harvest. Nevertheless they soon took root in the slums and suburbs of the cities, and, for better or worse, adapted to an environment that had disoriented and shocked them at first, ultimately bringing their families to join them or founding their own in the cities. The second generation would be unable even to imagine village life, but those first migrants had no choice but to radically transform their beliefs, concepts, and mentalities. Many came to reject everything that could symbolize the closed and stagnant village world. A quarter of a century later Chinese peasants underwent the same stressful uprooting and trauma—and for some, a feeling of liberation—when they went to find work in Shanghai or Tianjin. They were repeating the experience of their forerunners in Saint Petersburg or Moscow, even though they had never heard of them. As Stephen A. Smith wrote, "the growth and development of a working class in two areas of the globe outside the West" produced "striking similarities"—even though "different social, political and cultural contexts inflected the process of working-class formation."[6]

Since I know of no scholar other than Smith who has made a firsthand study of the Chinese and Russian proletariat and workers' movements,[7] I will summarize a few of his reflections and conclusions. The very location in which these two proletariats-in-the-making were concentrated reveals their intrinsic relationship, albeit with significant differences. Saint Petersburg and Shanghai were atypical in their respective countries and incarnated the capitalistic modernity of the future as well as presaging the future of their respective countries as a whole. Because of this, and also because both countries still retained numerous images of a past from which they had scarcely emerged, not everyone approved. Gogol and Fyodor Dostoyevsky condemned the vice in the capital, while for many Chinese intellectuals the very existence of Shanghai was a permanent affront to Confucian virtues. Shanghai, even more than Saint Petersburg, symbolized the consumer society, the lure of lucre, the rat race, and the dynamism and brutality of a youth with no respect for tradition. Last but not least, the modernity that had rubbed off on the inhabitants' way of life and their "cosmopolitan" habits was a foreign one. Shanghai, more than anywhere else in vast China, incarnated the dilemma, which, in the dawn of the last century had tortured those Chinese intellectuals most aware of the need to modernize their country: Just how far should modernization proceed before China risked losing its national identity? Was the "Westernization" of culture inevitable?

The workers' movements differed far more than the places in which the uprooted villagers had acquired their new identity. From 1925 what Smith calls "a class-infected anti-imperialist nationalism" prevailed in China, tantamount to subordinating the workers' movement to the struggle against imperialist domination of an entire people. That was not the case in Russia, where a veritable class consciousness had emerged a generation earlier. Of course on occasion the workers took part in a common struggle, as in China, but the designation of the adversary alone (Tsarist despotism/the enemy within) reveals the main orientations of the Russian and Chinese workers' movements. Far from being the result of a subjective choice by the parties concerned, this divergence reflects a fundamentally different objective situation; "semicolonial" China faced hostilities from incessant imperialist aggression, whereas Russia was a stakeholder to the entente among European powers. In addition to colonialism, there was anti-yellow racism, even though ultimately China's Japanese neighbor and brother turned out to be the more dangerous imperialist. Anti-Western sentiment was of a different nature for the Russians, who were as white as the Westerners themselves, so criticized and feared by the Slavophiles and their later emulators.

Being initially more proletarian than the worker component of the Chinese "proletarian nation,"[8] the workers of Saint Petersburg were more open to socialist ideas. These ideas had developed in a Europe that was fairly familiar to the Russians (the first volume of *Das Kapital* was published in Russian as early as 1872, before the English translation), whereas in China socialism was an imported theory. In 1905–1906, and again in 1912–1914, as well as in 1917 of course, the Russian proletariat, without necessarily being Marxist or revolutionary, led a workers' movement (especially in Saint Petersburg and its surroundings) that was unparalleled in the rest of Europe. In China, because of the time lag, the ideology of the first Russian Revolution, and the methods it exported, the CCP exerted a strong hold on the Shanghai (and Chinese) workers' movement from 1925–1926. This movement was a mere flash in the pan, its failure often explained by the betrayal of the Nationalist allies (Chiang Kai-shek) or the aberrations/betrayals of the strategy concocted in Moscow, which sacrificed the Canton workers for the creation of a short-lived commune. Neither explanation takes into account the small number of Chinese proletarians (0.5 percent of the population), admittedly concentrated. The Russian workers were not numerous either, representing only 2 percent of the total population on the eve of the revolution taking into account factory workers and miners (3.5 million), but far more (nearly 20 million) if workers in the crafts and traditional factories are included.

Different Degrees of Cultural Heterogeneity

The CCP's control over a large segment of the Chinese workers' movement does not mean that socialist ideas had penetrated as widely among Chinese workers in 1925 as among their Russian counterparts beginning in 1905. Among intellectuals, who were the sources and transmitters of socialist ideology, those ideas were more widely shared in Russia than in China. But in this case as in others, a comparable situation determined similar experiences, despite radically different cultural contexts. There is no need for me to elaborate on this, for while we can differentiate Russian culture from that of the rest of Europe ad infinitum, those distinctions pale as soon as that outlier—China—enters the game of comparisons. Whatever the situation (Russia being peripheral to "European" culture so conveniently placed at the center, or China completely outside of it), the reactions were the same, ranging from rejection to admiration, and from selective borrowing to justifications of their own culture—if only to preserve its identity, via the premise of a "third way."

How can one equate Russia's backwardness with "the great Russian century,"[9] lasting from the golden to the silver age via Pushkin, Dostoyevsky, Tolstoy, and so many others that we have appropriated as humanity's shared heritage, along with Socrates, Shakespeare, and (why not?) Marx. The backwardness lay in the penetration of ideas that had been introduced into Western Europe from the beginning of the eighteenth century and the emergence of what was not even a class, but a slim layer of educated people, for the intelligentsia emerged only during the 1860s. Because of that perceived backwardness, everything was absorbed at breakneck speed and a premium was placed on the latest imported novelties, which as often as not were also the most radical and at the time included socialism. The isolation of this flimsy stratum, cut off from both the illiterate masses and the elite, not to mention Western Europe, perceived as the hub of cultural debate, led to an extremist tendency. In Russia and China, awareness of the country's backwardness led to self-criticism and a desire to learn from Western Europe on the one hand, and reproof of a refuted Western model and admiration for national identity on the other—as for instance in the quarrel between "Westernizers" and Slavophiles.

This stance was reproduced in China during the May Fourth Movement (1919). "Chinese thinking is 1,000 years behind Western thinking," said Chen Duxiu in terms that echoed Pyotr Chaadayev's bitter observation that "we have not contributed anything to the advancement of the human spirit, ... not a single useful thought has germinated in the sterile earth of our fatherland, nor any lofty truth."[10] Before converting to Marxism, or rather adopting the Leninist recipe for conquering power and modernizing a backward country, Chen had admired the French Third Republic. At the time Chen could roughly be equated to a Chinese Herzen, an advocate of the West and the ideals it supposedly propagated, such as democracy, reason, science, and progress. The philosopher Liang Shuming (1893–1988), promoted Chinese replicas of the Slavophiles' themes by publishing *Dongxi wenhua ji qi zhexue* [Eastern and Western Civilizations and Their Philosophies] (1922).[11] He maintained that China was not lagging behind the West but had chosen a different path, one that the West would take in turn. The West's current domination was due to the fact that it had focused on man's basic necessities. Dry intellectual calculations that analyzed and dissected had produced science, while reliance on individual interest led to democracy. Once affluence was achieved, the West would begin to need the spiritual life denied by positivism and utilitarianism. It was discovering the virtues of intuition; witness Henri Bergson who was discovering what the Chinese had known all along. According to Liang Shuming, disinterested intuition, freed of all practical aims, the sense of and a taste for the incessant flow of life, a profound compatibility with the cosmos, harmony, compromise, contentment, and a love of life were just some of the virtues that Confucianism would teach the entire world. Once the first layer of problems was resolved (survival, immediate material needs), the West would discover the second one, which China alone had explored. Indeed, Liang Shuming predicted the imminent spiritual Sinicization of humanity.[12]

He was not alone in that belief. That as eminent a pioneer of Chinese modernization as Liang Qichao (1873–1929) had appealed to China as early as 1919 to ensure the West's spiritual salvation reveals the ambivalence of even the boldest "Westernizer."[13] The carnage of World War I had shocked Liang Qichao, just as the failure of the European revolutions in 1848 had disappointed Herzen, who, like Dostoyevsky and many "third world" intellectuals, became a harsh critic of Western Europe, corrupted by mercantilism and a bourgeois spirit. With the exception of Europe and its American offshoot, the entire world, not just Russia and China, was suffering in this way.

After this reminder of China and Russia's common condition—or historical situation—I must stress the obvious differences between them, starting with the most important. Chinese intellectuals were far more isolated from Western Europe than their Russian counterparts. Chaadayev, for instance, wrote his *Lettres philosophiques* (Philosophical Letters) (1836) in French, imploring his country to learn from the West, and his friend Pushkin replied in the same language, declaring, "pour rien au monde, je n'aurais voulu changer de patrie" (I would not change my fatherland for anything in the world).[14] Lin Shu (1852–1924), who introduced Chinese readers to Western literature, knew no foreign language at all, but that didn't prevent him from "translating" Montesquieu, Hugo, Dumas, Shakespeare, Swift, Dickens, Tolstoy, Ibsen, Cervantes, Homer, and Aesop. Colleagues selected the works for him and translated them into the vernacular (*baihua*). Lin then rendered what he understood (or imagined) into an elegant written Chinese (*wenyan*). It is no surprise that Lin Shu included Tolstoy among the Western authors to be introduced to China; it was as obvious to the Chinese intellectuals of the time as it is for us. Like literature, Western thought by which Chinese "Westernizers" and Sinophiles alike compared their views naturally encompassed Russia. They included Mikhail Bakunin and Peter Kropotkin as much as Marx or Darwin and quoted or interpreted them—often erroneously, with simplifications or approximations that were not to be found in the original works of the Russian authors. Liang Shuming compared Kropotkin to Mencius because he stressed man's natural goodness. His thought, even more than Bergson's, suggested that the West would imminently be won over to Chinese thought. Not only did the Chinese authors permit serious distortions, their lack of familiarity with Western culture enabled them to take any direction they wished. However I must not oversimplify. Many Chinese authors had a far better knowledge of the Western authors they quoted, starting with certain critics of Liang, and did not fail to pinpoint his errors.

The Chinese became aware of being alien to European culture far later than did the Russians. That was inevitable since they discovered the Western "other" only at the very end of the nineteenth century, and were less affected by it. The Russians deplored their country's backwardness, its shortcomings and failure to adjust, whereas the Chinese were fighting oppressors whose secrets, such as the efficiency of their weapons and industry, their government and ideology, they had to uncover. Anticolonialism and awareness of white racism were never far from any reference to the European model. Chinese intellectuals were better integrated into their own society than were their Russian counterparts. On a local level, the scholar often played an active role as a respected arbiter or organizer, and participated in village life. While not totally absent, the Russian nobility, and still more the intellectuals, generally left local affairs to be managed by the *mir*. The contrast was even greater on a national scale where there was a clear rift between members of the Russian intelligentsia and the civil and military establishment, poorly educated as a rule. Conversely, Chinese scholars shared the official ideology of the empire on the whole, and all administrators were recruited from their ranks. This situation lasted until the advent of the twentieth century and was challenged only after the imperial examinations were abolished in 1905. During the brief republican interlude (1912–1949), an embryonic intelligentsia gradually emerged, but only during the warlord period did it truly feel alienated from power. Even then, its skepticism and tendency to find a middle way mostly prevented any extremism. A Sergey Nechayev was hardly imaginable in China—something I have given up trying to remind anyone who remembers those images and sounds of screaming Red Guards. Indeed, that is my point, for the contrast between traditional representations of what is typically Russian and typically Chinese (or Korean) is pushed into the background as soon as a regime arises that is capable of manufacturing fanatics out of any psychological raw material.

Divergence and Ultimate Convergence

At the outset, different cultural traditions and comparable historic situations led to two separate paths that ultimately converged. In Russia, the revolutionary intelligentsia was often tempted by dogmatism, intransigence, sectarianism, and an illusion that it alone possessed the absolute truth (these remarks do not concern such subtle and sophisticated spirits as Anton Chekhov, who cared little for the intelligentsia). The Russian intelligentsia was far from being a unanimous body and defended opposite ideas with equal conviction; consider for instance partisans of a strong state versus the anarchists, the Marxists versus the populists, and so forth. However, many members of this intelligentsia shared a common aspiration for a national messianism, which sometimes united followers of the Westernizers and the Slavophiles (some individuals being both). That, supposedly, could reconcile the desire to adopt "European" rationality and science while rejecting the bourgeois path taken by the West. Russia would find an original third way, indeed had a mission to invent this new way and lead the rest of humanity onto it. We can find traces of this aspiration throughout the half century from 1861 to 1914, from the populists wanting to prevent the development of capitalism to the Socialist Revolutionaries (SR) who aspired to socialism but bypassing the capitalist phase.

To some extent, we can even find it in Lenin, who opposed the SR and scorned the naïveté of populists. The "Western" carried the day for Lenin—witness his sarcasm about "Russian idiots" and tirades against "Asian despotism." If he later returned to the concept of a separate way, which even the advocates of Russian messianism would not have sneered at, he showed not the slightest sympathy for nationalism; it was just his desire to act that gained the upper hand over theoretical coherence. That coherence was that of Georgi Plekhanov, Pavel Axelrod, and others (the makings of the Mensheviks), who, unlike the populists but like Lenin, believed that the development of capitalist industry was inevitable and essential, but hastened to add that it would take time for capitalism to mature and would first lead to a bourgeois revolution, a prerequisite for a proletarian revolution. Having posited against all evidence that "the development of capitalism in Russia" (the title of Lenin's first book) was already so advanced that it had led to the proletarianization of a good half of the peasantry, Lenin then claimed that because the bourgeoisie was so weak in Russia (by implication because capitalism had still not developed) Russia could therefore move directly to the proletarian revolution stage. That anticipated a specific route for Russia, distinct from the one conceived by Marxist tradition. If there was to be no national messianism, then at least there should be a wager on the advantages of lagging behind. Trotsky developed that point of view in a more systematic manner, but Pyotr Tkachev had preceded both of them for he too saw the nondevelopment of the bourgeoisie as an advantage for the revolution. Indeed, in many other respects, Tkachev and not Marx or Engels, was the true precursor of Lenin.[15] In this, as in his relationship with revolutionaries or prerevolutionaries from the preceding generation, Lenin was part of a national tradition (he borrowed the title of Nikolay Chernychevsky's novel *What Is to Be Done?*, his bedside book, which, together with Nechayev's *The Revolutionary Catechism*, formed the perfect Bolshevik's bible before its time). He, who was accused of being a Blanquist, succeeded in Russifying Marxism just as Mao later Sinicized it, albeit in a very different way since Mao substituted the workers with peasants but (like Lenin) for the purpose of adapting to the country's backwardness and turning it into an advantage.

The Russian intelligentsia went through contrasting phases with regard to the peasants. The populists idealized them and felt guilty about those whose labor enabled them to live a privileged life and, by extension, obtain an education. Thus they simultaneously expressed their faith in the Russian people, their aversion for the bourgeoisie, and their intention to prevent any capitalist intrusion in Russia. The populist illusion did not survive the shock of 1873–1874, when young Russians "went to the people" and discovered that the flesh-and-blood *mujik* bore no resemblance to the noble savage of their dreams, which were instinctively collectivist and anarchist. However, the SR later followed the same line.

The ebb of populism opened the way to terrorism and then to Marxism, another two schools of thought and practices whose followers were at loggerheads despite a shared hostility to populism. The penetration of Marxism then enabled revolutionary intellectuals to place their hopes and dreams on the nascent proletariat, while a more realistic perception, free of benevolence for the peasant masses, asserted itself from Chekhov's "The Mujiks" to Maxim Gorki and Ivan Bunin.

Despite my perhaps excessive insistence on the messianism of a fraction of the Russian intelligentsia in the nineteenth century, the social problems, as opposed to the political or even national ones, remained at the heart of the intelligentsia's concerns. That was not at all the case for the Chinese, even if the ultimate outcome (Communist revolution) might lead one to suppose the opposite. I will insist again that the revolutionary vocation of nearly all the radical intellectuals was triggered by imperialism and the need to resist it. They may have bemoaned China's backwardness and wanted to remedy it, but very few would have resorted to Chernychevsky's quip, "Better not to have been born at all than to be born a Russian."[16] Even the boldest and most iconoclastic Chinese were less likely to denigrate their country than their Russian counterparts.

These pioneers wrote and acted in the last years of the nineteenth century, a period comparable to that described in Daniel Mornet's *The Cultural Origins of the French Revolution*. From the start, these Chinese pioneers (I shall name four to match Montesquieu, Voltaire, Rousseau, and Diderot) were driven by a common desire to save their country and to that end remedy its backwardness. One exception, however, was Tan Sitong (1864–1898). His indignation about the "abysmal depravity of the traditional Chinese order" led him to call the imperialists "forces for humanity and justice" sent by Heaven to administer the punishment China deserved. Tan chose to die a martyr's death the day after the coup that ended the Hundred Days' Reform, even though he could have fled like Kang Youwei (1858–1927), who had inspired those same reforms.

Kang's disciple, and later right-hand man, Liang Qichao soon surpassed his master and all the others too. In 1902 he published *New Citizen*, which became a bible for Chinese students in Japan. Influenced by Rousseau, the new citizen in question assumed that a democratic regime would be established, but Liang used democracy and freedom as remedies for traditional Chinese despotism and the "servile" mentality of his contemporaries. In other words, they were the means to an end: the grandeur of the nation. *New Citizen* was an ode to the nation-state more than to democracy, a state that must urgently be erected and protected from destructive imperialism. Influenced by Herbert Spencer's social Darwinism, the fourth musketeer, Yan Fu (1853–1921), did everything possible to ensure that his country would, in turn, pass the natural selection test. In order to galvanize the Chinese, he introduced them to Montesquieu, Adam Smith, and Stuart Mill. Against the background of these various publications, released between 1895 and 1908, was a tireless search: "What do they have that we don't, and how can we get it?"

None of the three survivors (Kang, Liang, and Yan) followed the fifth pioneer, Sun Yat-sen (1866–1925), who was far more of a political leader than a thinker. In 1905 a revealing conversation was held in England between two critics of traditional Chinese civilization, each more impatient than the other to put their country on the right track to modernity (English modernity, of course). Yan Fu said to Sun Yat-sen, "Given the poor quality of our fellow citizens and their low level of knowledge, the most urgent task is to educate them. Perhaps after that we shall make some progress." Sun Yat-sen apparently replied, "How can we wait that long? You, Sir, are a thinker, I am a man of action."[17] Yan Fu believed that it was irresponsible to overthrow the existing regime just when it was finally promoting some reforms. Humanity's progress was the result of a very long, slow, and laborious process, according to the lesson Yan had learned from his evolutionist English masters.

The outcome of that revolution (a republican regime that proved to be even less capable of resisting the imperialists than the Manchu dynasty) confirmed Yan's fears and, he believed, Sun's mad recklessness. For our purpose, however, the importance of this lies less in the split between reformists and revolutionaries than in their common Nationalist fervor. As early as 1904, Yan had stated, "Once China becomes aware that its old laws can no longer be followed, once it realizes that its fixed views and evil customs are harmful, and once it sweeps away its corruption and pursues power earnestly, there will be no nation on the five continents like it."[18] Twenty years later, Sun echoed: "If China reaches the standard of Japan, she will be equal to ten great powers. ... She will then be able to recover her predominant national position."

The May Fourth Movement (1919), better known than its predecessors to which it owed a great deal, confirmed and highlighted those same premises. On the one hand, China's cultural heritage was challenged and supplanted by values borrowed from the West and made familiar through translations of English, French, German, and Russian works, including by great writers such as Lu Xun (1881–1936). On the other hand, there was a Nationalist reaction, which included infatuation with the West in order to resist it and, why not, surpass it. The movement got its name from the demonstration held on May 4, 1919, in which students in Beijing protested against the Paris Peace Conference's decision to transfer Germany's rights over Shandong province to Japan.

No sooner did the May Fourth Movement triumph, which it rapidly did, than it divided. The liberals were satisfied with a literary and cultural revolution, whereas the radicals supported a political and social revolution. That split the movement into two opposing factions, embodied by Chen Duxiu, founder of the CCP (in 1920–1921), and Hu Shi, who represented the Nationalist regime in Washington and died in Taiwan in 1962. The growing interest in Marxism in the 1920s and 1930s was less due to social concerns than the Nationalist quest. Since everything had failed in China and the country was more divided and powerless than it had ever been. Why not try something that had just succeeded—it was thought—in another backward country? Instead of stubbornly copying the West, discredited by the abuses of capitalism and the horrors of war, why not follow Lenin, who has just assimilated imperialism, the secular enemy of "semicolonial China," with the "ultimate stage of capitalism." The original goal was not abandoned, but a new path was found to achieve it: modernity *via* anticapitalist socialism. Russia led the way.

For now, I shall not insist on future divergence. To conquer power, it was the peasants, not the sacrosanct proletariat, who were now mobilized for a second revolution. This infringement of doctrine was not a result of ideas but imposed by the situation. China was far less industrialized than 1914 Russia (or 1917 Russia for that matter). When Chinese intellectuals became seriously interested in the peasants in the 1930s, the more radical among them, like the populists sixty years earlier, tended to confer their own revolutionary aspirations on the rural masses.

Most intellectuals disagreed with the radicals, whether in their Communist or Nationalist guise (the latter being the Guomindang, founded by Sun Yat-sen). After the 1927 split, only the Communists incarnated the revolution because the Guomindang identified with the government. However, the disillusionment and ultimately the disgust provoked by the government in place did not convert this majority to the Communist cause. Most intellectuals made their choice *in extremis*, when the only alternative left was between two powers and two armies. They chose to stay with the Reds even when there was still time for them to emigrate. Once again, the determining factor, apart from family or professional reasons or habit, was patriotism. The winner seemed better positioned than the loser to get the country back on its feet.

Tsarism: An Even More Desperate Case Than the Guomindang

In 1917, most Russian intellectuals did not hesitate in February (they supported the revolution) any more than in October (they were against the Bolshevik coup). At worst they feared that the February Revolution would fail. Zinaida Hippius was one whose fears were confirmed in October, but it didn't occur to any intellectual outside the circles of power to regret the old regime. It must be said that the regime strove to validate the point of view of the radical intelligentsia, namely that for something to change, everything had to change. In the eyes of educated Russians, the regime they endured was archaic and ill-suited to administer a vast empire with a population of 170 million. The patrimonial principle still prevailed; the army was considered the tsar's personal possession, the officers his vassals, and the bureaucrats (*chinovniki*) his private servants. The bureaucratic system itself, with the higher echelons reserved for the nobility, and quasi-automatic promotion based on the length of service, encouraged mediocrity, opportunism, corruption, and obsession with status and hierarchy. Yet for the tsar, politics amounted to the administration. Nicholas II lacked the intelligence and character to be an accomplished autocrat like his father, Alexander III, but he obstinately defended autocracy on principle as well as out of duty since it was the divine will. The empress encouraged him in this belief and his actions, both of them despising public opinion, perceived as a barrier between them and the people who supposedly revered them.

Conceptions of the tsar and the bureaucracy were gradually eroded and then belittled by the economic development of the last half century (1861–1914). Ironically, the tsar himself sought that development (even though it was opposed by the more conservative elements in his court and the bureaucracy) having been convinced by a few rare enlightened ministers (e.g., Witte) that military power and a balanced budget depended on it. Before industrialization, the nation's resources largely derived from (insufficient) taxation on the rural community. This contradiction between stated principles and the recurrent demands of the government of the world's fifth largest economy was never resolved. It even worsened until the war made it intolerable and devastating for one and all.

The despotism of Imperial China may roughly be compared to that of the Russian autocracy. It was equally archaic, comprehensive, religious, and essentially administrative. With the exception of the first epithet, the others need to be nuanced, since in both cases inefficiency was undermining that supposedly absolute power. A wide gulf separated Confucianism and the Orthodox Church, although the Son of Heaven enjoyed the same sort of legitimacy as that defender of orthodoxy and its bastion, Holy Russia. Above all both empires were undergoverned. Primitive communications and minimal fiscal resources prevented both emperor and tsar from maintaining local-level officials and intervening efficiently. There were plenty of other common features, starting with the venality and brutality of the civil servants, mocked and denounced in literature from *Rulin waishi* (The Scholars)[19] to Gogol's *Dead Souls*.

The imperial regime was overthrown by a first revolution (1911–1912), so that is not the one to assess. China's Nationalist regime (the ancien régime, overthrown by the Communists in 1949) was in many ways less obsolete than the Tsarist autocracy in 1914. It partially unified a continent-wide country, which was urgently required after the internecine wars and the ravages of the warlords. It established a government that, despite its numerous flaws, was the most modern one China had ever known and extended to the local level a corrupt yet more efficient administration than any previous one. And although Tsarist Russia was better than the Nationalist regime at pursuing industrialization, the latter nevertheless transmitted a reasonable legacy to its Communist victors. Conversely, agriculture stagnated and the Nationalists soon abandoned the agrarian reforms they had vaguely intended to implement at the outset. That failure allowed the rival Communists to occupy the rural ground and mobilize the peasant masses against the government. Fear of the same Communists also made the regime more conservative and authoritarian. Like Nicholas II, Chiang Kai-shek placed people loyal to him in key positions, rather than appointing able and competent leaders. On the whole, however, despite other shortcomings common to both regimes, the Nationalist regime in 1937 was less disastrous than the Tsarist autocracy in 1914, and had slightly more capacity to evolve.

However, the problems it faced were greater and even more pressing, giving China more "excuses" than Russia, with one exception. The Russians were a minority in their empire, whereas the Han represented 94 percent of the Chinese population. The Russification policy of the last two Tsars made enemies of peoples who might have been content with cultural or linguistic concessions. At Warsaw University, Polish students were obliged to study their own literature in Russian translation. Felix Dzerzhinsky, the future founder of the Cheka, was expelled from high school for having spoken Polish in the dormitory. In 1907, the medical commission in Kiev province refused to allow cholera epidemic notices to be published in Ukrainian, with the result that many peasants who could not read Russian died from drinking infected water.[20]

The Impact of World Wars and Civil Wars

One ultimate difference concerned the impact of the two world wars as well as their origin. The game of European alliances, to which Russia was party, transformed an Austro-Russian conflict in the Balkans into a world war. China was once again the victim of imperialist aggression that it was unable to prevent. Chiang Kai-shek played for time, to the extent that his appeasement policy with regard to Japan aroused the ire of a less well-informed public opinion. Nor was the Japanese invasion the cause of the Second World War; just a long, eight-year war, which China had to fight and endure alone from July 1937 to December 1941, a little longer than the duration of the entire First World War.

The effects of the war were catastrophic for Tsarism but devastating for the Nationalist regime in China. Without it the Chinese Communists would not have come to power. Mao himself admitted (in 1971) that Japanese imperialism had made his victory possible. The Chinese did not stand a chance, given the disproportionate strength of the Japanese and Chinese forces. It was a miracle that they held out as long as they did without collapsing or begging for grace. China paid excessively for its obstinate resistance. Chiang Kai-shek sacrificed his best troops in the early months of the war in the battle for Shanghai, after which he ruined himself trying to rebuild a less efficient army, triggering a level of inflation on par with that under the Weimar Republic. Had the war merely highlighted the regime's weaknesses and vices, it might have survived. Instead it enabled the Communist adversary to increase its forces, its territory, and the population under its control.

In comparison, the Russian military might did not cut such a sorry figure when confronting the Austro-Hungarian troops, twice repelled by Aleksei Brusilov (in 1914 and 1916). Germany, the more formidable enemy, was obliged to converge most of its forces on the western front against the British and the French. However, faced with a less impossible challenge than that confronting the Chinese, the Tsarist autocracy failed equally badly. The disastrous rout in East Prussia at the end of August 1914 contrasted with the heroic defense of Shanghai in the summer of 1937, but the Nanking Massacre carried out by the Japanese a few months later confirms that comparisons of the military performance of the belligerent in 1914 or the victim in 1937 are not what matter most. Among the many failures of the tsar's government was its inability to supply the troops due to chaotic transportation, leading to serious food shortages in the cities.[21] On the eve of the war, Russia had been the world's foremost exporter of wheat. Thirty months later, a bread shortage was the immediate trigger for the February Revolution.

The autocracy was blamed for many other things, not only by socialists and revolutionaries from all spectrums, but by the liberals and patriots and even ultimately the monarchists themselves, who tried to prevent the catastrophic situation facing their war-torn country. And yet during the emergency both the liberals and the monarchists did the impossible by collaborating with the government through para-governmental organizations.[22] They feared the revolution, which the regime finally imposed on them, more than they hoped for it—fears that were grounded since the revolution promptly swallowed them up. In a well-known parable used by the liberal lawyer Vasily Maklakov, the situation in Russia was comparable to a car driven by a mad driver at high speed down a steep slope bordered with precipices. Disaster is assured, whether or not the wheel is left in the driver's hands or snatched away from him. In September 1915, Maklakov still believed it necessary—or less irresponsible—to give advice to the driver, who was quite incapable of taking it. He may have changed his mind about that later.[23]

The final contrast between the two countries was that the February revolutionaries managed to reap the benefits for the Bolsheviks, who came to power through a coup, while the Chinese Communists did so as victors of a civil war—not really what one expects from a revolution in either case. The Bolsheviks would later have to deal with a civil war, which weighed heavily on the regime's future orientation. That was one disadvantage their Chinese emulators would not have, since their compatriots now accepted them as legitimate.

2. Catching Up

The Economy

Once they rose to power, the Russian and Chinese Communists did not forget their utopic objective (to construct a fair, egalitarian, and fraternal society), still less their more prosaic one (modernizing a backward country). Indeed, that was the one they had to tackle first and devote most of their efforts to. In addition to inheriting a backward country, they had to rectify a disastrous economic situation resulting from years of war and civil war. When Lenin launched his New Economic Policy (NEP) in 1921, Russian industrial production accounted for only 31 percent of production in 1913,[1] a time when Russia was also the world's leading wheat exporter. Now the country prepared to seek foreign aid to fight off famine. The NEP was efficient in making up those first shortfalls, and by 1926 industrial reconstruction was almost complete, making further investment necessary to maintain the pace of advancement. Repairs and reconstruction were no longer enough; new factories had to be built and industrial equipment replaced. Agriculture quickly recovered after the 1921–1922 famine, but remained primitive in many regions. In 1928, 5.5 million peasant households were tilling the fields with wooden ploughs "dating back to the Pharaohs," half the crops were harvested with scythes and sickles, and two fifths were threshed with a flail. In 1917, the vast majority of the population had yet to enter the industrial age,[2] yet that matched the level achieved by the successful NEP ten years after the October Revolution. In other words, once the preliminary work required by reconstruction was achieved, everything remained to be done. When Anton Ciliga traveled to Russia in 1926, he admitted that "in those first days, I was obsessed by the misery, Russia's backwardness compared to Europe. ... Like all foreigners I had no concrete and living knowledge of the immensity of that backwardness."[3]

China may have been more backward than Russia, but its preliminary reconstruction task was easier and accomplished faster, if only because the civil war occurred before the conquest of power. Moreover the mining and metal industries had peaked in the middle of the war, when the Japanese were developing industry in Manchuria and northern China, recaptured by China in 1945.[4] As early as 1952, that peak was surpassed, the cereal harvest returned to prewar levels, and the catastrophic inflation that had greatly contributed to the fall of the former regime was curbed. Within three years China was therefore in working order and facing the same colossal problem as Russia in 1928 (and many developing nations later): how to transform a country largely populated with peasants devoted to traditional agriculture, into a modern industrial nation.

This historical reminder has been just a prelude, a prologue to deal with as quickly as possible. The subject of this chapter is not the NEP or China's rapid reconstruction, but the "second revolution" following Stalin's Great Turn of 1929, the Five-Year Plans, and the Great Leap Forward in China. But that is no reason to forget Lenin. It was he who showed the way ("soviets plus electricity") and whose doctrine (Marxism adapted to a backward country and therefore crossed with voluntarism) made the task even more difficult once the Communists came to power because he did not wait for the economic and social conditions to mature, as Plekhanov, Julius Martov, and Karl Kautsky had advocated, but tried to speed things up. He was counting on the world revolution, supposed to be hastened by World War I, but its failure, or rather absence, transformed difficulties into near impossibilities. To go back even further than Lenin, Witte's task was comparable but less challenging since he could depend on foreign capital, which was not available to the revolutionaries. Without foreign capital, industrialization could be financed only by the peasants, who were by far the most numerous producers in 1920s Russia and 1950s China.

But industrialization at what pace? A snail's pace, Nikolai Bukharin advised in 1925, in order to preserve the precarious *smyčka*, the "peasant and worker alliance" that Lenin had established without consulting the parties concerned. Bukharin believed that, without demanding too much from the peasants, the regime would gradually improve their living conditions and the demand for manufactured goods would increase at the same pace. It was a case of playing the market economy card by constructing socialism at a rate the peasants could accept. "Get rich," he even advised them, but that quote from Guizot, the archetypal bourgeois politician, could provoke only the ire of his Bolshevik comrades. Stalin himself, still his ally at the time, deemed it wise to disassociate himself from such a sacrilegious slogan.[5] Most of the leaders could not accept such distant prospects of industrialization. Bukharin spoke of a generation, which was optimistic. After his U-turn, Stalin justified his refusal of that slow pace with a comment: "We are fifty or a hundred years behind the advanced countries. We must make good this distance in ten years. Either we do so, or we shall go under."[6] He said that in 1931, just ten years before the German invasion.

By then no one would dare contradict him, but in 1925 the subject was still debatable and Bukharin's critics had plenty of arguments. Leaders and economists faced a classic problem: how to develop a backward country. Yevgeni Preobrazhensky, the leading theoretician of the anti-Bukharin left, advocated implementing a "primitive socialist accumulation," in reference to the primitive (or initial) accumulation of capital achieved, according to Marx, by the British bourgeoisie through their exploitation of the peasants, the workers, and the British colonies. Since Russia had no colonies, that accumulation could come only from the private sector, essentially peasants. It was therefore necessary to impose a heavier income tax on rich peasants and, above all, to syphon off the farmers' resources unfairly by keeping agricultural prices artificially low and the prices of manufactured goods artificially high. That was possible since the state was the leading producer of industrial goods and held a monopoly on foreign trade.[7] This was a voluntarist and even brutal method, but not radically different from the one Witte had initiated.

As far as brutality was concerned Stalin did much better. He exceeded even the wildest dreams of the champions of primitive socialist accumulation. In relation to the positions advocated by the Trotsky-dominated left (incarnated by Preobrazhensky) in opposition to the Stalin-dominated right (incarnated by Bukharin in the mid-1920s),[8] the policy that Stalin imposed on the country after the Great Turn of 1929 can be qualified only as "ultra left," to use the official jargon. He carried out his U-turn in 1928 without duly warning Bukharin, his ally or duumvir

(Stephen Cohen) thereby also making it impossible for the duumvirate to continue. Bukharin now became a "right deviationist." At the same time Stalin delivered the coup de grâce to the NEP (already heavily distorted by infringements on market laws from above) and to the *smyčka*. The first Five-Year Plan, launched in 1929, favored massive investment to the detriment of consumption and living standards, for it was devoted mainly to producing capital goods, energy, and raw materials, and disadvantaged the consumption and services industries, considered unproductive. Once completed, the Magnitogorsk iron and steel works, built in the middle of the deserted Ural steppe, was to produce as much steel as the whole of Russia in 1913 or the Soviet Union in 1927.[9]

The first plan was rapidly revised upward, even though it was already optimistic to the point of being unrealistic. In the eight months from the Soviets' Fifth Congress in May 1929 to January 1930, the production objectives for the end of the five-year period were increased. The objective for coal was raised from 75 million metric tons to 120 and then 150 million, oil was increased from 22 million metric tons to 45 million, and cast iron from 10 million metric tons to 17 and then 20 million. That was just a phase, followed by other unachievable figures and percentages. Targets would indeed not be achieved even though the Five-Year Plan was declared completed in March 1933 after just four years and three months. National volition was to impose itself on reality and consequently war was declared on nature and time. "We must make up for centuries of backwardness in ten years." The term "teleological planning" was even used. All that mattered was the end, not the means. There were no objective difficulties for the Bolsheviks, and nothing was impossible for them: "there are no fortresses the Bolsheviks cannot storm."[10]

At first, the experts at Gosplan (the state planning committee) and other economists ventured objections or suggested that it might be preferable to maintain a balance between the various branches of the economy, or that revolutionary momentum alone could not accomplish miracles. Their arguments were promptly swept aside. Take the example of an oil industry specialist who dared to criticize the "purely arbitrary" nature of the goals. He advanced arguments, such as "over a third of the oil must come from unexplored areas ... the three cracking plants which now exist are to be turned into 120 plants by the end of the Five-Year Plan." A young woman activist promptly replied, "We do not doubt the knowledge or goodwill of the professor ... but we reject the fetishism of figures which holds him in thrall." During the first plan, "the testing of political and economic assertions against empirical evidence fell into desuetude; open discussion on the scientific model ceased." Later, when Stalin was informed that the Stakhanovites had broken all records thanks to the special conditions arranged by the foremen with the help of the other workers—frequently at the risk of damaging the machines— he refused to take that into account. The workers' enthusiasm created miracles and that was it. I have understated his ambition. "Catching up" is too weak an expression; he was aiming far higher. Soviet modernity was to be quite different from blind imitation of the advanced capitalist countries. It would raise humanity to a higher level by accomplishing novel feats unparalleled in the West.[11]

With the experts pushed aside or curbed, the most important decisions were taken by a highly restricted but not very competent group who consulted very little, deliberated in secret, and had a plethora of scapegoats at their disposal should anything go wrong. The command economy implied an all-powerful state, or "policy in command," a formula later faithfully copied by Mao. All policy decided at the summit was correct; errors and failures could only be the fault of the executors. That is what Moshe Lewin calls an "irresponsible dictatorship." Opposition was equated with treason and terror ensured that orders were obeyed blindly. And when the plans were misguided, disasters were sure to follow. Planning errors were frequent toward the end of the NEP; they even contributed to its demise. After that it became increasingly difficult to discuss the decisions of the leaders—soon to be "leader" in the singular.[12] At execution level loss and wastage were inevitable. Production costs in Magnitogorsk were all the higher since the leadership cared little for costs, buying equipment and raw goods anywhere and everywhere, gobbling up state credit in the process. In any case the state demanded higher and faster, but not profitable, production. When the price of energy, raw materials, and transport became too high, the planners unilaterally lowered the costs to make the purchase price of Magnitogorsk steel seem affordable. Like Magnitogorsk, the major state enterprises regularly demanded more raw materials and inputs than necessary because their first obligation was to achieve the plan's objectives and they were never certain of obtaining everything they needed to do so—or only after a lengthy delay: "Comprehensive central planning produced its own forms of 'anarchy'" (Kotkin). Furthermore orders rarely arrived complete.

In 1938, coking coal from the Kuzbass mines weighed 30 percent short of the order when it arrived at Magnitogorsk because enterprises less favored in the distribution of raw materials helped themselves on the way to compensate for their own shortfalls.[13] Transport itself was slow and irregular, leading to a chronic shortage of essential raw materials and chaotic production. The tyranny of quantity was such that neither the suppliers nor the Magnitogorsk industrial complex itself were greatly concerned about quality—but nor could they deliver just anything. In early 1937, Magnitogorsk had accumulated and scrapped the equivalent of 6.5 million rubles worth of pig iron and 9.7 million rubles worth of unusable steel—while nevertheless including it in the total production figures as reported to the leadership.[14]

The system may have been short on quality, the economical use of inputs, efficiency, and rationality, but certainly was not short of manpower, and a great deal of it was required to modernize a traditional economy at breakneck speed. In 1936, in the middle of the second Five-Year Plan, nearly two-thirds of all earthmoving work in Magnitogorsk was accomplished by hand. All-out industrialization solved urban unemployment, and the number of workers more than doubled from 3.7 to 8.5 million during the first plan. In addition, collectivization and dekulakization hastened the rural exodus, making manpower even more abundant, although these workers were inexperienced and suffered from low productivity. Where necessary, workers were obliged to maintain sixteen-hour shifts, but more often as not they were motivated by piecework.[15]

Propaganda was another tool, with endless campaigns geared to educating the workers and raising their political consciousness. Many did learn to read, acquire a trade, and improve their skills. They felt that they were taking part in a great exploit and were different from workers toiling under the capitalistic yoke. In Magnitogorsk even former kulaks—or many of them at least—felt they were carrying out a historic task. Workers who did not join in the collective enthusiasm or willingly carry out the exorbitant tasks demanded of them were labeled "class enemies" whatever their class of origin. Witness the Magnitogorsk metal worker who expressed dissatisfaction with the pay, equipment, food, and lodgings—despite having worked thirty years in the Donbass mine. Anyone daring to ask for better rations, an improvement in working conditions, or a less meager wage was treated as a threat to the enterprise or even to the revolution itself. Every new industrial site built in the 1930s was sacred, rather like the Red Army in the early 1920s. Its task was to forge steel and the New Soviet Man, in other words to transform the peasants who were recruited into the collective crusade. They were constructing socialism and building a new society. Every individual must have felt that he or she was fighting on the front line, and many were indeed convinced of it.[16] The first batch of steel produced at Magnitogorsk on 1 February 1932 was a triumph that received a unanimous ovation. A battle had been won, never mind a work accident that same day, followed by another shortly thereafter.[17]

Despite work accidents (which were neither more frequent nor more serious than those in China in 2013), machines breaking down, neglected maintenance (a waste of time), stagnating productivity—which improved during the second plan—disorder, waste, and irrational decision making, Russia did become industrialized. The process was not exactly painless but was achieved in record time. Needless to say, it mainly concerned the production of machine tools, turbines, tractors, metallurgical equipment, and so on, all of which advanced at high speed. During the first Five-Year Plan, heavy industry almost quadrupled in value according to official statistics, which were slightly overestimated. At the same time, and according to the same statistics, production of consumer goods rose by 64 percent. Conversely the textile industry fell slightly and transport remained a bottleneck, despite the construction of 5,500 kilometers of railway, just one-third of the 16,000 kilometers stipulated by the plan. The massive dam across the Dnieper River was built rapidly, and industrial centers and complexes developed at the same speed in Ukraine, the Volga Basin, the Ural Mountains, and the Kuzbass. The second Five-Year Plan was more modest, balanced, and reasonable. It curbed investment growth and obtained excellent results from 1934 to 1936, in part thanks to the completion of factories and plants that were started during the first plan. The Moscow Metro was inaugurated in 1935 during the second plan. All in all, industrial growth exceeded 10 percent per year during the decade 1928–1937, greater than in Japan, where industrial production grew just under 9 percent per year in the 1930s. In the twelve years from 1929 to the German invasion, the Soviet Union built nine thousand major industrial enterprises. The Red Army's resistance to the invader from 1942 would not have been possible without the metallurgical plants developed or established after 1928, especially in Siberia and the Ural Mountains. They helped to save Europe from Nazi domination that might have spread from Brest to Vladivostok.[18]

On the eve of the war a first stage had thus been achieved in a feverish and chaotic atmosphere and at a record speed. The result was impressive: backward Russia was in the process of modernizing itself. That feat came at a price, both monetary (due to financial irresponsibility) and, more still, in human suffering, including a decline in living standards. The Bolsheviks drove their workers harder and paid them less, all in the name of socialist construction. They lowered wages and raised targets. The childish fascination with machines ("we are becoming a nation of metal, motors and tractors," exulted Stalin) revealed the fact that revolutionary goals were identified with material progress. Socialist construction consisted of reversing backwardness, in other words, achieving primitive accumulation by doing as well or better than the capitalists at exploiting the workers. Or alternatively, achieving the work started by Peter the Great and pursued by none other than Nicolas II: "A powerful industrial state with a big army was what the Bolsheviks were building—a state project no different from the one they had rebelled against" (Vladimir Brovkin). A revolution to return to the past!

Indeed, despite the modernizing frenzy, the system continued to perpetrate archaic practices (such as obsolete social structures) and reinforce the more sinister aspects of Russia's past. The state's tentacles stretched out still further and oppression increased.[19] It was a "conservative modernization" (Anatoli Vichnevski) in another sense too. With the exception of cash crops, collectivized agriculture was stagnating. The blame lay not solely on the revolutionary entrepreneurs' decision to "advance on one leg" (to use a Maoist term). The extent of Russia's backwardness and the massive scale of the modernization project also explain why "Soviet modernity always remained moored to its agrarian legacy" (Lynne Viola). Nevertheless it was achieved so rapidly that it conferred not only considerable power to the regime but also a sort of legitimacy—as in postrevolutionary China at the dawn of the third millennium—but with one difference: in China, economic progress went hand in hand with an improvement in living standards.[20]

However, the subject of this book is not China today, but the China of yesterday and the day before that. As I have said, the Communists' revolutionary mission was triggered by the need to catch up with the imperialist West. That was therefore the priority once they came to power—or rather three years later, after they had dealt with reconstruction and the battle against inflation. China's backwardness was so flagrant and a desire to reestablish the country's grandeur and prosperity was so widely shared by the elite that any kind of nationalist coming to—or remaining in—power would have pursued the very same goal. The divergences were related to the means for achieving it. For the Communist victors of the civil war, the way was clear: follow the model of the pioneers, the "elder Soviet brothers," as the Chinese called them in the 1950s, before denouncing Soviet revisionism and imperialism.

To rise to power, Mao had innovated, confident of being able to Sinicize Marxism. In fact, like Lenin before him, he had simply adapted to the national situation: a country far less industrialized and with a greater proportion of peasants relative to Russia in 1917. He had no qualms about copying the Stalinist development model to construct a modern nation. The nagging question that had dogged both Lenin and Trotsky was, "why did the Jacobins fail and how can we avoid that?" In March 1921, Lenin compared the recent victory over the White Army with the Jacobin's "spring of victory" (1794)—as something not to rejoice in but to be concerned about (after all, these victories were closely followed by the fall of Maximilien Robespierre). Outside events (famine, peasant revolts, the Kronstadt rebellion, etc.) obliged him to abandon wartime communism in favor of the NEP, but the fear of repeating Robespierre's mistake was also a contributing factor. While the influence of the Bolshevik Revolution on Mao was clearer, and above all more direct, than that of Robespierre on Lenin, Mao did not linger on its failures, errors, or crimes.

Like the Soviets, Mao wasted no time in launching an initial Five-Year Plan (1953–1957). Based on the first Soviet plan, it stressed maximum effort, absolute priority toward heavy industry, and low investment in agriculture. Mao was unconcerned about the costs and setbacks of the Soviet experience, about which in any case he knew little. Nor did he linger on the contrast between the inherited demographic and economic situations in either country: there were nearly ten times more Chinese people per hectare of arable land in 1949 than Russians in 1917. The Chinese relied on a far slimmer food security margin than did the Russians, and the pace of economic growth was much more susceptible to climate. From the first Five-Year Plan (which was a success, compared to what followed or the Ukrainian famine of 1932–1933) the neglect of agriculture caused industry to advance unevenly and sometime even brought it to a standstill. A major consumer industry such as the cotton industry would at times be restrained from full capacity due to a lack of raw materials. The considerable fluctuations in the cotton harvest were due to the previous year's weather, and when these led to a shortfall in the grain harvest, cash crops (including cotton) had to be reduced in favor of cereals.

The lesson of the first Five-Year Plan was clear: economic growth depended on the levels and fluctuations of agricultural production. To neglect agriculture was to jeopardize key industrial expansion. To some extent, that was the lesson Mao learned from the first plan, since he then inaugurated a "Chinese way," supposedly free of the Soviet model. The goal of the Great Leap Forward (GLF) was to remedy the imbalance of the first plan by advancing on both legs: a rural one, using China's abundant labor force to build massive irrigation projects or produce steel in the countryside, and an industrial one, which would continue to drain off capital and technology, which were in far shorter supply.

The fact that the rural leg included steel and hydraulic construction projects showed that Mao's emancipation from the Soviet model was tenuous. Mao challenged one model but got bogged down in another, as witnessed by his successive statements: "The road taken by the Soviet Union is our model," he declared in 1955 during the first plan. This didn't prevent him from declaring ten years later, "We cannot continue to follow the old paths of economic development of other countries and crawl behind them."[21] Mao was perfectly entitled to factor in experiences and omissions—he should have done so earlier—but Stalin's trajectory is easier to understand than that of his disciple. As I mentioned earlier, from around 1934 Stalin changed his first Five-Year Plan strategy to allow better control of development, more methodical planning, and a less excessive imbalance among the various branches of the economy, with less brutal shocks. Stalin even authorized a relative easing compared with the earlier frenzy (or used it as a pretext) declaring that "life has improved." Mao, on the other hand, nurtured as he was on Soviet texts from the early 1930s, remained faithful to the "revolutionary Stalinism" of the first plan, which better suited his impatient nature. He saved his criticisms for the "bureaucratic Stalinism" of the second Five-Year Plan and later, if only because of the social implications, starting with the emergence of a new class, which ran counter to his egalitarian ideal.[22]

We should not be surprised therefore that despite some of its stated principles, the GLF continued to focus on heavy industry, in line with the first Soviet and Chinese plans. Heavy industry obtained even more investment, leading Mao to speculate that steel production might double within a year. As its name suggests, the GLF was not content with advancing but sought to leap. Even when Mao decided to distinguish himself from the Soviet model and pursue an original path to development, he continued to stress heavy industry and the fast pace of industrialization. The plan to catch up to and surpass the oldest capitalist nation (Great Britain) was reminiscent of Stalin's objectives in the early 1930s with regard to the advanced capitalist nations.

The similarities don't stop there. In 1958 as in 1929, planning obeyed voluntarist objectives dictated by ideology, which made a mockery of any obstacle. Mao frequently revised upward his steel production target, exactly as had occurred in Russia earlier, even though the objective had been utopic from the start. In addition to having similar goals, such as focusing at all costs on heavy industry, the plans shared many other identical features. Take for instance the enthusiastic (rather than resigned) acceptance of economic imbalance, the disregard for specialists and cautious planners, and the manipulation of statistics. Even the slogans were the same (the expression "great leap forward" had already been used to describe the second Stalinist revolution), except that Mao transferred the Bolsheviks' "nothing is impossible" to the Chinese people. In many ways and despite Mao's claims to originality, the GLF was a disastrous replica of the negative aspects of the first Soviet plan, failing even to take into account later Soviet corrections to it.

In other ways however, the GLF introduced pragmatic elements that ultimately might have been successful in a different political context. For instance the Chinese use of intermediate technology, the development of small rural industries, and the systematic use of the underemployed agricultural labor force during the slack season were all GLF prescriptions that had proved fruitful in Japan, Taiwan, and South Korea, and improved the fate of the next generation of Chinese. Unfortunately even sensible measures turned out to be detrimental and sometimes even disastrous because of incessantly higher targets, the lack of preparation, and the disorder and "statistical fiasco," about which Li Choh-ming devoted an entire chapter of his pioneering work.[23] One example is decentralization, necessary when the GLF strategies demanded it but, because of the nature of the regime, served only to exacerbate the imbalance, encouraging local and regional cadres to outdo each other on the principle that it was, "better to err on the left than on the right."

Following the failure of the GLF and the ensuing famine (see chapters 4 and 5 below), Mao drifted further still from the Stalinist economic development strategy, which he had applied to the letter until 1957. Stalin never lost sight of his goal to modernize Russia and continued to steer the course, except that the Nazi threat shifted the emphasis to the armaments industry. With Mao, the need to catch up contradicted (and conflicted with) the ideal of social equality. It was as though he sought to belittle, if not the extent of the GLF disaster (difficult to refute) for which he was first and foremost to blame, but its significance and impact. I am uncharitably attributing to him an ulterior motive along the lines of "We suffered a setback but our originality and our principal task lies on a higher plane, above mere material well-being."

To be fair, Mao's social concerns (which I shall attempt to analyze and assess in chapter 3) were sincere. Regarding economic development, which concerns us here, we should not forget that China began at a far lower level than Russia and that the GLF did later produce results. The industrial infrastructure built in haste during the GLF bore fruit some years after the disaster, rather as the second Soviet plan benefited from the accelerated pace of construction during the first. In the Mao years and under his aegis, heavy industry developed considerably, albeit at a slower pace than Soviet industry between 1929 and 1941—and even agriculture made modest progress, thanks first to irrigation and later to the "green revolution." This was adopted in China before the end of the Maoist era (in the full Cultural Revolution) and entailed a combination of mechanized irrigation, chemical fertilizers, and seed selection. The latter was very efficient and increased yields. Yet until the early 1980s the Chinese peasantry still lived by its ancient rhythm, "the water-buffalo pulling the plough in the rice paddy, women in rows transplanting each clump of rice by hand, and the harvesters cutting the stalks with a sickle," as Claude Aubert described it.[24]

Given the greater progress accomplished in other areas (health, education; see below), China did not stagnate during the Maoist era, but advanced less rapidly than the capitalist world. The hoped-for catching up did not occur, and the gap even grew wider. The contrast with the Taiwanese economic miracle is massive. The loser in 1949 won the next lap. Of course it is far harder to develop a continent than an island, especially since the island in question had benefitted from initial modernization under colonialism, despite its exploitative nature. To return to China, it is almost as though the modernization project that began under the Republic and was then interrupted by war and subsequently pursued by the Communists during the 1950s, suffered from the deadlock of revolutionary strategy. I admit that this somewhat offhand shortcut is short on compassion (China did after all modernize under Mao), but nevertheless something was lacking. Here was a backward country that embraced revolution in order to close the gap with the West, but so long as it stayed revolutionary (until 1978), that gap merely widened.

China has caught up today. While far from being as rich and powerful as Western public opinion would believe, the country is now on the right track with a solid base. The Chinese nationalists are thankful for this success, and the Chinese people have profited from and accrued the dividends of development, albeit in a very unequal fashion as this "Communist society" is one of the most inegalitarian in the world. One could be tempted to blame this on Mao's successors, so-called Thermidorians who betrayed Maoism and the revolution. In fact between 1978 and 1985, those successors began by reducing the most glaring inequality of all: the chasm between city and country dwellers, but then proceeded to increase it further. Contemporary inequality, in part inherited, is growing within a framework, and thanks to a system, erected by Mao. During his lifetime there had been relative equality within each of the two universes (the privileged urban one and the miserable rural one), which scarcely concealed the poverty in both cases. In all, Mao lost on both counts. At the time of his death China had not caught up with other nations and, as we shall see in chapter 4, the living standards of the poorest segment of the population (the peasants in the west and in the hinterland) were equal to or below those of their grandparents in 1933, under the former regime.

Qita

Qita in Chinese means "the remainder"—in this case everything related to catching up, without measuring it in tons of wheat or rice, or coal and steel. In some areas such as urbanization, catching up was simply a corollary to industrialization. Elsewhere it required deliberate effort and was pursued zealously with unequal results, depending on the period and the revolution in question. There remains one domain, education, where a voluntarist policy obtained remarkable and rapid results in the Soviet Union and China alike.

Urbanization as a consequence of economic development

Unsurprisingly, urbanization advanced far more slowly in China than in the Soviet Union. The cities developed fairly rapidly during the first Five-Year Plan, and faster still during the GLF, after which more than twenty million "new" city dwellers were sent back to their villages during and after the famine. Until Mao's death, the urban population stagnated as a percentage of the total population (at around 20 percent throughout the 1970s). The slow pace of economic development, particularly in the service sector, was not the sole cause of this stagnation. The *hukou*, a kind of domestic passport (similar to that instituted by the Soviet Union in December 1932), was codified during the GLF and forbade peasants from leaving the villages of their birth. Its alleged purpose was to prevent the emergence of slums (something Chinese propaganda boasted about throughout the 1960s), but the measure mainly checked the overload on the cities, which were unable to provide food and work for a massive inflow of immigrants. During the last Maoist decade, another measure with more modest demographic consequences relieved the cities of some seventeen million "educated youths" (high school pupils at the end of their secondary education) when they were packed off to the countryside.

Those young people returned to the cities after Mao's death, but there are other, less specific explanations for the rapid urban growth of the past decades. The first is administrative, since a far less rigid application of the *hukou* gave rise to a massive rural exodus. Next and more important was the economic takeoff, for the peasants would not have flocked to the cities had there been no work for them. Since Mao's death the urban population has more than doubled, and today China has slightly more urban (over 700 million) than rural residents (640 million). However, the definition of an urban population was changed several times, with the cities sometimes encompassing far more than the market gardens surrounding them.

These more numerous city dwellers are better housed than they were under Mao, with the exception of the *mingong* (young villagers seeking work in the cities), who would envy the conditions of the undocumented immigrants in France today. In 1978, the inhabitants of the fourteen largest cities in China (with a total population of around 100 million) lived in an average of three square meters per inhabitant versus six square meters in 1949 after the civil war. Constructing housing and developing the road infrastructure were not priorities for Mao, any more than they were for Stalin. What has grown far worse in the post-Mao era is the pollution in which those unfortunate citizens live.

In the Soviet Union, urbanization advanced far more rapidly. After the Great Turn it accelerated further but was imbalanced and poorly controlled, to the point of transposing to the cities the "idiocy" that Marx associated with rural life.[25] The urban population leaped from 26 to nearly 56 million between 1926 and 1939. Three-quarters or four-fifths of those 30 million new urban dwellers were peasants, many of whom wanted to escape dekulakization or collectivization. In 1926 the urban population accounted for only 18 percent of the total population, rising to just under one-third in 1939, but after that eighty-nine cities had a population of 100,000 or more, compared with only thirty-one in 1926. During the first Five-Year Plan, the Moscow and Leningrad regions each acquired 3.5 million new inhabitants, while the population in the new industrial centers such as Dnepropetrovsk, Chelyabinsk, Novosibirsk, and Kuznetsk, increased five- or sixfold in just a few years.[26] Unlike in China, this urbanization was permanent. It continued to advance during the Communist era (two-thirds of urbanites in 1990), whereas in China it really took off only after the revolution was finally laid to rest.

Magnitogorsk ("the magnetic mountain") was the symbol of these new industrial centers (see Box 1).

Box 1

Magnitogorsk, City of The Future

Magnitogorsk was supposed to incarnate the cities of the future, the first in the world to be planned from start to finish, boasting beautiful urban areas with large avenues, founded on education and science instead of ignorance, superstition, and exploitation. In actual fact Magnitogorsk developed despite of, rather than because of, preestablished plans. Most new arrivals lived in tents until they could be crammed into shacks, supposedly temporary but never replaced. Every day the train unloaded 400 or more immigrants, who were also squeezed 150 at a time into housing meant to hold 40. Some immigrants built huts in the middle of the countryside (the city spread over 100 square kilometers), which enabled them to raise chickens, pigs, or cows. Nevertheless buildings were erected at great speed, and would later have to be rebuilt because the taps leaked, toilets lacked flushing system, and the windows had no glass: they were mere openings stuffed with rags. Furthermore it was difficult to heat such buildings since coal was reserved for factory use. The shacks were even worse, with occupants complaining that it was colder inside than out, where the ground remained frozen for several months on end. Residents slept in their coats wearing fur hats. Yet central heating was available in the Kirov district, set aside for the specialists and the skilled workmen who had somehow deserved it, or knew how to win favor with the authorities. However, the most privileged were the foreign experts and senior cadres who had well-equipped individual houses in the center of a gated residential area, equipped with its own services.[*] Nor did such segregation in the homeland of egalitarianism stop there. The kulaks brought back from deportation to work on this new industrial project were placed in a "kulak gulag" in the suburbs, surrounded by barbed wire. Conversely, the gates were left open in the penal colony housing some ten thousand delinquents, for they were considered "class allies" and not class enemies like the kulaks. It was a short-lived illusion. The class allies escaped and perpetrated robberies and murders, so in 1932 barbed wire was erected around their housing.

The entire city can almost be described as a conglomeration of suburbs, mostly between eight to ten

---

[*] This description, borrowed from Kotkin (1995, pp. 125–127), reminds me, in a more luxurious vein, of the cadres' housing in Nanjing, which made a similar impression on me almost four decades ago.

kilometers away from the factory or the mine. These were reached by a long walk to a distant bus stop, where people had to wait for a slow bus, usually running late. Entire districts were served only by a single, poorly lit earthen road, dotted with large puddles of dirty water, scattered with piles of rubbish and open toilets. The drains were trenches open to the elements, and some districts suffered a ten-year water shortage. In 1931 there was a typhus epidemic, followed by malaria in 1932 and 1935. The hospital was ill-equipped, initially with only one doctor in charge. The schools had far too many pupils, so half attended in the morning, the other half in the afternoon. And despite the professed desire to eradicate "rural backwardness," the authorities turned a blind eye to the cows, pigs, and gardens surrounding the huts of the transplanted peasants, for they helped to alleviate a chronic food shortage.

Source: Kotkin, 1995, pp. 18, 20, and 33, as well as the entire chap. 3, pp. 106–146.

As a rule the situation was worse in "socialist building sites" such as Magnitogorsk than in the rest of the Soviet Union, but only just. City dwellers had an average living space of four square meters per inhabitant, or one room per family, often in a communal apartment. Cities other than Magnitogorsk, first and foremost Moscow, also became "ruralized." That was already the case before 1917, and intensified when so many urban areas sprung up in the countryside lacking any real urban environment or adequate infrastructure, giving an impression of unfinished urbanization. Usually cities take over their suburbs, but here the suburbs wormed their way right into the city center. Conditions worsened during the first plan when millions of immigrants flocked to the cities. The government was unconcerned with constructing housing, let alone water and sanitation infrastructure. That chronic shortage became a serious crisis when the Nazis destroyed the western Russian cities, resulting in waves of refugees fleeing east. During the last decade of Stalinism, the daily life of city dwellers in the hinterland, standing in line at water pumps and haggling with their neighbors over a bucket of dirty water, picking their way across mountains of excrement and garbage (collected only twice a year), was scarcely more enviable than the situation in Magnitogorsk ten or twenty years earlier.[27] Millions of Russian citizens would not have access to a family home with running water, gas, indoor plumbing, or (sometimes) central heating until the 1960s. Although the program launched by Nikita Khrushchev in 1957 failed to reach its objective of solving the housing shortage before 1970, it did give rise to massive urban construction projects.[28]

In this urban development model, natural economic relationships flourished in the twentieth century and competed with central planning. There was no real estate market as such, and housing was designated. Consequently city dwellers were not allowed to move to another city unless they managed to arrange a housing swap.[29] Despite all this, it was deemed a privilege to live in the city, and from December 1932 urbanites were granted domestic passports that were not available to country dwellers. Anatoli Vichnevski defined urban society at the time as "intermediary, semi-urban and semi-rural." That was no mean feat. The growth of the urban population and the rise in the number of cities were themselves factors of modernization and steps toward "catching up." Millions of people benefited from Soviet society's cumbersome urbanization process, but also from the other aspects of catching up mentioned in this chapter. "It could only be a matter of reducing the gap, and that is what occurred."[30]

Health and the demographic transition: More than a mere corollary to modernization, especially in China

While the pace of urbanization faithfully replicated the pace of economic development, the same did not hold true when a voluntarist policy boosted modernization. In China especially, modernization straggled in contrast with the impressive and speedy progress made in health and the demographic transition thanks to a targeted policy. Certainly, life expectancy rose worldwide after 1950 and decreasing mortality in the developing world preceded the fall in the birth rate. But this dual decline occurred more rapidly in China than elsewhere. Unlike the downturn in the birth rate, the fall in mortality did not wait until the last Maoist decade to make a decisive advance. Indeed, it was a spectacular falloff from the first decade. Health care and widespread prevention, mainly through vaccination campaigns, led to sharp reductions in most contagious and parasitic diseases such as tuberculosis, plague, leprosy, cholera, diphtheria, venereal diseases, malaria, and schistosomiasis, among others. Some were even eradicated. Measles mortality stood at 9 percent in 1950, falling to 2 percent in 1958.[31] Within ten years, infant mortality fell by two-thirds according to official estimates, which tended to exaggerate the progress made, but before the famine children certainly survived better than ever before in China. According to the same statistics, the rate today is a mere one-sixth of that around 1950. Even when China was far poorer than it is now, the country had more doctors per ten thousand inhabitants, more nurses, and more hospital beds than developing countries with "intermediary living conditions" and between three and four times more than the average in countries as poor as China was then. Furthermore, health care was cheap—at least for urbanites—as was medication. That is far less true today, but progress has continued on all other fronts. Life expectancy (officially at seventy-three years, almost twice the 1949 level) is nearly as high as in the West and, as in the West, people are now dying more of cancers (exacerbated by pollution, it is true) and cardiovascular disease than from infectious diseases, despite the ravages of AIDS.

The sudden and lasting improvement in health in China made the demographic transition all the more urgent. Here, as in other areas, ignorance and dogmatic illusions fed on Marxist anti-Malthusianism—not to mention national pride—wasted precious time. Mao's initial optimism was an extension of his predecessors' population theory, starting with Sun Yat-sen. In Sun's Three Principles of the People, he suggested that if China learned from Europe, as Japan had done, it might be worth ten major powers since China's population was ten times greater. For the more lucid Chinese, the results of the 1953 census were disturbing, yet with the exception of a few large cities, a birth control policy was not imposed until the early 1970s.

Since then, however, a sustained effort has been made, despite concessions to resistance among couples, especially in the countryside. The results have been spectacular. They were already impressive in the 1970s and noteworthy after that. The total fertility rate of between 1.5 and 1.6 children per woman is not as low as that in Germany, Spain, or Italy, but is below that of the United States and France. The official rate is an underestimate since censuses and published surveys play down the total population. Frequently, when the parents ran the risk of sanctions, births were not declared, often with the complicity of local Communist cadres who risked criticism if they declared too many excess births. Nevertheless, official statistical bias does not impact the overall assessment, which is that the demographic transition in China was very rapid, even brutal, and will continue albeit in a less punishing way. In the not-so-distant future, the aging of the population, already under way, will diminish natural growth by helping to raise the mortality rate and lower the birth rate. Within a few decades the most populated country on the earth will no longer be China but India, and the total Chinese population could even start to fall within about fifteen years. The numbers will continue to cause serious problems, if only for the economy and the environment, but the worst is over. That was one challenge, and no mean one at that, which the Chinese revolutionaries dealt with—although it was a pity that they had not conquered such an urgent problem sooner.

The manner in which it was dealt with is, of course, another matter. The methods used were restrictive, the best known being the one-child policy, imposed for thirty-five years, which led to countless tragedies such as forced abortions after the seventh month of pregnancy, compulsory sterilization, infanticide, and others. The policy was relaxed on several occasions and later became obsolete, if only because it was necessary to slow down the rapid aging of the population. Indeed the age pyramid will become inverted and the tricky unemployment issue solved, but a new problem is emerging: old-age pensions. That was the price to pay for the brutal fall in fertility and the longer life expectancy. Instead of a "demographic bonus," contributing to the economic boom of the past three decades (fewer old men and children to be fed by a large workforce, in better health), China must now confront a disadvantage in the decades to come. The workforce has peaked and is beginning to fall, with those over sixty-five becoming increasingly numerous. Unlike the situation in Europe and Japan, the Chinese population will grow old before getting rich.[32]

In contrast with birth control, the Chinese Communists did make an early attempt to modernize in a related area—marriage and the family—before backtracking in the face of tradition and people's mentalities. The new marriage law of May 1950 extended the freedoms acquired a generation earlier by the intelligentsia and a slim layer of the urban bourgeoisie to the population as a whole. The law banned child marriages, arranged marriages, concubines, and infanticide. The minimum age for marriage was set at eighteen years for women and twenty for men, and divorce by mutual consent was permitted. The measures met with strong resistance in the countryside, where the patriarchal family remained the rule, based as it was on a hierarchy of obligations and unequal rights. More willing to "disrupt the organization of public affairs than that of their private lives" (M.-C. Bergère), the Communist cadres found a hundred and one ways of getting around the law. The rural population they governed nicknamed the marriage law "the divorce law" or "the women's law," since women mainly resorted to it, sometimes risking their lives, being mistreated as they were or beaten by a husband they were obliged to marry by force.[33] Be that as it may, the number of divorces rose during the first years of the regime; the tyranny of mothers-in-law on their daughters-in-law decreased, and child marriages along with infanticide all but disappeared, before a new upsurge with the imposition of the one-child family. Until recently rich men supporting one or several concubines was an antiquated notion, yet that practice too has reappeared.

Arranged marriages resisted the best. The Party relaxed its efforts after 1953 because it had other urgent matters to deal with and did not want to battle peasants' prejudices in other areas than those relating to their attachment to the land, which was about to be collectivized. Similarly for divorce, which the Party did not forbid. However, being unavowedly Confucian, it continued to preach marital harmony, even as a prerequisite to gender equality. That equality was the official ideal, but, like so many other Maoist aphorisms, the well-known "Women hold up half of heaven" was an empty slogan. As in the Soviet Union, women were "liberated" to work, including to carry out heavy menial tasks, but rarely paid as much as their male counterparts. In collectivized agriculture most women earned fewer work points than men. Nevertheless, the authority of the *pater familias* declined—but to the benefit of the Party, which imposed its own mediation in the event of conjugal disputes, and set political and social origins for the selection of a spouse. A Party member could not even think of taking the daughter of a landlord as his wife! However, we should not lay the entire blame for the relative failure of women's emancipation on the Party. It was also due to social resistance, especially in the countryside. These difficulties were proportionate to the massive task of catching up, to which they were now inextricably linked. At the end of the three-decade revolutionary period, the tasks accomplished in this domain were as noticeable as they were incomplete.

While Chinese Communism inherited a population surplus, Soviet Communism bequeathed to postrevolutionary Russia a country in demographic decline. For almost half a century the fall in the birth rate had gone hand in hand with a decrease in life expectancy, especially in men,[34] even though the opposite was true worldwide. That had not always been the case. In 1917 the demographic transition had barely begun and was a long way from catching up to Western European levels. Before 1914, the total fertility rate (which stood at 7.1 children per woman in 1900) was as high as it was in China before 1937 and at least twice as high as in Western Europe. While mortality also remained well above European levels, early marriage (under twenty-one years for 47 percent of women) and the absence of any form of contraception led to an annual population increase of two million. Revolution, war, and civil war halted this growth, leading to a fall in fertility and birth rates, both of which began to decline rapidly and lastingly from the mid-1920s. Unlike in China, that fall was not the result of a deliberate policy, but belatedly followed a classic trajectory that was scarcely influenced by government decisions—except that divorce by mutual consent, legislation on abortion, literacy, and women's labor very quickly led to couples having fewer children.

In fact, in spite of localized overpopulation in the Central Black Earth Region, overpopulation was less of a problem for the Russians than it would be for the Chinese in the second half of the twentieth century. During the imperial period, "the vast Russian landmass was a greater concern than the size of a population that had no problems spreading out in it" (Alain Blum). Reducing mortality was considered more important than reducing fertility. As in China and numerous other countries, the epidemiological transition occurred rapidly thanks to mass vaccinations and numerous health and hygiene measures. Later, the number of doctors doubled while the number of hospital beds tripled between 1928 and 1940. Nevertheless, the Russian government did not fight death and disease with the same vigor as the Chinese; it was even largely responsible for the rise in the death rate in the early 1930s after the sharp fall of the previous decade. The cumulative impact of the famines of 1920–1921 and 1931–1933, the Great Terror, excess mortality due to gulags, World War II, and, more locally, the Ukrainian famine of 1946–1947 was more lasting than the 1958–1961 famine in China. In the years 1918–1922 and 1931–1949, ten million male deaths (nearly one-third of the total) were not from natural causes. In the long term, however, the demographic disaster could mainly be seen in the age pyramid. Blum rightly stressed "the incredible recovery mechanisms" of populations after the most violent crises and disturbances.

As with the decline in fertility, the fall in mortality began in the westernmost regions of the vast Soviet Union. From the Caucasus to Central Asia, the demographic transition lagged far behind that of Europe. As autonomy in social issues increased with regard to the Politburo's edicts (from the 1930s, propaganda increasingly failed to change mentalities and behavior), so geographic autonomy drew together fertile Muslim populations in a cultural space outside the Soviet Union. Indeed ethnic differences did not bow to political singularity, with all its impulses and constraints. Even in the European part of the Soviet Union, the 1936 law banning abortion led to only a passing and limited rise in fertility, which fell again after the war. The most blatant result of banning abortion, which had more ideological significance than any impact on demographic change, was that it became clandestine. The practice was first legalized in 1920, and the moral and nativistic about-turn in the second half of the 1930s led to it being banned again until Khrushchev's 1955 thaw. Before and after its abolition in 1936, abortion, rather than contraception, was key to the fall in fertility. Having no political freedoms, Soviet citizens felt at least that they had some demographic freedom, in other words a desire and ability to reduce births. Stalin's denial of the results of the 1937 census and his decision to include one million dead Kazaks from 1931, and five million dead Ukrainians, Caucasians, and Russians from 1932 to 1933, belong to another political/ideological chapter. It had no impact on the country's demographic evolution.[35]

Before the revolution, in rural Russia as in rural China, the patriarchal family constituted a kind of absolutist mini-state in which the *bolshak*, usually the father, played the role of czar. In line with the time lag we observed earlier, the revolt against paternal despotism began earlier in Russia than in China, at the end of the nineteenth century. Soon after the revolution and the civil war, there was a wave of attacks against the family, supposedly doomed, like prostitution, due to "disappear at the same time as ... private property and the oppression of women" (Bukharin). The turnaround of 1930 closed the door in authoritarian fashion on the sexual freedom of the 1920s. In the mid-1930s, "Thermidor in the Family," so criticized by Trotsky, rehabilitated the family unit, made divorce more difficult, imposed strict Victorian morals, and enforced modesty in artworks. As in China, but in a less fastidious way, the Party interfered in family issues, although without submitting people's private lives to such rigid control as their public lives. Neither the anti-family campaigns of the 1920s nor the conservative about-turn of the 1930s had a decisive influence on changes in mores. These, like demographic changes, were largely spontaneous. Overall they were influenced less by the government's contradictory directives (which in the early 1920s were not directives but, at best, exhortations by intellectuals and propagandists) than by factors such as the very large number of women in professional activities, as well as industrialization and urbanization.[36]

Education as a triumph of voluntarism

With the exception of Maoist health policy, voluntarist policies in China were either late in coming (e.g., birth control) or hesitant (in matters of mores). In the Soviet Union efforts were less sustained and results less brilliant. On the other hand both revolutions get good marks in education. The Soviet Union started from a higher level than China. In 1917, 43 percent of citizens aged nine or older could read, and books spread quite rapidly to the villages on the eve of the war. Nevertheless in the outer regions, such as the far north near Arkhangelsk, there were still villages in which no one had even heard of schools. With a few rare exceptions, that ceased to be the case from the 1920s on. The lack of cultural investment certainly delayed progress, especially in the countryside where 40 percent of the eight- to twelve-year-olds were still not in school at the end of the NEP. Ten years later, however, the education budget was seventeen times higher than in 1928, and one hundred times higher than in 1913. The following year (1939), if official statistics are to be believed, 81 percent of Soviet citizens aged between nine and fifty could read and write. Yet the education gap persisted or grew between the peasants (despite spectacular progress in supposedly backward rural areas such as Central Asia) and the workers who benefited from evening classes and had greater incentives to educate themselves. In Magnitogorsk in the 1930s, quite a few workers were reading Gorky, Tolstoy, and Turgenev, in addition to the newspapers, not to mention Nikolai Ostrovski's *How the Steel Was Tempered* and the translation of Henri Barbusse's biography of Stalin.[37]

Progress came later in high school education, where three million of eleven million children were enrolled at the end of the 1920s. It was then stymied at the beginning of the first Five-Year Plan by the need to rapidly train a large number of workers from the rural exodus. The number of high schools fell by two-thirds in 1930–1931 because they were converted into technical training centers. Gradually, however, the various industries opened their own professional schools, providing fast-track training until such time as the more traditional secondary school education could recover and develop. That occurred during the second Five-Year Plan, and in 1939 eighteen million children were enrolled in high school out of a total of thirty million in schooling. The emphasis, including in higher education, was mainly on professional training and technical skills, leading to the opening of many technological institutes. The number of students in all categories of schools grew spectacularly from 170,000 in 1928 to 810,000 in 1940, but of the eleven-million-strong "new people's intelligentsia" in 1939, barely two million had followed a complete higher or "specialized secondary" education cycle. On a more modest scale in the sphere of knowledge but higher in the spheres of power, the Stalin Industrial Academy in Moscow attempted to fill the educational lacunae of the more promising cadres with proletarian origins. These were almost all adults and included one Nikita Khrushchev, aged thirty-five when he was admitted to the academy in 1929 along with another hundred or so handpicked students.[38]

In addition to pursuing practical objectives, the promotion of education and cultural dissemination among the masses transformed the beneficiaries themselves, even though they were also subjected to incessant propaganda and zealous thought control (albeit less so than in China). By developing people's capacity for analysis and differentiating topics of knowledge, the highly specialized training gradually put an end to traditional syncretic mentalities. Ultimately, the "blend of propaganda, education and coercion" triggered an unstoppable trend.[39]

In China,[40] literacy and schooling made considerable advances right from the early Maoist period. In 1949 some 80 percent of people were illiterate, rising to 90 percent for women. During the GLF, 60 million people were mobilized to eradicate illiteracy within a period of three to five years. Nevertheless in 1990 there were 180 million illiterate people over the age of fifteen and only 85 million in 2000. That fall was a reflection less of (undeniable) progress than of the natural mortality of the older generation. Since official figures tend to underestimate, we can estimate that on the dawn of the twenty-five century the illiteracy rate stood at 8 percent, mainly among women, in rural areas, and in regions with ethnic minorities. That is ten times below the 1949 figure. The figures for school enrollment were comparable, the difference here being that progress occurred exclusively during the Maoist era. Only 25 percent of school-age children were in primary school in 1949, but more than 95 percent were when Mao died in 1976. The Maoist era may be subdivided into two stages: before and after the Cultural Revolution. Progress during the first stage was impressive. In 1966 about 36 percent of children completed primary school, against less than 7 percent in 1949, and over 10 percent finished junior middle school, compared with 2 percent in 1949. The proportions were far lower in the countryside, which was something the Cultural Revolution attempted to remedy, for in theory it made primary and even secondary education universal. In fact the years of schooling were cut and education standards declined.[41]

Since Mao's death, schooling has even regressed a little in the countryside, especially in the hinterland and the west of the country, which lag behind the rest of the country and where poor peasants hesitate to send their children to schools, which often require fees, are poorly equipped, and have improperly trained teachers. Whereas high school enrolment advanced enormously under Mao and has fallen back a little since, the reverse is true of higher education. Here progress occurred mainly during the reform period, and like China's economic takeoff, it was both considerable and rapid.

The result is an accepted inequality, an elitist choice that is the very opposite of Maoist egalitarianism. In Mao's lifetime, the avowed intention was to make education available to everyone, urban and rural populations alike. That claim, and the emphasis on technical and professional training, made China's educational policy very popular in the developing world. China's prestige declined sharply once that model was rejected and it became clear that egalitarianism under Mao had been flaunted far more than it had been practiced. From the early 1960s, schools and even kindergartens provided opportunities to the children of cadres and intellectuals that were denied to others, of one day being qualified for very selective higher education. Mao made the academic authorities responsible for this, but the system he had decreed during the GLF period had everything to do with it. The economy's "two legs" also held true for education: one oversized, neglected leg for teaching the masses to read and write, and another slender, well-nurtured one for training the elite.

The Cultural Revolution halted that inequality, but at the cost of leveling down, and even selection based on political and social criteria. In other words more children of workers, peasants, and cadres were admitted to higher education without exams. None of them really profited from that, given the considerable drop in standards and the duration of their studies—indeed if the schools opened at all, which was not often at the peak of the Cultural Revolution (1966–1969). As for research, it had languished prior to 1966 under the management of ignorant bureaucrats, and then ceased entirely until the end of the Maoist era. It has since had its revenge.

All in all, while higher education and research have developed mainly during the past three decades, quantitative progress in literacy and primary education largely occurred in Mao's time. The global results of sixty years of "Communism" (almost seventy years of Communism and over thirty-five years of rampant and unorthodox capitalism) nevertheless remain impressive. In access to higher education, the results are comparable to those of India and far better than most of the countries that used to be called "underdeveloped." The same is true in other areas, such as mass literacy and schooling, where China has outperformed India, even though the nine years of mandatory education decreed in 1998 are far from being respected. And of course we are not taking into account the very specific type of education and culture dispensed by a totalitarian regime. But that is true not just in China. The two revolutions will give me an opportunity to return to that.

The contradictory assessment of the two halves of this chapter is that Maoist China, while far more deficient in economic development, accomplished faster progress in education and health. Despite that, let us stress economic modernization: on Stalin's death Russia had partly caught up, whereas that was not the case in China on Mao's death. I will confront my privileged European viewpoint with one from the less privileged southern hemisphere. "For most of us, people of the South, China … remains one of the major success-stories of the century."[42] Nor did the author, Walden Bello, cofounder of Focus on the Global South, intend to restrict his comment to the last two decades of the century. In his overall assessment, Bello suggests that the achievements of Mao's successors were a continuation of his work—and made possible by Mao in the first place—rather than the result of a divergent trend. I do not share that viewpoint. I believe that it was *infidelity* to Mao's precepts that led to those achievements. The "revolutionaries" would have furthermore corrected my simplistic notion of "catching up" and transformed it into the more innovative and masterful concept of "modernization."

The problem is that they identify revolution with modernization. That was clear in the 1930s Soviet Union. It was precisely what Anton Ciliga deplored at the time, praised by Claude Lefort, because Ciliga did not "seek the growth of machines and factories in socialism, but rather the transformation of human relations." Instead Stalin pursued modernization from above, in the fashion of Peter the Great, which telescoped all the stages of development at great speed. That dislocated, fast-track model, together with an obsolete social structure, set the Party-state against the people.[43] As a result the state, which Marx and Engels had expected to decline (something Lenin repeated in his *The State and Revolution*), increased its powers and capacity for repression in order to impose its way—supposedly the only way true to the laws of history.

3. Politics

A regime that boasts about its emphasis on social issues requires everything to be political, right down to the last detail of social organization or technical equipment. From Leningrad to Guangzhou (Canton), the system operated in much the same way. The Chinese copied what Lenin had introduced and Stalin perfected. In this chapter, before identifying the inherent kinship between the two "brother" regimes, I review and compare the main features of their political developments from 1917 to 1953 and from 1949 to 1976, respectively. They diverged as a result of very different external circumstances, but nevertheless acquired a set of constants because of their shared Leninist matrix.

Stages ...

The most obvious contrast may be found in the first eleven years (1917–1928), which had no equivalent in China. Mao, who was China's Lenin and Stalin rolled into one, had supreme power from the very beginning, whereas Stalin had to take it little by little. The price of having recognized legitimacy as Supreme Leader, even before the regime was founded (from the Seventh Party Congress in 1945), was that the Chinese copy was immediately Stalinized, imitated the mature Soviet model. There was no equivalent in the People's Republic of China (PRC) of those early Soviet years during which Lenin had to fight to impose the Brest-Litovsk Treaty or the NEP on his reticent colleagues, nor of the relative freedom (compared to what followed) of the 1920s. There was no equivalent either for the civil war, since it had preceded the conquest of power, with its inevitable consequences on the methods used by the government in order to survive and conquer the enemy. Certainly the Chinese had to consolidate a victory that occurred almost too fast, put the finishing touches on it (in Tibet for instance), and lead a war on its borders (in Korea). Despite that, 1949–1952 was an easier and less dramatic period than the Bolsheviks' baptism by fire from 1918 to 1922, consisting as it did of civil war and peasant revolts, epidemics and famine. There was no need for an NEP in China, where the general sentiment was that the initial installation and consolidation had been successful. The new regime curbed the rampant inflation inherited from its predecessors, toppled the influence of the rural elite by promoting agricultural reform, and even resisted American imperialism in Korea. Consequently it was possible to get down to "socialist construction" immediately—at least that was what Mao, as usual more dogmatic and impatient than his lieutenants, believed.[1] The first Five-Year Plan (1953–1957) was a replica of the first Soviet plan (1929–1933), only Mao didn't have to wait twelve years to launch it. Nevertheless, it was at the end of that first plan that the PRC began to resemble its model even more dangerously, in this case the "second Soviet revolution." When Mao decided to launch the Great Leap Forward (GLF) in the fall of 1957, he made a break equal to that of Stalin's Great Turn in November 1929. The GLF, even more than the first Chinese plan, should be compared with the first Soviet plan, for they had in common excessive industrialization efforts and a shake-up of traditional rural life, and above all they triggered an even more serious crisis. In China, the rapid collectivization of land imposed from 1955 on a reluctant peasantry was only a foretaste of the trials and tribulations the peasants later suffered, further exacerbated by the GLF. First and foremost of these was the famine (1958–1962), a direct consequence of the GLF, even more so than the Soviet collectivization's impact on the 1931–1933 famine.

The two dictators suffered the repercussions. Even before the Ryutin affair there were murmurs in the Communist Party of the Soviet Union (CPSU) that "Bukharin, [Alexei] Rykov and [Mikhail] Tomsky were right."[2] In China, on the contrary, the Peng Dehuai Affair preceded Liu Shaoqi's belated 1961–1962 awakening. It would take more than that to shake the absolute domination of the two dictators, even though they still had to wait a few years before ridding themselves of anyone who had dared to express opinions that differed from theirs. And that leads us to another sinister similarity: 1937–1938 in the Soviet Union and 1966–1968 in China (see chapter 9).

After that the two regimes went their separate ways again, as during the civil war, but this time due to a foreign invasion. Whatever Maoist propaganda might have claimed, China was never threatened by American imperialism in the same way the Soviet Union was threatened by Hitler. There was no "Great Patriotic War" in China, at most threats and local incidents, such as the 1969 Sino-Soviet border conflict for which China was the main culprit and which drew China closer to "American imperialism"— despite having rebuked Khrushchev for attempting to build a "peaceful coexistence" with that very same imperialism. From 1945 to 1946, Stalin dashed all the hopes of opening and change desired by so many Soviet citizens after the hardships of a very bloody war. The final years (Zhdanov, followed by anti-cosmopolitanism and anti-Semitism), exacerbated by the personal powers and stubbornness of an aging tyrant, were a fairly good foretaste of Mao's own appalling last five years (1971–1976), when he proved to be totally unable to extricate his country from the mess of a poorly conceived and led Cultural Revolution. Late Maoism's inexorable degeneracy crudely evoked late Stalinism, with a similar wait for the almighty leader to depart. It was an interminable wait in China, but in Russia it occurred opportunely in the first days of March 1953, in a dacha near Moscow. Everyone was well aware that nothing would change so long as the obstacle to that change had not breathed his last.

... and Similarities

In that brief overview I gave a unilateral opinion, which I must now explain. I dated the moment when the Chinese regime dangerously began to resemble its Stalinist model as 1957. Yet it was in around 1956–1957 that the Chinese Communists, Mao first and foremost, began to harbor doubts, and then express criticisms, about the model they had unswervingly followed until then. It is indisputable (and it would be bad form to deny it) that the Soviets had the most direct and far-reaching influence during the initial 1950–1956 period and that the Chinese accepted it gratefully and unhesitatingly. The tenet of the propaganda's repeated declarations was that *laodage*, "elder brother," had acquired vast experience and was generously enabling China to benefit fromit.[3] Mao subjected the Communist cadres to intensive study sessions of the Communist bible, *The History of the Communist Party of the Soviet Union (Bolsheviks): Short Course* (1938). During the 1953 study campaign the cadres were divided into three levels, elementary, intermediary, and advanced, that level being reserved for ministers and other high-ranking leaders. All participants had to read and reread the book, learn that catechism of untruths by heart, convince themselves of the validity and virtues of the correct way that led from Lenin to Stalin and triumphed over the incorrect way that was incarnated in turn by the Plekhanovs, Trotskys, and Bukharins. When the Gao Gang Affair came to light in 1954, followed by Hu Feng in 1955, the practical application was automatic. The fallen leader (Gao Gang) and repressed intellectuals (Hu Feng and his clique) incarnated the successive manifestations of an incorrect line that had to be fought relentlessly. It was easy enough to find the correct line since it was always the one taught by Chairman Mao. It was therefore enough merely to wish him a long life.[4]

For their part the Soviets sent some ten thousand experts and advisors to China between 1953 and 1957 to inculcate the methods and processes of consolidated Stalinism, as well as to teach technologies the Chinese could only dream of. A Chinese delegation spent eight months in the Soviet Union from August 1952 to April 1953, headed at the outset by Zhou Enlai, only the prime minister could not be absent from his country for too long. They visited factories and building sites, listened to conferences by specialists, and absorbed the Soviet experience firsthand so as to be able to draw up a first Chinese Five-Year Plan in the image of its Soviet counterpart. At the core of the first plan were 156 priority projects launched and achieved with Soviet help. I therefore do not dispute the important Soviet contribution to the progress made during that first plan—the most important accomplished in Mao's entire lifetime, with the exception of the initial return to order in 1949–1952. That contribution led to the conversion, or strengthened support, of the beneficiaries. As Gilbert Rozman put it, "Rarely has one great power become such a testing ground for the wholesale importation of another society's organizational and ideological blueprint."[5]

So why did that unfortunate reproduction of a model occur in the period after 1957 when it is a known fact that by then the Chinese were no longer satisfied with indiscriminate imitation, and the following year even inaugurated a "Chinese way," which, by definition, was original? I shall attempt to demonstrate that this original way (imposed by Mao during the last two decades of his life, 1957–1976), which claimed to correct the Soviet model, was in fact inspired by the same ideals, radicalized by Mao. The Chinese way went further in the same direction and in doing so exacerbated the effects of the repeated traumas of the early 1930s: breakneck industrialization, dekulakization, famine, and the Great Purge. I shall not fail to point out that all the similarities reveal that Mao was tied to a model from which he never broke: maintaining the system and its organizational structures during the 1960s and 1970s, reproducing and even exaggerating its obsessive practices, and above all fanatically pursuing the stated goals (put aside once Stalinism was established and assured) and following an ideology that claimed to be different but in fact evolved just as Stalinism had before it, according to the political situation and the interests of the supreme guide.

That model was not a Leninist interpretation of Marxism but a Stalinist application of Leninism. Mao was inspired first and foremost by Stalinism, and that was the only model he was familiar with. In this brief reminder of the obvious similarities,[6] we will come to recognize the many Leninist traits inherited by Stalin, but the comparison really becomes essential when we consider the political system from 1929 to 1953. The preeminence of ideology, the osmosis between the Communist Party and the state, the control over the economy, the means of force and persuasion[7] —all these and other traits certainly refer to Leninism, but the reference was in fact to the ideology of the 1930s and the Party, which by now had become a mere conveyor belt. Add to that the economy during central planning phase and the fast-paced industrialization (the first Five-Year Plan), the NKVD rather than the Cheka, Andrey Zhdanov rather than Anatoly Lunacharsky, and a press mired in lies that made the leader writers in Lenin's time seem mere youthful amateurs.

I said in the beginning that everything was political, but I might just as well have said that nothing was political, for politics were forbidden and barely distinguishable from administration or government. In China as in the Soviet Union, administration was a façade, tightly controlled by the Party, which acted through it—or at least through the state institutions that played a real role. Those "real" institutions included the State Council (the government presided by Zhou Enlai), which was the Chinese equivalent of the Council of People's Commissars. The sole purpose of the "formal" institutions,[8] which included the National People's Congress (NPC), was to confer a democratic veneer on the Party's monopoly. As in its Soviet counterpart, NPC members were elected from a single list drawn up by the Party and served solely to ratify Party decisions. The plethora of other formal institutions included the presidency and the Chinese People's Political Consultative Conference, which was even more bogus than the NPC. Like the Stalinist constitution of 1936, the 1954 Chinese constitution guaranteed a full range of liberties. Alas, in real life the Chinese people could only dream of such freedoms and certainly did not benefit from them.

Even within the Party, the sole function of certain institutions, including at the central level, was to provide a semblance of democratic legitimacy to the absolute power of a handful of leaders. Convened on an irregular basis,[9] the national Party Congress "elected" the members of the Central Committee, preselected by the Party hierarchy. The same was true for the Central Committee's election of some twenty members to the Politburo. Everything occurred exactly as in the CPSU, except that after 1956 the Politburo itself was placed under a Permanent Committee. That four- to nine-member committee held all the remits of the Soviet Politburo. As suggested earlier, the two irremovable Party leaders respected their Party's statutes less and less. They convened Central Committee meetings whenever they wanted (which in China between 1962 and 1966 was never) and the same went for the Politburo meetings, when the leaders even bothered to show up. In the 1930s Stalin increasingly had his decisions approved by Vyacheslav Molotov and Lazar Kaganovich, whose signatures appeared at the bottom of documents alongside his. The (automatic) approval of the other members, consulted by telephone, was then added overleaf. After the war Stalin governed with the help of the Central Committee Secretariat, seconded by Georgy Malenkov, Zhdanov, and, after 1949, Khrushchev. But what is the point of lingering over those violations of norms and statutes by a regime that sent full and alternate members of the Politburo to the firing squad with as little regard as they might sweep leaves from the pavement, or a regime in which a Central Cultural Revolution Group, which had not the slightest legitimacy, regularly supplanted elected bodies (although of course the elections themselves …). Suffice it to say that in the Soviet Union the rules were increasingly cast aside during the 1930s, and the same was true of China in the 1960s.[10]

In addition to the redundancy of a dual Party-state, there were two more bodies that were independent of the state if not the Party: the army and the political police. The latter played an especially important role and was the leading instrument of terror, the very essence of totalitarianism according to Hannah Arendt. The political police was also the main source of private information for the leaders (and for historians of the Soviet Union today, as the OGPU archives become available). That information was circulated in a restricted manner and by degrees to the various levels of the nomenklatura. The information blackout to which the remainder of the population was subjected could not be as tight as the leadership wished, as inevitably some unimportant scraps of information reached the people, especially the more educated segments who probed for whatever truths they could glean between the lines and lies in the official press. It always came as a surprise that the "state secrets" revealed by dissidents were common knowledge. The charge of "revealing state secrets" was inevitably mentioned alongside the person's alleged crimes, however paltry the secret in question: revealing to the enemy that the earth is round, the Soviet Union vast, or China populated.

Was this the end of the façade? Not yet, but cracks were beginning to appear. In theory the politics behind every thought and deed were assessed in the light of ideology, that "secular religion"[11] that provided an answer to everything. In practice, monolithic power decided either according to the very ideology that was clouding its judgment, or depending on the opportunity of the moment, or else according to internal power struggles. The implied contradiction (a divided monolithic power) is easy to resolve. The party exercising that power was not only unique,[12] but united and unanimous and required total obedience and discipline from its members. It therefore displayed a façade of unanimity under all circumstances, each member adopting and defending the majority point of view without batting an eyelid, in accordance with Leninist theory. Or to be precise (and in accordance with good Stalinist/Maoist practice), they obeyed the orders of the supreme leadership of a highly hierarchical Party, which was content to echo the orders of its chief, the *vožd* or *helmsman* who was the sole interpreter of truth. When Trotsky unwisely proclaimed "the Party is always right ... we can only be right with and by the Party," he sanctioned in advance the more definitive "no man can be right against Stalin," which prevailed for nearly a quarter century. The same was true of Mao until his very last breath when he was in his eighties and people could no longer understand him when he spoke. The leader was infallible and thus ipso facto all-powerful, far more so than (let us stick to local traditions) Ivan the Terrible or Qin Shihuangdi. From the 1930s in the Soviet Union and from 1949 in China—even before the Communists came to power—no Party leader could rival the Party's Number One. Members of the Politburo and the Standing Committee were vassals, charged with ratifying and applying the decisions of an irremovable leader. It was the leader, be it Stalin or Mao, who declared the left or right policy shifts, as often as not giving the signal for more radical policies such as the Great Turn or Great Leap, but moderate decisions were also made by them and them alone. Consider, for instance, after the 1933–1934 famine when Stalin granted concessions and a few kind words to the kolkhoz peasants, or when Mao attempted to correct the excesses of the GLF in the spring of 1959. Contrary to claims made by Chinese propaganda—repeating Soviet propaganda— there was never a "two-line struggle," but at most muffled resistance to the only authorized line, the one drawn by the Supreme Leader. That was even clearer in the original version than in the copy. Unlike what was claimed in the canonical version of the history of Soviet politics in the 1930s, there was never a Politburo confrontation between a "moderate" line and a "hard" one.[13] No Politburo member contested the "general line," which was correct by definition since it emanated from the infallible leader. However, that line was a meandering one, given to detours and about-turns. It advanced in zigzags according to the tactics and successive choices of the sole decision maker.

On local and regional levels, numerous Party committee secretaries were small-time Maos and Stalins. They might be despotic to their subordinates but owed faultless obedience to their superiors. In theory they were elected but in fact were appointed on recommendation (*tuijian* in Chinese), or more often as not co-opted by the higher Party ranks. Clientelism and conformism played key roles in promotions. The intermediary and lower Party ranks did not always stick to executing orders and directives from above. Rather than reproduce an identical model they frequently made it even more brutal by exaggerating the radical aspect of the orientations set by the centers in Moscow and Beijing. Those zealots stood a good chance of being promoted, whereas anyone reticent to toe the line ran the risk of being sanctioned.

Going above or through their subordinates, the violence of the local Party despots was directed at the people as a whole, yet the famous "masses" (workers rather than peasants in the Soviet Union, primarily peasants in China) were supposed to be mobilized rather than terrorized. Their participation marked an important break from traditional tyranny. True believers were mostly recruited among the young, voluntarily mobilized outside of any class consideration.[14] Class itself was defined as much by origins and filiation than by individuals' work and role in the economy. Class became an objectivized notion and ended up looking much like the estates in France's ancien régime.[15] Or like the castes with their permanently ostracized "untouchables" (former aristocrats, priests, or kulaks in the Soviet Union, landowners and their descendants in China).[16] Together with other harmful elements, they were deemed to be the leading "parasites" to be purged from society. In addition to the gulf between those outcasts and the hallowed worker and peasant "masses," there was another equally important, if not more important, gulf between the people and the nomenklatura. The latter were the aristocrats of this new society of estates, which made the distinction between "them" and "us" and was a given from Leningrad (and Warsaw or Prague) to Guangzhou.[17]

Despite that, the Party's local and regional spin-offs succeed in controlling neither the vast Soviet territory, nor the massive Chinese population. Party auxiliaries (the Komsomol in the Soviet Union, the Communist Youth League in China) propagated its influence on young people. In other circles, that influence was relayed by mass organizations carefully controlled by the Party, whether they were for women, children, or trade unions. But even that was insufficient. Even though the regime was intentionally totalitarian, it never succeeded in being truly totalitarian in practice. That was correctly perceived in the criticisms of the totalitarian school by "revisionist historiography," as it was in the criticisms addressed to me over four decades ago, when one of my students grew angry at my use of the word "totalitarianism." According to Bernard Bruneteau, "A society is not just a passive area for the application of state coercion."[18] The subjects were not all subjugated or terrorized, some resisted, such as the Russian peasants in 1930 and the Chinese peasants in 1955, or else they got around the *ukase* by relying on friends, family, or the community. The State-party itself suffered from tensions between rival institutions or between the center and the periphery. The local Stalins and Maos allowed themselves considerable freedom of maneuver. As Merle Fainsod wrote as early as 1958, "the totalitarian façade concealed a host of inner contradictions."[19] In any case, the Party-state did not have the means to administer its vast empire lastingly and efficiently. In between mobilization campaigns, negligence (or abandonment), as much as constraint, was the order of the day. Worse, the Party believed itself omni-competent, but was not. There were failures in planning, since it was based on unreliable statistics, if not theoretical concepts that were refuted by a diverse and complex reality.[20] Applying Gosplan did not mean that it was applicable.

That was where the leaders' convenient use of the "anti-bureaucratic scenario"[21] came in, laying the blame for failures and malfunction on the bureaucrats (Party bureaucrats as much as state ones, supposing there is any point in that distinction). Administrators were inherited from Czarism or the Guomindang, whose skills were used for a time, necessarily disobeyed as a result of class hostility, whereas "our" administrators were lured by the sirens of the bourgeoisie (the experts, who warned of the dangers). They vacillated and were too weak to maintain a firm class line. Hatred and disdain for bureaucrats, those "chatterers," "crafty ones," "imbeciles," as Stalin variously described them,[22] anticipated Mao's own curses aimed at the Communist bureaucracy on the eve of, and during, the Cultural Revolution. Furious at not being obeyed in every way, the autocrats unleashed their spite on the first available scapegoats. Being calculating, they exploited the resentment felt by the people beneath their subordinates and encouraged their criticisms of the often arbitrary actions taken by the local and regional authorities. Stalin liked to play the good Czar, concerned with correcting the wrongdoings of the evil *boyar* (members of the nobility under the Tsars),[23] while Mao had no need for lessons from his master in this domain. But however calculating the two leaders may have been, they were sincere on occasion. Stalin's rage against the bureaucrat-saboteurs in his letters to Molotov was no pretense. In 1930 he truly believed them guilty of the sabotage he accused them of. Taken in by the biased explanations inspired by his ideology, he was blind to the proofs when "the logic of things" dictated another truth. He lost the intellectual capacity to grasp the causes of the problems he faced, as well as the consequences of his acts. The same was true of Mao; I shall return to that. To challenge their dogmatic faith was a capital crime against which the despots constantly protected themselves. According to Molotov the most serious affliction was lack of faith and the "ideology of incredulity" that gives rise to it.[24] We shall grant him that, even though he was a lapdog (or wolf!) devoted to his master, whom he served with the same loyalty as he served Marxism, which "makes utopia the motor for its scientistic assertions."[25]

Political life was marked by a similar frenzied pace, similar government methods, and the same desire to catch up in record time. That pace was marked by a series of political campaigns during which the state mobilized all means at its disposal in manpower and equipment to force nature to bend to human willpower. Not content with "abandoning the slow pace of the cart for … the rhythm of the machine" (Maurice Dobb), the respective governments imposed a military rhetoric, which some cautious individuals warned against (such as Groman in the Soviet Union or Chen Yun in China). The first Five-Year Plan (FFYP) in the Soviet Union and the GLF in China best illustrate this type of campaign, which Khrushchev still used in the 1950s to catch up with (and overtake) the United States. Thirty years before Khrushchev, agitprop was already launching campaigns in areas other than economic development, the first of which already took place in Lenin's lifetime, followed rapidly by many others in the 1920s (to stick to that decade alone). China was no exception, and in the space of six years, still during that initial period, it launched campaigns in fast succession that combined social transformation, ideological indoctrination, and, above all, political repression. As a rule, each campaign was followed by a pause, officially known as a "consolidation" phase, during which attempts were made to dress a few wounds and repair some damage. That is what Mao called "advancing in waves," alternating relentless struggle with periods of rest during which to recover.[26]

The same spirit inspired the quotas. Like the campaigns, the quotas switched easily between production objectives and the number of farms to collectivize or kulaks to deport in 1930, or counterrevolutionaries to crack down on or execute in 1937. Here too the Maoist response was disturbingly similar, whether in grain production during the FFYP or the percentage of landowners to execute per village or township during the agrarian reforms. The quotas, whether in production or in sentencing, were a minimum, freely increased by the authorities (or Mao himself on several occasions in 1958 with regard to steel production), or in response to demands by regional governments, keen to show their enthusiasm, for instance the allocated quotas of arrests during the Great Terror. Rather than ask the central authorities for an increase in quotas, the regional heads sometimes increased them on their own initiative, hoping to obtain bonuses or promotions or demand still more from the people they governed and be certain of achieving the norm. Therefore collectivization quotas, which Moscow set at 15 percent of households, rose to 25 percent at regional level in January 1930, before reaching 40 percent and ultimately 60 percent at the lower levels.[27] In 1958 that pattern was repeated endlessly in China for the quantity of rice to be produced per *mu* (one-fifteenth of a hectare).

Once the quotas were raised, people were urged to exceed them. Failure to do so was a sacrilege, as the regional and local Chinese cadres learned the hard way during the GLF. Any cadre unable to achieve his quotas—even on paper—immediately became a "negative example" to be stigmatized and "struggled against" in public criticism sessions, or even dismissed and sanctioned. This practice, constantly used in Maoist China for the edification of the masses and to serve as a warning to the cadres, was inspired by a process that Stalin regularly used to isolate and discredit his opponents, even virtual ones, such as the former oppositionists denounced by a unanimous Central Committee.

The risk, once the Trotskyists and their allies in the united opposition were vanquished, was to err on the right, and that was even more the case in China. The two primary historical "right deviationists" were Bukharin in 1929 and Peng Dehuai in 1959, but to be labeled a "deviationist" or a "right opportunist," it was enough to point out the obstacles. Among Peng's predecessors there was Deng Zihui, in charge of agriculture in the Central Committee (a higher-ranking position than that of minister for agriculture), criticized for having bravely resisted the acceleration of the agricultural collectivization advocated by Mao. Had that acceleration been advocated by anyone other than Mao it would have been labeled "adventurism"—which it certainly was. But having been recommended (or rather imposed) by Mao, it immediately became the correct line, and anyone straying from it was a deviationist. It was as simple as that. No one was to deviate to the right or to the left of the line set by Stalin or Mao. And since the path changed according to circumstances or the whims of the prophets, anyone not wanting to commit the sin of deviationism had to embrace every twist and turn.[28]

Like the term "deviation," or "deviationist," the entire Chinese (or rather Sino-Maoist) vocabulary was based on the Soviet one, beginning with "politics in command." Even the sacrosanct term "Cultural Revolution" had been used in the 1920s, and the "antagonistic contradictions" were taken from chapter 4 of the famous *Short Course*, published in 1938, as were the military terms ("brigade," etc.), the activist ones ("catching up" and "overtaking"), and "consolidation," which concealed an unavowed setback.[29]

Chinese Specificities?

This section does not deal with the period 1917–1929—even Stalinism is mentioned only as a reference. The question here is, how did Maoism differ from its model? We should bear in mind that there was only one model, Stalinism—we can forget Marx and even Lenin. Chinese policy will also be relegated to the background, in the massive shadow cast by a far less debonair Mao than his image suggested, greatly enhanced as it was by propaganda. From the moment Mao's model became Stalin, his policies can be summarized as autocrat's politics. From that point of view, Mao was a perfect replica of Stalin.

To use the expression that displeased Roland Lew, "a totalitarianism that was both public and more introspective than Stalinist totalitarianism, which remained the inevitable reference."[30] In the past I justified the public nature of Chinese totalitarianism by the recurrence of the political campaigns, mentioned above as being among the similarities—proof that at the time I had an oversimplified notion of the Soviet model. By "introspective" I mean in fact the desire to educate and persuade, and not depend on constraint alone, an aspect that I will discuss at greater length during the comparison between the *gulag* and *laogai*. While I agree with Jean-Luc Domenach's (1992) defense of Chinese originality in this domain, it is also easy to point out countless prior Soviet precedents to this Chinese concern with convincing without merely ordering. That is one of the conclusions I will try to prove in this section. Mao copied more than he invented, and quite a few of his so-called "innovations" may be boiled down to exaggerations of a trend that already existed in the original. And when that trend failed, he pushed it even further until it verged on, or triggered, a disaster.

One difference that has frequently been pointed out between the political practices of the two regimes may lead us back to the campaigns again, since it concerns the role allocated to mass movements—which resemble nothing more than mass campaigns. The difference lies in the emphasis placed on the masses, a term that is both more encompassing and yet far vaguer than in the Soviet Union, where the "masses" or "laboring masses" mainly designated the workers and such peasants as could be trusted. In China the masses composed more than nine-tenths of the population, broken down, it is true, into concentric layers with the working class at the center, followed by the peasants (the proletariat's most trustworthy ally), and then the petite bourgeoisie, which supported the movement but without taking any initiative, and finally the national bourgeoisie, which, because of its dual nature (patriotic and exploitative), could tilt into either camp. That arrangement was not very different from the "Four Class Bloc" put forward by Stalin in the 1920s. Among other features, the repeated utilization of mass movements, from agricultural reform to the Cultural Revolution, via the GLF and the Socialist Education Movement of 1962–1965, lent credence to the theory of the originality of the Chinese variant of Communist-style totalitarianism. For Mao, the "mass line" consisted of fishing for ideas that already existed in latent form among the masses, and then distilling and reorganizing them before preaching them back to the masses. The masses thus ended up embracing as their own some ideas that they would have been unable to develop themselves.

When enacted, the initial creativity of those ideas that originated with the masses (and which Lenin denied) was implicitly denied.[31] For Mao the masses could make history only if they benefited from a correct leadership dispensed by the Party (that was the rule before the Cultural Revolution), and, once the Party disappointed its leader, dispensed by the Great Helmsman himself. That the masses had been manipulated during the Cultural Revolution is too obvious to justify the least argument, but even before that (from 1949 to 1965, and even in Yan'an and in Jiangxi), no "mass movement" had ever spontaneously arisen among the masses. Such movements were all decided by leaders, and nearly all of them mobilized the masses in an authoritarian way by applying orders and directives transmitted top-down by the Party and the administrative hierarchy. At best, the mass movements were a travesty of people's enterprise, at worse—and that was not infrequent—they led to tragic consequences.[32]

Before the Cultural Revolution, those mass movements were more rural than urban and usually accompanied the idealization of the "peasant masses," on whom all the virtues, especially revolutionary ones, were conferred as a result of their poverty and availability, not to say their lack of sophistication. The Chinese people were "poor and white," and on that blank page the Supreme Leader, guided by Marxism-Leninism, could sketch out his utopia at his leisure. The people were required to have revolutionary virtues, but also ardor and enthusiasm in order to advance in leaps and bounds toward socialist construction, to produce in ever greater quantities, and transform the environment and their own condition. That was especially true in periods of revolutionary zeal, for instance the speeding up of agrarian collectivization in 1955 or in the early stages of the GLF, when the authoritarian mobilization of the masses was accompanied by eulogies to their glory. When it was necessary to slow down the movement during the so-called "pauses" or periods of "consolidation," the Supreme Leader, followed by the official press, would unveil some obvious facts: those peasants showed a certain attachment to their material interests after all, or had immediate, concrete concerns that prevented them from seeing further.[33] Nevertheless from the 1927 Report on the Peasant Movement in Hunan to the pioneering role assigned to rural People's Communes during the GLF, through to the famous comparison made between Asia, Africa, and the Latin America's underdeveloped countries with the world's "revolutionary countryside," which would triumph over the "cities" of Europe and North America, Mao's constant pre- and postrevolutionary "ruralism," as well as his almost equally tenacious antiurbanism, sharply contradict the basic orientations of Marxism-Leninism as well as the policies pursued and implemented by Stalin. The Cultural Revolution "was directed primarily against" urban elites, the "technological intelligentsia, and especially urban-based Party bureaucrats," in other words the very groups that Stalin favored.[34]

Another difference, related to Mao's partiality for the rural poor, was egalitarianism. While never actually achieved in China, it was pursued more single-mindedly and almost achieved between urbanites. That was even the case in the rural population (poverty for all, except for the cadres), but the average income in the countryside was barely one-third that in the cities, and urbanites also benefitted from far better services (not to mention cheaper or even free ones) such as health care, schools, and so forth. Be that as it may, inequality was more pronounced in the Soviet Union and the gap with China grew over the years, especially in the final period after the GLF (1958–1976) and the Great Terror (1938–1953). Whereas Mao never achieved equality, he did at least dream of it, whereas Stalin rejected it, assimilating it with petty-bourgeois deviationism.

That takes us back from political practices to the ideology behind them. In China, Marxism-Leninism was supposed to be enhanced by "Mao Zedong thought" (which from now on I call "Mao-thought"). Where does the originality of this addition lie? The "Sinicization of Marxism" that was claimed from the 1940s mostly refers to the adaptation to national conditions: mobilizing peasants for lack of workers (as others launched "revolution in one country," lacking revolutions elsewhere), and leading rural guerrilla warfare in regions where there was little risk of being dislodged. Once several rural bases had been consolidated, a mini Stalinist state was established, which reinforced the efficiency of Mao's formula but without adding to its originality. Last, he sought not to overexpose Communist troops to the Japanese invaders, who were being provoked at the time by a rash (in Mao's eyes) Peng Dehuai.[35] I am not claiming that the sycophants of that "Mao-thought," which had already been drawn up (and glorified) in Yan'an, would be satisfied with such an offhand summary, only saying that those commonsense decisions might lead one to conclude that Mao did not steal the Party leadership, quite apart from the countless intrigues and acts of cruelty that went into conquering and consolidating it.

Alas, any claims to originality in Mao-thought (and he must be placed alongside a comparable figure, such as Stalin, his preferred reference, rather than Marx or Lenin) may be found in the period after the conquest of power, and especially in the last two decades of his long life.

At the outset, he still had the kind of common sense that led him to compensate for the shortfall in the proletariat by the abundant peasantry. One example was when he reproached Stalin for placing excessive importance on pursuing the class struggle during the phase of transition to socialism once victory was consolidated. On 2 May 1957, Mao still believed that the principal contradiction in China was no longer between hostile classes (the proletariat and the bourgeoisie), but the chasm between the requirements for constructing an advanced industrial nation and the objective reality of a backward rural country. After his militant impulse in the summer of 1955, when Mao decided to attach greater importance to the class struggle in the countryside so as to speed up rural collectivization,[36] Mao was confirming the claim by the Eighth National Congress of the CCP in September 1956 that following the recent nationalization of trade and industry, the opposition of the bourgeoisie was no longer a major issue.

However, after the crucial Hundred Flowers episode, Mao suddenly deemed that placating judgment to be overoptimistic. He was disappointed by the trenchant criticisms from intellectuals as well as leaders of the democratic parties, some of whom he had appointed as ministers (albeit always flanked by a Communist deputy who held the real power). Consequently he decided that the bourgeoisie had not in fact truly surrendered, and that the class struggle remained alive and well and more virulent than ever. In actual fact he was aligning himself on the very position he had previously criticized in Stalin. He even adopted the Stalinist thesis of the class struggle intensifying with the progress and victories of the socialist regime. This contradictory thesis (despair will lead the capitalist phoenix to rise from its ashes) was repeated ad infinitum and ultimately accepted as truth. To the end of his life, Mao continued to stress the persistence of the class struggle during the socialist transition. And the only valid issue in the inexpiable two-line struggle was to choose the socialist way or the capitalist one. Mao even identified the leading culprit: the president of the Republic, Liu Shaoqi, "the number one capitalist roader."[37]

Once the class struggle involved the Party (where this particular Number One was Number Two), we can no longer diminish the originality of the Chinese position by pointing out the contradictions and palinodes of the person who had inspired it. From the summer of 1957 Mao's position (and consequently that of the PRC in the last two decades of his reign) was closer to that of Djilas or Trotsky, whom he took care never to quote, than to that of Stalin. While continuing to denounce the imaginary intrigues of a bourgeoisie that was already on its knees, Mao increasingly located the germs of this recurring infection within the Party he led. Privileges and power lead to bourgeois attitudes and mentalities: just look at the sons of the leaders who behave as though they are members of an hereditary nobility. The "blood princes" who monopolize many important management positions in China today (2013) would validate Mao's somewhat commonplace prediction, were it not that his concern (and hence the evolution of his thought on the subject) derived from extraintellectual roots.[38]

In the last twelve years of his life, Mao was no longer content to denounce the over-spoiled Communist potentates who had converted to bourgeois values, or even the infiltration of "bourgeois elements" in the Party. He saw the emergence of a "Goulash Communism" in China, similar to the one he found so despicable in Khrushchev's Soviet Union, and he located the danger (be it revisionist or capitalist, it was all the same) right in the heart of the Party, a veritable "bourgeois den" that he intended to combat first and foremost. In other words (still borrowed from his vocabulary), the "contradiction" between the Communist cadres—most of them, but not their infallible leader—and the people now acquired an "antagonistic" hue. The evil was thus totally unacceptable, and nothing less than a Cultural Revolution would rid China and its people of such a scourge. And since the same causes produce the same results, it would be necessary to renew the process, in other words to launch new cultural revolutions every ten or twenty years to purge the revolution of the gangrene that infected it.

It would be difficult to be any more unorthodox, especially in relation to Leninist theory (the Party had become the sick organ that was infecting the entire body), but also in Stalinist practice too, for the Great Terror did not target the Party itself. Mao's heterodoxy was reinforced by his definition of what made a bourgeois: it was less the individual's place and role in relation to production, than his behavior, mentality, and political choices. That explains why of two Communists exercising the same power and enjoying the same privileges, one might remain faithful to his revolutionary past and be devoted to the people he has served throughout his life, while another might become a traitor. Better still, even a designated bourgeois could be transformed from within by education and self-criticism. The Maoist definition of class and class struggle therefore generated another heresy: the importance and significance of subjective forces, conscious choices, and the superstructure, to the detriment of the infrastructure. Here Mao was diverging from Marxism, for materialism and determinism were replaced with the individual's free choice, his idealistic motivations, and, for the Supreme Leader as well as for the masses he led, a kind of voluntarism that resembled nothing less than a promethean impulse. True, that was also present in Marx himself, and even more so in Bolshevik practice. As Liss, the SS commander of the camp, reminded his prisoner, the old Communist Mostovskoy: "Do you really not recognize yourselves in us—yourselves and the strength of your will? Isn't it true that for you too the world is your will? Is there anything that can make you waver?"[39]

From the 1960s, as Mao gradually distanced himself from literal Marxism, he returned to national sources and values. As a young man, he had enjoyed reading anti-Confucian tirades by the May Fourth writers. For decades he—as much as if not more than anyone else—rose against tradition (e.g., the "four olds" denounced during the Cultural Revolution) and the pedants who reduced people to slavery on the pretext of honoring that tradition. In 1964, that same Mao admitted that Confucius had some qualities, then proceeded to define himself as a "native philosopher," unlike his Communist comrades, who still adhered to foreign philosophy.[40] That distance from the philosophy developed in Berlin, Paris, or London left a void that was rapidly filled by ideals inculcated during Mao's Hunanese childhood, confirmed by his schooling in Changsha, and kept alive throughout a lifetime of reading and rereading the Chinese classics (dynastic history, novels, and poems). Those were the ideals that inspired his idealistic take on Marxism, which I mentioned earlier, as well as the importance he placed on education and the state's educational role. Among the Great Helmsman's thoughts, Marxist reminiscences then became increasingly submerged by native wisdom. Whereas he had consistently rejected the famous axiom by the late Qing dynasty mandarin, Zhang Zhidong, "Chinese learning for fundamental principles and Western learning for practical applications" (a free translation of *zhongxue wei ti, xixue wei yong*), he now subscribed to it. That such a vacillating leader could, from one fluctuation to the next, be the permanent source of all truth and the salvation of his people hardly fits in with another, equally well-known quotation, "There are no supreme saviors."[41]

Instead of perpetuating the initial ambiguity (a nationalist revolution that officially, but quite incidentally, became a Communist one), Mao glorified the Communist incarnation and in doing so exacerbated the misunderstanding. However, he had only the most superficial knowledge of the Marxism he so praised and pontificated about. He had read very little Marx, but endlessly read and reread, as though it were a bible,[42] the Stalinist *Short Course*, published in 1938, that he so admired and likened to an encyclopedia of Marxism. "It is the best synthesis and summary of the world Communist movement of the past 100 years." He had no need to go on about *The Dream of the Red Chamber, The Water Margin,* or *The Comprehensive Mirror to Aid in Government* (Song dynasty), because those works accompanied him all his life. In order to discern what was Marxist and what was Han in Mao, I only need to refer to my own case. I could keep repeating the standard clichés about Confucius, but he will always remain less familiar to me than Socrates, Montaigne, Pascal, and a few others.

Appreciation of the Differences and Their Origins

To get the measure of Mao's thoughts (or practices), be they original, heterodox, or merely incongruous, we should remember that they occurred within an extremely narrow field, one that we cannot even call Marxist. Mao was no Bernstein or Kautsky, any more than he was a Rosa Luxemburg, a Trotsky, or even a Lenin. His field was the Stalinist *doxa* codified in that very same *Short Course* of 1938, and his Marxist culture was mainly acquired though that Stalinist prism. In such a circumscribed field, where "thought" and political practice intermingled, a part of what seemed to be new in fact related to themes and practices heard or observed in the Soviet Union, while another part reinforced what Mao claimed to correct, and in doing so betrayed his subjection to the Stalinist model.

There remains what was truly different, and even went against the development of that model. Let us start with a simple practical arrangement I didn't mention earlier, for it is light years away from differences in ideology or high politics. It concerns the distribution of tasks at the summit of power. In a political structure based on the Stalinist model, a Chinese innovation with many repercussions was the distinction between two layers of government. The first governed while the second outlined long-term policy.[43] Needless to say, Mao, who was as uninterested in day-to-day management as de Gaulle, reserved policy responsibility for himself, while his lieutenants busied themselves with implementing the broad line he defined. Before we return more systematically to the consequences in chapter 9, we can already get an inkling of the risks, or complementary risks, of this arrangement. The second government layer, concerned only with ideology and principles, might lose sight of the political problems caused by the application of an abstract general line decreed from above, while the players in the first government layer would mainly be concerned with solving the numerous difficulties they encountered in the field, starting with the contradictions in the very policies they were charged with implementing.

The Soviet Union never faced such risks, especially with the second layer. Stalin never took refuge in the ethereal heights of some second front, but involved himself in the nitty-gritty of governmental routine. His letters to Kaganovich and Molotov confirm the attention he paid to current matters, and when he took his studious holidays in Sochi, he deluged his correspondents with detailed instructions. The rest of the time he relayed his orders in person.

Another, more significant difference lies in Mao's obsessive egalitarianism. Here too there is no precedent in the Stalinist phase of the Russian revolution. That may be explained in part by the time lag (the revolution was already twelve years old when Stalin began to exert power comparable to that wielded by Mao from the very start). But only in part because that difference persisted, Mao was emphatic about it, and the goal of the Cultural Revolution was to place all the elite, old and new, into the same mold,[44] whereas from the early 1930s Stalin was making sarcastic remarks about the proponents of what he called "leveling." Had he lived long enough, he would certainly have directed those remarks at 1960s Mao. Stalin's wage differentiation, piecework, the well-known "life has improved comrades" from 1935, and, the following year, his ode to prosperity that inspired, among other things, the constitution reflect an untroubled acceptance of inequality, and even of the regime's first gentrification. After the war, reconstruction followed by the continuation of modernization, led Stalin to increase those inequalities and restrict the range of beneficiaries. Workers were excluded—even the Stakhanovites were not skilled enough to be profitable partners, unlike the engineers, specialists, technicians, factory managers, and, above all, Party administrators. This arrangement between the regime and the middle classes (which included many other professional categories) was what Vera Dunham called the Big Deal.[45] Such a deal that distributed material advantages and prestige in exchange for professional skills and apolitical conformism satisfied everyone whose aspirations could be summed up as career, comfort, and stability. In a way, it was the death of an early view and practice of revolution and pushed many of its ideals into the background. They were never actually disowned, but in practice that was the case. The aspiration to private happiness was rehabilitated, along with material satisfaction and soon the philistinism of the *kulturnost* (public behavior that complied with convention and etiquette), which was quite oblivious to real cultural concerns.

It was in signs such as these that Mao detected incipient revisionism, attributed to Khrushchev even though he merely inherited it. What

Khrushchev did revise was in an entirely different area (see below). Mao was right, however, to see this as the end of the heroic stage of the revolution, and it was that dreaded eventuality he wanted to prevent at all costs. Unfortunately the cost was beyond anyone's wildest fears. That flagrant contrast with the Stalinist model (dreamed-of equality versus imposed inequality) was therefore derived from a loyalty to Bolshevik ideals and places Maoist originality right back into the Bolshevik mold.

Other differences, such as the importance given to thought reform and, more broadly, to the superstructure in China, prospered on the fertile soil inherited from the previous revolution alongside obvious native roots (for instance, the state's educational role in Chinese tradition). That revolution believed that the spirit of capitalism had infected all mankind and that it was necessary to eradicate it—a belief that already foreshadowed Mao's emphasis on therapy and the healing of those corrupted by bourgeois decadence. More precisely, the second (Stalinist) revolution was also inclined to define the class status of individuals by their mentalities and political behavior rather than their objective condition. "Almost any peasant could be a kulak. The party increasingly judged a peasant's socioeconomic status on the basis of his political behavior," a judgment that the Party cadres used to justify as follows: "It's true that he is not economically a kulak, but his ideology is that of a kulak." Although both these quotations referred to the initial period (1929 and January 1930), they came from books published a quarter of a century apart.[46] In between, countless authors noted the practice of calling anyone a kulak or an "ideological kulak" if he or she was opposed to collectivization or protested against the expulsion and deportation of kulaks. So where is that originality claimed by Mao? He boasted about it, proclaimed it far and wide, and incorporated what he borrowed into his "thoughts"; but they were in most cases only the Stalinist-Maoist regime's customary deviations.

Another superficial and partial resemblance to Stalin conceals a more fundamental one to well-known Marxists who had become outcasts. As early as 1957, Mao had adopted the Stalinist thesis about class struggle intensifying as socialist construction advanced (see above), yet Stalin himself did not see the threat of capitalist restoration at the heart of the Party to the same extent. Rather than rail at the Party, he decimated it in 1937–1938.[47] I cannot however sidestep the question like this for there are no two ways about it: the new "bourgeoisie" that emerged within the Communist Party was Mao's addition to Stalinist political culture, not Djilas's or Trotsky's.

Other features that were perceived as being specific to China may be reduced to a difference of degree with a common base. If mass movements took on proportions in China that were unknown elsewhere, Nikolai Berdyaev and above all Bukharin had already observed the subjection of the masses by the Bolsheviks. In a final article, a kind of political testament written eighteen months before his execution, Bukharin denounced the "illusion of mass participation in government" purported by Stalinism, calling it "organized deception." That instrumentalization of the masses was not incompatible (far from it) with the celebration of symbolic figures representing anonymous and continuous self-denial. Lei Feng and all the others in whom Maoist devotion prompted humble sacrifice are reminiscent of the sorry heroes in Yevgeny Zamyatin's *We*, the "interchangeable cogs in the machinery of state." Stalin used those cogs carelessly, consuming them in vast quantities, like the chips that flew from the felled trees.[48]

Similarly for the native roots that Mao increasingly asserted during the 1960s and 1970s. As early as the mid-1930s Stalin exalted Russia's past. He later commissioned Sergei Eisenstein to make a film glorifying Ivan the Terrible and encouraged novelists to write about him in more amiable terms than was usual (the underlying message being, it was sometimes necessary to take harsh measures for the good of the country). Glorifying Ivan the Terrible as a "true socialist, a Stalinist of the 16th century" (Tucker) not only prefigured Mao's glorification of Qin Shihuangdi, but revealed the seeds of heresy in Stalin.[49] And finally, there was *The Internationale* ritually sung, with the words "there is no supreme savior" duly repeated in the Soviet Union, which had its very own Great Helmsman.

Finally? No, for I have yet to mention the most important affinity between Stalin's and Mao's regimes. Mao's sudden about-turn after the Hundred Flowers Movement, when he stressed the need for class struggle (even though prior to launching the movement he had claimed it was no longer relevant), showed the extraintellectual roots in the development of Mao-thought. Did the non-Communist intellectuals he had encouraged, or obliged, to express themselves make more forceful criticisms than he anticipated? Rather than admit that he had made a mistake, Mao concluded that intellectuals were incurable petit bourgeois and therefore the bourgeoisie had not disarmed. The class struggle was still virulent and vigilance was required. I have detailed the novel trends in his thoughts during the last two decades of Mao's life, but we should be aware of mistaking his gut reactions or bad faith for the intellectual quest of a thinker. Why did he believe that bourgeois weakening and the danger of a capitalist restoration lay within the Party? In part because the Party's Number Two, his very own second in command, Liu Shaoqi (more ascetic not only than Mao, which was not difficult, but than almost the entire Communist leadership), did not always agree with him. After all, was Liu not moved by the suffering of the starving and their numbers? That betrayed his sensitivity; sensitivity is a bourgeois luxury, ergo Liu was a bourgeois. And since he persisted in not always concurring with Mao's revolutionary way, he must be hatching the restoration of capitalism behind his back. Once again, Mao was less innovative than one might suppose. As Robert Tucker has pointed out: "If ideology influences Soviet policy via the minds of the policy-makers, it is also demonstrably true that policy influences ideology, that official interpretations of Marxism-Leninism develop and change in response to policy needs, political interest, and changes in the policy mind. This being so, we can view the ideological process in the Soviet Union as a kind of 'language of politics.'"[50]

Last, I must repeat that Mao's originality from 1957 onward (in other words from the time he criticized his model and decided to correct it) in part consisted of going further in the same direction and radicalizing policies that were already far too radical. He never questioned the doctrine itself, but remained a pure Stalinist even as he criticized such and such an aspect of his former master's action or thought.[51] In 1956, he reproached Stalin in a well-known text ("On the Ten Great Relationships") of having given absolute priority to heavy industry and exploiting the peasants too harshly. "In view of the grave mistakes made by the Soviet Union on this question ... the proportion [of investment] for agriculture and light industry must be increased." Was he then leaning toward a more moderate, more balanced policy, a Bukharin-style review, even a toned-down version but without any reference to him? No, for instead of that Mao launched the GLF in the fall of 1957, further increasing investment in heavy industry and exploiting the peasants as much as, if not more harshly than Stalin during his first Five-Year Plan, using methods that resembled wartime Communism even more than the FFYP. As for the social innovations of the GLF (People's Communes, mandatory canteens, etc.), the mobilization of millions of peasants sent to distant projects, and the backyard furnaces, all exceeded anything Stalin ever attempted to do or probably even dreamed of. During the 1960s, Mao's continued criticism of Stalinism and his inflammatory denunciation of revisionism went hand in hand with maintaining identical structures, identical practices, and an identical economic system to the one China inherited from Stalinism. As for the Cultural Revolution, though Mao's methods of mass mobilization and manipulation were far removed from the sinister legalism of the Great Terror, it yet again demonstrated a type of radicalism I can call only *conservative and defensive*. The real reformer, or apprentice reformer, who didn't go far enough but just sufficiently to encourage the Poles and the Hungarians to try to shake off their yolk, was Khrushchev. By criticizing him, Mao was merely shoring up the defenses of the system he was claiming to improve.[52]

***

To conclude, I must first make (and concede) two caveats. First, the significance of the various similarities I have pointed out between Mao's thought (and policies) and the Soviet model varies significantly. Mao's loyalty to initial Bolshevik ideals, and the link between Djilas's former criticisms and Mao's concerns about the emergence of a new privileged class of Party bureaucrats should not be equated with the more basic reproduction of the Stalinist regime. Even within that reproduction there is a notable difference between a regime that labels a poor peasant who objects to collectivization an "ideological kulak," thereby justifying repression, and Mao's sincere belief that an individual's thought, behavior, and political choices were more important in determining his class than his place in relation to production. This was, of course, blatantly *un*-Marxist, as was his partiality for the countryside at the expense of the more modernized (and therefore better-off) cities, the utopian dreams he promoted or favored during the GLF, or his praise of the advantages of backwardness as being (supposedly) more receptive to revolutionary changes. Maurice Meisner wisely observed: "As Marxism moved eastward from its Western European homeland, to the economically backward and underdeveloped lands, the doctrine tended to become increasingly infused with political activism and utopian purpose. A voluntaristic approach to historical change and a chiliastic utopian expectation were the necessary ingredients for Marxism to find meaningful political expression in economic backward lands."[53]

The voluntarist Lenin had indeed argued against Marx and Engels that revolution might be undertaken in "a backward productive system,"

even though "workers were not 'mature' in the traditional Marxist sense."
He therefore decided that revolutionary consciousness would be delivered
to the proletariat by the bourgeois (or, more often, petit bourgeois)
intellectuals.[54] Given that the Chinese economy was even more backward
and the Chinese proletariat far smaller and less revolutionary than in
Russia, it is little wonder that Mao was even more voluntarist, utopian,
and heterodox than Lenin. We have returned to the commonsense
observation made at the beginning of this book, namely that revolution
did not occur where Marx and Engels expected it.

A brief word concerning the second caveat: I have allowed myself
to be monopolized by Stalin's influence on Mao, but, more broadly, it
was the influence of the first revolution on the second that we should
bear in mind. The well-known article "Long Live the Victory of the
People's War" (1965), attributed to Lin Biao, compares the colonies,
semicolonies and underdeveloped countries in Asia, Africa, and South
America to the "rural areas of the world" preparing to encircle the "cities
of the world" (industrialized Europe and North America). At first sight,
this was simply extending the relevance of the Chinese Communists'
successful strategy to the entire world. In fact, Lin—or rather the staff
who wrote the article—plagiarized that unmentionable author, Bukharin,
who, forty years earlier, saw the "industrial metropolises" (Europe and
North America) as a "world city" doomed to be destroyed by the "world
countryside" (the "agrarian colonies").[55]

The two regimes were alike as two brothers but obviously not twins.
The younger one copied a great deal, far more than was suspected on
the basis of the so-called novelties (which they sometimes were). More
often as not, those originalities reproduced features of the model (or the
original model repudiated by Stalin without him actually admitting it) or,
as with the elder "brother," they were triggered by a reaction to a given
setback. Those reactions were justified, as was the use of a set of ready-
made replies (it's the fault of the kulaks, or the *fu nong*, the bourgeoisie
that refuses to accept defeat, or its hidden agents who have infiltrated
our very ranks and are plotting to restore capitalism) because the leaders
believed they were in line with history, helping to create the future. That
certainty and blind confidence, "that denial of reality" (Alain Besançon),
and hence that sincerity drowned in an ocean of lies, was already present
in Lenin. I have endeavored to attach Mao to Stalin, but let us not forget
to attach both of them to their common source.[56]

4. The Peasants

Russia

The peasants immediately became a thorny issue for the Bolsheviks, who were claiming to achieve a proletarian revolution in a peasant nation. In 1917, workers accounted for only between 2 and 3 percent of the Russian population, compared with between 80 and 85 percent of peasants (conversely in China in 1949, the rural population accounted for more than 89 percent, with only 1.5 percent workers). Theirs was an anticapitalist revolution in a backward country, and the Bolsheviks viewed the *mujiks* as the very symbol of backward and barbaric Russia. They were the main obstacle to modernization, which necessarily entailed urbanization and industrialization. In the early days before his exile, Gorky, who was hardly a Bolshevik, expressed their fears perfectly when he denounced "the overwhelming predominance of the illiterate village over the city, the zoological individualism of the peasantry and its almost complete lack of social consciousness." Marx, who also had a few things to say about the peasants on the other side of the European continent, did not exclude a happy union between a "peasant war and a proletarian revolution."[1] That is what occurred in 1917 if we agree to Soviet terminology, labeling a coup d'état carried out by mobilizing Petrograd workers as a "proletarian revolution."

By attacking the manors and confiscating the lands of the squires, the peasants helped the Bolsheviks come to power, but they did it for their own benefit in order to satisfy their "petit bourgeois" aspirations to become landowners and multiply the fragmented holdings. Lenin hastily sanctioned that division of land so as to ensure the support of the "allied" peasants, but never lost sight of the fact that individual property ownership contradicted the nationalization of land that he intended to carry out at an opportune moment. "The peasants," he deplored a few years later, "secrete capitalism every day and every hour."[2]

For their part the peasants may have appreciated that initial decree confirming the seizure of land from the large estates, but they retained their habitual wariness of any government. They had no regrets for Czarism—at least at first—but their new masters, like the preceding ones, were "strangers" from the city with an even stranger discourse. Did they not glorify and favor the *bedniak* (poor peasant), whom everyone in the village despised, and when even the *bedniak* himself failed to understand why he has been placed on a pedestal when he only aspired to raise himself to the same rank as the better-off farmers?

From 1918, the government tried to group the *bedniaks* together into committees of poor peasants (*kombedy*) in order to enlarge its social base in the countryside where the urban Bolsheviks were weak and isolated. The government also attempted, without much success, to pit the poor peasants against the rich ones (kulaks), but it was not so much that remote-controlled (and hastily abandoned) outburst of social warfare that turned the peasants away from the new regime, but the brutality of the armed squads who requisitioned their grain. In the government's favor it must be remembered that its predecessors, Czarism and the provisional government, had been unable to remedy the bread shortage that followed Russia's entry into the war, a shortage that was further exacerbated by the civil war and the loss of the rich wheat-growing lands in the south. The *kombedy* and squads, or "food brigades," triggered more than two hundred peasant riots between July and August 1918, and still more in November. The protest movement grew stronger still in the spring of 1919, when the government recruited a large army of conscripts. These were originally composed mainly of Red Army deserters who had hidden in the woods (hence their name, the Greens) and refused to fight for the Reds or for the Whites, yet by taking sides *against* one or the other, they succeeded in giving the other side an advantage. At the outset they were not hostile, and resisted only when driven out of their place of refuge or when their families were taken hostage. All they wanted was to be left alone and for the government to stop requisitioning their men, cart horses, and grain to feed the parasites in the city in the name of a war they felt did not concern them. Once the Whites were defeated and the Bolshevik presence in the countryside had become permanent instead of temporary (depending on the advances and retreats on the battlefront) and confined to the railroads, the Green movement intensified again, only this time in protest *against* the "normal" policies of the revolutionaries, with the plundering and violence inflicted on them by the local representatives of the new government. In 1920 and early 1921, the Green rebels were more numerous than the combatants of all the White armies put together. Repression was ruthless, but so were the peasant guerrillas, leaving the Bolsheviks with a lasting feeling of vulnerability faced with the "peasant barbarity" they had so welcomed in the summer of 1917.

The main ingredients for the tragedy that was to occur ten years later were thus assembled as early as 1918–1922.[3] At the heart of these was the battle between the government and the peasants for wheat. The peasants hated the idea of selling their cereals in exchange for rubles, which were as good as useless due to rampant inflation, not to mention the scarcity and expense of the consumer goods produced by a devastated industry. Some peasants reduced the acreage devoted to cereal crops and concentrated on the slightly more lucrative industrial crops, which did not come under state control. Others (or the same ones) transformed grain into vodka or used it for cattle feed since they earned far more from meat, milk, and eggs. Any residual grain left was hidden in barns or in the woods or buried in the ground. As for the state, it was more interested in abolishing the market than regulating it. On 9 May 1918, a government decree stated that any excess grain stored by the peasants would be considered state property. The requisitioning brigades dispatched to the countryside used every means possible to force the farmers to comply, if necessary even confiscating the grain set aside for seed. Right from the "Lenin years," the new-style *chinovniks* (tsarist bureaucrats) were greedy, brutal, and corrupt, helping themselves, as well as the army and the state, which in turn had set the quotas for farmers far too high. Abuses of power, violence, and terror led to local resistance, which grew and spread with the repression.

In August 1920 in the province of Tambov, there arose what a few months later was to become the largest peasant rebellion of the Soviet era. Several other insurrections (in Ukraine, Kuban, Volga, the Ural Mountains, and Western Siberia) and hundreds of smaller ones in all the other provinces led Lenin to make the alarmed observation (on 8 March 1921) that this was "the greatest threat the regime had ever faced." However, the threat was less dangerous than he feared, for those peasant wars were first and foremost defensive. They did not intend—as yet at least—to overthrow the central government, but only to protect the villages or regions from its encroachment and abuses of power, the local Soviets having rapidly become cogs in the Bolshevik bureaucratic machine. The peasants even demanded a return to their short-lived liberation of 1917–1918, with local autonomy and the "Black Repartition" of land. Their slogan was "power to the Soviets without the Communists," their emblem the red flag, and their leaders either an anarchist like Nestor Makhno, who had spent seven years in Tsarist goals, and then, during an early phase of the civil war, placed his fifteen thousand men at the disposal of the Reds before turning against them; or else a left-wing revolutionary socialist like Alexander Antonov, who, until the summer of 1918, had been district head of police in the new regime. That did not prevent the said regime (another warning sign of future Stalinist exuberance) from laying all the blame for a movement that united the entire peasantry solely on the kulaks.

The NEP

Lenin had no shame about altering truth and, like Trotsky, was inclined to spill blood freely, yet he was less rigid than Stalin. The Kronstadt rebellion, combined with the strikes and workers' uprisings that were spreading in the cities where food rationing was reduced still further, the dramatic decline in industrial production, the devastating epidemics, the wide-scale peasant revolts, all convinced Lenin that a retreat was inevitable. The New Economic Policy (NEP), promulgated in March 1921, marked a (temporary) victory for the peasants. Their goals were achieved and the Bolsheviks left them alone. They might have been relieved if the famine that hit at the same time had not killed many more of them than the half million Greens (and civilian peasants) massacred when their uprising was squashed between 1919 and 1921.[4]

The NEP replaced grain requisitioning with a tax in kind, and later in rubles, and legalized private trade, allowing farmers to sell their surplus crops on the town market. Thanks to such concessions, the NEP came to be seen as a blissful interlude, especially in retrospect, or at the very least a welcome pause between what occurred earlier and what was yet to come. Both the cultivated land area and yields recovered fairly quickly after the famine, but without reaching 1913 levels, as Table 1 demonstrates.[5]

Table 1. Cereal Production in Russia and the Soviet Union from 1913 to 1925

	1913	1922	1925
Sowed Land (in millions of hectares)	105	77.7	104.3
Cereal Production (in millions of tonnes)	80.1	50.3	72.5

The same was true of cattle. While livestock quantities were below those on the eve of the revolution, they nevertheless were far higher than in 1922. We must remember that 1925 was the year of the famous Bukharin and Yevgeni Preobrazhensky controversy, when Bukharin wanted to allow the peasants to become richer gradually and provide a market for industry, in the hope that balanced growth would finance slow but harmonious development. If the preference was to be for rapid industrialization—or if it were deemed essential—there would be no choice but to squeeze the peasants by means of heavy taxation, artificially low prices of agricultural products and grain exports, to finance the massive investment it required. The resources could come from nowhere else, since the peasants represented the overwhelming majority of the population. It was that last consideration (the weight of numbers) that convinced Lenin of the need for *smychka* (the proletariat/peasantry alliance or bloc), for as long as support from future revolutions in developed Europe failed to support the paradoxical and fragile revolution that had lost its way in backward Russia. He believed it would be necessary to maintain the *smychka* for at least a decade or two, which concurred with Bukharin's argument but did not fit in well with the legendary impatience of the Bolsheviks. Or for that matter, with Lenin's own impatience in other circumstances, when his imagination was not as cruelly fettered by the immovable boundaries of possibility as it was in the spring of 1921.

Furthermore it was difficult to reconcile the economic and social consequences of the NEP. While the revolutionaries were satisfied with the upturn in agriculture and the rural economy, they were less so with its corollary, since the more prosperous peasants grew richer. Whenever any attempt was made to confer a social rather than an ideological dimension on it, the *smychka* proved to be a somewhat hazy concept. Could the alliance with the peasantry include the rich peasants (kulaks), supposedly the enemies of the Soviet state? At the other end of the scale, the agricultural workers (*batraks*) were in a similar category to the proletarians, and the poor peasants (*bedniaks*) were considered dependable allies, but what about the vast majority of middle peasants who fell between the two? The alliance made no sense if they were excluded from the *smychka*, but Lenin himself had warned that the *seredniak* (middle peasants) vacillated between loyalty to the proletariat and collusion with the bourgeoisie, incarnated in the countryside by the kulaks. Their case and their fate were important for by reducing social inequalities, the 1917–1918 Black Repartition of land had considerably increased their numbers. On the eve of the revolution, social divisions within the peasantry, while not as clear-cut as Bolshevik analysis would have it, certainly existed. Poor peasants accounted for 65 percent, middle peasants 20 percent, and rich or well-off ones 15 percent, these having been reinforced by Stolypin's reforms. By reducing the kulaks' lands and giving plots to the poorest, this egalitarian division did far more than just clip the wings on both sides, leaving just 25 percent of the poor peasants and 3 percent of the kulaks at the end of the civil war. The middle peasants therefore now represented the vast majority. Were they to follow Bukharin's advice and get rich, the prosperous *seredniaks* would become kulaks, and be perceived as enemies of the regime. The regime's dilemma was reduced to a choice between its economic and its social objectives. If it did not help the *seredniaks* (middle peasants, but also an incarnation of the peasantry as a whole) or at the very least treat them considerately, how was it possible to avoid agricultural stagnation with its inevitable consequences on food supplies to the cities and exports of cereals? Yet if it did help them, they were bound to become "enemies." A similar contradiction could be found in the regime's dealings with the poorest peasants. Its social concerns entailed help for the *bedniaks*, who benefitted from a progressive taxation that exempted many of them entirely. In economic terms this was a waste of money; the *bedniaks* ate a little better but supplied no more to the market.

The regime was faced with a comparable dilemma when dealing with the other wing. The Black Repartition of land had dismantled the property of the really rich kulaks. The remaining properties were mostly modest in size and the landowners, depicted as capitalists, undoubtedly belonged to the peasant class. They earned on average five times more than a *bedniak*, which was the difference between being able to live from their labors and being constantly plagued by hunger. Despite that, while a *bedniak* may on occasion have been jealous of his more prosperous neighbor, he sometimes depended on him for help or advice. They had neighborly relations, if not actual family ties, and their mutual dependence was light years from the class hatred posited by the revolutionary government. United by intra-village solidarity, they shared the same resentment against the city and its privileged inhabitants. And not without reason, for any qualified worker was earning more than the majority of the kulaks—not even the peasants!—the difference being that workers had to pay for their food and lodgings, whereas the kulaks owned their isbas and consumed the own farm produce. Treating the kulaks as capitalists was pure ideological manipulation, and by expropriating them the state would deprive itself of a major asset for modernizing agriculture.

Because the landlords had disappeared and there were fewer kulaks in overall production and trade, it fell to the *seredniak* to feed the cities and supply grain for export in order to finance primitive accumulation. While claiming to target the kulaks alone, the regime had no choice but to squeeze the *seredniaks* as well—in other words the entire peasantry. When the government decided to extort more in order to industrialize faster, all the peasants were the victims, not just the kulaks who were a smokescreen for a far greater offensive. Under Stalin this became a veritable war that pitted the urban power against the rural majority.

How did it come to that? Simply by a conjunction of persistent objective problems and erroneous political decisions applied with criminal stubbornness and brutality. In 1926, after a five-year period of growth, cereal crops reached the high levels achieved before the war, yet the portion sold was far below that in 1913. In 1927 there was a serious shortage in state cereal procurement and insufficient supplies to the cities. There were short-term reasons for that: poor harvests after the good ones of the previous year, the fear of war that was sustained by the regime following several incidents, including the breaking off of diplomatic relations with Great Britain, all of which encouraged the peasants to stock more wheat than usual. Stalin preferred to blame the crisis on the scheming and ulterior political motives of his favorite targets, the kulaks who refused to sell (except perhaps on the black market) and their accomplices, the private merchants, or else that ever-available scapegoat, some local administration that Stalin believed to be colluding with the speculators.

The underlying causes of the crisis went far deeper and were far harder to control. The social leveling that resulted from the Black

Repartition led to a fragmentation of farms into multitudes of small holdings that did not produce a surplus. There were 16 million farms prior to 1917. By 1928 the number had increased to between 25 and 26 million.[6] Almost all of them (at least 95 percent) belonged to middle or poor peasants and produced 85 to 87 percent of the total harvest and consumed 80 percent of their own harvest. Before the war they harvested no more than half of the cereals grown in Russia and consumed only 60 percent of their own production, so they were now eating better and feeding their livestock. The kulaks, who represented between 4 and 5 percent of the farms in 1927 (there were slightly more of them thanks to the NEP), produced far less than their prewar predecessors. Together with the landowners they supplied half the national cereal production at the time and 71 percent of the portion of the harvest that was sold. Toward the end of the NEP, they were only producing 13 to 15 percent of the national harvest and surplus production for sale was very low compared with that of their predecessors (and especially the landlords) before the war.

What is more, every year half a million new peasant households made a further dent in the total production intended for trade. The urban population was growing even faster, so the total population was rising at a rate of 2 percent per year. Wheat production per inhabitant fell from 548 kilograms in 1914 to 484 kilograms in 1928. Yields stagnated, and agriculture became more backward after the civil war than it had been in Stolypin's time, for the revolution had wiped out the economically progressive effects of his reforms. In 1925, more than 90 percent of the farms were attached to the *mir*, which carried out a community-based distribution of land, maintained or reestablished the system of a three-yearly rotation of crops, eliminated or reduced the size of the more modern farms, and increased the number of farms broken up into some ten to twenty plots that mainly produced for the peasants' own consumption. In 1928, three-quarters of the wheat was still sowed by hand, nearly half the crops were harvested with a sickle or scythe, and 40 percent were threshed with a flail.

The result of those demographic, economic, and social changes was that in 1927 the state received less than half the wheat it had procured in 1913 and exported twenty times less. By buying this wheat at below-production cost and overestimating the peasants' reserves for tax purposes as well as procurement for export (assessed, according to

Bukharin, at "mythological" levels), and making only a trifling amount of manufactured goods available to rural producers and consumers, the government hardly encouraged farmers to sell what little grain they had. The left-leaning reorientation of government policy, once left-wing opposition had been crushed, wrecked the NEP, which became extinct at turn of the new year 1927–1928. In January 1928 after dispatching several leaders to the Ukraine, the Caucasus, the Urals, and other grain-producing regions in order to speed up the cereal harvest, Stalin went in person to Siberia to put the necessary pressure on the kulaks and the local administration. He felt it was urgent to teach the cadres "the art of Bolshevik politics." "Grain procurement … represents the fortress that we must capture at any cost. And we will certainly capture it if we do the job in a Bolshevik style, with Bolshevik pressure."[7]

That gave the signal. From now on the market, or what remained of it, was supplanted by "administrative measures," a euphemism to designate the exceptional actions that would be implemented throughout 1928. The crisis in state grain procurement was blamed on a strike by the kulaks, even though it was common knowledge that most of the unsold reserves were held by the middle peasants, who were labeled kulaks if they resisted or concealed their grain. The procurement campaigns soon came to resemble military requisitions. In one village an assembly was summoned with a revolver conspicuously placed on the table; in others there were night searches, with violence and illegal arrests, none of which were reported in the press. In most cases, grain procurement, now almost the only state activity in the countryside (along with espionage and repression), amounted to forced confiscation. Letters written by peasants (including poor peasants) to their soldier sons expressing their despair and hostility to "pure and simple robbery" and to the regime were intercepted by the OGPU. Bukharin proved to be quite moderate when he warned that if the policy were pursued there would be a risk of the *smychka* collapsing. That was confirmed by the murders of procurement officers and Communist cadres, attacks, and riots. Almost everywhere, the farmers reduced the portion of their fields sown with cereals, so that despite the exceptional measures, the 1928 grain procurement campaign fell below the already poor one of the previous year, obliging the government to increase wheat prices (in July 1928—too late!), a measure that had been considered until then as an inadmissible demand by the kulaks.

Collectivization and dekulakization

The year 1928 was a time of transition. For the peasants it was worse than the preceding year, but a godsend compared with what was to come.[8] On the twelfth anniversary of the revolution, Stalin named 1929 "the year of the Great Turn." It proved to be very apt, albeit not exactly in the way he intended it. What changed in 1929 was the definitive demise of the NEP and the *smychka*, since a major aspect of the Turn was the replacement of economic relations between the cities and countryside by what Stalin called "tributes" (in grain, taxes, manpower, and soldiers) to be levied, willingly or otherwise, on the peasantry. According to him, the grain procurement crisis had clearly shown the peasants to be an unacceptable partner for the *smychka*. He deemed it inadmissible that the regime should have to depend on the goodwill of the *mujik*, who supposedly suffocated the workers and the cities by holding "bread strikes." If there was to be no radical change to the policy (understood: Bukharin's "right-wing opportunist" policy), and if the kulaks were left to their own devices, Russia would head straight for the restoration of capitalism. The peasantry was the last remaining capitalist class. Stalin used the word "kulaks" but he meant "peasants," and it was that "peasant class" that he intended to bring to order, since his Marxism mainly pitted the city against the countryside. The peasants gave as good as they got by unanimously resisting his offensive—as a class—and considering the exploiter to be not the kulak but the city (and, for that matter, the state).

During the winter of 1929–1930, the Stalinist offensive shifted into a higher gear on two fronts: collectivization and dekulakization. Many Bolsheviks saw the collective farms (kolkhozes) as the road to progress since they would receive tractors and modern tools and thus make farming more rational than on private plots. Hence the threat, "If you don't join a kolkhoz, you won't get seeds or machines."[9] In actual fact it was a long time before the collective farms were equipped with tractors, and kolkhoz members continued to work with horses (confiscated from the kulaks) or oxen. That did not prevent the November 1929 plenary session of the Central Committee (the very one that expelled Bukharin from the Politburo and excommunicated right-wing opponents) from declaring its intention to achieve, by the spring of 1930, "a great leap forward" from the *mujik's* family farm to "combined sovkhozes/kolkhoz associations," veritable agricultural factories that were expected to produce incredible results. A few such enormous monsters were indeed established, but proved to be no more productive than numerous little kolkhozes, and far less so than the individual farms they replaced.

The main aim of collectivization was to supply the state with wheat. Farms were collectivized in the hope of freeing the state once and for all from its dependence on the peasants, and the goal of "dekulakization" was to ease collectivization. It soon became mandatory and advanced rapidly from 7.5 percent of rural households to 18.1 percent during the last quarter of 1929, before leaping to 57.2 percent on 1 March 1930. A minority of poor peasants joined the collective farms of their own volition, but the kulaks were forbidden to join for fear they would sabotage the collective labor. The vast majority of poor and middle peasants had to be coerced into joining, but the central government gave few instructions to the local authorities about the way to proceed. The local authorities knew only that they must be neither conciliatory nor accommodating, for those were far more serious errors than any excess of zeal, haste, or aggressiveness. To meet their target figures they resuscitated the worst aspects of wartime Communism and intensified repression. Recruitment was first placed in the hands of the *aktivy* (activists). Since there were rarely any Communists in the villages, one or two poor peasants were attached to a Komsomol member, thus creating a core of operational activists.[10] Charged only with "collectivizing as much as possible," the recruiters used threats—and often carried them out. Anyone refusing to join a collective farm was labeled "pro-kulak," or even a kulak, and "an enemy of the Soviet state." People who hesitated to sign the documents were threatened with deportation to the Solovetsky Islands (a far northern archipelago in the White Sea and the site of the Solovki prison camp, one of the first concentration camps). Some recruiters organized a vote at the village assembly to ask, "who is against the collective farm?" or, since the one implied the other, "who is against the Soviet government?" If no one raised a hand, they considered that the entire village was joining the kolkhoz. However, many of those hastily established kolkhozes existed only on paper in order to reach or exceed the quotas, or to do as well or better than the neighboring district, which in turn, not to be outdone, felt obliged to do better still ("socialist emulation" of that kind was responsible for even greater damage in China during the Great Leap Forward).

The kolkhozes depended on the acquisition of the kulaks' property in order to operate. It was understood that once the land was acquired, the kolkhozes were obliged to hand over their harvests to the state. That was the first reason for dekulakization, inaugurated in Stalin's speech of 27 December 1929, which announced the "liquidation of the kulaks as a class." The second reason was the desire to exploit the vast and inhospitable lands that were rich in natural resources. The third, which explains why the two campaigns (dekulakization and rapid collectivization) occurred simultaneously, was the most important: to prevent unrest among the peasants most liable to resist collectivization and intimidate the others so that they joined the kolkhoz (in fact many resigned themselves to joining so as not to suffer the same fate as the kulaks). The kulaks were divided into three categories, according to their supposed guilt or the danger they represented on the one hand, and their wealth on the other. The first category, the "counterrevolutionary activists," were dealt with by the OGPU, which arrested the household heads and either dispatched them to the gulag or executed them, the remainder of the family being deported. Deportation (especially to Siberia or the Great North, but also to the Ural Mountains and Kazakhstan) was also the fate reserved for families in the second category, a mix of "other activists" and the richer kulaks. The third and largest category suffered "only" partial expropriation and was settled on less fertile lands on the borders of their districts. The "dekulakized" included former village heads, shopkeepers, priests, teachers, former soldiers from the (Red!) army, as well as a large number of middle and poor peasants who were the victims of score settling, or selected because they refused to join the kolkhoz, or protested when the kulaks were evicted, or simply picked out to fulfill the quota for that particular village. In addition to having their land and their houses confiscated, the kulaks often lost their cattle, their kitchen utensils, and even their children's underwear, or the pillows from under their babies' heads. Dekulakization was accompanied by a stampede to obtain the confiscated goods, which were bought for a nominal price (sixty kopecks for a house) or divided up between the activists and the local Soviet members. Sometimes a kulak was left in his long johns and told by the person who had taken his warm clothing, his pelisse, and boots that, "It's my turn now, you've worn them long enough."

Many kulaks from the second category also lost their coats, shoes, and provisions, and left their southern regions barefoot, wearing light clothing in midwinter (February 1930) for a sixteen-day journey that would take many of them to the northern tundra, where they were supposed to build their own camps. Children separated from their mothers died on the way in what came to be called the "death trains." In the transit centers, such as those in Arkhangelsk and Vologda, the lack of hygiene, overpopulation (one square meter per person), the cold, the famine-level rations, and typhus pushed the mortality rates still further, especially among infants.[11] When the Party secretary of the Northern Region requested urgent medical aid, the only reply he received was not to mention typhus to the press. The starving went mad, others hung or suffocated themselves, mothers strangled their children and threw themselves into the icy river with them. When the river was not frozen, it was sometimes the only source of drinking water. Kulaks were registered and packed off in great haste (families in Crimea were given twenty minutes to prepare for their exile in the taiga) with no care given to their arrival point, which often proved to be inaccessible, or even uninhabitable. In the course of 1931, those who survived were joined by more than one million new deportees,[12] and others followed in 1932–1933. The negligence and chaos were such that in May 1931 the OGPU took over the management of this new type of settlement, which by now formed a string of islands in the "Gulag Archipelago." Some of the deportees were "rehabilitated" after 1935, but were not allowed to leave their place of exile before 1954—unless they succeeded in running away.

Peasant resistance

Some of the deportees rebelled, up to seven thousand of them on one occasion.[13] More tried to resist departure, and more still anticipated it and fled before they could be "dekulakized." This amounted to "self-dekulakization," a move for which they were punished if they were caught. If they had time before leaving, they killed their cattle, sold their property, and married off their daughters to poor peasants or Komsomol members to spare them the exile. The peasants who signed up to join the collective farms also got rid of their cattle and their agricultural implements as fast as they could rather than have them seized by the kolkhoz. The slaughterhouses worked overtime and prices slumped. It would be years before livestock numbers recovered.

The government may have called peasant resistance to collectivization and dekulakization "kulak terrorism," but it occurred across the peasantry. At first it consisted of rumors that were the exact reverse of official propaganda, with class war replaced by the fight between good and evil, or God and the Antichrist (the Soviet government). In official discourse this flood of rumors was labeled "kulak agitprop." In fact the kulaks were not the only ones, everyone was propagating alarmist rumors, for instance, that the kolkhoz was a return to serfdom or, on a more optimistic note, that war would break out and free them. The villagers even denied that there was any social stratification among them. Many deplored the departure of the kulaks, and they helped them or put them up, wrote petitions for them, or voted against the expulsion of the kulaks who had succeeded in joining a kolkhoz. When the dekulakization agents arrived in the villages they were often met with a standard response: "We have no kulaks here." Between the end of 1929 and the spring of 1930, Stalin received fifty thousand letters of complaint and denunciation of activists and local officials, while Mikhail Kalinin received eighty-five thousand.[14]

The peasants used violence only as a last resort. The intermediary stage was a Luddite response, which, in addition to breaking tools and instruments, included sabotaging those belonging to the kolkhoz and even killing horses and cows. The next stage consisted of making threats, "kolkhozniks, we will kill you all in a single night." Last of all came the violence, with both attempted and successful assassinations targeting Soviet officials and activists far more than the kolkhozniks, setting fire to official buildings or those belonging to kolkhozes (which were often the confiscated houses of the kulaks). These acts of individual or collective terror increased tenfold between 1928 and 1929, rising further the following year with 13,794 cases recorded by the OGPU, compared with 9,093 in 1929. In 1929, the majority were triggered by grain requisitioning, while in 1930 the main cause was collectivization and dekulakization. In both cases the peaks of peasant violence directly followed a surge in state violence. While young men carried out most of the assassinations, arson, and other attacks, women also played an important role in public demonstrations. It was hoped that they would be spared from the subsequent repression, but that was not always the case. They were the first to disrupt public meetings either by remaining silent when asked to participate, or else by kicking up a rumpus ("Down with the kolkhoz!"), insulting and thrashing the Party secretary and the president of the local Soviet. Women were also the most likely to protest against the closure and pillaging of the churches, as well as the collectivization of dairy cattle, which jeopardized the lives of their children. Overall this "terrorism" proved to be counterproductive. Although Communist cadres no longer dared to go out at night, the peasant's reign of terror served only to reinforce state terror.

The riots and uprisings were rather more dangerous to the regime. They were almost as numerous as the acts of violence, with 13,754 recorded in 1930, most of them at the start of the year. More than 70 percent were triggered by the simultaneous collectivization and dekulakization campaigns. According to OGPU statistics, these riots gathered ten times more participants than the previous year: 2,468,000 in 1930 versus 244,000 in 1929. This was the most massive (but also the last) wave of peasant resistance after the major uprisings of 1920–1921. Back then, the rebelling peasants had rifles and machine guns; ten years later they had to fight with spades, pitchforks, and axes. Resistance often occurred in the same regions and villages.[15] Although entire zones (near the Polish and Romanian borders of Ukraine, shaken by demands for independence) momentarily escaped Soviet control, most of the revolts remained local, limited to a handful of villages, or a single one, even though they rallied all the villagers, whatever their class. The rebels often made passionate proclamations, some of which circulated from village to village, such as "Down with the Communist tyrants, long live freedom of speech, long live the freedom to work the land," "Down with Communist autocracy, down with Stalin's dictatorship!" and even "Long live capitalism, the Czar and God!"

The unrest became so widespread and disruptive that Stalin was induced to write his famous article "Dizzy with Success," published in the 2 March 1930 edition of *Pravda*, in which he blamed the local authorities for the leadership errors. He claimed that they had become intoxicated by success—a success he claimed for his own: "A radical turn of the countryside towards socialism may be considered as already achieved." And he went on to reprimand the underlings, "Our collective-farm policy ... rests on the voluntary character of the collective-farm movement ... collective farms must not be established by force. That would be foolish and reactionary."[16]

The accused cadres took this badly, furious at being blamed for applying policy that had been decided on high. Furthermore they feared that this late about-turn would give the peasants dangerous ideas. In some regions, the cadres stopped the publication of Stalin's article, prevented it from being distributed, burned any copies in circulation, and punished peasants who gave public readings of it to their illiterate peers. The cadres' fears were justified, for peasant rebellions flared up again with renewed vigor, and even peaked in March and April 1930. The kolkhozniks who had been enrolled by force believed they had received the green light to withdraw their signatures and the collectivization rate fell by half in three months, from 57 percent on 1 March to 28 percent on 1 June, and subsequently plummeting to its lowest level of 20.6 percent in August. That was when the "March Fever" (Lynne Viola)[17] subsided, for the peasants believed they had achieved their objectives. In addition to the temporary dismantlement of the collective farms, they obtained—on paper at least—an end to the "socialization" of poultry, the reopening of free markets, a review of the list of dekulakized persons (although most of those who were wrongly declared to be kulaks never succeeded in recovering their property), and an end to the closure of churches, which had been carried out at great speed earlier in the year. The unrest started up again in the fall when the grain was requisitioned, but did not reach spring levels. When collectivization started up again shortly afterward, it was at a more moderate pace, the methods used were more discreet, and the peasants were too starved and weakened by repression to oppose it efficiently, particularly since the government took care to remove every last kulak from all the villages. A new collectivization drive was launched in early 1931, and this time progress was not stopped. At least 60 percent of farmers' households were collectivized by the summer harvest of 1931.

That was a Pyrrhic victory for both sides: March 1930 for the peasants, and the "second October" for the government, which "spread the pathology throughout the system," and triggered a "cascade of crises and imbalances" (Moshe Lewin). To paraphrase the same author, "premature nationalization of production capacity can cause serious political and social damage" when what is being nationalized is not "a large industrial society organized bureaucratically, where a mere change to the board of directors could be enough," but instead consists of "huts, cows and carts." Imposing "on small producers the forms and methods appropriate for a large-scale organization ... before they have the requisite technical means and the cadres required, and without passing through the necessary transition stages," led to "another considerable regression in the agricultural sector"[18] (the first dating back to 1914–1921). Agriculture

would be the Achilles' heel of the Soviet economy right to the very end—
just as it was of the Chinese economy until the death of Mao.

Collectivization, dekulakization, and excessively high grain
procurement were largely responsible for the famine of 1932–1933. The
way Stalin and his lackeys managed or manipulated the famine (see
chapter 5) confirmed that the regression diagnosed by Moshe Lewin
had spread beyond agriculture to other sectors. Regression or, as Andrea
Graziosi ironically wrote, "selection"; in other words the survival of the
fittest in order to advance in a Party that was becoming more of a "criminal
conspiracy" every step of the way. It was not easy for a committed
Communist in the field to be taken in by the "Stalin's crude evasion of
responsibility" (R. W. Davies).[19] Those excesses Stalin denounced were
practices imposed from above in order to collectivize as rapidly as possible
(and, Graziosi suggests, taught in the crash training courses given to the
cadres who were dispatched to the countryside). Those who, like Sergo
Ordzhonikidze, did not wait for the green light from the Supreme Leader
to deplore those excesses, and who asked if it was possible to "construct
socialism with chains and collectivize 25 million households in the space
of a few months," were unlikely to survive 1937. They were not the type
of Bolsheviks Stalin wanted—and yet had not that same Ordzhonikidze
proved himself to be a "real Bolshevik" (according to Stalin) by insulting
the Georgian Communists and then slapping one of them in the face, to
Lenin's great annoyance?[20]

Kolkhozes

By the 1930s the cause was understood, agriculture was collectivized,
and the peasants had become resigned.[21] Independent farmers who had
refused to join a kolkhoz changed their minds, for they were crippled
by state taxes they could not pay and subject to constant discrimination.
They become a rare species, representing only 7 percent of peasant
households in 1937. The following year a massive tax on horses forced
the last independent farmers to capitulate. Without a horse they could
not work their farms, so they joined the kolkhoz and handed over
their horses.

After an initial phase of gigantic state farms (that dream of large-
scale mechanized socialist agriculture), the average kolkhoz proved to
be little more than a collectivized village. It took the land from the *mir,*

which had been abolished or emptied of substance in 1930. To work the land the peasants had to make do with roughly half the number of horses they had before collectivization: fifteen million in 1934 versus thirty-three million in 1928. After the carnage of 1929–1930 the horses and the rest of the livestock only gradually began to recover after 1935. But at least the peasants could depend on the tractors that were slowly being delivered by Soviet industry—or could they? In fact the tractors were parked in the Machine and Tractor Stations (MTS), which charged a high cost for their use, based on a percentage of the crop. However, since the use of tractors and combine harvesters was still quite limited, the largest dent in the kolkhozes' budget came from the state procurement program, "the central hub in relations between the state and its kolkhozes."[22] It represented a good third of production on average, far more than the portion of agriculture that was being sold on the eve of collectivization. The state paid a purely symbolic price for this massive levy on agricultural production.

Because of state pressure, the kolkhoz allocated only a pittance to its members, amounting to less than one-tenth of their very modest monetary income. They also received—or were handed back—a portion of the cereals and potatoes they produced, but too little to feed their families. Such payment in kind was purely residual and the amount random. It was distributed from what little remained once the state had taken its share, and after the seeds and fodder had been set aside. Inevitably, there was a conflict of interests between the state and the kolkhozniks, with the state wanting to increase collective ownership and obtain more grain, while the kolkhozniks wanted to limit the expansion of collective property and deliver less grain. The government wanted to strengthen its control and impose detailed seed plans, while the peasants only sought to free themselves of state interference and ridiculed the detailed instructions drawn up by incompetent officials. The authorities depended on collective agriculture to carry out their leap forward, whereas the peasants considered it to be a leap backward, a return to serfdom and *barschina* (the obligation to work for a noble landlord).

The kolkhozniks discharged their duties in this "new serfdom" negligently. They dragged their heels before showing up for roll call, rested whenever the brigade chief had his back turned, left the fields early, or didn't even bother to show up (absenteeism reached record highs). They snubbed the Stakhanovites who "did wrong to all kolkhoz members," and shamelessly appropriated a portion of the collective property they considered to be theirs. They took no care of the tractors, and even destroyed a few, so that some kolkhoz fields ended up looking more like tractor cemeteries. Those huge machines were of no use whatsoever on private plots. Some crops weren't harvested but left to rot in the fields; next year's fodder was given to the cattle when prairies were left unmowed. At this level, the incompetent, corrupt, or drunkard kolkhoz directors were as much to blame as the kolkhozniks, who had become veritable serfs of the state and consequently measured their efforts according to whether they were working "for them" or for their own families.

Working for one's family meant working a private plot, something that was merely tolerated before it was legalized in 1935, when the government finally learned some lessons from the peasants' resistance. The plots, an average half hectare per household, enabled the peasants to grow vegetables and other foods and especially to raise a cow, calves, sheep, and pigs for their own consumption and even for sale, as well as chickens in larger quantities. For the kolkhozniks that meant being able to obtain two-thirds of the family's consumption of potatoes and all their vegetables, meat, eggs, and dairy products, which they could consume without making a dent in the portion they could sell on the market or that required by the state. In 1938, private plots represented 3.9 percent of the cultivated land and nearly 45 percent of the country's agricultural production. Those tiny private farms not only prevented the kolkhozniks from dying of hunger (they nevertheless ate less well in 1937–1938 than in 1923–1924), but made an appreciable contribution to feeding the urbanites by selling their produce on the kolkhoz markets. Of the three sectors, MTS (bureaucratic and smacking of the police), the kolkhoz, and the private plot, which coexisted uneasily and antagonistically, the one most despised by the government proved to be the most efficient by far. Those "amazing dwarves" formed a major economic sector and saved the system, despite itself.[23]

After tolerating the existence of private plots, the government led an economic and ideological war against them, which was tantamount to shooting itself in the foot, for the more the state intervened, the more production fell. The state demanded a quota of milk and meat from all kolkhozniks, including from those who had no cow to milk, and no sheep or pigs. The government saw private plots as incarnating the archaic methods and mentalities of the *mujiks*, confirming their exclusive attachment to their private interests. Ancestral practices were certainly used on the plots, indeed their small size hardly facilitated their entry into the technological era. How much time was wasted by the processions of kolkhozniks (usually men) carrying the produce grown and picked by their wives to the market! That market gardening business and resulting revenue were crucial, but it was the regime that obliged the peasants to work a double day (one on the kolkhoz fields, which in fact was not over-taxing) since it was unable to ensure either a minimum income or the social welfare the other classes enjoyed, and still imposed particularly high prices on the peasants for the purchase of manufactured goods. It was the state that reinforced the peasants' sense of property ownership by depriving them of it. It was the state that countered the spontaneous egalitarianism of the *mujiks* in the *mir*, by granting more *trudoden* (the measurement unit for payment in kind, calculated in work days) to the white-collar workers (the kolkhoz administrators) and the specialized blue-collar workers (tractor or truck drivers, machine operators, blacksmiths, etc.) than to the average farmers.

Agricultural production fell during the first Five-Year Plan and a good half of the second one, until the exceptional harvest of 1937. The improvement continued until the war, but even in 1940 the country produced less animal source foods than in 1916 and scarcely more cereals than under the NEP, for despite an increase in the acreage of fields sown the average yield of 770 kilos per hectare never surpassed the yields recorded before collectivization, and yet there was a growing number of mouths to feed. At the end of the decade, livestock had still not returned to previous numbers, but the near stagnation of cereal production was due more to the fact that productivity in the collective fields had ground to a halt since the kolkhozniks saw no point in working for such a pittance. The system conceived by the harbingers of progress was simply not rational.

However one thing did grow from year to year, and that was the tractor fleet and the number of combine harvesters made available to agriculture. Many young people, not content with simply learning to use them in order to earn more *trudoden*, left the collective farms to join the MTS, considered a springboard for a job in the cities. Others joined the rural exodus and discovered a more modern world while those left behind were the victims of legal as well as economic discrimination, forming a lower class, distinct from the rest of the population. That class ruminated on its loathing of the state and its officials, who reciprocated those sentiments. The gulf between the "two nations" had existed under the empire; collectivization served only to increase it.

China

The Chinese peasants were scarcely less badly treated by the revolution, even though Mao and his team were much better disposed toward them than the Bolsheviks had been to the *mujiks*. That is a sad paradox, for that greater proximity to the peasantry merely ended in the same way: they were sacrificed on the altar of modernization or of utopia. Most of the Chinese revolutionaries came from the countryside, although as often as not they were the children of scholars or landowners rather than simple peasants, but they were familiar with their villages since childhood. They were not the sort of people to make Marx or Gorky-type categorical rejections or abrupt condemnations. They sounded out the abyss of peasant ignorance, the weight of conservatism and superstition, the peasants' short-term particularistic and xenophobic view that considered anyone born forty *li* (twenty kilometers) away from their village as a foreigner—yet sympathy carried the day over contempt and often excluded it. "It's not their fault. They're not innately stupid, they didn't benefit from the same opportunities as we did." Or, "We have a lot to learn from the peasants, who are innocent, uncorrupt, uncontaminated by the city and civilization, yet work so hard for so little." Of course I am generalizing,[24] and in the early days that condemnation of ignorance did not always have a benevolent counterpart, witness the revulsion felt by Chen Duxiu, future cofounder of the Chinese Communist Party, for the largely peasant Boxer Rebellion. "How shameful China is! What a curse the Boxers are! ... Peasants all over China belong to this type ... wild, stupid people who are ignorant of ... the dismemberment of China that is going on."[25]

Chen was upset about the wrongs inflicted on the country by an insurrection that massacred missionaries. In fact the "powers," in other words the rival imperialist nations, for once unanimous, made China pay a heavy price for the Boxers' excesses. Chen's remarks illustrate yet again the nationalist origins of so many revolutionary vocations. As China's weakness was confirmed, national concerns fueled the revolutionary vocations. As China's weakness was confirmed, national concerns fueled the revolutionary intellectuals' growing interest in the peasant masses. They were perceived at one and the same time as a millstone (if we can't transform them we cannot save China) and an asset, because of their numbers and their poverty, which supposedly made them potential revolutionaries. Some twenty-five to thirty years after the Boxers, the asset aspect began to triumph over the millstone: "our hope, our strength lies in the countless peasantry." True, they were as powerless as they were numerous and oppressed, but it was up to the revolutionaries to inculcate class consciousness and organization into them (as Lenin did with the Russian workers). From the end of the 1920s, village characters were depicted in novels and short stories as "positive heroes," driven by a desire to revolt and the sentiments of the intellectuals who portrayed them. The enemy, for those intellectuals, was imperialism. For the villagers, it was more likely to have been the landlord or his steward, the tax collector or local despot who had his own militia. In any event, the scourge was far closer to home and more tangible. Nevertheless, the one was linked to the other: the local despots depended on more powerful militarists who joined forces with the imperialists or bought weapons from them; while the tax collectors and officials worked for a government that was constantly ceding territory to the insatiable Japanese, and so on.[26]

Without resorting to such arguments, numerous plays portrayed a village "elder" who explained to the audience that if poverty had grown worse and spread during the last three or four decades it was due to imperialism, which had not been prevalent in the region when he was a child.[27]

Not all intellectuals were satisfied by such one-sided explanations. Hu Shi (1891–1962) listed five scourges that urgently needed to be eradicated—poverty, sickness, ignorance, corruption, and disorder—adding that each of them was inherent to Chinese society and existed well before the arrival of the imperialists. The peasants' supposed conversion to the revolution hardly fitted with the characters (such as Ah Q, Xianglin's Wife, Runtu,[28] and many others) depicted during the 1920s by the greatest Chinese writer of the first half of the twentieth century, Lu Xun (1881–1936). No matter, a literary critic was found who declared in 1928 that Ah Q represented the peasants of a past era. From that time on Lu Xun's lucidity became politically disturbing, the more so since it was shared by people working in the field, starting with the reformer Yan

Yangchu (1893–1990). Yan had dedicated his long life to trying to educate peasants and improve their condition, first in his own country and then, once it had fallen into Communist hands, in destitute villages in Africa, Latin America, and Southeast Asia. In the model *xian* (county) of Ding Xian (Hebei province) that he strived to develop, Yan was confronted with conservatism and superstition sustained by ignorance and a very precarious existence.[29]

The sociologist Li Jinghan, who worked for many years with Yan carrying out surveys, had plenty to say on the subject. "If there is no rain, they [the peasants] pray to the dragon king; if the river floods, they pray to the river god; if they are poor and badly in need of money, they pray to the god of wealth; if their wives are sterile they pray to the goddess; if they are seriously ill, they pray to the god of medicine. They are quite indifferent to the common good of the village … , but as soon as it's a matter of renovating temples or statues and organizing ceremonies for gods and fairies, they contribute beyond their means."

Far from reassuring the peasants (at last, someone who was interested in them and wanted to help), Li's visits were perceived as an intrusion and troubled them. "Farmers suspected that Mass Education Movement workers might be army recruiters out for their sons, Communists out for their daughters, tax collectors for their cash or missionaries. … Male researchers could not talk with village women." Numerous families refused to reveal the number and age of their unmarried daughters, or their sons for fear of their being sent to a school or to the doctor. When the Mass Education Movement (MEM) established by Yan Yangchu attempted to disinfect the wells, the villagers objected, saying that food was poison until the flies had tasted it. One of MEM's priorities was to reduce infant mortality and the mortality of mothers in childbirth, but trying to persuade neighbors who came to help with a birth to respect the basic rules of hygiene proved to be so difficult that MEM hastily trained a few midwives. In vain as it turned out, for the villagers did not trust young women of twenty-five—and "foreign" to the village to boot.[30]

Even though the peasants considered those intellectuals with their strange ideas to be members of the ruling classes who lived off them, they were also capable of evolving and being won over by the sympathy they were shown, and inviting the intruders to their homes as guests. Little by little they even became convinced by the value of educating their children, and the use of hygiene in childbirth. Yan Yangchu willingly admitted that, despite the very modest successes of his work. Whether or not the peasants showed good will, the results of the efforts made by a small number of reformers could only be paltry. A handful of drops in the Chinese ocean, as their revolutionary competitors did not fail to point out, for they were far too impatient to adapt to such a frustratingly slow pace, and moreover were convinced that they alone held the key for solving all the problems of the peasant masses and the entire country as well. They used the peasants to their own ends, which they imagined—at least at the outset—to be the same. They created and developed a "peasant movement" with great effort and at considerable sacrifice to themselves (and to the villagers they recruited) that finally triumphed since it gave rise to the greatest "peasant revolution" in history. That expression is still in use, and yet it is nine-tenths misleading. I shall try to unravel the fragment of truth it encloses.

Essentially this was not an authentic peasant movement, but the ultimate manifestation of the nationalistic and anti-imperialistic movement that had moved the intellectuals—but not the peasants—since the end of the nineteenth century and, I must repeat, in many cases led to their revolutionary vocation. Take for instance Chen Duxiu's U-turn, after he reiterated his original denunciation of the Boxers' xenophobia, superstition, and barbarism in 1918, but went on to declare in 1924 "that the Boxer Rebellion was the solemn and stirring prelude to the Chinese national revolution."[31] In the meantime he had become secretary general of the Communist Party.

A peasant revolution?

After a fairly fruitless start, it was thanks to imperialism that the Communists finally succeeded in mobilizing the peasants. One-third of a century after the Japanese invasion of 1937, Mao admitted that without it, the Communist regime could not have imposed itself in China. Ten years prior to the invasion, the same Mao had nevertheless been enthusiastic about the revolutionary capabilities of the peasants in his native province. He was deluding himself somewhat, but his famous "Report into an Investigation of the Peasant Movement in Hunan" nevertheless pointed to a profitable course for the Communist movement, failing a peasant movement. In a country nine-tenths rural, where more than 95 percent of the poorest and most exploited segment were peasants, it made more sense to stir them up and mobilize them rather than to recruit from a scanty proletariat. As soon as Mao's report was published, and especially after Chiang Kai-shek's betrayal when he massacred his Communist allies in the cities, the rural refuge became in any case the best way to escape the urban White Terror. The Communists took refuge in their *guxiang* (region or village of birth) where many became active. They differed in this from the Bolsheviks, who ignored the countryside as much as they despised it. The 1917 Black Repartition of land was a spontaneous peasant movement. The Bolsheviks did not take part in it, but they benefited from it.

There was no such thing in China, where from 1927 to 1930, or even 1932, the riots and "peasant" uprisings provoked by the Communists proliferated. The Communists mobilized semi-owners and tenant farmers against the landlords, agricultural workers against their employers, taxpayers against the tax agents and the state. Nearly all these attempts failed or were quickly put down, often with bloodshed, after an initial but short-lived success that benefitted from the surprise factor and the very meager police presence in the countryside. The very rare cases that lasted long enough to serve as a core base for a local (and rural) Communist administration are duly recorded in the Chinese Communist bible. The most famous Communist base (not only because it was founded by Mao) was the Soviet Republic of Jiangxi (1931–1934), so-called in reference to the original bible, but that too was conquered in the end. Propaganda and legend have transformed the Long March (1934–1935) into an epic, but it was in fact an interminable and costly retreat following the headlong flight of the Red Army (revolutionary capital must be preserved at all costs!) from its Jiangxi sanctuary. It has endlessly been repeated that 100,000 left Jiangxi (in fact it was more like 86,000) but only 7,000 to 8,000 arrived at their destination on the other side of the country-continent, but we should not deduce that most were killed. On the contrary, desertion was far more frequent than losses in combat during the early stage of the Long March, since the Jiangxi peasants did not want to fight far from home.

Nevertheless the peasant mobilization in Jiangxi province did have a social base, in contrast to national mobilization that proved to be far more fruitful in wartime northern China. Mao's early efforts to differentiate (and if possible to oppose) classes in rural society testify to that. Whether or not he was at the helm (he was briefly pushed aside from the supreme leadership in Jiangxi), he and the other leaders were inspired by the Bolshevik precedent, although they allowed themselves numerous concessions and tactical reversals. The agricultural workers were authentic proletarians, the poor peasants were reliable allies, the middle peasants were hesitant allies or partners, while the rich ones were opposed to the revolution. The Chinese peasants were no more aware of such clear-cut, even antagonistic, divisions in their ranks than the *mujiks* were. Dividing the peasantry into friendly or antagonistic classes was not the only aspect reminiscent of the Russian revolution; there was also a sort of Chinese-type *smychka*: that mythical worker and peasant alliance. The workers were supposedly represented by the intellectual revolutionaries, so the term *smychka* comprised an alliance between the revolutionary intelligentsia and the peasantry. That theoretical and, more importantly, "unequal" alliance could be boiled down to the utilization of the peasant masses by leaders from another class,[32] which assigned to them the function of disciples (only a small minority of activist peasants were actually promoted Communist cadres) or loyal subordinates to the cause. By making them serve the national cause, which ultimately could be summed up as the conquest of power, they modeled and remodeled the peasant clay, the players in their revolutionary epic.

This transformation really took place on a large scale during the war and civil war (1937–1949), even though in Chinese terms it still concerned a minority for outside the Communist zones, with few very exceptions, the peasants did not take part in the revolution. If they were transformed despite that, it was due to the impact of war and the invasion, with the subsequent proliferation of killers and torturers.

Before examining in greater detail the collaboration between the minority residing in the Communist bases and the revolutionary intellectuals, we should remember that the real peasant movement, the one that was not organized and exploited by the Communists, remained defensive and particularistic throughout the four decades of the Chinese republic (1911–1949). Whether reacting to some abuse or injustice, or the local deterioration in the peasants' condition—for which the government was rarely responsible—the peasant movement only aimed to reestablish the previous status quo, if necessary by transferring the problem or burden to someone else, for instance the maintenance of some army rabble for which villagers in other areas could take their turn. That was light years away from any revolutionary action, implying as it does an overall goal and an offensive strategy. The villagers' collaboration in what was, to them, an insane enterprise was far from certain, as confirmed in early reports by revolutionary leaders claiming to be confronting "cold and reserved" rural masses wherever they went (the expression was Mao's very own).[33]

At the outset the Communists were reduced to launching a peasant movement without peasants—supposing that the term is appropriate for designating a resistance drive to the invader launched from the villages but without much help from the villagers. Fortunately for the Communists they found support elsewhere in rural society, among the cultural and social elite, mainly the teachers who had returned to their native villages after studying in the cities, and the educated offspring of the landlords. The Japanese invasion gave a second chance to a battered movement and many more sympathizers and recruits flocked to the Communists out of patriotic motivation rather than the social radicalism of the preceding period. Apart from these young patriots from privileged backgrounds, the revolutionaries found or negotiated more circumstantial support with military leaders or local despots, who, like they, wanted to preserve or increase their independence from the nationalist government. It was a case of "my enemy's enemies are my friends," but it was understood that the enemy in question was not the Japanese invader. Hence the lapidary conclusion of an impressive and well-informed study, that "armies, not classes, made the Chinese revolution."[34] To that I would add the (proto-Stalinist) political system established by the revolutionaries in the bases they controlled, and then the classes (read: the masses) relegated to third place.

In fact the masses did rally around, and very fast in some cases, because of the Japanese invasion, which they had no desire at all to fight. The threat of danger was the first reason for the peasants' abstention, but it had a reverse effect when it led to panic and they required the protection of the Communists (or any other anti-Japanese force) at all costs. Once placed, willingly or otherwise, under the "revolutionary" banner, the Communist militia endeavored to convince the recalcitrants. On the whole the peasants were satisfied with the social reforms implemented by the Communists (the reduction of land rents and usurious interest rates, and a very progressive tax rate). More receptive to material advantages than patriotic exhortations, they were nevertheless in no hurry to fight the social exploitation of which they themselves were the victims. At first many farmers secretly made up the difference to the landlord between the original land rent and the reduced one set by the Communists. That dogged reticence to take a position against the "master" was due to the uncertainty as to the duration of Communist rule, a fear of reprisals by the landlords, a desire to avoid confrontations and persisting paternalism, not to mention the links that connected neighbors or members of the same clan.[35]

The Communist bases survived and then consolidated and expanded at the end of the war once the Japanese had withdrawn their troops, required in the Pacific or transferred further south to fight the nationalist army. By now the majority of peasants had overcome their fear of landlords and local strongmen—sometimes too much so for the Communists, who were then at a loss as to how to deal with the anger that they themselves had provoked in the peasants. For once roused and egged on by the Communist cadres, some peasants attacked their masters or their oppressors in public and those meek and deferential peasants were suddenly transformed into aggressive zealots.[36] Having so long been defenseless against insults, extortion, and violence, knocked into shape as it were by the experience of life that was part of their destiny, the peasants were ill equipped to treat victims with compassion, especially when those victims had previously been so privileged. "Everyone has a turn," as the looter said, putting on the kulak's pelisse (see above). Whereas in the early days some farmers had secretly supplemented their rent to the landlords, now others, or the same ones, refused to pay any rent at all. After doing their utmost to prevent the farmers from paying more, the Communists cadres now had to prevent them from paying less than the legal rent. That was particularly important since the United Front against Japan did not allow the Communist party to fleece the landlords relentlessly, particularly since it comprised a number of patriots from that privileged class.

Peasant collaboration with the revolutionary government was not only on occasion too radical or too egalitarian, it was also fragile. The limitations of this precarious and regional government varied according to the fortunes of war. The Hundred Regiments Offensive, launched in August 1940 by the Communist general Peng Dehuai, provoked a rapid and violent counterattack by the Japanese, which undermined the peasants' trust in the Communist authorities, apparently no longer capable of defending them. In addition, the Communists were obliged to relax their social policy to prevent the defection of the members of the rural elite to the enemy-occupied zones, which were growing ever closer. During 1941–1942, when several Communist bases were fighting to survive, peasant support for the revolutionary regime declined spectacularly for the same reasons (fear and mistrust) that had explained the passivity of the peasants at the outset, after the invasion. That this combination prevailed again highlights the frailties and limitations of the peasants' support for their new masters. In the dark years during the middle of the war, the famous Maoist aphorism (about the guerrilla fighter among the masses being like a fish in water) was less true than ever. Far from the masses protecting the fighters, a small core of militiamen and activists were ensuring the safety of all and sundry.

And did most of that hard core of villagers who had become Party members, activists, soldiers, or militia come from poor peasant or agricultural proletarian backgrounds, as the revolutionary leaders claimed? That may have been true of the farmhands, mainly unmarried because they were too poor to marry, and therefore more available than those with family ties who might have been more reticent. But those bachelors apart, the agricultural workers and poor tenant farmers showed no more eagerness to join the ranks of the revolution (*canjia geming*) than the less poor. The only constant from one revolutionary base to the next was the predominance of young intellectuals among the original recruits to the movement. In the early phase, recruits had been so rare that the Party indiscriminately welcomed anyone wishing to join them. Once the Party had taken root and could be more selective, it got rid of a number of the vagrants and *liumang* (local hoodlums) who would participate in an ambush or the public denunciation of a local bigwig in exchange for money or food, but still be prepared to sell themselves to the highest bidder, in the manner of the lumpen proletariat, according to Marx.

Not content with purging itself of recruits with questionable loyalty, the Party was also wary of intellectuals because of their "bad" social origins. It accused them of monopolizing too many positions of responsibility in the new Communist administration. To fill the posts vacated by those undesirable elements, the Party set a quota of poor people and "proletarian" elements to be recruited and trained. In the Red Army there was a clearer majority of poor peasants, since the Party avoided enrolling and arming young people whose families were liable to pay the price of its social policies. Consequently the social composition of the Party, the army, and the Communist administration after the war and the civil war reflected the successive choices of the revolutionary leaders far more than any logic resulting from the preexisting social divides. In 1945 or in 1949 at village level, poor peasants often held the majority of the Communist cadre's posts, even in places where they represented a tiny minority of the early activists and members.

Whether they were poor, middle, or rich peasants, after the age of forty they merely obeyed and the activists were recruited from among their sons. Since the Communists needed soldiers and militia in good physical condition, they favored youth and it became a revolutionary criterion for membership that counted for far more than social origins. From 1937 to 1949, the generation gap was a permanent feature across all the Communist bases. Skepticism or caution may have prevailed among the older peasants, and not all the young people were enthusiastic, far from it, but all the enthusiasts were certainly young.[37]

Just a word to finish with the silent majority among the "large rural masses." We can roughly distinguish two concentric circles around the small core of unconditional devotees to the revolutionary cause. The first consisted of those who had been won over by the benefits of a regime that had pulled them out of poverty. For them, the exchange worked in a fairly satisfactory way, so long as the costs and the risks did not outweigh the benefits. The Party did not experience great difficulty in obtaining "the ad hoc support of particular groups or individuals for particular policies," and found it easier to extort grain and services from them than to recruit soldiers. The villagers who were won over in exchange for a given advantage, could return to the majority in the external circle at any time. People in that outer circle obeyed (as they had done since time immemorial) an administration armed with a secular branch (the army), and all the more so given "the Party's capacity to exert control by direct or, preferably, indirect coercion of those who would not comply on other grounds." Since the pioneering work by Chalmers Johnson (1962), historians have strived to determine how revolutionaries went about obtaining the massive support of the peasantry: through national resistance to the invader, social reforms, or revolution. The truth is that the revolutionaries often imposed themselves and ended up being accepted without obtaining that massive support.[38]

Distinguishing between the devoted support of a small minority and the more or less constrained support (obedience) or support motivated by self-interest (exchange) does not mean that the Communists achieved their victory solely by the use of force and trickery, or that the peasants were indifferent. The above-mentioned outbursts of rage and vengeance revealed the seriousness of the social tensions concealed behind the

Confucian façade of affection (*ganqing*). The Communists exploited and inflamed those tensions, but they did not create them.

Conversely they had their hands full in turning that peasant raw material into the rank and file of the revolution. This was a massive and complex enterprise that entailed obliging the peasants make a complete about-turn (*fanshen*) by exhorting them to confront a status quo they wanted to preserve. That the Communists succeeded in their enterprise, learning the difficult profession of "making revolution"[39] as they went, rehabilitates the role of the actors of the revolution to the detriment of the structural causes. True, the success of those actors owed a great deal to luck, in the form of the providential Japanese invasion. That contingency factor may serve as an argument against teleological determinism, even though anyone is free to integrate imperialism into the planetary order (or disorder) that gives rise to revolutions. In any case, where the actors are concerned, the cause was understood, for it was an elite outside the peasantry that conceived and led this revolution. The fact that it triumphed with the help of a fraction of the peasantry did not make the Chinese revolution a peasant revolution. The peasants participated, willingly or unwillingly, in a revolution that was undertaken and managed by others, and in doing so they gradually altered their conceptions and behavior. But with the exception of a minority of followers and believers, the arrival (or intrusion) of the Communists in the villages did not change the villagers to any great extent. Their reactions to the successive measures that concerned them, once the revolutionary strategy was extended to the country as a whole (agrarian reform, collectivization, People's Communes, retreat as a consequence of the failure of the Great Leap Forward, the agricultural radicalism of the Cultural Revolution, and so on), echoed those of their grandparents, bound to their scrap of "yellow earth." And those of their brothers in misfortune, the very first guinea pigs: the *mujiks* who became kolkhozniks.

From the regions (bianqu) to the country-continent (quanguo)

The *bianqu* were the border areas (between the northern provinces, not with other countries) administered by the Communists between 1937 and 1949. From 1949 and especially after 1950, the Communists were able to extend the experimental methods they had used in the northern Chinese countryside to the entire country (*quanguo*). But that was not enough.

Bound as they were to a twofold "superego" (Marxist doctrine and the Soviet model) they did not allow themselves too many deviations, at least during a good part of the first decade. The Chinese experiment continued to resemble a replica of the Soviet precedent, even when the players believed, or pretended to, that they were doing differently and better than the now disparaged model. It was as though the rural origins of many Chinese revolutionaries, the long years spent organizing and mobilizing the peasants and the CCP's strong foothold in most north Chinese villages, was less important than conforming to the model and complying with doctrine.

Yet the agrarian reform launched in the spring of 1950 (and a little later in southern China because of the time required to pacify the area following a later conquest) illustrates a contrast with the Bolshevik Revolution. In this case it was the Communists who gave the land to the peasants and not the peasants who seized it, as the Russian peasants had done in 1917. The violence that transformed this agrarian reform into a real agrarian revolution convinced the long-subjugated peasants that they no longer needed to fear possible reprisals from a rural elite, which was now far too broken and decimated to make any attempt to restore its ancestral domination. The Chinese peasants so appreciated this godsend that they came to identify the revolution with the sharing out of the land.

This initial gratitude of the peasants to the revolutionaries was matched by the sentiments of the revolutionaries themselves, who were far better disposed toward them than the Bolsheviks had been to the *mujiks*. They knew the peasants too well to accept a categorical rejection of their backwardness, and moreover were aware of the contribution made to the conquest of power by the peasant rank and file in the Red Army. Mao did not consign the peasants to a netherworld of obstacles to the revolution as Stalin had done. During the GLF, that utopia so dear to Mao, he declared that he understood the peasants who kept aside a portion of their harvest from the mandatory contribution. He interpreted that as "legitimate self-defense." Later, he protested against the treatment of the peasants by the regime under his own leadership, and deplored the fact that hospitals and good schools remained the privilege of the "Urban Gentlemen." Later still, he sent the *zhiqing* ("educated youth," in other words city dwellers with high-school diplomas or who were completing secondary education) to be "reeducated" by those honest, frugal, hardworking, and disinterested peasants—he conferred so many virtues on them a priori. None of that rang true for if the so-called educated youth learned one important thing in the countryside, it was just how backward their country was and the true extent of peasant poverty, rather than those Maoist virtues that were drummed into them far too often to be readily observed (with the exception of frugality, for which they had no choice). As to the glaring inequalities between the cities and the countryside, Mao railed against them far more than he actually remedied them.

However, we should not neglect tangible achievements, and there were a few in Mao's lifetime. Expensive and sophisticated health care may have been available only in the cities, but the peasants benefitted massively from the fall in infant mortality and the emergency health care provided by the "barefoot doctors." The same was true of schooling and the campaigns to eradicate illiteracy. While 80 percent of the population was illiterate in 1949, the percentage was down to just 12 percent at the time of Mao's death. Insofar as those tangible benefits were concerned, China was clearly in line with the Soviet Union, since both revolutions immediately made a priority of education, culture, and health care for the (mainly rural) masses. To illustrate the relationship, we therefore need to get to the heart of the matter: agricultural collectivization, which traumatized the Chinese peasants in 1955–1956, albeit to a far lesser extent than their Soviet predecessors a quarter of a century earlier.[40]

Less so maybe, but still a great deal, for how much do those initial remarks weigh, once they are drowned in descriptions of the distressing similarities between the two experiences? The recipe for modernizing an underdeveloped county was the same: priority to industrial development financed by the production of very poorly paid peasants, those slaves of primitive accumulation, even though they had no idea what that might be and nobody asked their opinion anyway. From the autumn of 1953, a "unified procurement and unified distribution" system obliged the peasants to sell to the state any surplus grain not consumed by the family, at a very low government price. That clearly resembles the state monopoly of the cereal trade established by the Bolsheviks as early as 1918, when they were facing civil war. Nor was that the end of it, for in China as in the Soviet Union, the revolutionaries (and Mao first and foremost) wanted to move fast and believed that collectivization was the best means of achieving their goal. The agrarian reform, necessary from both a social and a political point of view, led to a proliferation of tiny farms. The forty-seven million hectares that were transferred from the rich to the poor and destitute amounted to three-quarters of a hectare per beneficiary, barely enough to cover the family's subsistence and a very long way from freeing up the substantial grain quotas the planners dreamed of! The year after the compulsory procurement of cereals at fixed prices was established, the peasants were invited to group themselves together into production cooperatives. This was the prelude to collectivization, which was accelerated as early as 1955 in the hope of facilitating the grain requisitioning that was so essential to "socialist construction" (understood in China, as in the Soviet Union, as the industrialization of an agricultural country). The methods employed to encourage or force the peasants to join the newly formed cooperative were similar to those used in the Soviet Union, albeit less brutal. In one village in Hebei province, the Communist cadres set out two tables in the main street and told the peasants, "Now we'll see whether you follow the socialist road or the capitalist road. If you follow the socialist road, sign your name here to join a cooperative." Or, in a neighboring village, "Anyone who is refusing to join is taking the road of the landlords, rich peasants, capitalists, and Americans." And when the Hebei Party Provincial Committee attempted to moderate that type of coercion, it was criticized by none other than Mao himself.[41]

Until now I have attributed to the revolutionaries in general a desire to follow the path inaugurated by the Bolsheviks and advance very rapidly along that path. That was true of this model, for no leader could imagine that the future of agriculture would not transit through collectivization. The impatience was mainly due to Mao, who, in the summer of 1953, drew a similar conclusion about the cereal requisitioning crisis as Stalin had when he faced similar difficulties in 1928, which boiled down to: let's speed up land collectivization![42] Divergences emerged as the Communists ran into the inevitable calls to order by nature as well as humans (the farmers), less about the goal itself than the pace imposed to achieve it. These divergences were mostly discrete, for one opinion would eclipse the others before silencing them. That had been the case with Stalin, but Mao held all the power that Stalin took years to appropriate. Mao's personal responsibility in defining agricultural and agrarian policy was almost as massive as that of Stalin—which does not mean that he applied it with the same indifference and cruelty. He gave the impetus, then imposed the period of acceleration and finally the leaps.

In 1955, having agreed to "consolidate" the cooperative movement (which in Communist jargon signifies having a pause and placating the resistance before going even further), Mao changed his mind and imposed a proliferation of cooperatives at a pace that had never even been considered until then. The Party head of rural affairs (Deng Zihui, a revolutionary veteran who had supported Mao at the time of the Jiangxi Soviets) refused to condone this leap into the unknown. Mao sharply criticized him as a "rightist," and in a speech mocked those comrades who were lagging behind, "hobbling along like a women with bound feet." He succeeded in persuading first the provincial leaders and then other central leaders, who refrained from objecting, to approve his foolhardy venture. Yet there had been no shortage of warning signs. These of course came not from the mute inner circle—Deng Zihui had no emulators— but from the masses as well as from nature itself. As early as 1954, the peasants were putting up a peaceful and dissimulated resistance to the "most reasonable" procurement, and a violent resistance to excessive procurement.[43] They preferred to sell, maim, or kill their cattle rather than hand them over to the cooperative they had to join, willingly or otherwise. In 1955, if a survey commissioned by Mao himself is to be believed, the peasants in Henan were reduced to eating leaves. Certainly, that was a special case since the province had been hit by floods, but no more so than another survey observing a production increase in a newly established cooperative.

This was enough for Mao to conclude that the shortages were due to the small size of the private plots, and that collectivization must be speeded up. He accused the rich peasants of lacking in goodwill, dissenting, and sabotaging, and credited the poor peasants with unbound enthusiasm. He then recommended (still in 1955) that the management of the cooperatives be placed in their hands and that the rich peasants be shunted aside. As in Russia, there remained the majority category of middle peasants. The better-off among them, classified as "upper-middle peasants," were excluded from management, like the rich peasants, while the poorer "lower-middle peasants" were welcomed to such posts, alongside the poor peasants.

The tragedy of 1929–1930 was thus repeated a quarter century later, although less atrociously,[44] first and above all because the Chinese kulaks (*funong*, or rich peasants) were allowed to join the cooperatives, even though they weren't allowed to manage them. They were neither imprisoned nor sent off to farm the Central Asian desert or the Mongolian steppe. In the Soviet Union, the two campaigns (dekulakization and collectivization) were carried out simultaneously, which made them far more brutal. In China, agrarian reform had already "solved," so to speak, the problem of the rich. What is more, it enabled many poor peasants to join the Party, and consequently they were experienced and available when the new stage was tackled. They joined forces with the rural cadres who were trained prior to 1949 and incorporated the now well-honed practice of mobilizing the peasant masses. Directives such as the "Three Togethers" (living together, eating together, and working together) were more a matter of propaganda than actual observance, but it was still a long way from the troika or the twenty-five thousand workers,[45] who disembarked from the cities to speed up the establishment of the kolkhozes, or the absence of any CPSU cell in three out of five villages on 1 January 1930. However, those differences cannot conceal the similarities, or rather the relationship between the two collectivization campaigns (1930 and 1955). While less brutal, or more discrete, in China, the pressure on the villagers and rural cadres was also very strong, and downright coercion was never absent. The same illusions or pretensions prevailed, for instance about the enthusiasm for socialism regularly attributed to the poor and "lower-middle" peasants. In China there was less emphasis on the magic of tractors, for they were even more out of reach than in Russia in 1930, but that didn't prevent many wonderful promises from being made, such as the claim that 90 percent of peasant households would see an increase in their incomes once they joined the cooperatives.

There was no time for those promises to be forgotten before it became clear (as early as 1956) that they would not be kept. In that same year of 1956, despite the efficient use of pressure and constraint (91 percent of peasant households were collectivized within ten months!), the repercussions of such a massive transformation carried out in great haste and without the least improvement to agricultural production, led to a new "consolidation" phase, which continued and intensified in 1957. The authorities now tolerated withdrawals from the cooperatives and granted more "material incentives." The size of private plots was increased and secondary activities, such as crafts or specialized farming, were permitted again, free markets proliferated, and the prices of pigs and fertilizer sold by the peasants rose. The results followed immediately. As controls were eased in the cooperatives, members neglected their "adopted sons" (the collective fields) to devote their efforts to their "legitimate sons" (the private plots). There was widespread absenteeism on collective land, which delivered only a stagnating or lower amount of grain to the state. Some regions suffered grain shortages, and food shortages fueled the black market. As is well known a different segment of the population was offered an opening-up (the intellectuals invited to sow the "Hundred Flowers" of free speech), but that too failed to achieve the hoped-for results, and the concessions did not last. During the summer and fall of 1957, a rural "socialist education" campaign took action against the recalcitrant or skeptical peasants and attempted to reinforce the endangered cooperatives. That was just the start. The radical about-turn of the autumn of 1957 was a replica of the Great Turn of 1929 based on the premise that such measures were deemed necessary in order to modernize quickly.

From the Great Leap Forward to the "liberated" peasantry

That was not how Mao described things or imagined them. He dreamed of a peasantry walking cheerfully to the collective fields with banners held on high, in order to advance socialist construction.[46] The Great Leap Forward (GLF) launched in 1958, but already concocted in the fall of 1957, overturned the lives of millions of peasants, dispossessed them of their private plots, and cut them off from any form of family life since they were now obliged to eat in the communal canteen, and the men were mobilized far afield to dig or to build reservoirs, dams, or canals. "Liberated" from the kitchen, the women worked even harder, harvesting and reaping the good harvest of 1958 on their own, as well as feeding the small rural blast furnaces with scrap iron, and incidentally producing such mediocre steel that nine-tenths was discarded as scrap. Unusual development strategies and grandiose concepts required new institutions. Enter the People's Commune, which brought together between fifteen and twenty-five thousand people and broke all ties with the natural village, leading to a nostalgia for the neighborhood and kinship connections of yesteryear, or simply for the family plot granted to peasants during agrarian reform. Caught up briefly in the passing euphoria of canteens where they could eat their fill and not pay, the peasants rapidly became disillusioned, even before the shortages appeared. After that, how many were left to fall for the marvelous prospects opened up to them by the demiurge: yields will increase so much that we will reduce the area sown in rice or wheat and divide up the land into three, one-third for cereals, on to remain fallow, and one-third planted with trees: "China will then be a vast garden." That fall, the harvest rotted in the fields because manpower was needed elsewhere, but the same demiurge told the rural cadres not to worry about the abandoned cereal crops for, "by rotting they will provide fertilizer for future harvests." Those harvests would be so incredible that people wouldn't know how to dispose of them. Mao estimated that 1965 would see an almost fourfold increase of the good 1958 harvest, in other words up to 750 million tons of cereals, "or one ton per inhabitant," "which will enable peasants to rest for a year."

All that seemed simple enough, even quite clear if taken as a kind of daydream, but in fact things were far more complicated with Mao than they were with Stalin. We could start with an approximate but clear-cut comparison of their cases. Stalin mercilessly squeezed the peasants and in doing so killed them. Mao killed as many, if not more, by ignorance, arrogance, and insanity. But it was his madness that was lethal, even though it was interspaced with moments of lucidity in which he seemed momentarily aware of the country's headlong rush into the abyss of his own making. "I am seized ... with panic [when I see where] the blind adventurism I am guilty of [is leading]." He made that mea culpa in public—after a fashion, since of course the Chinese people were quite unaware of it—in the presence of the twenty or so Politburo members. This was December 1958, a time when the numbers of those who had died of hunger were being counted in tens of thousands, but not yet tens of millions. Learning a lesson from his belated—and transient— moment of lucidity—Mao declared himself to be a "rightist" over the following months and until the early summer of 1959 pursued a policy that could indeed be called "right-wing" in his jargon. Production targets were revised downward (albeit not sufficiently), as were the mandatory state procurement quotas for cereals. However, that scarcely benefited the peasants, for although Mao reduced the massive procurement levels from 40 percent of production down to 33 percent, and even 25 percent, he overestimated the national harvest at 375 million tons instead of 200 million tons, so procurement levels continued to be at unsustainable levels.

Mao's transitory lucidity, interspaced with outbursts of optimistic delirium, did not prevent him from imposing a new left-wing about-turn in the summer of 1959 that proved to be even more deadly. This was not the result of new illusions or some intellectual aberration. Mao was reacting to something far worse in his eyes than the slaughter that was decimating his people. A revolutionary veteran and comrade in arms of the past three decades expressed some criticisms in a private letter to Mao that were not unlike the very self-criticisms Mao himself had made (see chapter 5 below). Mao's revenge, which consisted of firing that member of the Politburo and minister of defense (until such time as he could obtain a far more virulent revenge during the Cultural Revolution), was not enough. He then launched a vast "anti-rightist" campaign against this "right-wing opportunist," in other words he relaunched a GLF that was far more deadly than the original. That particular Mao was certainly not unworthy of Stalin.

Both during and after the famine, Mao's lieutenants devoted themselves to the tasks at hand. They attempted to carry out some damage control and got the rural economy back on its feet. They introduced or implemented innovations that proved to be very fruitful twenty years later when Mao was no longer around to put a spanner in the works. The most revolutionary of these was the "contract" or "household responsibility system," which was de facto decollectivization. The production teams allocated a field to each of their members, in return for which they were required to hand back the major part of their production. However, once their quota was fulfilled they could dispose of any surplus as they wished: use it for the family's consumption or even sell it on the free market, now tolerated again. Another important concession was the greater autonomy of the production team in relation to the highest echelons of collectivized agriculture (the production brigades and the People's Commune). The peasants now had a clearer view of the connection between their work and their remuneration. However, the most revolutionary of these concessions never had the time to spread to the country as a whole. Mao saw the "responsibility system" as the start of a dreaded return to capitalism. He tolerated the other reforms (but without committing himself to them) even if it later meant becoming indignant about the social effects of that necessary policy, which he considered to be so harmful. This led to a to-and-fro between more flexible policies and a Mao-inspired authoritarian regain of control. The production brigades once again replaced the work teams, remuneration became more egalitarian, the private plots shrunk, and the free market became suspect once again. Sometimes two contradictory policies were applied at one and the same time, each pulling in different directions, or more specifically, Mao's second in commands would sabotage the application of his august directives (for which they later paid a heavy price during the Cultural Revolution). Did Mao and those subservient to him learn any lesson at all from the disaster caused by the GLF? In any case, agriculture recovered far more slowly and less comprehensively than industry.

Fortunately from the mid-1960s, industry started providing a growing quantity of chemical fertilizers and made advances in mechanized irrigation. These, together with seed selection, enabled the Green Revolution to take off in China.[47] Nor did policy interrupt any of these advances, although it did thwart them at times and in places, especially when the disturbances and atrocities of the Cultural Revolution spilled over into the countryside. It mainly prevented the peasants from benefiting from those advances as much as they would have liked, whenever the radicals promoted by Mao during the Cultural Revolution succeeded in imposing their views. The radicals believed that the course of China's glorious future was laid down and it was necessary to advance unremittingly toward a higher stage of socialism—and of course to get rid of any capitalist legacies that stood in their way, such as free markets and private plots. The peasants made pretense of obeying, but would, for instance, hide the couple of ducks intended for sale (illegal profits that betrayed an incurable capitalist mentality), sometimes with the collusion of the local cadres. Those cadres had become experts in creating theatrical stage sets that, while not quite the phantasmagoria the radicals dreamed of (that was impossible), did not belie it too much. Those stage sets did not always suffice, for the brigades in charge of uncovering and destroying the despicable tail end of capitalism spread desolation and terror, and the moral incentives for productivity (the only ones allowed) ill-concealed the constraints. They failed to stimulate production, and merely encouraged hypocrisy. So while the peasants were spared the utopia imposed on them by the radical directives (they would not have survived it), the suffering imposed by a predatory policy (that claimed to be pro-peasant) left them to vegetate, and agriculture with them. One might say that despite Mao's repeated declarations, the unrepentant theoreticians claiming to follow his line worked in good Marxist fashion to stamp out the peasantry. Yet even from that point of view, the modernizing epigones proved to be more efficient. Today rural industries and the rural exodus are drawing a growing number of people (but still not enough) away from agriculture. It is as though behind the "revolution or modernization" dilemma (with the latter sacrificed to the former until Mao's dying breath) there lies another, even more implacable one: utopia or real life.[48]

In 1977, one year after Mao's death, the peasants' average standard of living was still equal to or below the 1933 level under the old regime (although it is true that their numbers had greatly increased in the meantime). Seven years later, in 1984, it had tripled. How did this miracle occur, after decades of quasi-stagnation? All it took to liberate the energies of the peasants were a few simple measures, like the increase in agricultural prices (by 49 percent for cereals between 1978 and 1982, and similar levels for other products), which had been kept abnormally low, and allowing peasants to grow whatever crops they wanted (adapted to the soil, the climate, and a less-regulated market). Farmers could now specialize in tree cultivation, cattle breeding, fishing, or fish farming, and sell their produce on the market. Before that, the work teams and brigades were obliged to grow cereals first and foremost, and deliver them to the state at a very low price. The abolition of the People's Communes, carried out in stages (decollectivization in other words) speeded things up and freed up excess labor force, an obvious fact that was concealed in the time when the Chinese "kolkhozniks" worked very slowly and work points were earned in proportion to their presence (but speeded up when they were earned according to the work carried out).[49] That excess labor force was now free to work in rural industries and began to migrate to the cities to work in industry there. It was as if the energy of the Chinese peasants, so long curbed, had suddenly been liberated.[50]

Comparison

The Communists

I started with how the Russian peasants were treated by the 1917 revolution but went back to a much earlier era for their Chinese counterparts by mentioning the Boxers (1900)! For the Chinese Communists the 1949 victory was the culmination of a peasant epic that began in 1927, or even five years earlier with the first peasant union founded in Guangdong province by the pioneer Peng Pai. The Bolsheviks had no rural roots on the eve of the revolution, with only a total of four Party cells throughout the whole of Russia. If I had stuck to the Communists alone, that discrepancy would be justified, but I kept a place for rural reformers and even for the Chinese intellectuals' changing perception of the "other peasant" (Yitsi Feuerwerker). I should then have mentioned the abolition of serfdom in 1861, the disappointment of the Narodniks (Populists) in 1873–1874, Gleb Uspensky, Chekhov, and Bunin's village heroes, the 1891 famine and ensuing turmoil, the revolts of 1902 and 1905–1906, the village opposition to Stolypin's reforms, the Socialist Revolutionaries' solid rural presence, and finally the massive impact of World War I on a countryside bereft of men, all mobilized (before deserting massively in 1917) but filled with refugees and prisoners of war. I could put forward the excuse that since the unfortunate similarity in agrarian policy after the Communists came to power did not justify such a lengthy elaboration on China as on the pioneers, I made up for that by filling out the part about the period before the conquest. However, it is better to admit that I was simply unable to resist the temptation of giving a disproportionate place to the figure who has occupied me for a third of my life![51]

Nevertheless, the main point is that the Chinese Communists were far more familiar with rural life than the Bolsheviks. The feelings and attitudes of the Chinese revolutionaries were different since they were far better disposed toward the villagers than the Bolsheviks were to the *mujiks*, and they acted in response to their intentions (at least in the early days). The 1950 agrarian reform distributed the land of the rich to the poor peasants, whereas the *mujiks* seized it themselves. Any *funong* (the Chinese equivalent of the kulaks) could join the agricultural cooperatives founded in 1953–1954; they were excluded only from management. They were not sent off to cultivate virgin lands in the northern and western borderlands, indeed there was no dekulakization in China. Nor was there a flow of rich peasants to the "Chinese archipelago" (Jean-Luc Domenach) in 1955 when a far less traumatic collectivization than the 1930s one was hastily organized.[52] Last, in the few instances where we can give credit to both revolutions, the Chinese did better than their predecessors with more intensive and systematic literacy and vaccination campaigns, health care provided by "barefoot doctors," and so forth.

How then can we explain that good intentions and less brutal measures ended up causing as much misery and led to more deaths from starvation in China?

- First by taking into account China's demographic and economic vulnerability. The private plots made available to the kolkhozniks after 1935, while still too small, would have more than gratified the Chinese farmers. There were no boasts about the magical merits of tractors in China—and for good reason since they were even more inaccessible there than in 1930s Russia—and the famine that was dealt with in a rather less criminal fashion, proved to be even more devastating (see chapter 5 below).

- The second reason was the tragic fecklessness of the sole decision maker. Mao's flashes of lucidity and repentance were rapidly submerged by new aberrations, stoked by arrogance and stubbornness, to the extent that it is sometimes hard to believe that the same man was speaking (and acting, unfortunately) within the space of a few weeks.

- Last, and more important, was the twofold superego (the doctrine and the model; Marxism-Leninism and Stalinist development strategy), which left no room for differences of policies, at least during the first decade (or even before that, for instance naming the rural base in Jiangxi a Soviet Republic!). Or dividing a fairly consistent peasant class into *funong*-kulaks (rich peasants), *zhongnong-seredniaks* (middle peasants), *pinnong-bedniaks* (poor peasants), and *changgong-batraks* (farmhands and agricultural workers). But designations mattered less than the policies, distressing replicas of which had been experimented with, and failed, in the Soviet Union. Founded on the same but more glaring observation (the backwardness), a similar desire to modernize rapidly dictated the same imperative: primitive accumulation must be financed (to excess) by the peasants. There were the same excessive procurement quotas for the rice paddies as for the Black Lands, and an even greater rush to impose collectivization in the hope of facilitating that essential undertaking. And finally, the unified procurement and unified distribution system of 1953 recalls the state monopoly on the cereal trade the Bolsheviks established in 1918 when confronted with civil war.[53]

That war gave me the opportunity to temper my harsh diagnosis. From 1918 to 1921, the main grain-producing regions in the Russian empire escaped the grasp of the Bolsheviks. Without making excuses for the *kombedy* and the excesses of wartime Communism, that does explain how a hard-pressed regime, struggling for survival, resorted to exceptional measures to feed the Red Army soldiers. An additional problem, and a more lasting one than the civil war, was the national question. For the Chinese, who were nationalists above all else and Communists by chance, that problem never complicated the solution to the peasant issue to the same extent as it had in Ukraine between 1918 and 1933. The launch of the NEP suggests similar considerations to those of the civil war. It became a necessity because of the failure of wartime Communism and the peasant revolts that followed on from those of the Whites, Kronstadt, and so on, but nevertheless ran the risk of being rejected by unrepentant ideologues. As indeed it was, so we must admit that Lenin, and the Bolsheviks he finally rallied around, were able to free themselves from a rigid adherence to dogma, or at least show less pigheadedness than those who followed, namely Stalin and then Mao. With regard to Mao, I need to qualify the damning statement that I made earlier by pointing out the posthumous use of the infrastructure built during his lifetime, including some of the most daring projects of the GLF. The industrial boom of the 1980s did benefit from a base established under Mao.

Conversely, there is one excuse that is often made for him, or at least a good point in his favor, that I will not have the grace to admit, and that was his alleged emancipation from the Soviet model or, better still, his original Chinese way, as symbolized by the GLF. I will willingly admit that he had the best reasons in the world to worry about inappropriateness of Stalinist development strategy to the specific economic and, above all, demographic characteristics of the country he was attempting to modernize. In that respect he did learn the lesson of the first Chinese Five-Year Plan: to neglect agriculture is to compromise the pursuit of industrial expansion. I will therefore not reproach him for having criticized Stalin's manual of political economy (in 1958); still less for having tried to remedy the imbalances of the first plan by "advancing on two legs," the one fed by abundant manpower, the other consuming imported technology. But what I shall persist in deploring was his incapacity to free himself from the very core of the strategy he claimed to reject, in other words placing even greater emphasis on heavy industry than during the first Five-Year Plan, and thereby creating an even greater imbalance, which he enthusiastically, rather than resignedly, embraced.

The term "Great Leap Forward" was well chosen, for it was indeed the reproduction (only worse, far worse) of the Great Leap Forward of 1929–1930.

Peasants

Armed with better intentions, the Chinese Communists had no qualms about treating millions of peasants in much the same way as the Bolsheviks had treated the *mujiks*. The peasants reacted to the shock treatment in a similar way but with one important difference, for the Chinese peasants (*nongmin*) proved to be more docile, subjugated, and hardy than the *mujiks*. The few Communist leaders who at one time or another criticized the Party's agrarian policy (such as a Peng Dehuai or a Chen Yun) paid homage to the patience of the peasants, who were "kind enough not to revolt" when they were dying of hunger.[54] Before the famine, they certainly resisted grain procurement and collectivization: unrest and riots were frequent between 1954 and 1956, but were nowhere near the levels in the Soviet countryside a quarter century earlier. That was in part because the cereal requisitioning and land collectivization were not carried out simultaneously with dekulakization and the closure of churches, but even more so, it would seem, for cultural reasons. There was nothing in China comparable to the egalitarian practices of the *mir*, and the periodic redistribution of land according to family size. Some people in China, usually intellectuals rather than peasants, used the expression "the land belongs to he who cultivates it," but that originated in the Soviet Union. It never entered the mind of the *diannong* (tenant farmer) to challenge a distribution of land that had been decided by destiny and the behavior of the ancestors. In 1917 Russia, the memory of serfdom persisted and there was considerable resentment of the *barschina*, the unpaid corvées owed to the master. The *diannong* did not have such a clear-cut distinction between labor to feed their families and labor to pay the land rent. There was no equivalent of the Black Repartition of land in China, or of the triangular struggle between Reds, Whites, and Greens. In China's supposed peasant revolution the peasants were not independent players. The Communists mobilized and then recruited some of them in the zones under their control. Most of the intellectuals, heirs to the scholars who once aspired to a career in the administration, were themselves far more respectful of the power, the hierarchy, and the established order than their Russian counterparts, and, despite May Fourth, Confucianism still had its imprint on society, and on the peasants most of all.

Once that important difference in degree of resistance has been stressed, it is possible to list the similarities. The Chinese peasants behaved like that previous generation of *mujiks* and kolkhozniks. They too slaughtered their animals rather than hand them over to the cooperative, they too tended their private plots and neglected the collective fields. In other words, they dawdled, chatted, and rested while they were being paid according to the time spent at work, but as soon as they were paid piecework, they speeded up, worked in slapdash fashion, weeded in haste, and carelessly replanted the rice. They concealed and pilfered a portion of the harvest, and sent their children to filch in secret. A number of burlesque quatrains celebrated this type of *farniente*:

> Down in the fields in a line
> Huffing and puffing in time
> Looking good and doing less
> The iron rice bowl's still mine.

Or:

> However hard you work,
> You will never make it.
> The only way out is
> When you see it, take it.[55]

Were relations between the Communists and the peasants doomed to remain conflictual? As a general rule the peasants identified the state with the parasite city, which intruded into their villages only to collect taxes and recruit soldiers or a labor force. They viewed the Communists no differently, except that the Communists intervened more frequently and had a greater presence. They also invented strange concepts such as the class struggle between poor and rich peasants, when it was common knowledge that these were merely imperceptible gradations from the top to the bottom of village society, which could be torn by dissensions but remained unanimous and united against the foreigners from the city. Whether in the kolkhoz or the People's Commune, conflict was inevitable between producers who wanted to give up as little grain as possible to the state, and a state determined to collect as much as it could. Add bitter regret to that mix, for the farmers could no longer run their farms as they pleased and felt that they had lost their independence. They railed against intervention by the government agents, especially people who knew nothing about agriculture and yet imposed absurd farming methods on them.

5. Famines

The two revolutionary regimes triggered the greatest famines of the twentieth century. The ones I will compare here led to the deaths of some six to seven million people in the Soviet Union between 1931 and 1933, and between twenty and forty million in China between 1958 and 1962.[1] Among other things, the Chinese famine led to a comparable fall in the birth rate as a result of diminished sexual activity and famine-related amenorrhea.[2] Given that China's population was roughly four times that of the Soviet Union three decades earlier, the proportion of deaths was very similar. In the countryside, which paid a far heavier price than the cities, the proportions could sometimes be far higher, one in twenty, and even more (between one-tenth and one-third) in the most hard-hit regions, first and foremost Kazakhstan in 1931, and then in Ukraine, the Lower and Middle Volga, and the North Caucasus in 1932–1933; and Anhui, Henan, Sichuan, Shandong, and Gansu provinces between 1959 and 1961.

According to statistics that probably underestimate the figures, during the most deadly year in China (1960), the mortality rate was 54 per thousand in Sichuan province, more populated than France, and more than 68 per thousand in Anhui, or six times more than the estimated 11 per thousand birth rate. Those records pale in comparison with Soviet mortality rates, which, all regions taken together, reached 70 per thousand in 1933, and more still in Ukraine, where life expectancy at birth that same year fell to eleven years for females, less than eight years for males. To correct that contrast (supposing it is reliable), in Ukraine, the peak in mortality was concentrated in the spring and early summer of 1933, whereas in Sichuan it remained at more than double the normal levels for four entire years, from 1958 to 1961. Above all, in 1957 the average mortality in China had fallen to levels well below those recorded in the Soviet Union a generation earlier, so that excess mortality must have been roughly comparable.[3]

Overall figures, incidentally not very reliable, are less telling than their local impact or anecdotes: one or two survivors, if any, in many six- to eight-member families, empty villages (neighboring villagers were obliged to bury the dead), entire districts decimated. The few peasants who managed to escape to the city exchanged earrings, rings, or clothes for a piece of bread or a bowl of rice. Others abandoned their children in the cities in the hope that some kindly soul would take care of them, and then returned to their villages to die. In some farms peasants hid the dead in order to keep their rations, but in others the bodies lay on the ground where the dying had fallen, or were piled up, thick with flies and worms, for no one had the strength to bury them. Conversely, undertakers, who were paid by the body, threw living ones into pits. People lucky enough to be on top of the pile and not crushed by other bodies might miraculously escape, supposing that some kind benefactor would then feed them.[4]

The survivors extended their lives by a few weeks—or hastened their deaths—by eating anything that came to hand, cutting up carrion, fishing dead rats out of cesspits or maggots in cowpats. They fought the pigs over their slops (but the militia was supervising), ate toads, snakes, lizards, cockroaches, praying mantis eggs, chicken or duck feathers, the cotton in jackets and mattresses, or thatch from the roofs. Trees were stripped of their bark and their leaves, the poplars of their buds, sweet potatoes of their shoots, grain of its husk, oilseeds of their solid residue after pressing, the sea of its algae. Many people poisoned themselves or suffered in other ways as a result. In China a mixture of earth and weeds called "Guanyin's earth" (after the goddess of mercy) filled people's stomachs before blocking their intestines completely, since it could be neither digested nor evacuated.[5]

Needless to say people also ate the flesh from dead bodies found mutilated along the roadside or guarded by families to prevent others from dismembering them. Nor did people refrain from eating members of their own families who had died at home. Sometimes they even killed them. After necrophagy came infanticide and cannibalism. Children were not allowed to go out in case they were killed, yet mothers strangled, cut up, and boiled their own children, some losing their minds as a result, others were arrested, or survived unscathed from feasting on their children's flesh. Yet rather than eat their own children, most people preferred to exchange them with those of their neighbors, each surviving thanks to the others' offspring. In one district in Anhui province, it became common practice and was called *yi zi er shi* ("exchanging children for eating").[6] Even without killing to survive, people became hardened to the point of indifference by the deaths of their loved ones. Persistent hunger ultimately led to apathy, interrupted by bursts of unrestrained violence leading to the lynching of suspected thieves, rampant brutality and torture, a proliferation of wanton petty tyrants, and a subsequent rise in rural crime.[7]

That "regression" (Nicolas Werth) hit two countries in peacetime, with no enemy invasion, not even by grasshoppers, which could have destroyed the harvest, and with sufficiently developed means of communication to be able to rapidly transport supplies to regions with shortages. Furthermore, the disaster-stricken zones included regions that traditionally produced a surplus, from "heaven's granary" (Sichuan) to the fertile chernozem belt in the north of Ukraine, celebrated by grateful villagers as a place where you could "put a stick in the ground and it will grow."[8] So what provoked such terrible disasters? And first and foremost, were the revolutionaries to blame?

Innocent Revolutionaries?

I will not linger on the natural disasters used as an excuse in China. Some regions of the country did suffer from bad weather in 1959 and 1961, and others a drought in 1960, but one author (Yang Jisheng) found that within a twenty-seven-year period (1956–1983), there were eleven years of bad weather conditions and even natural disasters that affected more regions than in 1959–1960 without causing a famine or even a noteworthy drop in cereal production.[9]

What was true for China in 1960 and the Soviet Union in 1932–1933 was that agriculture in both countries was vulnerable to vagaries in the weather. That made agricultural production highly unstable since it depended on rainfall—and that was sufficiently unreliable in China for the government to think of using it as an excuse. Droughts were also a recurrent factor in Russia, although they were less frequent than in the North China Plain, and they were a prelude, and then a minor contributor to famine. During the winters of 1927–1928 and 1928–1929, an early thaw, leading to early germination, was followed by a late freeze that proved disastrous for the wheat sowed the previous fall. To offset that, fallow land was hastily planted, thus compromising yields for subsequent years—not the 1930 harvest, which benefited from excellent weather conditions, but the ones in 1931 and 1932. Furthermore in 1931 drought hit the Urals, the Volga Basin, and part of Siberia, while 1932 heralded a bitterly cold March in Ukraine followed by very hot weather in early June. That was followed by abundant rainfall, which, combined with the high temperatures, left young plants highly vulnerable during flowering. The weather was therefore partly responsible, but so were people, who took liberties with crop rotation because of the temperamental weather. Nevertheless, far worse freak, or even catastrophic, climatic conditions, such as those in 1946 and 1972, or in 1954 and 1978 in China, caused far less disastrous famines or even none at all.[10]

Another excuse that was used—only in China, and for good reason—was that it was Khrushchev's fault for having recalled the Soviet experts in the summer of 1960. Apart from the fact that Mao had done everything possible to provoke that recall, it had practically no incidence on agricultural production. Indeed there were very few agronomists among the specialists, and on two occasions Khrushchev had even offered to send help, but was haughtily turned down.[11]

One argument that would have carried some weight was not mentioned by propaganda, and that was the demographic transition, which had scarcely advanced in either country. It began in around 1900 in Russia, and a little later in China, but was still in its early stage with fertility rates at high levels whereas mortality rates were falling rapidly. Mortality fell far faster in China, if only because the fight against infectious diseases worldwide was far more efficient in the 1950s than in the 1920s. Apart from China's chronological advantage, the regime itself contributed to the fall in mortality rates during the eight years preceding the disaster of the Great Leap Forward. That spectacular fall makes the famine appear even more deadly, for had mortality remained at pre-1949 levels, many of those who died of hunger would not even have survived until 1958. The birth rate did not begin to decline noticeably until the 1970s, so the natural population increase was very rapid during the first phase of the demographic transition, at between 2 and 2.5 percent per year between 1955 and 1957.

The demographic transition in the Soviet Union was similar, only it was less advanced and less rapid. The birth and death rates, especially the latter, were far higher than in China a generation later, the natural population increase was slightly lower, albeit still considerable at around 2 percent per year between 1924 (after the extended crisis due to war, civil war, and famine) and 1928. The fundamental factor was the decline in the mortality rate, which while slower than in China (at about 10 percent over five years, from 1924 to 1928, versus 27 percent in China from 1953 to 1957) was nevertheless twice as fast as the fall in the birth rate. That explains the rapid population increase, a marked improvement in life expectancy (from thirty-four years in 1923 to thirty-nine in 1928) and a pronounced rural overpopulation. When Stalin put an end to the NEP, food production had hardly increased but was now required to feed forty-one million more people than had been counted in the 1897 census.[12]

The two revolutionary governments were not responsible for almost unmanageable population growth, even if (and it is to their credit) they contributed to the fall in mortality rates. As long as the birth rate did not follow the same downward trend as the death rate (in Russia, it ultimately fell even faster and mortality rose!), in other words, as long as the demographic transition was not sufficiently advanced to impose a period of relative stability, the issue of the number of mouths to feed and agriculture's capacity to deal with it would be problematic. That was the situation during the regime's first decade in China, as it was in the 1920s Soviet Union, and it was that very fragile base that was toppled by an ill thought-out policy.

Furthermore, urbanization grew even faster than the total population. It started from very low levels, with an urban population of 18 percent in the Soviet Union in 1927, and 15 percent in China in 1957. It rose by 5 percent per year at the end of the 1920s and by 10 percent in 1930 and 1931 in the Soviet Union. Over the total five-year period from 1928 to 1933, the urban population grew from 26 million to 38 million and the nonagricultural labor force from 12 million to 20 million. In China, the pace was even faster. It already stood at more than 8 percent in 1957, reaching 15 percent in 1959. In that year alone, China's urban population increased by 16.5 million (from 107.2 million to 123.7 million), a record that was surpassed the following year (1960).[13] That rapid urbanization was less due to natural growth, which was slower in the cities, than to a hasty rural exodus triggered by the blunders and brutality of the two regimes: collectivization and dekulakization in the Soviet Union, People's Communes and breakneck industrialization in China. Most of the migrants were young peasants. Because of the surplus rural labor force they could easily have been replaced in the fields had the GLF not mobilized the workforce for the great hydroelectric projects or the small backyard furnaces, and in Ukraine if the famine hadn't made formerly able-bodied men incapable of working.

Not innocent!

I have almost finished with the considerations that excused the two revolutionary regimes, although I will make the transition with a plea. Such rapid urbanization was the corollary of unrealistic development strategies, but development as such was an inevitable choice for both "backward" countries. The slow start to the demographic transition went hand in hand with economic underdevelopment and a chronic exposure to famine. From 1918 to 1922, the Soviet Union was hit by an earlier famine that was even more deadly than the one in 1932–1933.[14] Another had shaken the Czarist regime in 1891–1892, and that one was preceded and followed by less serious food crises in 1868, 1898, and again in 1901.[15] In China, a famine had killed some ten million people in the north and the northwest of the country between 1928 and 1930.[16] It occurred between the famines of 1920–1921 (already in north China) and 1943 (in Henan province), but none of those famines were equal in scope or gravity to the ones that hit imperial China in 1876 and 1879.

It is important to recognize the weight of historical legacy as much as it is to incriminate, as I was about to, the two cruel and misguided regimes. Édouard Herriot made himself ridiculous, if not odious, by boasting that the Ukrainian kolkhozes specially orchestrated for his 1933 visit were "blooming,"[17] but he did not run the risk of killing even one million of his compatriots, not because his Radical Socialist Party was cautious about extremes, but because even methods as extreme as Stalin's (and Mao's a quarter century later) would not have succeeded in starving a comparable proportion of forty million French people, even just after the Great Depression. They would not even have been conceivable: only desperate times lead to desperate measures.

The Great Turn

Those extreme measures included modernization at reckless speed (and therefore accelerated industrialization and urbanization), and ignoring the constraints of nature or the capacity of an underdeveloped agriculture to finance primitive accumulation at such a breakneck pace. To resume the "achievements" mentioned in the previous chapter: in the Soviet Union the agrarian revolution led to a considerable fall in the portion of the harvest that could be sold. Before 1914, the large landlords and rich peasants had accounted for 70 percent of that portion. The downgrading of the former kulaks and the promotion of poor farmers (*bedniaks*), resulted in a larger majority of middle peasants (*seredniaks*), but they had very little surplus for sale. The discrepancy between the very low price of cereals and the very high price of industrial goods meant that farmers preferred to plant better-paid cash crops, eat a little better, and feed the cattle, rather than sell their wheat. Thanks to the NEP, livestock numbers were up again, having fallen when peasants killed their animals out of necessity in 1921–1922. The use of artificial insemination had produced larger and stronger animals, only these ate more. Since the price of the animals, as well as of meat and milk, was quite high, farmers preferred to raise more cattle and feed them better, rather than sell their paltry amount of surplus grain at the low state price. Even if (and it is doubtful) cereal production in 1927 returned to 1913 levels as official statistics claimed, the amount was insufficient to feed a larger population as well as the cattle, and fulfill the export quotas, which the revolutionaries wanted to maintain at 1913 levels. The insufficient grain levy in the fall of 1927 was the prelude to the Great Turn.[18]

But not immediately. Before triggering—and imposing—rapid collectivization in 1929 by arguing that the economies of scale would increase production, and in the belief that it would be easier to collect grain from large units (such as kolkhozes or sovkhozes) than to search innumerable households, Stalin was content during this transition stage to blame the grain shortage on the "saboteur" and "striking" kulaks. He accused them of having stocks but refusing to sell them, making it necessary for the government to go and fetch the grain from the villages. And Stalin set the example himself during one of his very rare trips out of Moscow (with the exception of his summer vacations by the Black Sea). In February 1928, after what resembled a veritable police raid in the Urals and Western Siberia, he returned triumphantly to Moscow with wagon loads of cereals seized from "speculators" who were "stockpiling" them—in other words the kulaks and middle peasants who had been forced to hand over their grain. That, in short, was the famous "Ural-Siberian method" that Stalin's minions were then obliged to implement from the Volga to the Caucasus and in Ukraine. Stalin had thus decided to declare war on the peasants without mentioning it to Bukharin. Faced with this fait accompli, Bukharin warned against the "military-feudal exploitation" of the peasantry in his article "Notes of an Economist," but succeeded only in rousing Stalin's ire, for Stalin was now as relentlessly denouncing "the dangers of the right" as earlier (with Bukharin) he had denounced the illusions of the left. Since the kulaks would not give up their wheat voluntarily, it had to be seized. According to Stalin, if grain collection was in deficit again in 1928, it was due to kulak ill will, rather than to the drought and the late freeze. In 1929, impossible quotas were imposed on the rich peasants and their grain was expropriated if they did not fulfill them, the logic being that if they could not satisfy the state's requirements it was proof that they had carried out an act of opposition by reducing the number of fields sown. Everything was ready (the dictator was ready, the country would follow suit) for collectivization and dekulakization, those instruments of the Great Turn that would lead to the "second revolution": all-out industrialization at the expense of agriculture and the peasantry.[19]

Launched in the fall of 1929, the "kolkhoz movement," in other words collectivization, was anything but spontaneous. The "policy of liquidating the kulaks as a class" was carried out simultaneously as part and parcel of collectivization. It finally succeeded in convincing the middle peasants themselves that there was no longer a future in developing their family farms. In addition to the kulak category, there were now "ideological kulaks" (peasants who were reluctant to join the kolkhozes), and "henchmen" or "apologists" of kulaks, who took pity on them and deplored the treatment they were subjected to. Other peasants however, participated in the brutality, arrests, and pillage, further exacerbating the damage caused by official requisitioning. In all sixteen million tons were collected in 1929 from a harvest that was as mediocre as in 1928, the year the state had to make do with just eleven million tons.[20]

Terrorism, abuses of power, and forced collectivization led to many different reactions from the peasants. In Kazakhstan, the forced sedentarization of nomadic and seminomadic herdsmen was carried out at the same time as collectivization and dekulakization, resulting in a persistent guerrilla war (from 1929 to 1931) and veritable insurrections.[21] The government did not face such large-scale revolts elsewhere, but it had to deal with numerous other riots and even more day-to-day forms of resistance. James Scott (1985) has demonstrated that very often that was the only type of resistance possible under a Communist dictatorship, and took the form of, for instance, rejecting collectivization, concealing grain, refusing to work for the kolkhoz or working "with arms down," and killing cattle rather than making it collective property. Just when peasant protest peaked, Stalin ordered the collectivization agents to retreat and accused them of having grown "dizzy from success." After that, the percentage of collectivized farms fell by a good half in just three months.[22]

It was a short-lived pause. In the summer of 1930, the denunciation of a fictitious "Labor Peasant Party" as a counterrevolutionary organization headed by economists as well known as Alexander Chayanov and Kondratiev was a bad augur. However, favorable weather conditions produced an excellent harvest and grain collection was even better. Rather than give thanks to the weather, the leaders, Stalin first and foremost, attributed that success to collectivization (Mao did the same in 1958), and instead of building up stores that would sorely be needed later, they exported 5.8 million tons of the grain. The government then relaunched collectivization with a second wave spread over two years from September 1930 to July 1932. At the outset the collectivization agents were fairly passive, given the rebuff they had suffered in March, but from the spring of 1931 they were obliged to increase pressure. This time nobody could claim to associate progress with collectivization with progress in production—which in any case was compromised by the severe drought that then occurred in the Urals and in Siberia.[23]

Kazakhstan

The first famine occurred in Kazakhstan that same year. It started in 1930 and ended only in 1933, after killing at least one-third of the Kazak population, with an estimated 1.4 million dead and missing out of a population of around 4 million. The wide-scale revolts of 1929–1931 were an expression of people's despair. Cereal procurement was enforced in a climate of terror and was stepped up far more rapidly here than anywhere else with the exception of Ukraine and Kuban, rising from 33 percent of production in 1930 to 39.5 percent in 1931, despite production being in free fall (having dropped by one-third between 1928 and 1932). Meat requisitioning rose even more, from 31,200 tons in 1926 to 400,000 tons in 1929. That same year, herdsmen were obliged to deliver nearly 15 percent of all Kazak livestock to the state, and the percentage rose to 47 percent in 1931 and to 68 percent in 1932! That exorbitant share is partly explained by the spectacular fall in Kazak livestock numbers, once the largest in the entire Soviet Union. It dropped by nine-tenths between 1928 and 1934, and by 97.5 percent in the nomadic and seminomadic zones. Forced to become sedentary and hand over their animals to the kolkhozes, many Kazak herdsmen either killed their animals or fled with them. The livestock in the collective farms and the "industrial" meat production enterprises was also decimated during the winter of 1930, as a result of the neglect and disorganization that followed over-hasty collectivization. Forced sedentarization was even less well thought-out than collectivization. People were dumped on insalubrious sites on which it was impossible to grow any food crops, with only four hospitals for five hundred such sites. They were provided with one building for forty families, but no heating, water, soap, or blankets. The people had only worn-out, torn, and dirty clothes, or they covered themselves in roughly made, untanned sheepskin. Forced sedentarization made many of the nomads, and especially their children, subject to contagious diseases, all the more deadly to them because they were so undernourished. Many died from hunger and disease, others simply took flight. Nearly two million Kazaks (half the population) fled in order to survive, some to the interior of Kazakhstan, the others to various Asian Soviet Republics or even to Western Siberia, the Central Volga, or China. Many later returned, but emigration became permanent for six hundred thousand of them.[24]

Escalation in Ukraine (second half of 1932 to January 1933)[25]

The largest proportion of people who died from hunger was in Kazakhstan, but the carnage was greater in Ukraine where between 3 million and 3.5 million people died. Many more studies have been carried out on the Ukrainian famine (and it was more frequently mentioned in the press) for several reasons, not the least being that Ukraine is a European nation. The famine there raised a question that the Kazakhstan famine did not: the hypothesis of whether or not Stalin had deliberately aggravated the famine from the autumn of 1932.

If the government had stuck to two waves of collectivization and grain requisitioning (from the fall of 1929 to the summer of 1932, separated by the retreat and pause in the spring and summer of 1930), the worst might have been avoided, especially in Ukraine, but also in the Kuban and Volga regions and Western Siberia. True, the excessive levy (nearly 23 million tons in 1931, or one-third of what was already a poor harvest) and the pursuit of exports (4.8 million tons) led to a critical situation as early as the spring of 1932. Ukraine was obliged to give up 42 percent of its harvest to offset the deficit in the drought-stricken eastern regions, and the first food shortages occurred there in February and March. To fulfill the 1931 procurement plan, many kolkhozes even had to relinquish a portion of their seeds, thereby compromising their future. On 10 June 1932, Vlas Chubar, the head of the Ukrainian government, asked for emergency help in a long letter to Stalin and Molotov, in which he reported the peasants' complaints: "Why did you create an artificial famine? After all, we had a harvest. Why you confiscate it all?" He received no reply. Two days later Molotov, his opposite number in the Soviet government, declared, "Even if we face the specter of famine, especially in the cereal producing regions, the procurement plan must be fulfilled at any price." On 21 June, Stalin and Molotov confirmed Moscow's position in a telegram to the Ukrainian Communist Party: "No fall in deliveries due from the kolkhozes and sovkhozes will be tolerated, there will be no extension of delivery deadlines." Even though the majority of the delegates to the Ukrainian Communist Party conference held in Kharkov from 6 to 10 July deemed that Moscow's procurement plan was "impossible to achieve," they changed their minds and ratified it after Molotov and Kaganovich arrived to teach them a lesson. The procurement plan demanded 6 million tons from Ukraine, which it simply could not deliver.[26]

These exchanges in June and July 1932 heralded Sokoloff's famous "final escalade." He dated it at the beginning of the following month with the 7 August 1932 decree punishing by death, or ten years in a camp, anyone caught stealing public property. The peasants named the decree "the law of spikelets" from what the peasant women (nicknamed the "hairdressers") gleaned in the collective fields to feed their families, but the law mainly targeted peasants who were caught with grain reserves. Stalin himself pushed the law through, furious that grain requisitioning was coming in so poorly.[27] While he may have attributed imaginary motives to the farmers, he was not wrong in suspecting them of trying to boycott requisitioning by concealing a portion of their harvests. They buried wheat in "grain pits," hid it in secret warehouses, or diverted it during transportation to the silos. Some kolkhozniks complained of having less grain than before collectivization, others left the kolkhozes, taking collectivized tools and cattle with them, more still stole from the collective harvest, often with the complicity of the Communist cadres. They harvested and distributed the wheat before it was ripe, or came at night in groups armed with sickles to steal it in the field. Lastly, demonstrations and hunger riots grew increasingly frequent, with more than one thousand in Ukraine during the first half of 1932, for which the local authorities sometimes paid the price. Apart from these, what really troubled the OGPU informers was the fairly widespread complicity between kolkhoz members and leaders, including Party and Soviet officials, who were almost unanimous in condemning, and if possible sabotaging, the procurement plans.[28]

In fact, concealment, petty theft, and diversion hardly contributed to the growing deficit in the grain procurement plan. The "hunting tables" in the OGPU reports revealed mediocre spoils. There were simply not enough reserves to accomplish an unachievable procurement plan. That was so glaringly obvious for anyone living in the countryside, especially in the regions hardest hit by procurement, such as Ukraine and Kuban, that Party members handed in their cards out of disgust and despair, and regional leaders—not all, but the most courageous among them, or the momentarily courageous who later had second thoughts—grew bold enough to attempt behind-the-scenes negotiations to reduce the quotas imposed on them, or even beg for emergency food aid. They were rebuffed by Molotov or some other lackey and made Stalin even angrier. According to Stalin, the Ukrainian leaders were useless and must be replaced, they allowed themselves to be influenced by gossip or manipulated by kulaks or other enemies of the Soviet government, or even by foreign agents. "We could lose Ukraine," he wrote to Kaganovich in August 1932. Not lose Ukrainians by starvation, but lose Ukraine itself, which might break away. It was in Ukraine that the peasant revolts had been the most numerous some thirty months earlier, and Ukrainian nationalism had not abated. Józef Piłsudski's spies abounded, the Ukrainian Communist Party was rife with "rotten elements and conscious or inadvertent Petliurites whether they know it or not."[29] It was urgent to regain control, and oblige the Ukrainian peasants to obey the Soviet Union's priority global development objectives once and for all.

In the short term the regain of control proved to be efficient. The September procurement campaign was almost in line with the plan, but nearly half the annual collection had to take place in October and November, once the harvest was in. But that harvest proved to be even worse than the 1931 one, and consequently less than 60 percent of the procurement plan was collected in the entire Soviet Union, and less than 40 percent of the target in Ukraine.[30] Stalin was all the more indignant because he wanted to convince himself that the 1932 harvest was better than the 1931 one. As the harvest progressed he was obliged to revise his forecasts downward, but he was still far short of the target. In any case, the excesses of the 1931 procurement plan (42 percent of Ukraine's harvest, as we have seen, and up to 47 percent in Kuban, whereas under the NEP the peasants were selling just 15–20 percent of their harvest) made it impossible to repeat the exploit in 1932.

On the production front too, the peasants paid the price of the earlier constraints and imbalances. Yields fell for many reasons, starting with the abandonment of the traditional crop rotation system. Although that was not the most important reason, its impact was multiplied because of the increase in the cultivated land area, which reached record levels in 1931 and fell very little in 1932. The soil, which had not been left fallow long enough, grew poorer. Yields suffered even more from the unfavorable weather conditions and the shortage of seeds following the poor harvest of 1931, and more importantly, from shoddy and tardy work at all stages of agricultural production, from the plowing and sowing to the hoeing, harvesting, and threshing, carried out by poorly fed and badly paid kolkhozniks. Finally there was the sharp drop in cattle numbers since many animals were killed to prevent them being taken over by the kolkhoz, and later because there was nothing left to feed them. The horses lacked fodder, they were overworked and untended. The shortage of draft animals was partly offset by tractors, but these were no longer imported in 1932 because of the drastic and inevitable drop in grain exports. People therefore made do with those produced by Soviet industry, but since these were few and far between, they were used over-intensively, like the horses. Nor were they repaired, for there was a shortage of spare parts, the tractor drivers were inexperienced, and there was little or no maintenance.

Agricultural labor therefore grew slower and less efficient, falling behind in the process and further jeopardizing the success of the harvest. To cap it all there was a shortage of natural fertilizer because of the drop in livestock numbers.[31]

Soon men were in as short supply as the animals. Mendel Katayevich, first secretary of the Dnepropetrovsk region, warned prophetically, "We must care that the main production and consumer needs of the kolkhozy and the collective farmers are satisfied otherwise there will soon be nobody left to sow and ensure production."[32] Because the procurement plan was impossible to fulfill, the state was obliged to reduce its demands and increase pressure on local producers and authorities in order to attain the lower objectives at all costs. At the end of November, one week after the "friendly" exchange between Khatayevich and Molotov, the levy had brought in less than fifteen million tons of grain (compared with more than twenty-one million in the same period after the very mediocre levy in 1931) and the procurement plan was reduced by three million tons.[33]

By now the dramatic acceleration of the escalade had begun; in other words, this was the "final escalade," and the "desperate battle for grain" (Davies and Wheatcroft, 2004) took on a terrorist guise. From the end of October, Molotov and Kaganovich headed two independent commissions charged with speeding up procurement in Ukraine and Kuban. They compiled a blacklist of kolkhozes, villages, and districts that had fallen behind in their grain deliveries (and automatically deprived their shops of all products, including food).[34] They confiscated their last reserves, arrested and deported the "procurement plan saboteurs" (in some cases entire villages were packed off to Siberia), and dismissed and imprisoned thousands of local cadres.[35] Soon those commissions were feared even more than the fabled "shock brigades" that were formerly recruited among Communist city-dwellers and komsomol members to "take cereals" from the villages. Many peasants, individuals and kolkhozniks, abandoned their land without permission and flocked to the cities or the major infrastructure projects in search of work. Two or three years after the "self-dekulakization," a second "de-peasantization" wave occurred, but from now on it was carried out by the poor and middle peasants themselves. While Kaganovich left with others to deal with Ukraine, the year 1932 ended with a final and fatal measure imposed on the Ukrainian Communist Party leadership: the confiscation of so-called seed stores from the kolkhozes, a fairly logical move really, given that soon there would no longer be any able-bodied people left to sow them.

The Ukrainian exodus was logical too, since people abandoned a region in which there was nothing left to eat. By January 1933 the exodus was already massive and would have grown still further had the authorities not taken care to block departures "knowingly organized by the enemies of the Soviet state." They intercepted fugitives in train stations and on the roads and sent them back to their deaths. Not all of them though, the most suspect among them turned out to be luckier, since they were imprisoned or deported to the gulag. On 22 January, Stalin issued a secret circular ordering an immediate end to the massive exodus of peasants fleeing Ukraine and the Kuban "on the pretext of looking for bread." He blamed "the enemies of the Soviet state" for organizing the exodus, "in order to discredit ... the kolkhoz system in particular and the Soviet system in general."[36] On the very next day the sale of train ticket to Ukrainians was prohibited, twenty-five thousand fugitives were arrested in the last week of January 1933, and two hundred thousand others over the following months. The domestic passport was brought into force on 27 December 1932, based on its Czarist predecessor, making it possible to track non-urbanites who might have slipped through the net. "People who were swollen up through hunger were transported in goods trains to the countryside and abandoned some 50–60 kilometers from the city so that no one would see them die."[37]

The measures applied from November 1932 to January 1933 stripped Ukraine of its last reserves and were responsible for the extent of the catastrophe. Every day from February to July 1933, dozens of bodies were picked up on the streets of Kiev and Kharkov, but there were ten times more deaths in the surrounding countryside, right to the border of Moldavia (and ten times more deaths in June 1933 than in June 1932). There followed the usual consequences of an acute famine: rural banditry, the lynching of thieves, abandonment of children, necrophagy, and cannibalism. Since few survivors were left to work the land, tens of thousands of men, women, and teenagers were rounded up in the marketplace in Kharkov and in other towns and sent to work in their stead. Later, during the remainder of 1933 and in 1934, hundreds of thousands of demobilized soldiers and other Russians were settled on that depopulated land. After Ukraine, the Kuban, the Volga, and the Black Earth regions were the worst hit, but excess mortality spread right across the Soviet Union with at least four million dead from hunger in 1932–1933, which is three to four times more than died in the gulag over a twenty-five-year period. That same year, infant mortality exceeded 300 per thousand across the Soviet Union.[38]

The Great Leap Forward

Mao loved to praise the virtues of "negative examples," mercilessly pointing them out from among the ever-criticized class enemies in order to educate the heirs of the revolution. But did he learn the lesson from the profusion of negative examples provided by the tragedy of 1933 and the four preceding years? Apparently so, since in 1958 he inaugurated a Chinese way that ceased to be faithful to the model he had followed unswervingly until then. This claim to originality contributed to the emergence of the "Far Eastern Schism," which began during that period. It would have been praiseworthy had the new model corrected the aberrations of the original.

Alas it did not, or hardly at all. Mao criticized the Stalinist development strategy and altered his own, but this correction had nothing to do with factoring in a famine that was distant in both time and space, and about which he knew very little. He was content just to take into account the most recent vexations. We may credit the first Chinese Five-Year Plan (1953–1957) with accelerated industrial construction, but it also confirmed that it was no longer possible to continue neglecting agriculture. That sector had received only 7 percent of the government's total investment in the plan, compared with 46.5 percent for heavy industry. The emphasis on expensive technology had drawn abundantly on the country's meager capital resources but very little on the overabundant workforce. It was in part to remedy that imbalance that the GLF was concocted during the winter of 1957–1958.

In actual fact, Mao did not change tack. He claimed to be doing everything at once and faster than before, but the necessary readjustments carried out in agriculture and the consumer industries were not accomplished at the expense of heavy industry. If industry had benefitted too much in the past, it now benefited still more, obtaining 57 percent of total investment in 1958 versus 46.5 percent, the investment itself having increased disproportionately. In 1959 it was further increased to reach

a historic record of 43.4 percent of GNP! The god of steel, that symbol
of modernity and power, demanded maximum effort, as witnessed by
the cascade of quotas that followed one after the other in the space of
a few months: 6.2 million tons (annual production) in February 1958,
already a 16 percent increase in relation to the 5.35 million tons produced
in 1957, and then 8 million tons in May and 10.7 million in August. Mao
himself had seen to it that the objective (doubling production in one
year) was ratified by the Politburo before increasing it himself to 11 and
then 12 million tons in three speeches he made in early September.[39]
This additional production was to come in part from the small backyard
furnaces, which between 70 and 90 million (sources differ) peasants,
mostly peasant women, were busy stoking using very rudimentary
techniques. To keep those furnaces going, the local Communist cadres
seized saucepans, stoves, scissors, knives, spades, pickaxes, bicycles, iron
railings, door knockers, and temple bells—all to produce such mediocre
steel that nine-tenths had to be thrown away as scrap.[40]

Kitchen utensils and knives were in any case useless since people
could no longer cook in their own homes. Everyone ate in the canteens,
which served free food provided by the newly created People's
Communes. The agricultural cooperatives they replaced were, as the
name suggests, specialized in agricultural production. The far larger
Commune, created on the scale of the massive projects it was supposed
to undertake, was omnipotent. As the base-level administrative unit it
was charged with speeding up social evolution, and even carrying out a
veritable transition from a family framework to a community one. Was the
Commune the social counterpart to the economic GLF? That was hoped
a little and claimed a great deal. Preaching by example, many People's
Communes in Henan province (where the first Commune was founded)
ceased to distribute work points since everything was free, not only food
but clothing, education, medical care, weddings, and funerals. Without
going that far, other Communes abolished private plots, now as useless as
personal pots and pans, given that the advent of "each to his needs" was
imminent. Propaganda certainly did not contradict that prospect, even
hinting that the arrival of the Communist society was just around the
corner. The Party secretary of a town in Hubei province even announced
the date: the socialist era would end on 7 November 1958, forty-one
years after the October Revolution. The following day would mark the
advent of the Communist society.[41] The Soviets would take umbrage at

being overtaken by the Chinese. More seriously, the performance of the First Soviet Plan had suffered from the agrarian collectivization and its attendant reduction of the peasants' productivity. China did not repeat the error (it had already accomplished agrarian collectivization). Instead it made things worse by proposing to go further, from collectivization to "communization." China did indeed go faster than its model, quite oblivious to growing "dizzy with success," and within a few months 99.1 percent of the peasants had become members of People's Communes.

Those members were mobilized in almost military fashion. They went to work in squads, and the peasants were "soldiers on the agricultural front." That metaphor betrayed the true ambition of the Great Leap, which was less social (Communism) than economic: to mobilize the peasant masses to industrialize the nation and forge workers out of those peasant foot soldiers. Propaganda endeavored to make such taxing labor appear exciting, in order to arouse enthusiasm and inspire emulation. It sang relentlessly of selflessness in the hope of kindling that sentiment in the "poor white masses." For that was how Mao defined his compatriots in the spring of 1958, boasting that "the poor want to change the world," and the painter or calligrapher was now free to fill the blank sheet of paper. He could not have put it better, for the GLF was a utopia and the artist who conceived it was free to let his imagination to run wild, and to mold and remold human clay as he pleased.[42]

In fact the demiurge merely gave the initial signal that set off all the rest, the ceaseless activity and the distribution of tasks. That was how sixty million villagers were packed off to hydroelectric projects near and far, small and large. In no time at all they built numerous dams and dug countless irrigation ditches, all with the most rudimentary tools, working day and night in shifts to the sound of martial music blaring from loudspeakers. But since the projects were designed by peasants rather than engineers, and built from earth, corn cobs, and bamboo, rather than cement, many of the constructions were washed away in the first floods. The largest dams, inspired by the Dnieper dam, held out longer, but after the heavy rains of August 1975 two of them collapsed in Zhumadian, Henan province, killing three times as many people as the May 2008 earthquake in Sichuan.[43] Smaller dams and reservoirs merely reduced the yields they were supposed to improve with irrigation, for in their haste to get the job done faster, cadres and peasants often dispensed with drainage. As a result of the subsequent evaporation, salts in the water built up and led to the salinization of the soil.

The mobilization of a female labor force, now "liberated" from domestic tasks thanks to communal canteens, did little to offset the shortage of manpower that was the consequence of those projects and the rural furnaces. Add to that the exodus to the cities that boosted the workforce in modern industry from just over 9 million in 1957 to more than 25 million in 1958, while the agricultural workforce plummeted from 192 million in 1957 to 151 million in 1958. The Chairman ordered agriculture to become mechanized, but even fast-track industrialization cannot be carried out at the drop of a hat. And in the meanwhile sickles, spades, and pickaxes would have been most welcome had they not been melted down in the furnaces. Because of the shortage of labor, a portion of the bumper harvest of 1958 began to rot in the fields. Shock brigades were organized to work day and night to bring in the harvest. An editorial in the People's Daily (9 November 1958) thought it necessary to remind local cadres that peasant men and women must be allowed six hours of rest and sleep per day.[44]

The excellent harvest of 1958, the best since the revolution, was attributed to the People's Communes and the GLF rather than to the good weather. According to regional reports, a total 450 million tons of cereals was brought in that year, but Mao decided to be cautious and opt for 375 million tons. That is how, in the absence of reliable statistics, the official production figure for 1958 was arbitrarily decided by the head of state, and it was on that basis that the 1959 production target was set at 525 million tons, while taking care to reduce the land sown by 10 percent, and land sown with cereals by 13 percent. The leaders were now grappling with a thorny issue: what should they do with the surplus rice and wheat? Mao suggested that the peasants work only in the morning and devote the rest of the time to educating themselves. In actual fact the good harvest of 1958 exceeded the previous year's only by 1.33 percent, at 197.6 million tons compared with 195 million in 1957. With less land sown and less favorable weather conditions, the 1959 harvest fell to 170 million tons. People were growing disillusioned even before those poor results. By spring, in canteens where people had eaten their fill the previous fall, some foodstuffs were already running low. Matters grew worse after the harvest for, on the basis of those inflated forecasts, grain procurement reached record levels, far above all the other, equally excessive levies in Mao's lifetime: 67.4 million tons, nearly 20 million of which would later have to be returned to the starving peasants.[45]

144 | STALIN AND MAO

While not the sole cause, this pernicious process considerably aggravated the famine. The example for all the bragging came from above: "Let's produce more, faster, better, cheaper," "let's achieve the second Five-Year Plan in two years." Spoil-sport experts were silenced and timorous economists (in fact those who persisted in expressing objections were anything but timorous) were sanctioned, for instance Ma Yinchu, the rector of Beijing University, who was dismissed in 1958 for having dared to advocate birth control instead of trusting Mao's implacable wisdom that "every new mouth to feed is also a pair of arms and a pair of hands." In anticipation of future anti-Malthusian scientific conquests, an official communiqué drove the point home: "It will soon be proved that the arable land mass is not too small but too big, and the problem is not overpopulation but the shortage of manpower."[46] The GLF achieved the impossible feat of creating a labor force shortage in the largest peasantry in the world.

The leaders were taken in by the lies for which they, first and foremost, were to blame. The cadres were under such pressure that they were "tempted to inflate figures at every level" (Xue Muqiao, in charge of statistics, fired in 1959). The production figures were so fantastic that the regular increase in cereal procurement quotas appeared reasonable. Take, for instance, a county in Henan Province that, in 1958, doubled the state levies whereas production was supposed to have increased tenfold on the previous year. Competition between cadres constantly impelled them on to do better, to surpass the neighbor, to launch satellites (in reference to the Soviet Sputnik) ever higher into the skies. Those satellites might be the brilliant yields in the "sputnik" fields of Sichuan province, as much as the size and volume of the plants themselves: sixty-kilogram pumpkins, one-pound ears of corn, ears of wheat growing so densely that they could bear the weight of three children, and so on, and so on. In 1958, the convoy transporting Mao to the center of the Xushui model Commune in Hubei province, passed turnips, cabbages, carrots, and other vegetables lying piled up along the roadside for more than a *li* (a third of a mile). Mao was told in all seriousness that the peasants had thrown them there, not knowing what to do with such a food surplus. The Commune's Party secretary confirmed this, saying, "Here everybody eats five meals a day for free." In the words of Mao's personal doctor Li Zhisui, "the whole of China was a theatre, and everyone redoubled their efforts of exaggeration in order to please Mao."[47]

Despite that, Mao could not allow himself to be duped for long by the fantastical reports that came to him from the provinces. During the winter of 1958–1959, it became clear that despite the good harvest, grain procurement deliveries were below forecast and there was a risk of food shortages in the cities, where population numbers had risen considerably as a result of the rural exodus. In collusion with the local cadres, the peasants had held back a portion of the harvest. Some provincial leaders wanted to lead a merciless anticoncealment campaign, but Mao declared that he understood that the peasants had been driven to this kind of passive resistance by over-burdensome levies. "I now support conservatism. I stand on the side of right deviation. I am against egalitarianism and left adventurism."[48] As early as December 1958 he had warned that the advent of Communism would have to wait. The People's Communes should abstain from free food distribution and stick to the principle of "each according to his work." In 1958, the rich brigades, in other word the villages that were fortunate to have fertile soil and easily irrigated land, preferred to sit back with their arms crossed or hide their grain rather than share their surplus with the poorer brigades. From then on the previous system returned to the fore; egalitarianism lost out and productivity won the day.[49]

One sign of the changing times was the (provisional) return of Chen Yun (1905–1995), a member of the Permanent Committee of the Politburo and fifth in command in the regime. Chen was the person in charge of the economy and the only leader who opposed the GLF strategy from the start—which led to him being shunted aside. In the spring of 1959, he visited Henan, the vanguard province for utopic political activism, but did not believe a single word or number in the fairy tales spun by the regional leaders. Like Deng Xiaoping later, when he attempted to regain power, Chen Yun took cover behind a formula Mao used in Yan'an when advising his colleagues to "seek truth from facts" (shishi qiushi). Mao also came around to that sensible argument in a letter dated 29 April 1959 with instructions to the Party cadres: "Fixing production targets must be based on realities. Just do not pay any attention to these stipulations made in the instructions from higher levels. State exactly how much you have harvested and refrain from making false statements which are contrary to facts." In June, Mao accepted Chen Yun's proposal to reduce the steel production quota for 1959 without batting an eyelid.[50]

Lushan (summer 1959)

In all, a good half year, from November 1958 to June 1959, was devoted to "consolidation," the standard euphemism for a retreat. At the end of June, when Mao went to Lushan (Jiangxi province) to preside over the leadership's summer meeting, he seemed resolved to confirm his rejection of exaggerations, illusions, and imbalance, as symbolized by Chen Yun's return to favor. Another leader, Marshal Peng Dehuai, minister of defense, had also made some enquiries in the provinces and drawn the same conclusions as Chen. From October 1958, he visited Gansu, Hunan, Jiangxi, and Anhui provinces. The son of a poor peasant himself, something quite unusual in the Party leadership, Peng had seen famine as a child; it had even killed several of his own brothers. He had only two years of schooling before starting to work and had no special knowledge of, or responsibility for, the economy. But he learned enough during those four trips to understand what was coming. Furthermore, during a trip to Moscow and Poland from 24 April to 13 June, he had learned about the Soviet criticisms of the GLF and the People's Communes. He had not yet decided to take the step, or even to go to Lushan, but Mao insisted—that selfsame Mao who was constantly urging his colleagues to express their criticisms freely. Peng, with his bulldog physique, was tireless and austere, and had a reputation for not mincing his words. During the Eighth National Congress of the Chinese Communist Party, he had expressed his surprise to Anastas Mikoyan, the head of the Soviet delegation, that the CPSU had waited so long to criticize Stalin. Mikoyan apparently answered, "We didn't dare to advance our opinions at that time. To have done so would have means death." To which Peng retorted, "What kind of a Communist fears death?"[51]

So Peng plucked up his courage and on the afternoon of 13 July, went to see Mao in Lushan to persuade him to go further still in correcting his GLF strategy.[52] Unable to express his viewpoint face to face because Mao was asleep, Peng spent the following night writing him a letter, which he then had delivered. There was nothing really original in that letter, which expressed the unspoken opinions of the majority in the Party leadership. Peng was careful to balance profit and loss with great tact, even when mentioning the backyard furnaces that had made him particularly indignant during his trip, but he committed the sacrilege of changing the prescribed order: victories first, then the setbacks. And in the second part of his missive he committed the more flagrant crime of lèse-majesté by attempting to show what lessons could be drawn from the GLF experience—normally the prerogative of the Party leader. After criticizing the irresponsible slogans launched by Mao earlier, Peng attributed the leftwing errors of the past twelve months to "petit-bourgeois fanaticism," in terms resembling those used by Lenin to denounce *"Left-Wing Communism": An Infantile Disorder.*[53]

That was more than Mao could take. He could criticize himself but for someone else to criticize him, and even make him look ridiculous was perfectly intolerable—especially when those criticisms came from Peng Dehuai, with whom he had not always seen eye to eye, and had clashed with in Yan'an. They had even disagreed on the strategy to use in the Korean War, during which Mao's favorite son was killed. Peng, the commander of a Chinese expeditionary force, had been unable to protect him. Khrushchev's open criticism of the Chinese People's Communes (on 18 July, in Poznan) further fanned the flames, but by then this was just more ammunition for Mao, who had already made up his mind to bring Peng down and get his revenge.

Mao chose to view that private letter, written to urge him to pursue a retreat he had already begun, as a political attack against him. The majority of the leaders were as surprised as Peng by the ferocious attack that followed, but then sided with Mao in criticizing him. Mao gave them no choice; they could either support the president or follow the militaristic "plotter" Peng. While Mao accepted his share of the responsibility for the launch of the GLF (how could he do otherwise?), he said, "I was not alone, and anyway who can claim to have never made a mistake?" Confucius had made mistakes, as had Lenin. "Marx too was guilty of impetuousness. … Contrary to what Peng has said, successes have won over failures, so it is only a partial failure. We have paid a price … and enabled the people of the entire nation to learn a lesson."[54] Zhu De was the only member of the Permanent Committee of the Politburo to defend Peng. The army remained silent, but just to make sure, Mao sent an ultimatum to his generals: "If you take Peng's side I will place myself at the head of the peasants and lead a guerrilla warfare against you."

The Plenary Session of the Central Committee met on 2 August and condemned the right-wing opportunism of the anti-Party clique headed by Peng Dehuai—a "clique" composed of the very few people who had dared to speak up using the same arguments as Peng (Zhu De merely pleaded for clemency) and one provincial official who was guilty of having provided the information Peng used as an argument in his letter. The warning was clear: from now on anyone criticizing the GLF would be considered to be part of that clique of reprobates. Peng immediately made his own self-criticism, but hotly denied the existence of the "military club" of plotters invented by Mao. Marshal Lin Biao replaced Peng at the ministry of defense and Peng left Zhongnanhai (the official residence of the upper echelons of leadership). He spent the next six years in a suburb northwest of Beijing, but that was just a moment of respite compared with what would happen to him later.

The relaunch of the Great Leap Forward (end 1959) and the carnage (1960–1961)

Lushan was just one of the regime's turning points, which started in the fall of 1957 if not before that. It was however *the* turning point for the famine. "Had the leadership reversed course in the summer of 1959 at Lushan, the number of victims claimed by famine would have been counted in the millions, "and not in dozens of millions.""[55] Frank Dikötter's assessment illustrates the bitter truth: Peng's courage relaunched and aggravated the famine. The Plenum revised downward (drastically, but insufficiently) both the 1958 production figures and the 1959 objectives— was that not, after all, what Mao had in mind in a bygone era, before he received Peng Dehuai's sacrilegious letter? But to no avail, for the torrent of denunciations of right-wing opportunists and Peng Dehuai's henchmen was enough to discourage local cadres and provincial leaders from carrying out the adjustments they had begun earlier in the year. It was less dangerous to err on the left than to err on the right. Anyone wanting to avoid being labeled a right-wing opportunist had to be careful not to challenge the validity of the People's Communes or the communal canteens. As the *People's Daily* of 29 August 1959 insisted, "Despite internal and external enemies, right-wing opportunists, and natural disasters, the People's Communes have held up well. They will never collapse."[56] One unwise official who suspended the communal canteens in a county in Anhui province (22 September), in line with what was being done on a wide scale six months earlier with the center's blessing, was promptly labeled a right-wing opportunist by Mao. In Macheng, in the neighboring province of Hubei, the militia patrolled the streets in search of any smoke escaping from chimneys. Families guilty of having cooked at home were fined and their food and kitchen utensils confiscated. At the end of 1959, the canteens were feeding four hundred million people, or more than 72 percent of the members of People's Communes (and nearly 98 percent in Henan, one of the provinces in which the famine was most devastating).[57]

The lethal frenzy was launched again, but on a different scale than during the first phase of the GLF. As in the Soviet Union, compulsory grain requisitioning was responsible for the deaths of the largest number of peasants, but the main difference was that in China the official media were far more trusting of the most flagrant lies. Xinyang prefecture in southern Henan province is a good illustration of the process that led from fabrication to famine via terror. In the fall of 1959, the local authorities of Guangshan, a *xian* dependent on Xinyang, announced grain yields of 239 tons, which was closer to triple than to double the true harvest figure of 88.4 tons. The state's share was therefore set at 75.5 tons, but since the authorities received only 62.5 tons, which already represented 70 percent of the real harvest, the local cadres launched an extremely brutal anticoncealment campaign. True, the peasants had hidden a portion of their grain, but far less than was assumed by the authorities, who claimed to have detected an ideological conflict in which "little Peng Dehuais" reported that the harvest was not as good as in 1958 and that there was a food shortage. The cadres were told to report on the campaign up to three times a day. They were to smash the "three obstacles" attributed to the peasants, who (1) claimed they no longer had any grain, (2) demanded the closure of the canteens, and (3) tried to run away. They beat up, tortured, imprisoned, or killed the "enemies of socialism" suspected of hiding their grain.[58] In some places they knocked down walls and vied with each other in devising new forms of cruelty, in the hope that torture would finally lead to a confession about where the grain was concealed.

As in the preceding cases, local cadres were responsible for the most deadly violence. In a highly hierarchical system, they themselves were the victims of the upper echelons, who subjected them to such pressure to collect the grain quotas that they could not do so without resorting to violence. If they failed or objected, the Communist cadres not only faced political sanctions, demotion, dismissal, and arrest, but were themselves quite often thrashed, injured, and even beaten to death.[59] So they in turn resorted to thrashings, torture, and sham executions (and even real ones) on pilferers, escapees, or simply people who worked too slowly (see Box 2).

In all, violence leading to death contributed substantially to the excess mortality of 1959–1961.[60]

Box 2

Violence and Torture Inflicted on Chinese Peasants during the Famine

In the Wanxian region of Sichuan province, where the local cadres unlawfully set up private courts, jails and labor camps, methods of torture included, "hanging people up, beating them, forcing them to kneel on burning charcoal, piercing their mouths, clipping off their fingers, stitching their lips, pushing needles into nipples, force-feeding them with feces, stuffing dried beans down their throats, and so on" (Zhou Xun). Some torture victims died of their injuries, others committed suicide, and many were beaten to death, tied up and thrown into a pond while still alive, or else buried alive. In the People's Commune of Dahe, also in Sichuan, one cadre tortured 311 people from the same brigade, 8 of whom subsequently died. Children were beaten to death for stealing a handful of rice or merely looking at a cadre preparing a hearty meal. In the south of Yunnan province, people from the national minorities caught trying to escape to Vietnam, Laos, or Burma were beaten, a mother and her baby were killed with a bayonet, while other escapees were locked in a house and blown up with dynamite. When torture victims began dying in droves (as in 1961 in Fengle Commune, Sichuan), the Party secretary told his underlings not to overestimate the scope of the collateral damage: "A few deaths are nothing, there are too many people in our country, the more people die, the more food there is for us to eat."

Sources: Mainly Zhou Xun, 2012, pp. 21–22, 34, and 123; also Dikötter, 2010, pp. 239, 294, 296, 311, and 319. Other authors, from Jasper Becker to Ralph Thaxton, and from Yang Jisheng to Yang Xianhui, confirm the banality (to parody Hannah Arendt) of the brutality, torture, and summary executions.

By 1960, there was nothing left of the egalitarianism proclaimed two years earlier. The local Party secretaries and their families, other cadres too (and of course the cooks in the communal canteens), survived in far larger proportions than the remainder of the villagers. They frequently ate in separate refectories with better quality and more abundant food than the rations distributed to the peasants who lined up in front of the canteens with their bowls. The Communist cadres were occasionally invited to banquets, but urban cadres fared better than their rural counterparts, although rural cadres occasionally went to the cities for meetings they nicknamed "health-replenishing activities," which had the advantage of not arousing the jealousy of the villagers.[61] Some local cadres protected their flocks, for instance by concealing and redistributing part of the harvest. More often they would favor some people above others, and ultimately came to hold the lives of the Commune members in their hands. According to the principle that had already been experimented with in the gulag, healthier people, more able to work, were sometimes given more food, whereas "death rations" (si liang) were given to the weak, the uncooperative, and the shirkers. In several Sichuan xian, the authorities even deprived those too weak to work of any food at all in order to hasten their deaths.[62]

In any case, there was so little to share that the government began to promote food substitutes (daishipin). Among the "natural substitutes" (plant- and animal-based ones, as opposed to synthetic substitutes for meat, milk, artificial oils, etc.), the prize surely goes not to an insect species, rats or field mice, egret droppings, tree bark, cores, stalks, leaves, corn husks, rice straw, or roots, but to an algae called chlorella, which began to be used in Shanghai in the first half of 1960 for feeding pigs. By the end of July, twenty-seven provinces were growing it to feed humans (it was supposed to be more nourishing diluted in a little urine). At the end of 1960, the department of ideological propaganda attributed food substitutes with "a nutritional value ... even greater than of real grain," as a result of which many people poisoned themselves, and workers complained of having to eat what even the chickens used to turn down. Others reminisced ironically, "If only our lives were ... as good as working as a hired-hand for a landlord ... as good as it was for pigs and dogs back then."[63]

Such words may have provided a few seconds of comfort, but survival was a matter of action, preferably nonviolent, since the regime's repressive capacities could put an end to the slightest attempt at revolt.[64] Riots and collective violence were less widespread than in the Soviet Union in 1930, following the first round of collectivization and dekulakization. Conversely people made considerable use of what James Scott calls "the weapons of the weak,"[65] such as theft and petty thievery, underestimating harvests, botching up work, killing livestock, and so forth. Chinese historian Gao Wangling listed the thousand and one ways of "extracting food from the tiger's mouth." Most acts of resistance (fanxingwei) he catalogs are "everyday forms of resistance,"[66] one of the most common being to surreptitiously eat unripe plants before the harvest. In seven production brigades in Shandong province, 70 percent of the forthcoming harvest was eaten in this way. That practice may have prolonged many lives, but not those of children under the age of six, or elderly people, whose stomachs were unable to digest unripe cereals.[67] And even though this may have provided some short-term relief, it was one of the causes of the disastrous harvests that followed in 1960 and 1961. Among the survival strategies already mentioned, pure and simple theft appears to have been the most common. Large-scale theft took place at night as the harvesting drew near. The authorities increased the number of night patrols, but they were often inefficient, not least because those very same night watchmen were the following day's pillagers, and vice versa. Although large-scale thefts (da tou) were an exception, petty thievery increased, enabling many members of People's Communes to divert a hundred or so jin of grain (about fifty kilograms) from the collective sector, enough to enable a family to survive.[68]

The government, apparently incapable of imagining just how poor the 1960 harvest was (144 million tons [see Table 2]) levied an excessive amount, which meant that it later had to return 20 million tons to the starving farmers. The remaining 113 million tons left only 215 kilograms of grain per rural inhabitant, compared with 298 kilograms in 1957, on the eve of the GLF. Subsistence level is around 275 kilograms per person per year, and 300 kilograms leaves a slim surplus for seed and animal fodder. The following year's harvest proved to be even more catastrophic (136.5 million tons), the amount levied was a little less exorbitant, and the remainder (110.7 million tons) still very insufficient. However, it was now spread over fewer rural inhabitants, given the number of people who had died of starvation the previous year, so the result was 207 kilograms per inhabitant.[69] The three years 1959 to 1961 were by far the most deadly, especially 1960, since that year alone was about as lethal as the four years (1958, 1959, 1961, and 1962) taken together.[70] The 1962 harvest, while not as good as those from 1952 to 1959, was still better than the two previous ones in 1960 and 1961, and helped to put an end to the carnage. A more decisive factor in stopping it, however, was the two measures that helped to reduce grain procurement quotas in the countryside, namely increasing cereal imports, and sending back to their villages some twenty million recent arrivals to the cities.[71] The famine really peaked from 1959 to 1961.

Table 2. Grain Production and Extraction: The Food Availability of Rural Inhabitants (in millions of tons, except per inhabitant)

	Total Production	Extraction			Food Availability of Rural Inhabitants	
		Initial	Sold Back to Peasants	Net	Totals	Per Inhabitant (in kilos)
1957	195	48	14	34	161	298
1958	197.65	58.8	>17	41.7	156	290
1959	169.7	67.4	<20	47.6	122.1	227.6
1960	144	51	20	31	113	215
1961	136.5	40.5	14.7	25.8	110.7	207
1962	154.4	38.1	12.4	25.7	128.7	230

Source: Ash, 2006, pp. 970 and 973.
NB: I have rounded some of the figures up or down.

Comparisons

The comparisons lie essentially in the obvious relationship between the two famines. In the period preceding them, the beginnings of a demographic transition had led to a rapid population increase in both countries, while rapid urbanization led to a sharp increase in the number of non-cereal-producing consumers. Underdevelopment in both countries left their governments with no choice but to try to catch up in leaps and bounds, and both wanted to go too fast—far too fast. In accordance with Yevgeni Preobrazhenski's Law of Socialist Accumulation,[72] the two countries embarked on an accelerated industrialization program while the economy and rural societies paid the price. In both countries a similar development strategy led to excessive transfers from agriculture to heavy industry. While the first Chinese Five-Year Plan took the first Soviet plan as its model, the GLF, as we have seen, marked an attempt at shedding that model, but was made impracticable by the desire to surpass it and advance faster than the Soviet Union. In many respects, the GLF was an exaggerated reproduction of the first Soviet Plan. Unlike the aftershock of an earthquake, the GLF was far stronger and more deadly than the original.

A direct cause of the two famines was the excessive and ruthless grain requisitioning from producers that continued well after the famine had started. Similar methods were used, from steel probes to detect where grain was hidden (Ukraine, 1932) to smashed walls for the same purpose (Tibet, 1961–1963). In both countries there was veritable competition among units (Soviets or Communes) and neighboring districts to see which could extract the most grain, to the detriment of "rightists" or "dunce caps" (in China), or "blacklists" and "blackboards" (in the Soviet Union), honors that were conferred on anyone late in delivering the grain, or who posted only a meager catch at the end of the anticoncealment campaigns. Such a curse and disgrace was to be avoided at all costs, for as the leader of a *xian* in southeastern Henan province admitted, "Better to see a few hundred people die than to lose one's honor."[73]

In both countries, grain requisitioning plans were based on inflated harvest estimates—even more so in China than in the Soviet Union. Consequently the authorities ended up having to revise the plans, and thus their requirements, downward, as they lost a growing part of their illusions. Finally they were obliged not only to reduce grain levies but to return a portion of the levy to the starving producers. Help to the victims was too little, too late, albeit a little less derisory in China than in Ukraine. Another similarity lay in the decision to reserve food rations for those who worked or were still able to work. That selective aid was supposed to favor the working classes over the rest but mainly benefitted city dwellers over rural ones, workers over the peasants who produced the very grain that was denied them.[74] The Soviet internal passport, established in 1932 in full famine to stop the rural exodus, illustrates the priority given to supplying the cities, where food riots were deemed more threatening to the regime. The leaders had not forgotten that these had proved fatal to the old regime in Petrograd in February 1917. The Chinese *hukou* (residence certificate), which condemned anyone born in the countryside to remaining there for life, was established before the GLF, but applied more strictly and more systematically during the famine for the same reason. Apart from the key concern of ensuring the survival of the regime, there was the desire to conceal the famine from foreigners, which also explains the privileged treatment of urbanites, especially in Moscow, Leningrad, Beijing, Shanghai, and Tianjin.

Another trait common to both revolutions was the denial of famine, or rather of two episodes of it, since the Soviet Union did not hide the 1921–1922 famine, but concealed the one in 1946–1947. In both cases, doctors and local cadres were not allowed to report the cause of death; consider the secretary of a rural soviet near Kiev who was obliged "to put the same cause of death—old age—in front of each name; for the elderly as for the one-year-old child." In China, when the Jiabiangou camp on the fringes of the Gobi Desert was closed down, all the prisoners were freed, all but one, a doctor, who stayed on for six months to complete the medical files of all those who had starved to death by inventing a variety of pathologies.[75] And in both cases, the governments not only deprived themselves of international aid by not recognizing the disaster, but continued to export grain when numerous wheat or rice producers were dying of hunger—right until 1960 in the case of China, and until the end, albeit in increasingly smaller quantities, in the case of the Soviet Union.[76]

Actors and victims

There were also countless similarities in the attitudes of the actors and the victims, together with a few significant differences. The victims, peasants for the most part, hid or buried their grain, stole from the harvest or collective stores, tried to run away, and so on. In other words they tried to survive but hardly revolted, given what they had to endure. In Ukraine, there were many incidents of unrest, but fewer in the spring of 1933 than in the spring of 1930, and they were less widespread than during the peasant revolts of 1920–1921. In China, unrest was endemic during the famine, but provoked more pillaging of grain that actual riots, and any that did occur were no greater that those triggered by collectivization in 1954–1955.[77] "If our peasants and our workers were not so good [meaning subjugated], we would have had a Hungarian-style incident on our hand long ago and we would have had to ask the Soviet army to intervene" (Peng Dehuai).

Confronted with the same diktat from their superiors, the two Communist bureaucracies seem, overall, to have reacted in the same manner. That is especially clear in the way they dealt with the thefts carried out by the starving in order to survive. Just about everybody stole just about anything, or at least anything edible. With the exception of a few details, Gao Wangling's research (see above) could have been transposed from China to Ukraine and Siberia a quarter century earlier. One difference was the absence of emergency legislation in China, where there was no "spikelet law" (see above). The Communist cadres decided on the spot to whip, hit, or beat to death anyone who stole half a bowl of food or swiped a turnip from the collective fields. The banning of home cooking was a frequently used measure, but not an emergency law.

Flight away from the disaster areas was as inevitable as the pilfering, and even more harmless. The Ukrainians' exodus is the best known, but the population of Heilongjiang province grew by several million refugees during the GLF famine. In China as in the Soviet Union, there was a ban on ticket sales in stations or ferry ports, and road blocks were set up to prevent peasants from fleeing. Troops fired on escapees attempting to cross the Yangzi River to reach Nanjing.[78] Despite that, the hunt for fugitives and refugees was applied less systematically, massively or lethally in China than in the Soviet Union, where it was organized at the highest level.

We must admit the limits of our information regarding those recalled or presumed majority attitudes. The local cadres were at one and the same time victims and actors in the famine, and the appointed scapegoats when they were unable to meet the impossible objectives set by their superiors.[79] Because of their vulnerable position, many were tempted to be overzealous, while others (but in what proportion?) put the survival of their charges before their own fate and career concerns. It is difficult to explain the considerable variations in mortality rates between neighboring, equally poor or equally prosperous counties, other than by the zealousness of the local cadres in carrying out the deadly grain requisitioning, or diverting the agricultural labor force to ambitious industrial projects.[80]

That the survival or death of so many starving had depended on the behavior of local Communist cadres does nothing to diminish the responsibility of the higher echelons in the hierarchy. The behavior of the regional leaders in the Soviet Union conforms more to what might be expected of a totalitarian state. The Ukrainian leaders asked for food aid in June 1932 (which was refused); the following month they declared that the grain collection plan was not sustainable, but then promptly ratified it. Katayevich, first secretary of the Dnepropetrovsk region, did the same about-turn. He first pointed out (in November, in a letter to Molotov) how irrational it was to seize the last reserves of the kolkhozes, and then the following month, in the presence of the imperious Kaganovich, publicly supported the official line (with which he disagreed) and presented a mawkish report on the situation in the Odessa region.[81] During that December 1932 meeting, Roman Terekhov, head of the Kharkiv region, was the only one to distance himself a little from the official line. He dared to tell Stalin that there was famine in Ukraine, which triggered the famous response from the secretary general, "You have made up this fable about famine, you thought you would frighten us, but it won't happen. Wouldn't it be better for you to leave your post of regional Party secretary and central committee secretary and go to work in the Union of Writers: you will write stories and fools will read them." Yet a short while earlier, that same Terekhov had accused some of his subordinates of having sabotaged grain procurement and betrayed the Party. The same regional cadres fought behind the scenes to reduce or postpone the grain collection plans, which they knew were unachievable, and yet supported them in public, even to the extent of making apologies for their past "mistakes"— or should we say courage?[82] If by chance one of them (Terekhov) dared to venture his reservations in the presence of emissaries from Moscow and tell Stalin the truth, he also shamelessly bawled out the lower echelons for the insufficient amounts of grain levied in their sectors and ordered local Party committees to deal mercilessly with the black-listed kolkhozes.

"Flatterers, self-seekers and cowards," concluded an old Bolshevik in October 1932, while on a two-month assignment to Kharkov. "Afraid to lose their jobs and concealing the true situation. ... Not to report that the plans are unrealistic is worse than a right-wing deviation." His diatribe, deemed "anti-Party and intolerable," was at once transmitted to the Politburo in Ukraine. Around the same time, the case of a local Party secretary in the North Caucasus reveals just how dangerous deviation could be—for it could go far beyond losing one's post. True, this time it was a case of deviation in actions and not just in words. The Party secretary in question was condemned in October to ten years in prison for having taken it upon himself to advance one kilogram of grain per day worked to each kolkhoznik in addition to the 491 grams permitted by the authorities. In his defense he said that he wanted to encourage the kolkhozniks to produce more. Mikoyan compared that transgression to the Kronstadt revolt. Kaganovich treated the accused (named Kotov) of being an agitator. That was enough for the regional Party committee to order a retrial, the court having "underestimated the counterrevolutionary significance of Kotov's crime." He was promptly sentenced to death and executed.[83]

In China too many local cadres tried to protect their citizens and not all provincial leaders showed such excessive zeal in implementing lethal policies.[84] But among those who occasionally allowed themselves the luxury of holding more radical positions even than Mao, I shall mention Li Jingquan, Wu Zhipu, and Zeng Xisheng.[85] Why those three? Because the famine was most deadly in the provinces governed by those "radical" leaders (Sichuan, Henan, and Anhui). Their case differed from that of Ukraine and Kuban, which suffered the privilege of being the traditional wheat granaries and so were intensively exploited as soon as grain was in short supply.[86] When the situation grew worse, those leaders and many of their subordinates concealed a famine that would have revealed their lies. They collected and displayed what little grain remained, and brought out only the least poorly fed villagers during visits by senior officials. In 1961, when Liu Shaoqi and his wife, Wang Guangmei, came to report on Liu's native region, they found that the trees had been stripped of their bark and eaten by the starving, but the local leaders had taken care to cover the trunks with mud and straw to hide the fact. Liu discovered the truth only when some villagers grew bold enough to reveal that some twenty of them, including the Liu's nephew, had died of hunger. In this case, the regional leaders were trying to fool the president of the People's Republic, but the same procedure was carried out at all levels. One starving prefecture in southern Henan province arrogantly returned the grain sent as food aid by the provincial government. To accept it meant that they had exhausted their supposedly miraculous harvest.[87]

If lying was ubiquitous in the Soviet Union, it was even more so in China, where cadres were less likely to refrain from uttering the implausible. The regime itself was responsible for the one-upmanship in bragging: who could best accomplish the center's unrealistic demands. There was only one way to make oneself heard in the chorus of boasts, and that was to invent even more shamelessly. Nevertheless, that hardly explains how so many leaders allowed themselves to be taken in by such fantasies. I am rather skeptical about the explanatory value of cultural interpretations, although after a good half century of practice I still admire, as I did from the very first, the Chinese art of theater—not art or Peking Opera, but the omnipresent day-to-day staging for the heavens to bear witness, that can either amuse or arouse indignation. And of course its counterpart, disdain for lowly truth, which must be made presentable out of decency, or so as to learn lessons from it, and, under the Communist regime, to educate the masses.[88]

Without mentioning Chinese specificities, is it possible to suggest the hypothesis of a totalitarianism that had now reached maturity? The Soviets had to deal with all the original problems; the Chinese who followed apparently learned a lesson useful for bureaucracy, if not the revolution and the people. Rather than argue about unrealistic plans and then be obliged to capitulate under duress and later be executed during the Great Purge, was it not preferable to anticipate the center's desires and accomplish twice, or ten times the impossible norms, and attain heaven in one season instead of the five recommended by the supreme leaders?

A question remains: in 1959–1961, did the overzealous provincial leaders act out of conviction or careerism? Some were convinced radicals, and furthermore had climbed sufficiently high up the nomenklatura ladder not to hope for any further advancement. But that does not seem to be the case for the majority of those who carried out the most ruthless grain requisitioning and mobilized the maximum number of people for the radical construction products (hydroelectric and others) so dear to Mao's heart.[89]

Relations within the leading oligarchy (a misleading name since both dictators delegated only limited powers to their "colleagues") were somewhat different in Moscow and Beijing. Once Stalin was rid of the second Himalaya (Bukharin), he was surrounded only by his accomplices, Molotov and Kaganovich types, implacable and assiduous executors of his desires.[90] In China too, one is struck first and foremost by the submissive, follow-my-leader attitude of the central leaders. Their virulent criticisms of Peng Dehuai were all the more eloquent in that before Mao detected right-wing deviationism and conspiratorial machinations in Peng's letter, the other leaders had seen nothing to change in its contents.[91]

The discussions at the summit during a "realistic" period, such as in the six months preceding the Lushan conference, had a surreal aspect. The leaders suspected that something was up since grain procurement was not on a par with a harvest that supposedly had increased twofold. They correctly surmised that the peasants and cadres were concealing a part of the harvest, but nobody dared to question the official production figure. Not a single spokesman among those "realists" ventured a refreshing hypothesis along the lines of, "And what if the increase was only 50 percent instead of 100 percent?" (in that year of 1958, the best of the GLF, it did not reach even 1.4 percent). In Lushan, Politburo member Bo Yibo dismissed the critical report prepared by his experts at the last minute, as soon as he heard about Mao's "counterattack" against Peng Dehuai, and replaced it with a defense of, and apology for, the Great Leap. The following year, he insisted on a "far left" line in the industrial sector and imposed unreasonable objectives, contrary to his own firm moderate convictions. Deng Xiaoping himself hastened to remove any reference to the color of the cat in his famous speech,[92] and, for good measure, added strong support for the collective economy as soon as he got wind of Mao's political counteroffensive in the summer of 1962. Liu Shaoqi was one of the very few to show some courage in that same year (1962), and paid for it during the Cultural Revolution.

The phase that followed the Lushan summit meeting (from the fall of 1959) was more like the death knell of the summer of 1932, rather than the one in the fall of 1932: Lushan put Mao pretty close to Stalin on the podium of mass murderers. Even if Mao knew, from October 1958, that people were starving to death, and even if Stalin allowed himself to be misled on numerous occasions by what he wanted to believe, Stalin nevertheless could depend on more reliable statistics, and was better informed of the extent of the disaster and earlier on, than Mao had been.[93] He more deliberately allowed the peasants to die. Did he purposely doom them to death by starvation in Ukraine from the fall of 1932, as quite a few authors suggest? The problem was well put by Andrea Graziosi, who concluded that from the fall of 1932, Stalin used the famine and allowed it to get worse, letting the Ukrainian peasants pay the price. Stalin considered the Ukrainians, already guilty of having revolted more often that the others two years previously, to be very dangerous, and thought for years that "the national question is in essence a peasant one." Intellectuals could express themselves and spread dangerous ideas, but separatist troops were recruited from among the peasants. After 1917, Ukraine played a similar role to that conferred on Poland in the Czarist empire. Stalin always kept the national question in his sights, and that may have induced him to aggravate the famine, at the expense of the peasants in Ukraine and North Caucasus (where there were many Cossacks of Ukrainian origin). The famine was originally caused by his blunders, but it was not programmed as such. To add insult to injury, from the end of 1932 (and even more so in 1933 and 1934), the deadly terror that held sway in the villages was accompanied by sustained repression against Ukrainian cultural and educational institutions and their representatives. Teachers were sacked, intellectuals and writers were arrested, sent to the gulag, or driven to suicide. The Russification policy, which was also linguistic, and, to a lesser extent, the replacement of the Ukrainians who had starved to death with Russian settlers, tilted part of Ukraine's demographic balance in favor of the Russians.[94]

Without clearing Stalin's name, other historians put less emphasis on his "national" interpretation of the grain requisitioning shortage in Ukraine, and more on the political and economic crises resulting from the anti-peasant policy pursued since 1928. The kolkhozniks of 1932 were no longer the farmers of the NEP, or even those of 1928. They didn't give a fig about overgrown and invasive weeds and deliberately harvested as perfunctorily as possible so that they could return to glean once the collectors' backs were turned, and they organized collective strikes from July to October 1932, during the crucial season in the agricultural cycle. Convinced that excessive levies and not the drought would make famine inevitable, they challenged the authorities, "When you give us bread then we will show up at work. If you don't, then bring in the harvest yourselves." In January and February 1933, the kolkhozniks refused to prepare the sowing, "why work on a collective farm since they confiscated everything we harvested and earned last year?" They echoed the same dissent a month later, "in any case we won't be there (alive) to harvest what we have sown." It was to overcome this opposition once and for all that Stalin allegedly deprived the strikers or all means of subsistence and replaced them with workers from elsewhere, to show them that they weren't indispensable.[95]

Davies and Wheatcroft reach the opposite conclusion, even though recent research largely stresses the deliberate nature of the aggravation of the famine, despite the fact that the Soviet Union finally reduced its cereal exports, and even imported a little—far too little—and sent (belated and insufficient) food aid to Ukraine.[96] I cannot compare my profane musings with those of specialists engaged in, often lively, arguments;[97] nor can I shy away from expressing my own opinion. While I appreciate the soundness of Davies and Wheatcroft's arguments (and learned a great deal from their excellent study), I nevertheless tend to favor Graziosi's argumentation. He first reminds us that the 1.4-million-ton cereal reserves, estimated at their lowest level in early summer 1933, would have made it possible to feed between three and four million people for one year. That same year, the Soviet Union exported a further 220,000 tons of wheat. He then estimates the number of Ukrainians who died of starvation in 1932 at 100,000, and concludes that if Stalin had allowed the famine (or nature) to pursue its course, there would have been at most several hundred thousand deaths in 1933 and not some three million. Graziosi therefore attributes Ukrainian excess mortality in 1933 to the consequences of Stalin's "national" interpretation of the crisis. Ultimately, from November 1932, he utilized a famine caused by his mistakes to quell what he perceived as Ukrainian separatism, and at the same time transformed the federal Soviet state (Soviet Union) into a despotic empire.[98]

In China, the Tibetans and the Uighurs were not deliberately left to starve to death, but (as in the Soviet Union) the government refrained from distributing the reserves from the silos in neighboring Henan and Hubei provinces. These contained more than two million tons of cereals, which could have saved the millions who starved in Xinyang, on the border of the two provinces.[99] With Mao there was no intentionality, but total inability to recognize his errors as well as a dramatically irresponsible degree of inconsistency for a person invested with the highest office. In November 1960, at the peak of the famine, he stopped eating meat and lost a few pounds, but devoted the better part of a Politburo meeting to Sino-Soviet relations.[100] In all, the assessment of Mao's management of the famine is catastrophic, yet better than that of his counterpart who may deliberately have allowed a greater number of Ukrainian peasants to die.

Differences

The less important differences between the two famines (except for the last one) include mere differences of degree. Soviet collectivization was carried out too hastily, but the forced membership of the People's Communes was hastier still. As we have seen, in China the lies were far bigger and therefore more lethal. Conversely, the Soviet Union only reduced cereal exports but never stopped them altogether, whereas they did cease in China (albeit too late) and were replaced by imports.

Other differences lay in agricultural labor. In Ukraine, superficial digging compromised yields.[101] That sort of thing could be expected when there was a shortage of draft animals, the kolkhozniks were behind in their work and in any case had a tendency to botch up collective labor.

The complete opposite occurred in China, with even more catastrophic results. That is particularly ironic given that the idea of digging deep and planting close together was borrowed from none other than the Soviet Union. Mao was besotted by Trofim Lysenko's theories, which matched his own theory of class struggle: plants of the same "class" would not compete for light or food. Deep digging had already been tried out in the Soviet Union, but Mao wanted to surpass the model and had the peasants dig a meter deep, and sometimes even three or four meters deep. In Guizhou province, the trenches were so deep that the peasants had to tie ropes around themselves so as not to drown. In Anhui province, where there is very little topsoil in many areas, deep digging left the fields sterile for a number of years.[102]

In Ukraine, yields suffered from, among other things, the excessive increase in sown land, which peaked in 1931. The reduction in fallow land (already far less in normal years than in the rest of the Soviet Union) had a negative impact on soil fertility.[103] In China in 1959, the land sown with cereals was reduced even more recklessly. The 1958 harvest had been so abundant that it was believed that there would be no use for such mountains of cereals.

One of the more important differences, albeit less frequently mentioned, was the foothold and influence of the CCP in the countryside, which was far more solid, diffuse, and deep-seated that that of the Bolsheviks. While that is indisputable, the CCP's rural roots still left something to be desired and the center's control over the villages was highly variable. Urged to attain certain objectives, the rural cadres had a fair amount of latitude regarding the choice of means to achieve them. As for the empathy of the supreme leaders with the peasants, that ultimately proved to be very weak in China too. In the spring of 1959, Mao claimed to understand the peasants who were defending their class interests when they concealed their grain. Later experience confirmed that despite their rural origins, Mao and the other leaders hardly understood the peasants at all—albeit a little better than Stalin.

At least as important were the Chinese innovations, such as the canteens and People's Communes, which were a means to an end: industrialization. That was to be achieved by exploiting China's massive rural labor force, perceived as being the country's great advantage. The canteens alone may have been responsible for one-third of the deaths by starvation.[104]

Ethnic minorities, on the other hand, suffered far more from the famine in the Soviet Union than in China. Nearly 80 percent of the "Soviet" people who starved to death were Ukrainians or Kazakhs, the latter solely because of irresponsible policies brutally applied, and a total indifference to their fate. In China the famine hit provinces with a majority Han population (Anhui, Henan, and Shandong) more than those on the periphery, if only because the latter produced less grain and were harder to reach. Harshly-hit Qinghai, where many Tibetans live, was an exception, but even within Qinghai province Garnaut's findings apply quite well: grain surplus areas located in the eastern, relatively accessible part of the province, were especially hard hit. The real question posed by the geography of the famine in China is how to attribute the respective share of responsibility to the economic factors and to the behavior of the provincial leaders.[105] Unlike in the Soviet Union, national considerations never played a role.

Each of the two famines comprised three or four phases, but in China it pursued its course in fits and starts. In the Soviet Union it was inexorable. An initial or premonitory phase, during which the Kazakh slaughter foreshadowed what was developing elsewhere, was followed by a two-phase escalation: in the summer of 1932, and from October 1932 to January 1933. Last, after the already high February mortality rates, the crisis in Ukraine and North Caucasus lasted five months (from March to July 1933, the peak being in May). In China, the famine started in 1958, was managed with unequal results from November 1958 to June 1959, and then took off again from the fall of 1959, ending only as late as the spring of 1962. The crisis lasted not five months but two good years (what an epithet) from the fall of 1959 to the fall of 1961, with the peak in mortality rates occurring between the winter of 1959–1960 and the fall of 1960.

That interminable ordeal reflected the objective situation in China, where there was far less room for maneuver. Stalin (and his accomplices) were every bit as responsible as Mao for the causes and management of the two famines. Why then were the effects of the famine more catastrophic in China? Simply because in normal times (before the famine) the overpopulated country was living, or rather subsisting, on borderline rations: 307 kilograms of grain per inhabitant in 1956, a record since the foundation of the new regime, equaled and surpassed for the first time in 1975 (308 kilograms), just before Mao's death, an event that paved the way to decisive agricultural progress at last.

Even though Soviet agriculture was also in urgent need of modernization, every Soviet citizen could depend on an average of nearly 500 kilograms of cereals. Horses consumed some of that, but in periods of food shortages the slaughter of cattle did provide people with a safety margin that was not available to the Chinese, while the cattle, dead or alive, also provided a considerable supplement of meat and dairy products compared to the (very slim) resources available to the Chinese consumer. To illustrate the contrast in the conditions that prevailed in the two countries, it is enough to compare the food substitutes, detailed by Davies and Wheatcroft to the *daishipin* (same meaning) studied by Gao Hua.[106] The former, which appear almost harmless, were similar to those the Chinese resorted to during the first phase of the famine, before things got even worse.

***

Two causes then, the first obvious, but the second more important:

- The same development strategy (accelerated industrialization at the cost of agriculture) provoked both famines. Grain requisitioning starved the peasants who were the main victims of the two largest famines of the century.
- The nature and operating method of the regimes transformed requisitioning into ruthless extortion. The extremely hierarchical organization prevented anyone from challenging the arbitrary orders of the two dictators, and encouraged or obliged the local and regional authorities to plunder their charges relentlessly until they simply gave up the ghost. That the regime was to blame as much as the strategy was confirmed by the pragmatic aspects of some GLF innovations. One of these (greater decentralization) had beneficial effects in Japan, Taiwan, and South Korea, but proved to be disastrous in China because of the nature of the regime. It gave local and regional cadres greater powers and was responsible for the deadly one-upmanship. Those cadres had learned from experience, and the GLF, with its succession of political labels and sanctions, was a reminder to them that it was better "to err to the left than to the right," and to pretend to exceed the quotas, rather than speak out and say that they were totally unachievable.

However, in the last moments of the famine, leaders at various levels (from cadres in Anhui province to the president of the People's Republic) showed that they were capable of independence and courage; independence for innovating on the spot, courage for freeing themselves from the dogma. In 1961 and 1962, Liu Shaoqi applied the "three liberties, one guarantee" (*san zi yi bao*) formula for which he would be severely criticized during the Cultural Revolution. The three liberties consisted of owning livestock, growing vegetables, and selling them on the market. That was equivalent to expanding private economic activities and went hand in hand with the "guarantee" of a minimum production per household. Before Zeng Xisheng (see above), other cadres in Anhui province (and even cadres in Zhejiang province from 1956) took the initiative of increasing the peasants' private plots and, more importantly, offering them a "responsibility contract" that authorized them to work a plot of land as they wished, after deducting the portion reserved for growing grain for the state. That was the veritable prelude to the decollectivization that was carried out two decades later.[107] The need to end the famine obliged the dictator to tolerate, momentarily, this bending of rules. In 1962, as soon as he glimpsed the prospect of a good harvest, he put an end to these measures, which did not reappear until after his death, when they subsequently spread across the country with the success we know. Thus one injudicious man was able to impose his will on everyone else. This, like the Stalinist dictatorship, substantiates the noxiousness of the formula concocted by Lenin at the turn of the century.

Nevertheless, let us end as we began, certainly not by exonerating the two revolutionary regimes, but by recalling, after Felix Wemheuer, that both countries were ancestral "lands of famine," and that the two regimes tried, after the fact, to draw lessons from the disaster.[108] From 1963, birth control was imposed on the major Chinese cities and the peasants were less badly treated—at least under Stalin and Mao's successors. Last, and more importantly, let us forget for one moment the two regimes that are the subject of this book, and remind ourselves to what depths human beings may sink when faced with disasters on such a scale and of such intensity. Rather than provide more examples of humanity becoming inhuman under such tribulations, let the Ukrainian poet, Vasyl Barka, have the last word: "Mothers with several children killed the smaller ones and fed the older ones with cutlets made of their flesh."[109]

6. Bureaucracy

The workers, having conquered political power, will smash the old bureaucratic apparatus, shatter it to its very foundations, until not a stone is left standing upon another; and they will replace it by a new one, consisting of the very same workers and office employees, against whose transformation into bureaucrats the measures will at once be taken which were specified in detail by Marx and Engels: (1) not only election, but also recall at any time; (2) pay not exceeding that of a workman; (3) immediate introduction of control and supervision by all, so that all shall become "bureaucrats" for a time and that, therefore, nobody may be able to become a "bureaucrat."

—Lenin, "State and Revolution"

"The greatest illusion was that industrialization and collectivization ... and destruction of capitalist ownership, would result in a classless society" (Milovan Djilas). Good Marxist that he was, Djilas emphasized the social aspects of the experiment in which he was a player, but later criticized. He drove the point home, "More than anything else, the essential aspect of contemporary Communism is the new class of owners and exploiters." "Exploiters" was indeed how the subjects of Stalin, Mao, or Tito viewed the members of this new class. But how was it possible to be a factory owner in a country where all the means of production belonged to the state? Djilas foresaw the objection: "As defined by Roman law, property constitutes the use, enjoyment, and disposition of material goods." The law allowed the Communist political bureaucracy to "use, enjoy, and dispose of nationalized property." And clearer still, "The new class obtains its power, privileges ... from one specific form of ownership—collective ownership—which the class administers and distributes in the name of the nation and society." That roughly sums up Michael Voslensky's (1980) argument, which he illustrates with numerous details, and since both works are classics in the canon of critical literature on Communism, we need to go into the matter in greater detail.[1]

A first paradox is that the class "administering" the nation's assets was not restricted to that role alone. In a democratic regime, high-ranking civil servants obey—or are supposed to obey—the politicians, whereas this new class comprised both administrators and decision makers. True, the bureaucracy obeyed the supreme leadership, which was only the top of the pyramid of this new class, but made decisions at its own level or sector at the same time as performing administrative tasks. The second paradox is that Marxists usually held the bureaucracy in low esteem, believing it to be subservient to the dominant class. They mocked its cult of secrecy, its routine, the paperwork, and the slow pace of bureaucratic procedures. They were not the sort of people to be taken in by a Max Weber–type analysis, which stresses the rationality of modern bureaucracy, its professional competence and impartiality. They deemed it to be "formal." Not for nothing, however, has contemporary Communism been defined as a "civilization of reports." Bureaucracy is essential to the functioning of Communist regimes. It never ceases to proliferate within them because the state aspires to control everything and therefore cannot do without it for managing the economy, planning, and distributing production.

Well before five-year plans, Lenin was already concerned about the rampant growth of a body of apparatchiks, often vulgar and incompetent, ever ready to take advantage of their prerogatives. Instead of seeking the roots of bureaucratization in the system he created, starting with a party of professional revolutionaries who formed the embryonic future "new class," Lenin saw it as an inheritance from the Czarist past or a resurgence of Asian despotism. It was certainly natural for the revolutionary heirs to the protesting intelligentsia of the nineteenth century to connect present ills with those of the nation's past, the Czar's well-known *chinovnik* state." Bukharin had the same reaction when he later accused Stalin of transforming the Soviet Union into a direct descendent of old Russia.

It is even harder to forget the Mandarins than the *chinovniks*. In the Middle Kingdom, hell was often depicted as being peopled with bureaucrats torturing the dead. The first instinct of the nineteenth-century

Taiping, the Communists' agrarian predecessors, was to bring down the officials (*da guan*, or "hit the officials"). Communist propaganda under the old (nationalist) regime never failed to mention the wrongdoings of the *guanliao* (bureaucrats), who were servile to their superiors but dealt with the people arbitrarily and brutally. Lenin may have decided that it was impossible to entrust a backward people with the task of governing itself ("we're not utopian"), but the Chinese Communists didn't even consider the issue. They had to administer a larger rural population with a greater population density that was also more illiterate and more glued to the village universe than the one in Russia. They immediately resolved not only to administer, but to overturn and transform society by controlling it very tightly.

Numbers

Independently of the novel ambition of overturning and remodeling the social structure, the vast expanse of the Soviet Union (as later the immensity of the Chinese subcontinent and its population) made it impossible for a small elite of revolutionary professionals to occupy all the key posts. The pyramid base had already incorporated the mass of permanent employees from the Soviets, the factories, district committees, as well as the trade union activists and the Red Guards who, after 1917, formed an embryonic new social group, the future apparatchiks.[2] The state and Party apparatus recruited massively, leading to frequent replications of posts in both and rapidly created a "colossal, invasive bureaucracy that covered the whole country like a spider's web" (Nicolas Berdiaev). From 1921, the Soviet Union had ten times more bureaucrats than the Czarists regime had ever succeeded in amassing (2.4 million), twice the number of the working class, which had been severely depleted by war and civil war. In Moscow, which, according to Lenin, was "bloated with civil servants," bureaucrats already accounted for one-third of the city's working population.[3]

The bureaucracy overlapped the ranks of the new class, even though its members were largely recruited from it. At the outset anyway, that class could not be identified with the caste of more selective, privileged Party members, any more than it could with the bureaucracy. The trouble was that it was harder to estimate the numbers in the new class, which was also highly hierarchical, than the numbers in the bureaucracy or the Party. Where the Party was concerned, Lenin's death provided the secretary general with the opportunity, or pretext, to swell its ranks with his own cronies, by recruiting numerous careerists in the well-known "class of Lenin." Between the Twelfth Congress in May 1923 and the Thirteenth in May 1924, the Party membership almost doubled from 386,000 to 736,000. During the NEP, the new class grew further and took root, but it was from the Great Turn that it really boomed. The abolition of private trade made it necessary to establish a state-controlled trading bureaucracy, rapid industrialization required a specialized industrialized bureaucracy, and the collectivization of agriculture went hand in hand with the recruitment of an army of agricultural bureaucrats. Between 1926 and 1939 the number of Party and state officials, including upper-level managers of industrial enterprises and collective and state farms, more than quadrupled (from 266,000 to 1,416,000), while the number of engineers and agronomists increased six- or sevenfold (from 249,000 to 1,915,000).[4]

In 1931, in Magnitogorsk, 30 percent of the mainly peasant labor force was illiterate or semi-illiterate. Charged with rapidly supplying qualified technicians, the local authorities understood their objective to be a battle to form new cadres in every factory. The local authorities themselves were redundant, for the factory administration had numerous responsibilities outside the factory, and their relations with the city soviet, which represented the state, were not always easy. The two (soviet and factory) had their own Party committees, which depended neither on the soviet nor on the factory but on the *gorkom*, the city Party committee. It goes without saying that that the ultimate decision lay with that body, but the state-Party duality meant that before taking the slightest measure, the real decision makers were obliged to meet twice, first as Party members, and then as members of the managing committee of the institution in question. Five years later we see the same duplication of bodies (Party and state) in Smolensk, when the *nomenklatura* alone (which depended on the Party) occupied 3,085 posts.[5] The state, under the Party's control, also grew from the 1930s on, with all services from tailoring to shoe repair provided by the state or the cooperative, essentially the same thing. Repression required greater numbers of secret police, and the establishment of domestic passports (at the end of 1932) and residence permits necessitated still more civil servants.

The increase was comparable in China but started from a different situation at the outset. The Communists has already started to establish a bureaucracy in their regional north China bases, and they did not subsequently disperse it. Or rather they did, by displacing it from the north to the south of the continent they had just conquered, in order to manage the new bureaucrats they now needed to recruit. Because they were in such a hurry, they transferred Red Army cadres to carry out civilian tasks that very few were able to accomplish, for some were even illiterate and the majority lacked any qualifications or administrative experience whatsoever. The government therefore had to recruit massively and very fast elsewhere. The shortage of managers in the major cities, where the Communists faced novel problems, was especially blatant. In Beijing there were about two Communists for every thousand inhabitants, in Guangzhou one for fourteen thousand. Necessity knows no law, and Mao, the person who incarnated the revolutionaries' antibureaucratic sentiment, had no compunction about using the administrative personnel from the old regime (as occurred in the Soviet Union). He rapidly hired a multitude of activist workers and peasants, but backed them up with an educated minority from less perfect social backgrounds. Between October 1949, the date the regime was founded, and September 1952, the ranks of cadres swelled from 720,000 to 3.3 million. They grew further over the following years, during the first Five-Year Plan. By 1957, there was approximately one cadre for every twenty city dwellers. During that period, there was a plethora of bureaucrats, certainly far more than there were members of the new class. Even if we choose to put the new class (an approximate equivalence I'll admit) in the same category as the "state cadres" (those who drew their salaries from the state budget, as opposed to the local rural cadres who were paid in work points), the increase was still of the same order. The state cadres were eight times more numerous in 1958 than in 1949. As for Party members, their numbers doubled from 4.5 million to 9.4 million between 1949 and 1955, and then again over the following decade (18.7 million in 1965 on the eve of the Cultural Revolution). As Andrew Walder remarked, "There was no other path to the top."[6] The government tried to purge their ranks by dismissing incompetent cadres or, during the Cultural Revolution, those suspected of anti-Maoist conservatism. Nevertheless, overall this bureaucratic inflation remained more or less constant after the regime was consolidated. Over time, that excess reached the top of the hierarchy, leading one cartoonist to represent the bureaucracy as a reverse-pyramid-shaped building, in which the upper floors towered over the lower ones. Needless to say, this occurred during the post-Maoist thaw when it became possible to mock such things. To anyone remarking on this anomaly he would explain, "Officials can only go up, not down!"[7]

Working Class Origins

The "plebeanization" (Marc Ferro) of the government and the administration occurred very early on in what was to become the Soviet Union. Until September 1917, the radicalization of the masses benefitted the Bolsheviks, who were initially in the minority in the Petrograd soviet. By voting against the agreement with the Duma on the formation of a provisional government and then against various unpopular measures that Soviet had to take because of the continuing war, the Bolsheviks gathered the support of the discontented. That was what Ferro called the "Bolshevization from below," the democratic way. Just before and after October, the process was speeded up with the help of some manipulation. That was the bureaucratic way, the main form of "Bolshevization from above." It was rapidly superseded by the authoritarian way, when the Bolsheviks eliminated their socialist and anarchist rivals from the soviets and other organizations established after February. Next, but also very quickly, the need to create a state machine sanctioned the rise of an apparatus with working class origins that submerged the small number of "old Bolsheviks," who were mainly intellectuals or "petit bourgeois." In February and March 1917, frock coats and cravats held the place of honor among the deputies in the Petrograd Soviet, and they were sported by Bolsheviks, Mensheviks, and Socialist Revolutionaries alike.[8]

This rapid promotion of a lower social class accelerated after the Great Turn. How else was it possible to manage the new institutions that had been patched together to ensure state control over the economy? The kolkhoz president and his assistants were peasants just like its members. The administration of the kolkhozes was backed but above all controlled and managed by a bevy of cadres and administrative posts that had never previously existed in agriculture, including during the NEP. The same was true of the factories, where many workers were promoted to foreman or workshop head. The number of workers doubled in industry during the first Five-Year Plan, from 3.1 million in 1928 to 6 million in 1932, while management tripled, from 236,000 to 700,000. For the most part it was incompetent, numerous so-called accountants or economists who were promoted to the job only because they could read and write, unlike most of the *mastera* (foremen). The lack of professionalism, the inefficiency, and even the stupidity and vulgarity of the new bureaucrats provided stimulating material for the satirical review *Krokodill*.[9]

The leaders were well aware of this, Stalin first and foremost. He did not mind that the mass of new bureaucrats and Party members had as little political baggage as they had culture and education, for their lack of education made them more docile than the old Bolsheviks.[10] What worried him was the lack of training among the higher level managers, particularly the factory directors. Convinced that malicious bourgeois experts were making all the important decisions in the names of their masters (former workers promoted to head a given sector they did not understand), Stalin launched the famous Shakhty Trial in 1928 against the mining engineers in the Donbas region, accusing them of sabotage and cooperating with foreign powers. He was no less concerned by the ignorance of the directors who blindly approved decisions taken by others, than by the treason he accused the experts of. The first plan was not just about producing more steel and machines, but also about producing a new technical intelligentsia with proletarian origins. Mao had opposed the "red" versus the "expert" on many occasions, always to the benefit of the former, especially during the Great Leap Forward. Stalin wanted a new elite that was both red and expert, trained for the most part in the engineering schools. The successors to the victims of the Great Purge were mainly recruited from among the graduate working-class *vydvizhentsy*, who had entered higher education as adults during the first Five-Year Plan. At the end of Stalin's reign in 1952, half of the ministers in the Soviet government (57 out of 115, including Leonid Brezhnev, Alexei Kosygin, and Gromyko) were *vydvizhentsy* from the first Five-Year Plan. A generation later, in 1979, half the Politburo members (the same three plus four others, or seven out of fourteen) were *vydvizhentsy*. This was also true of Khrushchev, but here I am less interested in the people at the summit than in the battalions of new graduates who, from 1938 on, flooded all the managerial positions from one end of the Soviet Union to the other. From that time on, Stalin, who had wanted to create a new proletarian intelligentsia, ceased to be interested in workers as such. He needed educated communists, preferably engineers. The workers, with their anti-intellectual sentiment, were no longer as useful to him, although they had been only recently when he encouraged the Stakhanovites to protest against "bourgeois" management. Now they were even potentially harmful because they hampered the actions of the new elite that Stalin boasted of having created and that he so badly needed.

Two lessons, complementary rather than antithetical, may be learned from this. The same leader who, in the 1930s, gradually abandoned the concept of the dictatorship of the proletariat had strived throughout the first plan to give the dictatorship of the proletariat the substance that it lacked. At the very least he educated some of its members in order to make them leaders or minor leaders. The breakneck industrialization of the first plan would in any case have led to upward social mobility and Stalin ensured that the beneficiaries were working-class. In 1934, 60 percent of Party members were working-class, but only 9.3 percent of them were allocated to production tasks. The others were "permanent" and held positions within the Party apparatus, the factories, or the administration. The Communist Party was gradually being transformed into a party of civil servants. Only 7.6 percent of the delegates to the Nineteenth Party Congress in 1952, the last in Stalin's lifetime, were workers (for workers remained workers), and 7.8 percent were peasants.[11]

The beneficiaries knew very well that they owed their promotion to the very nature of the regime. They were proud of having advanced by their own means and grateful to the regime. This reinforced its legitimacy, at least in the eyes of those former members of the proletariat, but not the proletarians themselves, who, had they been better informed, might have envied their exploited brothers in the capitalist West.

And this brings me to the other lesson. The alliance that Stalin concluded with the new class in the second half of the 1930s, which Vera Dunham called the Big Deal, was reinforced after the war, pushing the Stakhanovites out from the privileged class for not being expert enough.[12] War had proved that ideology can neither build tanks nor conduct battlefield operations. It had also devastated the country that now needed to be rebuilt, and that required not only hands, but specialists and organizers—in other words the white-collar workers, whom Stalin expected to be zealous, productive, and efficient. He expected that army of experts and administrators to work hard as professionals. They were given a small dose of the official history of the revolution, even if it

BUREAUCRACY | 175

meant forgetting its ideals. The important thing was that they were to be unperturbedly apolitical and conformist, diehard nationalists, and unfailingly loyal to the *vožd*. In exchange Stalin spoiled them with material prosperity, security, and prestige. From the early 1930s on, he began granting them a growing number of privileges, making a mockery of the egalitarian ideals of the early years. In February 1932 he abolished the "Party maximum" introduced by Lenin, which set a ceiling for the earnings of all Party members. The 1917 veterans now formed only a tiny minority of the new class, which now had indisputable proletarian or peasant roots. That new class lost no time in reproducing the taste and values of all philistines since time immemorial, the very same tastes and values the revolutionary intelligentsia had revolted against. Being attached to material values, comforts, and possessions, members of the new bourgeoisie dressed and decorated their homes with care, showed off their distinction and their *kulturnost*, as opposed to *kultura*, true culture, which was suspect since it was far too dissatisfied and attached to ideals, serving to produce only dreamers and eternal discontents. Asceticism was also suspect. The new class produced and manufactured, and consequently believed that it deserved to benefit from that—and benefit their descendants too, once the regime no longer killed off its servants. In short, Stalin had created a new bureaucracy that was loyal to him because it owed him everything; a new service class as under Peter the Great. The revolutionary regime had transformed itself into a conservative establishment. It was easier to found and consolidate a new regime than it was to change people. And Stalin had no cure for men, their nature, or their souls, as those alienated by the opium of the people used to say. He was concerned only about what men built or had others build for them.

Mao and the New Chinese Class

So, long live Mao?[13] The ideals and practices of mature Stalinism, or "achieved Stalinism," were everything that Mao detested: the preeminence of material values, comfort, luxury, distinction, privileges, and prejudices. He at least was faithful to the revolutionary values, or thought he was; his revolt was authentic, he did not compromise. Nor did he come to terms with the Communist hierarchy exploiting or scorning the masses. He worried on many occasions about inequalities within a socialist regime and the rise of a new privileged class and he had endeavored to keep them at far more modest levels than in the Soviet Union. Stalin had re-created a privileged layer of society and depended on it to modernize the country. Mao was as impatient as Stalin to modernize a country that was even poorer, but he never tolerated the inequalities that resulted from such an enterprise. Despite that, he perpetuated them.

The real and even flagrant inequalities that Mao most deplored, those between the cities and the countryside, and between intellectuals and manual workers, were only indirectly related to the privileges and power of the new class. Yet Mao seemed to have them in mind when he imposed the unfortunate Hundred Flowers episode on his reticent colleagues. When he launched the campaign in February 1957, he took care to distinguish "antagonistic contradictions" from "non-antagonistic contradictions" (see above). Antagonistic contradictions were between the people and the former exploiting classes (landlords, capitalists, etc.) and were no longer of concern given that the last means of production had been nationalized the previous year, and before that, agrarian reform had confiscated the landlords' land. Consequently Mao now stressed the "non-antagonistic contradictions" that existed within the people, in other words within the four classes Mao recognized as representing the people: the workers, peasants, the national bourgeoisie, and the intellectuals. There was no new class in this setup as yet, but since it was understood that the Party represented the proletarian avant-garde, one might, in a pinch, concede that those famous "non-antagonist contradictions" also encompassed the contradictions between the people and those who governed them. In other words, that the new class in the process of being created was already in his sights.

That may be crediting Mao with too much foresight, for he challenged only the "working style" of the Party members and not the monopoly they had on power. His motives were less fundamental (the new class's power and privileges, its exploitation or oppression of the masses), than related to circumstances. He reacted to the events that were troubling the Communist bloc (in Warsaw and Budapest) and hoped to improve cooperation with the intellectuals by listening to their complaints. However their protests went much further than the incurable optimist ever imagined and he concluded that the class struggle (the *old* one, between capitalists and proletarians) continued even under the dictatorship of the proletariat. Very soon Mao claimed Stalin's discovery as his own: that strange premise whereby class struggle intensifies as socialism progresses.

So even though Mao never renounced the fictional class struggle (the antagonistic contradictions) I still believe that he suspected the existence of the real class struggle, the one that opposed the people to the new class. It goes without saying that he never used the term (to refer to Djilas would have been as incongruous as to refer to Bernstein or Trotsky), but his repeated diatribes against the "bourgeois elements" that had infiltrated the Party or the bourgeois tendencies of Party members who were corrupted by comfort and luxury, betrayed his unease or anxiety in the face of the emerging new class nesting in the very heart of the socialist institutions. A new difficulty immediately arose: how to define this "new bourgeoisie" (which, in his vocabulary, was the closest to the "new class")? Should it be defined in social terms? Our Marxist had never ventured down that path. A social criterion ran the risk of bringing the high-ranking cadres, that privileged layer of the new class, into conflict with the mass of rural cadres, who had the best possible reasons to be jealous of their urban colleagues.

Failing to come up with a social definition of the "new bourgeoisie," Mao had long suggested a definition (or an approximation) in moral and behavioral terms. The new bourgeois tendencies existed and had to be fought, but they concerned only a minority of bad cadres. The frugal cadres, faithful to the revolutionary ideal and devoted to public service were deemed to be good (or revolutionary, it was the same thing). The bad ones were the profiteers who thought only to grow their personal interests. Objective social criteria (the cadre's place in the hierarchy, the salary and privileges it entailed) were less important than the subjective attitude of the beneficiary. It is not certain that Mao, whose personal physician described his own sybaritic leanings,[14] was aware that such a criterion might make him a target, rather than Liu Shaoqi, the austere president of the People's Republic. Yet Liu was the main victim of the Cultural Revolution, accused of having plotted to restore capitalism. Lifestyle was therefore not yet the correct, or at least not the sole criterion for sorting the wheat from the chaff.

Mao's concerns and considerations were of a different order, for they were political. All cadres who remained faithful to the line (understood: the Maoist line) in all circumstances were considered revolutionary.[15] Anyone opposed to that line, or, since no one dared openly oppose it, anyone who dared to implement their own pragmatic convictions rather than execute Maoist directives to the letter, was reputed to be bourgeois, and later revisionist, and later still, of paving the way to capitalist restoration and being a counterrevolutionary. Did Mao still have the new class in mind when he made such accusations, or had he returned once again to the Hydra (however many heads are cut off the classes condemned by history, they will constantly reform)? In the last twelve years of his life, Mao's increasingly used political criteria to define the new class. He admitted that power, rather than money, was key to this "new bourgeoisie" located in the heart of the Party—yet continued to favor the subjective factors to becoming bourgeois, which he now located less in the weakening that occurred as a corollary to bourgeois comforts, than in the uses and abuses of power. Better still, he shifted the contradictions up a notch. During the Hundred Flowers period he had defined them as "non-antagonistic." He later came to see the relationship between the leaders and the people as "antagonistic."[16] In short they had become the famous "us and them" of citizens and subjects, be they Soviet or Chinese.

Nevertheless, let us agree on the real scope and significance of those terms. The leaders of the "new bourgeoisie" were concealed among "my adversaries within the Party leadership." This "antagonistic" contradiction between "them and me," and therefore between them and the people, left them open to merciless repression. Two years after the Hundred Flowers movement, the minister of defense, Peng Dehuai, was bold enough to criticize the GLF at a meeting of the Party leaders in Lushan. Mao drew the lesson from that episode: "The struggle that arose in Lushan is a class struggle."[17] That's all well and good, though Peng Dehuai was hardly a representative of the former exploiting classes. He was considered "one of us" who has been led astray and thus a representative of the "new bourgeoisie" who must be sacked until such time as the Cultural Revolution would settle the score. Meanwhile, the famine Peng warned about really took off. When it finally ended, it was again in terms of class struggle that Mao interpreted the muted conflict between him and other leaders, who were less concerned with orthodoxy than kick-starting the economy. When the plenary session of the Central Committee met in September 1962, he warned them, "Comrades, never forget the class struggle!" It also continued in the Soviet Union but the Soviets stubbornly refused to recognize the fact. Mao now mainly analyzed his—by now repudiated—model in terms of the class struggle. If it had infected the

Soviet Union, revisionism might well poison China too. The concern that haunted Mao (might the Chinese revolution in turn run the risk of degenerating?) increasingly focused on that twofold danger: revisionism as the harbinger of the restoration of capitalism. Here was the link between the degeneracy of the new class (Liu, the Chinese Khrushchev) and the specter of the former exploiter (capitalism).

His enemies within the Party—alleged or timid opponents, or more likely some lieutenants who were bold enough to try and temper the dictators' excesses—were in Mao's eyes incarnations of the cursed bureaucracy he targeted when he launched the Cultural Revolution. This was an antibureaucratic revolution that tolerated both the manipulation of the apparatus (the Central Cultural Revolution Group that directed the students to the prey identified by Mao) and the use of the army once the Red Guards began to take their revolt seriously. It was a revolution that fought bureaucracy as though it were a deformation of the regime, whereas it was consubstantial with it, since the regime confided all the means of production to a bureaucracy appointed by the single Party, in line with a model that Mao had unscrupulously copied. A so-called revolution against bureaucracy ordered by the very person who headed that bureaucracy.[18]

Despite the instrumental confusion of ideas, and the social, if not moral, veneer of the political disagreements (whoever does not obey me to the letter is a vile intriguer), we cannot contest Mao's flashes of lucidity, which were rapidly forgotten, if not actually contradicted by an ulterior action. Nor can we deny his greater awareness (in comparison with Stalin) and concern about the return of inequalities in a "socialist" society, with a greater tenacity to pursue the egalitarian dream. Greater, but also more irresponsible, if not downright disastrous when that tenacity tilted into senile obsession. Unlike Stalin in the 1930s, Mao did not dare to get rid of everything that might hinder the forced march toward modernization. He blindly and zealously served the ideology (Marxism, or what he had retained and understood of it) as a substitute for the original nationalism. He stressed the avatar (the egalitarian country) over the earlier enterprise, which was to modernize a country that was so badly in need of it.[19]

The social composition of the two new classes differed far less than the attitude of the two dictators toward them. In China, even more than in the Soviet Union, the new class was largely composed of people from working-class or (mostly) peasant origins. Unlike Lenin's professional revolutionaries, they initially included few intellectuals. Since it is impossible to know the precise numbers of a new class in the process of consolidation, I shall stick to the numbers of Party members. In 1949, 80 percent were peasants who had been recruited over the previous decade in the northern revolutionary bases. By 1961, peasants accounted for only 66 percent, whereas the number of intellectuals had tripled, from 5 to 15 percent. The workers accounted for 15 percent of CCP members in 1961, whereas they were practically nonexistent in 1949. This redistribution was the result of a parallel development among the workers, but inverse where intellectuals were concerned, that occurred in the Soviet Union during the first two decades of the regime. In the Soviet Union quite a few old Bolsheviks, intellectuals for the most part, had been purged, and this was followed by a massive recruitment of proletarian elements. Many of the new arrivals filled the ranks of the secretariat and supplanted the old guard of revolutionary professionals. In 1930, more than two-thirds (69 percent) of the secretaries and members of the Central Committee of the Federated Republics were members of the Communist Party of the Soviet Union (CPSU) before October 1917 (rather like the Chinese *lao ganbu* who had joined the CCP before 1949). In 1939, at the end of the decade, four out of five (80.5 percent) had joined the Party after Lenin's death.

In China, as in the Soviet Union on the eve of the first plan, many of the newly appointed cadres were incompetent. Not all of them of course, far from it. I had many opportunities to appreciate the intelligence and dynamism of the young rural cadres who welcomed me. The Party's choice was not restricted to careerists, it sometimes fell on the most open and enterprising young people. Yet invariably the majority of rural cadres had only a very basic education. The few peasants with more than a primary school education were from well-off families and therefore suspect. While the regime's considerable efforts in education, especially after the GLF and under Mao's personal impetus (see chapter 2), did not entirely make up for this, it did make the shortcomings less blatant. In any case only a minority of rural cadres belonged to the new class. This was more problematic in the higher echelons of the Party, where everyone was a fully fledged member of the new class, but few had any of the necessary technical and administrative skills. During the Hundred Flowers movement the criticisms flew and professors complained of being placed under ignoramuses: *waihang lingdao neihang* ("those who know nothing are leading those who know"). The repression that followed put an end to the complaints—until speech was freed again after Mao's death (like Stalin's) and the Twentieth Party Congress. One foreigner in Mao's lifetime did mock on their behalf "the fruitless stupidity of a narrow, dogmatic bureaucratic apparatus, that is also mediocre, arrogant, complexed and rigid in its conformity, terrorized at having to take the slightest initiative."[20]

Behavior and Corruption:
The Caste and Its Privileges

Although the regional and local Party heads enjoyed privileges during the period of the Five-Year Plan, they nevertheless lived in a constant state of urgency and tension, and were subjected to continual pressure. Being obliged to achieve virtually impossible objectives come what may, they had to be prepared to dash off anywhere their subordinates encountered difficulties and certainly did not use kid gloves to urge them to be more zealous and dynamic. "The ideal leader of the 1930s was no office worker. ... [He] spent his life in the open in the mud on construction sites. He was hard on himself and on others, even brutal when he had to be, indefatigable and gifted with great common sense. ... Obsessed by their duty to produce results, the leaders frequently spoke sharply to others, shouted their orders and demanded instant obedience, with no discussion."[21] In 1929, a grain requisitioning agent convened the village assembly and addressed the audience by first placing his revolver on the table. Another warned the peasants that Soviet power was like having "a hand on one's throat and a knee on one's chest" (Moshe Lewin). As far as brutality and authoritarianism were concerned, the soviet cadre was much like the *chinovnik* under Nicolas 1st (or in Gogol). What was the point, however, of stressing the weight of tradition? The model was far closer to home and from one end of the Soviet Union to the other, thousands of autocrats behaved like little Stalins; *vožd* in their own kingdoms. One factory director forbade people from getting a haircut anywhere else but at the factory hairdresser's and ordered "criminal proceedings" to be started against anyone breaking the rule. A kolkhoz president in the Voronej region fined his kolkhozniks if they failed to attend a class on eradicating illiteracy, used impolite language, neglected to tie up their dog or wash the floors in their homes, and so forth.[22]

Given that a portion of those fines remained in their pockets, the dictatorship of small-time leaders often went hand in hand with corruption. That was commonplace at the kolkhoz and factory levels, and frequently involved Party members with the collusion of civil servants and high-level inspectors. Despite being severely punished, corruption continued to flourish. Meanwhile the caste spirit took root in the new class even faster than corruption. Anton Ciliga, once a lecturer at the Communist University of Leningrad, found that his students considered their privileged situation to be normal and felt alienated from the working class from which they originated. For Ciliga, they represented not so much a working-class elite, but a "young guard in the bureaucracy." When Stalingrad was being bombarded in 1942, one young member of the *nomenklatura* described by Vasily Grossman wanted to chase neighbors out of an antiaircraft shelter designated for a building in which only scientists and company directors were housed.[23]

During Ciliga's last year of freedom in the Soviet Union (he was arrested on 21 May 1930, and was freed and deported only at the end of 1935), he lived in the Leningrad Party Residence, where the Communist Party elite lived, starting with Kirov. There he met an aristocracy of nouveaux riches, mainly with working-class and artisan origins. Nearly all flaunted their prerogatives and were obsessed with their precedence in relation to each other. Men continued to observe convention; they tried to maintain the proletarian and revolutionary appearance that had been instilled in them. Aware of belonging to "society," their wives thought only of dazzling with their appearance, or their boxes in the theater, the elegance of their interior decor, and their photographs, in which they could be seen on summer holiday in the Caucasus, in the company of someone like Semyon Budyonny or Kliment Voroshilov. The salaries of these nouveaux riches were still fairly modest, but they paid very little in rent and/or on furniture, while their cars, theater tickets, holidays and children's schooling cost nothing at all.[24] In Magnitogorsk, the Kirov district was set aside for those who had won favor with the authorities, but even those privileges paled in comparison to those enjoyed by the leaders, who lived in a far more luxurious residential enclave set in splendid isolation in the middle of the woods. The house belonging to the Party first secretary cost a quarter million rubles, which was several hundred times the average annual wage in Magnitogorsk.

The privileges were more restricted under Mao than under Stalin. Was this a socialism of the poor? Undeniably so, but that still does not explain everything. The fact that China was far more underdeveloped than the Soviet Union a generation earlier was not enough to account for the narrower range of salaries—with the exception, nevertheless, of the high-ranking bureaucrats who were quite richly rewarded.[25] While they may not have enjoyed such comfortable salaries, other cadres benefitted from all kinds of advantages, both symbolic and substantial, dosed out according to their rank (twenty-six of them, or even thirty if we include the lowliest servants of the state). Even in Yan'an days, Wang Shiwei was astonished to find five quality levels for food alone. Fifteen years later, when the Hundred Flowers campaign allowed people to voice their grievances, these included complaints that the first rows of theater seats were always reserved for Communists, that a bus in Nanjing made a detour rather than take the direct route in order to serve the residence of a VIP, that a bevy of servants was ever ready to wait hand and foot on high-ranking Party cadres in rest homes, that admittance to the Beijing Hospital was reserved for families in ranks one to seven, that elite schools were reserved for children of high-ranking cadres, that only the children of Party members and members of the Communist Youth League could ever study abroad, and so on, and so on.[26]

High-ranking cadres and their families lived in the residences of former bureaucrats or rich families under the old regime. Called *dayuan* (for instance, *shengwei dayuan* was the residence of the Provincial Party Committee), the residences were usually surrounded by red walls, much like the ones in Zhongnanhai in Beijing, where the national leaders lived. Both lodgings and offices were located in the *dayuan* and they too were organized hierarchically. The service staff lived apart in far less grandeur and did not enjoy the material advantages, or very few. These advantages and the various prerogatives that went with them were strictly hierarchical, the divide being in the eighth, thirteenth, and seventeenth echelons of the cadres' thirty grades. From the fourteenth to the seventeenth, cadres were deemed "ordinary," and inferior after the seventeenth, and therefore not the subject of this chapter. Children of high-ranking cadres (from the first to the thirteenth grade) grew up together cut off from the real world and from poverty. Sentries stood guard at the gates and they never left the *dayuan* alone. They frequented the same (excellent) schools and when, in a bout of Cultural Revolution egalitarianism, a school for the children of cadres was merged with a one in a nearby suburb or a village, they were astonished to find pupils with chapped hands and feet, often bleeding and covered in chilblains. The system therefore remained elitist and hierarchical, but one or several notches beneath the Stalinist model.[27]

The inequalities in access to schooling and the nepotism that persisted throughout Mao's reign did not always disadvantage the same classes. When school performance was a criterion for admission to high school or university (for instance in 1960–1963), it was the working-class children who were affected, whereas when political criteria were stressed again (in 1964–1965), it was the former "exploiting class." But the offspring of high-ranking cadres benefitted in all cases and were as aware of their status as the young people observed by Ciliga a generation earlier. Schoolchildren would for instance quarrel about the number of cars made available to their respective families. The use of a car was one of the most valued privileges in a country, where, as Simon Leys pointed out, seriously ill people were taken to hospital in a wheelbarrow or a cart. Here, even more than in the Soviet Union, "there were only Mandarin cars," the "model, color and size varied according to the rank of the user," the topmost being "the long black limousines, ... windows covered in tulle to spare the passenger from being seen by the vulgar masses ... spacious black hearses, the blind windows of which radiated an aura of respectful mystery."[28]

As in the Soviet Union, it was the system that fabricated a privileged class, but Liu Binyan, that *lao ganbu* (who joined the Party in 1943), was punished for having naïvely said as much in 1957. Cadres were expected to be zealous and conformist, and that conformism was both prying and fastidious, far more oppressive than in the Soviet Union. That difference in degree changed nothing to the outcome, a litany of practices, failings, and vices mocked or denounced by writers during both countries' political thaws: the opportunism of the yes-men and the triumph of the sycophants, the day-to-day spying, the exchanges of good practice between powerful people who had become masters in the "art of relationships" (*guanxixue*).[29] The hero of Sha Yexin et al.'s *If I Were Real* (1980) got just about everything he wanted by passing for the son of a high-ranking Communist official.[30] The comparison required here (Gogol's *The Inspector General*) is not a Soviet one, I'll admit. On the other hand, where else but in the two sister regimes would holding a tiny portion of power allow a person to mistreat the "masses" (who allegedly hold all the power) with impunity? By making people depend on the state for all goods and services, those regimes conferred exorbitant powers on the new class, which was the only one authorized to distribute them. During the famine, the local cadres held the power of life and death on the peasants. As we saw, they even used food as a weapon by reducing rations for people who were uncooperative or shirkers: the crumbs they were given to survive were called "death rations" (*si liang*). It was not rare for people to be beaten to death, even small children who had stolen a handful of rice to assuage their hunger. I'll concede the exceptional nature of the circumstances (famine), but those horrific practices, like so many others observed at the time throughout the country, appeared to be a normal resort for numerous cadres only because in the previous "normal" period they had grown used to bullying, accusations, thrashing, and jailing with impunity.

Let us jump from one extreme to another, from the beatings, tortures, hangings, and massacres that led to a million more victims during the famine, to the day-to-day, in some ways trivial, violence. Here is one very banal example that has been engraved on my memory for a good third of century: the authoritarian cadre who ordered my chauffeur to drive at full speed to the entrance of a theater where hundreds of people were lining up outside, waiting for the same performance I was to attend. I will never forget the flurried scattering of startled people. Was the manoeuver intended to spare the foreign Sinologist (who was, of course, to be seated in the front row) from having to walk a single step or wait for a single minute? Or was it to prevent him from having any contact with the masses?

A fear of displeasing one's superiors, or not executing orders to the letter, often had the opposite effect to the brutality I have just mentioned, leading instead to administrative paralysis. Panic can also be a reason for inaction and endless delays. The important thing is not to displease one's superiors and to avoid making any mistakes that you could be blamed for. And the best way to do that is to do nothing. This was marvelously illustrated in Zhang Jie's short stories published in the English translation under the title *As Long as Nothing Happens, Nothing Will.*[31] Corruption poisoned the entire apparatus from the top to the bottom of the hierarchy, right down to the civil servant who was supposed to provide some necessary authorization but only provided (as the saying went) the same answer, *yanjiu yanjiu* ("we'll look into the matter"). Using different Chinese tones, the second *yanjiu* suggests that the solution may be found in cigarettes and alcohol, in other words, in the cadre's "sweetener."

Even in its earliest years, the regime found it necessary to launch a campaign (*san fan*, or The Three Antis) against the urban cadres who had granted favors to industrialists and businessmen in exchange for bribes. A decade later, the Four Purifications campaign (*siqing*) targeted rural cadres guilty of embezzlement and accepting bribes. Did the regime fight a merciless battle against a recurrent ill when it suited it? It did fight it in its own way, by confusing rivalries or political deviation with alleged dishonesty. That only made matters worse, especially after the GLF. Blamed and punished for the disastrous consequences of a policy they were forced to apply, the cadres learned a lesson at some cost to themselves—one that was not taught in the Party schools—namely, how to protect themselves by using relationships and the very same informal, particularistic strategies that the revolution wanted to abolish. The Cultural Revolution drove the point home by revealing to the Communist cadres, "the insecurity of their positions and the precariousness of their power" (Lü Xiaobo). Lü attributed the origins of the corruption to the involute process that threatens any revolutionary regime. Those "neo-traditionalist" Communist cadres (Kenneth Jowitt and Andrew Walder) were neither the revolutionary militants Mao dreamed of, nor Weber-type modern bureaucrats. They preferred informal operational methods, particularistic networks, clientelism, and rituals (together with the dissimulation and lies that went with it) over rules and faith. Lü Xiaobo's premise (a little systematic to my liking)[32] about the "involution of organization" threatening Communist regimes has the merit of transcending "a narrowly-defined corruption study *per se*." By going beyond the purely monographic, he suggests a link between "permanent revolution" (Mao's, not Parvus's or Trotsky's) and permanent involution.

The connection between a socialist economy and the corruption of the new class was highlighted in Liu Binyan's "People or Monsters," a classic essay of post-Maoist "reportage literature." I mentioned his misadventures earlier: his sincerity led to him being condemned as a rightist and he spent the better part of the next twenty years in forced labor or a May Seventh School until he was rehabilitated in 1978, after Mao's death.[33] The book (see Box 3) reveals the mechanisms of corruption illustrated in a county where it was particularly widespread. When it was published in 1979, Liu Binyan received thousands of enthusiastic letters from readers, a similar response to the one received by Vladimir Dudintsev after he published *Not by Bread Alone*, also three years after the death of the dictator. Dudintsev mocked the "cult of incompetence" incarnated by Leonid Drozdov, at the "beck and call of the Party" called upon to manage anything and everything, public baths today, culture tomorrow, the aeronautical industry after that. Perry Link establishes a parallel between the two "artists" Drozdov and Wang Shouxin. With his deadpan humor he calls Wang Shouxin "the back-door artist" (*houmen* in Chinese), able to pay for, or sell, all the privileges that were not available to ordinary people.

Box 3

Two Examples of Careerist and Corrupt Cadres

Three years after the death of each of the two dictators, two descriptions of members of the new class delighted countless readers from Leningrad to Canton. Not that they told them anything they didn't already know, readers were simply relieved that these things had been brought out into the open and grateful to the authors for daring to speak the truth.

Far from being a work of imagination, the novel published by Liu Binyan in 1979 reads like a journalistic report. "People or Monsters" narrates the actions of a woman sentenced to death for corruption. The woman, Wang Shouxin, was secretary of a Communist Party cell and director of a power company in a district of Heilongjiang province.

To get rich at the state's expense, Wang Shouxin used a typical practice in the socialist economy. The selling price of coal extracted from the state mines (24.8 yuan per ton) scarcely differed from the cost price after it left the mines. It was part of the "Plan supply" as opposed to the "extra-Plan supply," which concerned the coal produced in small mines (39.9 yuan per ton) that was far more expensive because the price included transport and various other costs. Wang's trick consisted of selling part of the "Plan" coal at the "extra-Plan" price. That required the complicity of the director of the department of trade and the accountant of the state enterprise under her management. She got both of them to join the Party along with nine others of her very own "special crop" all devoted to her, by virtue of the adage "to support the Party secretary is to support the Party, to protect the Party secretary is to protect the Party." The accountant, a widower who hoped to remarry, was forbidden from doing so (and he obeyed), to prevent another pair of ears (and more importantly, another mouth) from being in on the secret and running the risk of divulging it.

But this was only one aspect of the power company director's tireless activity. She held countless receptions, offered gifts, and contributed to charities to ensure that she received substantial returns from just about all the local political elite. She delivered first-rate coal to the secretary of the Binxian Party Committee and to members of the Permanent Committee, the highest-ranking local Party body. Nor did she neglect the directors of the weapons department (at the time the army had not yet lost the dominant influence it acquired during the Cultural Revolution), as well as to the directors of organization, labor, and other departments. She soon realized that those wealthy local potentates were short of very little, except where their children's careers were concerned. These were threatened by the obligation for "educated youth" (*zhiqing*) to go down to the countryside and be reeducated by poor peasants. Never mind that, Wang Shouxin set up an "educated youth district" in a People's Commune, open to the children of cadres, for whom she negotiated a rapid return to the city, a prelude to being admitted to university and obtaining a decent job. To thank her for bringing his three children back to town, the vice-secretary of the CCP's economic Committee for Heilongjiang province sent her a free plane ticket for Canton and Shanghai, where she stayed in the best hotels. When her plane took off from the airport in Harbin, the provincial capital, three high-ranking provincial cadres came by car to see her off. By then (1978), she was already the subject of anonymous denunciations, about which she was warned by a member of the local Commission for Discipline Inspection, who hastily hushed up the complaint. That failed to reassure Wang, however, who organized a poetry competition among her employees in order to compare their handwriting with that of the whistle-blower.

At first glance, the exploits of this former cashier in the power company, promoted director because the secretary of the Binxian Party Committee had taken her under his wing, beggar belief. In just over a decade she amassed the tidy sum of 450,000 yuan, the equivalent of a thousand years of salary (the average wage at the time being 37 yuan per month), not to mention the nine hundred other types of goods she generously distributed to whoever could be useful to her. Yet as the revelations emerge, the reader becomes convinced that her exploits were hardly miraculous, for the book does not limit itself to one individual's actions but dismantles an entire system. As the author suggests (p. 232 of the French translation), "this type of 'socialist' trade is far superior to capitalist exchange for neither party requires capital, neither party has to compromise their personal assets and neither party runs the risk of going bankrupt." The source of Wang's wealth is her position, and the powerful are connected by a network of interested relationships (*guanxi* [see above, note 29]), corruption is not the exception but the rule, but the rule itself conforms to the popular saying, "if you don't grease somebody's palm it won't work." Ten other people were charged and imprisoned in the Wang Shouxin case, all of them Party members. As one worker wrote to the author, "the Binxian you describe is a microcosm of the country as a whole." Intermarriage between members of the new class succeeded in transforming that class into a hereditary caste in which members were afraid of displeasing their fellows but had no compunction about mistreating the people, the theoretical "masters" of the People's Republic.

While "People or Monsters" reveals how the system functioned at base level, *Not by Bread Alone* brings us closer to the summit, in this case the director of a giant industrial complex in Siberia. The "hero," Drozdov, is posted to Moscow where he becomes vice-minister before the end of the book. However, in the first part of the story the reader catches a glimpse of the local *vožd*, his psychology, and the way he "rules." Drozdov's wife is a geography teacher, but he refuses to invite his wife's friends and colleagues because "our home would make them jealous." Members of the new class only invite each other and that is simplified by the fact that the senior management of the complex live in the same neighborhood on Stalin Avenue, where the director, Drozdov, actually has two apartments. They entertain each other but Drozdov warns his wife that "here we cannot have friends. ... One will envy me, the other will fear me, a third will be wary of me and the fourth will want a favor. ... Isolation my darling! And the higher we get, the greater our isolation." Endless advancement means endless isolation. The ambitious and cunning Drozdov feels that holding responsibilities beyond a person's capacities is both healthy and stimulating.

This cult of incompetence was not enough to make someone a vice-minister. It was also necessary (as Drozdov's wife ended up reproaching him) to throw spanners into other people's works. "You put the noose around the person's neck and you tighten it! You strangle him, you strangle him!"[*] The victim in this instance was an inventor. Drozdov had promised to promote his invention (a centrifuge), but once he learns about an inferior machine produced by a high official with friends in the right places, Drozdov drops the inventor. He reproaches him for working on his own, "Our new machines are the fruit of collective thought." Drozdov takes part in the production of the rival machine, but leaves when it proves to be unsuitable and

---

[*]   Doudintsev, 1957, p. 287.

wasteful of raw material. When the authorities discover the merits of the inventor who had been passed over, Drozdov briskly opens an enquiry on the reason for the eight lost years for which he alone was responsible. The inventor had submitted his project in 1945 but only obtained justice in 1953, having been condemned to the gulag and then recalled in the meantime. The zealous enquiry, which allows Drozdov to pose as a brave defender of truth, enables him to topple and supplant his superior vice-minister, another crook but a less cunning one than Drozdov. Aware that "by taking a few risks, it would have been possible to support this inventor as early as 1946," Drozdov immediately corrects himself, "No, no, no! At the time it made no sense. ... Both of us would have lost out. Whereas now. ..."[†] No one is right in relation to the authorities, except when the time has come to make one's direct superior take the blame for ones' own mistakes and crimes. Normally such a reversal of situations would have been inconceivable. The state would have continued to waste its money and the inventor would have stayed in the gulag, like Nikolai Vavilov and so many other of Lysenko and Stalin's victims. Perhaps Dudintsev added that last part for the sole purpose of getting the book published.[‡] Even after the Twentieth Congress, everything under a socialist regime must have a happy end.

Liu Binyan had no need to alter the truth since he was dealing with a case of embezzlement that was taken to court. Even so, he thought it necessary to hammer the point home: the reasons why Wang Shouxin got so rich were still very much present. His book aroused the ire of Wang's accomplices who were still in place and determined to get their revenge if Liu so much as set foot in Heilongjiang. Across the country their emulators loudly denounced the "poisonous weed." The author who had distilled the venom was not surprised by the hostility of the powerful, and

---

[†]   Doudintsev, 1957, p. 549.

[‡]   Ibid., pp. 479–610.

concluded that although Wang Shouxin's corruption had been uncovered, it was "not yet the time to cry victory."

Both authors' works met with the same reception. In 1956 as in 1979, the readers were enthusiastic while the official reaction was critical, but, in the case of *Not by Bread Alone*, kept at bay by a firm public defense from Constantine Paoustovski and a dozen other writers. Although I would certainly not compare Dudintsev or Liu Binyan with Molière, I am not surprised that thousands of our contemporaries in those countries referred to a Drozdov or a Wang Shouxin in the same way that French people allude to a Harpagon or a Tartuffe.

Sources: Doudintsev, 1957; Béja and Zafanolli, 1981, pp. 203–293. English translation in *People and Monsters. And Other Stories and Reportage from China after Mao*, ed. Perry Link, Bloomington, Indiana University Press, 1983.

After the Purge: The Transformation of the Elite and the Consolidation of Its Privileges

The Great Terror and the Cultural Revolution marked a brutal end to the prosperity and security of the new class, but the death of the two dictators allowed them to raise themselves far higher, quite undisturbed. I have now exceeded (or will shortly) the chronological limit I set for myself!

The most severe criticisms of bureaucracy sometimes came from the leaders themselves. From the mid-1930s the government encouraged citizens to denounce abuses of power by civil servants—which was a risky business for the plaintiff when the very person he or she was denouncing was in charge of the case. Or if not that person then his accomplices, patrons, or clients, for the apparatchiks protected themselves by forming "families" of the faithful, bound together to defend their common interests, if necessary by hiding the failures, difficulties, and abuses from the center in Moscow (and later, in Beijing). Between 1929 and 1937, the efficiency of the barrier erected by his "family circle" allowed the First Secretary of Party in Smolensk to have more or less a free hand in that western *oblast*. This exploit was facilitated by the difficulties central leaders had in following in detail what was going on from one end to the other of their enormous empire, and the priority they gave to the regional leaders' political and economic performance. If these were considered satisfactory the central leaders weren't going to linger on the brutality (or worse) of the methods used to achieve it.[34] The gradual consolidation of the hold regional potentates had acquired on their satrapy, was one of the causes of the Great Terror, for wary Stalin soon became aware of the flaws in his (insufficiently docile) bureaucracy.

During and after the war, the control exercised by the apparatus (the Central Committee) on the appointment of officials became even less efficient. Ministries and administrations increasingly selected their cadres without asking the Central Committee, or indeed, even without informing it.[35] Faced with the growing independence of a network of well-entrenched bureaucrats, the control procedures established in the 1920s proved to be inadequate. From the top to the bottom of the hierarchy, government representatives plied Party secretaries with gifts and bonuses, so that they in turn allowed them to appoint whoever they wanted (relatives, patrons, or flatterers), or allowed them to be sold to the highest bidder. The reforms carried out by Alexey Kuznetsov in 1947 were an attempt to deal with this growing corruption and the weakening power of the central apparatus, but had little success.

The widespread idea that the Party management systematically recruited a certain type of member who complied with a predetermined model (zealous fanatics, sectarian ideologues little inclined to ask uncomfortable questions) is a legend. Moshe Lewin, my main source for this paragraph, met many an idiot, but also some talented people among a majority of conformist careerists. Even under Stalin, the Party had to relinquish a portion of its power to the bureaucracy, which was skilled in scheming, using contacts, putting pressure on people, and bribing (out of state funds) in order to place its own candidates in key positions. If the recent memory of the Great Terror could not prevent this development in Stalin's lifetime, it is understandable that bureaucracy won the day under Brezhnev: a flourishing bureaucracy, peopled by privileged parasites, and a weakened state.

This better educated elite no longer risked the gulag or death, nor did it risk losing its position for by now membership of the new class was for life, and that life would not be cut short before time. Membership even became increasingly hereditary. Indeed, education became linked to the hereditary transmission of privilege. "From 1945 to 1950, the number of students in universities and higher schools doubled, giving rise to a young professional class of technicians and managers who would become the leading functionaries and beneficiaries of the Soviet system over the next few decades."[36] By the 1960s, most children attended secondary classes up to eighth grade (age fourteen or fifteen), but "a high-achieving child of semi-skilled or unskilled parents had less chance of moving to grades 9 and 10—and from there to higher education and a privileged job— than a less able child of better-educated and more affluent parents."[37] By 1970, the children of specialists made up over three-quarters of science postgraduate students at the Leningrad branch of the Soviet Academy of Sciences. The first generation of specialists trained under Stalin thus "proved able to pass its privileges on to its offspring."[38] Hereditary privilege via education applied not only to the intelligentsia and the technical elite, but even to the elite in power, which was increasingly recruited from among the graduates, as "professional capacity began to take the place of proletarian values in the ruling principles of the Soviet elite."[39]

As Joel Andreas brilliantly demonstrates, ultimately developments were fairly similar in post-Maoist China.[40] The elite that Mao fought not only survived the Cultural Revolution, but reformed and perpetuated the regime that had been so battered by Mao, and continues to dominate it to this day. As Andreas reminds us, it comprised two elites that were frequently in opposition: the educated elite, inherited from the old regime, and the political or Communist elite that came to power after 1949. By attacking the two simultaneously, the Cultural Revolution finally drew them closer together and then united the two, originally hostile, groups. Deng Xiaoping, who had persecuted the intellectuals in 1957, now favored their recruitment in the Party and appointed them to responsible positions.[41] They were necessary to the Four Modernizations, and "scientific management" replaced mass mobilization.[42] In the twenty-first century it is common knowledge that engineers are especially in demand and promoted to the summit of the Party. In 1982, not a single member of the Politburo held a science or engineering degree, but 50 percent had such degrees in 1987, and 75 percent in 1998. By the 1990s, promotion to the ranks of the upper stratum of the top 345,000 leadership positions typically required a university degree.[43] With this political and cultural capital in their hands, the new class was able to consolidate its hold, even in Deng Xiaoping's lifetime—indeed he forced the old "non-expert" cadres (*lao ganbu*) into retirement. From 1990, Cheng Li and Lynn White diagnosed, "the largest peaceful turnover in the leadership of modern China, and probably the most massive elite transformation in history."[44]

This transformation clearly improved the skills of the elite, now composed of experts who were or claimed to be red. They turned their backs on Chairman Mao and reverted into the imperial mandarins of yesteryear, with one difference: Confucian culture was replaced by the specialized expertise of engineers, while access to higher education, which opened all the doors, now depended not on the parents' land ownership, but on their position. The new class was emancipating itself, and today a class of careerists continues to claim that it follows a dogma in which it no longer believes. Some strive for the grandeur of the nation—in this case they have turned their backs on Marx—while others (or the same ones) strive for their personal and family interests.

Since I have now gone beyond the limits I set for myself (both under Stalin and under Mao), I may as well linger on the privileges of the new class during its apogee under Brezhnev, a time when, as Moshe Lewin has written, the system was sick and bureaucracy flourished. Those privileges were already notorious in the 1930s, but far greater three or four decades later, when Michael Voslensky collected those observations for his book.[45]

Taking into account advantages and various bonuses (such as a thirteenth month of salary, a special "treatment" benefit, a "housewife's shopping basket," food coupons, etc.), Voslensky estimated the salary of a section head in the Central Committee to be five times that of an average worker or employee. As Ciliga had pointed out earlier, as had Ilf and Petrov (and as was the case in China), the amount of the salary was less important than the many privileges conferred on the *nomenklatura*. And those privileges continued to grow after the death of the two satirists. While Soviet citizens had to stand in line to buy mediocre quality produce, the section heads were able to buy good food at low prices, not to mention delicatessen produce. They occasionally enjoyed free meals in the Central Committee's "guest houses" and unlike ordinary Soviet citizens, they could travel abroad and purchase goods that were simply not available in the Soviet Union. They could adorn their wives with them (since they had to live up to their status), or else sell them on the black market. Similar goods could be found in the Soviet Union but in special stores where payment was in foreign currency only. That was not usually a problem since they would have brought plenty back from their latest escapade to Berlin, London, or Paris. Although trains and planes were always full and there were long lines at the booking counters, their tickets were handled by the Central Committee. They were driven to the station or the airport in their black Volga cars where they had their own VIP waiting room, which they left before the other travelers so as to avoid being jostled or getting too close to the sacrosanct "masses."

Nor did they have to put up with the long waiting lists for obtaining a small apartment with a communal kitchen, for they were attributed housing in buildings belonging to the Central Committee. In East Berlin, the Berliners called such residential blocks Volga German Estates. Was that in reference to the settlers repatriated from Russia during the war? Certainly not, as Stalin made sure they were deported to the east. No, the name referred to the *nomenklatura*'s Volga-brand office cars! Above a certain rank, the senior cadres were entitled to not only an office car, maintained and repaired by the state, and a driver, but also a dacha, which they could fit out without spending a penny of their own.

Certain higher learning establishments were reserved for the *nomenklatura*'s offspring. If they wanted to earn a Ph.D. they could register with the Academy of Social Sciences where the criteria were political and not scientific. The living conditions were excellent, and the student grants almost equal to the salaries of the teachers. If they should fail to obtain their Ph.D., which in principle almost never happened, the blame would fall on the doctoral supervisors and not on the candidates, who would look down on their supervisors the day after their dissertation, knowing that they were now certain to obtain a managerial position within the Party apparatus.[46]

Once Stalin's death made people less fearful, scarcely disguised chains of collusion increased the possibilities for bribes. In some of the Federal Republics, these could represent colossal amounts. According to a confidential report presented in 1970 by the First Secretary of the Central Committee of Azerbaijan's Communist Party, in 1969 it was possible to acquire the post of District Chief of the Militia for 50,000 rubles, the directorship of a kolkhoz for 80,000 rubles, and the position of Second Secretary of the Azerbaijan district committee for 100,000 rubles (double the amount for the post of First Secretary). The price of a pardon for someone with a long prison sentence was set by the president of the Supreme Soviet of the Soviet Republic of Azerbaijan at 100,000 rubles. At the time an employee or worker earned an average of 150 rubles per month.[47]

Where corruption is concerned, the Brezhnev-era collapse is best compared with contemporary China. Was it a collapse or an advancement? The amounts "diverted" from the tax department continued to rise, reaching $5.6 billion in smuggled goods in the port of Xiamen alone at the end of the 1990s, after an illiterate businessman succeeded in corrupting just about the entire civil and military administration of the town. The amounts diverted or paid out in bribes between 1991 and 2011 were estimated at more than $100 billion.[48] That amount concerned only the goings-on of the high-ranking cadres, but corruption flourished at all levels of the hierarchy, to the extent that, according to the former leader Hu Jintao, it became a "time bomb" waiting to go off, as much of a threat to the stability of the regime and long-term growth as social inequality of environmental damage. A good indicator of the most lucrative positions is their quotation in the detailed index of the most lucrative posts: to become a customs officer, tax officer, or head of land sales, infrastructure, or public markets cost far more than a prestigious position in diplomacy or the central administration. Since the late 1990s, nontransactional administrative corruption (embezzlement and misappropriation) has receded because of successive reforms, but transactional corruption, namely bribery, has increased sharply.[49]

The law is indecisive about dealing with corruption. The judges are appointed and paid by the very same local or regional administrators they would have to judge and, more importantly, only the Party Central Discipline Inspection Commission is authorized to convene, question, and sanction a Communist leader. Only after the offender had been expelled from the Party can it decide to refer the case to the courts, which generally merely ratify the guilty verdict issued by the Party and set the duration of the sentence. Until recently, the members of the Permanent Committee of the Politburo were virtually untouchable since only the highest Party echelon could take the initiative to launch an inquiry into the behavior of a Communist. In line with that custom, Bo Xilai, the former First Secretary of the Chongqing Party Committee, was accused (among other things) of having sold the deputy mayor's position for 30 million yuan (over $4 million) only after he was expelled from the Politburo. As a rule, corruption allegations target a fallen politician and almost never an ally. They linger in the files, ready to be taken out if the person in question becomes a little too independent or if his or her protectors fall in the faction war, which would make an army of patrons equally vulnerable.

***

I have not always used the same terminology to define the subject of this chapter: I have referred to the "new class," like Djilas, the *nomenklatura* like Voslensky, or alternatively used bureaucracy, elite, cadres, leaders and petty leaders, and so forth. Mao spoke of a new bourgeoisie, Christian Rakovski of a managing class; Vera Dunham merely calls it a middle class but suggests that Stalin, like Peter the Great, created a service class. Annie Kriegel compares the "meticulously hierarchical" and stratified Communist society, with an estate or "rank" society.[50] That brings to mind the privileged orders of the French ancien régime and suggests that this chapter might just as well have been called "The Nobility,"[51] or "The Castes," since the revolutionaries replaced the class society they claimed to have abolished with an even more hierarchical society, with more rigid distinctions conferred by a status that distributes privileges. I decided not to use the word "caste" however, for as Louis Dumont has said, we may talk of caste only where there is a separation between status and power, which is certainly not the case with Communist regimes.[52]

In the end I chose the most controversial term. According to Vincent Dubois and his colleagues, a bureaucratic characterization of Communist regimes that combines politics with analysis is implicitly accusatory, and highlights the failures of the Soviet administrative system. Instead of which, those authors prefer an empirical analysis of its day-to-day operating methods and concrete relationships, the tensions and internal rivalries that prevent that complex organism from becoming a monolithic block when faced with colossal tasks.[53] I take full responsibility for the choice I made nearly a half century ago, and I have therefore used partial or subjective accounts, and even literary ones, of a priori and long-held convictions. At least I have kept as closely as possible to the empirical and I have placed myself in the hands of Merle Fainsod, among others, who investigated the Smolensk archives. Where possible I have avoided steering the discussion to more abstract terrain, but I shall do so now that it is time to conclude, and the methodological point of view expressed in the article by those three colleagues encourages me to be as clear as possible. The bureaucracy that is the subject of this chapter is indeed the new dominant social class described by Djilas, Aron, Lefort, Castoriadis, and others.[54] In other words, this chapter laboriously attempts to confirm Max Weber's warning, "In a capitalist economy the state and the private economy balance each other, but in socialism there will be just one vast power elite that decides everything." Or, if you prefer, his 1918 prophecy, made just a few months after October, that instead of the dictatorship of the proletariat, there would be "the dictatorship of the official."[55]

The following chapter will reveal an additional argument against my choice of the word "bureaucracy" to designate the privileged elite, for many writers, artists, and intellectuals were fully a part of it, especially in the Soviet Union. In China, most writers were far less privileged. As for the rest, the differences of degree identified in this chapter, starting with the far greater inequalities in the Soviet Union, did not affect how the Soviet and Chinese bureaucracies were related. The difference and even the contrast (except during the first years, when China copied its model) lay mostly in the attitudes of the two dictators toward them, rather than in their sociology and behavior.

7. Culture

We can, at a pinch, distinguish roughly comparable phases in the development of the two regimes' cultural policies. A first period would correspond to the first eight (1949–1957) or twelve (1917–1929) years. If there is a slight resemblance in those early periods, it is only in relation to what followed; later, the artists and writers would have much time to regret it. A second period ran from 1929 to June 1941 in the Soviet Union, and from 1957 to 1966 in China. The Cultural Revolution at the end of the 1920s, the Great Turn in 1929, the campaigns against Isaac Babel, Boris Pilniak, and Yevgeny Zamyatin the same year, and the trials of the scientists, intellectuals, and Mensheviks in 1930–1931 all showed a desire to homogenize ideology and society. Socialist realism, fabricated in 1932, was defined and imposed in 1934 during the first Congress of the Union of Writers. Writers could no longer be content with describing contemporary society; they now had to anticipate and depict the workers' paradise that would be created by revolutionary development.[1] I am not inclined to divide up this second period from the mid-1930s, with a return to more traditional ideals (the motherland, the family, and the state), since constraints and repression intensified instead of diminished. The real break and respite came with the war.

China spread the second Soviet phase over two phases, which I shall detail for they are less well known. They ran from 1957 to 1966 and from 1966 to 1976. The initial period was less repressive than the two decades that followed, and the spring of 1957 was crowned with the ill-advised Hundred Flowers bouquet. Mao took the initiative for this campaign against the advice of leaders who were less prepared to bet on the Marxist-Leninist flower winning the day once the competition was open, however little. When the intellectuals were finally reassured and dared to speak out, the extent of their criticisms confirmed the wisdom of Mao's lieutenants. Those who had trusted the Party's guarantees were punished. More than half a million intellectuals were labeled "rightists" and sent to the countryside for reeducation or to *laojiao* (labor camps).[2] Most moldered there for two good decades until 1979, the year when it finally became possible to start rectifying the "errors" that have yet to be attributed to the late dictator.

The GLF frenzy further stifled thought and creation. The "rightists" arrested were far from being the only creators condemned to twenty years of silence. No, I'm being unfair, for during the GLF millions of poems were written, more than in the entire five thousand years (the official and extensive number) of Chinese history. In 1958, Mao wanted a collective production of folk songs, so the "worker and peasant masses" carried out his orders—or if not the masses, then various committees supposed to represent them. A selection of those poems, *The Red Flag Ballads*, was the great literary event of 1958. The events that punctuated this second phase, which lasted from mid-1957 to mid-1966 (and included the "mini" Hundred Flowers of 1961–1962, which occurred when the gravity of the famine made concessions a necessity) do not justify dividing it up, any more than the second Soviet phase.

People who believed that they had already been subjected to everything that could possibly happen to them during this phase were far off the mark, for the Cultural Revolution (1966–1976) ushered in the real cultural desert. You could count on one hand the number of writers who were still able to publish. The writers' and artists' associations no longer met, and literary reviews ceased to be published. Writers now had to describe a "higher, more intense, life, better focused, more typical and more idealistic than ordinary life," and the heroic characters they depicted had to be sublime, perfect, without the slightest weakness of character or thought. Authorized literary creation and politics were almost one and the same. Cultural exchanges abroad ceased and classical works were denounced, including the socialist "classics" that had been praised until then.[3] Traditional theater was no longer staged, including Peking Opera with its feudal connotations. The public could always fall back on (and was even obliged to assist) the eight revolutionary operas selected by

Mao's wife. In short, the copy now surpassed the model, for even at the peak of Stalinism the Soviet Union had never seen that.

Four phases in the Soviet Union correspond to three phases in China. The German invasion halted the second phase, while the third, from June 1941 to May 1945, did not outlive victory, and the hopes that had been kindled during the turmoil of war were soon dashed. The war had resulted in a kind of respite, despite the lies (or the silence) of propaganda. Government and patriots grew closer together by force of circumstance in defense of a "just cause."[4] So long as the regime incarnated and led the struggle for survival (and did so better than in 1941), most writers put aside their grievances. For the first time, Anna Akhmatova used the first person plural when writing about the Soviet people and in 1945 she sang about "my land," "delivered from foreign fire," and even Bunin, the émigré, sang of the Red Army's exploits!

The historians' late Stalinism corresponds to the ultimate phase (1945–1953), before the thaw, which the deaths of the irremovable dictators finally bestowed on the two revolutions. Dashing the postvictory hopes ("it can never again be as it was"), the regain of control intensified from 1946 with the sentencing of Mikhail Zoshchenko and Anna Akhmatova (see Box 4), a prelude to the "cosmopolitan" writers and other witch hunts that were unleashed after 1948. The brief period of harmony in 1942–1944 even made Akhmatova nostalgic, whereas her friend Boris Pasternak recalled a time when "the spell of the dead letter was broken."[5] China, spared from a foreign invasion, did not benefit from the cautious revival of freedom during the Great Patriotic War. Nevertheless, there are some similarities in the two lackluster final periods (1948–1953 and 1971–1976) when everything was suspended until the very last breath of the one person who blocked all change. Although Jews were not persecuted in China (there were very few of them), people withdrew into themselves, and denunciations of "cosmopolitanism" and foreign culture were rife.

The two regimes' trajectories resembled each other more in the years following the death of the two dictators. The Chinese already used seasonal metaphors during the Hundred Flower spring. They borrowed the word "thaw" from the Soviet Union, but had no need to imitate the post-Stalin precedent. The reaction in both empires, decapitated at last, was the same. In all it took just three years for a timid thaw to be transformed into a liberating rout (1956 and 1979). From Vladimir Pomerantsev's article, comparing Soviet literary drivel to the sincerity of authentic literature, to the novel by Ilya Ehrenburg, which gave its name to the period, the first literary fruits from Russia were nevertheless earlier or more mature than the short stories by Lu Xinhua and Liu Xinwu.[6] Nor did China benefit from a bombshell comparable to the Twentieth Party Congress. The "Resolution of Certain Questions in the History of Our Party" did not see the day until 1981, and that had more lacunae and was even more biased than Khrushchev's secret speech. But the Chinese writers had no need to wait for the green light, let alone the indicator. The stories by Wang Meng and Liu Binyan that had been sanctioned by the authorities after the Hundred Flowers now seem timid in relation to the many works published since 1979, including by Liu Binyan himself. Chinese literature had never known such an exuberant blossoming since the May Fourth Movement (1919) that shook Confucian tradition sixty years earlier. In their own way, the authorities went along with this sudden emancipation, for instance by allowing people to purchase individual tickets for the cinema in 1979 (although not yet to see a foreign film). Until then the Chinese were allowed to attend only in groups, with the head of the *danwei* (the unit every person was attached to depending on where he or she lived or his or her place of work) who chose the film and the performance for everyone else.[7]

On occasion the authorities were more reticent, as witnessed by the brutal condemnation by the People's Liberation Army of a work by the poet Bai Hua (at the time, Bai belonged to a military *danwei*). The bloody repression on Tiananmen Square in the spring of 1989 put a brutal end to these events, but the repressed Democracy Movement was itself the result of a decade of thaw. Chinese writers had not seen anything comparable since 1949. Nonetheless, as in the Soviet Union, it was political events that made the news in literary, artistic, and intellectual spheres in general.

Now that we have recalled the events, we can proceed to the essential task of comparing the two regimes' cultural policies, and the response of the writers, artists, scholars, and other intellectuals to those policies.

Cultural Policies: Some Differences among the Massive Similarities

I mentioned both regimes' impressive progress in literacy and education in general in chapter 2. I will not return to that, but it should be taken into account to correct the overall negative impression that the reader will be left with from what follows.

Although the two cultural policies were fundamentally the same, there were a few differences. The most important ones can be found in the rough comparison I touched on earlier, and occurred in the very first phases: 1917–1929 and 1949–1957. Since China was already Stalinized, it could not enjoy a slightly protected initial period, like the 1920s in the Soviet Union. But would that "protected" claim have convinced Zamyatin, Babel, Pilniak, Andrei Platonov, Akhmatova, Osip Mandelstam, or Pasternak? Or the poets who were shot (like Nikolay Gumilyov) or committed suicide (like Sergei Esenin and Vladimir Mayakovsky)? There is only one answer to that. In China socialist realism immediately held sway instead of waiting for some fifteen years. Immediately? Mao pronounced his famous "Talks at the Yan'an Forum on Literature and Art" in 1942 and imposed a rigid version of socialist realism right until his death. The Chinese revolution was Stalinized even before it won the day, as the writers and intellectuals who flocked to mythical Yan'an to resist the Japanese invader, were to learn the hard way (see Appendix).

A second major difference was that some Soviet writers benefitted from privileges comparable to those mentioned in the previous chapter. Chinese writers and artists lived in more precarious material circumstances. The opulence of a Konstantin Simonov, with his villa overlooking the Black Sea, his *dacha* in Peredelkino, his big apartment on Gorky Street, and his limousine, driver, two servants, and a steward, would have been quite inconceivable in Mao's China. Furthermore, some Soviet writers and artists had relations of patronage with a leader, whom they could appeal to if, for instance, they wanted a bigger apartment. Aleksey Tolstoy, for instance, was granted an eight- to ten-room *dacha*.[8] In that kind of situation it was preferable to be in cahoots with Molotov rather than with Mikhail Tukhachevsky, Genrikh Yagoda, or Bukharin—a privilege that would be paid for heavily between 1936 and 1938. However, it goes without saying that the majority of Soviet writers and artists displayed nowhere near the same level of opulence as the intelligentsia that rubbed shoulders with the political elite. Nevertheless, the advantages and pay granted to all its members by the Union of Writers (or the Union of Musicians, etc.) would have made their Chinese counterparts envious.

With a few exceptions, Chinese writers had very modest incomes. A literary prizewinner would obtain a bonus that was between ten and one hundred times less that the one obtained by a Soviet prizewinner. The rest was in keeping with that. The *danwei* (the system was the same, even if the pay was not) paid authors the same wage as workers. As in the Soviet Union, the political or bureaucratic authorities decided the print runs without taking into account the popularity of a manuscript; by contrast, royalties allowed only some twenty to thirty writers to feed their families, at best. And those were mainly old writers (thanks to reprints of books published before the revolution) and only for the period 1949–1966, after which it became almost impossible to live from one's writing. In the early 1970s, anyone who succeeded in getting published received only a symbolic payment. When the author handed in the manuscript,[9] he or she would receive a "present" of a few books, a pen, or some tea. That made the exceptions all the more fantastic, such as Du Pengcheng's 107,000 yuan (see below) or the 230,000 yuan in royalties that Mao received every year (nearly forty-eight times his annual salary). The *danwei* provided access to health care and provided its writers with low-rent lodgings, just as it did for the rest of its employees. Zhang Jie, one of the best-known post-Maoist writers, lived for years in one small room in Shanghai.

Some differences in degree in China were due to the more zealous application of common principles. The discrepancies between the Zhdanovian socialist realism and the one that held sway over Yan'an and then over the whole of China were not immediately apparent, but basically went along the same lines: Mao intended to surpass his model, especially after the two Communist regimes fell out. Instead of merely describing the projected or dreamed-of future, literary works had to combine revolutionary realism with revolutionary romanticism. Now they also had to add a layer of daydream (see Box 4 on Page 218). As they grew further away from a myth-biased realism, the romanticism they were required to stress demanded ever more perfect heroes. The peak was reached with the rules of the "Three Prominences" (*san tuchu*) imposed under the Cultural Revolution, which obliged writers to emphasize positive characters, identify the heroes among them, and focus on the central hero above all. The Soviet Union took the opposite path, for the ideals of the 1920s were forgotten, neglected, or scoffed at after the mid-1930s, while elitism and nationalism took over and the difference in degree now became more of difference of type.[10]

In the Soviet Union, censorship and control were carried out by a far more substantial and specialized bureaucracy, which issued more explicit orders and prohibitions than in China. Compared with the directives drawn up and transmitted by the seventy thousand employees of *Glavlit* (the censorship administration), the Chinese equivalent issued fairly vague instructions, tinged with Confucian paternalism. The writers' task was certainly not made easier, for it was up to them to guess which way the wind was blowing, as well as the type and intensity (a gentle breeze or a hurricane) and draw their own conclusions as to the degree of self-censorship to apply.[11]

A final difference is less related to the regimes, both careful not to allow any deviances to attract the attention of foreigners, than to the foreigners themselves. The West was far better informed about (and was far more interested in) what was going on in the Soviet Union than in China. Pasternak, Alexandr Solzhenitsyn, and Grossman became familiar names abroad quite early on—though only after Grossman's death. In China the events in Tiananmen Square in the spring of 1989 finally prompted Westerners to pay some attention to the Chinese Democracy Movement, if not Chinese dissident (or simply independent) literature.

Resemblances

The first reason for the similarity between the two policies was simply that cultural organization in China was based on that of the Soviet Union. Both had monopolistic writers' associations (there was no salvation without them, if salvation was understood to mean a career and fame in one's own country), headed by a powerful cultural bureaucracy with regional branches.[12] There were the national and provincial literary reviews, also headed by cultural bureaucrats or favored writers. Over and above those institutions, on a more personal level, Soviet literature had a considerable influence in China. It had been popular among the left-wing intelligentsia in the 1930s and twenty years later was systematically disseminated and taught in schools and even held up as a model. Things changed after Mao criticized its revisionist degeneracy, and even more so when the trauma he inflicted on his people altered the way the Chinese perceived Soviet literature.

A good illustration of that is how two generations of Chinese readers understood Nikolai Ostrovsky's edifying classic, *How the Steel Was Tempered*.[13] André Gide paid a visit to the author when he was suffering from an incurable disease that left him blind and paralyzed, but nevertheless devoting his last efforts to describe the ideal Communist. Gide described his own emotions in *Return from the USSR* ("If we were not in the USSR, I should say he was a saint"). The hero of Ostrovsky's book, Pavel Korchagin, is the incarnation of a "Soviet saint" (Michel Heller) or of a "martyr for an idea" (Evgeny Dobrenko). He renounces the love of Tonia Tumanova, which represents a form of personal happiness that he rejects as being selfish, in order to devote himself entirely to the revolution. Korchagin was often held up as a model to Chinese schoolchildren and teenagers, rather than some romantic hero from the literature of the May Fourth Movement, when the slogan was "the Soviet Union today is our tomorrow!" and the ideal of the "new socialist man" was copied from the "new Soviet man." *How the Steel Was Tempered* was the most published foreign work in China before the Cultural Revolution, with a new print run every six months (twenty-five in a thirteen-year period from 1952 to 1965). Significant extracts were reproduced in teachers' manuals to be read and commented on in class. Any pupil who thought that Tonia was "depicted in a lively manner" was immediately reprimanded for living in the old bourgeois world. It was then up to the other students to "help" their classmate until collective harassment resulted in a uniform understanding of the work.

Between 1950 and 1966, this bible for an apprenticeship in heroism was instilled in all Chinese adolescents in school. It remained popular after the Sino-Soviet split, and even today many Chinese retirees will claim that *How the Steel Was Tempered* was one of two or three books that marked them during their lifetimes. The book was not reprinted in the decade from 1966–1976; nor was it banned, a fate reserved for native socialist classics, once praised to the skies and then identified with Zhou Yang's "black revisionist line" (see Box 4 on Page 218). It was simply that the schools closed down and the bookshops no longer sold any novels since their shelves were now filled 60 percent with Mao's works, 30 percent with works by Marx, Engels, Lenin, and Stalin, and 10 percent with reference material for political criticism. The few books people kept hidden in their homes had to be devoured in secret, first and foremost being *How the Steel Was Tempered*. Once the Cultural Revolution had destroyed their faith or dissipated their illusions, Chinese teenagers acquired a different take on their elders' bible. They considered Pavel's farewell speech to Tonia as insensitive ("I would be a poor husband to you if you expect me to put you before the Party. For I shall always put the Party first, and you and my other loved ones second").[14] Those clandestine young readers believed that Tonia had a deeper understanding of life than Pavel and the Bolsheviks, for she did not preach, she simply understood.

After Mao, Ostrovsky's novel ceased to be special, if only because by then it was in competition with so many others. Chinese intellectuals have described the ten Cultural Revolution years as a *shuhuang*, or "book famine." And all the people who had been starved of books had only one concern, and that was to get up to date in every domain. Ostrovsky's star waned in consequence.

The influence of Soviet literature, the adaptation of Soviet institutions, and the imitation of Soviet behavior should not conceal the similarities that arose from the same base, in other words the shared faith of the two regimes. In the north as well as to the south of the Great Wall and even as far west as the Vistula River, this "new faith" (Miłosz)[15] wreaked the same havoc. Denounced as a "false conscience" by Marx and Engels, the ideology ruled undivided in the universe created by their disciples. However its impact may be assessed, it is hard to exaggerate the importance of ideology. It produced a unilateral and exclusive interpretation of reality, triumphant conformism, and a superior abstraction of the concrete, as opposed to real life, human beings— the nuts and bolts, or cogs and screws according to Stalin's formula— and the ideal that Lei Feng would attempt to achieve.[16] As Solzhenitsyn pointed out, that ideology made it possible to do so much better than Shakespeare's villains, who couldn't exceed a dozen corpses at best. It was only necessary to start chipping it at the corners, even indirectly like Khrushchev in 1956, to trigger a chain of revolts. The ideology never recovered from that, but since it was vital to the system a pretense of faith was required for a long third of a century. That is how things still stand in China today. A comparable, even longer lapse of time has passed since "de-Maoization," but the younger brother still thinks he can teach big brother a thing or two.

The nationalist reorientation of an internationalist ideology ("workers of the world") was useful to offset an unavowed loss of faith. The nationalist element of revolutionary momentum had been so predominant in China that this new veneer was easily accepted. Stalin had carried out the same feat in the mid-1930s and thanks to Hitler the travesty acquired authenticity. Once the nationalistic veneer had concealed much of what remained, the pathological distrust of foreign influence (*wuran*, or pollution in Chinese) could be openly expressed. Witness the "spiritual pollution" campaign of 1983, which came in the wake of foreign technology and capital, a worthy echo of the campaign against cosmopolitanism carried out thirty-five years earlier in the Soviet Union, when the writer Vladimir Tendriakov could not understand "how internationalism (which was above all praise) was any different from cosmopolitanism (which was quite simply considered criminal)."[17] It was not enough to contain foreign pollution; endogenous attacks on purity and unanimity had to be concealed from foreign eyes. If foreigners had the bad taste to honor the deviants, similar campaigns would attack the recipients of that disgrace. In 2010, the Chinese mimicked the 1958 campaign against Pasternak with Liu Xiaobo as the target.

Ideology was therefore free to evolve as long as the additions were Stalin's creations, later enriched by Mao. It could also accommodate itself to the parallel existence of a body of political truths emanating from the same august sources: the criminal nature of Trotskyism (or Hitlerism/ Trotskyism, or Bukharinism/Trotskyism), pernicious revisionism and Liu-type conspiracy (from the president of the People's Republic, Liu Shaoqi) aiming to restore capitalism, and so on. As with ideology, such assertions could not tolerate the slightest denial or time discrepancy. The price to pay for continuing to praise Lin Biao, Mao's former closest companion in arms turned traitor, was the same as abstaining from praising him before his fall. To be correct too soon was unpardonable, as the unwise were to find out when they voiced their reservations about the Soviet elder brother as early as the spring of 1957, instead of waiting for Mao to give the signal.

Writers (and artists)

Writers were more exposed than others to such blunders. The imposed truths were clear-cut, whereas literature depicts complexity and ambivalence, which led critics obedient to the government to condemn insufficiently unambiguous development. In China the "Mist" poetry of the 1980s aroused suspicion and disapproval. In Russia as in China, the cultural leaders and bureaucrats boasted of expressing the point of view of the masses. In the name of the masses they handed out praise and criticism, and obliged writers to revise their manuscripts. Even the most conformist writers were not spared. Aleksey Tolstoy (1883–1945), "attentive to the voice of Soviet opinion," rewrote *The Death of Ivan the Terrible* several times, having already altered *Peter the Great* at Stalin's request. In 1949, Alexander Fadeyev (1901–1956) was obliged to revise *The*

Young Guard, which had earned him the Stalin Prize in 1945 (see below). One example on the Chinese side is enough: the reworking of *Song of Youth* by Yang Mo (1914–1995). Widely acclaimed when it was published in 1958, it became the subject of a criticism campaign the following year, which obliged the author to make considerable changes to her book. The 1960 edition removed the heroine's "petit bourgeois" aspirations and added ten chapters, seven of which were devoted to the heroine's stay in the countryside, because "the masses" had regretted their absence in the first draft of the book, which was devoted to the student movement in the cities. Despite those changes, which were critically well received, the 1958 best seller (1.3 million copies sold in six months), also made into a popular film, was nevertheless listed among the "poisonous weeds" during the Cultural Revolution.[18]

Another mishap that could befall a writer far more frequently than being obliged to rewrite a work was quite simply a bad review that could escalate and develop into a fully fledged campaign. It mattered little if the criticism of a work was motivated by purely nonliterary considerations; a zealous critic knew exactly how to detect the artistic shortcomings in any nonconformist work, starting with its formalistic nature or its darkness. Among the very many Soviet writers who were criticized (and this was just a first stage until appropriate sanctions could be found) were Platonov, Mikhail Bulgakov, Ilf and Petrov, and later Aleksandr Tvardovsky and Vasily Grossman. Satirists and humorists (I might add Zoshchenko to the authors of *Twelve Chairs* and *The Golden Calf*) were more vulnerable than others. They mocked or lambasted what they were supposed to praise or turn a blind eye to. As Ilf explained to Ilya Ehrenburg in Paris, "in chronicles for newspapers it is possible to show despotic bureaucrats, thieves and scoundrels ... but if you write a story about them, it immediately causes an uproar; 'you are generalizing, that is an atypical situation, it's calumny.'" Behind the closed doors of ad hoc meetings of the Union of Soviet Writers, such criticisms could give rise to a form of chastisement called *prorabotka*, whereby everyone denounced the errors of the guilty party, who "recognized his/her mistakes and rolled about in the mud in front of them, swearing that he/she will never do it again."[19]

China set the tone in 1950. The film *The Life of Wu Xun* was one of the regime's first great popular hits. The edifying subject dealt with a poor orphan who was forced to leave school because he could not afford to pay the fees. Wu Xun, a peasant, begged for thirty years and was able to save some money, which he then lent out and ultimately made enough to become a landlord. Once he was comfortable, Wu Xun founded three free schools and was honored by the emperor in an official ceremony (the story takes place in the nineteenth century). Some forty articles praised the film, until in March 1951 the Party Central Committee made public a request by Mao for a wide public debate on how saving the country through education was just "bourgeois idealism." The "defeatist reformer" Wu Xun was accused of perpetuating the social order instead of overthrowing it. For nearly two months the newspapers devoted one-fourth of their columns to denouncing the film; the critics who had praised it retracted and accused themselves of having indulged in "petit-bourgeois sentiments." The film was withdrawn, and the director was obliged to make his self-criticism in due form in the *People's Daily*.[20]

Apart from the purpose behind the criticism (Mao wanting to inculcate liberal intellectuals with Marxism-Leninism), this event recalls how Dmitri Shostakovich was treated some fifteen years earlier. Shostakovich reached his artistic maturity with *Lady Macbeth from Mtsensk*, composed between 1930 and 1932. Audiences in Leningrad and Moscow enthusiastically applauded the opera in 1934 and 1935—but only in the first few weeks of 1936, for the 28 January edition of *Pravda* abruptly challenged this "muddle instead of music ... a confused stream of sound," before concluding that it was "all that is coarse, primitive and vulgar."

The reason for this about-turn was that Stalin had just seen a performance of the opera and did not like it. As a result it was removed from the repertoire of all the country's opera houses. The ballet *The Clear Stream*, for which Shostakovich composed the music, met with the same fate. Stalin endured one performance of this "implausible and absurd ballet," "rubbish in guise of ballet," with music that made a lot of noise but "expressed nothing." The critics immediately took up these accusations, and neither of the two works was ever mentioned again in Stalin's lifetime.

Stalin's taste was much like that of the majority of leaders, Party members, and the concertgoing public. Good, healthy music was inspired by classical principles, a musical tradition that "complied with natural harmony," and a harmony that destroyed any "formalism." And any composer, painter, or poet open to an avant-garde aesthetic was reputed to be a formalist or a modernist. Like Shostakovich, such artists were far too appreciative of decadent Western music (or art or literature)—products of the last phases of doomed capitalism. Published two months after the *Lady Macbeth* scandal, Gorki's article (*On Formalism*) described the use of formalism as a mask that attempted to conceal mediocrity or emptiness of spirit. Anyone comparing formalists (such as Proust or Joyce) to Shakespeare, Pushkin, or Tolstoy would immediately be told that nothing equaled realism and simplicity, and that ornamentation and superfluous elaboration served only to weaken a work. There was nothing specifically Marxist in those reactions (apart from the last convulsions of capitalism) for they were as common elsewhere as they were in the Soviet Union. As Sheila Fitzpatrick suggests, Mayakovsky himself would have run the posthumous risk of being charged with "formalism" had Stalin not consecrated him as the greatest Soviet poet. What was specific to the system was not Stalin's (banal) taste, or Lenin's (even more traditional) taste, but the automatic sanctions on anyone who did not comply with the majority "good" taste. The rest was just a matter of jargon. In other latitudes that majority, or traditional, good taste was reputed to be bourgeois; here it was the reverse. The bourgeois (and decadent) was anything that went against inherited taste and models. The avant-garde, condemned for being formalistic in Germany as well as in the Soviet Union at the time, showed the pernicious influence of decadent capitalism in one country, and of the international Jewry in the other.[21]

When the criticism of a work was transformed into a campaign, anyone who did not take part in that campaign was suspect and ran the risk of becoming the target of an ancillary one.[22] At that stage, a criticism campaign soon raised the issue of the author's personality and political status. That was the case with Bulgakov, Platonov, Zamyatin, and Pilniak as early as 1929, Vsevolod Meyerhold in 1936, Akhmatova and Zoshchenko in 1946, Pasternak in 1958, Solzhenitsyn in 1967, and so on. China was not content with simply importing this type of campaign, but resorted to it far more frequently than the Soviet Union. Unlike in the Soviet Union and the cases of the above-mentioned authors, the Chinese campaigns preferred to target writers reputed to be close to the Party. Among the notable exceptions, however, were the literary critic Yu Pingbo (attacked for his interpretation of a great Chinese classic, *The Dream of the Red Chamber*) and exiles, like Hu Shi. Otherwise the targets of the "literary" campaigns were for the most part Marxist theoreticians, or even members of the CCP charged with heterodoxy, or writers whose works had initially been praised for their revolutionary good health.[23]

After the campaign against him (and formalism) in 1936, Shostakovich ceased to compose operas and returned to grace fairly quickly after 1938, though he was criticized again and dismissed from his teaching posts in 1948.[24] However, he received unanimous praise during the war for the "tragic heroism" of the Seventh Symphony. Above all he did not have the misfortune to die on 5 March 1953, like his elder, Sergei Prokofiev, on the very same day as their suspicious critic. As a result he was able to stage his opera again in 1963, in a more "sensible" version. Prokofiev, like Shostakovich, Aram Khachaturian, Dmitry Kabalevsky, Nikolai Myaskovsky, and other composers with "formalistic and anti-worker tendencies," were subjected to Zhdanov's same sententious admonitions and, like them, was condemned by the famous February 1948 Central Committee resolution. Yet he had conscientiously celebrated the resistance to the Nazi invader by filling his Fifth Symphony (1944) with heroic themes. Earlier, in 1941, when composing the opera of *War and Peace* he even suggested comparing the war against Hitler with the war against Napoleon. Following criticisms from the Soviet Arts Committee in 1942, he revised the opera by praising "in direct contravention to Tolstoy's intentions, the heroic leadership and military genius of (Stalin-like) Kutzov" (Orlando Figes). Before the war, in the same spirit, Prokofiev composed the score of Eisenstein's film, *Alexander Nevsky*, which narrated the medieval victory over the Teutonic knights and their failure to Germanize the Slavs. That was a welcome celebration of Russian patriotism at a time (1938) when propaganda was preparing people for the possibility of a German invasion, but the film was withdrawn the very next year as a result of the German-Soviet pact.[25] From works criticized for themselves (and their bourgeois stench), that film illustrates how the vagaries in the fortunes of artistic works could also depend on historical circumstances.

Even a work such as the sentimental and patriotic novella *Smoke of the Fatherland* by Konstantin Simonov (1915–1979), which at first sight, appears harmless and perfectly ideologically correct, became the target of orchestrated attacks at the end of 1947 as an "immature and erroneous" novel that represented Soviet patriotism in too passive a manner. As a well-known eulogist of patriotism, Simonov was astonished by the criticisms and demanded to see Zhdanov, who had written a criticism praising the novel before revoking it once Stalin set him straight. Simonov was received by Zhdanov's deputy, who immediately asked him what progress he was making on his play about the Kliueva-Roskin affair. That seemingly innocent question revealed the nature of the attack on *Smoke of the Fatherland*. Six months earlier, Stalin had met with the two leading lights of the Union of Writers, Fadeyev and Simonov, for three long hours, in the presence of Zhdanov and Molotov. Stalin suggested that they develop the theme of Soviet patriotism and servility to the West. As an example he showed them a letter detailing the crime of the two scientists, Nina Kliueva and Grigorii Roskin, who had communicated an article to their American colleagues in which they mentioned a possible cure for cancer. Both of them were fired from their research institute, and the secretary of the Academy of Medicine who had sent the article was sentenced to twenty-five years of forced labor for spying. Stalin thought that a novel should be written about this incident, but Simonov suggested a play—which was still unwritten six months later. He immediately learned his lesson, asked the Central Committee to send him an expert in microbiology, was received the very next day by the health minister, and two days later met the academician who was to be his scientific advisor. The play was finished in the spring of 1948, but Simonov never included it in any edition of his complete works.[26]

Among similar tribulations on the Chinese side, I will mention two cases, although it is paying them a great honor to place them on the same level as Fadeyev and Simonov, and even more so alongside Eisenstein and Prokofiev. In *The Song of Ouyang Hai*, published in 1965, Jin Jingmai (1930–) praised the sacrifice of a young soldier who had given his life to prevent a train accident. The author embellished this incident, which had occurred two years earlier, by attributing the soldier with a difficult childhood under the old regime, and his devotion to Liu Shaoqi's edifying opuscule *How to Be a Good Communist*. Jin could not foresee that Liu would fall the following year for attempting to restore capitalism. No matter, for a new edition replaced the references to Liu with "Mao Zedong thought" and, for good measure, added praise for Lin Biao, who, in the meantime, had been promoted to Chairman Mao's "closest comrade-in-arms." Four years later, when it was Lin Biao's turn to be accused of treachery, the author had to alter his novel once again. He brought out a new edition in 1979, but too early to pay his dues to Liu Shaoqi, who was rehabilitated posthumously in 1980.

After fate had smiled on Du Pengcheng (1921–1991), his fall from grace hit him all the harder. His novel, *Defend Yan'an*, published in 1954, made him rich and famous, exceptionally rich for a Chinese writer, with 107,400 yuan in royalties, the equivalent of more than two centuries of wages for a worker and five hundred years of peasant income. Du had a perfect pedigree and past. The son of a poor peasant family who lost his father at the age of three, Du went to Yan'an when he was still a teenager. His best-selling book was also faultless. He narrated with meticulous precision every detail of the counterattack that led to the reconquest of Yan'an after it had been occupied by the Nationalist forces in 1947, making the book less of a history and more of a hagiography. Every page exalts not only heroism, but the goodness, bordering on saintliness, of an "old" twenty-nine-year-old revolutionary, who had been a beggar before signing up with the Red Army, along with his two comrades, a machine gunner and a cook who died in battle. Yan'an deserved those sacrifices, at least according to history transformed into myth and using a quasi-religious tone to describe the holy town. The author's only mistake was to pay homage to General Peng Dehuai, who led the resistance and later the counterattack. Du and his novel had enjoyed a long period of glory, but after the Lushan episode (see above) the veteran Peng was transformed into a plotter leading an anti-Party clique (a term probably borrowed from the one conferred on Molotov and others in 1957). At first, *Defend Yan'an* was called an antihistorical poisonous weed, and was no longer published. Shortly afterward, two secret circulars issued by the Ministry of Culture banned the sale or loan of the book and ordered all remaining copies to be destroyed. During the Cultural Revolution, Du Pengcheng was accused of plotting against Chairman Mao. Three years after Mao's death, Peng Dehuai was rehabilitated posthumously and this epic to his glory returned to favor.[27]

At least the books demolished by critics got published in the first place; many authors were unable to get that far because they could never overcome the prior obstacle of censorship. Plays, such as Bulgakov's *Flight*, failed to make it to the stage, and many magazines were prevented from being published or sold. Since films reached a wider audience than literature, and a cinema audience could react collectively, they were even more tightly controlled than books. The producers of the film *In a Twinkling* (1980) lost one million yuan after it was banned, the equivalent of eight hundred years of an average wage. The prospects of such losses, not to mention possible political sanctions, were persuasive enough for the majority of film directors to apply self-censorship.[28]

Rather than practice self-censorship, many writers wrote for their desk drawers, without any hope of being published in their lifetimes (Bulgakov or Platonov, for example), or at least in Stalin's lifetime.[29] Some manuscripts reputed to be unpublishable could be confiscated, such as Solzhenitsyn's *The First Circle* and Grossman's *Life and Fate*. As Suslov explained to him, it would be some two hundred years before a work like that could be published.

If an author who submitted an unpublishable manuscript was a CP member, he or she ran the risk of being expelled from the Party. That happened to Viktor Nekrasov, the Stalin Prizewinner for *In the Stalingrad Trenches*. Authors who were members of the Union of Writers, such as Akhmatova and Zoshchenko in 1946 or Solzhenitsyn in 1969, were expelled from the union.[30] Some writers were deported, such as Aleksey Remizov in 1921, Sergei Melgunov and others in 1922. It was mainly after the thaw (under Brezhnev in the Soviet Union, and in the 1990s in China) that deportation became a way of getting rid of troublesome people. Vasily Aksionov and Georgii Vladimov were stripped of their citizenship and forced to emigrate, as were many others, Solzhenitsyn included. In China the banished included Liu Binyan, Su Xiaokang, Wang Ruowang, and Zheng Yi.

Then there were the arrests, the deportation to the gulag or *laogai*, and death. The cases that came after the Twentieth Congress, from Joseph Brodsky to Yuli Daniel and Andrei Sinyavsky, Andrei Amalrik to Anatoly Kuznetsov and Eugenia Ginzburg, were the ones that mainly attracted the attention of the West (and then more for the psychiatric hospitals than for the gulag). After that Congress we learned that more than six hundred members of the Union of Writers (nearly one-third of the total number of members) had been arrested or deported to the gulag between 1934 and 1943. The union's presidium was even worse hit, for sixteen of its thirty-seven members did not survive the purges.[31] Mandelstam was arrested and banished, then arrested again in 1938 and deported to the gulag, where he died almost immediately. The son of Anna Akhmatova and the poet Gumilyov (executed in 1921) was arrested and deported three times. Among the writers who died in prison or the gulag, as the result of mistreatment or shot, I should mention at the very least Nikolai Kliuyev in 1937, Pilniak in 1938, Meyerhold in 1940, Babel in 1941, and the critic Aleksandr Voronsky in 1943.

Predictably, the largest number of executions and deportations to the gulag took place during the Great Terror. In China there was an even

218 | STALIN AND MAO

more clear-cut concentration of "extreme measures" during the Cultural Revolution. Some people, such as Deng Tuo, preempted inevitable punishment by committing suicide, but more died of ill treatment, such as his collaborator Wu Han (they had dared to mock Mao). Alongside the rare authors who stayed aloof from Marxism, such as Zhou Zuoren, there were many who were believers and even Party members who had been targeted by criticism campaigns in the past (Shao Quanlin, Xiao Yemu). Others still were celebrated and applauded for works deemed to comply but later repudiated during the Cultural Revolution (Zhao Shuli). Lao She (1898–1966), the famous writer of the 1920s, deserves a special mention, for he threw himself into a lake in Beijing in the early days of the Cultural Revolution.[32] Like Deng Tuo, he was in good company. On the rostrum of the Fourth National Congress of Chinese Writers and Artists (the first post-Mao congress, held in October 1979), the names were read out of two hundred writers and artists who had been beaten to death, forced to commit suicide, or killed during the Cultural Revolution. However that did not beat the record established by the Great Terror. Of the 597 delegates to the inaugural congress of the Union of Writers in 1934, 180 were repressed in one way or another in 1937–1938, but a total of nearly two thousand Soviet writers were victims of the Great Terror.[33]

Box 4

Watchdogs

Zhou Yang (1908–1989) was known in his lifetime as the czar of culture. The reference was so obvious to us that some French Sinologists simply called him the Chinese Zhdanov. Andrei Zhdanov (1896–1948) gave his name to *Zhdanovtchina*, the search for formalistic and cosmopolitan tendencies, a euphemism for the late 1940s witch hunt that targeted (among others) writers and artists open to foreign influence in their works and, less openly, to Jews. Like Nikolai Yezhov and *Yezhovshchina* (to designate the Great Terror) a decade earlier, it is giving Zhdanov too much credit, for both were zealous lackeys. For all that I won't deny him his accomplishments. It was he who defined socialist realism, a triumphalist vision of utopia under construction, as early as 1934 at the first Soviet Writers Congress. The year after that, Zhdanov accompanied his master's "great retreat" by warning, "If we educate our young people on the model of *Narodnaya Volya*, we will produce terrorists."

Two decades earlier, a young revolutionary militant Zhdanov would have replied sarcastically to such a remark. One decade later he would save his sarcasm for the most popular satirists and one of that century's great woman poets, calling Zoshchenko "a petty soul, trivial and lowly … , a literary thug, shameless and without principles" and Akhmatova "with her petty, narrow personal life, her paltry experiences, and her religiously mystical eroticism," "now a nun, now a whore, or rather a whore and a nun at the same time, combining prayer and debauchery." Zhdanov's diatribe was accompanied by a Central Committee decree on 14 August 1946, and was the prelude to the two authors' expulsion from the Union of Writers. Little did Zhdanov know, a year and a half later, when he reprimanded composers with a "formalistic anti-people tendency," that he would die of a heart attack six months later, but *Zhdanovshchina* would outlive its eponym.

Zhou Yang makes Zhdanov seem like a nice man. He was not lying when he said, "I exert every effort to succeed in being the interpreter, the propagandist as well as the practitioner of Mao Zedong's ideas and policies in cultural matters." He followed every twist and turn in the Party line, not without credit. When Mao gave his blessing to the competing "hundred flowers," Zhou Yang said the very opposite of what he had been repeating a few months earlier, and denounced a litany of misdeeds that he himself was guilty of, first and foremost. He even went as far as to suggest, in April 1957, that the administrative ukase and the bureaucratic management of everything related to the domain of art, literature, and science were detrimental to those disciplines, including for good measure sectarianism and assessments founded on ideological criteria (he actually said "doctrinaire"). Zhou revealed his own sectarianism the very first time he blacklisted a work (the film *The Life of Wu Xun* [see above), denying people the right to show the least independence, or even to abstain in politics. One of his associates confirmed that "a person's ideas at present are either progressive or reactionary—there is no third way."

The reader may object: it was not Zhou but one of his associates. There lies the core of the problem. Zhdanov brought some of his Leningrad colleagues "up" to Moscow. Unlike Zhou Yang, he did not build a clique around himself. Zhou was more concerned with eliminating his rivals than suppressing unorthodox ideas. Once his adversaries or simply his competitors were excluded from the few literary reviews that were not yet under his clique's control, he quickly replaced them with people loyal to himself. Zhou selected his targets from among the deviants who were potential models for "negative examples," according to the danger a given writer might represent to his authority (Ding Ling in 1957), or because of a grudge or to settle old accounts (Hu Feng in 1954), or for both reasons at the same time (Feng Xuefeng, also in 1954). By representing the Party and orthodoxy he was sure to succeed in his offensives. He had shown his worth very young, long before the Communist victory. The line adopted by the Comintern's Seventh Congress obliged the CCP to declare a united front, and it resigned itself to that in December 1935. Charged with applying this about-turn in culture, Zhou Yang dissolved the League of Left Wing Writers without warning its chairman, the great writer Lu Xun. It is true that as the league's (Communist) secretary general, Zhou was the real boss, just as later he would run the ministry of culture with a title of deputy to the minister, another non-Communist writer. For good measure, and still as second in command, he controlled the Union of Writers, but his real source of influence was elsewhere, in the Central Committee's propaganda department, where he held his usual position of deputy director—the difference here being that the director here was, by definition, a Communist like himself.

During the GLF, Zhou Yang responded to Mao's desire to produce more rice, steel, and poetry. He and his theoretical superior at the Union of Writers (Guo Moruo, president of the pan-Chinese Federation of Writers and Artists [see Box 5 on Page 233]) led the mass poetry movement. The two of them complied a selection for this work called, unsurprisingly, *Songs of the Red Flag*. It was Zhou Yang, rather than Guo Moruo, who pushed the exaltation of the worker-writer the furthest: "In the new epoch of the Great Leap Forward, the experience of old writers can give us little help. ... Poems written by the masses are better than those written by poets." The poetry of the masses illustrated the superiority of the Chinese Way, like the People's Communes, at a time when Mao had decided to surpass the Soviet model. Mao even wanted to "perfect" venerable socialist realism by combining revolutionary realism with revolutionary romanticism—and Zhou Yang followed suit. This new doctrine was a perfect replica of the original, expounded and imposed by Zhdanov, who, what is more, had advocated that literature by the masses exist alongside literature for the masses. Mao—and therefore Zhou Yang—had invented nothing; they merely made their findings a little more ridiculous. They would have done better to allow them to fade into oblivion—as happened after the death of the two dictators.

However, there were some important differences between Zhdanov and Zhou Yang. Zhou Yang's authority was confined to culture. Shortly after Kirov's assassination, Stalin made Zhdanov the Party first secretary in Leningrad, where he remained in that position during the siege. In 1941, Zhdanov became deputy secretary general of the CPSU, and therefore deputy to the irremovable secretary general himself. In 1946 he appeared to be the heir apparent within the Politburo, to the great displeasure of his rival Malenkov. He carried out other important missions in the Baltic States, in Finland, and finally in Poland, where in 1947 he announced the creation of Cominform, and in 1948 the excommunication of Tito.

Even though Zhdanov fell out of favor in the last months of his life, he was long a favorite. Stalin enjoyed talking to him and even considered that he was the only member of his entourage worthy of pursuing an intellectual conversation with him. Zhdanov's mother was a well-known pianist, and as a pianist himself, he accompanied Stalin, Molotov, and Voroshilov when they sang. During a meeting with artists, he played a few notes on the piano to show Shostakovich the type of melody that was easy to sing and accessible to the masses. His son Yuri, whom Stalin had known since he was a five-year-old boy, was only twenty-eight when Stalin thrust him to the head of the Central Committee's Department of Science. Yuri disappointed his benefactor when he publicly criticized Trofim Lysenko, which did not prevent Stalin from persuading a reticent Svetlana to marry him.

Zhou Yang was never part of the inner circle and was never a member of the Politburo. Furthermore he was violently attacked and criticized in the early days of the Cultural Revolution, after which Mao called the Central Committee's propaganda department, which Zhou Yang presided, "the palace of hell." When Mao attacked the "dictatorship of the black revisionist line," which had persistently held sway from 1949 to 1966, he was specifically targeting Zhou Yang. Through Zhou, Mao was criticizing the Party's cultural bureaucracy for having failed to bring the intellectuals on board. Zhou's methods and the directives he implemented, had only alienated the creators, artists, and writers. And having failed to bring them on board, at the very least Zhou and his clique should have made the intellectuals more docile! In classic fashion, Mao made Zhou Yang the scapegoat for his own failure. He even accused Zhou of laxity and lacking in principles during the Hundred Flowers, when in fact the zealous parrot had retracted by repeating slogans fished out of Mao's speech of 27 February 1957 to encourage the intellectuals to speak out.

But was Zhou Yang only a scapegoat? During the "little hundred flowers" of 1961–1962, he went as far as to proffer run-of-the-mill counterrevolutionary statements such as, "If we train all students to be political activists ... they will become empty-headed politicians without professional knowledge." Why take the opposite view of the eternal truths of Mao-thought, recently taken to its pinnacle during the GLF? Did that disaster and famine allow the scales to fall from Zhou's eyes? Or, having rediscovered his youthful infatuation with nineteenth-century European literature—that same bourgeois realism that he later so decried—did Zhou end up developing an allergy to Maoist oversimplification? And what if the unfortunate *apparatchik* simply decided that it was less dangerous to follow the same course as the majority of his hierarchical superiors, starting with the president of the People's Republic, Liu Shaoqi?

Zhou Yang was spared more than Liu and survived the Cultural Revolution. Mao released him in 1975. After Mao's death he once again held important responsibilities, always in the cultural domain. In the early 1980s, he praised the very literary genre he had criticized and repressed relentlessly from Yan'an days to the eve of the Cultural Revolution. During the 1983 campaign against spiritual pollution, Zhou Yang seized the opportunity of the centenary celebrations of Marx's death to declare that alienation existed not only in capitalist countries, but could also exist in a socialist society when government officials abused their powers, and that those powers were undemocratic. Even though he was criticized by guardians of Mao's word, more fastidious and faithful than he, his speech was published in the *People's Daily* and had a considerable impact. I must point out one final difference between the two watchdogs: one died in his fifties, before his master; the other lived on until his eighties. He survived the master who had punished him, and by disowning him disowned himself.

Sources: Many details on Zhdanov may be found in Montefiore, 2005. See also, among others, Brown, Edward J., 1969, pp. 224–230; Graziosi, 2010, p. 130; Etkind et al., 1990, pp. 387 and 513 (those pages will allow the reader to find precise quotes or borrowings). The essential source for Zhou is Goldman, 1967 (quotations or precise details pp. 48, 92, 191, and 247) and 1981, pp. 52–53. See also Goldman, 1966; Bianco and Chevrier, 1985, pp. 783–787; Hong, 2007, pp. 278–279; Hsia, 1961, pp. 291–300; Link, 2000, pp. 30–32; Vogel, 2011, pp. 134–135, 558, and 563–564; Zhang Yinde, 2003, pp. 51, 56–57, and 60–64.

Scholars (and charlatans)

Because writers are the most vulnerable I have said little about artists and nothing at all about scholars. Even in domains about which he knew nothing, Stalin, like Mao later, imposed his own preferences and prejudices. That was why, in 1938, he appointed Trofim Lysenko (1898–1976) to direct the Lenin All-Union Academy of Agricultural Science. After all, did not that inspired inventor claim to have created a new variety of wheat that could be grown in permafrost? Lysenko believed that if man carefully adapted the environment, the nature of plants could be altered. The hereditary transmission of acquired characteristics was one of the founding principles of Lysenko's new genetics. Nikolai Vavilov, the most famous Russian geneticist, protested but Lysenko simply pooh-poohed decades of studies proving that plants did not transmit acquired characteristics to future generations. As a result Vavilov was driven out of the academy before being arrested in 1940. He died in prison in 1943. Five years later, at the opening of a session at the academy on 31 July 1948, director Lysenko made a triumphant speech (previously edited by Stalin) banning the "bourgeois" genetics of Gregor Mendel and Thomas Morgan, by which genes were the medium for heredity. There were now two sciences: an idealistic pseudo-science (in the West) and true Marxist, materialist, practical science. Lysenkoism not only destroyed vast stretches of newly planted forest, but caused Soviet biology to fall behind for many years.

And not only Soviet biology but Chinese biology too. Lysenko's theories and practices were introduced to China in the first months of the new regime and they prevailed until 1956. They even had a "posthumous" revival after Lysenko had been unmasked, thanks to the GLF, which exalted the same values (the creativity of the masses and mistrust of bourgeois scholars) and rehabilitated some of his practices, such as dense sowing that depleted the soil and made the plants rot. China embraced not only Lysenko's theories but those of Ivan Michurin (1855–1935), the horticulturalist who had so pleased Lenin. After all, he claimed to have created new species of robust and resistant plants that could not only acclimatize to the Great North but would produce miraculous yields in a less hostile climate. "Don't wait for favors from nature; we must triumph over nature," repeated first Michurin, and then Lysenko. Did the *Communist Party Manifesto* not urge philosophers to change the world rather than limit themselves to studying it? It was necessary to carry out Marx's instructions and to do better than Darwin. Michurin's "creative Darwinism," as adapted by Lysenko, could not be satisfied with a slow evolutionary process and the accumulation of very small changes over extremely long periods of time. Darwin should have paid more attention to Marx; they were contemporaries after all. A more interventionist Darwin, more concerned with changing the world rather than merely observing nature, would have recognized man's capacity to alter the species and rapidly create new ones without waiting for thousands of years.

It was that Michurinism revised by Lysenko that prevailed in China throughout the first Five-Year Plan. During that initial period China fervently copied the Soviet model, for surely what worked for the northern pioneers would work even better on the yellow earth cultivated by more frugal and hardworking farmers. The Stalinist development strategy allocated the financial burden of industrial development to its investment-strapped agricultural little sister. According to the Soviet "missionaries," Michurinism as revised by Lysenko, was an inexpensive way of rapidly obtaining fantastic yields. It never appears to have crossed the minds of the Chinese leaders to test the validity of those claims; indeed, there was not a single biologist or geneticist in their ranks, and they paid no attention to the opinions of specialists trained in Europe or North America; that would be doubting the Soviet big brother and causing him to lose face.

It was not until the Soviet Union started to debate the issue and then disavow Lysenko that China grew concerned—but even then, not immediately. At first China banned the dissemination of the critical assessments that began even in Stalin's lifetime. But the nuclear physicists who built the atomic bomb were influenced by Western science. Was it possible that the "Party spirit" could prevail over scientific truth in biology but not in physics? Khrushchev, who was more at ease with the former peasant Lysenko than the other academicians, briefly supported him, but when Lysenko was finally obliged to step down as director of the Academy of Agricultural Science in April 1956, China was quickly informed about it by a Soviet biologist who was invited to help implement the twelve-year agricultural plan. The Russian's vehement public criticisms of Lysenko finally convinced the Party that it should abandon the Lysenko model it had imposed in 1952. In August 1956, a geneticists' symposium put the Chinese Michurinists to the test for the first time. Their adversaries were authorized to report on the role and nature of DNA and other Western discoveries in genetics they had recently learned about, thanks to the political about-turn. Genetics was not the only sector concerned. In this new climate, where discredited Lyssenkoism went together with the first doubts about blind imitation of the Soviet Union, the editors of a leading Chinese scientific journal revealed that only 11 of the 330 scholarly articles published during the previous five years had not come from the Soviet bloc. Others, or the same ones, revealed the subterfuge they had to use in order to secretly introduce European or American scientific articles by dissimulating them under Russian covers. Others still dared to protest against the systematic use of Soviet manuals and the exaggerated esteem for Soviet experts.[34]

At the end of this first section I will repeat my initial warning. I selected the charlatan who held sway in one revolution, and therefore in the other as well, but the case of Lysenko and biology was an exception. Unlike the geneticists who "had no ready response to the agricultural crisis,"[35] the physicists could help with the industrial modernization of the Soviet Union. Lenin despised the Russian intelligentsia and in 1922 deported some two hundred writers and intellectuals, but was careful never to banish scientists. His goal, and one that Stalin achieved, was to create a new intelligentsia with worker and peasant origins—but how could they be trained if the only people capable of educating them had been deported? Specialized institutes began to proliferate from the 1920s, and by 1925, seventy-three of the eighty-eight existing research institutes had been established after 1917. Although scientists and Bolsheviks were wary of each other, they cooperated in the belief that science would play a vital role in Russia's future. Scientific development accelerated again after 1928 with investment increasing threefold until 1933, and almost doubling between 1933 and 1940.

That money could have been put to more efficient use. At the end of the 1920s, governmental control strengthened and now eight Communists had to be elected to the Academy of Sciences. Since the academicians themselves elected only three, the authorities imposed a second vote. The five others were elected under pressure, despite numerous abstentions. The newly elected members took over the management of the Academy and imposed the government's objectives, which emphasized the training of engineers rather than scientific researchers, with orders to give priority to applied research. The academy's publications were censured, foreign publications became increasingly hard to obtain, and foreign travel became nearly impossible. After the Shakhty Trial, the equally fabricated show trials of the so-called Peasant Worker Party and the Industrial Party led to the arrest of scientists as eminent as Chayanov and Nikolai Kondratiev. Both were shot during the Great Terror, when tens of thousands of scientific researchers and engineers were arrested and many research institutes were closed down. Despite that, scientists and specialists unhesitatingly devoted their skills to the service of the nation after the Nazi invasion. From 1945, it was the turn of German science and technology to be pillaged by brigades of Soviet specialists dispatched for the purpose of borrowing wholesale from the Germans. After 20 August 1945, two weeks after Hiroshima, absolute priority was given to nuclear research, with some help from industrial espionage. That resulted in the launch of the first Soviet atomic bomb in 1949, followed by other exploits every four years: the thermonuclear bomb (1953), the Sputnik (1957), and Yuri Gagarin's flight (1961). Under Khrushchev, or to be precise between 1953 and 1968, expenditures devoted to science doubled again and the number of researchers increased fourfold. At the end of the 1960s, more resources were poured into research and development in the Soviet Union than anywhere else, and Soviet mathematicians and physicists were among the best in the world.

Despite those ups and downs (what a euphemism!) Stalin can claim credit for the result because, like Lenin, he was convinced that Marxism was a science, and given that the Soviet Union was a child of the

Enlightenment, science must play a vital role in enabling the country to "catch up and surpass the technology of the advanced capitalist nations."[36] Mao later adopted both the phrase and the ambition for himself, starting from a lower point and with far less success. In the 1950s, priority was given to training engineers, but that training was more frequently interrupted with political activities and continual meetings than in the Soviet Union. The failure of the GLF finally convinced the government (in 1961–1962) of the need to listen to scientists and provide science students with a broader theoretical training. The Cultural Revolution interrupted this timid revival for a full decade. Research institutes were closed down and tens of thousands of researchers and scientific technicians were persecuted. In 1975, Deng Xiaoping insisted on the need to develop science and expertise and to train real specialists, before being overthrown a second time a few months later. Deng was able to implement his program only after Mao's death, and by 1981 China already had twice as many scientific institutions and more than twice the number of science and technology students as in 1976. That, as we know, was only the first step. So while scientific and technical development in China could not be compared with what Stalin accomplished in his lifetime, we should remember that China did better in literacy and primary education during the earlier stage.

Inevitable Similarities and Notable Differences in the Face of a Revolutionary Regime

The two regimes' cultural and anticultural policies resembled each other far more than the responses they triggered in the writers and artists.

"There was no Soviet literature between 1929 and 1953," joked Solzhenitsyn, who presumably considered that Bulgakov's *The Master and Margarita* (among others)[37] published in 1964, did not belong to the period in which he wrote it. The same is true, with fewer reservations, for the 1949–1978 period in China. The differences between the two countries' immediate heritage (the Silver Age and May Fourth) or between the people's cultural characteristics—with the additional complication in the Soviet Union of the multitude of different ethnic groups—are not as great as the responses from writers and artists facing similar oppression.

The amenable writers

At the top of the list are the many people in all countries who choose comfort, conformism, and even complicity with a regime that pays them (richly in the case of the Soviet Union), as well as the many true believers. Some have no compunction about embellishing truth by adding flourishes to please the censor. That was true for Hao Ran (1932–2008), one of the very few writers authorized to write and publish during the Cultural Revolution. The son of a landless peasant, orphaned at the age of thirteen, he only had three and a half years of primary schooling but completed his education as a reporter and propagandist for the Red Army. A peasant writer if ever there was one, Hao Ran spent the better part of his life writing about peasants, but always toeing the Party line. The three volumes of *Bright, Sunny Skies* (1964, 1966, and 1971) depict the class struggle in an agricultural cooperative during the summer of 1957. The starting point for the story was an incident the author had witnessed firsthand: the raid by a group of robbers on a cooperative's cereal stores. In the novel, this episode becomes a deliberate attack by reactionary classes led by a former landlord and backed by "rightist" Communists and anti-Communists around the world, including Soviet revisionists. Hao Ran's two-volume *The Golden Road* (1972 and 1974) portrays such a black-and-white vision of the class struggle during collectivization that it is almost a caricature. The class struggle is incarnated by the golden road that the novel's hero describes to the peasants. The hero's name alone is a feat of propaganda: Gao Daquan, high, meaning "lofty," "tall," "complete." In fact he is so perfect that that he loses any human dimension, largely as a result of the three golden rules (*san tuchu*) imposed on the few writers allowed to practice their craft during the Cultural Revolution.

Among the hundred or so short stories by this prolific writer, "Dawns Clouds Red as a Flame" (1959) is a romance about love at the backyard furnaces during the GLF. Needless to say, the lovers are exemplary. He is the son of a "revolutionary martyr" (a generic term to designate Communists who were executed or died in combat) and proved his own heroism fighting a flood. His beloved throws herself on some explosives during a work accident to save her comrades. She survives but suffers severe injuries and is disfigured. Despite that, as might be expected, the hero declares his undying love for her at the hospital bedside. A few months before Hao Ran wrote this edifying tale, a friend had warned him: official claims relating to the GLF are "nothing but a pack of lies! ... Those above and those below are lying and boasting, it's bound to end in disaster. ... If you write your story, you'll be colluding in the deception."[38]

Even orthodox writers like Hao Ran who were well viewed by the authorities could provoke governmental ire; no one was spared. Alexander Fadeyev was far above Hao Ran in the official hierarchy since he had presided over the Union of Soviet Writers for more than ten years (1939–1943 and 1946–1953) and furthermore was a member of the Party Central Committee and later a deputy to the Supreme Soviet. A more complex personality than Hao Ran, Fadeyev criticized or persecuted the authors he admired, such as Pasternak (whom he denounced in public while reciting his poems in private), as well as Anna Akhmatova and Mikhail Zoshchenko in 1946. That same year he obtained the leading Stalin Prize for his most famous novel, *The Young Guard*. The Komsomol Central Committee had commissioned the book, based on the true story of a group of resisters aged between sixteen and nineteen who were captured, tortured, and executed in Nazi-occupied Ukraine in 1943. Critics praised the meticulous way Fadeyev had researched the stories of the young partisans by interviewing their friends and family. The praise continued until October 1947, when Stalin saw a film adaptation of *The Young Guard* and immediately started a campaign against the novel. Who else could attack the leading light of Soviet literature for a work that received a prize named after himself? The attack was launched at the end of October, two years after the book first came out, claiming that it did not show "the leadership role of the Party organs working underground" and gave the erroneous impression that the young people had acted spontaneously. In December Fadeyev admitted that the criticisms were well-founded and announced that he would rewrite parts of *The Young Guard* based on those "justified" reproofs. He removed some characters and episodes that he liked and added a dozen chapters in order to "age" the young guards in question. They now became adult Communists leading the young resisters. "A good book has become even better," stated *Pravda* approvingly in an article hailing Fadeyev's public submission. Was that painful rewrite a purely calculated move? Not according to one eyewitness. "He did not pretend, he did not cheat; he loved Stalin. He tortured himself, suffered and promised" to rewrite the book. Two and a half months after the Twentieth Congress, Fadeyev committed suicide, leaving a letter addressed to the Central Committee, rather than to his wife and son.[39]

Like Fadeyev, other Soviet writers chose to make a career of their writing and pay the price, even if they died old and covered in medals. They sacrificed their talent and, more than that, their vocations as writers. In his youth, Konstantin Fedin (1892–1977) had joined a literary group called the Serapion Brothers, which believed that literature should be independent of government.[40] In his novel *The Brothers* (1927–1928), Fedin narrates the story of a musician who sacrifices his art for the revolution. Both Boris Pasternak and Stefan Zweig congratulated him, but the critics called him a "class enemy." "Life demands that I destroy everything! Even what is most important to me, my understanding of the art and my feeling for it," he wrote in despair in his *Journal*.[41] But what life was that? Certainly not the artistic life as understood by the Serapion Brothers, for that required nothing of the sort, and certainly not to make additions to a manuscript and spoil it by pandering to official criticism. It was from this period that the "process of surrender and adaptation" (Cécile Vaissié) began. Fedin's *Journal* reveals a complex and subtle man, who was sure of his taste and despised the official literary production and its dogmas. "Can it be a matter of realism when a writer must represent a desired reality and not the existing one?" Soviet authors "have become phonographs."[42] Leonid Leonov for one. Fedin was underwhelmed by his prizewinning play: "Clearly it was necessary to grovel. He did so by adding the last tableau, which was nothing but an ode (to Stalin) and he was paid for bowing and scraping."[43] Arrested and brutally interrogated, Pilniak and later Babel had to admit to sharing the same viewpoints, feelings and fears as Fedin. In his book *Gorky Among Us*, Fedin depicts that belated exalter of Stalin as a "complex intellectual who preached freedom and individualism" and thought that nothing could be obtained "by persecution alone."[44] Accused of defending "apolitical art," Fedin was attacked and persecuted for a while but protected. It was more of a warning than a definitive condemnation, and the way was open for him to redeem himself. And so he did. The Party willingly courted people they had a hold over, thanks to some kind of stain against their name. In Fedin's case it was his poor social background; his mother, the daughter of a priest, had aristocratic origins. So Fedin gradually rose in the hierarchy of those who Cécile Vaissié called "engineers of the human soul," giving the authorities guarantees, including in writing, while maintaining ties and a close friendship with Pasternak, his dacha neighbor in Peredelkino, who for years had been reading chapters of *Doctor Zhivago* to him. In early

1958, the year in which the "Nobel scandal" broke out, Fedin was still saying, "Don't expect me to attack Pasternak, I would never do that."[45]

But he did, and that very fall, with no further ado. The two ceased to have any contact, and the dacha neighbor pleaded illness rather than attend Pasternak's funeral. He was rewarded for that (appointed secretary of the Union of Soviet Writers in May 1959 and on four occasions received the Order of Lenin). The people who rejoiced that the union would be headed by a writer who knew what good literature was and whose venerable age would protect him from trouble were to be disappointed on every count, although the troubles in question would be less terrible under Khrushchev and later under Brezhnev, than they were in Stalin's lifetime. Fedin refused to intervene in favor of Brodsky, approved of the trial of Sinyavsky and Daniel, prevented the publication of *Cancer Ward,* and presided over Solzhenitsyn's expulsion, each time using the very same methods that had made him so indignant when he himself had been the victim. He died replete with honors at the age of eighty-five, and his death was announced jointly by the Central Committee, the Presidium of the Supreme Soviet, and the Council of Ministers. But as a writer he had died long before that, even though the print runs of his final works ensured that his income was proportionate to his rank. Did he first cease to displease out of fear, before acquiring a taste for "the advantages obtained in return from his submission"?[46] Those who knew him when he was young hated him even more than they hated those among the "engineers of the human soul" who had no need to renounce their talents or vocations.

Another of Solzhenitsyn's barbs appears more justified than the one about nonexistent Russian literature between 1929 and 1953, namely his skepticism about Ehrenburg drawing the winning number in the lottery of fate. I found it hard to select a single pair of authors for Box 5. In the end I decided on Guo Moruo for his opportunism, even though the works of other authors are more representative of 1950s and 1960s "conformist" literature, starting with Hao Ran (see above), Du Pengcheng (see above), Zhao Shuli, and Zhou Libo. On the Soviet side, Fadeyev, Fedin, Feodor Gladkov, Leonov, Simonov, Aleksey Tolstoy, and others could, in various ways, be a match for Guo Moruo, but I settled on the Nobel Prize-winner and author of *And Quiet Flows the Don.*

Box 5

The Favored Writers

As with Zhdanov and Zhou Yang, there are many differences between Guo Moruo (1892–1978) and Mikhail Sholokhov (1905–1984). Guo was born to a family of landlords and rich merchants, Sholokhov to a poor family. His mother was illiterate and he had to leave school at the age of thirteen, the age at which Guo had finished not with school, but with the study of the classics, taught at home by a private tutor. After the imperial examination system was abolished, his family decided that he should have a more modern education so he learned English and completed his studies in Japan, where his two elder brothers had already studied—a privilege that was available only to a tiny minority of rich families. At the age of eighteen, Sholokhov returned to his *stanitsa* (Cossack village) in the Don region to write *And Quiet Flows the Don*. He was to remain a novelist above all and, incidentally, a journalist. Guo Moruo was a nonpracticing doctor and a born polygraph. He was also a novelist and a journalist, but at the same time he was a poet, playwright, essayist, writer of memoirs, historian, paleographer, translator, and … propagandist. His four-volume, two-thousand-page biography is, in turn, "a memoir, a chronicle, a travel story, poetic prose and even a play" (Zhang Yinde). He was not only a prolific writer but a very busy dignitary who made numerous official trips abroad in the 1950s and 1960s, and welcomed many famous guests to Beijing, especially Japanese ones since he was one of few Chinese dignitaries to speak the language, but also Russian and European visitors. The regime was happy to put forward this sensible fellow traveler (who only became a Communist in 1958), an expert in the art of employing or fabricating the appropriate discourse for the occasion.

Because of that aptitude and role, I shall set aside the differences between our two writers for a while. Sholokhov obtained the Nobel Prize (in between Pasternak and

Solzhenitsyn!) but no Chinese writer obtained it before the dissident Gao Xingjian, exiled in France, and both received national honors. Guo was the chairman of the All-China Federation of Literary and Art Circles of the Academy of Sciences, the Chinese Peace Committee (and obtained the Stalin peace prize in 1952), was vice–prime minister from 1949 to 1954, member of the Central Committee, vice-president of the Chinese People's Political Consultative Conference, and so on. As for Sholokhov, he was a permanent deputy of the Supreme Soviet and member of the Central Committee, a Stalin as well as a Lenin Prize-winner, twice named hero of socialist labor, and that's not all. Those honors were certainly deserved because during *Zhdanovshchina*, Sholokhov repeatedly made virulent criticisms about the West while extolling the Party and the Soviet people. During the thaw and then the Brezhnev ice age, he stood out for the crudeness of his attacks against Pasternak, Solzhenitsyn, Daniel, and Sinyavsky. When commenting the accusations made against the latter, Sholokhov was applauded by the tribune of the Twenty-Third Party Congress in April 1966 for saying: "If these chaps with a black conscience had been brought to trial during our memorable 1920s ... , the scoundrels would have had a very different punishment!" This led to the famous response in an open letter by Lydia Chukovskaya. "You spoke like a literary traitor. Your shameful speech will go down in history. As for literature, it will get its own revenge ... for it will sentence you to the most serious punishment for an artist: creative sterility."

That sentence had already been passed on Sholokhov, for he was both the "standard-bearer and victim of the Soviet government" (Herman Ermolaev). During the last twenty-five years of his life, while the press unanimously extolled him as a "living treasure," he wrote almost nothing at all and what little he did publish was not up to *The Don*'s standard. There were two Russias, the Chukovskys used to conclude, Sholokhov's one and Solzhenitsyn's one. Sholokhov confirmed that the following year when he felt he could no longer tolerate rubbing shoulders with an anti-Soviet writer in his Union, and demanded that Solzhenitsyn no longer be permitted to write. Solzhenitsyn returned the compliment when he refused a dinner invitation in Moscow from a foreign guest (Sartre), because "by giving the (Nobel) prize to Sholokhov he could not have more cruelly insulted Russian literature."*

As for Guo Moruo, he took part in every campaign to denounce as "rightists," any liberal, unorthodox Marxist or progressive writers, from Yu Pingbo to Feng Xuefeng, Hu Feng, Ding Ling, and He Qifang. All those names were mentioned in Box 4 on Page 218, bar one (He, Zhou Yang's lieutenant who went astray by disparaging the poetry of the Great Leap Forward). Guo Moruo was less distinguished for his criticisms of designated targets, required of him as chairman of the All-China Federation of Literary and Art Circles, than for his zealous support of pet idols ("our master, the great scholar Michurin") and the regime's slogans: "Cultural work must be led by amateurs who have mastered Marxism-Leninism." Not to mention his flattery. After Chiang Kai-shek received him in Nanjing in 1937, he promptly wrote an article expressing the emotions that the personality of the supreme leader aroused in him. His later poems and writings celebrated Stalin, Mao, and Mao's wife Jiang Qing, on two occasions. He praised her to the skies at the start of the Cultural Revolution, before tearing that "old skeletal devil" to pieces ten years later, when she was arrested and denounced. When the first of these poems (to the glory of "dear comrade" Jiang Qing) was published, Guo Moruo made a resounding self-criticism, "Everything that I wrote in the past deserves to be burnt, it does not have the least worth for I had not understood Mao Zedong thought or worked with my hands." That enabled him to get through the Cultural Revolution without mishap, and even continue to publish, unlike 99 percent of Chinese writers. Whether that was an excuse or an explanation, Guo was less affected by those palinodes than the others.

---

* When Jean-Paul Sartre turned down the Nobel Prize in 1964, he deplored that it had been attributed to Pasternak rather than Sholokhov.

After making a sensational entry into literature with romantic poems exalting his ego, he quickly became a convert to revolutionary literature, and preached it with the same confidence and the same sectarianism. The writer who had denounced Lu Xun's "conservatism" in 1928, ended up as a court poet, exchanging verses with Mao Zedong.

In fact he survived Mao by two years. He died at the right time, before the great upheavals that would have led to yet another repudiation. Sholokov also died in time, one year before Mikhail Gorbachev came to power. Less flexible than Guo Moruo, he stopped writing for six months at the peak of the 1932–1933 famine and even wrote a sixteen-page letter to Stalin describing the horrors of grain requisitioning in the Don region. He urged Stalin to deliver grain to the starving people in the North Caucasus. For once, that request was granted, but Stalin snubbed Sholokhov, considering that he had been duped by "saboteurs" who refused to feed the workers and soldiers of the Red Army. Five years later, the publication of the final volume of *The Don* was delayed by two years because Sholokhov refused to make his hero, Grigory Melekhov, a Red Cossack as Stalin had requested. In the same period, the NKVD was preparing to arrest Sholokhov because of his defense of local Communists who had been expelled in 1937. Sholokhov demanded, and obtained, Stalin's support. Sholokhov was grateful for that and never criticized Stalin under Khrushchev.

Standing alone, *And Quiet Flows the Don* (which according to some was partly plagiarized)[†] can withstand

---

[†]   When the first two volumes of *And Quiet Flows the Don* were published in
        1928, Sholokhov was accused of having appropriated the work of a dead
        writer, Fyodor Kryukov, and merely completing it. In 1974, those rumors
        were taken up again by Roy Medvedev, as well as by a critic, by then
        deceased, in an unfinished work that was published in Paris thanks to
        Solzhenitsyn. However, neither of them drew any conclusions and a
        graphological study of the original manuscript of *The Don* found in 1991,
        apparently confirmed that it was indeed written by Sholokhov (see
        Vaissié, 2008, pp. 134, 136, and 397–399, and Medvedev, 1975, for the
        French translation).

a comparison with Guo Moruo's entire exuberant output. We'll forget the 1953 edition, spoiled by the cuts and additions imposed by Stalin. The two first volumes, which caused a sensation in 1928, did not comply with the rules of socialist realism decreed six years later, for there were no clear-cut White (or rather Red) characters, but crude descriptions of rape, violence, and vendettas, dialogue scattered with swear words and obscenities, that would make puritan Zhdanov blush. The tone is set in the very first pages, when a soldier's wife glimpses the Turkish woman brought back by the hero's grandfather, the Cossack, Prokofy Melekhov: "If she'd been a woman now, but a creature like her! Our girls are far better covered. Why you could pull her apart like a wasp." An outbreak of cattle disease was blamed on that witch, the Turkish woman, so the villagers went to Prokofy's house to "Drag the bitch out into the yard." She died that evening of her injuries, and beside her lay, "a squealing little ball— the prematurely born infant." For having used his sword to avenge her, "with a diagonal sweep down across the left shoulder from behind … to the belt," Prokofy was sentenced to twelve years of "penal servitude." All this occurs in the first five pages of the book (out of fifteen hundred or two thousand depending on the edition) and by the seventh page, his grandson Grigory is born, the spitting image of his father, "the swarthy Turkish-looking boy," who survived the massacre. Grigory had "the same pendulous hawk nose … the whites of his burning eyes blueish in their slightly oblique slits, … and even in his smile there was a similar, rather savage quality." Grigory's passion for a neighbor's wife, the almost ethnographic description of a Cossack *stanitsa*, were far more important to the author—and to the reader—than any proletarian saga. The advent of war, and then the revolution, led to upheavals in the village, comparable to the effects of more commonplace disasters such as drought and flooding. At first Grigory follows the Reds and then the Whites, and then no party at all, but the reader is attached to him, not his contingent allegiances, and still less to the ruses of triumphant Reason. Attached to him but also to his wife, Natalia, whom he neglects[‡] and then leaves, and who tries to commit suicide.[§] And also the soldiers of "August 1914" who confront each other for the first time.[**] In its way, *The Don* invalidates the "binary" code (Katerina Clark) that so long distorted our critical judgment about Soviet literature (mine included), whereby it either toed the line or criticized the regime. In *Cancer Ward* Russanov perfectly incarnates the kind of negative hero that socialist realism demanded in opposition to good heroes or the martyrs of the revolution.

To make honorable amends I must now praise Guo Moruo's talent. Indeed, he was a tireless and fast worker with a broad range of talents that he deployed in a wide variety of fields. As a cultured scholar he was familiar with all the Chinese classics and he loved European and American romantic poetry. However, I am as underwhelmed by the versatility of this literary barometer, as I am by his imperturbable dogmatism that, already back in the

---

‡   "That night, in the steppe some eight *versts* from the village ... Grigory said wistfully to Natalia, 'You're a stranger somehow! You're like that moon, you neither chill a man, nor warm him. I don't love you Natalya; you mustn't be angry'" (in the French translation: Cholokhov, 1959, pp. 222–223).

§   "There she picked up a scythe by the handle, removed the blade (her movements were deliberately assured and precise); and throwing back her head, in a sudden joyous fire of resolution slashed her throat with its point" (ibid., p. 320).

**   "Men who had not yet acquired the knack of killing their own kind, had clashed on the field of death, and in the mortal terror that embraced them, had charged, and struck, and battered blindly at each other, mutilating one another and their horses: then they had turned and fled, frightened by a shot which had killed one of their number. They had ridden away morally crippled. And that was called a heroic exploit" (ibid., p. 454). August 1914 refers to the first "knot" of *The Red Wheel* by Sholokhov's enemy, Solzhenitsyn.

1920s, transformed him from an uncompromising harbinger of art for art's sake and frenzied romanticism, into an intransigent apologist for revolutionary literature as "the only authentic literature."

Sources: Volumes and volumes have been written on Guo and Sholokhov. I will only mention the authors who shed the most light on the subject for me, or the works from which I have taken precise facts or quotations. First and foremost Clark, pp. 136–137, 140–142, and 150; then Vaissié, 2008, pp. 16, 133–136, 183, 217, 244–245, 308, 317, 343, 397–399, and passim;Edward J. Brown, 1969, pp. 179–189 and 296–299; Saraskina, 2010, pp. 563, 603, and 616; Solzhenitsyn, 1975, pp. 121 and 185; Ermolaev, 1990, pp. 87 and 96; Davies and Wheatcroft, 2004, p. 217; Cholokhov, 1959. For Guo Moruo, see first Hsia, 1961, pp. 93–102 and 319–320; Goldman, 1967, pp. 65–66, 90, 117, and 241; Goldman, 1981, pp. 91 and 133; Zhang Yinde, 2003, pp. 207–221 (quotation p. 218); then, more sporadically, Kouo, 1970; Lee, 1986, pp. 422–423; McDougall, 1977, p. 39; Liu Zaifu, 2000, p. 6; Graziosi, 2013, p. 18; Rohlf, 2010, p. 200; Michel Bonnin's notice on Guo in Bianco and Chevrier, 1985, pp. 223–226; Boorman, 1968, pp. 271–276.

... and the others

The prolific works of compliant writers who were celebrated for a time and then denounced and silenced contrast with the silence of the older writers. Anna Akhmatova remained silent for nearly twenty years after publishing *Anno Domini* (1922), and Boris Pasternak stopped writing in 1936, turning instead to translations of Shakespeare, Goethe, Schiller, and the Georgian poets. However, one writer who would not be silenced was Yevgeny Zamyatin. Was it because, as a former Bolshevik (in his student youth), he could count on a little indulgence? He left the Party early on and criticized the revolutionaries. Unlike all the other enthusiasts who became disillusioned (Alexander Blok, Vladimir Mayakovski, and so many others), he had no need to sober up. He had already been arrested and imprisoned under the old regime in 1905, was banished from the capital, and had a writ served against him because he ridiculed Russian officers in a Far Eastern garrison with a sarcasm worthy of Gogol (in *A Godforsaken Hole*, written in 1914 but unable to be published before 1917). Then in 1919 the new regime arrested him, and again in 1922 (but to his great disappointment removed his name from a compulsory deportation list at the last minute). The previous year he had expressed his fear that "the only future for Russian literature is its past," and denounced those "skillful writers" who know "when to celebrate the arrival of the Czar and when to celebrate the hammer and sickle."

During that same period (1920–1921) he wrote *We*. It was not published in the Soviet Union before 1988, but it inspired both Huxley and Orwell. *We"* was even more prophetic than *Brave New World* and *1984*, if only because of when it was written, in Lenin's lifetime. The Benefactor who presides over the dystopian society depicted in *We* is reelected unanimously on the day of the Feast of Unanimity, and conjures up Stalin of the 1930s and Mao in 1966. The Benefactor obliges his subjects, named only by numbers (such as D-503 or I-330) to undergo the Great Operation to cure them of the very last sickness that prevents them from being as perfect as machines: their imaginations. Much of Zamyatin's work belonged to what he called "the catalogue that most honors a writer: the forbidden books catalogue," but when *We* was published abroad (in English in 1924, in Czech in 1927) it fueled (or served as a pretext for) a campaign against both him and Pilniak (guilty of the same "betrayal") in 1929. The persecution of Zamyatin, who had begun the decade as one of the leading Russian writers and one of the most influential (notably on the Serapion Brothers) continued almost incessantly, to the extent that in 1931 Zamyatin wrote a dignified and frank letter to Stalin asking for permission to emigrate: "I have a bad habit of not saying what it is in my interest to say, but what seems to me to be the truth." Against all expectations, Stalin granted his request, and Zamyatin spent his last years (1932–1937) in Paris, where his screenplay adaptation of a Gorky's *The Lower Depths* was made into a film by Renoir (*Les Bas-Fonds*).[47]

With no Chinese equivalent of a Zamyatin, I would suggest that Qian Zhongshu and Shen Congwen would be among the ready matches for Akhmatova and Pasternak's silence. Both were already atypical writers before 1949, who refused to join any political party or movement. When Qian Zhongshu's *Fortress Besieged* was published at the start of the civil war, nobody paid much attention to it. The book describes Chinese society during the Sino-Japanese War (the equivalent of the Russians'

Great Patriotic War), but since it was not very favorable to Chinese society, it met with a poor reception. However, it is one of the first books I would recommend to anyone wishing to dive into modern Chinese literature.[48] The book was banned after 1949 and published again only during the unacknowledged "de-Maoization" era. Qian never wrote another novel, for the anti-rightist repression of 1957 definitively convinced him that it would be a vain enterprise. However, he did not remain silent but buried himself in literary research, which led this cultivated polyglot to "confront the theories of Kierkegaard and Valéry with themes in classical Chinese literature" (N. Chapuis). An important and original work, certainly, but the world lost a Juvenal (or Swift, La Bruyère, or Molière) able to satirize Chinese society. Instead of mocking others, Qian Zhongshu mocked himself. In the preface to his wife's book, Yang Jiang's *Six Chapters in a Cadre's School*, in which she describes her experience as a "stinking" intellectual undergoing reeducation during the Cultural Revolution, Qian deplored that she did not add a seventh account devoted to the "shame of having taken part in political campaigns." He added, "the shame, in my case, is of being a coward who, having understood that injustice was being done, did not have the courage to protest against it, and merely participated unenthusiastically."

Shen Congwen (1902–1988) expressed his cautious attitude to political parties very early on, and no faction ever forgave him for that. During the winter of 1948–1949 when the Communists besieged Beijing, he refused to flee, even though he had no illusions about what to expect. "I might not be able to accomplish such a transformation (from contemplation to conviction, from thinking to believing). Before long I will stop writing, even if I am not forced to. This is the predestined fate of certain people of our generation."[49] At a time when the majority of intellectuals were sympathetic to, or enthusiastic about, the Communists, and when many writers were prepared to alter their esthetic concepts, Shen was one of very few to state his fears about seeing literature hijacked by propaganda. As a result he was accused of being an obsolete supporter of art for art's sake who ignored reality. Shen resisted a vicious attack by Guo Moruo (our hero in Box 5 on Page 233) but found it increasingly hard to endure the growing criticisms that assailed him from all sides. In January 1949, his students in Peking University started a petition demanding that he be fired and posted Guo's article to back their demand. Shen found himself isolated, alienated, misunderstood, and desperate.

"Nobody understands anything I say. Not a single friend is willing to understand or has the courage to understand, that I am not mad." In March 1949 he attempted suicide. He was saved and treated, and then spent several months in a psychiatric hospital.

While Pasternak escaped by translating Shakespeare and Qian Zhongshu by burying himself in literary theory, Shen found release in an art that was deemed a minor one. He finished his *Studies on Traditional Chinese Costumes* in 1964, but the book was published only during the post-Mao thaw. Even before it was published it was immediately denounced as a "poisonous weed" and a reactionary "black book." True, he could hardly have devoted himself to a more frivolous distraction or, worse, prepared a more malicious counterpoint to the universe of unisex uniforms. With regard to his previous works, there was a general pretense of forgetting that he had once been a writer, and his publisher in Shanghai told him in 1953 that every last copy of his books had been pulped. At the time his works were also banned in Taiwan for their "Communist tendencies"— for he had sympathetically depicted the ethnic minorities of his native region (western Hunan province), whose nebulous separatist desires were repressed equally harshly by both the old and the new regimes.

It would be easy to complete the list of writers who became silent in 1949 or a few years later, starting with Zhang Tianyi or Ba Jin, who finally took up his pen again during the post-Mao thaw to write his memoirs. Some, like Lu Ling, were silenced following an irrevocable criticism. However, on the Chinese side I know of only one example of a novel that was written "for the desk drawer," and that was Cong Weixi's *The Children*. He wrote the book, largely devoted to the GLF, in the early 1960s, but no one will ever be able to judge its literary qualities for his mother thought it wise to burn the manuscript.[50] On the Soviet side, Bulgakov's *The Master and Margarita* is the most famous example of a book published long after the author's death. But from the thaw, so many works were nurtured and written in secret, even if some authors occasionally took the risk of asking for it to be published, usually abroad. From either secrecy or the desk drawer, we have acquired, among others, *Doctor Zhivago*, *Life and Fate*, *The Faculty of Useless Knowledge*, and almost all of Solzhenitsyn's works.

Solzhenitsyn might have accused Cong Weixi's mother of being fainthearted—or perhaps not, for he had many opportunities to observe and pity our frailty, from the gulag to Elizaveta Voronianskaya's suicide.[51] "Oh the shame of having been afraid," repented Tvardovsky, whose parents were deported to Siberia two years after he joined the Party. Or Olga Bergoltz, "As, in interrogations, with clenched teeth / we renounce ourselves." Those who, like the two poets, looked back in shame and bitterness were just a minority, like that other poet who assigned art with the task of "killing fear in man" (Mandelstam). Others, like Nicolas Andreyevich, who allowed fear to "feed their convictions," were more numerous.[52] That fear, even for the less cowardly, was a leitmotif for Shostakovich's "Life Symphony," and explains a great deal of the commitment, the belief in the myth, and ultimately the unanimity that Zinoviev so mocked: "You vote Yea together …, they you vote Nay together. Together … together" (*Yawning Heights*).

Tvardovsky admitted, shortly before dying, that constant fear is debasing, and that the habit of pretending in order to avoid "inconveniences"—or worse—destroys the soul: "My body drags itself about without a master, for its soul did not survive." Millions of resigned people ceased to be aware of that, their serenity, "reveals something incredibly dry, hard, and even ossified" (Dombrowsky). As a result: "Smerdiakov has invaded Russia! Make way for His Majesty Smerdiakov! Everything is possible, everything is permitted! … The whole world, the entire universe, should bless Russia to the end of time, because she has shown, through her atrocious example, what must *not* be done!" (Maximov). What a pity that China did not learn that lesson.

Differences

The Russian intelligentsia welcomed the fall of Czarism but shunned October. Before he became the eulogist of Stalinism, Gorky did not spare his *Untimely Thoughts* until the day Lenin closed down his paper, *Novaya Zhizn*. In China, many intellectuals had long been convinced of the need for a revolutionary upheaval, seeing it as the only way China could regain independence and recover its greatness. The majority of them therefore welcomed the new regime with considerable optimism, all the more so since they shared the same principal objective, which was to get China back on its feet.

Only a very small minority followed the nationalist regime to Taiwan and a handful of people emigrated to the United States or Hong Kong, but conversely exiled Chinese flocked home to help with national reconstruction. Even the very few with some knowledge of the Stalinist precedent overcame their reticence and apprehension to enroll in the service of the nation. That was the case for Xiao Qian, who had met Orwell in Paris and had a long-standing suspicion of ideologies.[53] For others, apart from Xiao, who was well integrated in Europe, the desire to take part in the great work of national regeneration was not the only motive, even though it was the leading one. These "new intellectuals" were less liberated from Confucian tradition than they thought, and believed that the state must use their talent and skills. Mandarins were recruited from the scholars; that honor was therefore theirs and they could not escape it. Without going as far as to suggest Chernyshevsky or Nechayev, just imagine Tolstoy serving the autocracy and the Orthodox Church.

Intellectuals, artists, and scholars were soon disillusioned (the unfortunate Xiao Qian as early as 1950), but few challenged the validity of the goal that was being pursued. The safety valve of the Hundred Flowers enabled them to express their disappointment and make their demands (which were not met). The repression of intellectuals during the "anti-rightist" campaign of 1957 established a decisive deterioration in their relationship with the regime, but the final break occurred only with the Cultural Revolution. The contrast is not absolute with the Soviet Union, where there remained a certain support for the regime. The aims of the first Five-Year Plan were quite popular, and even Akhmatova and Pasternak had faith in some lies of propaganda. The "keeper of antiquities" (the future Zybin in *The Faculty of Useless Knowledge*) admitted that "like just about everyone, I believed in anything then, including these trials." However, I do not know a Chinese equivalent of a poem as sacrilegious as the one that dispatched Mandelstam to the gulag and his death.[54]

Once the Chinese revolution was finally rid of its founder and grave digger, the Chinese writers' national "obsession"[55] led to a different development to the one exemplified by Pasternak, Solzhenitsyn, Grossman, and so many others, although the feeling of liberation was the same. In China during 1978–1980, people felt as though they were back in Russia in 1956, that blessed time when it suddenly became possible to say and read everything that had been concealed from others for so long. A sarcastic laugh interrupted the performance of a play in 1980 (in which a guerrilla rises, and declares "I am a Communist"), yet in the 1950s the same play was met with an emotional silence from a spellbound audience. There was even talk of a "second liberation" (Perry Link), with reference to the first in 1949. And there's the rub, for in 1956, it would not have occurred to anybody in the Soviet Union to describe as a "second" liberation, what was perceived as deliverance from the Stalinist-Zhdanovian yoke. If anyone had any memories of a previous liberation, it would have been February 1917, not October.

The Chinese thaw started on a minor note compared with the Soviet one. Lu Xinhua's *The Scar* (1978) was a pioneering novel that had the merit of bluntly exposing what had been forbidden up to then. However, it is mediocre and melodramatic, and hardly stands up to Ehrenburg's *The Thaw*, which was actually one of the author's minor works. Nevertheless *The Scar* gave its name to the first post-Mao literary trend, "Scar Literature" or "literature of the wounded," with reference to those marks left on the bodies and souls of the victims after suffering ten years of the Cultural Revolution, not to mention the ten years before that, from the 1957 anti-rightist campaign. In denouncing Maoism, Scar Literature took up a recurrent theme since the very early Maoist era (when the "wounds" were inflicted by the Japanese army rabble) and was the continuation of the unambiguous recounting of epic tales that was so esteemed in Mao's lifetime. "Reform literature" was scarcely more original (*gaige*, or reform, was the official name for the new turn Deng Xiaoping gave to the Chinese revolution), nor was "reportage literature," as illustrated by the veteran rightist Liu Binyan. He condemned corruption in the CCP and, like the preceding generation in Moscow, the "somber aspects" of society, but only for the purpose of improving them. He did not challenge the historic optimism that continued to prevail under Deng. It was a matter of correcting an erroneous—and occasionally criminal—trajectory (that of the Gang of Four—Mao was still hardly called into question) and then building a modern and fraternal society.[56]

Celebrated at the time as "the literature of a new age," the dominant literary production of the first half of the 1980s may have been more critical and more forceful than the literature of the previous thirty years, but it still conferred legitimacy on the "new era" of reform and extended the previous tradition in one vital area: it maintained the link between politics and literature that had been implicit in China since the early twentieth century. For the majority of Chinese writers from the May Fourth period to Yan'an and Maoist China, literary and national renaissance went hand in hand, for the first must serve the second. That correlation and that function extrinsic to creation was what a new generation of writers finally rejected in the second half of the 1980s. Their most accomplished works clearly mark a break with those of the early post-Mao era and eclipse everything written since 1949—even, according to many critics, the gems of May Fourth literature.[57] That did not prevent those writers from steering a different course to that of their Russian counterparts during the Khrushchev thaw, and still less to that of the Brezhnev era dissidents.

Maoism, the Great Leap Forward, and the Cultural Revolution certainly merited a Shakespeare, a Tolstoy, or a Dostoyevsky—or at the very least a Grossman. To truly understand totalitarianism in its Communist version, and therefore the twentieth century, we will be eternally grateful to the Russians and not, or not yet, to the Chinese, who lived through the same tribulations.[58] The Khrushchev report did not have the same impact on China as on the Soviet Union or Eastern Europe. For while Khrushchev's revelations were only partial and incomplete, they nevertheless sapped the ideology that lay at the very heart of the system. Was Chinese skepticism a protection against too great a shake-up? Many intellectuals were not believers but were putting on a show (*biaoxian*), pretending in order to survive. Of course the Russians were obliged to do the same; we have countless accounts of that. If we were plunged, as they were, into totalitarian hell, we too would give a pretense of conformity. Of the Russian and Chinese victims, however, the Russians gave the impression of having been more affected. In an article titled "Literature and the Awareness of Repentance," published in 1986, the literary critic Liu Zaifu deplored the absence in Chinese culture of the religious notion of sin and repentance, which he deemed essential for apprehending a moral disaster like the Cultural Revolution ("Oh if only we had had a Dostoyevsky or a Tolstoy!"). Another author wrote ironically, "Is it possible that four individuals (the Gang of Four) managed to manipulate 800 million others?" inferring that those millions also had a share of responsibility.[59] The old writer Ba Jin, famous for more than half a century, wondered in his memoirs *Random Thoughts, 1978–1986*, "How can an entire people, masses of several hundred thousand persons, have been able to participate in this turmoil in an atmosphere of superstition and adoration?" Ba Jin did not exempt himself from those who should be held to account. Among other acts of cowardice, he regretted not having defended his friend Shen Congwen when he was harassed by the regime. But if Ba Jin was elected president of the Association of Writers in 1984 and Liu Binyan the vice-president, it was because their peers were aware of their courage and honesty, however belated in the case of Ba.

My description of an entire people bowing down or applauding the injustices and excesses of the Cultural Revolution is cavalier and unfair to the thousands of Chinese who dared to express their nonconformist views publicly, or showed their disagreement by committing suicide.[60] I should add that Chinese intellectuals and writers may have felt as much of a need to protect their country's cultural integrity as their leaders, and more than the Russians, for China had suffered from a century of imperialist domination. In any case, the cultural distance was far greater for them than for the Russians; they even tended to consider Russia as part and parcel of the European other (and long-standing adversary). Nor, European that I am, can I exclude that I may more spontaneously feel what a Russian might feel.[61]

The process in China appeared to be slower than for the Soviet dissidents, but the Chinese writers became no less disenchanted for all that. Not only did they refute utopia, as well as Chinese (Mencius) and Western humanism (reputed to be "bourgeois" and individualistic), but also the utopia that Mao believed, or claimed to, would result from Marxism.[62] During the first Scar Literature stage, many writers displayed their wounds—in other words depicted what intellectuals were subjected to after the Hundred Flowers, and especially during the Cultural Revolution.[63] From the 1990s, the initial leniency was challenged again, and people realized that many intellectuals were simultaneously victims and accomplices of the regime, and moreover that those intellectuals were not the sole victims, or indeed the principal ones. On the eve of the twenty-first century, there was a growing focus of interest in the Great Leap Forward and its victims, peasants rather than intellectuals and urbanites.[64] The change of victims went with a no less significant change in the people's attitude to the regime. At first nobody challenged Deng Xiaoping's modernization program, everyone supported it. Then came a transition from the rejection of Mao-thought to a more global doubt of historical optimism, still connected to the Deng consensus. Next, and better still, once it had stepped over the Maoist era, the living literature of the past twenty-five years was released from all the century's modernity from May Fourth to the Four Modernizations. Writing ceased to be a political action—which did not prevent the writer from mocking the myths conveyed by history, or revealing their sinister outcomes. It was sufficient to record the succession of violence and tragedy epitomized by the modern history of China and its people once and for all. Not only the revolutionaries in power but the vocation twentieth-century Chinese writers attributed to themselves and their old and lasting obsession (China) now provoked bitter laughter. Zamyatin had reacted much earlier—in Lenin's lifetime—but China too would have its period of dystopia.[65]

The subject of this book leads me to refer to Zamyatin, but neither Zamyatin nor Huxley nor Orwell was the primary inspiration for the contemporary dystopic novelists studied by Jeffrey Kinkley.[66] They referred to Gabriel García Márquez, or even Hobbes: Man is Wolf to Man, his primitive instincts lead to fighting and violence that has not the slightest political, ethic, or ideological significance. One should not be surprised then if the lives of characters in novels are "poor, nasty, brutish and short."[67] Even if such widespread disenchantment was the result of the Chinese revolutionary experience, rekindled by youthful memories of dystopic writers (many of whom were the rusticated youths of the "lost generation"),[68] it did not refer as explicitly to the Communist leaders themselves, or their deeds and crimes, as that of their Soviet predecessors.[69]

If contemporary Chinese literature does not enable us to "feel" totalitarianism to the same extent as post-Stalinist Russian literature (including that written for the desk drawer or published abroad under Stalin), it does make us aware of a classic effect of totalitarianism, in other words, the extent of the trauma caused by Maoism and the Cultural Revolution. That trauma disconnected the literary avant-garde, not only from the revolutionary regime and its ideals, but also from the most deep-rooted ideals of modern Chinese literature.

8. The Camps

I know more about the Soviet camps than I do about the Chinese ones. The Sinologist's limited knowledge is a clue, for the Chinese themselves do not seem to have gauged the extent and significance of their own "archipelago." Thanks to Solzhenitsyn and others, foreign opinion is far more aware of the living (or rather, survival) conditions of gulag prisoners than of their counterparts in *laogai*.[1] The name Auschwitz is universally known, but has one Westerner in a hundred ever heard of Kolyma? And that would be one hundred times more than the number of people who have heard of Jiabiangou (I have deliberately chosen a camp that was the subject of a book that has been translated into French and made into a film).[2]

And yet there are comparisons to be made between the two archipelagos. Not only did they last far longer than the Nazi camps, but the Chinese archipelago still exists. They also held more people, an average of a million and a half to two million *zeks* between 1938 and 1953,[3] and nearly ten million Chinese prisoners between 1952 and 1977. The differences here are misleading, for they do not show the turnover in prisoners, which was extremely high in the Soviet Union. In 1943, 2,421,000 prisoners passed through the gulag, or nearly 1 million more than the official figure of 1,484,000 prisoners at 1 January 1943. That is largely because many prisoners were mobilized into the Red Army and the prison population suffered a 22 percent mortality rate that year. Between 1929 and 1955, nearly 20 million men and women were sent to the gulag or to prison, nearly 6 million others were deported to distant colonies in the far north, Siberia, or Kazakhstan, or closer ones in the Ural region.[4] The *laogai* population was more stable, with a lower annual number of people entering or leaving the camps (whether dead or freed). The total percentage of prisoners (in camps and prisons) declined from a maximum of 1.75 percent of the total population in 1952 to 1.05 percent in 1977.[5] While the annual percentage of prisoners in the gulag were scarcely more than that, the proportion of Soviets sent to the camps at one time or another was far greater because of a higher annual renewal rate. Between 1929 and 1953, that may have reached one adult out of six.

The gulag also wins as far as the expanse is concerned—assuming we set aside the land mass denominator (less than ten million square kilometers for China versus one-sixth of the land mass for the Soviet Union). The main gulag camps and "complexes" were on a more massive scale. While the Chinese camps were not as large as the Dalstroy or BAMLAG camps or those in the Komi Republic,[6] those in the northwest (Xinjiang and Qinghai) and the northeast (Heilongjiang) and as well as others, sometimes closer to the big cities, like the Qinghe Farm northeast of Tianjin, were hardly small affairs. Close to the Siberian border, the discreetly named Xingkaihu Farm, where Jean Pasqualini spent time clearing virgin land, comprised nine ancillary camps, and its Mishan neighbor apparently held sixty thousand prisoners over several hundred square kilometers. Not only were the Chinese camps less vast than the Soviet ones, but there were fewer of them: around one thousand,[7] compared with thousands and thousands of camps and *lagpunkts* (small, sometimes temporary camps) spread over 476 complexes. But there is no point in quibbling for there are many more similarities between the Chinese and Soviet archipelagoes.

And all the more because the gulag served as a reference, if not the model, for *laogai*. As early as 1949–1950, NKVD specialists came to lend their Chinese brothers a hand in this domain and Luo Ruiqing, minister for public security during the first decade (1949–1959), had spent two years in the Soviet Union in the early 1930s. He studied the relevant Soviet organs closely and admired the work of Felix Dzerjinski, founder of the Cheka, whose portrait hung in Luo's offices in Beijing. The Chinese, like their Soviet predecessors, found it expedient to use slave labor to exploit the inhospitable outer regions of their empire. They were also attracted by the romantic aspect of the "new frontier" and, like Stalin, they chose to disperse their camps in this virgin territory, where both the climate and the distance made escape extremely difficult. The camps the Chinese prisoners feared the most were those in the far northeast and (especially) the northwest, just as the Russians most feared Kolyma and Vorkuta.[8]

There were nevertheless a few differences between the two massive undertakings. In Confucian China, law never held the role that it played in Europe, Russia included. What mattered was the moral code that each individual was supposed to observe, and given that virtue was acquired through study, the scholars, rather than the state, were supposed to inculcate and respect it. The purpose of putting people behind bars was as much to reform criminals as to punish them. Mao exploited that tradition, as well as the use of torture for extracting confessions and the harsh sentences imposed in Imperial China, but both practices were also inherited from the Soviet model.[9] A second difference was that *laogai* camps were constructed immediately, not only because the Chinese were inspired by their predecessors, but also because they had already acquired a solid experience in repression in the Jiangxi Soviet during the 1930s, which they consolidated in the guerrilla zones of northern China over the following decade. The first Soviet camps were ad hoc creations, built in haste. It would be many years before the gulag system emerged from the chaos of improvisation.[10] In 1923, the camps on Solovetsky Islands were paradise compared with those in the 1930s and 1940s. Even after the Great Turn, the prisoners suffered far less in the camps in 1930–1931 than during the famine, the Great Purge, or the war. Between the famine and Purge, the prisoners had a (very relative) reprieve lasting from 1934 to 1936. They became aware of that only after the fact, rather like that young German Jew imprisoned in an "ordinary" camp in the Soviet Union who became nostalgic for prewar Dachau.[11]

In China there was no need to wait for any Great Turn. From 1952, the Chinese archipelago began to take shape and would only grow a little more. In 1959, some two million prisoners were held in *laogai* and especially in *laojiao*, including the rightists imprisoned since 1957. The utopic campaigns (GLF) and the repressive ones (Cultural Revolution) destabilized the Chinese archipelago rather than reinforced it. After 1958, the new contingents were not numerous enough to replace the prisoners who had died of starvation. In the Soviet Union too, the utopic campaigns (insomuch as we can call Stalin's Great Turn utopic) and the repressive ones (the Great Terror) also disorganized the gulag while at the same time providing it with an additional labor force. Lavrenty Beria's so-called reforms attempted to establish a "new order" in the camps. Another shared characteristic regarding the upsurge in repression in both countries was that they provided opportunities to reimprison former prisoners who had already served their sentences. In the eyes of the authorities seeking to fulfill their quotas, once an "enemy of the people," always a scapegoat.[12]

As I mentioned previously, there was another difference between the two systems. In addition to *laogai* (reform through labor) the Chinese had *laojiao* (reeducation through labor). The latter punished offenses deemed to be less serious and had the advantage of not requiring any legal procedure. A mere administrative or police decision could send someone to *laojiao* for an undetermined period, albeit in principle limited to three years. Today that limit is respected (or was until the recent abolition of *laojiao*), but that was not the case in Mao's day. Wu Hongda, one of the most famous "prisoners of Mao" (to borrow the expression used by Jean Pasqualini, another famous prisoner), was sentenced to three years of *laojiao* but in fact served ten, and was scarcely better off than anyone sentenced to *laogai*. In 1965, one year after his 1961 sentence should have come to an end, Wu and two fellow prisoners managed to get a letter to Chairman Mao posted outside the camp, in which they asked the chairman when the rightists sentenced to reeducation might hope to be freed. The result was predictable: Wu got eight days in a punishment cell, which left him at death's door. Over time the differences between *laogai* and *laojiao* camps, often located close by or even within the same compound, gradually disappeared. Conditions were equally harsh, and the diet was the same. However, *laojiao* prisoners were, in theory, paid a paltry wage, and some of them obtained (short and rare) furloughs. That did not prevent some prisoners from preferring *laogai* to *laojiao*, where they were more likely to have to do agricultural work, which as a rule was more exhausting than most artisanal or industrial tasks, and where the duration of their imprisonment could be prolonged indefinitely. The term *laojiao* does not, however, cover all the varieties of "peripheral confinements" (Jean-Luc Domenach), which ranged from the overcrowded holding centers to the "stables" where many Cultural Revolution victims were held, and the "May Seventh Cadre Schools" where intellectuals and urban bureaucrats were sent to learn from unqualified and indifferent peasants.[13] These innovations were formal rather than significant in relation to the Stalinist precedent, since a summary judgment by an obedient *troika* was no better than a police measure or a whim on the part of a local authority.

Categories of Prisoners

From Arkhangelsk to Guangzhou, the majority of political prisoners were the "class enemies," "enemies of the people," "counterrevolutionaries," and "rightists," sentenced more for who they were than for what they did[14]—unlike the delinquents and common criminals.

The social breakdown of the "political" prisoners varied from one archipelago to the other. In the Soviet Union, there was a good chance that the early prisoners belonged to the elite or the former urban elite, such as the erstwhile White Army officers, Czarist officials and nobility, Menshevik or Socialist Revolutionary militants, Shakhty "saboteurs" (engineers and technicians) or saboteurs from the "industrial party," Trotskyists, and other species of counterrevolutionaries targeted by a broad interpretation of Article 58. However, after 1930 they were submerged by the inflow of kulaks, or alleged kulaks, and the majority of *zeks* were then peasants. The Chinese archipelago was different in that the urban elite was far better represented than the rural one (former landlords), and the latter was more frequently imprisoned than peasants. In China, collectivization in the second half of 1955 was faster and a little less brutal than in the Soviet Union. It triggered less of an opposition and led to fewer people being sentenced to *laogai*. The agrarian reform of 1950–1952, which was in fact an agrarian revolution launched and led by the government, had already decimated the landlords. More than 1 million of them were executed and 1.29 million sent to prison or to *laogai*. There were therefore very few peasants in the prison population, unlike the Russian gulag, where it was common knowledge that many peasants who were labeled kulaks were actually *seredniaks* (middle peasants) punished for their reticence to join a collective farm, or listed as kulaks by a local soviet in order to provide the required quota to the administration.

There were also peasants among the common-law criminals, and again more in the Soviet Union than in China, if only because they had violated that famous 7 August 1932 "spikelet law" (see chapters 4 and 5). Those gleaners sentenced to ten years in the gulag were often just teenagers or mothers. There were similar Jean Valjean–type "criminals" in the Chinese archipelago when famine forced people to pilfer,[15] or the Cultural Revolution left children abandoned and without support while their fathers and mothers moldered in some camp, farm, or May Seventh Cadre School. Conversely, before the GLF and the ensuing disruptions, there was only a very small minority of ordinary criminals in the Chinese archipelago, around 20 percent during the first years of the regime. They received the same treatment as the others, particularly since the Communist authorities tended to assign political connotations to the least misdemeanor, whether it was a case of stealing an egg or tearing Chairman Mao's photo in the newspaper by mistake. There was not the slightest vestige of Lenin's ambivalence about punishing common-law criminals, perceived as potential allies of the regime. Once the social exploitation inherited from Czarism was eradicated, common-law crime no longer had any reason to exist and was supposed to disappear. During most of the 1930s, "socially correct" petty criminals continued to be seen as potentially "correctable." And failing that, they could serve to control and intimidate the "counterrevolutionaries" and other "socially dangerous" political prisoners. At its peak there was no equivalent in the Chinese archipelago to this repugnant pecking order, which allowed mobster bosses to exploit, steal, rape, or mutilate their unfortunate fellow prisoners. For one thing, as we have seen, all crime was deemed to be political, and for another, any prisoner who dared, for instance, to fornicate in public like Eugenia Ginzburg's fellow inmates on Saturday evenings in the quarry,[16] or simply played cards for clothes and other meager possessions belonging to the "enemies of the people" imprisoned with them, would immediately be disqualified from their position in the eyes of both the guards and the authorities. They would be considered "un-reformable" and therefore guilty twice over, despite all the efforts deployed by the Party to help them see the light.

It was not until the 1970s and the turmoil of the Cultural Revolution that the common-law criminals in *laogai*, now rather more numerous,[17] began to boast of their good social origins, which supposedly gave them a superior status to that of the political prisoners. In the early 1990s, the poet Liao Yiwu was often the sole political prisoner in his cell. The cell head, always a criminal, would impose a rule that was greatly appreciated by the *laogai* administration, despite the fact that even the most imaginative sadist would have trouble conceiving of such cruelty. Liao feigned to describe the "menu" of tortures inflicted by the cell head's henchmen in admiring tones. One consisted of hanging a prisoner over the toilet and repeatedly plunging his head into excrement until he was gorged on it. The poet, understandably, resorted to the Chinese adage that "you must stick to the animal as a fly sticks to shit," since "hog bristles grow on pig skins." He was equally detached in describing the brutality inflicted on him by the criminal "red-heads" who had served their sentence and worked as assistants to the *laogai* officers. Have I been misled by the distance that Liao succeeded in keeping between the victim and the observer (himself in both cases)? The fact remains that the freedom granted to those criminals to harass, rob, and torture the political prisoners at will, or sign the required false testimony against them, appears to have been a little less systematic in the Chinese archipelago, which claimed to be moral, especially at the peak of Maoism. Back in those stirring times, Liao was still "free" but already fighting for survival, not yet among prison thugs, but as a starved baby with "a small body bloated with malnutrition," before turning into an impudent youth a few years later, who wriggled his way into the front row of a public execution performance.

Nor will I forget the hundreds of juvenile delinquents—not even criminals, but children aged between nine and seventeen, who inspired the same revulsion in Jean Pasqualini ("they were the meanest and most terrifying little bastard that I have ever had the misfortune to meet") as those in the gulag did in Solzhenitsyn or Eugenia Ginzburg. Or forget Wu Hongda's fights with two fellow prisoners. He survived by returning blow for blow, thanks to the lesson learned from a common-law criminal, an illiterate young peasant arrested for filching food in order to survive (in 1960, when the GLF famine reached its peak). Because he had no money to pay for his mother's burial after she died of starvation, the young man was obliged to leave her corpse behind. Big-Mouth Xing (the name Wu gave to this twenty-year-old "guru" of his) explained, "Here the strongest wins, intelligence counts for nothing, so you must take yourself in hand." Hunger certainly helped, and Wu learned his lesson so well that he even devoured a turnip found by another man, after punching him to stop the weaker man's protests. "I never even gave a thought to the hound mentality I had adopted" in order to survive. At this point Varlam Shalamov's lapidary eloquence comes to mind: "In a discussion, the fist or the stick constitute the argument ... physical strength becomes moral strength; ... the intellectual becomes a coward, and his own brain prompts him with alibis; ... everything dear to him is reduced to ashes, civilization and culture disappear in record time that may be counted in weeks; ... the camp is a negative school of life; ... the prisoner learns to loathe work; ... he learns how to fawn and lie, to indulge in low deeds (great or small);

becomes selfish; ... his focus of interest grows shoddy and primitive. The moral barriers have been pushed back out of sight."[18]

The other major sociological difference between the two archipelagos concerns the foreigners, who were numerous in the gulag at the end of the 1930s, and more numerous still during and just after World War II. Foreigners were rare in the Chinese archipelago. Apart from the Japanese prisoners of war in the early 1950s, labeled "war criminals," there were Koreans who had escaped from North Korea (such as the clever Rhee to whom Pasqualini paid tribute), Western missionaries, White Russians like Constantin Rissov, and half-Chinese like Pasqualini himself. Foreigners became increasingly rare as the years passed, with exceptions triggered by the Cultural Revolution (fervent Maoists and "Foreign Friends," such as Sidney Rittenberg, were imprisoned).[19] China never faced a foreign threat comparable to the one posed by Nazi Germany, and the foreigners living in the country were but a tiny minority. The ethnic minorities themselves (Tibetans, Uighurs, Mongols, etc.) scarcely accounted for 6 percent of the population (more than 8 percent today). That proportion cannot be compared with that of the non-Russians in the Soviet Union. Tens of thousands of Tibetans died in *laogai* or because they could not adapt to the diet and climate, a tragic loss to the Tibetan population but a drop of water in the Chinese ocean. The slave-driving guards in China never had to deal with a resistance comparable to that of the united clans of Estonians, western Ukrainians, or Poles, chased out of their country after the German-Soviet Pact. I won't even mention the Volga Germans or the Chechens deported under dreadful conditions (seventy-eight thousand of them died during the transfer), before being massacred half a century later by the successors to the Soviet state. There is a great deal more to be said on the subject of the treatment of foreigners (from Koreans to Moldavians) and the ethnic minorities in the Soviet Union, but my intention here is not to say that the Chinese were less cruel—they are easily xenophobic, and the regime showed the same suspicion of any Chinese who came from (or returned from) abroad as Stalin showed to anyone who so much as corresponded with a Pole. I shall merely repeat that, not having faced the same dangers as their Soviet predecessors, the Chinese did not feel the need or temptation to lock up so many foreigners.

Aside from the greater proportion of foreigners and peasants in the gulag, the other differences between the two archipelagos were less important and varied according to the period. Women appeared to have been more numerous in the gulag, but my opinion is based on uncertain estimates for *laogai* (5 percent of female prisoners under Mao, only 2 percent in the 1990s). Estimates for the gulag are scarcely more reliable and vary still more, ranging from 6 percent to 15 percent of female *zeks* before the war, with more later. According to the official statistics made available since 1991, the percentage of female prisoners varied from 5.9 percent to 8.4 percent between 1934 and 1941. Numbers rose during the war because of the large number of male *zeks* sent to the front and the almost equal number of women arrested and sent to camps for absenteeism from the factories they worked in. Nevertheless, did they really reach 30 percent in 1945, as one serious author has claimed?[20] The arrests of "wives of enemies of the people" remained a Soviet specificity. That could not be said for the exploitation of freed workers and prisoners obliged to remain where they were, even after they completed their sentences. That occurred frequently in the gulag but less so than in *laogai*, where many former prisoners ended their days in the very place where they had been imprisoned.[21] "*Laogai* and *laojiao* have an end, but *jiuye* [keeping 'freed' prisoners at work] is for life," according to a popular saying in the camps, when most convicts were obliged to carry out this "second *laogai*" (*er laogai*) once they finished serving their sentences. Among the survivors was Wu Hongda who, after his sentence of nine and a half years, remained for an equal number of years as a "freed prisoner" in the Wangzhuang coal mine (Shanxi province), managed by the public security bureau. Ama Adhe Tapontsang, a Tibetan woman arrested in 1958 and sentenced to sixteen years for "counterrevolutionary rebellion," was obliged to carry out an additional eleven years of labor from 1974 to 1985, almost achieving the sad records held by Mandela and Blanqui.

From Arrest to the Camp

The fact that there were mainly Chinese males and proportionately more city dwellers than rural ones in *laogai*, whereas the gulag population was far more mixed (in 1937–1938 the NKVD arrested everyone and anyone,[22] unlike the more selective Chinese public security)[23] alters nothing to the underlying factor. From the knock on the door in the dead of night to being sentenced to forced labor, the two regimes' operating methods were very similar (and all the more so since the Chinese had borrowed a great deal from their predecessors). Once the prisoners arrived in the camps, whether in the Arctic Circle or in the tropics, they joined the millions of slaves who toiled, starved, rotted, and died before their time.

Box 6

China's Repeat Offenders—Stalin's Wide Net

First, here are three extraordinary accounts to illustrate what I mean by arrests being more selective in China, as opposed to Anna Akhmatova's "for nothing" (see note 22).

Before the revolution, Lin Zhao, a teenager, ran away from home to enroll in a Communist school of journalism. An ardent supporter of the revolution and the Party, she participated in agrarian reform and even rejoiced in the execution of landlords, but in 1957 she made the mistake of expressing sympathy for a "rightist" comrade. She was promptly labeled a rightist herself, and spent three years being reeducated in *laojiao*. After her release in 1960, she began to criticize Mao's policies and sent him a petition in support of Peng Dehuai. Subsequently sentenced to twenty years, Lin continued to write in prison and as a result was sentenced to death and executed in 1968, at the age of thirty-six. After she was shot, the police went to her mother's home and presented her with a bill for the bullet that had killed her daughter.

Wang Shenyou was a university physics student in Shanghai. In June 1966 he wrote in his diary, "The Cultural Revolution [which had just begun] will plunge the country into a massive recession." For that, he got two years in prison, but was arrested again in 1976 for criticizing Mao in a letter to a friend (as was the case with Solzhenitsyn with regard to Stalinist strategy in 1945). Since Wang refused to make the slightest self-criticism, a public trial was held in the Shanghai stadium and he was sentenced to death in April 1977. He was executed at the age of thirty-one.

Those two "incurables" (the people's justice aimed at "curing" the patient, as Mao never tired of repeating) were sentenced to death. Many others were "only" sentenced to *laogai*. That was the case for Cai Zhongxian, a priest in Shanghai's Xuhui parish. He was arrested a first time in 1953 for refusing to denounce the Catholic Church. After he was freed in 1956, he would not encourage the faithful to join the Patriotic Catholic Church (the official one, similar to the Constitutional Church during the French Revolution). He was sentenced to fifteen years in prison as a counterrevolutionary, and in 1969 he was sent to a labor camp to complete the final years of his sentence. Because he received a (forbidden) visit by another Shanghai priest, he was sentenced yet again, this time to ten years. When he was finally released in 1988, thirty-five years after he was first arrested (although he did enjoy a brief episode of freedom in between) he emigrated to the United States, where he died in 1999.

On the Soviet side, I have selected the cases of two Europeans who survived the camps or deportation. Jan Bohdan was born in sub-Carpathian Russia, which used to belong to Czechoslovakia until the Hungarian invasion of March 1939. He believed in the propaganda that described the Soviet Union as a "prosperous and anti-fascist" nation and was just eighteen years old when he decided to make a clandestine crossing into the Soviet Union in order to fight the Hungarians. He was immediately arrested but failed to convince the border guards or the NKVD of his good faith. He was sentenced to three years in a camp and was freed in his thirty-ninth month of imprisonment thanks to a 1943 ruling that permitted Czechs aged between eighteen and fifty-two to join the Red Army. His wish was finally granted, after a detour via the gulag.

Silvia Linarte was not eighteen but less than two years old when she was deported from Latvia, incorporated into the Soviet Union a year previously, in 1940. Her parents were teachers and her father, who headed a Catholic organization, was sent to a camp in 1941 where he died almost immediately. The rest of the family was given twenty-five minutes to pack. Silvia's little sister, aged eleven months, died on the way. On arrival in Siberia, they stumbled upon a veritable labor market. The teacher mother and her three small daughters (Silvia's two older sisters were aged six and nine) were sent into a distant kolkhoz. Silvia's childhood memories were not of Latvia but of the Taiga, the cold, and the wolves. However, they were able to return to Latvia in 1946, when children who had lost a parent were authorized to return home. A new wave of banishments then sent the family to Siberia in 1950 until in 1955–1956 the Latvians were authorized to return home, this time for good. Silvia, whose mother died and was buried near Krasnoyarsk, was one of the first to benefit from this measure but remained stigmatized as the daughter of a convict and former deportee to the "special colonies."

Sources: China: Kempton and Richardson, 2009, pp. 87, 91 and 96; on Lin Zhao, see also, Wang Youqin, 2007, p. 76; Dikötter, 2013, p. 180; Mühlhahn, 2000, p. 273; and above all, Pan, 2008, pp. 24–78. URSS: Mayer, 2012; Denis, 2012.

In 1937–1938, a joke used to do the rounds Moscow. It described a couple woken by sharp knocks on the door in the middle of the night, and the relief they felt when they learned that "it was only because the building was on fire." Many people were resigned to their arrest in advance and kept a bag ready under their beds in case the NKVD came to take them away. Unfortunately, since they never knew their destination, they rarely had sufficient warm clothing that was so essential in the far north. Eugenia Ginzburg was fortunate to be arrested during the day, but she was promised that she would only be kept "for some 40 minutes, possibly one hour." Because of that, she sent her son outside to skate and never said goodbye to her children. In China, Lai Ying was also arrested in broad daylight, in the train taking her from Guangzhou back to Hong Kong where she lived. The train was stopped in the middle of nowhere and she was pushed into a car that immediately returned to Guangzhou at high speed. The norm, however, was more like Bu Ning's case. He was woken at half past midnight by eight policemen who searched his home. They did not require a warrant to do so, and they handcuffed him and took him away. His family had to wait for weeks and months before learning where he was held. In the Soviet Union even relatives sometimes cautiously kept clear of such tainted families, as did their neighbors and colleagues, more frequently. In China, the authorities often insisted that the wife divorce if she did not want to compromise her career and the future of her children.[24]

In China, the detention centers were even more overcrowded and uncomfortable than in the Soviet Union and the interrogation was a more formidable affair. The prisoner being interrogated would sit on the floor or on a low stool, while the interrogator was placed on a high platform. This symbolic humiliation was not as amusing as in Chaplin's *The Dictator*, and was just the first step for conditioning the suspect. In both countries the interrogation had one purpose, or rather two: to obtain a full confession from the accused and for the accused to denounce other "guilty" parties. The confession played a key role in this strange form of justice, which often lacked the slightest material element. That was especially true in the Soviet Union, where fabrication was more flagrant. In China, the examining magistrate often mentioned precise facts and details, assembled in such a way as to provide damning evidence against the accused.[25] A similar principle was applied in both dictatorships, the Soviet term for it being "privileges for prisoners who cooperate," repeated in a variety of ways in China: "indulgence for those who confess" (with a variation, "clemency for those who repent"), "severe sentences for those who persist" (with a variation for "those who resist reform"). If the prisoner still failed to see the light and if the torturers were unable to persuade him or her to see reason, sleep deprivation might do the trick. Interrogations were nearly always held at night and could follow on, one after the other, all night long, after which the prisoner had to remain standing in his cell, and was forbidden to sleep—a measure reinforced with the help of a blinding light. Most of the time, the accused ended up "confessing" and regretting that he had not done so earlier. It wasn't worth "holding out," which only prolonged the interrogation. In the end nearly everyone was sentenced equally severely, and more severely still if they failed to confess.

As a foreigner (a Polish Jew), Julius Margolin was unaware of the rule (which would later be drummed into him in the camps) that "with the NKVD, if you argue or persist it will be worse still." He therefore persisted, "I had not understood that the real trial was already over ... and the sentence passed. We were all sentenced to three or five years. ... If I had not persisted, I would have received three years instead of five." There was no certainty of that though, for as a polyglot, Zionist, and doctor of philosophy, there were many reasons for him to receive special treatment.

People also hoped that by confessing they might at last be tried and sentenced, and then dispatched to a camp. Many saw that prospect as a liberation, especially in China where interrogations were followed by the writing up of autobiographical confessions, which were never considered sufficiently sincere or detailed. Prisoners grew fed up with stagnating in insalubrious cells and yearned to be in the open air of the countryside. Such illusions were quickly dissipated, but the camps did at least have one small advantage. Because the cell or brigade heads were obliged to draw up reports (daily in China), they were easily recognized and therefore less feared than the prison informers, who were harder to identify. There was nearly always one informer per cell. In the camps they were found out sooner or later,[26] but since people were not as well acquainted with each other in the prisons, they were constantly on their guard.

In both countries the trials were almost always parodies of justice. Occasionally in the Soviet Union, local judges might reduce a sentence, or even invalidate a groundless accusation, but from the summer of 1937 people could no longer cling to such a hope. Most prisoners taken during the mass arrests appeared for just a few minutes before a *troika*, a special court comprising three judges representing the NKVD, the public prosecutor, and the Party. Others did not even get that, but were sentenced in absentia without being aware of it, including to the "supreme punishment." The *troika* regularly passed sentences decided in advance by its superiors behind closed doors. The name of one of those superiors, Edward Salyn, head of the NKVD in Omsk province, deserves be remembered however. During a conference held by Stalin and Yezhov in July 1937, he declared that there were insufficient Trotskyists and enemies of the people in the region to justify a campaign of repression, and that it was an aberration to decide on the number of arrests and executions in advance. He was promptly added to that number as he was immediately arrested, sentenced, and shot.

There was no *troika* in China, but the result was the same. The judges were not independent from the Party and issued sentences in line with what had been decided for them, applying the *xian pan hou shen* (first the sentence, then the trial) formula. The lawyers were no more independent than the judges. Liao Yiwu's lawyer urged him to cooperate with the government and admit to his guilt. Pasqualini's lawyer made a speech for the defense that was exactly two sentences long: "The accused has, of his own volition, admitted to having committed those crimes. No defense is therefore necessary." Pasqualini, who had indeed written his "self-accusation," was astonished by the naïveté of those who appealed. They had not yet learned that to appeal was to reveal that they had not yet "reformed" and reconstructed themselves! And they consequently required a heavier sentence, which the judges would hasten to impose, in the interest of the accused, in accordance with Chairman Mao's teaching: "the guilty person is sick, we must heal him."[27] This concerns those condemned to *laogai*. As I said earlier, a decision by a local authority (police or administrative) was enough to send a person to *laojiao* without any kind of trial whatsoever.

In China, the transfer from prison to camp seems to have been less interminable and cruel than the *etap*, which terrified the Soviet prisoners and delivered the few survivors to their destination in such a state of exhaustion that they were unfit to work.[28] The transit prisons were equally filthy and overpopulated and the food was as bad, but the common-law prisoners were generally less violent and predatory. There are fewer accounts of this aspect of the archipelago in China, compared with those haunting accounts of torture and thirst throughout the interminable Siberian crossing (one month for Eugenia Ginzburg and her companions in wagon number 7 from Yaroslavl to Vladivostok). The prisoners lived on dried fish or salted dishwater with a few herring tails, and were given only one glass of water per day to drink. Of course it is only a matter of degree. In his train from Shanghai to Gansu in northwest China, Han Weitian also suffered from thirst, putrid air, and filth, with miserable prisoners often vomiting over each other in wagons carrying between seventy and eighty of them, piled one on top of another. The ten-day journey did not even take them to their destination. Another train then transported them to Xining, the capital of Qinghai, after which they still had a three-day walk to cover the hundred kilometers to the camp in the middle of nowhere, where the prisoners would have to build a road.[29] Whether they suffered a long journey from a transit prison to a camp, or a camp-to-camp transfer, the Chinese prisoners and Soviet *zeks* alike had no idea where they were going.[30]

The transfer of prisoners seems to me to be more horrifying on the Soviet side of the archipelago, but I do not exclude that someone with access to more abundant documentation than mine would reveal a Chinese equivalent to the exhausting deadly march of the *zeks*, without food in a heat wave, from the transit camp to the ships that would transport them to Kolyma, the laggards being kicked or shot for "attempting to flee." Or the Heilongjiang, Xinjiang, or Qinghai equivalent of the frozen prisoners piled up in open trucks transporting them from Magadan to Elgen. That was not the case during the heroic period when Kolyma was being developed. At the outset at least, most of the *zeks* worked on building the road from Magadan to the gold mines, and very few were sent to extract gold there with whatever paltry means were available. Nor was it the case in the winter of 1938, once Kolyma was "motorized." It may have been because of the exceptional influx of prisoners following the Great Terror that "the authorities decided that the prisoners would have to walk from Magadan to the gold deposits in the north. After the 500 kilometer-long walk only 30–40 prisoners arrived at their destination out of a column of 500. The others died on the way, frozen, starved or shot."[31]

The decision, in 1939, to allow more than one thousand *zeks* to die off the coast of Hokkaido when the ship transporting them from Kolyma to the mainland struck a reef (it would have been easy to ask for help from the foreign ships in the region, but there was no question of revealing the content of the cargo) is similar to the secrecy surrounding the GLF famine in China. The loss of face resulting from an admission of failure was far more important than the lives of millions of people. The *laogai* and *laojiao* prisoners contributed more than their share of lives to that number, with only some five hundred survivors out of nearly three thousand rightists imprisoned in Jiabiangou in the Gobi Desert between 1957 and 1961. One of the five hundred, a doctor was obliged to remain six months longer in the camps in order to fake the files of those who had died of hunger, by providing a medical case history for each of them. As a result, the official register states only death from natural causes such as heart failure, cirrhosis of the liver, dysentery, stomach cancer, and so forth.[32]

The Camps

The ways the camps were organized, as well as the techniques perfected to supervise the prisoners and knock them into shape, were similar in both countries, particularly since the Chinese public security borrowed a great deal from the NKVD. To save on wage-paying employees, who were usually in short supply, many tasks including supervision were given to the prisoners, divided up in military fashion into groups (squads) and brigades. At first, prisoners familiar with management and authority were placed as heads of cells, squads, or brigades. They were usually White or Chekist guards who had been sent to Solovetsky Islands (the archipelago in which the Solovki camp was located) for some abuse or crime, or, in China, nationalist officials or Japanese "spies." The cell and squad heads, and the brigade head in particular, benefitted from minor privileges and were allowed to delegate some of their tasks. It was up to them to ensure that their "units" fulfilled their quotas. Some tyrannical cell heads would report the slightest offense committed by a member of their group. That was rare, although perhaps a little less so in 1950s China, but even then it was usually the activists or the stool pigeons who did such things.[33]

The sacrosanct "quota," in other words the amount of labor the *zeks* or Chinese convicts were obliged to carry out, would be hard enough for healthy, well-fed, and experienced men to accomplish.[34] For intellectuals and urbanites unused to physical labor, and, furthermore, very undernourished and living in indescribable filth, such labor was nearly impossible and could rapidly kill the prisoners.

Hunger, cold, and exhaustion

"What did I feel above all in the reform-though-labor camp? The answer can be summed up in one word: hunger."[35] Survivors of both the gulag and *laogai* were unanimous about that. The authorities allocated rations in proportion to the work accomplished during the day. The type of food rations allocated to *zeks* were divided into "reinforced," "work," "basic," or "punishment" categories, depending on the difficulty of the work carried out and the prisoners' performance in relation to their quota. Eugenia Ginzburg and Galya, her fellow prisoner, achieved only 18 percent of their quota on the first day and ate in consequence, after which they survived by cheating, which was made easier in Kolyma by the laziness of the guards, than it was in 1950s China.[36] The system was the same in *laogai*,[37] except that the rations were leaner still (between 13.5 and 22.5 kilograms of poor quality corn and sorghum per month in the Beijing region), but even the "free" Chinese ate less than their Soviet counterparts. Chinese prisoners lost weight less rapidly than the foreign priests, for instance, 30 kilograms in six months for Father Pollio, 34 (from 72 to 38 kilograms) in eighteen months of prison (and not camp) for Reverend Vasquez. Zhang Xianliang, who came from a well-to-do family, grew almost as thin as the Westerners, and only weighed 44 kilograms in his third year of camp. He carried clumps of earth that weighed more than his bodyweight, but preferred doing that to other, more exhausting tasks.[38]

Every miner and woodcutter in Kolyma was obsessed with his daily bread, a precious commodity that people dreamed about, cared for, and even bequeathed to others when they died. Of course, for that bequest to be respected, it was necessary to conceal the testator's death for as long as possible to continue receiving his rations. The body would be placed on the topmost bunk, and raised for the roll call, propped up between the shoulders of two prisoners, one of whom would provide his "basic details," in other words his registration number and so on.[39] The descriptions of famine in *laogai* and *laojiao* camps are even more forthright and cruel, especially for the years 1960 and 1961, the hardest of the GLF famine. In May 1961, one prisoner paid scant attention when informed of his three-year prison sentence, for "I was unable to project myself three years' ahead, I was only concerned with my next *wotou*," "I wasn't even sure that I would live another month."[40] He was able to recover his strength thanks to a few discoveries he made in his ceaseless foraging for food in nearby fields; for instance a few bits of cabbage root the size of a crust of bread, or carrots planted too late the previous year that had never ripened, and, being frozen, were impossible to dig up. One prisoner, who only succeeded in scraping away enough earth to reveal half a carrot, lay on his belly to eat the part that he had uncovered. However, two more important discoveries saved our hero. After following the meandering traces of a burrow in a ditch, he used a spade and pickaxe to dig a hole more than six meters deep and eventually found a rat's winter stores: nearly a kilo of corn and soy, as well as a pound of rice. His other find was even more valuable: a dozen snakes in hibernation. He grabbed them one by one, bit off their heads and then boiled them: "The spade at my feet was a reminder to others that no one else was invited to my feast." Other prisoners who were less cunning, or simply too weak to carry a spade and a pickaxe, made do with eating toothpaste to assuage their hunger. That worked only for a minute before an edema would spread from their legs up to their waist and they collapsed in the toilets. Dysentery killed off the others, or tetanus caused by the slightest scratch on a severely weakened body.

In January 1960 the already poor rations in two Gobi Desert camps were further reduced. In exchange the prisoners were no longer required to work and permitted to explore the fields in search of field mice, worms, and wild herbs, some of which blocked their digestive systems. Others preferred to search for undigested peas in horse droppings. Some prisoners rejoiced when they were sent to load trucks with potatoes, but their "potato feast" resulted in terrible stomach pains, leading to death for one of them. Another prisoner suffered the same fate after he was released and fed by a kindly and brave Communist official. The practice of necrophagy spread, and when the wife of a "rightist" urologist made the long journey from Shanghai to the Gobi Desert to see her husband (who, unknown to her, had died nine days previously), everyone did their utmost to hide his body from her—or what was left of it, for it no longer had any buttocks, thighs, or calves.[41]

In the gulag, the ravages of hunger were fatal not only in periods of famine. Although there were numerous deaths due to work accidents, diseases (poorly treated, if at all), and recurrent epidemics, not to mention the deadly freezing cold and effortless suicide (anyone walking in the "death zone," that no-man's-land outside the fence, was immediately shot), it was hunger that killed the most people. Gnawing hunger rid the starving of their last shreds of dignity, as they lingered near the kitchen with a maniacal look in their eyes, licking any soup that might have spilled onto the floor and swarming about the garbage ditches in the hope of finding some little scrap of cabbage. Some used their last strength to fight for a fish head or bone, or vegetable peelings. But even that was not the dreaded final phase experienced by the "candles," when one of the goners fell prostrate during a roll call, and was immediately surrounded by a circle of necrophageous fellow prisoners who ripped off his coat, leaving the dying man in rags, so that ultimately it was the cold and not hunger that put an end to his agony.[42]

The Russians couldn't be blamed for the climate, but it greatly contributed to the suffering and deaths of the *zeks*, when, for instance, just touching a metal tool with bare hands could tear off their skin, and their hair froze in their beds in their barracks in winter. The only measure that was not humanitarian but common sense (and not always observed at that) was that the *zeks* were not required to carry out "general work" (in the woods, mines, etc.) when temperatures fell below –50°C (–58°F). Imagine the disappointment on mornings when temperatures hovered around the –45 to –48°C mark (–49 to –54.5°F) without dropping to that hoped-for level. But the Russian administration was responsible for the interminable roll calls, often followed by another, which the *zeks* had to endure outside in the Siberian cold. And for the lack of warm clothing, or heating in the barracks, "bare bedsteads, cracks in all the walls, sleeping prisoners covered in snow and no wood. Muddy rags ... holes in their shoes ... and no mittens. No hot food either."[43] That observation was made by a guard after carrying out his tour of inspection of the camp, and was for himself and not for the camp administration, which would have been far too risky. When he mentioned muddy rags, it was out of compassion, not in mockery.

Compassion was unusual, needless to say. The brutality of the guards (and the executions) appear to have been a little more frequent in the gulag than in *laogai* camps during the 1950s, and the labor harder. The *zeks* preferred agricultural labor or cattle breeding, sometimes perceived as quasi-sinecures. In *laogai*, that same agricultural labor was dreaded, even though it was carried out in a less harsh climate. The other tasks (working in quarries, at road work or construction sites, in mines and various industries) may have been carried out with primitive tools, but they were less exhausting than cutting down trees in the Taiga, or working in the mines of Vorkuta or Kolyma. It goes without saying that the barracks were no better heated in *laogai* camps than in gulag ones, and that it can be extremely cold in northern Heilongjiang province, western Qinghai, and Xinjiang, ($-30°C$, or $-22°F$). In the big camps in northwest China (Qinghai and Xinjiang) where the desert environment did little to improve a runaway's chances of survival, roll calls were rare. Even where they were more frequent, in camps such as the New Life United Enterprises where Lai Ying was held, the climate was less trying and the number of roll calls bore no comparison with the repeated ones endured by Shukhov and his companions in misfortune in a single day.[44]

Such differences did nothing to conceal the one thing that nobody could ever forget in either archipelago, and that was the constant, nagging hunger. In *laogai* too, the struggle for survival was the cause of many fights about food, or the theft of money and other items or of tobacco, which were traded for anything that might assuage hunger. As Zhang Xianliang observed soberly, "It was not *laogai* that made people lose all human feeling, it was hunger," and he immediately illustrated that by describing the arrival in the camp of a prisoner's wife and young daughter, who had traveled far to see him. The prisoner cut short the wife's greetings and snatched the parcel of provisions she had bought and promptly gulped everything down. Once replete, he cut his veins with the sickle he had been using to cut grass before his wife and child arrived. Did he do that because he suddenly became aware of their presence and the fact that they too were starving? That was one of the explanations suggested by the other prisoners.[45]

Hygiene, health care, overcrowding, and death

Perhaps because of the effect of different climatic conditions and slightly less arduous labor, it seems that fewer died in *laogai* camps than in the gulag—except possibly during the first years (1949–1952) and certainly a decade later (1959–1961) during the famine, when Zhang Xianliang estimated that approximately one-third of his fellow prisoners died. With the exception of those "black years" (to use the Chinese media's hypocritical euphemism) the mortality rate may have fallen from 3.5 percent to 2 percent per year from the mid-1950s to the end of the 1970s. We know less about those rates than about the considerable variations over time and place. In contrast with the two peaks in mortality mentioned above (the initial period and, more importantly, the famine), the rates fell considerably in the post-Mao era (below 0.1 percent in Qinghai in 1994 and 1995), but nevertheless with peaks at 10 percent in the Xinjiang uranium mines.[46]

There were similar fluctuations in the gulag but we know more about them because we have access to official statistics, although these certainly tend to be underestimates. They mainly provide the number of deaths that occurred in the infirmary or hospital. Those resulting from the brutality of the guards are less reliable. These tend to be labeled "shot for attempting to escape" and fail to include the many *zeks* who died on the way to the camps or during a transfer from one camp to another. Since the camps received bad marks or even sanctions if their mortality rates were too high, the camp commandants also tended to underestimate the number of dead. They even freed prisoners who were at death's door in order to lower the camp's mortality statistics. However, since they could not falsify statistics on a very large scale, the official mortality rates were both below reality and, on the whole, fairly reliable, or shall we say as reliable as the average secret Soviet statistic (for domestic use only) could be, unlike the public statistics that were far more likely to be false. Nevertheless we would be happy to have as many statistics for *laogai*. In the Soviet Union, even the years with seemingly abnormally low mortality rates (at below 1 percent between 1950 and 1953, less than that for the entire Soviet population) are not entirely unlikely given that the population mostly comprised young adults. The mortality fell in the gulag (1949) just at the time when *laogai* began to kill more people in China. Overall, however, the gulag seems to have been more deadly between 1930 and 1945 than *laogai* between 1954 and 1976, except of course in the period from 1958 to 1962.[47]

Hygiene was as poor if not more disastrous in *laogai* than in the gulag. Fleas and bedbugs abounded in most camps; mosquitos were as plentiful in the Arctic Circle as they were in the tropics, as were the filth and overcrowding. The Chinese prisoners sometimes slept on the ground, often head to foot. The situation was no better in the Russia, where children born in the gulag slept and defecated on the ground and adult *zeks* sometimes slept one on top of the other, syphilitics next to those suffering from tuberculosis. Running water was possibly scarcer in *laogai* camps than in the gulag, and prisoners sometimes washed in backwater, but more often in a little dirty water in a tub shared with many others.[48] In January 1938, the stench in the overcrowded camp of Ukhta-Pechora became unbearable because the *zeks* were almost never allowed to shower and could not wash their underclothes for months on end. The arrival of new prisoners (in full Great Terror) doubtless contributed to the shortage of space, clothing, and underwear—let alone sheets!—as well as soap, shoes, and other articles, and reports by the health departments and other official documents for the years 1939–1941 suggest the situation had hardly improved then. Very few Chinese camps had hospitals, and those few were equipped to treat only minor ailments but almost never the skin diseases transmitted by the vermin, the serious cases of diarrhea or constipation, tuberculosis, hepatitis, beriberi, and edema. In the gulag there were repeated epidemics of typhus and scurvy, and, with the exception of large camps such as Magadan for Dalstroy, the hospitals and infirmaries were scarcely better equipped as those in *laogai* camps. Competent doctors were thin on the ground; others learned how to administer a glucose drip to a dying prisoner. As for the male nurses, they were mainly privileged prisoners without training who (at least those who had any sense of fairness) merely handed out dispensations from labor in rotation, without taking the condition of the "patient" into account. More frequently, they demanded bribes for the dispensations but did not dare refuse them to the criminals, as Eugenia Ginzburg scornfully recalled, having become a nurse herself, by fluke.[49]

Survival strategies

To become one of the "aristocrats," who didn't have to work in the mines or fell trees, build roads or dig the earth (in China), was a prisoner's best chance of survival. In the Soviet Union, the majority of *zeks* who survived long sentences were probably *pridourki* or "trusties" at one time or another. That was true for the most famous among them: Varlam Shalamov, Eugenia Ginzburg, Lev Razgon, and Alexandr Solzhenitsyn. The disdain for those trusties as depicted in *One Day in the Life of Ivan Denisovich* triggered lively debates among the escapees. Unlike Shukhov (and therefore Solzhenitsyn) Razgon maintained that choosing to become a trusty when the opportunity arose was to choose life at a time when the rations for a healthy woodcutter would not allow him to live for more than a few months. To escape from "general work," which led to death in the long or short term, a prisoner had to obtain one of a wide range of cushy positions such as being a dishwasher, launderer, child minder for the prisoners' children, cook, hairdresser, accountant, sword sharpener, nurse or nurse's assistant, doctor, "quota-setter," who established the amount of work per day to be carried out by each brigade, or *starosta*, those in charge of keeping order in the barracks, if not an entire "zone." Such cushy jobs were given in preference to criminals, as being "socially close," but many ended up with the educated *zeks* and a few with the political prisoners. Doctors were a case apart, but under the pressure from the plan, it was no longer possible to employ illiterate thieves as accountants and it became necessary to recruit engineers, preferably with experience, and honest storekeepers. Ultimately a *nomenklatura* sprung up among the *zeks*. Anyone who had been a "task allocator," or worked in the cultural and educational section, had every chance of obtaining another cushy job sooner or later, assuming that he or she survived "general work" in the meantime. Even among the latter some jobs were cushier than others (such as transplanting cabbages or collecting the dwarf pine needles used to make a disgusting potion that allegedly prevented scurvy), and preserved people's lives for longer than mining or felling trees in the taiga.[50]

It goes without saying that there were easy jobs in *laogai* camps too. It was far cheaper to get the prisoners to carry out a wide range of tasks and services (the same ones as in the gulag, but with the addition of calligraphy, manure collection, irrigation, guarding warehouses or stables, etc.) rather than the staff. That was lucky for anyone with a skill or the required professional know-how. In 1954, in western Qinghai province, the people holding such jobs were Communists who had "made mistakes" and were treated as first-class prisoners, but the *laogai* authorities also knew how to exploit skills. Wu Hongda was able to obtain a number of "cushy" jobs because he was a student and knew about file management, and Zhang Xianliang, a writer, was put in charge of writing an article devoted to the glory of the "commissar," an old Communist cadre, whom he actually preferred to the others. Zhang even saw an opposition between "outside" (the camp) where the authorities were far more wary of the political dissidents (rightists, counterrevolutionaries, etc.) and "inside" where the camp authorities relied on them, in the belief that the common-law criminals would never rid themselves of their ingrained bad ways. That same Zhang not only was promoted head of a twelve-prisoner squadron and then a sixty-four-man brigade, but at other times was allowed to carry out little jobs that anyone could have done, like fetching clods of earth rather than breaking up rocks and stones, or better still, picking edible plants, a restful task that had the added benefit of allowing him to eat in secret. The former Guomindang (Kuomintang) colonel Han Weitian had the good fortune to be put in charge of boiling water in the kitchen for a fairly long time. But Lai Ying may have won the "cushy job" record, as she was placed in the "cultural squadron" (the camp's theater troop) for nearly half of her five-year *laogai* sentence. Because she could paint, play the flute, and sing, she was ordered to draw propaganda posters, paint decors, and even play a number of roles when the troupe staged revolutionary operas. "The camp tailor made two outfits for me, which made me look like a free citizen [when we played in the villages], we were privileged ... and ate exactly the same food as the cadres."[51]

The counterpart to Lai Ying was Vasily Shukhaev, the Russian émigré painter who unfortunately gave in to his desire to return to his homeland in 1935. He was packed off to Kolyma in 1937 where he became the chief set designer for the Magadan theater. Or the popular singer, Vadim Kozin, whom Stalin brought over by plane from Moscow to Teheran for the surprise concert he organized for Churchill's birthday on 30 November 1943. Kozin was arrested less than six months later and sentenced to eight years in the gulag, where the "Queen of Kolyma" (the wife of the

Dalstroy commandant) took him under her wing. She had him transported from Moscow to Magadan in conditions that bore no resemblance to those of the *etap* described by Eugenia Ginzburg (see above). Kozin led a fairly privileged existence throughout his six years of detention—six and not eight, for he was freed for "exemplary behavior" before finishing his sentence.[52] Few rose to that star's lofty heights, but the gulag organization was certainly based on an "hierarchical pyramid" (Luba Jurgenson). Julius Margolin is more explicit: "Nowhere in the USSR was social inequality more flagrant than in the camps, where the difference between a cook and a vulgar *zeka* (*zek*) who was hounded in the forest every day, was far greater than the one in New York that separates a millionaire from a shoe-polisher."

As diverse as those cushy jobs may have been, by definition they affected only a minority. How then did the others manage to survive? First and foremost thanks to the sacrosanct *tufta* ("truffle") that was invariably practiced in and outside the camps, from Warsaw to Vladivostok and Kolyma to Ho Chi Minh City. That consisted of working as little as possible, or pretending to work and deceiving the foremen and supervisors. In one quarry in the northern Ural Mountains at the end of the 1940s, the brigade head organized the workload very fairly. He moved the *zeks* in turn from the visible part of the quarry at the top, where all the guards were posted, to the invisible part at the bottom, where they could rest a little, even if they had to hammer the ground from time to time to make a noise. *Tufta* existed at all levels and everyone knew about it, from the "quota-setter" who fiddled the quotas by lowering them or pretending not to notice when they had not been filled (as though it were even possible to extract the quota requirement of five tons and more of coal per day!) to the accountant who fiddled the production figures. As a result, the official statistics provide only a very exaggerated picture of the true productivity of the camps. "Horses die from such work," observed Ivan Denisovich, who then tried to obtain sick leave from the doctor, even though he got caught up in the game later and toiled again, rather than waste bricks and mortar.[53]

Supervision

Ivan Denisovich trusts Tyurin, his gang leader, and knows that "he will not give him away." Tyurin is a *zek* like himself, the equivalent to a *kapo* in the Nazi camps. Conversely, gang leader Xie in Zhang Xianliang's *Mimosa* is a Communist cadre, and even braver than Tyurin, for he sends search parties out in all directions to bring back a runaway—except for the one direction he thinks he might have taken. Xie is not the only Communist cadre depicted in a favorable light by Zhang Xianliang, who admitted to have a good recollection of several of them, something that he has been reproached for. In China, many former prisoners also remembered a good cadre, from Bu Ning's Old Shen to Han Weitian's Boss Xu.[54] A certain Captain Chen even won the respect and admiration of the prisoners, admittedly privileged ones, under his orders. The gulf between the cadres and the prisoners appears to have narrowed after the 1950s, when a kind of solidarity sprung up between the victims of the disaster that swept over the entire country. After the famine, nothing would ever be the same again in the Chinese gulag, which subsequently "deteriorated." The chaos of the Cultural Revolution further accentuated this contrast with the "golden age" of *laogai*, the one of the first Five-Year Plan.[55]

In the Soviet Union, such accounts were far rarer. The few Chekists who were liked by the *zeks* were on the prison staff rather than in the camps. Solzhenitsyn made an exception for the head of the Marfino special prison, who was rapidly dismissed. Lev Razgon had a sympathetic recollection of the head of Georgievsk prison as well as the female supervisor of the Stavropol prison.[56]

The "good" guards remained a small minority among the managerial staff who were basically hostile to "class enemies." Ivan Chistiakov himself recognized that his compassion finally waned after the appalling living conditions of the *zeks* led to a growing number of escapes, which obliged him to be woken at night to go off in search of them. There were as many or more bloody brutes proud of their exploits, as there were "good" guards or commandants. In a camp on the island of Anzer, one of the smallest in the Solovetski Archipelago, the Chekist, Vanka Potapov, boasted of having killed more than 400 *zeks* with his own hands. Liang Ruoban, commandant of the Yanchang camp, near the hallowed Yan'an, was never seen without his riding boots and leather crop, and was reputed to have executed or buried alive 1,320 prisoners in one year, before being murdered by a prisoner whose wife he had taken. He stole and raped almost as many as he killed. Sadists flourished in all latitudes, from southern China to northern Siberia. Ivan Bogdanov was an NKVD delegate to a coal-prospecting venture in Kolyma in 1938 and beat his wife as much as the prisoners. The first thing he did when he arrived in the Taiga was to build a punishment cell. He tore up and burned the first letters sent to Shalamov by his wife, and consequently Shalamov had no news of her or their daughter for two years ("That's what I do with your letters, you filthy fascist!"). Being ignorant about production, Bogdanov cared nothing for quotas, unlike Colonel Tarasiuk, whose sole concern was to increase them. Briefly the head of the Ustvymlag camp, Tarasiuk treated *zeks* as slaves, who consumed merely in order to increase productivity, like fuel in an engine. When the camp doctor advised him to attribute supplementary rations to convalescents to prevent them from getting pellagra, which leads to desquamation and inflammatory diarrhea, he was interrupted by Tarasiuk who asked, "How many of them will go into the forest and when?"

"None," was the reply, "but they could live and, once they have recovered, carry out light tasks."

"Then stop the anti-pellagra diet and put them on an invalid's diet."

All 246 convalescents died within a month. In his own way, Colonel Tarasiuk was a "fair boss," neither corrupt not a sadist, yet "no officer was detested as much as he was."[57]

While disdain for the lives of the prisoners wreaked more devastation in the gulag than in *laogai*, corruption occurred in both archipelagos, or at least from the 1960s where *laogai* was concerned. In both countries, the guards held back a sizeable share of the food delivered to the camp, helped themselves to a portion of the contents of any parcel addressed to a prisoner, and traded and bullied at their leisure. Anyone arriving in the gulag wearing decent clothes, or who hadn't managed to conceal that they had some money on their person, was liable to be shot in the back for "attempting to escape."[58] The head of the clinic at the Jiabiangou camp pocketed the prisoners' possessions when they died (such as a watch worth three times his monthly salary, as well as treasury bonds, etc.), and had no compunction about sending a patient to the morgue in order to appropriate his goods before time. If necessary, the prisoners carried out the dirty jobs for their bosses and shared the crumbs left over from the catch, such as the "rightists" who worked as sheep herders and declared every week that a goat had been killed by a jackal. After removing and sharing out the entrails, they would carry the dead animal back to the camp leaders who divided up the meat without asking too many questions. Others might obtain a day's leave to go into the neighboring town in exchange for a bottle of liquor purchased there—a fairly harmless form of corruption compared with the sale of a pardon. After Mao's death, corruption among cadres became widespread, as did the theft of agricultural and industrial equipment perpetrated by the guards. Such thievery was less severely punished than the slightest petty theft by an inmate, and was also less risky than at the apogee of totalitarianism, when fear of very severe sanctions restrained the guards, who were duly indoctrinated, just like the prisoners. I must however be wary of exaggerating the contrast between the two archipelagos, or of the Chinese archipelago past and present. In the early 1960s, Lai Ying was already shocked by the luxurious apartments of the camp commandants whose floors she polished. Such luxury remained modest compared with that enjoyed by Ivan Nikichov, who ran Dalstroy from 1939 to 1948, with the caviar, "exchanges of experience," and gifts between the commandants of the neighboring camps, who rivaled with each other in their ostentatious demonstrations of luxury and art.

Both archipelagos boasted of their cultural and educational activities, even theatrical performances. In China, Pu Yi, the former emperor of Manzhouguo (Manchukuo), played his own role in a supposedly historical play, while the New Life United Enterprises theater troop put on edifying performances in Guangdong province villages. In the gulag, *Uncle Vanya* or *The Seagull* or even *Camellia* (*La Dame aux Camelias*) were occasionally slipped into the repertoire, along with Gorky and other playwrights who "toed the line," or a selection of songs and dances that toured the camps. Foreign visitors were permitted to attend these plays and ballets, as well as to view special flowerbed arrangements prepared for them by the "cushy" *zeks*. In 1944 Nikichov and the "Queen of Kolyma" organized such a successful visit to Magadan for American vice president Henry Wallace that he declared the labor camps in the Soviet Union to be "fabrications." Not content with boasting about how cultured he found the Nikichov couple, Wallace's special advisor, Owen Lattimore, compared Dalstroy to "a successful blend of the American Hudson Bay Company and the Tennessee Valley Authority."[59]

Just as every Chinese province was obliged to maintain its model prison, so every camp had its solitary confinement cell (*CHIZO*, abbreviation for *chirafnoï izoliator*, or "disciplinary isolation" in the gulag), carefully concealed from outside eyes. In the forty-eighth Kvadrat camp located somewhere between Karelia and Arkhangelsk, between forty and fifty men were locked up in turn every evening during the winter of 1940–1941. In October of the previous year, near Krasnoyarsk, several thousand kilometers to the east, 285 prisoners out of 800 tasted that pleasure at one time or another. No bright lights here, just a small cell without windows or shutters, usually damp and never heated (in Siberia it was almost as cold inside as outside). The distance between the edge of the bed and the latrines near the door could be as little as half a step, but the cell could also be a mere pit without a roof (in the Soviet Union). In 1965 near Beijing, Wu Hongda was locked up in a cell 1.8 meters long by 80 centimeters wide, "scarcely larger than a coffin." He spent nine days in it, three of which without eating or drinking, and six without being allowed to go to the toilet. Other prisoners lived in huts the size of a sentry box, with no seat, bunk, or light, others in a sort of cupboard in which it was impossible to lie down. Others still were enclosed in wells, like Han Weitian, who moldered at the bottom of a dried-up well for nearly two years (1966–1968), somewhere in distant northwest China. Before he managed to dig a shelter for himself in the wall of the well with his nails, he lived in the middle of his excrement. He had no water to wash with and saw daylight for only a few minutes three times a day when one of the flaps covering the well was lifted to send down his subsistence rations. When he was finally allowed out of his well, he looked like a shaggy, skeletal ghost. It took nearly a year for him to recover his sight.[60]

Lai Ying may have broken the "cushy job" record by spending twenty-eight pampered months in her cultural squadron (see above), but Han did not break the punishment record (he was accused of setting fire to a grain warehouse, whereas he had merely been aware of the plot).[61] The competition came from another well/cell, in which no one could survive a single day, let alone two years. "It was a wooden construction resembling a well. The guilty party was placed in it, his head tightly bound to his knees. There was no door, just a round lid that was lifted in order to lower the prisoner, and then closed and blocked with wooded wedges. You could only fit one prisoner in the hole at a time, but since there was no heating in the winter, the cell freed up pretty fast. After an hour or two the punished *zek* was nothing more than a stiff, frozen corpse. We buried him as we found him, all curled up. The graves we dug for those corpses were special because they were round. During our first winter, the worst threat we could ever get was, 'You'll see if I don't send you to the round hole!'"

Being sent to the punishment cell, which often included being handcuffed, was one of the most feared punishments. In China, inside the cell or out, handcuffs could be twisted and placed with one arm bent under the arm pit and the other tied to the waist, or be replaced with a cangue, or more frequently with irons carrying weights of five, ten, or sometimes nearly twenty kilograms. Prisoners could also be whipped with a riding crop or dragged around in circles with a leash around their necks like a dog or donkey, their heads bent low. Zhang Xianliang, who was punished in this way, called it "photography," a name often given to another form of harassment in which the prisoner posed, as though for a photo, bare-chested (or sometimes entirely naked) and tied to a tree or a cement post, where he was left to be burned by the sun and devoured by mosquitos.[62] Such a session could last for several days, without food or water. Or prisoners might be deprived of blankets at night, or have to stand to attention without eating or sleeping for two days and two nights (a punishment nicknamed "repenting quietly"). Or be tied by their hands and hang in the air, a punishment called "catching a chicken by its feet," which was less painful than the "airplane," in which the prisoner was always bent at the waist and hanging by the hands, except that in this case they were tied behind his back. Even worse than the punishment cell was to have the duration of one's sentence extended—but how many prisoners had their sentences extended indefinitely without even the pretext of a punishment? A freed worker might be publicly executed as readily as a prisoner, though such executions were rarer than in the gulag. A certain Yang Baoying was executed in 1970 however, and his brain was taken by the executioner to be eaten raw by the captain's father, who was convinced it had therapeutic virtues.

Did the prisoners never revolt? That question has been asked countless times including with a hint of a reproach when addressed to the Jews who had no idea that they were being sent to the gas chambers. I will merely refer those people interested in the question to chapter 24 of the comprehensive survey of the gulag by Anne Applebaum and the more specific study by Martha Craveri.[63] Major revolts shook the gulag, ten years after those in Treblinka and Sobibor. Stalin's death, Beria's reforms and fall, the massive strikes in East Berlin, and the presence of united colonies of Ukrainians, Balts, and Poles among the *zeks* provided fertile ground for triggering a series of protest movements, some of them lasting, which, in May and June 1954, culminated in the Kengir revolt in Kazakhstan.[64] On the Chinese side, far smaller revolts and riots broke out, especially in the early days, including even before the regime was founded, in the Communist-controlled zones of Manchuria. They erupted again with the

Hundred Flowers and later the Cultural Revolution. Wei Jingsheng's refusal to allow himself to be indoctrinated, as admirable as it was obstinate, illustrates the summits that can be achieved by the spirit of resistance.[65] In order to understand that, we must delve into a final section on hell.

Thought Reform

I may have given the impression that the living conditions in *laogai* were slightly less inhumane than in the gulag, and that prisoners there had a better chance of survival for longer.[66] The only comparison that could give some substance to that impression is the one I spontaneously made when reading Zhang Xianliang, Wu Hongda (Harry Wu), Liao Yiwu (despite repeated executions), and even Pu Ning. I would sometimes say to myself, "Now that reminds me of Varlam Shalamov and Eugenia Ginzburg's Kolyma," or, more frequently, "That is really a little less terrible," and exceptionally, "That's worse." There was one exception however, and a massive and recurrent one, and that was "thought reform," or to put it more crudely, brain washing.

Expressions such as reform, reeducation, remolding, or correction through labor were already present in Bolshevik propaganda as well as in the writings of its founders. In the *Critique of the Gotha Program*, Marx and Engels viewed forced labor as the sole means of improving criminals. Dzerzhinsky, the founder of the Cheka, immediately confirmed that: the camps would be nothing like the capitalist prisons and penal colonies, they would be "schools of labor." During Dzerzhinsky's lifetime, Bogdanov theorized about the ethical aspect of the gulag, "Early penal policy focused on re-education, rather than punishment, at least for common criminals and those with minor offenses."[67] That ambition faded after the Great Turn, but that was no reason to stop boasting about its merits. The same year as the Great Turn (1929), Gorky took up the subject in his essay on the Solovetsky Islands, where he had just visited a camp—sorry, an institution for education and rehabilitation—which, needless to say, was shown in its very best light. In the long term, Gorky claimed, such a system, and incidentally one that capitalistic and so-called cultivated Europe would be well advised to adopt, would make prisons unnecessary. They would quite simply be abolished. The "transformation of human nature" (still Gorky) supposedly carried out in the camps would remain a good propaganda argument for the outside world. For internal usage, Yagoda was far more frank: "Soviet policy will not allow the construction of new prisons. ... The construction of large camps, ... which will make rational usage of labor, is another matter. We have a great difficulty in attracting workers to the north. If we send thousands of prisoners we would be able to exploit the resources of the north. ... The Solovetski experiment shows what we could do in this domain."[68] It soon became a priority for such camps to be self-financing and to contribute to national production—apologies again, I mean "socialist construction"—but that was rarely achieved; the gulag was simply not profitable. The spiritual transformation of the *zek* into a *Homo Sovieticus* nevertheless continued to be brandished in articles and works of propaganda, such as the infamous collective work (for which Gorky was editor-in-chief) called *The I.V. Stalin White Sea—Baltic Sea Canal*, about the canal that had been dug solely by prisoners. Some of the prisoners had even surpassed themselves and were given the title of *udarniks* ("dynamic workers"), which entitled them to be rewarded with extra food.

When the canal was completed, more than twelve thousand prisoners were even granted early freedom, something that was celebrated in the media, although not as much as Stalin's triumphant journey down the "canal named after him" in a steamer. That was the last event to trigger such media frenzy. After that the camps continued to be known as "corrective labor" camps, and *zeks* were even encouraged to be Stakhanovite workers and earn their brigades a red flag, but there was less emphasis on the spiritual transformation of the "fascist degenerates" and other Trotskyist terrorists. Instead there was a tendency to conceal the existence of the camps. It cannot however be claimed that the concept of rehabilitating prisoners was a Chinese invention. It coexisted, like so many other things, in an assortment of imported recipes. But in the gulag, reform through labor aimed at the very most, in the words of a disciple of Vishinski, to transform "human material of a lesser quality" (which recalls, "man, the most precious capital") into fully qualified, active builders, informed about socialism.[69]

The Chinese, however, aimed far higher, even if the obstinate pursuit of reeducation went hand in hand with a good dose of hypocrisy. A dual indigenous influence was superimposed onto the Soviet model. First, there was the Chinese concept of malleable human nature that could be shaped through indoctrination sessions that were supposed to inculcate each participant with respect for, and the practice of, Confucian ethics. In addition to this age-old tradition, the Chinese Communists added another, more recent one, inherited from the iconoclastic thinkers during the end of the Chinese Empire and the beginning of the Republic. As early as 1906, Liang Qichao advocated the purge and reconstruction of the spirit of the Chinese masses, bogged down as they were in Chinese practices that were as deep-rooted as they were pernicious. A decade later, the harbinger of the May Fourth Movement and future founder of the Chinese Communist Party, Chen Duxiu, similarly insisted on the urgent need to "reform" or "overhaul" the minds of Chinese youth. Neither Liang nor Chen meant using force to achieve their goal. By adding coercion, the CCP intended to combine Bolshevik methods with Chinese moralism.

As with so many Soviet institutions, the name gulag is an acronym. It condenses three words meaning quite simply chief administration of corrective labor camps. In China the purpose was stated right away. As we have seen, *laodong gaizao*, condensed to *laogai*, means to reform or reforge through labor (see above). That was merely an extension of "thought reform" (*sixiang gaizao*), carried out in prisons for as long as necessary to make criminals aware of their crimes. After that, as new men or women, they could leave for *laogai* to be rehabilitated. In the camps themselves, the brigade or cell chiefs were seconded by study chiefs, which was never the case in the gulag.[70]

Prison may have been hell in the Soviet Union,[71] but in China. ... Thought reform lasted on average between seven and eight hours a day, sometimes more. Even in the camps, it occupied another half hour to two hours per evening after the meal. The working day was therefore a little shorter in *laogai* camps than in the gulag. Once the prisoners' thoughts had been reformed in prison and they recognized their errors, they could rest a little, if not relax, during study sessions in the camp. Much of the time in prison not devoted to thought reform was spent in study (*xuexi*). The "criminals" were also students, to be inculcated with theory (or have it drummed into them). That simply consisted of reading out loud and discussing a body of works comprising the sacred texts of Marxism-Leninism and Maoism, and the equally sacrosanct history of the CCP, to which were added various propaganda brochures, newspaper articles, recent statements by the Politburo, and so forth, depending on current events. Since the levels of the so-called students varied enormously, a text could be repeated ad nauseam until the very last prisoner knew it more or less by heart.

Study was merely a tedious pastime compared with the other integral parts of thought reform: criticism, self-criticism, and mutual criticism for the purpose of improvement. That is what was known as "mutual assistance" (marvelous euphemism!) and one of the worst ordeals of imprisonment. If a prisoner did not give in immediately and recognize his crimes, he would be endlessly harassed by the cell head, "Admit to your crimes!" and then the other prisoners would take over and continue the interrogation in a highly charged atmosphere of shouts and threats. Since the criminals were also patients, it was not enough for them to admit to their errors; they had to undergo a thorough transformation of their concepts, their moral or religious values, and in fact their very "conscience." In other words, a prisoner had to "participate in the destruction of his personality."[72] That's all well and good for the political prisoners, you might say, but what about ordinary criminals, the mere thieves or pickpockets? Well they too had to be made aware of the fact that their behavior was, in essence, capitalistic, antisocialist, and counterrevolutionary. The source of all crime lies in pernicious ideology, and laziness or simply negligence in laogai was proof that the prisoner had not changed his bad ways.

Once the "criminals" confessed and completed all the interminable stations of the cross, or "gone through the pass" (that was the term used) and glimpsed the radiant light on the other side, then everything became easier.[73] They were then ripe for the trial, which was a mere formality. As in the Soviet Union, the sentence was decided in advance. The accused merely had to recall their crimes and thank the socialist state for delivering them from their evil mistakes, killing the "old" in them and allowing them to be born again and discover a new life. Should they deny or underestimate the seriousness of their crimes, the judge immediately reminded them of the "correct" version and threatened them with an even heavier sentence. In theory the accused could appeal, but to do so would be proof (as we saw above) that even more reeducation was required and therefore a harsher sentence.

In appearance at least, the dehumanization enterprise was successful. It kneaded and shaped individuals until they renounced their values and adopted others ... or feigned to do so. Once Lai Ying had served her sentence, she spouted all the expected balderdash: "I was wrong to claim that no relationship existed between politics and religion"; "the Catholic Church is the secret weapon of the imperialists." When her judges were satisfied with her correct replies they asked her to spy on her fellow Catholics, both priests and laypersons, but she immediately disappointed them. In his memoires, Wu Hongda described himself and his fellow prisoners as zealous, eager to praise the Communist Party's latest exploits and persecute the wretches whose turn it was to be criticized, displaying a compliant attitude in all circumstances in order to survive. Liu Binyan described the "struggle sessions" (*pidou hui*) during which every participant contributed to the mutual criticisms. Yet scarcely was the struggle session over than the prisoners got back together again quite happily, like tolerant, affable accomplices, or old friends who had been subjected to similar ordeals. If we are to believe Constantin Risov, who was imprisoned in China first under the Nationalists and then under the Communists, "The Chinese have an infinite capacity for resistance. They are like a branch that bends without breaking, and can patiently tolerate the worst ordeals. They are blessed with a more flexible and passive character than Westerners, and perfectly play their roles in criticism and self-criticism, shouting and swearing when they have to, but also able to show imperceptible signs of friendship to the very person they have just dressed down."[74]

Up to now, we have discussed apparent submission, where the attitude on display complied in every way with the prescribed standards, but did not affect the person playing the required role. Each person's integrity was respected. The case of Zhang Xianliang, to stick with that example, although it was far from the only one, was more troubling.[75] No one was more vehement than he in condemning the violence carried out by the authorities in their relentless attempts to flush out a person's most intimate thoughts; scraping and scouring his brains and scrutinizing them under a microscope, even denouncing and punishing the "stinking capitalist complacency" of a prisoner merely caught cooking a rat to eat. Thanks to Zhang we have a description, even a mocking one, that is clear yet discreet, of certain rites such as the "ranking" (or "alignment") of thought. Once a month or every two months, the prisoners were placed in new categories depending on the improvement in their thinking. The worst in class were pushed to the back of the group and would stay there until the next "alignment" when some other offender to the standards of pure reason (apologies to Kant) would replace them in disgrace. It was Zhang too who sympathetically described a Muslim fellow prisoner who felt protected by his faith and confided to him, "A man like me can never be reformed in his lifetime"; "I will never be like them, dogs who bite dogs." At the same time, Zhang or prisoner Zhang Yonglin, the character who takes on his own reactions, does not emerge unscathed from the experience he was subjected to. Since the author describes the hero's mind-set ironically and at a distance, the reader is never quite certain of what is sincere and what is simply survival strategy. After managing to escape from the camp, Zhang returns to it the very same day. "My 'thoughts' told me that I should return to the labor camp. After all those study sessions, my thoughts were on such an elevated level that they refused to think it was wrong to send me in to do hard labor" (he had been imprisoned because of a poem composed in 1957 in response to Mao's appeal to intellectuals to express themselves). "I could only think that my unwillingness to do labor reform was wrong." As soon as he was back in the camp, the self-interest and irony that had been perceptible from the start returned to the fore, "My thoughts informed me that I should write a self-examination."

Nevertheless both his labor camp memoirs and the novels based on his camp experience are littered with expressions of the guilt he felt (sham, ironic, or contrite?) at having been born into a privileged class condemned by history, and of being a twisted intellectual.[76] In comparison, the descriptions, which incidentally are very moving, of the goodness of simple people (carters, agricultural workers) illustrate a popular Maoist theme far more efficiently than the best sellers of official literature. The reader sometimes feels that Zhang has gone through his own thoughts with a fine-tooth comb in order to purge them of any bad (i.e., bourgeois) tendencies with the same energy that he might have devoted to delousing himself or scraping the mud off his shoes. Which is the real Zhang Xianliang, one sometimes wonders: that acutely perceptive master of sarcasm who acutely discerns every disguised lie and rebels against what he is being turned into; or that poor, crushed, and masochistic wretch, who appears to have been converted? I believe that the first description carries the day and that his exceptional memory and writer's sensitivity enabled him to recall with great clarity the trials that he endured as well as his feelings at various moments during his twenty years of captivity. Yenna Wu diagnoses a fault line in one of his characters, a dislocation reminiscent of the "fragmentation" identified by Tzvetan Todorov, not in the victims but in the torturers, who "subdivide their lives into sealed compartments."[77] The author, doubtless also momentarily broken and fractured by the experience, later came to believe, rather like

Primo Levi, that the experience had given him a deeper understanding of human nature and the relationships between human beings.

Some Westerners who were imprisoned in the first years of the regime also felt that they had been "improved" and even regenerated in prison. The Rickett couple arrived in China in October 1948, three months before Beijing surrendered to the Communists, so they saw only the collapse of the old order, which confirmed their dislike of Chiang Kai-shek and his regime. At the university where they were studying under a Fulbright scholarship, they were less surprised by the students' enthusiasm for the revolution than by the speed with which numerous teachers and intellectuals, whom they had perceived as liberal, rallied to the new regime's views. They gave accounts of this as well as the students' poor diet, to the US Consulate, and after it had closed down, to the British Consulate. That was what their "spying" consisted of. Allyn Rickett, who was an intelligence officer during the Pacific War, spoke Chinese and Japanese. He was arrested during the Korean War and spent a little over four years in prison (1951–1955), while his wife spent two and a half years (1952–1955), preceded by fourteen months of house arrest. Their imprisonment convinced them not only that they had committed a crime (by "interfering in internal Chinese affairs"), but that they were egotistic (living in the intellectuals' ivory tower). *Prisoners of Liberation*, the book the subsequently wrote, expressed their gratitude to their jailers, who had made them into better and happier people.

Did brainwashing therefore work for them, at least for a time? It was a fairly long period of time in fact, since they didn't deny it in the second edition of their book (1973), originally published in 1957, albeit with some subtle differences. On rereading their book, "We were both struck by how much we are still in agreement with its content";[78] "what we learned during our prison experience had made us far happier and more active people than we otherwise would have been."[79] Moral improvement and disinterest were mentioned throughout the original edition. They described their jailers, who were avowed atheists, in the garb—the cassock—of new preachers who inculcate and practice Christian values. The reader constantly sees the comparison and finds confirmation of it when Adele Rickett writes, "From childhood I had attended church ... I called myself a Christian. But now I wondered: had I ever lived as a Christian? ... In the new China people were urged to put the common good ahead of personal interests. This was the whole basis of our thought reform in prison. Here was a concept of Christianity being put into practice as I had never seen it done at home."[80]

I can't be content with the spontaneous sarcasm I have allowed to slip through here and there. However much I feel that the two authors sometimes uttered absurdities,[81] I have to admit that they were sincere. They were also courageous, since they were reporting under jeers and sometimes insults in a country that had barely recovered from McCarthyism. I'll even go further and admit that in the very early days of the regime, many Chinese, moved by nationalism (they could hold their heads high at last), and by adding faith to the "serve the people" concept that was being drummed into them, may have truly felt that they were starting a new life. It pains me to agree that at the outset everything was not reduced to the posturing and play-acting that China has endured in abundance for half a century, but I'll resign myself to that. In turn, I will allow that terrible and frustrating account to "brainwash" me.

But what have I conceded in fact? First a banality that was just as valid for the preceding revolution. In the early days many Russians, even Pasternak himself, believed in it or were enthusiastic about it in one way or another. Then, with regard to the Chinese revolution, which, as I have insisted from the outset, was, "closely inspired by the Soviet model, ... Chinese totalitarianism [was] both more public and more internalized than Stalinist totalitarianism, which remained the inevitable reference."[82] The Chinese revolution was therefore more ambitious, since it aimed to change man rather than merely pretend to. The greater the ambition, the harder the fall. I am quoting myself again, this time from Mao's obituary, where I accused the "great educator" of having "fabricated bitter and skeptical people at a productivity rate worthy of the official statistics during the Great Leap Forward." The loss of fervor and the rise of rampant cynicism were on a par with the original expectations, and that is still the case in China today. Nothing surprising here, a prisoner subjected to the same treatment as Allyn Rickett during his first weeks in captivity may be taken in for a while—but after four years? Those whose eyes were not opened by the deadly hecatomb of the GLF had a harder time keeping them closed during the manipulations, about-turns, brutality, and crimes of the Cultural Revolution.

Up to a point however, and for a time, totalitarianism "works."[83] It even worked in the gulag, where Eugenia Ginzburg grew irritated by the aggressive faith of some prisoners, convinced they were the sole victims of an error that Stalin was quite unaware of. They belonged to the impenetrable "iron front" species, of whom Solzhenitsyn said that they "went around the ironworks only to return as ignorant as when they set out."[84] Even more so in China, not only in *laogai* but beyond the camp walls. Recalling the classic joke among *zeks* about how the "little zone" of the camp was set inside the "big zone" in which the supposedly free Soviet citizens lived, Jean-Luc Domenach rightly observed that the "free" were far more tightly trammeled in China. There was no equivalent in the Soviet model to the ambition and efficiency of the control carried out by the *danwei*, the work units to which each and every citizen was attached. This meticulous control over a population of 600 million (at the time) was further reinforced inside the camp. In support of the degree of perfection achieved by *laogai*, which he believes superior to that of its Soviet model, Domenach mentions how rare it was for the prisoners to have conversations with each other (they were forbidden to exchange the slightest information about the crimes they had supposedly committed) as well as the limited scope of the few revolts that were hardly comparable with those that shook the gulag in 1953–1954 (see above). While admitting that after the initial success, the Maoist prisoner dehumanization enterprise failed, Domenach regards *laogai* to be worse than the gulag because it was more ambitious in scale, and more personal, entailing worse horror. That is one of the very rare conclusions of this valuable study that I don't agree with, which does not mean that I believe the opposite to be true. The two systems evolved. From 1923 to 1930, there was only a pre-gulag, far less terrible than what followed or the Chinese *laogai*. The real comparison must be made for 1930–1953, even 1956, and 1950–1978. During those years hunger, terror, and war were the criteria for "worse" or "less bad" that were as decisive factors, or more so, as thought reform, the worse periods being 1933, 1938, and 1942–1943 in the Soviet Union, and 1950–1952, and especially 1959–1962, in China. Having made that point, I willingly admit that the hermetically sealed universe in which prisoners could either "die or survive by renouncing their very being"[85] had never been as perfected as it was in the *laogai* camps between 1952 and 1959. And it is thanks to Domenach again that I owe my understanding of the crisis in *laogai*, and its decline in the 1960s and 1970s, during Mao's lifetime. After the death of the two dictators the camps survived—and still exist in China today, although *laojiao* was recently abolished, but in a very watered-down version, albeit still a deadly one.

***

Whether the gulag or *laogai*, a far more serious disagreement than the one previously mentioned on the morality of the prisoners with the "cushy" jobs, pits Solzhenitsyn yet again against most former convicts. Nearly all of them would unhesitatingly concur with the lesson Varlam Shalamov learned during his long years as a convict: "the camp is a negative school of life; … the prisoner learns to loathe work; … he learns how to fawn and lie, to indulge in low deeds (great or small); becomes selfish; … his focus of interest grows shoddy and primitive. The moral barriers have been pushed back out of sight" (see above). Eugenia Ginzburg echoed this when she was arrested for a second time in October 1949 (just as the "new era" was dawning in China). "In '37, I became aware for the first time of my personal responsibility in all the crimes perpetrated, and I dreamed of purifying myself through suffering. Now in '49, I knew that suffering can only serve to purify below a certain dose. When it stretches out over dozens of years and becomes an integral part of your life, it no longer purifies you. It transforms you into a piece of wood." And in the other archipelago, "Jin Hua looked at me with pity but also with disgust. I deserved that look, so full of reproach. Those years of living side-by-side with thieves, murderers and rapists had transformed me." Or simply "Morals my ass, there aren't any morals in the camps!" Let us return to the *zeks* and allow Margolin, a doctor in philosophy, to present us with a paradox: "To be here, a person must not have committed a crime; a person's mere presence in those places, made each of us a criminal." Even a guard, after supervising the Bamlag *zeks* and chasing escapees at night, said, "The BAM (abbreviation of Baikal-Amur) reeducated me. I saw things differently. The BAM turned me into a criminal. … It's a job that leads to crime. … The past seemed like dream. I could not even believe that I had once lived in Moscow and been free." Free—he sounds like one of his prisoners! Finally, let us return to a century before the gulag to hear the complaints of one of the most famous former convicts, "Who has ever been corrected by hard labor?"; or escape to another totalitarian hell: when the women of Birkenau were given enamel basins, they had three uses for it: their daily bowl of soup, to relieve themselves in at night, and to wash themselves when there was water. As Primo Levi observed, "the transformation of humans into animals was on the right track," before concluding that "an inhuman regime extends and spreads its inhumanity …

especially downwards, and unless it meets with resistance and exceptional personalities, it corrupts even its victims and opponents."[86]

Primo Levi's exception for "exceptional characters" is precisely what Solzhenitsyn claimed. He recognized that "Yes, the depravation in the camps was a mass phenomenon"; "Experience taught the convict that in the struggle to survive, the best method is cheating"; "Your head grows full of miserly calculations"; "Compared with prison, our camps are damaging and pernicious"; they are "the scabies of the soul"; "If you treat a man like a pig for seven year, he'll end up grunting" (Dmitry Pisarev). Nevertheless, Solzhenitsyn held that no camp would deprave a person with a steadfast personality, that "losing one's freedom is less hard for a person with a rich inner life," and that "detention is a good place to think," and being deprived of everything confers a "fundamental freedom: no one can deprive you of your family or your possessions, you have already been deprived of them"; "your dried-up former soul, is irrigated by suffering," "you no longer make categorical judgments, ... you have measured your weaknesses so you can understand those of others." That a minority may benefit from imprisonment and find that it "profoundly regenerates man" and "enriches one's being," according to Solzhenitsyn, seems to have been confirmed by Eduard Kuznetsov, who wrote to his fiancée from the camp, "Here there are far fewer frivolities and less agitation. I feel a veritable transformation. Here we can listen to the voices that come from our inner selves and which, in comfort and ambition, are stifled by the external racket."[87]

Like Nicolas Werth, quoting a former *zek* interviewed in Magadan ("the camp is a school of decomposition for all, and people leave it irremediably damaged"), I remain more receptive to the arguments of almost all the former convicts quoted above. But what does our opinion matter, and are we even permitted to confront it with the viewpoints of those who know what they are talking about? Who would refute Solzhenitsyn when he says that he was improved by his years in the gulag, without which, he assures us, he could have remained an ordinary Soviet man? "Throughout my conscious life [before the gulag], I had never understood either my own being or my aspirations. ... In my worst actions, armed with the best arguments, I was convinced that I was acting correctly. ... When people talk to me about the insensitivity of our high-ranking officials or the cruelty of the torturers, I can see myself with my captain's stripes leading my battery of men across Prussia ravaged by fire, and I say: ... blessed are you prison, blessed is the role that you played in my life!" Whether or not we agree with him, how can we not find him endearing when he then adds, "But a voice answers me from the tombs: you can talk, you who stayed alive!" Which brings us back to Primo Levi, who believed that the best people did not survive the Nazi camps. I mentioned Primo Levi with regard to the majority viewpoint, but I should now add that like Solzhenitsyn, he drew up a "clearly positive" balance sheet of his deportation to Auschwitz. "What happened to me enriched my inner soul and strengthened me. ... Living, and then writing about and meditating on this experience, I have learnt a great deal about man and the world." So much so that he committed suicide?[88]

Mentioning Primo Levi leads me—obliges me—to correct an impression I may have given. The gulag and *laogai* were not extermination camps like those of the Nazis. Rather than the famous Arbeit macht frei (Work sets you free), it was Vernichtung durch Arbeit (Physical destruction through work) that characterized the Nazi concentration camps.[89] "While the Nazi institutions served as places of concerted, well-organized mass execution, their Soviet counterparts operated with more of a 'revolving door' mechanism. Millions died in the camp during the era of Josif Stalin, but even at the worst of times millions of others managed to survive them, with 20–40 percent of all convicts being released every year from 1934 through 1953."[90] Even though the numbers could on occasion be ten times those of civilians, the mortality in the camps was on average only four times higher than that of the Soviet citizens overall. "Sometimes, the soon-to-be-dead even received medical help, which supported them for a while or even enabled them to survive."[91] There was nothing in the gulag or the *laogai* camps that resembled the "selection" followed by the extermination of the weak and the sick, as practiced in the Nazi camps. And even more so during the Holocaust.

The "de-convoyed (unescorted or un-guarded) status" was inconceivable in a Nazi camp, but concerned at least 10 percent of *zeks* in one Soviet institution during the postwar years, and up to 30 to 40 percent in several large camp complexes. Prisoners benefiting from that status "had the right to unescorted movement outside of the camp zone, usually along a defined route" (Bell). For instance, they might go to Novosibirsk's largest factory complex, Combine No. 179, which they helped to construct. "Some looked at it simply as a taste of freedom, a respite from the Gulag's harsh conditions; others clandestinely visited stores and even movie theaters; and still others engaged in limited black-market or criminal activities in local towns. De-convoyed status could also facilitate escapes."[92]

The shortage of personnel following the inflow of prisoners to the camps in 1938, exacerbated by the enrolment of many guards into the Red Army during the war, were among the reasons for resorting to the practice of de-convoyed prisoners. More broadly, "the prewar Soviet bureaucracy was hardly modern. It was a ramshackle collection of inefficient, overlapping personal fiefdoms inherently incapable of developing a single strategy or even outlook."[93] Incapable too of competing with German hierarchy, discipline, and efficiency? Certainly, as well as with the inhumanity of the Aryan superman with regard to the Slavic, Jewish, or Gypsy *Untermensch*.

9. Dictators

"Marxism-Leninism recognizes that leaders play a considerable role in history. To deny the role of the individual or of forward-looking people and guides would be a great mistake" (*People's Daily*, 5 April 1956). That belated Chinese reaction to Khrushchev's speech at the Twentieth Congress of the CPSU was inspired, if not dictated, by Mao.[1] While defending his own record, Mao was confirming his tendency to attribute anything he wanted to a doctrine that, rather than celebrate great men, preferred to celebrate the masses, who at best could accelerate the course of history.

Let us forget the Marxist reference. The disdain for a history that focused on kings and battles, which the Annals School was suggesting to the apprentice historian that I was at the time, should have prevented me from ever emulating Plutarch. Nevertheless I shall devote an entire chapter to the parallel lives of two illustrious monsters.

I will start anecdotally with their appearance and presence. Mao's height, which made him stand a head higher than most of his rivals, was an advantage, as was the romantic appearance conferred on him by his penetrating gaze, long hair, and slim body—before middle-age spread dissipated any hint of romanticism. Stalin suffered from being short and having a pockmarked face as a result of smallpox, as well as a crippled left arm due to an accident during his teens in Gori.[2] Official photos and portraits were touched up to remedy those imperfections. They made him appear taller than Lenin and gave substance to the image of a good-natured and benevolent "father of the people."

Both were night owls. They slept for part of the day and imposed their rhythm on their entourage. Mao could easily call a meeting in the evening, read and write all night, and then sleep until two or three in the afternoon. He could also stay awake for twenty-four hours at a time if not more, and fall asleep at any time of the day. Those long evenings sometimes ended in drinking binges for the one (when drunk Kliment Vorochilov, Anastas Mikoyan, and the others might conceivably reveal their true feelings) and in debauchery for the other, whether in Zhongnanhai (the Chinese leaders' residence in Beijing), the provinces, or Mao's special train.[3] Mao was born in the south and disliked both Beijing and its climate. He traveled as much as he could to the provinces but rarely to the northern ones, and spent months on end in Hangzhou—especially when he did not want to ratify measures taken by his subordinates. Or alternatively when he was hatching a plot against them, as for instance during his absence from Beijing from November 1965 to July 1966, on the eve of the Cultural Revolution. Stalin, the Georgian, was even more of a southerner, but traveled less frequently. When he left Moscow it was for a long summer working vacation by the Black Sea. The way the two leaders traveled and their lifestyle in their various residences cut them off from the daily lives of their people, and for their part they made no attempt to get in touch with them. Stalin exempted himself from kolkhoz and factory visits, and a Russian cliché ("Potemkin visits") best describes Mao's "field surveys"[4] during which he was told exactly what he wanted to hear, until he finally stopped visiting any Commune or factory at all. But he didn't stop visiting altogether, for when he was seventy-seven he found the strength to travel to five provincial capitals in order to find out more about (and undermine) the relationship between his appointed successor, Lin Biao, and the regional officials and military commanders.

Neither leader was a good orator, and their strong regional accents (Georgian and Hunanese) made matters worse. At least Stalin's straightforward didacticism was appreciated by those he sought to mobilize. He was able, on occasion, to find the right words to sway his audience and spur crowds to action, as during his famous speech of 4 February 1931 when he repeatedly hammered in his leitmotif, "To slacken the tempo would be to fall behind, and the backward get beaten. ... We have fallen behind the advanced countries by fifty to a hundred years. We must close that gap in ten years. Either we do this or we'll be crushed."[5] The Chinese were not prone to admitting that their country was even more backward than Russia, but at times, or on a whim, Mao was capable of doing so.

Most of the early Bolshevik leaders would have concurred with the summary judgment by one of the most brilliant and arrogant among them:[6] "Stalin? The most eminent mediocrity in the Party." A statement as lapidary as it was unfair, as they would discover to their cost. A little later, in 1919, the Peking University library assistant Mao Zedong was mixing somewhat uneasily with brilliant professors and thinkers, some of whose articles had reached his distant province of Hunan. Later, the Moscow-trained Communists would boast about their theoretical training, something that Mao himself lacked and tried to acquire in Yan'an by getting the Marxist classics translated. That effort, more assiduous and prolonged in Stalin's case, was just the bookish aspect of their intellectual research, underestimated by rivals who had benefitted from a more advanced education in their youth. Stalin first had to learn Russian before going to school in Gori. At least the Tiflis seminary, reserved for the most brilliant Georgian students, provided him with better schooling than any that Mao received. Mao graduated at the age of twenty-five from teachers' training school having first heard of America at the age of seventeen and read his first newspaper when he arrived in the provincial capital at the age of eighteen. At the age when Trotsky was writing *Results and Prospects*, Mao was still hesitating between Bolshevism, anarchism, and liberalism. He even dreamed of independence for his home province.[7]

Despite that, each of them was an intellectual—intellectuals who claimed to theorize without being theoreticians. Stalin read and reread a great deal, rapidly assimilated his reading and ended up with considerable knowledge in many domains. As he grew older, Mao was increasingly handicapped by the numerous lacunae in his narrowly Chinese education, and when his failures highlighted his limitations he preferred to return to the classics rather than broaden his culture. What limited and ossified both Stalin's and Mao's thinking, or caused it to deviate seriously, was first and foremost their doctrinal stubbornness and the self-assurance of those who have "succeeded." But both constantly sought to find meaning in the world, endlessly asking questions that others did not (e.g., the majority of Stalin's lieutenants or accomplices in the Moscow Politburo in the 1930s and the members of the Permanent Committee of the Chinese Politburo two decades later). Yet an apparatchik such as Liu Shaoqi learned from the disastrous experiences, and thanks to common sense, could see more clearly than the stubborn theoretician who wielded supreme power. The fact that Stalin's determination to acquire knowledge and skills enabled him to diversify,[8] albeit without altering entrenched views, was due to beliefs or failings that were not solely the result of intellectual aptitude. Proof of that can be found in Trotsky and how he locked himself into his almost immutable worldview, impressive to read about in Trotsky's journal of his period in France in 1934–1935. Access to education was easier for the son of a Georgian cobbler than it was for the Hunanese peasant, but both shared a concern for abstract reasoning about the situations facing the Communist movement, as well as a desire to understand the world and its future.

So both were intellectuals—*Lumpen-intellektuellen*, Marx might have claimed, especially with regard to Mao—but how many disasters and tragedies have resulted from the doctrinaire arrogance of intellectuals! Neither of them knew much about foreign countries, and had hardly traveled, Mao even less than Stalin. They knew more about their own countries—and Stalin more than Mao, thanks to regular and detailed reports by the political police—but their documentation was skewed by unreliable statistics, arbitrary prices, and so on. Consequently the two dictators were inclined to see the world through ideologically tinted glasses and to promote ideologically inspired projects without bothering with empirical verification. In 1929 as in 1958, planification had to obey voluntarist objectives dictated by an ideology that paid no attention to obstacles of any kind. That ideology altered the leaders' perceptions of reality, Mao's even more and for longer than Stalin's. Mao was doubly a slave, a slave to Marxist doctrine and to the Soviet model that he copied. Mao integrated Stalin lock, stock, and barrel, and repeated the dogma Stalin had revised or manipulated. True, he drifted further and further from the model because he claimed to be doing better. Stalin's frame of reference lay in the advanced capitalist nations he wanted first and foremost to catch up with, and then to surpass. Mao's frame of reference was mainly the Soviet forerunners, and the same optimism—and arrogance—required him to outstrip them while correcting their defects. Stalin the realist was the victim of his own illusions, as in 1929 when he set the objectives for the first Five-Year Plan.[9] Despite his cunning and the detours of his *realpolitik*, he too was a true believer, convinced that he was constructing the world of the future. Both were hungry for absolute power but neither wanted power for power's sake. They believed in their mission and thought they were working for a happy future by inflicting suffering or death on the living. Lenin was already prone to seeing the hand of the enemy behind any hitch or failure, but Stalin saw a traitor to punish. Every decision, every action that was later "rectified" required a guilty party, someone to blame for sabotage—or for having too perfectly executed the orders of the immoveable dictator who, by definition, was never wrong. Mao was never wrong either. He too was an expert in the art of finding scapegoats, such as the local cadres who were "responsible" for the failure of the GLF.

As a result of breakneck voluntarism and the haste with which those builders of a new world acted, the past resurfaced, having been renounced and condemned by the Bolsheviks, or, in China, by the precursors of the May Fourth period. It was clearer and more deliberate in Stalin, that admirer of Ivan the Terrible and Peter the Great, but even there it was mainly the logical consequence of his way of ruling and increasing centralization from the 1930s onward, for an autocracy requires an army and a secret police.[10] Mao didn't revert to the celebration of national glories and traditions as Stalin did, but he behaved like an emperor. We could (if only to appear to be invoking Marxist doxa or the sacred trust the two leaders conveyed) use a frequently proffered but ineffective excuse, and blame that return to archaism on the primitive society they were endeavoring to transform (and in doing so, violating). Mao did not shrink from using extreme means, for he was "as stubborn as a mule, and a steel rod of pride and determination ran through his nature," according to Agnes Smedley, a journalist sympathetic to the revolutionaries, who added after she first met the Master of Yan'an, that "an instinctive hostility sprang up inside me." Mao's model in the Kremlin had even fewer scruples, since he acted, as one of his best biographers has assured us, "with a barbaric determination that had few parallels in world history."[11]

What is the point in distinguishing between the two personalities? We cannot avoid taking them into account, starting with Stalin, "as wicked a man as has ever lived,"[12] but the close relationship between two regimes forged from a common matrix, enabled dissimilar personalities to mold themselves into a system in which everything leads to the fabrication of a dictator. In line with the Leninist logic, the Leninist regimes evolved as Trotsky had predicted back in 1904: "finally the dictator will act as a substitute for the Central Committee" to such an extent that the term "oligarch" is no longer appropriate for designating the other members of the leadership. Once the Number One has been invested with supreme power he is irremovable and takes increasing liberties even with "Leninist norms" (Frederick Teiwes). The ideology confers an undisputed prestige equivalent to that of the Czar or the Son of Heaven in the past.

On the pretext of celebrating their personality, the cult devoted to them was actually devoted to the position they held; it was the cult of the Number One, whoever he may be. That did not prevent the cult from reaching extravagant proportions, even at Lenin's expense, as in the official paintings depicting Stalin as taller than Lenin (they were roughly the same height) and lecturing the latter on political strategy, with Lenin apparently listening intently, unfazed by his professor's pipe (although he hated people smoking in his presence). *Pravda* quoted Stalin's works every day, all public meetings began with praise to his glory, his (embellished) photographic portraits hung everywhere, in homes, workshops, and offices, his biography was given as presents to children on festivals, birthdays, or memorial events—rather like a solemn communion ceremony for those addicts of the opium of the people. "Short of being called God on earth, Stalin has deified himself" (Service). He became an impersonal, catchall, icon, the greatest genius in universal history as well as the best and the most benevolent. Furthermore he was modest. Did not the "man with the head of a scholar, the body of a worker and the clothing of a simple soldier" (Henri Barbusse), endlessly protest against the excessive personality cult devoted to him? Robert Service concludes, "His cult had been the most grandiose in history."[13] Was Stalin's biographer blind and deaf to the still more fantastical paeans to the glory of Mao, and even to his thoughts? Since thought is immortal, that cult survived the author's death.[14] Adoration of the idol was so perfectly internalized by millions of Chinese that a future dissident like Dai Qing dreamed of being able to sacrifice her life in order to prolong the Chairman's even for one minute, and one young man, on the point of saving his mother from the ruins of the Tangshan earthquake, changed his mind when he noticed a portrait of the Chairman on the ground, and took the time to save the holy picture first. Let me repeat that in both cases, from Guangzhou to Leningrad, the cult was detached from the attributes of the person being glorified. The same qualities would have been conferred on whoever occupied that position.

That was not originally the case for Mao. His cult, initiated right from the Yan'an prelude, was a deliberate one, copied from the Stalinist model, which also paid justified homage to his strategic perceptiveness. His legitimacy was comparable to Lenin's, and Mao broached his governance with advantages that Stalin lacked. He did not need to plot and fight to impose his authority, still less to liquidate the old guard. At the same time, as I mentioned in an earlier chapter, the ten or twelve years prior to Stalin's supremacy preserved a degree of freedom in the Russian revolution that the Chinese never experienced. The Chinese revolution immediately started out with an additional disadvantage: it was Stalinist from the very beginning.

Before getting to the main point (the prize for monstrosity for Stalin and the one for inconsistency for Mao), I must briefly discuss the usually difficult relations between my two protagonists, since their "parallel" paths did cross (see Box 7).

Box 7

The Number One and His Emulator

It would be tempting to exalt the rise of the guerrilla fighter whose clear-sightedness finally enabled him to assert himself despite obstructions from a Comintern that was under Stalin's orders. But that would be incorrect, as would be the reverse. Depending on what seemed to be dictated by the Soviet Union's priorities and according to the snippets of information that reached him,[*] Stalin sometimes supported Mao, and sometimes his chiefs or his rivals. When the threats from Hitler and Japan convinced Stalin that he should consider setting up anti-fascist popular fronts, the CCP obeyed, but reluctantly. Mao first conceived of an anti-Japanese front *without* and against Chiang Kai-shek, whereas Stalin saw the latter as the best rampart against the Japanese advance on the Asian continent. Aware of China's weakness, Chiang wanted to

---

[*] In March 1930, the *Inprecorr*, the weekly organ of the Communist International, devoted a laudatory obituary to the peasant leader Mau (Mao Zedong), who died of tuberculosis.

strengthen his army and get rid of his internal enemies before facing external ones. When, in December 1936 in Xi'an, one of his generals (Zhang Xueliang) arrested Chiang in order to convince him that he must oppose the Japanese rather than his compatriots, Mao was exultant. The CCP praised Zhang's patriotism, whereas Moscow considered him a traitor in the pay of the Japanese. When Chiang was freed, probably against an oral promise to change tack, he was less inclined to tolerate repeated imperialist Japanese attacks on Chinese sovereignty, and the war broke out seven months later.

Throughout that interminable war, Stalin was far more preoccupied with ensuring the security of the Soviet Far East than supporting the Chinese revolution. He relied on the government in place to deal with the Japanese threat. At the end of the war (14 August 1945) he signed a Sino-Soviet Treaty of Friendship, Alliance and Mutual Assistance with the Nationalist Chinese government, which Mao considered treason to the revolutionary cause. One week after the signature, Mao felt betrayed again when he received two telegrams from Stalin, one after the other, urging him to negotiate with Chiang. Three months later, the Soviet Red Army ordered the Chinese Red Army to evacuate the territory along the Chinese Eastern Railway (returned to Soviet control under the 1945 treaty) as well as the large Manchu cities it occupied. The Soviet Red Army continued to occupy those towns until 1946 when the Nationalist army was ready to take over, which did not prevent the Soviet Red Army from covertly delivering weapons and ammunition to the Chinese Communists. Two and a half years later, when the Communists had almost won the civil war, Stalin sent Mikoyan to see Mao and advise him not to cross the Yangzi but to leave south China to Chiang Kai-shek. As far as Stalin was concerned, preventing a possible American military intervention (which did not occur) prevailed over the spread of Communism to the most densely populated nation in the world. When, in dire straits, the Nationalist government abandoned its capital in Nanjing and fled to Guangzhou, the Soviet ambassador was the only member of the diplomatic corps to follow suit.

As soon as he was victorious, Mao pursued his resolution to push China "to one side," in other words into the socialist camp. He had no choice, for the Chinese army and economy were too weak for him to manage without a Soviet shield at a time when he feared an American attack. On 8 December 1949, just over two months after he proclaimed the People's Republic of China, Mao (who had never left Chinese soil before) took the train to Moscow. However, Stalin first refused to repeal the treaty signed with Chiang in 1945 and replace it with a treaty of friendship and alliance between two fraternal Communist nations. Mao was kept waiting for three weeks and said impatiently to the Soviet general escorting him, "I've only three things to do here, sleep, eat and shit." Stalin gave in, possibly as a result of the recognition of the PRC by Great Britain on 6 January 1950. The treaty of "friendship and alliance" was signed on 14 February 1950, but Mao complained for a long time that he had to extract his subsistence from a tiger's mouth. At least the considerable technological and financial assistance granted by the "older brother" (the expression used at the time) enabled Mao to launch an ambitious first Five-Year Plan. In early 1950, Stalin authorized Kim Il-sung to invade South Korea, promising weapons but not soldiers. As soon as things took a bad turn, Stalin sent Mao a telegram asking him to supply the soldiers. He thus dragged a regime that had barely put down its roots into an external campaign, but was in no haste to provide the Chinese expeditionary forces with the promised air support.

Once Stalin had left the scene, Mao considered that he was the most prestigious revolutionary leader on the planet. As early as 1956, he put the Soviets in their place when they started making their disturbing (for him) revelations without even consulting him. That same year he inaugurated the Eighth National Congress of the Chinese

Communist Party by specifying that "in the course of its 20th Congress, the CPSU ... criticized its insufficiencies." The Chinese were not to assume that the posthumous criticisms being addressed to Stalin could be applied to other, living, Communist leaders! Mao now aspired to the title of master thinker of world Communism. I will not go into the voluminous material about Mao's maneuvers against Khrushchev's "revisionism," but many of his criticisms did not spare the late departed Stalin, starting with those targeting the manual of political economy published under his aegis and, more importantly, the development strategy Stalin put in place during his second Five-Year Plan. That strategy was implicitly attacked in the statement mentioned in chapter 2 (see above): "We cannot continue to follow the old paths of economic development of other countries and crawl behind them." At the time (the winter of 1964–1965), Mao was no longer content to assert the specificity of the Chinese way, he was preparing to show humanity the path that true Communism must take. The Cultural Revolution would proclaim that loud and clear to the rest of the world.

Whether embarrassed, reserved, or deferential toward Stalin, Mao still resented his treachery—even though he did not immediately understand the extent of it—and the fact that he promoted the interests of the Soviet Union above all. Mao considered himself to be far more internationalist than his master, which gave him a feeling of moral superiority. He even felt rivalry with Stalin and nationalist rivalry with the Soviet Union. Stalin appeared more concerned with sizing up this new client: would Mao be deferential and subjugated like the others, or would he be a potential Tito?

Sources: Roux, 2009, pp. 418–425, 535–538, 541–545, 593, and 732; Pantsov, 2012, pp. 299–301, 369–371, 376–381, and 426; Chen Jian, 2001, pp. 21–28, 32, 36, 49–61, and 85–90; Short, [1999] 2005, pp. 367–376; Westad, 2003, pp. 310–325; Li Huayu, 2006, pp. 3 and passim; Lüthi, 2010, pp. 35 and 38. More details on the Korean affair can be found in Chen Jian, 1994.

The Most Cruel

"Stalin is the greatest torturer in History. Genghis Khan and Hitler were altar boys compared with him."[15] I don't know about Hitler but Mao certainly. I'm exaggerating as Anna Akhmatova did, but less so than when I'll compare Kang Sheng (see Appendix) with Yezhov (usually he's compared with Beria). That's just a matter of degree, and if disagreements with many of my Sinologist colleagues are anything to go by, I'll doubtless have trouble convincing my reader. Mao inflicted indescribable suffering on his people, and his reign was a disaster for China (especially the last two decades, which is considerable for a total of twenty-seven years). Nevertheless I think it is necessary to qualify the equation that I have so often read or heard: Mao = Stalin = Hitler = Pol Pot. I'll stick to the first two in a defense that will stretch my capacity for persuasion to its limits.

Mao was responsible for the death of millions of people during the Great Famine. Two-thirds of them could have been saved if Mao had not relaunched the Great Leap Forward in the summer of 1959 in reaction to Peng Dehuai's justified criticisms. The Cultural Revolution killed more than a million people and persecuted dozens of millions of others. In addition to the victims of the Red Guards (teachers, the "bourgeois," Communist officials beaten to death, etc.) were the Red Guards themselves, killed by other Red Guards and later by the army, and lastly the "class enemies" massacred by the militia in 1967–1968. While Mao did not order those executions directly, he was nevertheless ultimately responsible, as he was for the quotas of national minorities (Tibetans and others) to be executed per city and per area following a revolt in western Sichuan during the winter of 1958–1959,[16] and (more conventional and on a far wider scale) the death of landlords and rich peasants during the Land Reform. He accepted responsibility for that and was even proud of it on occasion, as in his famous speech of 8 May 1958, when he nevertheless took care to incorporate the Party in a collective responsibility for the revolutionary movement as a whole: "You call us Qin Shihuang as an insult, but we've surpassed Qin Shihuang a hundredfold. ... He only buried 460 scholars but we buried 46,000 scholars."[17]

There is therefore no doubt about Mao's cruelty, and above all his insensitivity. They appeared right from the earliest stage of the revolutionary saga, during the creation and consolidation of the agrarian bases that gave rise to the Soviet Republic of Jiangxi (1931–1934). The silences and the fabrications of the Party's official history have long concealed the causes of the Futian mutiny of December 1930 and the extent of the repression that followed. In that small town in Jiangxi province, Communist officers revolted against what they called Mao's dictatorship and executed about a hundred of their Maoist comrades. Strategic disagreements and resentment between indigenous Communists and the Hunanese ones from Mao's entourage (two bordering provinces) explain in part—but only in part—the hostility of the mutineers to Mao's agents and their methods. The repression, which ended only in the spring of 1932, led to the execution of approximately one-tenth of the Red Army soldiers and officers and perhaps one-quarter of the political cadres, most of whom were innocent. All of them either confessed under torture to belonging to the Anti-Communist League or were denounced by others who were also tortured. Mao was not in charge throughout the entire period, but the purge slackened once a succession of emissaries from the Party's Shanghai leadership (which included Zhou Enlai) supplanted him at the head of the Communist base. It seems clear that both before and after the mutiny Mao left it to his officers to apply those "Stalinist" methods in order to implicate his adversaries and rivals.[18]

Let us fast-forward from the young Mao to an aging emperor (see Box 8).

Box 8

Exit a President of the Republic

On 5 August 1966, Mao scribbled these words on an old newspaper: "Bombard the headquarters: my *dazibao.*" They were immediately copied, reproduced, and disseminated around the country. That *dazibao* (big character poster) called on the Party and the masses to bombard the headquarters and free it from the bourgeois dictatorship that had infiltrated the Party summit. It was his way of letting people know that he had broken off with his Number Two, Liu Shaoqi, guilty of having tried to destroy the marvelous impetus of the Great Proletarian Cultural Revolution by sending working groups to contain student agitation on the campuses. Dispatching working groups into the field was the usual procedure every time the government had to deal with popular discontent or promote an official campaign. Liu had taken care to send Mao a telegram asking for orders (Mao had been away from Beijing since November 1965) but had received no reply. In July, Liu went to Hangzhou with Zhou Enlai, Deng Xiaoping, and a few others, to consult with Mao and beg him to come to Beijing and settle the problem himself. Mao preferred to leave the matter in Liu's hands. He returned to Beijing on 19 July without informing Liu and called a meeting on the 23rd in which he publicly criticized both Liu and Deng, whose working groups had sabotaged the great revolution under way. During the Eleventh Plenary Session of the Eighth Central Committee that ended on 12 August, Lin Biao replaced Liu as the Party's Number Two. Relegated to eighth place and therefore disowned, Liu offered his resignation but Mao turned it down. The Great Cultural Revolution needed an existing enemy on which to unleash its energies.

From that time on (August 1966), all Liu could do was to proffer his self-criticisms, appear before the "rebels," or endure the criticism of those around him, including his servants and his own daughter, under pressure from Jiang Qing who urged her to revive a denunciation that she considered to be insufficiently ferocious. During his last meeting with Mao on 13 January 1967, Liu asked to be relieved of all his functions and permitted to return to Yan'an or to his native village in Hunan to work with the peasants in a People's Commune. Mao did not reply. In August 1967, Liu was summoned to a large meeting to answer questions from the rebels, where he saw another defendant, his wife Wang Guangmei. That was the last time he saw her, for she was imprisoned the following month and released only in December 1978, two years after Mao's death. In September 1967, Liu lost the custody of his children (two of whom met with tragic ends during the Cultural Revolution). In the summer of 1968, while under house arrest, Liu contracted pneumonia and then learned a month after the event that the Twelfth Plenary Session (October 1968) had expelled him from the Party and dismissed him from all his posts. He was given medical care until the Ninth Congress (April 1969) because a live target was required, but that ceased immediately afterward, leading to an aggravation of his diabetes and high blood pressure and worsening his ongoing pneumonia. He survived, bedridden and covered in bedsores, until he was transported to Kaifeng where he was imprisoned in October 1969. His new guards didn't even know who he was; his physician was not permitted to give Liu the medication he needed, and Liu died of pneumonia in November the same year.

So who was this supposed incarnation of evil, held in contempt by millions of Chinese? He was a gray apparatchik, not particularly outgoing or affable, who had supported or flattered Mao on numerous occasions. Yet it would be hard to find a more decent man among all those who played an important role in any revolution since 1917. Mao had more charisma and was more interested in general ideas. Liu was more gifted for organization and governing, more methodical and conscientious. He was a hard worker, and was also more frugal than Mao (which wasn't difficult, but also more than any other leader), even ascetic. Liu enjoyed considerable prestige among everyone who had worked with him, and therefore with most high-ranking Communist cadres, which greatly perturbed Mao. What if the Chinese Khrushchev turned out to be a Brezhnev and obtained a majority thanks to his support in the hateful bureaucracy? Instead of which Liu never rebelled against the ukase that denounced him. Mao, after being criticized by Peng Dehuai in 1959, threatened to revolt and take part of the Red Army with him if his colleagues did not follow.

Liu suffered his martyr's fate in silence, but what exactly was he guilty of (by which I mean according to Mao; history would tend to reproach Liu for being too submissive)? He mostly obeyed, but being in change of the "first front" (see chapter 3), he was unable to apply the "second front" directives the way Mao wanted and with the results he required—or rather dreamed of. I believe Mao to have been sincere when he thought the policy followed by Li Shaoqi and Deng Xiaoping from the end of the GLF to the Cultural Revolution was a rightist deviation of the "line."[*]

Who was Liu and what was he trying to do?[†] "Far more orthodox than the ideological renegade denounced during the Cultural Revolution," he was also more pragmatic and flexible than the "iron Bolshevik depicted in the pre–Cultural Revolution and post-1980 media" (Dittmer). A partisan of socializing the means of production in 1949, an orthodox Leninist in matters of ideology and organization, Liu nevertheless tried to reconcile order and revolution, efficiency and equality. He was an engineer by training and stuck to technical tasks; he set up the institutions and endeavored to make them work. While in charge of the "first front," he pursued attainable goals. He first supported the launch of the GLF, before disasters and famine made him more flexible and open to experimentation in economic matters. That was how, at the head of a team that provided good support, he was able to pull the country out of stagnation. Mao left him alone, before denouncing him after the fact for the inevitable social consequences of a more flexible policy. Even after his fall, Liu remained faithful to his principles

---

[*]   I am endeavoring to use Mao's own misleading vocabulary when he described a struggle as being between two lines; that of the proletariat, which he led, and the bourgeoisie, incarnated by Liu. In fact no such struggle existed for the simple reason that there was only one political line (his), and it was not obtaining the fanciful results he hoped for. Circumstance and the wisdom of his lieutenants were equally to blame for this "deviation."

[†]   This paragraph owes a great deal to Dittmer, [1974] 1998, especially pp. 23, 99, 153, and 289.

and continued to comply with the standards—standards that were abolished in the Cultural Revolution. A criticized leader must make his self-criticism and accept the sanctions the Party deems appropriate, without betting an eyelid. Collective interest prevails over that of the individual, and Liu submitted uncomplainingly.

Ultimately, Liu Shaoqi's real fault (apart from being more moderate than his overradical leader) was to be the Number Two; his successor would also suffer from that. The disproportionate importance conferred on the army by the Cultural Revolution, like the precedent in the French Revolution, made a Bonapartist deviation feasible— but with one difference: Lin Biao was incapable of playing that role and probably did not aspire to it. Mao finally began to feel imprisoned by the scaffolding he himself had set up. Lin, who knew him from early days, fled to his death, terrified by the realization that Mao had decided to get rid of the successor he himself had designated.

Sources: Above all Dittmer, [1974] 1998 and 1981, then MacFarquhar and Schoenhals, 2006. On the Lin Biao affair, Teiwes and Sun, 1996; Jin, 1999.

That is the man I'm portraying as a choirboy in comparison with Stalin! In his thirties Mao let his agents take care of torturing his adversaries to make them confess to fictitious crimes and then execute them. In his early seventies, in Beijing and at the peak of his powers, Mao persecuted Liu Shaoqi and killed him slowly but refrained from having him shot. Marshal He Long, an early revolutionary veteran, died in prison the same year as Liu Shaoqi. The following words by Mao probably hastened his demise: "We used to say as far as He Long was concerned that he should (a) be denounced, and (b) be protected. ... Now it seems we can no longer protect him, because of the things he did that we did not know about." What he allegedly did, or to be precise, the fabricated accusation against him that Mao feigned to believe, was to have wrecked a people's army. The Central Case Examination Group (a body established in 1966 and comparable to the Cheka or the Gestapo) immediately prescribed medical treatment for patient He Long, which hastened his death. The only difference here with the physical "liquidation" of Stalin's adversaries is that Mao was happy to let others do the job and he abandoned his former companion He Long to his henchmen.[19]

I shall begin the impossible demonstration (Mao less monstrous than Stalin) with the most subjective, and therefore the most debatable aspect: a rough comparison of their personalities. Lucian Pye has described Mao as "a narcissist with a borderline personality."[20] He pointed out his extreme sensitivity to rivalry and criticisms, his implacable grudges, his lack of human warmth, and his inability to develop any significant human attachments. Stalin's character was even less "normal" and many traits identified by Pye could just as easily be applied to him: solitariness, pride, the feeling that his worth was insufficiently appreciated,[21] resentment, and an implacable holding of grudges and desire for vengeance. Stalin was even more pathologically distrustful than Mao; ultimately he wanted to "liquidate" everyone he was suspicious of. Add rudeness and brutality to that, along with disloyalty—in other words all the warning signs that Lenin saw, and was repelled by, in 1922. Mao was easily coarse, more deliberately so too, in order to demonstrate his disdain for politeness and convention. Last, as far as I know Mao never showed the same sadistic traits as Stalin, who enjoyed reading the NKVD reports about the last days of former allies he had sentenced to death. All in all they were both paranoid, if not depraved, with "the Kremlin Mountaineer" (Mandelstam) slightly more so than his Chinese counterpart.

As a transition between their characters, acts, and massacres, I have to concede that the indoctrination of their subjects was as monstrous (or more so) in China. Jean-Luc Domenach suggests that it was more so (see above), with *laogai* worse than the gulag. Similarly, Pierre Souyri wrote succinctly that "Maoism is the bureaucratic manipulation of crowds and a state instrument for reshaping thought in the most extreme form of totalitarianism." I'll admit that the Maoist relentless remolding of consciousness to purge patients of their reactionary thinking and cure them, often degenerated into a shared cynicism by which the patient pretended to see the light, and the doctor of souls pretended to believe his playacting. For the Stalinist NKVD, cynicism was acquired early on. There was no intention to forge a "new man," but rather to fabricate a "docile cripple," a "yapping dog, obedient, dull and cowardly" (Malte Griesse), which Griesse immediately qualifies: "Blackmail is never explicit, people are 'made to understand.' The Stalinist regime ... does not want free and aware actors who collaborate willingly and out of conviction. It prefers compromised persons who collaborate out of fear of being unmasked and punished. It relied on weakness and corruption rather than on moral strength."[22]

In China, execution quotas were more frequent in the early days, during the agrarian reform. They were more reminiscent of Lenin in 1918 ordering one out of ten hostages be killed, rather than Stalin in 1938, daily signing lists of people sentenced to death. In 1918 as in 1950, merciless leaders deemed such measures necessary to protect the fragile realm they had just acquired. Two decades later, in 1938, it was a matter of consolidating undisputed personal power and "liquidating" potential adversaries or enemies "just in case." Objection! Twenty (or nineteen) years later people were still being massacred in China. I mentioned earlier the executions of former landlords' children. Why did they occur? Since the tumult provoked by the Cultural Revolution continued unabated, Mao, the person ultimately responsible for it, used the army to put an end to the anarchy and set up "revolutionary committees" ready to replace the overthrown Communist Party at a moment's notice. In the capitals and main cities of two southern provinces (Guangdong and Guangxi), rival rebel organizations, each claiming to be following Chairman Mao, continued to fight, causing the establishment of Revolutionary Committees to lag behind. The central government consequently invented the myth of a clandestine counterrevolutionary army aiming to restore Chiang Kai-shek to power. Since such counterrevolutionaries were inevitably class enemies, the militia undertook to exterminate them, along with their male descendants.[23] That crime, almost as stupid as it was monstrous, was the consequence of the chaos induced first and foremost by Mao Zedong. The executioners' concern with killing offspring because they may one day be tempted to take revenge on the death of their fathers is comparable to the Stalinist preventative measures as protection against a hypothetical danger in the future.

So what enables me to distinguish between the crimes committed by two monsters? I believe that it was the appalling chaos that prevented Mao from controlling the details of the "operations" (I'm talking about massacres here) with the cold meticulousness of a Stalin. Ultimately Mao was responsible for them, but let us suppose something that has not been proven, namely that he ordered Zhou Enlai and Kang Sheng to spread the tale to the provincial Guangdong and Guangxi authorities, about a clandestine army striving to restore a regime that had been overthrown nineteen years earlier. The provincial leaders battling with the rebel armies in the cities then preferred to hand over the task of driving out and repressing the alleged plotters to the local authorities. After which the local militia, boosted by fanatical or careerist activists, went around the villages arresting and massacring the usual scapegoats dragged out at every political campaign, that is, their neighbors with bad social origins. They murdered unhesitatingly to protect themselves from any possible later vengeance from those people's sons when they grew up. This reconstruction of mine is as hypothetical as the sons' vengeance. I based it on research by Su Yang and what we know about the anarchy that reigned in China in 1967–1968. Conversely, reliable documents show that Stalin dictated Andrey Vyshinsky's brief to him during the Moscow trials, drew up Mátyás Rákosi's accusation against László Rajk, and wrote the editorial in *Pravda* denouncing the Doctors' Plot.[24] I'll admit that for the victims it was six of one and half a dozen of the other, but since we're comparing two dictators I must include their methods. On the one hand premeditated massacre, rigorous, bureaucratic, and meticulous control of a process launched and controlled by a single man (it being understood, however, that in 1937–1938 the execution of his orders and Yezhov's directives in the field soon escaped Stalin's control, and that the nature of the regime led the provincial and local leaders to compete in zealousness and execution quotas). On the other, a government in dire straits, overtaken by the cataclysm it had launched and local initiatives for which it was responsible but could not control. And, hovering above the disaster, an irritated and then angry Great Helmsman, "Good-for-nothings ... who cannot be trusted."[25]

In 1930s Soviet Union, "violence was used to profoundly transform Soviet society by means of an aggressive policy of social engineering, but also *in response* to a series of crises triggered by that same policy in a period of extreme tension" (Nicolas Werth). The second aspect described by Werth *in response* (the italics were in the original) to that "series of non-anticipated crises ... demanding an urgent response, usually totally improvised" could apply just as well to Maoist violence. In contrast, there is no Maoist equivalent to social engineering, that "vast prophylactic operation of social 'purification'" decided and planned by Stalin himself. That aimed to "eliminate by preventive action, all the 'socially harmful' and 'ethnically suspect' elements ... as so many potential recruits for a mythical 'fifth column' of saboteurs." Stalin cleaned up the cities, the showcases of socialism, purging them of the troublesome dregs (only instead of using that term he spoke of ("lumpen and socially harmful elements")) by deporting them to the refuse regions of western Siberia, the Great North, the Urals or Kazakhstan. A composite rabble that included hooligans, prisoners, peasants in search of work (or bread) in the cities, elderly invalids (room had to be made in the hospitals as well as in the prisons), and ordinary citizens who may have simply forgotten to carry their passports, were all packed off to some uninhabited (and uninhabitable) island in the Great North without having time to take any provisions or warm clothing with them.[26]

In addition to the "socially harmful" elements, Stalin was after any potential enemies (such as the Polish officers massacred in Katyn) in order to liquidate them before they harmed the homeland of socialism. In occupied western Ukraine (after September 1939), NKVD agents went through lists and report cards of pupils in school before the war broke out, and drew up "lists of individuals for preventative arrest, with at the top, the names of the most gifted pupils (whom they considered to be) potentially hostile to the Soviet government" (Nicolas Werth again).

Mao's concern with caring for souls and consciences inflicted infinite suffering and miseries, but did not derive from a project comparable to the Stalinist cure, which was the preventative elimination of anyone who could conceivably do harm one day (it happened in China too, but far less systematically and on an incomparably less massive scale).[27]

The "special populations" mentioned above, like the (nonexistent) "special villages" where the second-category kulaks ended up (see above) in 1930–1931 and all the other deportation locations for social and national undesirables sent to colonize the vast and inhospitable outer regions formed a kind of second gulag,[28] almost as densely populated as the other. One adult out of six was sent to the gulag at one time or another between 1930 and 1953 (see above), a proportion far higher than for *laogai* (including *laojiao*).

Of all the crises resulting from the two regimes' aggressive policies (the second aspect identified by Nicolas Werth), the most disastrous were the famines. There were many similarities in famine management; for instance, both regimes prevented starving peasants from fleeing their village or sent them back to a certain death, but there was one difference that concurs with my earlier observations. Most specialists agree that Stalin used (and aggravated) the famine in order to kill more Ukrainian peasants, whom he suspected of separatist nationalist tendencies (see above).

The end of the two "reigns" (a sinister one for Stalin, a horrific one for Mao) seems symbolic of each of their specific characters and historical

records. Stalin's opportune death may have prevented a new Great Terror
from being unleashed in the Soviet Union, yet the crowds flocked to pay
homage to the person they had just been liberated from, including Polina
Molotov, who wept when the news reached her in Siberia where that
same Stalin had deported her. Conversely Stalin would never have gotten
bogged down by the pathetic Lin Biao affair (see Box 8 on Page 304) nor
would the mass demonstrations of 5 April 1976 have even been possible
under him. Those demonstrations obliquely targeted Mao himself and
he certainly deserved it, but the fact that such a "counterrevolutionary
rebellion" (which was how he called it, once he learned about it the
following day) could occur *in his lifetime*, is enough to distinguish the
terror Mao inspired from the terror that prevented millions of Soviet
people from taking action between 1929 and 1953. In April 1976 in Beijing,
it was not a Ryutin affair,[29] but a demonstration by ordinary citizens who
were tired of being subjects. Among the countless homages, flowers,
and poems, ostensibly placed in honor of the late Zhou Enlai, were bold
slogans suggesting that the era of Qin Shihuangdi was over, as well as
allusions to Mao's boast (see above) about having massacred one hundred
times more scholars than that cruel dynastic founder.

Almost two decades earlier, in full Hundred Flowers campaign, Mao
had praised the discipline of the Nanking students who demonstrated
against his regime. "When they went through the doors of the official
building they stood in rows and chanted, 'Down with bureaucracy!'[30] Had
they behaved like that in front of Stalin, heads would have rolled. Yet not
one of them was a counterrevolutionary. They were good students and
there was indeed a bureaucracy!" Mao was showing himself in a good
light, but he was not wrong. Was it possible to imagine for one minute
that heads would not have rolled under Stalin?

From the "masses"[31] (in 1957 and 1976 in China, but silent in the
Soviet Union), let us turn to the lieutenants. In 1944, Mao asked to be
forgiven—or feigned his mea culpa—for the excesses of the 1943 witch
hunt (see Appendix). However his first instinct was not to put all the
blame on Kang Sheng and have him executed. Instead Kang was relegated
to less important posts for a time, for he could prove useful again before
and during the Cultural Revolution. Mao devoured fewer torturers
(Yagoda, Yezhov) and fewer innocent people than Stalin.

Even when he wasn't wallowing in the suffering he caused, Stalin's
lack of sensitivity to the "chips" ("when you cut wood, chips fly")[32] makes

it pointless to draw up a list of collaborators who were executed—instead of dying of ill-treatment or for lack of healthcare, like the unfortunate Peng Dehuai and Liu Shaoqi. He executed hard and fast Stalinists, not members of the old guard who might have become rivals. Many people in his entourage feared they were on a suspended death sentence, which made them even more obsequious. Kaganovich for one, whose three brothers were executed. Or Alexei Kosygin, who, when he said goodbye to his wife every morning between 1948 and 1950, reminded her of what she must do if he did not return that evening. The president of the Soviet Republic, Mikhail Kalinin, humiliated himself in front of Stalin and begged him to free his wife, who spent ten years in the gulag (she was freed after the war, just in time to see her husband die in 1946).[33] Polina Molotov had to wait for Stalin to die before she could leave the gulag. Her husband, who loved her dearly (a major criminal is capable of human feelings), abstained from voting when the Politburo expelled her from the Party. He then retracted and begged Stalin to forgive him, "I declare that, having thought over this question, I vote for this Central Committee decision, which corresponds to the interests of Party and state. ... Moreover, I confess my heavy guilt in not restraining Zhemchuzhina (his wife) a person close to me, from erroneous steps."[34] Stalin's death not only freed Polina Molotov and thousands of others, it may well have saved Molotov himself, as well as Beria (but not for long), Mikoyan, and a few others. I abandoned the idea of including a "Russian" box to act as a counterpoint to Box 8 devoted to Liu Shaoqi's last years. I was tempted by Bukharin and there was no shortage of source material, but was it right to favor any one of Stalin's victims over another and risk silencing countless martyrs who made Liu's suffering seem almost trifling?

Did that make Mao a good-natured tyrant? Certainly not—but compared with Stalin. ... The Cultural Revolution persecuted leaders who disagreed with his policies, but most, including Deng Xiaoping, Chen Yun, Peng Zhen, and many more, survived the ordeal and outlived Mao himself. One might feel that history has decided in Stalin's favor, making him effective and respected. But what about the unwitting posthumous historical effectiveness of the less cruel of the two? Deng Xiaoping changed China and therefore the world; history will recognize the importance of his role as being more beneficial and less harmful that Mao's.[35] He is thanked for that, as is Mao who allowed him to live, for is it possible to imagine for one minute that a confirmed sinner like Deng, a repeat offender of capitalist restoration, might have survived under Stalin?

The Most Inconsistent

As a prelude to the Divagations of a Faun, here is a final box by Shen Congwen again.

Box 9

Decapitation in Shen Congwen's Work

"As a child, Shen saw thousands of heads hung out for display on the city wall or simply dumped on the riverbank for family members to sort out. More appalling is his recollection that soldiers often arrested innocent peasants to fulfill their daily quota, and after too many killings, they let their captives gamble for their lives in a lottery-like religious ritual. The winners were set free, while the losers had to resign their lives to fate. Thus it was not unusual to see an unlucky peasant bid farewell to his cellmates and ask them to settle for him things unfinished at home, a sad child carrying baskets containing the heads of his father and his brother, walking home along a mountain path, or more gruesomely, dogs fighting for decomposed bodies left on the riverbank."

Sources: David Der-wei Wang, 2004, p. 25, who quotes those of Shen Congwen's works that include such episodes, and highlights the author's decision to reproduce them without indignation about the near-daily routine he experienced or observed during his childhood.

Shen Congwen's horror of the tragedy that was his country's modern destiny is understandable. It is also understandable that repeated spectacles of that kind might lead to revolutionary vocations. One cannot disregard a heritage of that nature in the inglorious assessment of the Chinese revolution (1949–1976). The executions and decapitations to which David Wang devoted the first chapter of his tragic study are just one aspect, along with others that are scarcely less sinister. Because the assessment of Mao's actions in power (after 1949, and especially from 1955 onward) is so disastrous, a concern for fairness has led many historians to include what the revolution supposedly brought to China: independence, unity, guaranteed order, and a respected central power. With regard to the last two, the situation in Maoist China was not as wonderful as they suppose, for the government was obeyed rather than respected, and then mainly because it terrorized. Nevertheless, the legacy is such a weighty one that it is easy to compile an inventory of achievements.

By attributing the supposed benefits of the Chinese revolution to Mao, those historians base themselves on a well-known fact, which is Mao's decisive role in the conquest of power. On several occasions during the two decades that preceded that conquest, Mao was more lucid than the other CCP leaders. The strategy he conceived, and then enforced, paid off for his Party and the revolutionary movement as a whole. Even if the demography, the economy, and the circumstances (White Terror in the cities) imposed the decision to turn to the disinherited rural masses, that rural turning point in 1927 owed more to Mao than to anyone else—with the exception of Peng Pai, the pioneer shot in 1929. Furthermore, it was Mao who declared early on that "power lies in the barrel of a gun," warning his comrades that the Communist movement needed to have an army. In the decisive phase of the Sino-Japanese War (1937–1945), he imposed the selfish but fruitful choice of halfheartedly fighting the Japanese in order to preserve the Communist forces for the decisive battle with the Guomindang. Better still, he rapidly sent troops to the rural zones where the Japanese army had driven away representatives of the Nationalist administration and left the zones unoccupied due to a shortage of men. He then provided the revolution with an embryonic state by promoting, and then supervising, the creation of autonomous Communist bases. Those mini-Stalinist states prefigured the regime that was to be established over the entire country-continent. After the military victory he altered the scale but kept the matrix.

The point here is not to say that Mao contributed far more to the 1949 victory than Stalin to the 1917 one, otherwise I would compare Mao to Lenin. What I am attempting here is to compare what results Stalin and Mao can show to "justify" the monstrous dictatorship they wielded for a quarter of a century (1928–1953) or, in Mao's case, a little longer (1949–1976). Stalin kept Lenin's frail barque afloat. He not only kept the Soviet Union going, he transformed it by creating a modern industry and an army that was able (after his initial blunders) to stand up to the Wehrmacht. In

Mao's lifetime, the gap between China and the "imperialist" West grew wider and the Chinese people remained poor or destitute. The country took off only once it was delivered from his imperious rule and hundreds of millions of Chinese were able to benefit from post-Maoist development.

The relative advantage of the more efficient Stalin (although agriculture stagnated in both countries) may be explained in part by his task being less difficult. China was far more underdeveloped in 1949 than Russia in 1917. And that advantage concerned only the preliminary task of economic modernization. But let us linger on that prerequisite for a moment, for while it may have been a deviation from the initial revolutionary goal (building sites, factories, and cities as a substitute for a fair and fraternal society), it was nevertheless essential.

Stalin more serious, more efficient

A comparative assessment of the two revolutions is eloquent (see chapter 2). Stalin laid down the foundations of a modern economy, whereas the gap between China and the West grew under Mao's reign. Mao's failure was due in part to his character and temperament. His doctor's memoirs provide us with a glimpse of the chaotic existence he led. Contradiction was not only one of his favorite topics, it was also a way of life. He hated routine and convention, but also order, despising discipline and caution. He improvised on a whim and reigned rather than governed. He often went to bed when the Chinese workers were setting off for work and woke in the afternoon. He lived in isolation and confided in no one, except in jest. He made decisions casually, based on his pride and stubbornness. He was an intelligent man but cared not a fig for experts, and, depending on the case, resorted to the Confucian maxims of his childhood or the ideological dictates he assimilated (and venerated) later. Those dictates prevented him, for instance, from concurring with Zeng Xisheng's commonsense arguments about the beneficial effects of the "responsibility fields" in Anhui province (only after Mao's death could those methods prove themselves on a national level), while the Confucian maxims led him to resort to age-old wisdom for solving the most advanced technical problems. "What is accomplished by technology is inferior, what is accomplished by virtue is superior" (*The Book of Rites*). Thus his regular preference for the Red over the expert miraculously reconciled imported militancy and inherited wisdom.[36]

Stalin too was capable of getting misled by ideology, as well as his own arrogant and narrow certitudes, and proud optimism: "There are no fortresses that the working class, the Bolsheviks, cannot capture."[37] In 1929 as in 1958, planification bowed to voluntarist objectives dictated by ideology, which paid no attention to obstacles of any kind. Like Mao, Stalin relied too much on his own intuition. That led him to make terrible blunders, which, because of his stubbornness, became catastrophic, as, for instance, on the eve of the German invasion and shortly afterward.[38] He knew practically nothing about agriculture and ceased to visit farms after 1928.

It is possible to add to the list of Stalin's errors and shortcomings, but they seem almost benign compared with Mao's. Stalin was more regular and diligent in his work, paid more attention to detail in matters of state, and was more realistic. Stalin also pursued ideologically inspired diversions, and he too was convinced that he was right, only in Stalin that certitude coexisted with a cunning caution that was all too rare and short-lived in Mao. In Mao, every belated awareness of a hard-to-conceal reality was rapidly obfuscated by his persistent illusions. Although Stalin was misled more than once by the ideology that supposedly could explain everything, he nevertheless knew how to be pragmatic, and he was so in a more resolute and coherent way than Mao. As Vera Dunham put it so well, "consequences mattered to him" and he was concerned with the consequences of his actions. And she went on to say that (unlike Mao), "His concern was not thought reform among his subjects, but reform of their reflexes, their actions, and their reactions. ... He was not trying to shape a new man. He was molding, lethally and furiously, the Stalinist social order." He achieved that by sending the revolution to the scrap heap, prefiguring contemporary China, as made possible by Mao's death—and Deng Xiaoping's pragmatism, learned from his experience of Mao's disasters. Stalin's massive ambition (to establish a new political regime, change society, and develop the economy) was less excessive (and less inaccessible) than Mao's, which was to create a new man. He was therefore less concerned with education than with bureaucracy and organization. Let us feign for one moment to forget the suffering (Dunham's "lethally" molding): Stalin avoided the Maoist fiasco.[39]

The two fronts

As mentioned in chapter 3, at the summit the CCP was divided into a two-tier leadership, the second tier or "front" being reserved for Mao, who kept aloof from day-to-day management. That was typical of how he reigned rather than governed, and this allocation of tasks limped along because of the very person who instigated it. Dividing the leadership into two fronts was a constraint only for the actors in the first layer, who were supposed to carry out all the supreme leader's decisions, even though he himself had no quandaries about intervening at will in the first front, breaking the rule he himself had made. Conversely, Mao took refuge in the second front when he did not want to accept responsibility for a policy he knew was necessary but that he disapproved of for ideological reasons. He would later blame his lieutenants in the first front, who had endeavored to carry out urgent repairs to the damage.[40]

Stalin had no second front to deal with and got far more involved in governmental routine, as repeatedly illustrated by the frequent and insistent letters he sent to Molotov or Kaganovich during his working summer vacation. While it may have been easier for Stalin to work with his faithful followers than it was for Mao to impose his viewpoints on an old guard, however subjugated, he nevertheless did not immediately have the absolute power (at least once he brought down the other Himalaya)[41] that he would have ten years later. In 1929, a defeated Bukharin, fired from his position as editor-in-chief of *Pravda*, managed to avoid getting the uncomfortable post of People's Commissar for Public Education that Stalin had earmarked for him, and obtained instead, by an almost unanimous Politburo vote (the only vote against being Stalin's), his preferred job directing the scientific and technical management of the economy. In the early 1930s Stalin's power was less assured than Mao's when he obliged his colleagues to sack and vilify Peng Dehuai. The Politburo was managed collectively, but with one major restriction, which was that the general secretary dominated his colleagues. No more Himalayas, just one crocodile in the backwater. Still, in early 1934, during the Seventeenth Party Congress, the fallen Himalaya, in his required self-criticism, managed to advocate a foreign policy stance that was diametrically opposed to Stalin's. For Bukharin the main enemy was Hitler, not France or Great Britain, and their capitalists and "social traitors." During that same Congress, Preobrazhensky, the former Trotskyite who had rallied around and was now reintegrated, peppered his self-criticism with ironic innuendos mocking the Stalinist dogma by which everyone blindly followed the line laid out by the Guide. And the participants laughed, which they would have been ill-advised to do at the next Congress, five years later.[42]

Nor would they have laughed at Lushan in 1959, which suggests that Stalin's power in early 1934 was not yet equal to Mao's during the GLF, still less to the power he would have after the Great Terror. Stalin consolidated his power in the 1930s, whereas Mao's two fronts eroded his power—at least until the Cultural Revolution sorted that matter out. Having conquered authority by removing his rivals in the Bolshevik old guard, Stalin constantly reinforced his power at the expense of his own henchmen. Mao started from higher but fell lower during the first half of the 1960s, a time when he would have had trouble sacking Liu Shaoqi or Deng Xiaoping. Mao's loss of authority (back in 1949, everyone thought his position to be rock solid) symbolized a more serious failure that concerned the core of his political action, inspired and undermined by his own dreams.

Ideology

Mao's character and working methods are not the only causes of his aberrations. His disdain for routine, discipline, and regular work, as well as his self-made-man's pride, which convinced him that he had grasped all the fundamentals, served only to reinforce his ideological assumptions. The aphorisms he loved to serve up to intellectuals (such as "the more books you read, the more stupid you become"; "Clearly studying too much can seriously harm the people")[43] betrayed his feelings about them. They had humiliated him when he was young, and later, during the Hundred Flowers, they tried to teach him a lesson again (that was how he perceived it). His distrust of overeducation nevertheless tied in with his broader fear of specialization and expertise, easier to acquire in the cities where there was a danger of re-creating a privileged caste. The confidence he so often displayed in the creativity of the masses who could accomplish the impossible, and even make scientific discoveries that defied the scientists, was a corollary to his egalitarianism. During the last two-thirds of Mao's reign, he increasingly identified the end that supposedly justified the means prescribed by Leninism (the Party's unshared power), with his own egalitarian vision. But that end changed much less than the means. In Mao's eyes there were too many privileged people in the Party, unable to understand the spontaneous socialism of the masses.

Now that requires a few explanations! The initial goal of the Chinese revolutionaries was the grandeur of the nation, not the well-being of the masses. Their primary motivation was closer to Hitler's than that of Marx or Lenin—bearing in mind that China was on the defensive, a victim of the imperialist powers, whereas Hitler's Germany was offensive. The Chinese revolutionaries' crusade was not universal, like that of Marx, Engels, and Lenin, but specific, relating to a single nation. They didn't need to see the failure of the world revolution before converting themselves to a variant of their original aim, namely the construction of socialism "in one country." A minority of revolutionaries converted less readily to Marxism, which they understood poorly, than to the Leninist path to power and development, which was allegedly proving itself in another backward country. In doing so, the converts absorbed the Marxist potion and its ambition to end the exploitation of the masses without renouncing their original nationalism.

Mao rightly Sinicized Marxism by using the peasant masses rather than a minimal proletariat to conquer power. After that, as we saw, he obediently followed Stalin's first development strategy. However, since it wasn't adapted to the demographic and economic situation of the country he wanted to modernize, the recipe didn't work as well as in the Soviet Union, where it had already raised more difficulties than Mao imagined. Nor did Mao stick with that, for he took the egalitarian ideal more seriously than Stalin and never abandoned it. True, he denounced the inequality between urban and rural dwellers (just to mention the most obvious one) far more than he fought it, and his criticism was less concerned with income than with health and education. However, given that today those two very sectors illustrate the tragic price of unequal modernization, he had the best reasons in the world to be concerned. Let us at least give him credit for having denounced those very real scourges.

It is to his honor then that he was a revolutionary dissatisfied with his work and faithful to the ideal of social equality that the Communists claimed to represent. And there's the snag: Mao was not unfaithful to Communism, he even worked hard at keeping the flame alive. But he took on board the substitute ideology. Instead of perpetuating the initial ambiguity (a fundamentally nationalist project that became, officially but incidentally, a Communist one), Mao got carried away by the Communist metamorphosis and exacerbated the misunderstanding. So he deviated the Chinese revolution from its initial trajectory, and why not? He may, like others, have sought to find a way out of his country's misfortunes, and, once exposed to Marxist teachings, discovered the misery of the peasants, who certainly deserved that a life be devoted to getting them out of poverty. The trouble was that by brandishing calls to egalitarian order at all times and out of context, he lost on both fronts. China remained poor and the Chinese people destitute. The neglected preliminary issue obtained its revenge.

Conversely, inegalitarian modernization is now getting people out of poverty and proving to be far more efficient than leveling equality in combating the social scourges Mao inveighed against without correcting them. By claiming to reconcile the original (national) aim with the added (social) objective, Mao spoilt the whole enterprise. It was not only his ideological superego that altered the trajectory, it was also the pride that led him to magnify his work (the revolution) to the extent of being occasionally tempted to prefer revolutionary fervor to improvements in the living condition of the masses. Overwhelmed by trivial material considerations, those masses ceased to be the "white page" on which the demiurge was free to project his extravagant designs[44] —or in other words, his dreams. The severity of my judgment requires further, more empirical, explanations. During the first Five-Year Plan, and even later, Mao had no compunction about exploiting the peasants, just as Stalin had before him (with more determination, I'll admit) when he implemented the Preobrazhensky program by which the peasants' efforts financed "primitive Socialist accumulation." It was in part to this end that, after establishing compulsory cereal procurement at a fixed (low) price in 1953, Mao accelerated agricultural collectivization (as early as 1955) in the hope that it would facilitate the collection of grain, which the peasants were reluctant to part with. To achieve that prerequisite (development) Mao therefore thought to exploit the vast reservoir of (peasant) discontent that he had once mobilized to combat the former regime, and transform it into a massive labor pool, mercilessly exploited in order to "construct the country" (*jianguo* was the expression used at the time to designate the great national project, and even the era inaugurated in 1949). But it wasn't only the (*jianguo*'s) nationalist Mao who collectivized the land a breakneck pace, it was equally the socialist Mao. Egalitarian, you might ask? Yes, on the condition that we agree on what the term implies, for he did accept the state's exploitation of the poorest segment of the population, which resulted in the urbanites having three times the incomes of their rural counterparts. What he hoped to prevent was the emergence of a new social differentiation within the countryside that would allow rich peasants to exploit poorer ones.

In that he succeeded, for there were no rich peasants under Mao. The very first ones emerged six years after his death, thanks to a policy that broke away from the equality in misery that had been maintained until then. Mao always emphasized revolutionary fervor over any improvement in the masses' living standards, and leveling equality over inegalitarian modernization. As a result, a year after Mao died (in 1977), 150 million villagers lived below the poverty line and the average income per capita in rural China was slightly below what it was in 1933, under the discredited former regime. I have restricted myself to discussing the condition of the peasants, since they were the most numerous and unfortunate by far, but the entire Chinese population was still massively poor when the founder's return to his maker (Marx!) finally paved the way to a more prosperous future.

Stalin's evolution was more pedestrian and conventional in its inhumanity. The failure of the European revolution did not yet imply that the preliminary path toward economic modernization would triumph, but did encourage it. Catching up backwardness as fast as possible meant being able to resist the inevitable imperialist aggression. Stalin decided to build socialism in one country a few months after Lenin's death, but it was Lenin himself who had pointed the way (revolution reduced to modernization) with the famous equation, "socialism is electricity plus soviets." Since the soviets were mere tokenism, almost nothing stood in the way. It is hardly worth lingering on an appraisal of anything that was not an absolute priority (i.e., rapid development). Even if we take into account progress in education and health (see chapter 2), together with a handful of other measures from the social or egalitarian catalogue, the evidence remains the same: the revolutionaries constructed a more unfair society than the capitalist ones they denounced. The Soviet version of Marxism did not anticipate Mao's future warning, "Economic development and the existence of 'socialist relations of production' do not by themselves automatically guarantee the future realization of Communist goals."[45]

The October ideals, which flourished in the early 1920s, gradually came to be questioned or ignored in the 1930s. From the first Five-Year Plan onward, development took over. Unlike Mao, Stalin gave himself the means to achieve his ends. He did not just come to terms with social stratification, he reinforced it by creating a new intelligentsia, a technical one above all, with worker and peasant origins. Another necessity was a strong state, so Stalin consolidated it by making it increasingly despotic (which had already been the case since the Civil War), and crowning it himself, rather like a modern Peter the Great: "Asserting affinity with the ... czars, the cruel builders of the Russian state, enabled him to no longer feel obligated by his initial commitments, his promises to construct socialist, and above all, to close once and for all the Bolshevik chapter, whose founders had become his enemies" (Moshe Lewin). "Lenin had called Stalin a 'Russian brute,'" and the brute lived up to his name perfectly, which led to a 'change of ideology.'"[46] Before the end of the second plan, internationalism had joined egalitarianism in the cemetery of ideals abandoned by Stalin. In exchange, he rehabilitated traditional values, the family and everything that the Bolsheviks had repudiated or fought against.

Mao was more faithful to the October ideals. Faithful and inconsistent, for he wanted everything at once: a great powerful and egalitarian nation. He copied the Great Turn of 1929 (while claiming to do better than his model) but missed the second turn, that of "mature" Stalinism, which repelled him and which he blamed on Khrushchev. He treated the man who tried to reform—but not hard enough—as a revisionist. The difference with China was also due to the postrevolutionary time lag. At the time when Mao was deriding "Goulash Communism," the Soviet Union was already benefitting from what it had constructed whereas China had yet to take off. Instead of catching up, the disparity persisted and grew worse in Mao's lifetime. Unlike Stalin, Mao did not subordinate one end (social equality) to another (development), instead he tended to emphasize the former to the detriment of the latter. More often as not, wanting to believe that everything was possible, he gave up nothing and got nowhere.

"In all totalitarian regimes, the ideologues, guardians of the dogma, clash ... with politicians, who are obviously more realistic" (Krzysztof Pomian).[47] Stalin incarnated a form of realism, which seems obvious as soon as he is compared with Mao, caught up as he was in observing dogma and the religion of egalitarianism. That became even more fatal because his pride and stubbornness led him to impose harebrained ideas on his more realistic collaborators. The fact that during his lifetime they were powerless to cast out the scourge that Mao had become illustrates once again the defects in the system conceived and established by Lenin. And the same goes for his Georgian counterpart, whose growing paranoia distorted reality, but not cruelty.

Grand Terror and Cultural Revolution

The foremost crimes of the two dictators perfectly illustrate the contrast between their temperaments and their political choices. It is hard to imagine two more different episodes. The Cultural Revolution succeeded in galvanizing millions of gullible people, but it is impossible to imagine the Great Terror rousing the crowds, even if we restrict it to the tip of the iceberg (the Moscow trials) that was emerging at the time.

Let us start then with what illusions could be created by the Cultural Revolution, a revolution launched by an old revolutionary against his own life's work, so that it might regain its original purity.[48] That was unheard of, something that was really quite difficult to conceive. A revolution within and against a revolution; against what it had become (routinized) in order to turn it back into something it no longer was (revolutionary). Mao's dissatisfaction with the regime he had brought about was as founded as the criticism of the social inequalities he used as a pretext for his attacks against his subordinates' efforts to end the famine. That dissatisfaction did not lead him to the root of the evil since he merely diagnosed a degeneracy that had to be stopped before it led to a restoration of capitalism, just as the earlier revolution was betrayed by Khrushchev's "pseudo-Communism." Mao was careful not to challenge the regime itself, he merely wanted to restore it to its original pristine state out of loyalty to its very essence, which he deemed above reproach. The fact that the target of his denunciations (the Communist bureaucracy) was not specific to Chinese Communism conferred a universalist aura on "Mao thought." His criticism of the Communist bureaucracy was vehement rather than radical and contained nothing really new. However it was heartwarming—and promising for anyone naïve enough to believe it—to see that the arguments expressed for so long (and more coherently) by the liberals, anarchists, and Trotskyists had been rediscovered by the very person who controlled the summit of the bureaucratic hierarchy.

Mao's position should, in fact, have made them skeptical. His immediate target was not so much the regime but his opponents within the CCP's leadership, or, if we want to expand the debate and make it more abstract, his ultimate target became the bureaucracy, and specifically the Communist bureaucracy, which exasperated him just as it had exasperated Stalin, and generally does exasperate despots. His solidarity with the regime he was criticizing mercilessly, albeit in an oblique way, led him to abruptly interrupt the campaigns he himself launched, something he did every time they proved (predictably) dangerous to the established order, or in other words, to the perpetuation of the system he presided over while undermining it with his sarcasm. By placing himself above the fray, Mao accepted responsibility for neither the risks he inflicted on his regime, nor the constraints of the manager who fights with the fray, accepting responsibility for the imperfections and inequalities in order to transform and construct.

To prevent the Chinese revolution from degenerating, Mao had already shown that he was quite prepared to push his original goal (to make China rich and strong) into the background. After all, the poor were more inclined to revolution than the rich and he considered it more important to preserve the revolutionary fervor of the Chinese than to improve their living conditions. With the Cultural Revolution Mao took a large step sideways, from the individual to the universal. Since the Russians had failed, it was now up to him to take up the torch and confer a universal aim on a revolution originally intended to overcome the country's backwardness. In an earlier life he might have pursued that goal, but now the time had come to transcend it.

The end justifies the means. To achieve his grandiose goal, Mao first prepared the way. In the greatest secrecy, his wife Jiang Qing asked Yao Wenyuan, a pen pusher in Shanghai, to draw up a diatribe that Mao corrected three times, and which sparked off the event. It attacked Wu Han, the deputy mayor of Beijing, but through him the mayor himself, as the intermediate target leading to the final one, the president of the Republic Liu Shaoqi. I'll pass on the intrigues, lies, and traps that Mao concocted between the time the pamphlet was published in a Shanghai newspaper in November 1965 and the student agitation in the summer of 1966, which signaled to the world that spectacular events were in motion in Beijing. The student agitation was triggered by a *dazibao* (big character wall poster) pasted on a wall in a Beijing university canteen. It accused the rector of the university of being a capitalist roader. The author of this inflammatory denunciation was a mere assistant, a secretary of the CCP cell in the philosophy department. Immediately four hundred more *dazibao* denounced the denunciation, calling it counterrevolutionary, until Mao rapidly settled the issue. The *dazibao* causing all the rumpus was nothing less than the "manifesto of the Beijing Commune of the 1960s," and "even more significant than the Paris Commune." What nobody knew at the time, but might easily have suspected, was that the brave person denouncing her superior was controlled from afar by none other than Kang Sheng's wife. She asked the young woman to write that *dazibao*, and promised that she would obtain support at a very high level. Later, the manipulated Red Guards were asked to change their targets and aim higher than their professors in order to overthrow the "stronghold of capitalist restoration," which Mao was about to identify with his heir, Liu Shaoqi. And so on, and so on; there is no point in going into the details of Mao's intrigues,[49] it's all there.

But do they amount to another Great Terror? I might as well admit from the outset that my comparison is inappropriate. The Cultural Revolution *could* fire the imagination. It contributed more than any other event to making the Maoist era "one of the great utopian episodes in world history."[50] But could a deliberate, coldly organized massacre such as the Great Terror ever be the stuff of dreams? Let us first return to the obvious differences that make a comparison between two unusual episodes very difficult. First there was the "social engineering" identified by Nicolas Werth, after being overshadowed for many years by the purge of the elite—the only aspect criticized by Khrushchev in his secret report. That "engineering" also consisted of purging and discarding everything that Stalin wanted to get rid of, the difference being that it concerned not just the leading Communist Party cadres but society as a whole. First came all the regime's supposed enemies targeted by "operation kulak," launched by Stalin on 2 July 1937, a few weeks before the Grand Terror started. Kulak here was a generic term, for, in addition to the former kulaks, it included the "people of the past" (aristocrats, Czarist bureaucrats, the elite of the former regime) and "socially harmful elements," such as louts, hooligans, and others. To those were added members of the clergy and of any sects, White army officers, former participants in peasant uprisings, former members of non-Bolshevik political parties, and more importantly among the latter, the Socialist Revolutionaries, guilty of having obtained far more representatives than the Bolsheviks at the stillborn Constituent Assembly of January 1918. All in all, that was a lot of people. They had been silent and quiet for a long time, but just to be on the safe side … it was better get rid of all that vermin once and for all. "Operation kulak" was by far the most deadly of the secret operations that made up the Grand Terror.

Nor was it the only one. A series of "national operations" or "national lines" completed the kulak purge. These targeted foreigners who might potentially spy for their countries or even back a foreign invasion. Here too it was necessary to cast the net wide enough to include the Russians living on the borders who might plot with the Poles, and anyone who had been a prisoner of war in Germany during World War I, not to mention anyone who had family living abroad and wrote to them, or received parcels from them, and so on. Given the international power struggle in 1937–1938 and what followed, the "German line" may conceivably have been the bloodiest of the "national lines." Indeed, the descendants of the German colonists recruited by Catherine II and their compatriots residing in the Soviet Union paid a heavy tribute for 55,000 of them received a range of sentences, and more than three-quarters were executed (nearly 42,000). Yet the "Polish line" was even more lethal, with 140,000 sentences, 110,000 of them to death. Not that Poland was particularly dangerous, it was more of a prey than a threat, as the German-Soviet Pact and what followed soon confirmed. But simply being a neighboring country was incriminating enough. "That's excellent comrade Yezhov! Continue to look into this and eradicate this Polish filth. Liquidate it completely in the name of the interests of the USSR."[51] For the same reason as the Polish operation, the Finish, Estonian, Latvian, Romanian, and even Greek operations were also deemed necessary (in total there were some ten national operations). And what about the Japanese, for were they not neighbors in the Soviet Far East, and signed the Anti-Comintern Pact to boot? Since there were few Japanese residents in the Soviet Union, a special operation targeted the "Harbinians," the former railroad workers and other employees of the (Russian-owned) Chinese Eastern Railway Company based in Harbin, northern Manchuria. After the railway was handed over to the Japanese, the workers were repatriated to the Soviet Union. Yezhov and Stalin both believed there must surely be a few Japanese spies lurking in their midst, and once again it was safer to cast the net wide.[52] And last but not least among the victims of the Great Terror were the many foreign Communists either from the Comintern administration or who Stalin had summoned to Moscow—but they come under the purge of the elite.

Here there is certainly a common denominator to be found between the Great Terror and the Cultural Revolution, but otherwise there was nothing comparable in China to Stalin's social engineering and "purification." Mao did not specifically target the landlords or the other historical "counterrevolutionaries," nor the ethnic minorities—but that did not spare them from having to foot their share of the bill (and I'll return to that later). The external threats that worried Stalin in 1937–1938 were no more pressing for China in 1966 than they had been five or ten years earlier. There was no Hitler emulator in Tokyo, New Delhi, or Washington. At the end of the Cultural Revolution Mao even drew closer to the United States after he had made an enemy of the Soviet Union.

While the targets of the two movements (Moscow in 1937, Beijing in 1966) were not the same (apart from purging the elite), the means the two dictators used to achieve them differed even more. The Great Terror, despite its inevitable excesses,[53] was more controlled, more bureaucratic, and better managed than the Cultural Revolution; in short it was closer to Nazi formalism. Stalin would never have risked inflaming the masses against the Party he led, and he allowed no one else (apart from the NKVD, which he controlled) to decimate Party members. The Great Terror began when Stalin decided it should and ended sixteen months later when he thought the time had come to put an end to it. Mao had all the trouble in the world trying to stop the mayhem he had so unwisely unleashed, having provoked a situation of near anarchy and then civil war in the regime he had fought so hard to found. Because he lost control of the situation he had created, he too had to resort to more traditional means, first the army, that classical secular branch, and then the local militia and the Party cadres, whom he now had to reintegrate. The traditional means (e.g., the army) were, in principle,[54] tried and tested, but together with the local militia, over which Mao had less control but had to tolerate for a while, perpetuated the worst massacres of the Cultural Revolution. The fratricidal battles between Red Guards are better known but were less deadly, often serving (rather like the Moscow trials and the purge of the regional CPSU leaders) to conceal the most sinister but less spectacular aspects of the Cultural Revolution.[55]

Mao's tortuous and adventurous methods were, in part, responsible for the failure of the Cultural Revolution. Only in part though, since this failure owed even more to the contradictory nature of the goals he was trying to achieve. And also, incidentally, to Mao's less zealous cruelty than Stalin's more watchful one. Once we have taken Mao's inconsistency into account, along with his need to use the services of old cadres, especially after a large number of his loyal supporters had been arrested and dispatched to the deepest countryside for not having followed his every about-turn fast enough, one obvious fact remains.

Unlike Stalin, Mao did not "liquidate" anyone who might have put him in the shade (see above).

At first glance the Cultural Revolution was responsible for more victims than the Great Terror. About 750,000 Soviet citizens were executed between August 1937 and November 1938, while between 1.1 million and 1.6 million died as a result of the Cultural Revolution.[56] The second estimate is an approximation and comprises several categories of violent death, rather as though for the Soviet Union tally we included the number of people who had died under the torture used to extract their confessions to fictitious crimes; and we included excess mortality in the gulag in 1937–1938, or prisoners who, like Osip Mandelstam, died in the Russian Far East or elsewhere during transfer. Furthermore, the Russian population in 1937 was just under one-fourth of the Chinese population three decades later. The gap between the two is illustrated in the following remark by Nicolas Werth: "During the Great Terror, one Soviet adult in a hundred was executed with a bullet in the neck" at an average rate of 1,600 executions per day, or more than one per minute.[57] During the Cultural Revolution, executions and massacres were neither controlled nor regular. There were several peaks when the pack of Red Guards was unleashed in August and September 1966, during the civil war in 1967, and especially when the Revolutionary Committees took control in 1968.[58] Furthermore, the Great Terror supplied many more prisoners to the gulag (more than 800,000 sentences to ten years of hard labor) than the Cultural Revolution did to *laogai*.

Last, there were two essential differences besides the more coldly exterminating nature of the Russian model in 1937 (the "liquidator"). The first in particular, for while the historian may, with hindsight, condemn the gratuitousness of the Cultural Revolution, Mao deemed it crucial. Stalin launched the purges after declaring that the revolution had triumphed and life had improved. He wanted the administration to apply Moscow's *ukase* far more efficiently and, in addition, reinforce and preserve his personal power. Mao believed that the Chinese revolution was threatened and was ready to do the impossible to prevent its "revisionist" degeneration and stave off the restoration of capitalism. History, he believed, can reverse itself; nothing is acquired permanently. To that end (which went beyond the mere preservation of his own powers) he was ready to kill as much as necessary. For him, as for many revolutionaries, politics was a battle until death and had to be led in the same way as a war: by destroying the adversary once and for all. The second difference between the model and the copy was that while Mao was indifferent to the suffering he caused, he did not enjoy wallowing in it and was less directly involved than Stalin in the minutiae of his wrongdoings. His method was to inflict damage from above, like a deus ex machina flicking the switch.

None of this excuses Mao or justifies him. It was not necessary to equal Stalin in order to join the limited circle of the worst monsters in a century that abounded in them. But the Cultural Revolution was debatable in terms of ideas, if only to underline its heterodoxy in relation to Marxism-Leninism. It attacked the sacrosanct Leninist Party and, more broadly, the elite who, like Lenin, were aware of the limitations of the masses' revolutionary spontaneity. We could endlessly try to identify the causes of the Great Terror, but it belongs to a different category, namely that of the mechanisms and methods of tyranny.

Despite the fundamental difference, or contrast, I have just emphasized, the Cultural Revolution reproduced numerous traits of the Grand Terror. I shall try to identify some of the similarities, while taking care not to place them on the same level as the above-mentioned facts.

The two "movements," if we can call them that, had a preventative, almost defensive aspect. That comes out more clearly in the Cultural Revolution, in which Maurice Meisner discerns a "partially dystopian strain." The Great Leap Forward was utopic, since it aimed to put Communism within reach. Its failure put the Communist bureaucracy back in place, and for Mao that made it more of a threat than ever. However, such reversals are in the nature of things, "disequilibrium is normal and absolute" whereas "equilibrium is temporary and relative." Conflict must be ongoing, and every generation would have to renew and relaunch its own cultural revolution.[59] The Grand Terror also aimed to prevent a possible threat from hypothetical enemies within and without. Stalin had better control of the domestic situation than Mao, but the threat of imminent war was more pressing.

The origin or prehistory of the two cataclysms is comparable: agrarian collectivization, dekulakization and famine in the Soviet Union; the GLF and famine in China. As Boris Pasternak wrote in *Doctor Zhivago* (as recalled by Nicolas Werth), the unprecedented cruelty of the Great Terror was part of the "extraordinary brutality of the cursed decade," with forced expropriations, the deportation of millions of peasants to distant and inhospitable regions, the military blockade of disaster-stricken areas to prevent the starving from fleeing, the cult of statistics, coded political discourse increasingly removed from reality, progressively more brutal relations between the state and society—all so many practices and trends that were already experimented with during the 1930–1933 upheavals before coming into their own in 1937–1938 (see chapters 4 and 5). In China, the famine was comparable, if not worse, and the practices of the state and the Communist cadres similar, but sometimes less merciless. There was one difference however: the person mainly responsible for the disaster lost some of his authority in the process. Mao's errors and stubbornness tarnished his prestige, but only, I must repeat, among his henchmen and the very small number of informed persons in the top layer of government. That was sufficient reason for him to want to get rid of all those who had "failed him," an offense that mainly consisted of recognizing the responsibility of the Center in a disaster that he persisted in denying, and learning—too late—the lessons required to stop it. Stalin, on the other hand, despite a few disturbing episodes that occurred before the Great Terror (the most notable being the Ryutin affair; see above), suffered less than Mao from the torments he inflicted on his people.

Mao's desire to do battle with his own lieutenants and the first of them above all was a factor that triggered the Cultural Revolution and had no equivalent in the Great Terror.[60] At a lower, broader level, the responsibility of the two Communist bureaucracies and the two dictators' perception of them played a similar role. In both cases, the practices denounced by the two dictators go back to that prehistory I just mentioned. Since the objectives required by the Moscow Center during the first Five-Year Plan, and the Beijing Center during the GLF, were unrealistic and there was no question of challenging them, the regional and local leaders got by with lies, dissimulation, and falsified balance sheets (see chapters 4 and 5). In the Soviet Union, Stalin's growing distrust of the "family circles" of the provincial *nomenklatura*, his frustration at being obeyed verbally whereas his instructions were circumvented, was a foretaste of the themes Mao would reiterate thirty years later, before and during the Cultural Revolution. Even the expression "cultural revolution" was in widespread use in the Soviet Union from the late 1920s and already conveyed concepts later used by Beijing and disseminated across the world thirty-five to forty years later: the fight against bureaucracy with its routine and privileges, "bourgeois" theater, and cultural elitism.

If I must introduce a difference, let me say that there was slightly more paranoia on Stalin's side, as was often the case (those provincial cliques were deliberately "sabotaging" the economy), while on Mao's there was a more abstract and theoretical analysis, rather than rantings and ravings against specific people. But for the most part, under Mao's pen there really was a repetition of the themes launched by his predecessor, with the same populist appeal to grassroots militants, and even to the victims of bad bureaucrats. Fortunately, the Master (the *vožd* first and then the Helmsman) was there to watch over them, concerned even for the most humble of his ... I was about to say subjects, for like the Czars, Stalin punished the wicked *boyar* who oppressed the people.

There were some similarities even in the way the two "campaigns" were carried out. That is, assuming we can use that word to designate what was boastfully called a revolution in the second episode, whereas in the first Stalin abstained from naming something he was careful to conceal from the public. Similarities despite the contrast I stressed earlier between the riskier means (using high school and university students to purge the Party) and the safer one (charging the political police with the task for forging accusations, and then having a *troika* hold a production line of trials to issue sentences decided in advance.[61] With the exception of the most important similarity (in both cases the terror came from above; the dictator started everything), comparable events often occurred in different time sequences and illustrated recurrent tendencies common to both regimes, for instance the supreme leader's manipulation of young people's iconoclastic tendencies and their hostility to authority and institutions. That practice, typical of the Cultural Revolution, was ignored during the Great Terror but was used in Russia eight or nine years earlier when the cultural revolution theme was launched there. Conversely, the competition between the provincial branches of the NKVD, which led them to exceed their quotas for arrests, sentences, and executions, even requesting authorization from the Center (almost always granted) to increase those quotas, in other words that devotion to statistics that multiplied the number of victims, was more notorious in China during the GLF than during the Cultural Revolution. It goes without saying that this had already occurred in the Soviet Union in the early 1930s with regard to the number of kolkhozes created on paper, and later the tons of steel (still on paper) during the first plan. It was a compulsive habit in both regimes, which led subordinates to outdo each other relentlessly in order to catch up with or surpass their neighbors and, in all cases, to please, or not displease, their superiors. That frenzy spun out of control in the Soviet Union during the spring of 1937, as it did in China during the fall of 1959. At a pinch, it mattered little to those leaders whether, in the first case, it was the number of heads falling, or, in the second case, yields rising—or at other times illiteracy dropping, malaria being eradicated, sparrows killed, or "rightists" unmasked.[62]

Another shared trait was that both dictators used the Great Terror and the Cultural Revolution to settle old scores, having waited for the right moment and hatched their revenge. Just as the Great Terror provided the opportunity to get thousands of former Trotskyites, rightists, and other kulaks out of the camps in order to shoot them on the spot (and make room for new *zeks*), so during the Cultural Revolution former "counterrevolutionaries" or Peng Dehuai–type rightists, class enemies, and others were dragged out for criticism, arrest, torture, or death by beating. The dictators' emulators were not to be outdone. All mobilization campaigns led to an escalation of military ardor and witch hunts, and the Great Terror and the Cultural Revolution provided opportunities for their agents to unearth lists of former suspects or simply to drag out the usual locally available scapegoats. Obliged to meet the prescribed arrest quotas rapidly, the NKVD first fell back on long-standing "enemies," such as those from the civil war or the peasant uprising of 1920–1921.[63] Similarly in China, the militia drew on the local representatives of the "Five Black Categories": landlords, rich peasants, counterrevolutionaries, rightists, and "bad elements"—a species that comprised (in addition to the Chinese equivalent of the Soviet hooligans) vagabonds or rebels who had the courage to say out loud what most people were thinking.

Collective responsibility was another feature that was not specific to the Great Terror or the Cultural Revolution, but was used again at the time, and implicated everyone close to the condemned person, starting with family members. "We will eliminate all the enemies of the state … , we will also eliminate … their families and their descendants!" (speech by Stalin on 7 November 1937 on the twentieth anniversary of the October Revolution, quoted by Nicolas Werth). Nearly twenty thousand wives of victims of the Great Terror received long sentences in the camps. For its part, China promoted the saying "If the father is a revolutionary hero, the son is also a hero; if the father is a reactionary, the son is a bastard." In the early days of the Cultural Revolution, a young intellectual called Yu Luoke who had "bad" social origins (his father was an engineer) exposed the stupidity of that blood law (*xuetonglun*) in an essay titled "On Class Origins." He was arrested in January 1968, sentenced, and executed two years later for refusing to "confess to his errors." Another tragic incident illustrates both the preceding cases concerning the class enemies dragged out again during the Cultural Revolution, and their descendants' "guilt." In 1968, in Guangxi province, a former landlord was ordered to jump off a cliff with his two children aged one and three. Since his wife, the daughter of a poor peasant, was not sentenced, he pleaded with the head of the local militia, "Could not the government consider that one of the two babies belongs to my wife? In that case I'll jump with the other." His request was refused.[64]

The beneficiaries of the two cataclysms had different fates, simply because the Cultural Revolution failed and the epigones rapidly took the opposite course from the one Mao had attempted. Many people promoted during the Cultural Revolution, left-wing ideologues or mere workers such as Wang Hongwen, ended up in prison. On the other hand, Brezhnev, Kosygin, Gromyko, and many others stepped into the shoes of those who had been executed (or the new *zeks*) in 1937–1938 and were destined to have long careers.

The "success" of the Great Terror and the failure of the Cultural Revolution epitomize their differences. To demonstrate their similarity I would add one final remark. The 1929 "second revolution" and the Great Leap Forward were typical of both Promethean regimes. What could be more absurd than the purge of dozens of thousands of Stalinist cadres, if not the dismantlement of the Maoist instrument of dictatorship?

✳✳✳

I have not spared the two dictators, but I cannot end without conceding their remarkable gift for political intrigue. It was thanks to that talent that they carried the day over their adversaries and rivals, Stalin in the 1920s and Mao in the 1930s (after which any talent was superfluous since the Number One imposed his will or his whims). I'll also admit, or repeat, that they both believed in their ultimate goal. Robert Tucker mentions the providential nature of Stalin's death, and immediately insists that "Stalin in his macabre way remained to the end a revolutionary, albeit from above."

The same was true of Mao, if not more so. He was a revolutionary to the end. Hannah Arendt confirmed that "the leaders took ideology dead seriously," those ideologies that "always assume that one idea is sufficient to explain everything in the development from the premise."[65] She was talking about Hitler and Stalin, but also Lenin before them, and Mao later. They believed and thought they knew, and men paid the price for that deadly certitude: "the devil seems very pallid in comparison to someone who possesses a truth, *his* truth" (Cioran).

Conclusion

Stalinism and Maoism are not aberrations of Leninism but manifestations of it, a result of "What is to be done?" that was neither unavoidable nor surprising. The personalities of the two dictators, Stalin's in particular, stamped their marks on the Leninist construction. In Mao's case it was absolute power (for which Lenin was responsible) that perverted it, or at the very least exacerbated its defects. Mao intrigued and massacred from the very outset (see above), but in my first book I praised the common sense of the strategist and the practitioner of the "peasant way." The portrait I drew of the sorcerer's apprentice during the Cultural Revolution that held sway at the time showed anything but common sense—a contradiction my students were quick to point out. At first glance, we seem to be dealing with two different men.[1] To be sure, the obstinate tyrant of the 1960s was already visible in the guerrilla fighter of the 1920s and 1930s. Yet adulation and being used to imposing his will, whims, and harebrained ideas without meeting with any real resistance were decisive factors in the catastrophic development of Mao's personality and its disastrous effect on the revolution, the country, and the people.

Lenin …

It is the omnipotence of the Egocrat, a term popularized by Solzhenitsyn and Claude Lefort, that may be attributed to Lenin. That was due in part to his way of governing, but much more to the system he put in place. Its future development was already predicted at the beginning of the century, by Rosa Luxemburg and Trotsky to start with, although the latter finally rallied around in the heat of the action in 1917.[2] With regard to Lenin's way of governing, it is easy to demonstrate how it differed from that of Stalin (and Mao), but equally easy to point out the solid bases on which Stalin could depend in order to reinforce—not found—a dictatorship. On the one hand there was Isaac Deutscher's *primus inter pares* Lenin, whose policy was criticized from almost every aspect at the Eighth Party Congress in March 1919 and even more bitterly at the Party Conference in May 1921. He had to fight hard to impose the signature of the Brest-Litovsk Treaty in 1918 (his critics were considering excluding him from Sovnarkom) or the introduction of the NEP three years later. Faced with grueling conflicts with Trotsky, Stalin, Bukharin, and other lesser grandees, he did not always get his way.

On the other hand, mentioning those lesser leaders unravels another facet. The offensive by Alexandra Kollontai and Alexander Shliapnikov prompted Lenin to push through the ban on factions, which Stalin later put to good use. Add to that the formation of the Cheka, the dissolution of the Constituent Assembly, the establishment of the first camps, the executions of hostages, the merciless requisitions of War Communism, state control over the economy (far greater than anything Lenin had suggested prior to October 1917), the confiscation of church property and the execution of the Metropolitans, the trial of the Socialist Revolutionaries (although Lenin did not obtain the death penalty or the organization of a similar trial against the Mensheviks, which Stalin would have imposed), the expulsion of writers and intellectuals, and so on and so forth. It is a classic litany albeit incomplete; the corollary of a dictatorship about which Lenin was quite candid. And there's more: Lenin simultaneously held the posts of president of the Politburo, of the Central Committee, and of Sovnarkom. He occasionally made decisions without referring to members of the Politburo; even before Stalin and Mao, he inaugurated the practice of giving mandates to his followers, and his excessive optimism prevented him from seeing reality (just as it did to the two others later on), which led him into such ventures as the invasion of Poland. He was loath to accept the sole responsibility for his mistakes (Poland again), and his stubbornness sometimes bordered on the absurd. Many of those traits that were later found ad nauseam in Stalin and Mao were there from the very start.

That Lenin behaved as a dictator is indisputable, but the gulf between the revolution's Leninist childhood and its Stalinist adulthood is almost as great as that between Maoism and what the Chinese dictatorship was transformed into in the twenty-first century—a veritable paradise for the older Chinese who had seen so much worse in their youths. Lenin's (very relative) humanity was not the only reason for that. The dictatorship did not yet have the time to strengthen its foundations, as many incidents confirm. Take, for instance, the employee at the Commissariat of the People for Education (the equivalent of a ministry for education) who informed Lenin's wife that she would not be coming in to the office because, since the workers were now the masters, she had decided to stay at home. Lenin himself, having briefly left his coat in the office, discovered that one of his bodyguards had stolen his Browning and had to raise hell to get it back again.[3] Finally let us compare the treatment of the two dictators when they were ill, as illustrated first by the famous Politburo decision, which stated that "Vladimir Ilyich [Lenin] may dictate every day for 5 to 10 minutes, but this cannot have the character of correspondence and Vladimir Ilyich may not expect to receive any answers. It is forbidden for him to receive any [political] visitors."[4] True, the purpose of this decision, dated December 1922, was to protect Lenin's failing health. It is however quite unimaginable to think of Chinese leaders doing any such thing for Mao during the summer of 1976, a time when only his nephew (on occasion) and his mistress (a little more frequently) managed to decipher the mumblings that emerged from his august lips and were immediately transformed into Party orders and decisions.

The sick Lenin, haunted by fears about his succession, devoted those five to ten minutes a day (and more) to dictating letters, his last articles, and his "testament" (an inappropriate term but an accepted one). Ten days later, he broke with the uneasy equilibrium of that testament with his famous addendum: "Stalin is too rude and this defect although quite tolerable in our midst and in dealing among us Communists, becomes intolerable in a Secretary-General. That is why I suggest the comrades think about a way of removing Stalin from that post and appointing another man in his stead … more tolerant, more loyal, more polite, and more considerate to the comrades, less capricious, etc." Nothing apparently too serious, except the lack of loyalty. Lenin seemingly stressed good manners; the veneer of the reputedly exploitative ruling glasses.[5] The key, however, lies in the proposal to remove Stalin from the post of secretary-general, eight months after he himself had sanctioned it: King Lear regretting belated choices! The remedies that Lenin suggested for dealing with the very real issues at stake, such as the nature of the regime and its bureaucracy, which had become "the government's real social basis" (Moshe Lewin), would not have been feasible even if his colleagues had agreed to implement them.[6] Although Lenin was aware of Russia's economic, cultural, and other backwardness, which threatened to doom the revolutionary project from the start, he never challenged either the project's validity or the strategy (the single, tyrannical, "avant-garde" party of a working class that was bogged down in revolutionary spontaneity) that was diverting it from everything he had dreamed of. The fact that the personality of the "marvelous Georgian" ultimately repelled Lenin does not invalidate Leninism's filiation to Stalinism—and indirectly to Maoism.[7] Dominique Colas eloquently resumed Lenin's viewpoint, when he said that the Revolution of 1917 was achieved by the "miracle of the inter-imperialist war," and "was an advance of politics over the economy, a happy anticipation of the development of productive forces." It is therefore possible to "explain Stalinism either as a negative effect of the backwardness of the productive forces, or as an heroic attempt to make them catch them up. In that respect, Stalin's barbarism was an historical stipulation that enabled Russia to be snatched away from barbarity according to Lenin's very own principle: do not hesitate to use barbarity against barbarity."[8]

This takes us a long way from the laborious confrontation between Lenin and Stalin/Mao's governing methods that I outlined above! It brings us far closer to the untenable promises of *The State and Revolution*, written just before the conquest of power and Lenin's rampant demagoguery of April to October 1917, which paid off. The book announced the decline of the state, which he immediately set about to reinforce; his speeches and articles celebrated the revolutionary spontaneity of the masses, in which he did not believe. That mistrust was part and parcel of his heresy. Because he denied the proletariat the historical capability Marx had conferred on it, Lenin transferred the task originally allotted to that chosen class, to a party of professional revolutionaries. Right from the very beginning of the century, in *What Is to Be Done* (1902), he therefore laid down "the foundations of modern totalitarianism" (Kostas Papaioannou).[9] If the Party's absolute preeminence appears to consecrate the shift from the social (Marx) to the political (Lenin), that is just an illusion since "its organizational structure ... reduced its political nature to the utmost, ... allied it with the church (by its dogmatized ideology), with the bureaucracy (by its centralized and hierarchical organization) and with the army (by the monolithic obedience he demanded from his grass-roots militants)."[10] Even if the mommy in his mausoleum cursed the monstrosities perpetuated in his name from Moscow to Beijing, and from Pyongyang to Prague, he could not disown his progeny.

... and Marx

Some followers might have seen Stalin as a Hegelian hero, the driving force of history who "necessarily crushes countless innocent flowers and destroys many things in its passage."[11] In between Hegel and Lenin, Marx's heretical disciple, there is no avoiding the one in between, the former young Hegelian who was only partly freed from the realization of philosophy (Hegelianism) that men must "achieve" in order to change the world instead of restricting themselves to simply interpreting it. Marx too was a party to that. Marx, far more than Lenin, loathed servility, revolted against injustice, was ready to defy all the religious, social, and political authorities, and lived for his ideas and for the revolution with a supreme indifference to creature comforts. We can imagine everything that he would have detested and condemned in Stalin and Mao, along with their sycophants and their nomenklatura.[12] Then one might imagine Marx defending the Mensheviks against Lenin, for how could a socialist revolution be possible in a country where the forces of capitalist production were so underdeveloped? And with what sarcasm would the man who opposed Bakunin, Blanquism, and terrorism, disown the new-style Blanquis, Bakunins, Chernychevskys, Nechayevs, and others, created by his so-called disciple: an elitist party of conspirators claiming the right to decide in the name of a class that was never consulted! Imagine the horror that he would have felt at all-powerful terrorist states imposing blind orthodox obedience.

Nevertheless, Marx cannot be exonerated any more than Lenin. He presented a prophecy and a philosophy of history as a science that claimed to explain the whole of human history by a single force: the class struggle. That could not be applied to the past, if only because it is impossible to account for slavery or the feudal society without taking into account military might, conquest, and politics, and it was rapidly refuted by the development of capitalism, which did not conform to the inexorable hurtle of increasingly insoluble and deadly contradictions that his *Capital* had assigned to it. Among other consequences, the proletariat did not become increasingly poor and revolutionary—to that extent that it proved Lenin right against Marx. Thus Marx's hypothetical deductions led him to conclude that the proletariat had a revolutionary vocation (it had to) before he launched into serious political-economic studies—which is what they later undeniably became. As for the decline of the state following the end of prehistory, in other words in the classless society, do we need to confront *Anti-Dühring*[13] with what I have attempted to document in chapter 3 and what is common knowledge? Or better still, with Leszek Kołakowski's ironic tirade, which Gomulka's censorship deprived the Poles from reading, and which stated that Socialism is not:

> A state whose neighbors curse geography; ... a state that is not very good at distinguishing between social revolution and armed invasion; ... a state where a nation can be transplanted in its entirety from one place to another, willy-nilly; ... a society whose leaders appoint themselves; a state that wants all its citizens to have the same views on philosophy, foreign policy, the economy, literature, and morality; ... a state where the results of parliamentary elections can always be unerringly predicted; a state that is always exceedingly pleased with itself; ... a state that produces excellent jet planes but bad shoes; ... a state where people are compelled to lie; ... a state where cowards are better off than the courageous; ... a society that is very sad.[14]

This list of examples or anecdotes confirms that Marx—far more than Lenin—detested what was accomplished/perpetuated in his name, but he was not entirely blameless either, as suggested by the same author when he endeavors to "trace back from Stalinism to Marxism."[15]

Let us leave Lenin and his origins and masters and return to the subject of this book: his Chinese heirs: the Maoist copy of Stalinism. Not that we are really abandoning the subject since the "Marxist-Leninist" affiliation spawned two related revolutions in two very different universes (briefly touched upon in the first chapter). Similarities can always be found in the breeding ground of revolutionary fauna, indeed I mention a few in the first chapter, and Bertrand Badie suggests another. While taking care to refute the existence of any pre-totalitarian filiation, he applies the criteria suggested by Raymond Aron to the Confucian and Orthodox traditions. The Confucian tradition neither postulates, nor indeed conceives of, the least conflict between God and the temporal power of the Son of Heaven. All well and good for China, but what about Christian Russia? Badie points out that in the Byzantine tradition, the Eastern Christian culture does not oppose temporal and spiritual authorities in such a decisive way as in Roman Christianity. The nonexistence of judicial institutions independent of political power is another tie between Russian and Soviet history. Nevertheless, Badie admits that Marxism itself arose in a cultural tradition that was extraneous to the values of the Third Rome, and still more so to those of Confucianism.[16]

Assessment

The breeding ground matters little, the faithful will reply, what is important is to put an end to prehistory everywhere, whatever the obstacles. Since man's exploitation of man was not eradicated but exacerbated, some other merit had to be found for the revolution. I can see only the early progress in health and education in both countries, and there the prize goes to China. True, that was thanks to the chronological time difference (the fight against infectious diseases was far more efficient worldwide in the 1950s than it was in the 1920s), but also to sustained efforts by the Maoist regime from the 1950s, which decisively pushed back the mortality rates (especially infant mortality) and reduced illiteracy still further. With regard to gender equality, the changes did not live up to the stated intentions, although they were far from negligible given the resistance of mentalities. I shall not expound on the about-turns in legislation in the Stalinist Soviet Union, but in China the 1950 marriage law could easily have been in the program of any reforming and modernizing team.

Health and education improve the workers' productivity and consequently could serve to illustrate the modernization enterprise as much as the departure from prehistory. That is why I included them in chapter 2, devoted not to the proletariat's presumed historical responsibility (getting humanity out of prehistory), but to the prerequisite enterprise ("primitive accumulation" as it were), namely getting a country (or two in this case) out of backwardness. It is in this area and no other that we must identify the main achievements.

As Anton Ciliga said mockingly, "If we were to judge according to the number of factories, socialism would long have been achieved in the United States." He agreed that the first Five-Year Plan could be called progressive "but in no way socialist." The frenzy it generated simply intensified the fascination for machinery, movement, and construction. That fascination was clear from the early years of the NEP, and confirmed a generation later when the hero of *Not by Bread Alone* declares, "I am among those who create material values. The main spiritual value in our time is to know how to work well and produce as many useful goods as possible." Some twelve to fifteen years before Dudintsev, Sigmund Neumann already observed that "the quasi-childish admiration for technical progress ... emerged in the 19th century. Lenin became Peter the Great of the 20th century." Without going that far back, Lenin, and above all Stalin, pursued the enterprise started by Count Witte with the blessing of Nicolas II.[17]

Lynne Viola compares the Soviet Union to "a Leviathan in bast shoes": "Soviet modernity always remained moored to its agrarian legacy." Despite that, Stalin accomplished far more than Mao, but Mao's task, faced as he was with greater backwardness, was far harder. Above all let us grant Mao the fact that never, even at the outset when he believed that he had no choice but to "copy the Soviets," did he confuse the industrial revolution with the socialist revolution so dear to his heart. Dissatisfied, he tried to promote the socialist revolution of his dreams, but met with no more success than with the industrial revolution. The Chinese leaders today are concerned with preventing the idol from being demolished. Since they cannot attribute the economic development and improvements in living standards that occurred after Mao's death, and thanks to his death, to the idol, they stress that he achieved the nation's independence and unity. That brings us back to the nationalist sources of the Chinese revolution far more than to its Marxist manifestation. When scholars such as Harry Harding credit the Communist Party for having transformed, under Mao, a society that Sun Yat-sen deplored as just "a sheet of loose sand" into "one of the most highly organized societies in the world," they remain in the same vein.[18]

It has been suggested on occasion that the spectacular growth of the Chinese economy in the past three and half decades was the result of a reaction against the waste of the Cultural Revolution, which had the merit of exploring a new way—and was the only way to demonstrate that it would lead to an impasse. Just how far can people go in their desire to attribute merit to the founder who went astray! I willingly admit that quite a few foundations for the subsequent industrial development were established in Mao's lifetime, including during the frenzy of the Great Leap Forward. Clearly nobody was prepared to discard anything that was salvageable from the reckless production of the so-called "leap forward" in order to achieve the phenomenal leap that occurred at the end of the century. And I'm even more willing to admit that Mao's misguided leap sprang from the desire (and belief) that it was for the good of the masses, even though it condemned them to famine.

That is the sad lesson of the revolutionary experience. The cynicism of today' post-totalitarian Chinese leaders, who believe in nothing more than nationalism and clinging to their own power, has proved much more beneficial than Mao's (and even Stalin's) stubborn conviction that he was acting for the future good of humanity. The same was true of their master: "While [Machiavelli's] The Prince was lucid and knew the truth, Lenin was blinded by ideology and saw only a falsified truth … ; he deceived himself."[19]

Gulag survivor Eugenia Ginzburg echoed that original sincerity in her recollections of her Communist youth: "We were the children of our time, that time of great illusions, … out-and-out idealists, despite our youthful enthusiasm for the cold constructions of dialectical materialism." In "looking back at my life with disgust," she regretted sharing responsibility for murders and massacres (by unthinkingly repeating dangerous theoretical formulas, by raising her right hand but not her voice, by cowardly writing half-truths). "18 years of hell on earth are not yet enough to atone for such an offense."[20] That deterioration must be explained: "How into worthless lead pure gold is changed!"[21]

Lies, Fear, and Debasement

First to blame were the lies that Hannah Arendt defined thus: "Preventing anything whatsoever from disturbing the macabre tranquility of an entirely imaginary world, with the slightest grain of truth."[22] It would be easy to provide numerous quotes from Ginzburg (yes, her again!) to Grossman and from Mandelstam to Miłosz,[23] but from my comparative perspective I will just add one last quote: "Russia is driven by the will to want and not see." Boris Pilniak claimed that this type of lie was "unique in the world," yet it would become even more applicable to Mao, the voluntarist who refused to see.[24]

Lenin's successors placed no more hope than he did in the workers, "coarse, egotistical, drunkards, cruel to their wives and distant with regard to the Party." That is what they read in their only reliable source of information: the secret reports compiled by the OGPU exclusively for them. In their agitprop discourse, the same leaders praised the revolutionary battalions of proletarians, driven by their class consciousness, the best sons of the motherland marching behind the Party in the vanguard. From that time on they lived in lies as willing schizophrenics. The OGPU told them about workers living in conditions worse than pigs and the strikes led by those desperate people, and, since it is impossible to strike in a worker state, they denounced the counterrevolutionary provocations of Mensheviks, white guards, and other class enemies. Any striking worker was therefore a secret Menshevik, a peasant who demanded a union was a kulak, a student who criticized bureaucracy was a rioter. The leaders did not believe this representation of the truth, nor did the people continue to believe in the truths that were served up to them. There were three levels of discourse: the official one, which celebrated the victories and unmasked the enemies; the confidential OGPU reports, which provided firsthand information to a handful of leaders; and private conversations within the confines of the family or between very close friends, which attempted to decrypt the scraps of truth concealed among the mass of lies poured out by propaganda.[25]

That third level of discourse declined or disappeared altogether in the 1930s as the secret police spread its branches. People limited their number of reliable friends to one or two at most—and the safest bet was to do without completely. People ceased to speak in front of their children, or lied to them in order to protect themselves (in case those young pioneers were ever transformed into apprentice Pavlik Morozovs) or to protect their children by presenting "the lies as truths right away (to make life easier for them)."[26] After the death of the dictator, Yevtushenko could well proclaim, "Fears are dying out in Russia, like the ghosts of bygone years," but, if we are to believe Chichibabin, those same fears that obliged everyone to embrace the lies for a quarter of a century, did not evaporate so easily:

As long as we don't stop the lies
And don't unlearn to fear
Stalin is not dead.[27]

In this post-totalitarian phase, "man has not the least obligation to believe in all these mystifications," he must only "behave as though he believes in them, or at least tolerate them in silence" (Václav Havel). This was therefore not the end of hypocrisy and lies. In 1978 Mikhail Gorbachev sent reports to Moscow praising the extraordinary energy of Comrade Brezhnev, even though everyone knew that he had all but stopped working altogether. That same Gorbachev was sincere when he declared, "I want to make the Soviet people a normal people." He attempted it and by doing so brought about the final collapse. The oligarchs, at least the more honest among them, began by confessing, "We wallowed in our lies, we gave each other medals."[28] In fact *glasnost*, which Gorbachev hoped would "fill the blanks" in Soviet history, led to such a cascade of revelations that the pace of them left no room for the lies—and consequently the regime—to survive.

China has not reached that stage, and the lies remain rife. So long as the parents or grandparents do not confide (and caution keeps them mum), a Chinese youngster will know even less about the Cultural Revolution, the Great Leap Forward, and the famine than his or her counterpart in the West—in other words, nothing. Not only have the lies persisted for longer but they started earlier, before becoming even bigger and more meticulous. During the GLF factories were supposedly built at a pace unequalled in world history: in a certain corner of the southwestern province of Yunnan, they were churned out one a minute, at a cost of just two yuan (just a few cents), while just fifteen hundred kilometers farther to the north, in Gansu province, ten thousand factories were built in a fortnight. So-called Sputniks sprouted everywhere,[29] those fields that produced miraculous yields. Such "records" proved fatal, for it was on the basis of those spectacular yields that the Communist leadership set the grain requisitioning quotas that caused the farmers to starve that winter and the following spring.

Some local leaders lied in order to appear to be doing better than their neighbors, others because any Communist cadre who failed to embellish local production results ran the risk of being beaten or tortured. Lies were a means for survival. As in Ukraine back in 1933, the Chinese police and the army intercepted starving people who were attempting to flee the disaster areas, in order to prevent the truth from getting out. Letters begging for help never reached their addressees, and the writers were arrested. That happened frequently in Xinyang, a southern prefecture in Henan province, where a record number of people died of hunger (more than one million out of a population of eight million). Yet even when hunger and cannibalism were rampant in Xinyang, the *Henan Daily* published a series of seven articles titled "Marching towards Communism" that described the excellent situation there. When it finally became impossible to deny the horror any longer, Mao settled the matter by saying, "The Xinyang incident is a restoration of the landlord class and counterrevolutionary class retaliation."[30]

The remedy for lies is quite simple, but it took more than a half century for a man to find the strength to advocate it. In 1974, Solzhenitsyn called on the intellectuals and the entire country to "live outside of lies." "What does it matter if the lies cover everything, if they are the masters of everything, but let us be uncompromising at least on that point: that it does not originate with me." And Liu Xiaobo in 2003: "In post-totalitarian China … , the system's only resource for remaining in place, are lies." There is only one solution to that, "to refuse to lie … not to take part in the lies, nor use lies in order to survive."[31]

What may have been obvious to those two Nobel Prize–winners for bravery was baffling for others, who remained rooted in their fear. In Moscow, almost every night between 1937 and 1938 people feared arrest and consequently tried to prevent the slightest little blot on the empire of lies from being attributed to them. Two decades later, in *The Quenching of Thirst*, Yuri Trifonov ironically portrayed Soviet citizens as having "rabbit hearts" and Vasily Grossman asked, "Who was the joker who said, 'Man! The word has such a proud ring!'" That poor joker was Gorky, whom Grossman regretted ever having admired in the past.[32] Those who felt shame were at one and the same time more affected and less so. More so because they could not forgive themselves their cowardice, and less so for they were still human beings, capable of repenting. The others, as they were described by Zybine to a policewoman, in Yuri Dombrovski's *The Keeper of Antiquities*: "Remember your witnesses. They confirm everything you asked. They deliver everything you demand … the lives of others, their honor, anything. And with what pleasure! They ooze the desire to please. Abjection flows in their veins. They are ready to do anything, so long as they can get out of your mousetrap. And once they get out,

Lord what joy! I'm alive! Free!"[33] The deterioration of the human species under the very socialism that was supposed to make it reach new summits was deplored countless times by its lucid victims.[34] They denounced conformism, the blind brutal selfishness, "something incredibly dry, hard and even ossified" (Dombrovski).

I can say the same of China, although there were fewer torments of the "will-I-manage-not-to-lie?" type. Lying meant surviving: that was an undisputed truth. Life was too precarious for any concern whatsoever to matter more than self-preservation. It was rather as though Russia, already European, belonged to that universe of privileged people who have the leisure to raise questions about moral and other issues. The shame came later, once the lies and deception accumulated, having been proffered or perpetuated unhesitatingly. Take the case of a privileged member of the former regime: a student in the United States at the time the Communists came to power. He returned to Shanghai out of patriotism, and taught political economy, before the government named him a "national capitalist" and put him at the head of three flourmills. He learned his lesson as early as 1951, during the Campaign to Suppress Counter-Revolutionaries. "Friends had to betray friends" and human relations immediately paid the price. As a result he decided to gain the trust of the Communists in order to obtain permission to go to Hong Kong on the pretext of visiting his family. He worked hard at confirming the official image of the United States in a seventy-page autobiography, in which he invented terrible scenes in which the American police massacred striking workers and racial minorities. He suffered from constantly having to debase himself, but he persisted and was ultimately successful since he was the only person to obtain a permit for Hong Kong.[35]

Can we doubt the account of an émigré who denounces the regime he has fled? Might a given anecdote not have been invented, like the massacre of strikers and blacks by the U.S. Police? Conversely there is no reason not to trust the well-argued and balanced paper by a Sinologist titled "From Friendship to Comradeship: The Change in Personal Relations in Communist China." He analyzes the decline of friendship, which was replaced by sacrosanct "universalist" friendship—except where landlords, capitalists, and their progeny were concerned. It became increasingly difficult for friendship to survive in a climate of mistrust, and the danger of confiding in someone who might be interrogated about you all the more persistently if it is known that you are that person's friend. People stopped inviting friends over for dinner, especially if a given item of furniture or dish of food were considered bourgeois, for the guests would be forced to describe your interior decor and the dishes you served.[36]

Everyone submitted themselves to this, including leaders, even if it meant that they were cut off from the masses even more. In 1971, for the first time there were no festivities at the anniversary of the founding of the People's Republic of China, so as to conceal the absence of "Chairman Mao's closest comrade in arms," the appointed successor, Lin Biao. Revealing a secret was such a serious crime that none of the leaders who knew about it dared to reveal it. That would be tantamount to divulging a secret to a foreign nation, which was a mortal sin. If the leaders were afraid of the slightest transgression, imagine what it was like for the rest of the population. "Everyone is afraid, including young people, and the older ones even more," remarked Deng Xiaoping in 1975 during his brief return to power.[37]

This recalls the Stalinist terror, when "obedience ... bypassed the brain, aiming at lower organs. Obedience turned blind, reflexive, visceral" (Vera Dunham). That fear was transmitted right down to the peasants, as described by Alexandre Iachine in Levers. Like everyone else, they adopted the official Newspeak whenever they took part in a meeting.[38]

***

This book seems to have given itself the task of dispelling any illusions about revolution, but it is a natural recourse given the abominable injustice in our world, the boundless misery, and the deadly scheming of the powerful. These constantly trigger new revolutionary vocations, which I believe should be resisted. As an old killjoy historian myself, I agree with a contemporary Chinese historian who, in the evening of his life, remarked, "If at all possible, it is best to avoid revolutions altogether,"[39] for as Berdyaev put it, "Judging the Russian revolution implies judging revolutions in general"—and that is all the more true if we include the Chinese one.

Appendix
Before and After: Yan'an, 1942–1943

The aim of this appendix, which concerns only China (since there was no Bolshevik government before 1917), is to show that China was already a faithful copy of the model—hence the title of this appendix—before the People's Republic was created but after the 1930s in the Soviet Union, which formed the embryo.

In two speeches made in February 1942, Mao called for the "rectification of the Party's style of work." He especially criticized dogmatism and those who embodied it; in other words the former students at Moscow's Sun Yat-sen University. I'll pass over the abstractions of the apprentice philosopher,[1] who only started to read Marx and have it explained to him in Yan'an in order to acquire the necessary theoretical veneer. Instead I'll go straight to the point. Those Moscow-trained Communists, known as "the 28 Bolsheviks" or the "internationalists," had supplanted Mao in his little Soviet kingdom in Jiangxi province. During the Long March and then in Yan'an, Mao had succeeded in reconquering most of the power, but they retained solid positions in the cadre training institutes and other propaganda departments. Mao therefore decided to consolidate his position by launching an "intellectual" offensive against the dogmatic abstractions that allegedly misled people if not applied to a reality that had been diligently studied in the field. Mao was especially targeting those leaders who might contest his supremacy, and, incidentally, the writers and intellectuals who flocked to Yan'an after the Japanese invasion. Mao wanted to use their skills but he needed to discipline them beforehand and reinforce their "proletarian" class-consciousness.

He succeeded in silencing the Soviet Union–trained students, but not the writers and intellectuals. In March and April 1942, a series of critical or satirical articles, essays, short stories, and poems appeared on the half page devoted to literature of the very official *Jiefang Ribao* (Liberation Daily) as well as in other publications. On International Women's Day, Ding Ling, the editor of the literary section (1904–1986), opened fire with an article titled, "Thoughts on March 8th" in which she protested against the situation of women in Yan'an society, who were mocked if they did not marry but criticized if they did and held on to their political positions rather than raise their children. If, on the contrary, they gave up their jobs to raise their children, they ran the risk of being mocked again for their "backwardness." The article also attacked the privileges of the (all-male) Party leadership—a topic that was followed up so eloquently by Wang Shiwei (1906–1947). In an essay called "The Wild Lily," Wang criticized the inequalities of Yan'an society and the behavior of the high-ranking Communist cadres who did not practice the ideals they professed. A second article by Wang, called "Statesmen and Artists," distinguished the roles held by the two. The politicians and revolutionary strategists had the task of increasing the revolutionary movement's material forces and changing the social system. They should therefore leave it to the artists to take care of the spiritual forces, and to form and reform human minds. The poet Ai Qing (1910–1996), a former student of the École des Beaux Arts in Paris (the French National college of art and architecture) and father of the contemporary artist and dissident Ai Weiwei, hammered the same point home in an article titled "Understand and Respect Writers." A handful of others, Communists or fellow travelers, contributed to those heresies, but publication of their works was brutally interrupted in early April 1942.

The danger those troublemakers represented led Mao and the Party leadership to temporarily adjust the target of the "rectification." Their priority was now to reeducate the intellectuals, victims of their petit-bourgeois mentality. A new directive "rectified" the goals and methods of the rectification. It was vital to insist upon unified thought in all Party members, who were invited to make their own self-criticisms rather than criticize their leadership. That they hastened to do by disavowing everything they had published a few weeks earlier—all but the stubborn Wang Shiwei, who maintained his stand and replied in writing to the criticisms made about him. Wang Shiwei's refusal to confess was not appreciated at all. He was already guilty of having aroused the enthusiasm of many people in the Party, who rushed to read his latest contributions to the wall-poster newspaper, *Arrow and Target*. It was necessary to destroy the poison that Wang had inculcated into so many foolish youngsters and, if he refused, he had to be dealt with. That was the subject of an almost daily series of meetings between 27 May and 11 June 1942, which started with a fairly harmless discussion of democracy in the Party (which got lost in the "extreme democracy" of the early stages in the rectification movement), before turning into a public trial of Wang Shiwei, a Trotskyist in disguise, then a Guomindang spy. Since his deeds must be incriminated as well as his thoughts and writings, a five-member anti-Party clique was concocted, consisting of Wang's accomplices in his counterrevolutionary work to undermine the Party and its historical mission. The Central Research Institute voted unanimously to expel Wang Shiwei, even though three months earlier it had approved Wang's proposal to elect the members of the "rectification committee" for the institute (which the management had intended to designate itself), by eighty-four votes to twenty-eight.

Rather than linger on this episode, Communist historiography has endlessly celebrated the "Yan'an Forum on Literature and Art" that preceded it. Above all it has stressed Mao's two "Talks on Literature and Art" (the official title of the speeches that have been quoted thousands of times) that opened and closed the forum on 2 and 23 May, respectively. The speeches were made to an audience of two hundred writers and cadres in charge of cultural matters, and at first were just a way of refuting Wang Shiwei and reeducating the fools he had misled. To criticize the Party leaders was to attack the masses who were the beneficiaries of the correct policies devised by those leaders. The said masses were the privileged public of the creators, and it was for them that they must write, paint, and compose. By subordinating art and literature to politics ("We must have a cultural army ... for uniting our own ranks and defeating the enemy") Mao identified once and for all what was permitted and, more importantly, what was forbidden to artist and writers. There is no point in expounding on that; anyone familiar with the socialist realism imposed in the Soviet Union from 1934 and Stalin's directives to the "engineers of the soul" will imagine the contents of the 1942 "Talks," which were never challenged over the entire Chinese subcontinent between 1949 and 1980.

I am detailing that first episode in the relations between the CCP and the writers for two reasons. One, it clearly shows the influence of the Soviet precedent on Chinese cultural polity and, over and above that, the close relationship between the two as shown by parallel spontaneous reactions. Two, it provides a prototype for later "campaigns" dealing with ideology or culture.

First, the Soviet precedent and the common ancestry of the two regimes. Mao boasted that he had Sinicized Marxism but remembered Stalin's lessons. He defined and exposed the principles, but as soon as it came to accusations and sentencing, he confided the tasks to others. His own Yezhov (or, to respect a more classic comparison, Beria) was called Kang Sheng (1899–1975), whom Wang Ming (the best known of the "28 Bolsheviks") had brought with him from Moscow in 1937. During a stay of several years in the Soviet Union, Kang Sheng had first studied the Soviet intelligence system and then served as a deputy to Wang Ming in the Comintern. Mao entrusted him with the joint management of intelligence and the secret police services, ingenuously called the Central Department of Social Affairs. Incidentally (except for what concerns us here!), he became deputy director (the titular director being Mao) of the committee supervising the rectification movement. It was in that position the he "revealed" Wang Shiwei's Trotskyism and fabricated the tale about the Guomindang spy, and for good measure added Wang's membership of the Blue Shirts Society, an organization of Chiang Kai-shek devotees who took more than just their name from Mussolini's Black Shirts.

The increasingly insistent leitmotif of the anti-Wang campaign was his "Trotskyism," based on clues that he himself had revealed to the Party when he arrived Yan'an in 1937—and which Kang Sheng found in Wang's file. Like so many Chinese Communists, Wang largely blamed the Komintern for the defeat of the 1927 Chinese revolution. He was friendly with two young Chinese Trotskyites who, like him, were critical of Stalin's Chinese strategy. He translated (from the English, since he did not speak Russian) Lenin's "testament" and two chapters of Trotsky's autobiography, less out of militancy than to earn a living, just as he also translated Thomas Hardy, Eugene O'Neill, and the English translation of Daudet's *Sapho*. One of the two Trotskyites was killed while still young by the Japanese, while the other testified in writing that Wang had refused to join the Trotskyites for fear of contributing to a split in the revolutionary movement.[2] The trouble with Wang Shiwei was his candor, which led him to confirm each of the accusations made against him without batting an eyelid. Yes, he believed that not everything in Trotsky's thinking was wrong, that the charges against Zinoviev were not proven, that the purges of Communists in Moscow went too far, that Stalin was too brutal—all statements that aroused the indignation of the audience: "He praises Trotsky and slanders Comrade Stalin." That was exactly what the Party needed to counter Wang Shiwei's influence. Wang proved to be so cooperative that it was necessary for him to take part in his own trial on only one occasion, 4 June. After that, during the last week of his trial from 4 to 11 June (a public trial, even if it did not comply with legal procedure), accusations, lies, insults, and abuse poured down on the absent defendant. Wang's friends, Ai Qing and Ding Ling, also took part in the assault in order to protect themselves. Despite that, there happened to be a Pasternak in the audience,[3] the writer Xiao Jun (1908–1988), who could not resist writing to Mao to express his disagreement over the way the trial was conducted. The Party never forgave him for that, and in 1948 Xiao was accused of hostility toward the Soviet Union (he had merely said out loud what most of the inhabitants of Manchuria were thinking during the Soviet occupation of 1945–1946). As little inclined as Wang to write an acceptable confession, Xiao Jun was sentenced to forced labor in a Manchurian coal mine, and his novel *A Village in August* was denounced in all the schools and factories, as well as among the "broad masses."

Given that all of the above clearly establishes China's relationship with the Soviet precedent, there is no need for me to add lengthy commentaries. Mao's manipulations, even though he did not intervene directly, and the growing number of accusations that went from ideological deviation to counterrevolutionary actions, "proven" by orchestrated lies (the Blue Shirts, the five-member anti-Party clique, etc.). Last of all, the crescendo in tone that started full of apparent concern for the comrades who had lost their way in egalitarianism and ultra-democracy, but ended in fury, insults, and total dehumanization. Chen Boda, who was about to become one of Mao's secretaries (and ghost writers), compared Wang Shiwei to a spineless bloodsucker. If only Wang had had a flexible backbone! The four other members of the alleged five-member anti-Party clique were freed, but not Wang, who was beheaded by axe on 1 July 1947 in Xing Xian (Shanxi province), shortly after Yan'an was recaptured by the Nationalists and evacuated. Mao claimed to have disapproved of the execution, but the order to execute Wang was transmitted orally by Kang Sheng, then a member of the Politburo.

The connection with what followed (in China) was as flagrant as with what preceded it (in the Soviet Union), just as though the draft of 1942 had provided the canvas for the tragedies to come. The first comparison that comes to mind is with the Hundred Flowers fifteen years later. The "rectification movement" of February 1942 prefigured Mao's repeated efforts in 1956 and 1957 to incite non-Communist intellectuals to criticize the Party and help it to "rectify its style of work."[4] The resemblance between the consequences of those two episodes is most striking. The "rectification" launched in 1942 led to a witch hunt in 1943 resulting in the interrogation, harassment, exclusion, imprisonment, or forced suicide of thousands of Communists or their sympathizers. In 1957, having failed to "rectify the Party's style of work," Mao corrected the intelligentsia, whose "calumnies" confirmed their bourgeois heritage. The deviants of 1942, first and foremost Ding Ling (even though she had obtained the Stalin prize in the meantime) and Ai Qing, were labeled rightists in 1957 and punished, even though they had both been very cautious during the Hundred Flowers, having had their fingers burned in 1942.

During a session to criticize Ding Ling held in Mao's presence, Kang Sheng's wife, Cao Yi'ou, opened fire against the pernicious "Thoughts on March 8th." Twenty-four years later, that same Cao Yi'ou sparked off the fateful events at Beijing University by inciting a Party secretary to write a big character poster (*dazibao*) attacking the university's president. That "coincidence" shows the parallel between the 1942 forerunner and the 1966 tragedy. Another similarity may be found in the *dazibao* itself. Those wall posters were "discovered" during the Cultural Revolution, despite the fact that Wang Shiwei and his friends had experimented with them (under different names) in 1942 with *Arrow and Target* and other wall-poster newspapers. There was, however, one important difference: the 1942 wall posters expressed sincere criticisms, whereas those in 1966–1967 expressed a choreographed indignation, controlled from above.

More importantly, the man who mounted the accusation against Wang Shiwei in 1942 was Kang Sheng, the very same person who planned the repression in 1943, and then carried out Mao's dirty work during the Cultural Revolution. In August 1943, with the commendable aim of training secret police cadres, Kang crudely revealed the methods he used to follow, segregate, and bring down Wang Shiwei and his alleged accomplices. He detailed the various phases of the secret police action, how they first encouraged "comrades" to talk (he admitted that at the outset of the "rectification," 95 percent of the comrades from the Central Research Institute had approved of *Wild Lilies*), identified the deviants, then concentrated their fire on Wang Shiwei by investigating his every deed and gesture, and in good time revealing his "Trotskyism." At the time when Kang made this report to his flock, he was fully engaged in his witch hunt for the Guomindang spies who had infiltrated Communist ranks and other subversive elements. He flushed out so many of them that in the end an enquiry was held into his methods. In December 1943, Kang admitted that more than 90 percent of those who had confessed to being traitors were in fact innocent and should be rehabilitated, some posthumously.

Several methods experimented with in Yan'an in 1942–1943 heralded those that would be carried out on a far wider scale in the People's Republic, such as accusing ideological deviants of subversive intrigues or even betrayal, or the public "struggle" sessions that attacked and condemned the prey, whose writings were distributed like so many exhibits in a trial (Peng Dehuai's letter to Mao was given to all the participants in the Lushan meeting in 1959). Or dividing up comrades and other people in need of reeducation into small study groups, in which they were obliged to read and memorize a selection of randomly chosen texts, examine and criticize themselves, and then criticize others. Or fabricating nonexistent anti-Party organizations, such as the Clique of Five in 1942. In 1955, the dissident writer Hu Feng was accused of heading a vast underground network on behalf of the Guomindang and the imperialists. Some of those good habits even survived Mao. We heard a muffled echo on several occasions in the 1980s and after, right until Liu Xiaobo was charged with subversion in December 2009. In short the very uncultural debates of 1942 were key moments in the turbulent relations between the so-called people's regime and its writers, artists, and intellectuals. Since they occurred or prevailed fifteen years before the Hundred Flowers, a comparison could be made with the debates that arose after *What Is to Be Done?* and the reflections by Boris Souvarine and Claude Lefort on "the development of a Party, the embryo of which already contained all of its fundamental characteristics nearly 15 years before the revolution."[5]

Sources: The most important is Dai, 1994, including the excellent introduction by Apter and Cheek. See also Fabre, 1990; Seybolt, 1986; Teiwes, 1993, pp. 58–60; 1995, pp. 362–365, 370–377; as well as Barmé, 1991; Goldman, 1967, chapter 2, and passim; Kuo, 1971, pp. 557–594, 610–647; Leys, 1974, pp. 183–189; Mao (I'm afraid so!), 1959, pp. 34–113; Roux, 2009, pp. 430–450; Rubin, 1981, pp. 508–510; Saich, 1996, pp. 978–985, 1240; Wylie, 1980, pp. 162–194. My thanks to Jean-Luc Domenach, who gave me the June 2013 issue of *Yanhuang chunqiu* (sometimes translated as *Annals of the Red Crag*), my source (Qiu Shipian's article on pp. 8–10) for the revelations concerning Wang's execution (the spoken order transmitted by Kang Sheng on behalf of the Politburo). *Yanhuang chunqiu* used to disclose a fair number of historical facts that enabled us to correct the official PRC historiography, at least until this summer (2016), when authorities removed the director and placed a more compliant staff in charge of the journal.

Notes

Introduction

1. Even though I have a book on the subject in my mother tongue: Depretto, 1997.

2. See Blum, 1994, p. 120; Yang Jisheng [2008], 2012, p. 194. English edition (*Tombstone*, 2012), p. 24

3. Lewin, 2003a, p. 367.

4. Gauchet, 2010, p. 304 (and p. 302 for "façade federalism"). For a more comprehensive treatment, see Martin, 2001.

Chapter 1   The Laggards

1. Estimates should be considered with caution; see Vichnevski, 2000, pp. 15–16. The other data are taken from chapter 1 of the same book and chapter 1 of Nove, 1992.

2. While usually overlapping with the village, the commune (*mir* or *obshchina*) was "a legal institution, a collective arrangement for the distribution among its members of land and taxes" (Pipes). Non-peasant residents such as the priest or the schoolteacher were not members of the *mir*. A *mir* could exceptionally encompass several small villages, or contrariwise represent only a part of a very large village (see Pipes, 1990, pp. 92, 97–99).

3. See Dumont, 1977, pp. 12–13. Conversely, by calling my first two chapters "The Laggards" and "Catching Up," I have betrayed my own internalization of the values of modern society.

4. Figes, 2007a, pp. 143–145; Berelowitch, 2005, p. 106; Werth [1990], 2004, p. 64.

5. That China was more backward was obvious to Witte. When summarizing his memorandum to Nicholas II (1899) he denied jeopardizing national independence by resorting to foreign capital: "Only decaying nations can fear enslavement by immigrant foreigners ... But Russia is not China" (quoted in Werth, [1990], 2004, p. 14).

6. S. A. Smith, 2008, p. 6.

7. See, among others, S. A. Smith, 1983, 2000, and 2002.

8. From Moussa, 1959, who labeled what were then called underdeveloped countries as "proletarian nations."

9. Berelowitch's title, 2005.

10. Quoted in ibid., p. 137; Chen Duxiu, quoted in Bianco [1967], 2007, p. 80 [English edition 1971, p. 40].

11. Others writers incarnate the reaction to the May Fourth Westernization trend better than Liang. Indeed Liang always vigorously refused to be placed in the category of supporters of that reaction, and praised Chen Duxiu's lucidity on many occasions. In his youth he had even participated in Tongmenghui (the secret society founded by Sun Yat-sen). Nevertheless I chose him because he is representative of the Sinophiles (a term I have hijacked in reference to the Slavophiles) and because his book is the most detailed of that period and, above all, because it was the most influential by far.

12. Alitto, 1979, pp. 82–125.

13. "On the other shore of the ocean are millions of people bewailing the bankruptcy of [their] material civilization and crying piteously for help, waiting for us to save them" (Liang Qichao, *Reflections on a European Journey*, p. 38, English translation in Alitto, 1979, p. 116). I provide a brief introduction to Liang in Bianco [1967], 2007, pp. 329–331.

14. Berelowitch, 2005, pp. 138–139.

15. Berdiaev [1938], 1951, p. 140.

16. Quoted in Figes, 2007a, p. 190.

17. Schwartz, 1964, pp. 146–147.

18. Ibid., pp. 182–183. The following quote in Sun Yat-sen, 1927, p. 146.

19. English translation by Yang Xianyi and Gladys Yang (Peking Foreign Languages Press, 1957). The French translation by Tchang Fou-jouei is titled *Chronique indiscrète des mandarins*. The book was written by Wu Jingzi around 1750, and seriously came to people's attention only more than a century after the author's death. In the meantime the dynasty was no longer at its apogee (when already lent itself to satire) but had grown decadent, and Gogol had lived, been praised, and then been disparaged.

20. Figes, 2007a, pp. 129–130.

21. Holquist, 2002, chap. 1.

22. Ibid., p. 46 and passim.

23. Details in Coquin, 1965, p. 21, and Figes, 2007a, p. 362.

Chapter 2   Catching Up

1. Other elucidating figures and percentages may be found in Nove, 1992, p. 62.

2. Lewin, [1966] 1976, p. 29, and 2003a, p. 371. The mention of the pharaohs was by the academician Vavilov, who died in prison in 1943 for having opposed Lyssenko's theories.

3. Ciliga, [1938] 1977, pp. 24–25.

4. Bergère, 2000, p. 44.

5. Deng Xiaoping later used the same concept and even specified that "some people will get rich first," which was tantamount to advance acceptance of at least temporary inequality. With this he sealed the fate of the Chinese revolution, to the joy of the Chinese people, and in the process achieved China's greatness and prosperity, which were the revolutionaries' original goals.

6. Quoted in Nove, 1992, p. 190, and Werth, [1990] 2004, p. 247.

7. That important and well-known debate in which many other leaders and theoreticians took part, in addition to Preobrazhensky and Bukharin, is discussed in Nove, 1992, chap. 5 and Cohen, Stephen, [1971] 1980, chap. 6. Cf. also Werth, [1990] 2004, pp. 207–209; Vichnevski, 2000, pp. 61–63.

8. Stalin professed to be an impartial centrist above partisan quarrels, but his moderate policy during the peak phase of the NEP (1924–1925) provided critics on the Trotskyist left with ample arguments.

9. Kotkin, 1995, pp. 47 and 66. On the duumvirate, cf. Cohen, Stephen, [1971] 1980, chap. 7.

10. Sources and studies abound: production objectives: Werth, [1995] 1998, p. 54; unrealistic and unachievable: Nove, 1992, pp. 190–191; war on nature: Vichnevski, 2000, p. 82, and Kotkin, 1995, pp. 31 and 50, who compare the Stalinist economy to a "war economy in peace time"; war on time: "We must make good this distance in ten years" (ibid., p. 69; "teleological planning": Cohen, Stephen, [1971] 1980, p. 319; there's no such thing as objective difficulties, nothing is impossible: Lewin, 2003a, p. 57, Schapiro, 1967, p. 412; no fortress: Nove, 1992, p. 146; Cohen, Stephen, [1971] 1980, pp. 266 and 314.

11. Expert in thrall to figures: Nove, 1992, pp. 191–192; scientific discussion ends and what follows: Service, 2005, pp. 300, 309, 317.

12. Small, incompetent groups: Kotkin, 1995, p. 41: irresponsible dictatorships: Lewin, 2003a, p. 52; mistakes toward the end of the NEP: Nove, 1992, pp. 137–146 and passim.

13. Kotkin, 1995, pp. 58–59, 67–69.

14. Ibid., pp. 45, 64–65, 422.

15. Ibid., pp. 89, 92, 420, and 424 for the entire paragraph, except for the number of workers, which more than doubled: Werth, [1990] 2004, p. 249.

16. Kotkin, 1995, pp. 35, 93, 215, and epilogue. Stephen Kotkin's thesis ("Stalinism as a Civilization") mentioned in the epilogue may not immediately suggest the gray or sinister reality, but his study of one of the most symbolic industrial sites of the effervescent 1930s sheds remarkable light on many facets of life in, around, and related to, the industrial plant.

17. Ibid., pp. 50–51. I will allow myself a recollection from some thirty-six years back, when I was being driven from Guangzhou to Haifeng, in eastern Guangdong province. I can still remember the joy and enthusiasm with which my guides greeted the completion of a bridge on the Dongjiang (East River), which had been inaugurated during our short absence. While they applauded enthusiastically their foreign guest regretted, in private, the spectacle that had delayed us for a good hour during the outward journey: a lively bustle of pedestrians, trucks, carts, pigs, and chickens, not to mention a few cars transporting cadres, who were obliged to wait like everyone else until the preceding ferry had discharged its passengers on the other bank.

18. Annual growth above 10 percent: Werth, [1990] 2004, p. 280; from Brest to Vladivostok: Lewin, 2003a, p. 467; the remainder of the paragraph: Nove, 1992, pp. 194, 196, 224, 228, 231–232, 260.

19. New stage achieved: Lewin, 2003a, p. 97; fall in living standards: Nove, 1992, p. 210; socialist construction and legitimacy: Kotkin, 1995, pp. 70–71; "We are becoming a nation of metal ...": Figes, 2007b, p. 111; also Gauchet, 2010, p. 315; Peter the Great and the reinvention of the imperial past: ibid., pp. 296 and 314; Bruneteau, 2010, p. 483. And above all, for the entire paragraph: Brovkin, 1998, pp. 15, 214, and 217.

20. Conservative modernization: subtitle in Vichnevski, 2000; agricultural stagnation, except for industrial cultivation: Nove, 1992, pp. 194 and 242–243; Werth, [1990] 2004, p. 280; moored to its agrarian legacy: Viola, 2007, p. 192.

21. 1955: Lüthi, in Bernstein and Li, 2010, p. 36; December 1964: Roux, 2009, p. 732.

22. Stalinist strategy during the second plan: Nove, 1992, p. 226 and chap. 9 passim; Mao nurtured on Soviet texts from the early 1930s: Wylie, 1980; criticism of post-1934 "bureaucratic Stalinism": Lüthi, in Bernstein and Li, 2010, p. 35.

23. Li Choh-ming, 1962.

24. Aubert, 1990.

25. The title of chap. 3 of the marvelous book by Kotkin, 1995: "The Idiocy of Urban Life."

26. Werth, [1990] 2004, p. 281; Vichnevski, 2000, pp. 123, 126, and 128.

27. Filtzer, 2010, pp. 56–57 and 337–340. On the small size of living space, see also Fitzpatrick, 2002, pp. 75–81.

28. Smith, Mark B., 2010. I only know this book through thirdhand reviews.

29. On the "misery of urban life" (Sheila Fitzpatrick), cf. Fitzpatrick, 2002, pp. 82–86; Figes, 2007b, pp. 119–120; Graziosi, 2010, p. 101; Nove, 1992, p. 200; Werth, [1990] 2004, pp. 281–282.

30. This quotation and the preceding one can be found in Vichnevski, 2000, pp. 159 and 451.

31. Banister, 1987, p. 56, and the entire chapter 3, as well as Walder, 2015, p. 320, for the remainder of this paragraph.

32. Some Chinese demographers raised concerns about the aging population, the decline of an available labor force, and the gender imbalance following selective abortion practiced by parents wanting a male heir, believing that the one-child policy was a serious mistake, if not a catastrophe (Wang, Cai, and Gu, 2013). It was indeed catastrophic because of the terrorist methods used and the tragedies they caused. However, even if a young and abundant labor force may benefit the Indian economy over the next decades, the day India becomes the most overpopulated country on the planet will hardly be an endorsement of a successful democracy. Conversely, I willingly concede that the most important part of the demographic transition was accomplished during the 1970s with what were restrictive methods even then, albeit less traumatizing than the one-child policy has been in China. When that policy was launched in 1979 it was intended to last for one generation. It was repealed only in 2015, after the publication of the French edition of this book.

33. Bergère, 2000, pp. 34–35.

34. Largely as a result of alcoholism and violent death (alcohol-related suicide, murder, and accidents). Mikhail Gorbachev's 1985 prohibition law undermined the regime's popularity and reduced its financial resources, but it did raise the life expectancy curve until 1988. It then plummeted again after the fall of the regime (Graziosi, 2010, p. 509).

35. The main source for these three paragraphs is Blum, 2004. In addition, but more sporadically, see another demographer: Vichnevski, 2000, pp. 167–169 and 183, and the review of one of his more recent books: Wood, 2013. Additional details on the 1920s may be found in Graziosi, 2010, pp. 50–51; on the final demographic decline and the prohibitionist regime adopted in 1985 in ibid., pp. 508–509; on the number of doctors and hospital beds in Nove, 1992, p. 259; and on their scarcity in the countryside in Fitzpatrick, 1994, p. 217.

36. See, among others, Vichnevski, 2000, pp. 178–180, 191–192, and 219.

37. In order: 43 percent of children could read books circulating in the villages: Berelowitch, 2005, pp. 106–107; northern villages without schools: Bertaux and

Garros, 1998, p. 45; school budget increased seventeenfold in ten years (from 1928 to 1938) and 81 percent literacy: Laran and Regemorter, 1996, p. 312; Fitzpatrick, 2002, pp. 109 and 354; illiteracy almost conquered at the end of the 1930s: Werth, [1990] 2004, p. 206; Nove, 1992, p. 250; reading in Magnitogorsk: Kotkin, 1995, p. 191.

38. The fall in the number of high schools and accelerated technical training for workers from the countryside in the early 1930s: Nove, 1992, pp. 198–199 and 234; increase in the number of students and numbers of the "new intelligentsia": Werth, [1990] 2004, p. 285; Khrushchev's studies: Taubman, 2003, pp. 72–73.

39. Vichnevski, 2000, pp. 262–264; also Linz, 2000, pp. 44 and 69.

40. On the spectacular progress of education in China, see Pepper, 1987 and 1991; Hayhoe, 1984; Andreas, 2009; also Bastid-Bruguière, 2009.

41. Andreas, 2009, pp. 44, 166.

42. *Far Eastern Economic Review*, 1999, p. 60.

43. Lewin, 1987, p. 379. Above: Lefort, 1971, p. 124.

Chapter 3   Politics

1. Li, 2006, pp. 48, 175, and passim.

2. Khlevniouk, 1996, p. 29. In 1932, the old Bolshevik Martemyan Ryutin, a local cadre in the Moscow district, circulated a manifesto among his friends demanding Stalin's deposition from his post as secretary general. He was sentenced to ten years of forced labor, even though Stalin had demanded his execution. He did not survive the Great Purge.

3. Bernstein, 2010, "Introduction," in Bernstein and Li, eds., p. 1. During my first visit to China in 1954, any success, be it in production, education, or the eradication of prostitution, was attributed to the masses' devotion to work, the correct policy line as defined by the Party and Chairman Mao, and "the unselfish and generous help of the Soviet elder brother." In 1953 I had only just begun to study Chinese, and barely recognized a few words, but I eagerly awaited the predictable peroration that inevitably concluded the translation.

4. Li Hua-yu, 2006 and 2010. The Gao Gang Affair (or Gao-Rao Affair) was the first major internal struggle of the new regime. Allied to Rao Shushi, and like him an important provincial cadre transferred to Beijing in 1952, Gao Gang was accused of attempting to overthrow Liu Shaoqi and Zhou Enlai, and plotting to become the Party's Number Two. Disowned by Mao after apparently having been encouraged by him at the outset, Gao Gang committed suicide in 1954.

5. Rozman, 2010, in Bernstein and Li, eds., p. 517.

6. Obvious, or at least notorious, and pointed out by many authors since Hannah Arendt, and even before her in the 1930s, when the comparison between various forms of totalitarianism became necessary (Bruneteau, 2010).

7. See, among others, Aron, 1965, p. 287, and the definition of "high Stalinism" by V. Kiselev, quoted in Nove, 1993, p. 10.

8. On the "real" and "formal" institutions, see Cabestan, 1994, p. 275.

9. Three times in twenty-seven years: 1956, 1969, 1973. It was only after Mao's death that the Chinese Communist Party Congress started to meet regularly every five years, from the Eleventh Congress in 1977, to the Nineteenth, scheduled for the fall 2017. The same atypical thirteen-year gap separated the two last "Stalinist" Congresses (1939–1952) and the CCP's Eighth and Ninth (1956–1969), the CPSU at least having the excuse of the Great Patriotic War, whereas Mao did not deem it useful to convene and consult a congress before introducing the two major upheavals of his reign: the Great Leap Forward and the Cultural Revolution. Or rather he did, further violating the Party's statutes. In the spring of 1958 he convened a second session of the Eighth Congress and asked it to ratify the very opposite of what it had decided at the 1956 session, which had been in principle, a one-off session.

10. See, among others, Huang, 2000, p. 257; MacFarquhar and Schoenhals, 2006 for China; and Khlevniouk, 1996, pp. 123, 138, 231–243, and 314–315 for the Soviet Union.

11. Gauchet, 2010, p. 545.

12. In China, the leading party was not technically a single party since it tolerated the existence of eight small parties from the "united" democratic front, all of which were completely powerless and served more to conceal the Party's monopoly.

13. Khlevniouk, 1996, pp. 82, 277.

14. Bruneteau, 2010, p. 194; Bianco, 2005, pp. 449–452.

15. Graziosi, 2010, p. 60. I should stress here, before returning to the subject in greater detail, that this was much more the case for the Soviet Union than for China, where, from the 1960s on, the definition of class increasingly tended to incorporate subjective criteria.

16. I must add that depending on the circumstances, those pariahs or suspects could include many other categories, especially political ones, such as the former SR (Socialist Revolutionaries) or the Mensheviks (and later former Trotskyists) in the Soviet Union. In China, those outcasts were grouped together under the humiliating name of *wulei* (the Five Categories), which applied a jumble of social and political criteria with a touch of common-law crime to former landlords and their sons, rich peasants, capitalists, counterrevolutionaries, and "bad elements," which could designate delinquents as much as protestors. From 1957 on, the list of pariahs often included the "rightists."

17. Besançon, 1977, p. 298.

18. Bruneteau, 2011, p. 145. Revisionist historiography from the 1970s, led by Sheila Fitzpatrick among others, attempted to rehabilitate social history and play down

the leadership struggle, which the dominant "totalitarian" historiography had focused on until then. I mentioned the name of my student not because of this disagreement, but because his name is worthy of mention. Roland Lew (1944–2004) was a politically committed man and a true intellectual, rather than a mere specialist. He would have been the first reader—presumably a critical one—I would have liked for this book.

19. Quoted by Davies, 1993, p. 67. See also Getty, 1993, pp. 127–129.

20. See, among many others, Bruneteau, 2011, pp. 144–145; Edele, 2012; Gauchet, 2010, pp. 324 and 522; Graziosi, 2010, p. 440; Pomian, 1995, p. 20; Viola, 2007, p. 190.

21. Lih, Naumov, and Khlevniouk, 1995, p. 59.

22. For example, in the letters to Kaganovitch, quoted in Yves Cohen, 1997, p. 329.

23. Getty and Naumov, 1999, pp. 266–267. See also Gauchet, 2010, pp. 331 and 334; Khlevniouk, 1996, p. 235.

24. Speech to the Party Congress, 1926, quoted and summarized in his letter 29 to Stalin, in Lih, Naumov, and Khlevniouk, 1995, pp. 53–54. For the remainder of the paragraph, see ibid., pp. 45, 47, 48, 62, and 63.

25. Bruneteau, 2010, p. 30.

26. Some examples (not exhaustive): the campaigns against the Mensheviks and the SR in 1921 to oblige the allies to withdraw their sanctions against the first "worker and peasant state," or to confiscate valuables from the Orthodox Church in 1922. A new campaign against the SR followed in 1923, and then others for "new morals in daily life," to "eradicate illiteracy," to enroll the "Lenin generation" in the Party, over the "Trotsky heresy," before arriving at a more classical campaign to boost production toward the end of the NEP and promote so-called "rationalization." The aim was to improve worker productivity without increasing workers' wages (see, among others, Brovkin, 1998, pp. 86 and 122; Gatrell, 2006, pp. 385, 394–395, and 402). China had a succession of campaigns as varied as those for agricultural reform, "Help Korea, Resist America," which was the prelude to sending "volunteers" to North Korea, two campaigns against counterrevolutionaries (*zhenfan* and *sufan*), the "Three Antis" campaign that targeted cadres in the Communist government, the "Five Antis" that targeted capitalists, thought reform (aimed at intellectuals), rural collectivization, and the nationalization of industry and trade (see Bianco, 1973, pp. 866–868; Roderick MacFarquhar, in Cheek, 2010, p. 348; Schram, 1974, pp. 106–107).

27. Davies, 1980, p. 218. On the quotas, see, among others, ibid., p. 402; Blum, 1994, p. 112; Khlevniouk, 1996, pp. 208 and 210; Lewin, 2003a, pp. 140 and 144; Sokoloff, 2000, pp. 30, 210 and 251; Viola, 2007, pp. 35, 98–99, and 165; Werth, 1997, pp. 165, 206, and 209–213; Werth and Berelowitch, 2011, pp. 244, 246, and 601. On China, rather than drown the reader in still more references, I would stress Yang Jisheng, [2008], 2012, translated into English and French. As the most detailed study of the great famine, it deserves to be widely read.

28. Among many other sources, Davies, 1980, p. 408; Fainsod, [1958] 1963, p. 142; Viola, 2007, p. 21; Teiwes and Sun, 1999; Teiwes, 2010, p. 38.

29. In addition to Fitzpatrick, 1978, see, among others, Brovkin, 1998, p. 106; Davies, 1980, p. 414; Davies, 1993, p. 55; Fainsod, [1958] 1963, pp. 270 and 305; Malia, 1995, p. 268; Werth, 1984, pp. 174–175, 241–242, and 273. These sources reflect only the Soviet side. I have confined myself to the origins of a vocabulary that is all too familiar to the student of Maoist China. Regarding the most famous of these expressions or appellations, I have disregarded, according to common practice, the emphasis ("great") and the inevitable Homeric epithet ("proletarian"). I will restore them just once to provide the exact title: the Great Proletarian Cultural Revolution.

30. Bianco, 1973, p. 866.

31. Let us summarize Leninist denial: If the revolutionary intellectuals, mostly from the petty bourgeoisie, did not introduce ideas about revolution and socialism into the minds of the workers, those workers would stick to purely concrete demands and never go beyond the limits of traditional trade unionism.

32. The best guide to Mao-thought is Stuart Schram. I refer here to Schram, 1991, pp. 3–7. See also Jiang Yihua, 2010, p. 338.

33. Bianco, 1970, reproduced in Bianco, 2010, pp. 17–52; Bianco, 1973, p. 875; Schram, 1991, pp. 20 and 38.

34. Meisner, 1982, p. 100 (quotation), as well as pp. 28, 35, 63–65, 67–68, 177, and passim. Also Dunham, [1976] 1990. On the world's "revolutionary countryside," see below.

35. General Peng Dehuai's Hundred Regiments Offensive in August 1940 triggered a bloody reprisal from the Japanese army, which considerably reduced the expanse of Communist bases in North China and apparently provoked Mao's ire. On the development of Mao-thought before 1949, see Schram, 1986, esp. pp. 818–870. Interested readers will find many more details in the multivolume *Mao's Road to Power: Revolutionary Writings 1912–1949*, edited by Stuart Schram, Armonk, N.Y., Sharpe.

36. Mao then subdivided the majority of middle peasants (the equivalent of the Russian *seredniaks*) into "lower middle peasants," who were with "us," and "upper middle peasants who were sabotaging collectivization."

37. Schram, 1991, pp. 25, 27, 32, and 68–71.

38. I attempt to analyze them below. On the "Capua syndrome" that affected the veterans themselves (the equivalent of the Bolshevik "old guard"), see Domenach, 2012.

39. Grossman, 1980, p. 371. In this celebrated passage of *Life and Fate,* Grossman quite naturally stressed the kinship between Nazis and Bolsheviks. My comparison between Communist brothers inevitably calls to mind the more frequent comparison between fascist and communist totalitarianism. The

similarities I have painstakingly compiled within the same (Communist) branch of totalitarianism should surprise no one, given the relationship between both the fascist and communist branches that has so often been pointed out. See also Schram, 1991, pp. 2, 20, 48, and 75–76; Cheek, 2010, p. 13.

40. Schram, 1974, pp. 208, 215, and 225.

41. Schram, 1991, pp. 42–43, 49–52, 67, and 97 (quotation from "The Internationale" anthem, p. 101).

42. Not even completely at that. Mao admitted in the 1940s that he had never read the entire *Short Course*, "just the concluding sections of each chapter," which provided him with a guide to action (Li Hua-yu, 2006, p. 101). On Mao's admiration for this book, see ibid., chap. 3; Li Hua-yu, 2010, chap. 4; Jiang Yihua, 2010, p. 340. On the beginning of the paragraph, see Bianco, [1994] 1997, p. 93.

43. Huang, 2000, pp. 12–13.

44. Andreas, 2009, p. 103 and passim.

45. Dunham, [1976] 1990. The author analyzes traces of it in official literature, comparing the literature of "late Stalinism" with that of the 1920s.

46. Viola, 2007, p. 18; Davies, 1980, p. 231. On the spirit of capitalism that corrupted everyone creeping into the Communist Party itself, see Besançon, 1977, pp. 239–240; Besançon, [1998] 2005, p. 155.

47. Which he didn't hesitate to do, as though justifying the decimation of Communists in advance (during that famous Central Committee Plenum of February–March 1937) by claiming that the main danger lay in the enemies holding Party cards. Mao could have said the very same thing thirty years later. Quoted in Heller and Nekrich, 1982, p. 252. See also Getty, 1993, pp. 131–132.

48. Berdiaev, [1938] 1951, p. 264; Bukharin: Stephen Cohen, [1971] 1980, p. 367. Of course, Bukharin used only veiled terms to imply Stalinist-type regimes. Zamyatin: Heller, Leonid, 1988, p. 469. Before Lei Feng's ambition to become a small screw in the great socialist machine, Stalin had already talked of screws and, with philosophical detachment, of lives crushed by socialist construction: "When you chop wood, the chips fly" (Besançon, [1998] 2005, p. 55).

49. Tucker, 1963, p. 37. Qin Shihuangdi unified China and founded the empire (in 221 BC). He allegedly governed in a very authoritarian and cruel manner, helped by a minister informed by the Legalist school of philosophy. As a result he was vilified by the Confucians and admired by an aging Mao.

50. Ibid., introduction, p. x.

51. Li, Hua-yu, 2006, p. 7.

52. Walder, 1991.

53. Meisner, 1982, p. 26.

54. This is at the heart of A. James Gregor's analysis of Lenin's heterodox Marxism. See Gregor, 2009, pp. 129, 166–167.

55. Stephen Cohen, [1971] 1980, pp. 253, 258, and 440. Bukharin situated himself in the line of *Imperialism, the Highest Stage of Capitalism* (Lenin), which was lawful and advisable to quote. On how the famous article attributed to Lin Biao was fabricated, see Teiwes and Sun, 1996, pp. 27 and 208.

56. Besançon, 1977, chaps. 13 and 15.

Chapter 4   The Peasants

1. Lewin, [1966] 1976, p. 22, for Gorky, and p. 296, for Marx.

2. Ibid., p. 39. Lewin, [1966] 1976, has scarcely aged, even with the opening up of the archives in 1991. For these first pages (until the NEP) I have mainly used Brovkin, 1995, pp. 129, 134–140, 145–148, 318, 323–325, 327–388, 418, and passim; Davies, 1980, pp. 1–3 and 51; Evans, 1988; Figes, 2007a, pp. 749–767, 814–815, and 922–931; Holquist, 2002, pp. 16–46; Shanin, 1971, pp. 369–371; Viola, 1996, pp. 13 and 30–31; Werth, 2007, pp. 50 and 509–510; and again Lewin, [1966] 1976, p. 34.

3. Graziosi, 1994, pp. 438–439, connects the two episodes (1918–1922 and 1929–1933), especially in Ukraine and what had been the southern front in the civil war. He sees them as "two indissociable acts in the largest European peasant war of the 20th century."

4. I have used the following sources on the NEP: Brovkin, 1995, p. 421; Davies, 1980, pp. 4–55 and 419–420; Fainsod, [1958] 1963, pp. 138–141; Fitzpatrick, 1994, pp. 28–33; Lewin, [1966] 1976, pp. 29, 66–74, 157–160, and 196–222; Lewin, 1987, pp. 167, 174–207, 214, 426–428, and 431–432; Nove, 1992, pp. 102 and 106; Viola et al., 2005, pp. 11, 18–19, 21–22, 56–64, and 89–91.

5. Taken from Nove, 1992, p. 106.

6. Lewin, [1966] 1976, p. 159. Nove, 1992, p. 102, has a slightly different assessment but the same trend: 17–18 million farms before 1917, 25 million in 1927.

7. Stalin, quoted in Viola et al., 2005, p. 56; see also Lewin, [1966] 1976, p. 196.

8. Unless otherwise mentioned or specified, the handling of collectivization and dekulakization is based on Davies, 1980, pp. 147–275 and 442–443; Fainsod, [1958] 1963, pp. 141–152 and 238–264; Fitzpatrick, 1994, pp. 64–65; Fitzpatrick, [1999] 2002, p. 52; Graziosi, 1994; Lewin, [1966] 1976, pp. 223–229, 323, 332, 342–351, 367, 387, and 402–403, chap. 17 as a whole (pp. 423–452, quotation on 443); Khlevniuk, 2004, pp. 12–18; Nove, 1992; Viola, 1996, pp. 23–24, 70, and 78; Viola, 2007; Viola et al., 2005, pp. 118–122, 175–176, 205, 215, 217, 259, 266, 268–279, 283–285, 313–314, 316–318, and 345–346; Werth, 2011b.

9. Lewin, [1966] 1976, p. 383.

10. Graziosi, 1994, p. 449.

11. In some places, child mortality rates for those under eight years in early 1932 reached 10 percent per month (Khlevniuk, 2004, p. 18).

12. According to the OGPU's statistics, there were 1,244,000 deportees in the first nine months of 1931, more than double the 1930 number of 560,000 (Werth and Berelowitch, 2011, p. 440). Twenty minutes for families in Crimea (previous sentence): Khlevniuk, 2004, pp. 12–13.

13. Viola et al., 2005, pp. 313–314.

14. Kalinin was of peasant stock, reputed to be a protector of peasants in the Soviet leadership. At first he opposed the use of violence and the exceptional measures, before doing a U-turn like so many others and supporting Stalin against Bukharin at the crucial moment.

15. Graziosi, 1994, p. 456, and ibid. for the mothers' exasperation against the collectivization of dairy cattle.

16. Viola et al., 2005, chap. 6, esp. pp. 276–277.

17. That is the title of chapter 5 in Viola, 1996.

18. Lewin, 1987, pp. 431–433.

19. Davies, 1980, p. 312; see also p. 410.

20. Graziosi, 1994, pp. 437, 459–460, 462, and 471, n. 69. On the slap in Georgia, see Service, 2012, p. 496. On Ordzhonikidze's suicide in February 1937, following a violent quarrel with Stalin and the day after his deputy Piatakov was sentenced to death, see, Service, 2005, p. 349.

21. All the more resigned since in the meantime they had suffered a famine. This paragraph largely relies on Fainsod, [1958] 1963, chaps. 13 and 14; Fitzpatrick, 1994, chaps. 4–7; Lewin, 1987, pp. 226–273 and 384–389.

22. Lewin, 1987, p. 265.

23. Ibid., pp. 262 and 267–268.

24. Nevertheless, this is based on Han, 2005, pp. 19–27. For the period prior to the conquest of power, I mainly have used Benton, 1999; Bianco, 1986 and 2005; Chen Yung-fa, 1986; Han, 2005; Hartford, 1980; Hayford, 1990; Hinton, 1971; Johnson, 1962.

25. Quoted in Han, 2005, p. 20.

26. A reference to Chiang Kai-shek's "appeasement policy." He was just as nationalistic as his critics only better informed than they were about the balance of power. He tried to play for time in order to postpone the inevitable clash and began by reinforcing his army and his control over the country. He hoped that further aggressions by the Japanese would ultimately bring China some allies better able than China to settle their differences. That assessment proved to be correct but too late for Chiang.

27. Adapted from Han, 2005, p. 33.

28. These are the heroes of three short stories. An odd kind of hero in the case of "The True Story of Ah Q," a poor wretch and the butt of repeated humiliations,

which he transforms into moral victories, rather as his compatriots attempted to conquer imperialism by praising the spiritual superiority of Chinese civilization. After becoming impassioned for a revolution he quite misunderstands, he is executed for a theft he did not commit. In "The New Year's Sacrifice" Xianglin's Wife commits suicide out of despair. The widow of a husband who was not of her choosing, she is remarried by force (resold might be more apt) by her former mother-in-law. Soon widowed yet again she exasperates the villagers by endlessly repeating how her baby, the only being dear to her, was carried off by a wolf. A sanctimonious old woman proceeds to taunt her by pointing out her inexpiable sin: "The two men's ghosts will fight over you. To which will you go? The King of Hell will have no choice but to cut you in two and divide you between them." In "My Old Home" the author meets up with a childhood friend, Runtu, after thirty years. When they were children, Runtu had taught him all the countryside, the animals and plants. Now a poor peasant with a large family, Runtu addresses his former close friend with a respectful *laoye* (master or lord). *All three stories are collected in *Selected Stories of Lu Xun*, translated by Gladys Yang/Yang Xianyi, Peking Foreign Languages Press, 1972.

29. Poor farmers "have not suffered nearly so much from their poverty as from their ignorance," noted Yan in 1925 (Hayford, 1990, p. 57).

30. Hayford, 1990, pp. 94–95.

31. Han, 2005, p. 59.

32. Bianco, 1986, p. 305.

33. Bianco, 2005, pp. 431–432.

34. Benton, 1999, p. 729.

35. Chen, Yung-fa, 1986, p. 220.

36. Ibid., p. 187.

37. Bianco, 2005, pp. 449–452.

38. Hartford, 1980, p. 41 and quotation on p. 56.

39. The title of one of the best works on the subject: *Making Revolution*, by Chen Yung-fa (1986).

40. Bernstein, 1967.

41. Yang Jisheng, [2008] 2012, p. 70. English edition (*Tombstone*), 2012, p. 157.

42. Li Hua-yu, 2006, p. 121.

43. Li Huaiyin, 2006. On Deng Zihui's courageous resistance, see Teiwes and Sun, 1993. That resistance persisted during the GLF: see Rohlf, 2010, in Bernstein and Li, eds., pp. 201–203 and 207; Xiao-Planès, 2013.

44. Far less atrociously. The pioneering comparison made a half century ago by Thomas Bernstein has stood up well to present broader knowledge on the subject (Bernstein, 1967).

45. These were the twenty-five thousand workers sent to the countryside in early 1930 to help or replace the *aktivy* who had failed, and to speed up collectivization. See Lewin, [1966] 1976, pp. 409–410; Graziosi, 1994, p. 453; Bernstein, 1967, pp. 29–30.

46. There is a solid guide in French to what follows: Roux, 2009 (my borrowings are to be found on pp. 636, 642, and 644–645).

47. Aubert, 1990, pp. 163–165.

48. For all the preceding paragraphs, the best guide is Zweig, 1989.

49. Bianco, 2005, p. 476.

50. "Liberated" here comes from a reminiscence. While I was working on the Nanjing archives in the summer of 1981 I would take a bus on Sundays and go as far as possible, usually to the neighboring province of Anhui, returning the same evening, since it was impossible to sleep anywhere except in a hotel for foreign guests. On the very first Sunday I walked several kilometers from the bus stop and found myself in the middle of the countryside, among a group of villagers working happily. I was surprised that they were working so hard on a Sunday afternoon. There was none of the usual nonchalance observed in the fields and building sites of the People's Republic of China. Instead they reminded me of the fisherwomen in Gaoxiong (Kaohsiung, in southern Taiwan) singing as they cleaned the fish that had been caught the previous night to have it ready to sell in the market at six in the morning. Here I felt that I was the very first "long nose," or foreigner, those villagers had ever seen, and they welcomed me warmly and offered me tea (in fact hot water) to drink from an old can—a detail I have added not to disparage their hospitality but to show their poverty. In line with tradition, they questioned me about my nationality and then asked me if French agriculture was as liberated (i.e., decollectivized) as theirs.

51. Feuerwerker, 1998, has analyzed with great subtlety the Chinese intellectuals' fascination for a peasantry they hardly knew. In Russia between 1873 and 1874, thousands of Populists (Narodniks) went off to the countryside to offer their services to the peasants as teachers, accountants, nurses, midwives, and agricultural workers. The peasants received them badly and did not appreciate them, sometimes even reporting to the police any who called on them to revolt (see Laran, 1973, pp. 18–19). Those pitiful "heroes" were the destitute, dirty, and often obtuse peasants, as described in *The Power of the Land* by Gleb Uspensky (1843–1902), Chekhov's "The Mujiks" (1897), and Ivan Bunin's *The Village* (1909) (Bounine, 2011).

52. Domenach, 1992, p. 120. On the rapid collectivization in 1955–1956, see Bernstein, 1967.

53. Li Hua-yu, 2006, richly documents Mao's "economic Stalinization of China."

54. Peng Dehuai in 1959, Chen Yun in the early 1960s, quoted in Domenach, 2012, p. 225.

55. First quatrain: Yang Jisheng, [2008] 2012, p. 417, English translation *Tombstone*, 2012, p. 315; second quatrain: Hinton, 1983, p. 250.

Chapter 5   Famines

1.   Estimates of excess mortality in China vary between 15 and 46 million, the most frequent being in the 30–36 million range.

2.   A record birth rate in 1963 (between 43 and 44 per thousand according to official figures), which remained very high in 1964 and 1965, began to offset the deficit in births (see Manning and Wemheuer, 2011, pp. 1 and 21–22; Banister, 1987, p. 235). In the Soviet Union, the birth rate had not reached half of its usual rate by the spring of 1934, still less the Ukraine and North Caucasus (Davies and Wheatcroft, 2004, p. 411).

3.   The Chinese levels can be found in Yang Dali, 1996, p. 38; Lardy, 1987, pp. 374 and 377; examples of record levels in Bramall, 2011, pp. 1004–1005 (one person in six dead in three counties in Sichuan) and Yang Jisheng, [2008] 2012, p. 286/English edition *Tombstone*, 2012, p. 137 (nearly one in three in Tongwei, Gansu province). Soviet levels are to be found in Blum, [1994] 2004, pp. 102 and 106; Graziosi, 2005, p. 461; Graziosi, 2013, p. 18; Davies and Wheatcroft, 2004, p. 511.

4.   For Ukraine, see Sokoloff, 2000; families and villages were decimated or disappeared: pp. 206, 225, 239, 241, 299, 402, and passim; exchanges: pp. 308–309; children abandoned: pp. 288, 312, and 315; unburied bodies: p. 369; buried alive: pp. 279, 359, 379, and 381. For China, see Yang Jisheng, [2008] 2012, p. 354; Becker, 1998; abandoned villages, without a living soul: p. 171; abandonment: pp. 216–217; hidden bodies: p. 173.

5.   For the Soviet Union, see Sokoloff, 2000, pp. 204, 217 and 403. For China, see Gao Hua, 2011; Becker, 1998, pp. 165–166, 243 and 290–291; Yang Jisheng, [2008] 2012, pp. 209 and 485–487; Dikötter, 2010, p. 284.

6.   Becker, 1998, pp. 196–197. I should add however that in China, a "land of famine" (Mallory, 1926), the expression had been in use for centuries, so much so that it may have been used more often than it actually occurred. Among the fairly frequent cases of cannibalism is the account by a Ukrainian defendant explaining how she cut up her child: "I put the child on the chopping board, and he asked me, 'What are you going to do Mummy?'" (Sokoloff, 2000, p. 105) and the example of the parents in Gansu province who "ordered their seven-year old daughter to boil water to cook her younger brother. Once the baby was eaten, the sister was asked to put the water on to boil again. Realizing that she would be next, the little girl knelt down and begged her father not to eat her, saying 'I will do anything you want if you don't eat me'" (Becker, 1998, p. 226). Many other cases of anthropophagy can be found in Werth and Berelowitch, 2011, pp. 498, 501, 510 and 534; Yang Jisheng, [2008] 2012, pp. 212, 283, 290, 292, 323, 371, 384–385, 399–404, 412, 425, 437, 455, 457, and 492; Zhou, 2012, pp. 61–64 and 67. On the human flesh trade in Kiev in 1933, see Sokoloff, 2000, p. 264; in Henan province in 1959, see Yang Jisheng, [2008] 2012, p. 215. A great deal of partial

quantitative data on the regions of Kharkov, Kiev, and Vinnitsa in the spring of 1933 may be found in Davies and Wheatcroft, 2004, p. 423; and on China in Dikötter, 2010, p. 322; Zhou, 2012, pp. 59–71.

7. "My mother said to me 'My daughter, we will say our goodbyes now because I'm going to die'. She lay down on the bench and I climbed onto the stove. I felt no pity, I wasn't frightened, I was just very hungry. At dawn a man woke me, 'Wake up, your mother is dying'" (Sokoloff, 2000, p. 221). See also Werth, 2007, p. 131; Werth, 1997, p. 187; Dikötter, 2010, pp. 225–226.

8. Sokoloff, 2000, p. 443.

9. Further details by the same author may be found in Yang Jisheng, [2008] 2012, pp. 541–544.

10. Davies and Wheatcroft, 2004, pp. 119–123, 437, 439 and 458; Wheatcroft, 2008, pp. 5 and 28–30; Penner, 1998, pp. 29–30; Yang Jisheng, [2008] 2012, p. 541; Bramall, 2011, pp. 999–1001.

11. Dikötter, 2010, p. 111.

12. For China, see Banister, 1987, pp. 56 and 352; For the Soviet Union, see Blum, [1994] 2004, pp. 90–97; Nove, 1992, pp. 12 and 110; Sokoloff, 2000, p. 16; Wheatcroft, 2008, pp. 20–22.

13. For the Soviet Union, see Davies and Wheatcroft, 2004, p. 434, note; Wheatcroft, 2008, pp. 22–24; for China, see Banister, 1987, pp. 330–331; Lardy, 1987, p. 369; Yang Jisheng, [2008] 2012, pp. 461, 484, and 531.

14. It was more the conjunction of two famines, an urban one during and just after the civil war (1918–1920), and a rural one in 1920–1922. After that, typhus and other epidemics killed more people than hunger, given that poorly nourished people have far less resistance to disease (see Davies and Wheatcroft, 2004, pp. 403–405, 431; Blum, [1994] 2004, pp. 93–96).

15. Bensidoun, 1975, p. 3 and chap. 5. The revolutionary student Ulianov (the future Lenin) refused to support the fight against the 1891–1892 famine, which in his eyes was a factor of progress (Service, 2012, pp. 105–106).

16. Lillian Li, 2007, p. 304.

17. Kupferman, 2007, pp. 73–75. See also Cœuré, 1999, pp. 171–182; Klid and Motyl, 2012, pp. 146–149; Mazuy, 2002, p. 163; Snyder, [2010] 2012, pp. 107–109.

18. Additional details may be found in Sokoloff, 2000, pp. 16–17; Wheatcroft, 2008, pp. 15–16.

19. Service, 2005, pp. 257–258; Sokoloff, 2000, pp. 21–25; Werth, 1997, p. 178.

20. See Sokoloff, 2000, pp. 26–32; Wheatcroft, 2008, p. 29.

21. Ohayon, 2006, pp. 179–206.

22. Lewin, [1966] 1976, pp. 453–454.

23. Davies and Wheatcroft, 2004, pp. 48–78 and 471.

24. In the nomadic and seminomadic zones, each family owned an average of 41.6 animals in 1929; in 1933 they owned only 2.2 (Pianciola, 2004, p. 165). On the Kazak famine, see ibid., pp. 137–191; Ohayon, 2006. See also Davies and Wheatcroft, 2004, pp. 321–326, 391, 408–409, 412, and 414; Naimark, 2010, pp. 75–76; Service, 2005, pp. 326–328; Werth, 2003, pp. 42–43; Werth, 2010a, pp. 144–145.

25. Sokoloff, 2000, p. 38, describes a "final escalade" of the famine from the summer of 1932. I have borrowed the expression from him but I have identified two phases in that escalade, on the basis of, among others, ibid.; Werth and Berelowitch, 2011, pp. 280–283.

26. Davies and Wheatcroft, 2004, pp. 79–123, 448 and 471; Sokoloff, 2000, pp. 33–38; Werth, 2007, pp. 116–118; Wheatcroft, 2008, p. 30.

27. The famous "7/8 decree" was applied in unequal fashion for a very simple reason: it was so brutal that it was almost impossible to apply short of executing dozens, if not hundreds of thousands, of starving pilferers. Nevertheless more than 200,000 people were sentenced to between five and ten years in a camp as a result, and at least 5,400 were sentenced to death between August 1932 and December 1933 (Ellman, 2007, pp. 668–669; Sokoloff, 2000, p. 38; Davies and Wheatcroft, 2004, pp. 162, 167, 198, and 202; Werth, 1997, p. 181).

28. By 22 September 1932, 446 village Soviets in Ukraine had refused the procurement plan assigned to them (Davies and Wheatcroft, 2004, pp. 153–154). Detailed in ibid., pp. 152–159, rural resistance—and that of local authorities as well as the *kolkhozniks* and individual peasants—is analyzed in Penner, 1998, pp. 37–42 and summarized in Werth, 2007. See also Werth, 1997 and 2003; Werth and Moulhec, 1994, pp. 91–92 and 151–159; Werth and Berelowitch, 2011, pp. 539–542, 549, and 562–565.

29. Petliurites is from the Hetman Symon Petliura, who briefly fought in Ukraine against the Reds during the civil war, as anyone who has read *The White Guard* may perhaps remember (Boulgakov, 1970). Extracts from Stalin's letter can be found in Werth, 2007, pp. 120–121; Davies and Wheatcroft, 2004, pp. 169–170. The OGPU's "hunting tables" are in Werth and Berelowitch, 2011, p. 283.

30. Werth, 2007, p. 121; Davies and Wheatcroft, 2004, pp. 170–171, 444–446, and 448–449.

31. Davies and Wheatcroft, 2004, pp. 108–123, 127–133, 434–439, and 449–452; Wheatcroft, 2008, pp. 30–31.

32. The letter to Molotov of 23 November 1932 is quoted among others in Werth, 2007, p. 125, and Davies and Wheatcroft, 2004, p. 150. Molotov rebuffed in it no uncertain terms: "Your position is fundamentally incorrect, non-Bolshevik."

33. Davies and Wheatcroft, 2004, pp. 181 and 185.

34. This boycott was extended to 88 entire districts out of Ukraine's total of 385 (Davies and Wheatcroft, 2004, p. 175; see also Werth, 2010a, p. 147, and Snyder,

[2010] 2012, pp. 85–90, who provide details of yet more deadly measures taken at the end of 1932 and in early 1933.

35. In Kuban, half the Party secretaries (358 out of 716) were excluded, and 46 percent of the 25,000 Party members. Within a three-week period in Ukraine, the courts passed 34,000 sentences for theft of grain or failure to deliver it. They included 480 death sentences and nearly 20,000 people being dispatched to the gulag (Davies and Wheatcroft, 2004, pp. 173, 178, and 198).

36. Werth, 2010a, p. 147.

37. Graziosi, 1989, pp. 59–60. See also Werth, 1997, p. 184; Werth, 2003, pp. 38–39; Werth, 2007, pp. 126–127; Werth, 2010a, p. 147; Penner, 1998, p. 49; Davies and Wheatcroft, 2004, pp. 426–428; Sokoloff, 2000, p. 326.

38. For the peak of the crisis I refer to Blum, [1994] 2004, p. 153; Davies and Wheatcroft, 2004, pp. 413–416 and 511; Graziosi, 1989; Penner, 1998; Werth, 1997, p. 185; Werth, 2008, p. 13; Werth, 2010a, pp. 144 and 149. See also Werth and Berelowitch, 2011, pp. 284–288, 496, 498, 533, and 535–536.

39. MacFarquhar, 1983, pp. 89–90.

40. Yang Jisheng, [2008] 2012, pp. 95, 198, and 309.

41. Becker, 1998, pp. 157 and 160.

42. Bianco, 1970; republished in Bianco, 2010, pp. 18–51.

43. Becker, 1998, p. 119.

44. MacFarquhar, 1983, pp. 119–120.

45. Ash, 2006, p. 970.

46. Communiqué from the Sixth Plenum of the Eighth Central Committee, Wuchang, December 1958, quoted in Becker, 1998, pp. 125–126.

47. Li Zhisui, 1994, p. 302. On what preceded that, see Bernstein, 1984, p. 354 (the *xian* in Henan province); Becker, 1998, pp. 110, 121–122, and 176; Teiwes and Sun, 1999, p. 123 (pumpkins and ears of corn, Mao's visit to Xushui); MacFarquhar, 1983, p. 127 ("sputnik" fields: Deng Xiaoping himself believed a peasant who claimed to have harvested 35 tons of rice on one *mu* of land, in other words on 660 square meters). A trick photograph published in *China Pictorial* in 1958 and reproduced in Manning and Wemheuer, 2011, p. 55, shows not three but four children standing on rice plants (the stool beneath them artfully concealed).

48. Speech on 5 March 1959, quoted in Dikötter, 2010, p. 86.

49. MacFarquhar, 1983, pp. 148, 154–155, and 162.

50. To please Mao, quotas had been raised above the objectives he had set a few months earlier. See MacFarquhar, 1983, pp. 169 and 171.

51. Ibid., p. 194. There are at least three substantial accounts and analyses on the decisive turning point at Lushan: MacFarquhar, 1983, pp. 187–251; Teiwes and Sun, 1999, pp. 202–212; Yang Jisheng, [2008] 2012, pp. 145–190.

52. Peng had good reason to believe that Mao was not sufficiently motivated to correct his errors, for even as he was calling on his troops to be more realistic, he persisted in distinguishing the "work style" that need to be rectified, from the GLF that must be pursued, since "the general line is correct and must not be changed, the errors concern only one finger out of ten" (Teiwes and Sun, 1999, pp. 119–164, especially pp. 121, 141–142, 151–152, 160, and 163). See also Yang Jisheng, [2008] 2012, p. 147.

53. Teiwes and Sun, 1999, pp. 202–212; MacFarquhar, 1983, pp. 212–216; Yang Jisheng, [2008] 2012, pp. 153–156; Union Research Institute, 1968, pp. 7–13.

54. I have resumed or paraphrased Mao's arguments. The quotations are from MacFarquhar, 1983, p. 221. See also Teiwes and Sun, 1999, p. 206; Yang Jisheng, [2008] 2012, pp. 161–164.

55. Dikötter, 2010, p. 103, Yang Jisheng, [2008] 2012, p. 145, suggests that as a result of Lushan, the number of dead from starvation may have tripled, from a dozen million to thirty-six million.

56. I'm summarizing the quotation used by MacFarquhar, 1983, p. 249.

57. Dikötter, 2010, p. 54; Xin, 2011, p. 139.

58. Becker, 1998, pp. 164–167; Yang Jisheng, [2008] 2012, p. 361.

59. For examples, see Yang Jisheng, [2008] 2012, pp. 232–239, 266, and passim; and also Thaxton, 2008, pp. 191 and 193.

60. Dikötter, 2010, pp. xi and 304, estimates the number killed or tortured to death at 2.5 million between 1958 and 1962 and a minimum of one million suicides, but he was extrapolating from local or regional archive data, which are not always reliable.

61. Thaxton, 2008, pp. 232–234; Dikötter, 2010, p. 193; Gao Hua, 2011, p. 192. See also Zhou, 2012, pp. 115–124; Yang Jisheng, [2008] 2012, p. 117.

62. Dikötter, 2010, pp. 248, 264, 301–302 and 304; Wemheuer, 2011, p. 126; Thaxton, 2008, p. 335; Yang Jisheng, [2008] 2012, pp. 109–111.

63. Gao Hua, 2011, pp. 184–185, 188, and 190; Yang Jisheng, [2008] 2012, pp. 209 and 485–487. See also Dikötter, 2010, p. 140.

64. Scott, 1989, p. 15.

65. Scott, 1985. "Everyday Forms of (Peasant) Resistance," used above, is the subtitle of this classic work.

66. Gao Wangling, 2011, pp. 272–294 (quotation, p. 285). The same author has devoted an entire book to the subject, Gao Wangling, 2006.

67. Thaxton, 2008, pp. 199–230; Thaxton, 2011, pp. 259–263. In Ukraine in 1932, and in the North Caucasus in 1933, many starving peasants also cut down unripe ears of corn to eat them (Dolot, 1985, p. 156; Werth and Berelowitch, 2011, p. 540).

68. Gao Wangling, 2011, pp. 285–289.

69. Ash, 2006, pp. 970–973.

70. Two otherwise contrasting estimates concur on this: Yang Jisheng, [2008] 2012, pp. 498–501; English edition (*Tombstone*), pp. 411–415; Li Che, 2012. "Unnatural death" figures compiled from provincial data by Yang Jisheng are much lower than Li's estimates. Yang, who estimated the total death toll at some 36 million (p. 516, *Tombstone*, p. 430) was aware that he worked on reduced figures. Where both sets of figures agree, however, is that about half the famine victims died in the single year of 1960, in other words 11,090,000 out of a total of 20,980,000 "unnatural deaths" from 1958 to 1962 according to Yang's calculations, and 17,002,000 out of a total of 34,568,000 famine victims according to Li's estimate.

71. Wemheuer, 2014, chap. 4. The author provided this chapter of an as yet unpublished book, to participants at a study session organized by the EHESS and INALCO (The National Institute of Oriental Languages and Civilizations) in Paris, October 2013.

72. Explained in, among others, Stephen Cohen, [1971] 1980, pp. 163–165; Nove, 1992, chap. 5.

73. Becker, 1998, pp. 167 and 238; Sokoloff, 2000, p. 306. See also Yang Jisheng, [2008] 2012, p. 296.

74. In 1960, the leaders in Sichuan repeated endlessly, "Better to have people die of hunger in Sichuan than in Beijing, Tianjin, and Shanghai." See Yang Jisheng, [2008] 2012, p. 322; see also ibid., p. 484. The case of Tianjin and the region around it is illustrated in Brown, Jeremy, 2011. In 1933 too, as we have seen, fewer people died of hunger in Kiev or in Kharkov than in rural Ukraine.

75. Sokoloff, 2000, p. 301; Yang Xianhui, 2010, pp. 368–369. In China, merely counting the dead was considered a political crime (Becker, 1998, pp. 273, 279, and passim).

76. Imports began to exceed exports only in 1961 (Ash, 2006, pp. 972 and 982); for the Soviet Union, see Davies and Wheatcroft, 2004, pp. 85–86, 185, 440, and 471. See also Werth, 2007, p. 130, and on the disastrous effects of the exports, Wemheuer, 2014, pp. 61 and 247.

77. Li Huaiyin, 2006; Yang Jisheng, [2008] 2012, pp. 72–75, 463, and 477.

78. Becker, 1998, pp. 202–203; Yang Jisheng, [2008] 2012, pp. 381 and 394; for the Soviet Union: Davies and Wheatcroft, 2004, pp. 426–429; Werth, 2007, pp. 126–128.

79. See, among others, Yang Jisheng, [2008] 2012, pp. 232–239, 266 (English edition *Tombstone*, 2012, pp. 61–68, 118); Thaxton, 2008, pp. 191, 193. In the Soviet Union, see below, for the case of Kotov, who was executed for giving the *kolkhozniks* a grain advance.

80. We are reduced to postulating about differences in cadres' attitudes to account for the contrasts in mortality at the height of the famine (in 1960) between neighboring counties (located on the plain of Chengdu in Sichuan province), equally prosperous and close to the railroad (and therefore accessible to the grain collectors): 175 per thousand in Pixian, 50 per thousand in Guanxian, and 37 per

thousand in Shuangliu. Comparable contrasts were found in a poor district in the same province, badly hit by drought during that same year of 1960: three counties with mortality rates of 31, 41, and 55 per thousand respectively, located next to two counties with rates of 163 and 168 per thousand (Bramall, 2011, pp. 1004–1005).

81. Werth, 2007, pp. 124–125 and 131; Davies and Wheatcroft, 2004, pp. 150, 152, and 193.

82. Davies and Wheatcroft, 2004, pp. 151–152, 190, 193, 197, and 199–200.

83. Ibid., pp. 157 and 177–178.

84. As a general rule, leaders who came from the provinces they administered were more concerned with saving the lives of their compatriots than were leaders from different provinces. The first secretary of Jiangxi province (where 180,000 died from starvation, or 1.06 percent of the population) and his three leading right-hand men were born in that province. Anhui province (6.33 million dead from starvation, or 18.37 percent of the population) was managed by a Hunanese; Sichuan province (9.4 million dead from starvation, more than 10 million according to another source—or 13.07 percent of the population) was governed by a native of Jiangxi province (Chen Yixin, 2011, pp. 197 and 212–220).

85. Zeng Xisheng later changed his mind and embarked on a "rightist" policy, which led to him being sacked in 1962 and beaten to death by the Red Guards in 1967 (Yang Jisheng, [2008] 2012, pp. 416–422; Teiwes and Sun, 1999, pp. 216–217; Teiwes, 1993, p. 367; Becker, 1998, pp. 210–211).

86. See below for other reasons for the Ukrainian carnage, which also hit the Ukrainians living in Kuban. Of the three Chinese provinces mentioned, only Sichuan was a traditional cereal exporter, but without being rich for all that. Anhui province had experienced difficulties in feeding its population for centuries.

87. Becker, 1998, pp. 173–174 and 325–326; Dikötter, 2010, pp. 119–120.

88. I will allow myself another anecdote. In September 1979, I was researching family planning in Guangxi province. I was taken to a People's Commune near Liuzhou, a pioneer in birth control. Because they had recorded 148 births between January and August of that year, compared with 161 for 1978, I asked the interpreter in English if the birth rate might not be set to rise a little for 1979. I tried to be tactful by adding that the growing number of better cared for children after Liberation might result in more age groups reaching marriageable age, so that a higher birth rate could well be combined with a fall in fertility. It was a waste of time. The vexed interpreter asked me how I could possibly foresee the future and know the number of births for a year that was still under way. I refrained from reminding him that the family planning committee had a precise record of the number of pregnancies in their fifth or sixth month, and therefore of the estimated number of births by year end. Instead I consulted the woman director of the committee, but that too proved to be a waste of time since she answered in the local dialect,

which I couldn't understand. Only one person in the room spoke Mandarin, and she held the highest "rank," being a *lao ganbu* (veteran of the revolution) who was sent there from North China after Liberation. It took her less than a minute to grasp the question and its implications, and to find the answer, "We expect some 180 births this year, which is noteworthy progress on the 190 the previous year." And to prove her point, she went to the board of this model commune, placed there for the edification of the masses (and nitpicking foreigners!) and promptly changed the 161 births noted for 1978 to 190 (Bianco, 1981, p. 128).

89. Kung and Chen, 2011. The two authors suggest that during the GLF, provincial first secretaries who were also full members of the Central Committee could expect no further promotion. The few Politburo members who had not taken part in the Long March had many years of guerilla warfare behind them and were therefore irremovable (the Cultural Revolution would change that). Consequently, however zealous they might be, no candidate's postrevolutionary loyalty could compete with the rights of those *lao ganbu*. Conversely, to become a fully fledged member of the Central Committee was a logical aspiration for an alternate member. By comparing twenty-four provinces and taking into account other variables (such as the province's natural resources, agricultural production, industrialization, hydrography, natural disasters, etc.), the authors estimated that those alternate members collected and exported more grain to other provinces and undertook more of Mao's beloved large-scale (hydraulic and other) projects, and thereby contributed to the excess mortality of that province.

90. Khlevniouk, 1996, chaps. 1 and 2.

91. Yang Jisheng, [2008] 2012, pp. 164, 174, and passim; Teiwes and Sun, 1999, p. 212.

92. Teiwes, 1993, p. 341; Teiwes and Sun, 1999, pp. 227–228. I should add that Bo Yibo's memoirs, published after Mao's death, described and confirmed numerous examples of the chairman's aberrational behavior and "leftist" stubbornness. Deng's hastily repudiated remark ("It doesn't matter if a cat is white or black, as long as it catches the mice") was made shortly before he suppressed it.

93. Blum, [1994] 2004, p. 104.

94. On the national question, see the essential Martin, 2001, pp. 292–308. On what preceded that, see Graziosi, 2005, pp. 459, 464, and passim. See also Werth, 2008, pp. 6–10 and 15–17; 2007, p. 133. On the demographic balance, see Snyder, [2010] 2012, p. 100.

95. Penner, 1998 (quotations on p. 39). The author's research covered not Ukraine but the neighboring Don region, in other words the northernmost region of North Caucasus, which includes a part of the Kuban where there were many villagers of Ukrainian origin. The government sent the greatest number of settlers to the Kuban.

96. Davies and Wheatcroft, 2004, p. 441; Wheatcroft, 2008, pp. 3 and 34; Werth, 2010a, pp. 146–151.

97. In, among others, *Europe-Asia Studies* in 2005 (vol. 57, no. 6. pp. 823–841), 2006 (vol. 58, no. 4, pp. 625–633; no. 6, pp. 973–984; no. 7, pp. 1141–1156), 2007 (vol. 59, no. 4, pp. 663–693), and 2008 (vol. 60, no. 4, pp. 663–675).

98. Graziosi, 2005; 2010, p. 115; 2013, pp. 16, 19, and 24. Furthermore I benefitted from attending the public lecture "Stalin and Hunger as a Nation-Destroying Tool" given by Andrea Graziosi on 27 September 2014 at the Toronto Conference on "Communism and Hunger: The Ukrainian, Chinese, Kazakh, and Soviet Famines in Comparative Perspective."

99. Yang Jisheng, [2008] 2012, pp. 217 and 537–538, English edition (*Tombstone*), pp. 48 and 449–450.

100. Li Zhisui, 1994, p. 360; Roux, 2009, p. 676. The same author (pp. 675, 682–683, and 687, among others) provides some edifying examples of Mao's irresponsible, overoptimistic, and even boastful (a poem!) statements during the bleakest hours (1959–1961). On Mao's "vegetarian" menu at the end of 1960 and in 1961, see the details provided by his cook in Yang Jisheng, [2008] 2012, p. 550.

101. In many kolkhozes, "they did not plough, but merely scratched the land on the surface" (Khataevich, 16 August 1932, quoted in Davies and Wheatcroft, 2004, p. 108). See also ibid., p. 438.

102. Becker, 1998, pp. 107 and 113–114; Yang Jisheng, [2008] 2012, pp. 133–134, 249, and 268, who mentions five-meter-deep furrows in Gansu province.

103. Davies and Wheatcroft, 2004, pp. 436–437 and 452.

104. Yang Jisheng, [2008] 2012, p. 111.

105. Garnaut, 2014, sheds light on the economic factors, Chen Yixin, 2011, on the behavior of the regional leaders. On Qinghai, see Yang Jisheng, [2008] 2012, pp. 455–458, English edition *Tombstone*, p. 394; also Wemheuer, 2014, chapters 5–7: "Famines on the Periphery."

106. Davies and Wheatcroft, 2004, pp. 400, 421, 433, n. 129, and 503–504; Gao Hua, 2011, pp. 182–196. See also, Yang Jisheng, [2008] 2012, pp. 485–490.

107. Teiwes, 1993, p. 348; Yang Dali, 1996, chaps. 3 and 6; Becker, 1998, pp. 330 and 334; Yang Jisheng, [2008] 2012, pp. 528–530.

108. Wemheuer, 2014, pp. 26–33 and 221–239. The author extrapolates Walter Mallory's classic work, *China, Land of Famine* (Mallory, 1926), to Russia.

109. Klid and Motyl, 2012, p. 310.

Chapter 6 Bureaucracy

1. This introduction is mainly based on Djilas, [1957] 1962, pp. 37, 44–45, 58, and passim; as well as on Courtois, 2007, p. 123; Fitzpatrick, 2002, p. 65; Lewin, [1966] 1976, p. 304; Cohen, Stephen [1971], 1980, pp. 320–321. Here, once and for all,

are my principal sources for the Soviet part of this chapter: Ciliga, [1938, 1950] 1977; Djilas, [1957] 1962; Dunham, [1976] 1990; Fainsod, [1958] 1963; Ferro, 1980; Figes, 2007a and 2007b; Filtzer, 2014; Fitzpatrick, 1992, pp. 149–182; Fitzpatrick, 2002; Kotkin, 1995; Lewin, [1966] 1976; Lewin, 1987; Lewin, 2003a and 2003b; Voslensky, 1980. See also a few occasional sources: Berdiaev, [1938] 1951; Blum and Mespoulet, 2003; Brovkin, 1998; Bruneteau, 2011; Graziosi, 2010; Grossman, 2008; Haupt, 1972; Heller and Nekrich, 1982; Kriegel, 1972; Lefort, 1971; Lefort, 1999; Soljenitsyne, 1968 and 1975; Sumpf, 2013; Svirski, 1981; Tucker, 1963; Werth, [1990] 2004. From now on I will mention only the author of a quotation or a little-known source. I will also specify the reference when I have borrowed massively.

2. Ferro, 1980, pp. 121 and 124–127.

3. Figes, 2007b, p. 32; 2007a, p. 845

4. Filtzer, 2014, p. 508.

5. Magnitogorsk: Kotkin, 1995, pp. 86–87 and 286–293; Smolensk: Fainsod, [1958] 1963, pp. 62–66.

6. Walder, 2015, pp. 100, 103.

7. Link, 2000, p. 268. This paragraph mainly relies on Kau, 1971. Unless another reference is specified, the developments relating to the new Chinese class are based on Harding, 1981; Kau, 1971; Kraus, 1981; Lü, 2000; and, in specific instances, on Andreas, 2009; Barnett, 1967; Bernstein, 1970; Bernstein and Li, 2010; Bianco, [1994] 1997; Dikötter, 2010; Economist, 2012; Huang, 2000; Lew, 1986 and 1997; Leys, 1974; Li Zhisui, 1994; Link, 2000; MacFarquhar, [1960] 1974; McGregor, 2010; Oksenberg, 1968; Scalapino, 1972; Schram, 1991; Schurmann, 1968; Townsend, 1969; Tung and Evans, 1967; Vogel, 1967a and 1967b; Walder, 2015; Xiao-Planès, 2013a; Yang Jisheng, [2008] 2012; Zhou, 2012.

8. Ferro, 1980, p. 72 for this specific reference; for the remainder of the paragraph, pp. 59, 119, 121, 124, 129–130, 138–140, 151–153, 157, 160, 174, and 236–238.

9. Lewin, 1987, p. 351; Courtois, 2007, p. 123.

10. Figes, 2007a, pp. 849–851. The remainder of the paragraph mainly relies on Fitzpatrick, 1992, pp. 149–182.

11. Heller and Nekrich, 1982, p. 400. Also Sumpf, 2013, p. 474; Figes, 2007b, p. 155.

12. This paragraph is based on Dunham, [1976] 1990.

13. With the exception of any references mentioned in the text, this section is mainly based on Kraus, 1981, except that I am far more critical of Mao than he, which does not prevent me from appreciating his sophisticated and well-informed analyses.

14. Li Zhisui, 1994.

15. I am satirizing but it comes to the same: in Mao-speak one would refer to two ways, the socialist one and the capitalist one, followed by the supporters of the two lines, the correct, socialist line being defined by Chairman Mao.

16. Schram, 1991, p. 80. At the end of his life, Mao unhesitatingly situated "the new bourgeoisie" within the Party; see ibid., pp. 93–94; Xian, 2010, p. 282; Pantsov, [2007] 2012, p. 492.

17. Kraus, 1981, p. 67; Schram, 1991, p. 71.

18. In order of appearance, Lew, 1986, pp. 47–53; Walder, 2015, p. 340; Bianco, [1994] 1997, p. 96.

19. Bianco, [1994] 1997, p. 93.

20. Leys, 1974, p. 289. On what preceded this, see Harding, 1981, pp. 348–349; MacFarquhar, [1960] 1974, pp. 44 and 68.

21. Fitzpatrick, 2002, pp. 54–55.

22. Ibid., p. 58; *Pravda*, 3 July 1929, quoted in Lewin, [1966] 1976, p. 208.

23. Anton Ciliga, quoted in Lefort, 1971, p. 128; Grossman, 2008, p. 634. Cases of corruption described in Fainsod, [1958] 1963, pp. 201–205; of arrogance and caste spirit in Figes, 2007b, pp. 32–33.

24. Ciliga, [1938, 1950] 1977, pp. 98–102. Kotkin, 1995, pp. 123–127, is the source of the brief observations that follow. They are all the more relevant with reference to the housing conditions of ordinary mortals in Magnitogorsk in the same period (see chapter 2 above).

25. The salaries of the Party cadres and other officials are detailed in Kraus, 1981, p. 186. See also Vogel, 1967a, p. 51.

26. MacFarquhar, [1960] 1974, pp. 55, 65–66, 93, 211, 222, and 230.

27. Xiao-Planès, 2013a.

28. Leys, 1974, pp. 172–173. The Red Guards found two such black limousines in the garage of the First Secretary of the Fujian Party Committee. His home was twenty times larger than that of an average worker (Ken Ling, 1972, p. 136). Kraus, 1981, p. 128 for the preceding paragraph (on admission to university).

29. To remain faithful to the Chinese, one should translate "the science of relationships" as a discipline that had to be learned by anyone ambitious, or indeed by everyone. It consists of increasing one's network of relationships: *guanxi*, the multiplied equivalent of the Soviet *blat*.

30. Link, 2000, p. 23.

31. Ibid., p. 265.

32. Lü, 2000, pp. 106, 140, and 229. I am more convinced by the author when he makes the more modest proposal of suggesting, "a possible, but not necessarily the sole, cause of official corruption in a Communist regime" (p. 228).

33. "Entre Hommes et Demons" was translated into French in 1981 by Jean-Philippe Béja and Wojtek Zafanolli in *La Face cachée de la Chine* (Béja and Zafanolli, 1981). For the remainder of the paragraph, see Link, 2000, p. 263; Svirski, 1981, p. 162.

34. Fainsod, [1958] 1963, p. 85.

35. This paragraph is mainly based on Lewin, 2003b.

36. Figes, 2007b, p. 470.

37. According to a survey carried out in Leningrad in the mid-1960s, 89 percent of children whose parents were in a job that required higher education reached ninth grade if they had marks equal to or above 3.5 out of 5, as well as 77 percent of those who obtained only marks below 3.5. Conversely only 41 percent of children whose parents were unskilled workers got into ninth grade if they obtained 3.5 and above, and 19 percent of those who obtained marks below 3.5 (Filtzer, 2014, p. 511 and Table 29.1)

38. Ibid., p. 510.

39. Figes, 2007b, p. 470.

40. This entire paragraph is mainly based on Andreas, 2009, chap. 10 (pp. 233–247).

41. "The proportion of new members classified as intellectuals grew from 8% in 1979 to about 50% in 1985" (ibid., p. 235).

42. Ibid., p. 238.

43. Ibid., pp. 241–242; previous sentence: ibid., p. 246.

44. Li and White, 1990, pp. 15–16, quoted in Andreas, 2009, p. 239.

45. The following paragraph is based on Voslensky, 1980, pp. 217–282.

46. In China, the privileges of the well-born were less institutionalized but equally glaring; take, for instance, the school in Shanghai where a general's son obtained the best marks in Russian even though he was a poor student. A few years later, having failed all his exams (except for those he didn't even bother to take) he was accepted by the best university in China (Tung and Evans, 1967, pp. 44 and 62–63).

47. One may gauge the increase in the amounts involved within a single generation by comparing the corruption cases mentioned in Voslensky, 1980, pp. 229, 231–232, and Fainsod, [1958] 1963, pp. 201–205.

48. McGregor, 2010, p. 139; Bergère, 2013, p. 195. See also McGregor, 2010, pp. 135–169; Wedeman, 2012; Bergère, 2013, pp. 194–203.

49. Ko and Weng, 2012. See also Osburg, 2013.

50. Kriegel, 1972, p. 50.

51. I can hear the protests already: what nobility and refinement would such upstarts have, proud as they are to show off their *nouveau riche* success. Take the Shanghainese billionaire, Zhou Zhengyi, who had solid gold bathroom fittings but forgot the name of the boarding school he sent his son to in England—but not the reason for sending him there, which was that "it was the most expensive one" (McGregor, 2010, pp. 157–158). Solzhenitsyn (1974, vol. 2, p. 206) marveled that "these Himalayas of self-importance have been assimilated by a first generation Soviet general."

52. Dumont, 1966, p. 269.

53. Dubois, Lozac'h, and Rowell, 2005. I willingly concede that the joint analysis of the budget surveys carried out by the statistical administration and the trade unions before and after Stalin's death (Moine, 2005) or that on the East German officials' perception of their West German colleagues' "bureaucratism" after unification (Lozac'h, 2005) are a good illustration of what such dispassionate analysis can achieve. These two articles, published in the same edition of the same review, used the approach recommended by Vincent Dubois and his colleagues.

54. Djilas, [1957] 1962; Aron, 1962; Aron, 1965; Lefort, 1971; Castoriadis, 1973.

55. Swedberg, 2005, p. 253.

Chapter 7   Culture

1. In other words "socialist romanticism" might better suggest the role permitted to the imagination in the works of the ideal Soviet writer, since "socialism is a goal, an aspiration, a hope" (Dobrenko, 2011, p. 109). See also Strada, 1990, p. 26; Aucouturier, 1998.

2. For a more precise definition of *laojiao*, see below chapter 8.

3. That was the case, among others, of Zhao Shuli (1906–1970). Born to a family of poor peasants, Zhao started working in the fields when he was very young. The cultural authorities praised his way of describing the peasants and telling simple stories that could be read to illiterate people. But now they accused Zhao of having praised an incorrect political line and portrayed "intermediary" characters (i.e., not revolutionary enough). In the end they persecuted and killed this zealous depicter of history as it should be, now superseded and rejected in favor of a new manifestation of utopia.

4. Vasily Grossman's *For a Just Cause* was published only after the war (and severely criticized), but his premonitory articles and his more "conformist" novel, *The People Are Immortal*, were published without the censors having much to quibble about—so long as they were in line with the union against the invader.

5. Pasternak, [1958] 2009, p. 647. Also Link, 2000, p. 67.

6. "On Sincerity in Literature" was published in *Novy Mir* in December 1953, while Ehrenburg's *The Thaw* came out the following year. Lu Xinhua's *The Scar* (or *The Wounded*), published in 1978, also gave its name to the first wave of post-Mao literature (Scar Literature or Literature of the Wounded). Liu Xinwu's short story, "The Class Counselor" (or "The Class Teacher"), inaugurated the same wave.

7. Link, 2000, pp. 39, 126, 203, and 253. This excellent study inspired me as much as it taught me. I admire the author's intelligence, sensitivity, and culture, and I am not surprised that this accomplished Sinologist is no longer able to obtain a Chinese visa.

8. Simonov: Figes, 2007a, p. 484; Tolstoy: Fitzpatrick, 2002, p. 169. See also Dobrenko, 2011, p. 99; Vaissié, pp. 97–101 and 374–375.

9. At the end of 1979, 2,450,000 copies of a speech made by Marshal Ye Jianying on the national holiday were circulating in the city of Beijing alone (or remained unopened on tables across the various *danwei*). A few weeks later, in January 1980, the play *If I Were Real*, by three young playwrights, was neither published nor produced, despite widespread enthusiasm following the debates about it in the press. The play was about a young man who pretended to be the son of a high-level Communist official and immediately received favors and gifts from other bureaucrats (Link, 2000, pp. 23 and 186). For the remainder of the paragraph, see ibid., pp. 130–131, 124, and 137.

10. Dunham, [1976] 1990, sheds a great deal of light on this point. For what precedes, see Birch, 1991, pp. 790–791; Giafferri-Huang, 1991, p. 145; Zhang, 2003, pp. 49–68.

11. Link, 2000, pp. 56, 65, and 101.

12. With some very small differences: the Chinese Association of Writers included only romantic poets and novelists. It was part of the China Federation of Literary and Art Circles (and, of course, there were sister associations in the cinema, music, dance, art, etc.).

13. With the exception of a few borrowings from Heller, Michel, 1990, p. 161; and Dobrenko, 2011, p. 105, I have mostly relied on He, 2010, in Bernstein and Li, eds.

14. He, 2010, p. 410.

15. Milosz, 1953, p. 90.

16. See above. The young soldier, Lei Feng, died in an accident in 1962. He is the best-known revolutionary model, held up for the masses to emulate. As disinterested as he was devoted, the only aspiration of this obscure hero and avid reader of Mao's works was to be a cog at the service of the people and the revolution—or at least that is what transpires from his diary (authentic or fabricated) and the eponymous campaign launched in 1963. For Lei Feng, see, Pantsov, [2007] 2012, p. 488; for the following sentence, see Solzhenitsyn, 1974, vol. 1, p. 131.

17. Vaissié, 2008, p. 125.

18. Giafferri-Huang, 1991, pp. 87–90; Hong, 2007, pp. 135–139. On the misadventures of Aleksey Tolstoy, see Svirski, 1990, pp. 348–349.

19. On Ilf in Paris: Ehrenburg's Memoirs, quoted by Ilyia Serman, in Etkind et al., 1990, p. 174; *prorabotka*: Vaissié, 2008, pp. 56–57 and 75–77.

20. Goldman, 1967, pp. 90–93; Giafferri-Huang, 1991, pp. 21–22.

21. Fitzpatrick, 1992, pp. 183–215; Gorki is quoted on p. 199, and Mayakowsky's imagined posthumous fate, p. 214. See also Roziner, 1990, pp. 269–272.

22. On two occasions in March 1936 (less than two months after the inflammatory editorial in *Pravda*), Meyerhold publicly praised Shostakovich instead of criticizing

him (Fitzpatrick, 1992, pp. 200–201 and 208). The audience, at first speechless with astonishment, greeted that courageous stance with thunderous applause. It was not the only reason Meyerhold was arrested in 1939 and executed in 1940 (Stalin had that "formalist" in his sights for years), but it may have contributed. See also Figes, 2003, p. 480.

23. That was the also case for Hu Feng, and his friends and members of his entourage, Feng Xuefeng, Lu Ling, and Liu Qing, for Wang Meng and Liu Binyan during the Hundred Flowers, Ding Ling and Ai Qing after the Hundred Flowers; Zhao Shuli and Zhou Libo later. Shao Quanlin, close to Zhou Yang, was attacked even before his patron for having advocated the depiction of "intermediary" characters (i.e., neither all white nor all black) and showing unpardonable boldness by wanting to "go deeper into realism" and "write the truth."

24. On the later relationship between Shostakovich and the disciples of "Karlo-Marlo," and more generally on the collision between art and power and the pernicious effects of compromise and cowardice, a recent novel (Barnes, 2016) is both despairing and salutary.

25. Fitzpatrick, 1992, pp. 210–213; Roziner, 1990, pp. 284–285; Figes, 2003, pp. 494–495, 503–504, 510.

26. Vaissié, 2008, pp. 103–108.

27. Link, 2000, p. 130; Giafferri-Huang, 1991, pp. 28–30; David Der-wei Wang, 2000, pp. 42–44; Hong, 2007, pp. 123–124.

28. Link, 2000, p. 95.

29. And even composers such as Shostakovich (Figes, 2003, p. 511).

30. Solzhenitsyn gives a lively account of his expulsion from the Union of Writers in *The Oak and the Calf* (Solzhenitsyn, 1975, pp. 255–261 and 471–480).

31. Ibid., p. 445; Heller, Michel, 1990, p. 155; Vaissié, 2008, p. 46; Aucouturier, 1998, p. 83.

32. In a premonitory essay ("The New Society Is a Great School," 1951), Lao She describes the self-criticism sessions and blows that were meant to re-educate intellectuals in "the great school of Mao Zedong Thought": "other intellectuals standing beside me and I, involuntarily also began to shout, 'Beat him! Why don't you beat him!'" The pack of Red Guards yelled the very same thing ("Beat him!") when they chased Lao She and forced him to commit suicide (Su Wei, 2000, pp. 71–72).

33. Hong, 2007, pp. 56 and 214; Dobrenko and Balina, 2011, pp. 100 and 259–260. On the problems writers faced with the authorities, nothing can replace Solzhenitsyn, 1975. Albeit less caustic, Liu Xiaobo, 2011, and Liu Xiaobo [2003], 2012a and 2012b, is almost as edifying.

34. On Lysenko, my main source is Schneider, 2010, in Bernstein and Li eds., which condenses Schneider, 2003, chaps. 4 and 5. See also, Pollock, 2009 (borrowings

from pp. 100 and 110) and Courtois, 2007, p. 509; Graziosi, 2010, pp. 82, 122, and 461; Service, 2005, p. 307; Figes, 2007b, p. 488; Becker, 1996, pp. 102–113; Roux, 2009, p. 632; Rohlf, 2010, in Bernstein and Li eds., pp. 200 and 220; Tucker, 1963, pp. 91–101.

35. Holloway, 2006, pp. 559 and 569. David Holloway's contribution to *The Cambridge History of Russia* (ibid., pp. 549–578) is my main source for this paragraph.

36. See the provocative title chosen intentionally by Alexey Kojevnikov: *Stalin's Great Science: The Times and Adventures of Soviet Physicists* (2004). I have only secondhand knowledge of this book through reviews.

37. Platonov, Zoshchenko, Ilf and Petrov, Mandelstam, and Pasternak's clandestine—or not so clandestine—poems, Akhmatova's Requiem, even Cholokhov, etc.

38. King, 2011, pp. 58–61 and 66.

39. Vaissié, 2008, pp. 49, 80–82, 104–105, 107, and 139–140. Translated into French by Cécile Vaissié (ibid., pp. 187–188), Fadeyev's last letter expressed more bitterness than remorse.

40. "We do not write for propaganda. Art is real, as is life itself. And like life, it has neither purpose nor sense" (extract of a manifesto quoted in Vaissié, 2008, p. 29). This book is my sole source for this long paragraph devoted to Fedin.

41. *Rousskaia Literatoura*, no. 1, 1998, p. 171, quoted in ibid., p. 61.

42. Ibid., pp. 77–78.

43. Ibid., p. 63.

44. Ibid., p. 63.

45. Ibid., p. 217.

46. Ibid., p. 413.

47. On Zamyatin, see Heller, Leonid, 1988, pp. 457–474 (quotations, p. 457); Bullock, Philip Ross, 2011, pp. 79–96; Brown, Edward J., 1969, pp. 69–83; Vaissié, 2008; pp. 28 and 30; and of course Zamyatin, 1971, pp. 169–171 of the French translation, for the Great Operation.

48. The French translation (*La Forteresse assiégée*) is by Sylvie Servan-Schreiber and Wang Lou (Qian, 1987a) (the English translation, *Fortress Besieged*, is by Jeanne Kelly and Nathan K. Mao, Penguin Classics, 2004). For the remainder of the paragraph, see Nicolas Chapuis's introduction to Qian, 1987b, p. 16; Yang, Jiang, 1983, p. 14.

49. Wang Xiaojue, 2011, p. 134. This study is my main source on the agony suffered by Shen in 1949 and later. The following quotation is found on page 140. On the life and works of Shen Congwen, see Kinkley, 1987; David Der-wei Wang, 1992 and 2000, passim; Hsia, 1961, chap. 8, pp. 189–211.

50. Link, 2000, pp. 162–163. At the time, and for many years more, the author was still held in a camp.

51. After being interrogated by the KGB for five days and five nights, Elisabeth Voronianskaya finally confessed to where she had hidden a copy of *The Gulag Archipelago* that she could not bring herself to burn the previous year when Solzhenitsyn had asked her to do so. When she was finally released she hung herself (on 23 August 1973), considering herself a Judas (Saraskina, 2010, pp. 688–689; Solzhenitsyn, 1975, pp. 339–340 and 523).

52. "He had spent his life bowing, obeying, fearing, being afraid of hunger, or torture, of hard labor in Siberia. … And the dreams of his youth … were now at the service of this vile fear. He should never have had doubts, should have voted without turning back, signed. Yes, he had been afraid for himself, and it was that fear that had fed his convictions" (Grossman, 1972, p. 52). Nicolai Andreyevich was the cousin that Ivan visited, the *zek* who was freed after Stalin died. For the rest of the paragraph see mainly Etkind et al., 1990, pp. 235 (Mandelstam), 268 (Shostakovich), 370 and 376 (Tvardovski), 778 (Zinoviev), 816 (Bergoltz), 833 (Dombrowsky); and, to a lesser extent, Svirski, 1981, p. 442 (Maximov). Smerdiakov was the illegitimate son (and parricide) of Fyodor Karamazov, in Dostoyevsky's *The Brothers Karamazov*. On Shostakovich (and cowardice), see as well Barnes, 2016, pp. 157–158 and passim.

53. Vidal, 2006, pp. 177–179 and 307.

54. Osip Mandelstam's famous poem about Stalin, the "Stalin Epigram," written in November 1933, was the reason for his first arrest in May 1934. It has frequently been reproduced, especially in the first volume of Nadezhda Mandelstam's memoirs, Nadejda, 1972, p. 415. For the preceding sentence, see Dombrovsky, 2005, p. 208. Nevertheless, Zybin adds, "With increasing frequency, a timorous doubt wormed its way into my faith."

55. The expression "obsession with China" comes from the author of one of the best studies of Chinese twentieth-century (pre-Communist) fiction: Hsia, 1961. It is no surprise that he dates that obsession to the May Fourth period and before that, to the early twentieth century. The fact that the "obsession" survived the trials and tribulations of Maoism and the Cultural Revolution is illustrated by Bai Hua among others, in his patriotic profession of faith, when he declared in 1984: "A true Chinese writer must be, first and foremost, a true son of China." The same Bai Hua had twice been the target of official campaigns (by the army and the government), as he was criticized for his "bourgeois liberalism" even during the thaw. Deng Xiaoping himself had given the signal for criticism of Bai Hua's *Bitter Love*, a play describing the trials of an intellectual badly treated by the country he loved and so devotedly served. Bai Hua did not run the risk of being criticized under Mao, since his poems were never published but remained as secret as Bulgakov's *The Master and Margarita*. On Bai Hua, see Link, 2000, p. 140.

56. Dutrait, 2006, pp. 27–28; Yang Xiaobin, 2000, pp. 195–196. For Scar Literature, see Link, 2000, p. 51; David Der-wei Wang, 2000, pp. 53–54.

57. I maintain my preference for Lu Xun.

58. As a reader devoid of any talent for literary criticism, I would nevertheless be tempted to compare Yan Lianke's *Four Books* with Bulgakov's *The Master and Margarita*, which is comparing a work that appeared a good one-third of a century after Mao's death, with one written in Stalin's lifetime (Bulgakov, 1968; Yan, [2010] 2012).

59. Link, 2000, pp. 45 and 54.

60. David Der-wei Wang, 2000, p. xxvi. On the preceding sentences, see, Dutrait, 2006, pp. 35–36; Link, 2000, p. 33.

61. I feel instant sympathy for the participants at the First Congress of Soviet Writers who signed a leaflet destined for foreign guests, "the Soviet prostitutes of the mind." "We prostitute ourselves out of necessity ... But you ..." (Graziosi, 2010, pp. 124–125). Conversely, despite having devoted my life to studying China, I required an explanation when I read that a Chinese student crossed the campus in a downpour without sharing his umbrella with the female student he was talking to before the storm broke. "If we share the same umbrella," the student said, "everyone will think we're a couple ... That would be very embarrassing, especially for her" (Link, 2000, pp. 311–312). On the previous sentence, my bible, as ever (ibid., pp. 61–62).

62. Kinkley, 2014, p. 198. In one of the works analyzed by that author, someone mockingly suggests a negative interpretation (men capable of doing the worst) of the famous Maoist aphorism, which summarized the ambition of the GLF: "There is nothing that the people cannot accomplish" (ibid., p. 85).

63. I have summarized the developments outlined in Veg, 2014, pp. 9–10, and added a few details of my own that Sebastian Veg might not necessarily agree with.

64. It had been the subject of several literary works from the start of the post-Mao thaw (Link, 2000, pp. 254–255), but it was not until the twenty-first century that Yan Lianke's *Four Books* (Sishu) provided the best example in literature, and Yang Jisheng became recognized as the most comprehensive historian of the famine, while the film directed by Yang Xianhui and Wang Bing (*The Ditch*) shed light on it through fiction. See respectively, Yan, [2010] 2012; Yang Jisheng, [2008] 2012; Yang Xianhui, 2010.

65. Kinkley, 2014.

66. I should add that Kinkley excluded epic critical works such as Yan Lianke's *Sishu* from his study.

67. Kinkley, 2014, pp. 67, 175. Violence lacking any moral or ideological inspiration: ibid., pp. 169, 172–173, and passim.

68. Bonnin, [2004] 2013; Bernstein, 1977.

69. As Jeffrey Kinkley rightly asks, "Why is Big Brother still invisible in the Chinese novels when the storyline reaches the Mao era?" (Kinkley, 2014, p. 123). See also p. 124 ("Mao Zedong's *utopia* and the ideas of revolution and making revolution are missing") and p. 128 for the replies the author suggests to this pertinent question.

Chapter 8 The Camps

1. *Laogai*, the abbreviation of *laodong gaizao*, means "reform through labor," as opposed to *laojiao*, "reform through education." One of the best guides to the subject is Domenach, 1992, along with three more recent studies: Seymour and Anderson, 1998; Williams and Wu, 2004; Kempton and Richardson, 2009. Domenach, 1992, pp. 552–560, lists sources prior to 1992.

2. Located in northeastern Siberia, Kolyma was one of *the* symbols, if not the symbol, of the gulag. See, among others, Applebaum, 2005, pp. 180–188; Chalamov, 2003; Conquest, 1970; Guinzbourg, 1980; Solzhenitsyn, 1974, vol. 2, pp. 101, 289–290, and 298; Khlevniuk, 2004; Werth, 2012; Yang, Xianhui, 2010. Wang Bing's film *The Ditch* describes the lives of prisoners in the Jiabiangou camp, in the Gobi Desert in northwest Gansu province, one of the poorest in China.

3. *Zek* (or Z-K or *zeka*) is the abbreviation of *zaklyuchennyi*, meaning prisoner in the former Soviet Union. See, among others, Solzhenitsyn, 1974, vol. 2, p. 501; Guinzbourg, 1980, p. 596; Blum, Craveri, and Nivelon, 2012, p. 301. See also Chalamov, 2003, pp. 599 and 601; Khlevniuk; 2004; Margolin, 2010.

4. I should add, however, that the usual figure of 20 million is only an estimate. Between 1930 and 1941 alone, some 20 million sentences were passed, and the same person may have been condemned twice or even several times over. In other countries they might be called "recidivists," but would that term be appropriate for a political dissident condemned to three years in a prison camp at the end of the 1920s, arrested again during the Great Purge, and then sentenced yet again after he had served his sentence, if not before? That is more or less what happened to Varlam Shalamov, who after doing time in the camps was placed under house arrest in Magadan, the capital of Kolyma. He was finally allowed to return to European Russia after Stalin's death, but not to Moscow until he was rehabilitated after the Twentieth Congress. It is impossible to know precisely how many *zeks* there were, or how many people were deported (kulaks first and foremost, but also Koreans, Poles, Ukrainians, Byelorussians, Moldavians, Balts, Germans, Chechens, and many more). See Khlevniuk, 2004, pp. 288–292 and 328; Werth, 2012, p. 6. For the rest of the paragraph, see Applebaum, 2005, p. 925, and on the Chinese side, Domenach, 1992, p. 491; Seymour and Anderson, 1998, p. 206.

5. And 0.17 percent in 1995: yet another reason for us to pay more attention to *laogai* in its Maoist heyday, especially since today only a tiny minority are political prisoners. That is no reason to forget the Nobel Prize–winner Liu Xiaobo and many others, starting with the numerous human rights lawyers who are still imprisoned, and will be for many years to come (Liu unfortunately died before the publication of this book). I must add Li Bifeng at the very least, who was accused of helping the poet Liao Yiwu to escape from China. Li was sentenced to twelve years in November 2012, just twenty years after he first met the poet in prison, having already been familiar with his work (see Liao, 2013, p. 572). In terms of absolute values, the number of prisoners fell in similar proportions

after the deaths of the two dictators: from 10 to 2 million in China between 1977 and the 1990s, and from 2.5 million to 0.5 million in the Soviet Union between 1953 and 1960. Regarding the percentage of prisoners, see the references in the preceding note: Domenach, 1992, p. 491; Seymour and Anderson 1998, p. 206.

6.   The Dalstroy industrial complex used slave labor to extract gold, and incidentally, cobalt, tin, tungsten, and uranium, as well as to carry out other grueling tasks such as road construction (the famous 500-kilometer "Kolyma highway") using pick axes, spades, and wheelbarrows. The Komi Republic, east of Arkhangelsk, was less freezing than Kolyma (where "winter is 12 months and the rest is summer") and closer to Moscow and Leningrad. It has lead and zinc deposits, and, more importantly, coal around Vorkuta, a town built in the permafrost. In 1938, the BAM camp sent more than 200,000 *zeks* (one-ninth of the total) to construct a 2,000-kilometer railroad connecting the Baikal Lake to Amur. They were given saws in addition to the primitive tools used to construct the Kolyma highway, but work was interrupted by war. It was pursued again, and with more efficient means, in the 1970s and completed on the eve of Perestroika. See Werth, 2012, passim; Khlevniuk, 2004, pp. 30–31, 107–108, 203–204, 333–334, 336–337, and 359; Applebaum, 2005, pp. 169–180; Irina Shcherbakova's introduction to Tchistiakov, 2012, pp. 40–42 and 44.

7.   Kempton and Richardson, 2009, p. 63, list 909 camps today, but repression is less rigorous in the post-totalitarian era. For the remainder of the paragraph, see Seymour and Anderson 1998, pp. 44–174; for the camps in Xinjiang and Qinghai, for Qinghe, the northeast, northwest, etc., see Wu Hongda (Harry), 1992, pp. 161, 183, 185, 205, 209, 211, and 218; Xingkaihu and Mishan: Domenach, 1992, p. 540; 476 complexes: Applebaum, 2005, pp. 13 and 325.

8.   Domenach, 1992, pp. 17, 42, and 479; Faligot and Kauffer, 1987, pp. 164 and 452; Williams and Wu, 2004, pp. 48–49; Seymour and Anderson, 1998, pp. 8, 128, and passim.

9.   Domenach, 1992, pp. 34–37; Michael, 1962, pp. 124–134.

10. Solzhenitsyn devoted no fewer than half a dozen chapters to this gradual development. The titles are revealing: "The History of Our Sewage Disposal System," "The Law as a Child," "The Law Becomes a Man," "The Law Matures," "The Archipelago Rises from the Sea," "The Archipelago Metastizes." Solzhenitsyn, 1974, vol. 1, pp. 25–75 and 219–308; ibid., vol. 2, pp. 21–94). Khlevniuk, 2004, retraces very clearly the vicissitudes of the history of the gulag during the peak of Stalinism, between 1930 and 1941.

11. Julius Margolin defines the forty-eighth Kvadrat camp in which he is imprisoned near the White Sea-Baltic Canal as an "ordinary camp in the USSR." That is where he heard his fellow sufferer, a Jew like himself, declare in the winter of 1940–1941: "Oh how wonderful life was in Dachau before the war! No quotas! After 45 minutes of work we had a quarter of an hour's rest; 1,300 grams of bread, sausage, jam and, for dinner, Goulash, real Goulash. And everyone had their own bed!" (Margolin, 2010, pp. 171 and 351; see also p. 240 on the Solovki "paradise" in

1924). See also the contemporary account of a Solovki escapee: Malsagov, 1926, as well as Duguet, [1927] 2004. For the remainder of the paragraph, see Domenach, 1992, pp. 63, 101; Williams and Wu, 2004, pp. 35–47.

12. Kempton and Richardson, 2009, p. 29; the GLF and the Cultural Revolution destabilized the Chinese archipelago: Domenach, 1992, pp. 242, 490; and for the Soviets (Great Terror and Beria's "reforms"): Khlevniuk, 2004, chaps. 4 and 5.

13. From 1968, many intellectuals, urban cadres, and government employees were sent to the countryside for two or three years. They were supposed to reeducate themselves there by carrying out manual labor in May Seventh Cadre Schools, so called because of a famous letter Mao wrote on 7 May 1966 to Lin Biao, his future successor, later turned "traitor." See "The Thousand Dollar Pig," the first chapter in Frolic, 1982; Yang Jiang, 1983; Barmé and Minford, 1988, p. 88–98. For the remainder of the paragraph, see Fu, 2005; Williams and Wu, 2004, pp. 55–58; Zhang Xianliang, 1994, pp. 124–125; Wu Hongda (Harry), 1992, pp. 81–107; Wu Hongda (Harry), 1995, pp. 76, 159, and 240–254; Domenach, 1992, pp. 459–467.

14. Witness the former *laogai* prisoner who was ordered to carry a distinctive sign that brings to mind the yellow star, in this case a 13- by 18-centimeter sign stating her "counterrevolutionary" identity marked in large characters. This being 1966, it meant that she could not leave her home for fear of being targeted by the Red Guards. But was she in fact sentenced to *laogai* only for being a Catholic? She was constantly reminded that Catholics spied for the Vatican and the Vatican was a known agent of American imperialism (Lai, 1970, pp. 234 and passim). Witness also those children and adolescents executed in 1967 and 1968 for belonging to the "black categories," even though their parents, former landlords, gave birth to them after the revolution and after they had been dispossessed of their land (Su, Yang, 2011).

15. Nor all of them; some fled to the cities in search of food. That was the case for some of the three thousand children who were picked up in the streets of Shanghai one day in June 1960. Most were "street children" or primary school pupils. All were packed off to Shanxi, where they spent two decades, many working in the Wangzhuang coal mines, which was in fact the Number 4 *laogai* camp in Shanxi. Those children who did not work in the mines built the offices and dormitories for the police officers guarding them (Kempton and Richardson, 2009, pp. 26–27). For the remainder of this paragraph and the preceding one, see Applebaum, 2005, pp. 122 and 471–487; Chalamov, 2003, pp. 536, 577, 861–862, 927–929, and 936; Domenach, 1992, pp. 73, 81, 500, and 502; Kempton and Richardson, 2009, p. 28; Solzhenitsyn, 1974, vol. 1, pp. 352–361 and 402; ibid., vol. 2, pp. 315–333; Solzhenitsyn, [1976] 2010, pp. 209–210; Williams and Wu, 2004, p. 53.

16. The limestone quarries, or "penitentiary of penitentiaries" in the Kolyma, where Eugenia Ginzburg was sent in her eighth year in the camp (Guinzbourg, 1980, pp. 138, 142, 145, and 147–149).

17. Today they represent more than 90 percent or even 99 percent of the *laogai* prisoners, except in the northwest, where quite a few Tibetans in Qinghai, along with Uighurs and Kazakhs in Xinjiang, are detained for political reasons. They are usually accused of leading "separatist" or "counterrevolutionary" intrigues (Williams and Wu, 2004, pp. 19–20; Seymour and Anderson, 1998, pp. 119 and 181–183). For the remainder of the paragraph, see Domenach, 1992, p. 325; Liao, 2013, pp. 27–28, 175–176, 189–199, 207, and 448. For insight into the morals of the *urki* (criminals) in the gulag and an anthology of their exploits, a good start would be Chalamov, 2003, pp. 219–223 and 869–989; then Guinzbourg, [1967] 1997, pp. 392–394; Guinzbourg, 1980, pp. 79–83, 114, 145–149, and passim; Margolin, 2010, pp. 382–384 and 666–673; Razgon, 1991, p. 127.

18. See, in order of appearance, Pasqualini, 1975, p. 255; Solzhenitsyn, 1974, vol. 2, pp. 334–349; Wu, Hongda (Harry), 1995, pp. 104, 121–123, 140 and 219–220; Chalamov, 2003, pp. 221–223.

19. Imprisonment did not shake his revolutionary faith, as confirmed by his memoirs *The Man Who Stayed Behind* (Rittenberg and Bennett, 1993). For the rest of the paragraph, see, in order of appearance, Pasqualini, 1975, pp. 68 and 274–276; Domenach, 1992, pp. 228 and 494–497 (Tibetans and foreigners); Applebaum, 2005, p. 691 (Chechens).

20. Women accounted for between one-seventh and one-eighth of gulag prisoners in the 1920s (Solzhenitsyn, 1974, vol. 2, pp. 174–175). Khlevniuk, 2004, p. 315, provides their numbers year by year and the percentage they represented in relation to the total number of *zeks* between 1934 and 1941: from 5.9 percent in 1934 to 7.6 percent in 1941, with a maximum of 8.4 percent in 1939. Applebaum, 2005, p. 517, pursues that by reproducing percentages that are far higher for the period 1942–1952, at between 13 and 22 percent, with the exception of a record 30 percent of women in 1945. Werth, 2012, p. 115, believes that the contingent of women varied year to year, ranging between 15 and 25 percent of the prisoners, a number that was almost reached in 1949. He describes (ibid., pp. 313–315) the almost exclusively female camp of Elgen. Eugenia Ginzburg, who was held there, devotes an entire chapter to it in her memoirs *Journey into the Whirlwind* (Guinzbourg [1967], 1997, pp. 438–447 in the French translation). The picture is less complicated for the Chinese archipelago, but only because there are far fewer studies and sources available. See Domenach, 1992, p. 498; Seymour and Anderson, 1998, p. 10.

21. At least in Mao's lifetime: the survivors were freed on a massive scale between 1980 and 1985. For *jiuye* and the end of this paragraph, see, in order of appearance, Seymour and Anderson, 1998, pp. 189–198; Williams and Wu, 2004, pp. 58–60 and 148; Domenach, 1992, pp. 156–159 and 323–324; Wu Hongda (Harry), 1992, pp. 18 and 108–118; Pasqualini, 1975, pp. 11, 282 and 295; Wu Hongda (Harry), 1995, pp. 306–315 and passim; Kempton and Richardson, 2009, p. 86; Yang Xianhui, 2010, p. 189.

22. "'Why did they arrest him?' became a forbidden question for us. 'Why?' cried Anna Andreievna (Akhmatova) angrily when one of ours, contaminated by the general mood, asked that question. 'Why? It's time to understand that people are arrested for nothing'" (Mandelstam, 1972, pp. i and 9).

23. The Chinese bodies were as free about sending people to *laojiao* as their Soviet predecessors. They too thought it better to lock up ten innocent people rather than let one guilty party go free. But they targeted *laogai*, prison, and death in a more meticulous manner and were especially unrelenting to anyone who refused to cooperate. Apart from famous dissidents such as Wei Jingsheng, Xu Wenli, or Liu Xiaobo, who were notorious repeat offenders, Box 6 on Page 258 deals with three lesser-known cases. Even though there were countless cases similar to that of a prisoner treated as a pariah until 1979 because as a high school student back in 1951 he added a bushy moustache to a portrait of Mao cut out of a newspaper to make him appear as virile as Stalin (Yang Xianhui, 2010, pp. 202–225), they were no match for Stalin's concern with casting the net wide, whether in Leningrad, among the Poles, Ukrainians, the Balts, the Chinese Eastern Railway workers, etc. Not to mention all those who were arrested and sentenced by pure fluke. "Stalin's lethal scythe cut everyone down, without distinction" (Chalamov, 2003, p. 610; Solzhenitsyn, 1974, vol. 2, pp. 221–233).

24. See, in order of appearance, Applebaum, 2005, p. 243; Figes, 2007b, p. 242; Guinzbourg, [1967] 1997, pp. 55–57; Lai, 1970; Solzhenitsyn, 1974, vol. 1, pp. 76 and 83–92; Pu, 1985, pp. 8–11. On the arrests in general, see, among others, Applebaum, 2005, pp. 240–251; Solzhenitsyn, 1974, vol. 1, pp. 10–24; Williams and Wu, 2004, pp. 62–67; Domenach, 1992, pp. 165–166.

25. Both the Gestapo and the Chinese *gong'an* (public security) had a need for proof, clues, and presumptions, which mattered little to the NKVD (Buber-Neumann, 1986, p. 322). For the paragraph as a whole, see Williams and Wu, 2004, p. 67; Applebaum, 2005, pp. 257, 259, 264–268, 271, 280, and 285; Pasqualini, 1975, pp. 35, 41, 72–75, and 77; Seymour and Anderson, 1998, p. 181; Wu Hongda (Harry), 1995, pp. 83, 243, 340, and passim; Domenach, 1992, p. 180; Rickett and Rickett, [1957] 1973, p. 108; Solzhenitsyn, 1974, vol. 1, pp. 76 and 83–92; Margolin, 2010, p. 122.

26. "Two stool pigeons had had their throats slit at reveille. Then the same thing happened to an innocent working prisoner—whoever did it must have got the wrong bed" (Solzhenitsyn, [1976] 2010, p. 92). English translation by H. T. Willetts. See also Solzhenitsyn, 1974, vol. 2, pp. 267–282; Wu Hongda (Harry), 1995, pp. 220–231; Yang Xianhui, 2010, p. 388; Pasqualini, 1975, p. 289; Applebaum, 2005, p. 281.

27. This description applied only to revolutionary China (during Mao's lifetime and just after, until 1978 or 1979). Since the 1980s, people have been able to appeal sentences and have, on occasion, won. For the rest of the paragraph, see Figes, 2007b, pp. 282–283; Liao, 2013, p. 376; Pasqualini, 1975, p. 85.

28. The second part of *The Gulag Archipelago* (Solzhenitsyn, 1974, vol. 1, "Perpetual Motion," pp. 346–432 in the French translation) is entirely devoted to the transport and transfer of prisoners, including transfer stations and prisons. Solzhenitsyn's transfer to a special camp in Kazakhstan took three months: "... in the 19th century one could go faster on horseback" (ibid., vol. 3, p. 34). See also, among others, Williams and Wu, 2004, pp. 76–81; Domenach, 1992, pp. 199–200 and 468; Applebaum, 2005, pp. 290 and 309.

29. Pu, 1994, pp. 58–63. Han Weitian, the Guomindang spy who was locked up for twenty-six years, wrote a diary that he gave to the writer Pu Ning in 1987. Pu himself had been arrested twice in the PRC. The diary, with the addition of many interviews, formed Pu's documentary base. For the sources about the transportation to the gulag, see Guinzbourg, [1967] 1997, pp. 333–334, 341, and 365; Razgon, 1991, pp. 101–102; Applebaum, 2005, pp. 296–297.

30. Williams and Wu, 2004, p. 79; Lai, 1970, p. 142; Chalamov, 2003, p. 237.

31. Chalamov, 2003, p. 1015. See also Werth, 2012, p. 79, and for what preceded that, Guinzbourg, [1967] 1997, pp. 385 and 438.

32. Yang Xianhui, 2010, pp. 9, 353, and 368–369; see also Pasqualini, 1975, p. 262. For the beginning of the paragraph, see Applebaum, 2005, p. 305.

33. In the novel, *Half of Man Is Woman*, the hero, Zhang Yonglin, is wary about what he says in front of the informer, Zhou Ruicheng. Zhou's final repentance is more of a case of self-pity, once he becomes aware of how abject he has become (Zhang Xianliang, 1986a, pp. 192–195). Among the survivors of Maoist *laojiao*, I think that Zhang provides the most original account.

34. Varlam Shalamov diverted himself by comparing the daily mineral extraction quotas imposed on the Decembrists (3 *poods*, or 49 kilograms) with those imposed on the *zeks* in Kolyma (800 *poods*, or 13,104.5 kilograms). The difference shows the colossal progress of socialism in matters of quotas (Chalamov, 2003, p. 533).

35. Zhang Yihe, 2013, p. 9. See, among others, Solzhenitsyn, 1974, vol. 2, pp. 160–163.

36. Guinzbourg, [1967] 1997, pp. 452 and 455–456; Guinzbourg, 1980, p. 146. On the rations, see, among others, Applebaum, 2005, p. 320; Solzhenitsyn, 1974, vol. 2, pp. 147 and 155; Razgon, 1991, pp. 98 and 112–113.

37. In November 1961, the eleven brigade members in the Qinghe farm near Tianjin, received three different rations: first class (2.5 *wotou* per meal), second class (2 *wotou*), and third class (1.5 *wotou*). A *wotou* is a conical shaped bun that may be steamed or fried (Wu Hongda [Harry], 1995, p. 135). In a farm several thousand miles west of Qinghe, the same ration hierarchy applied according to the work carried out, as it did in a Guangdong province quarry several thousand miles to the south (Pu, 1994, pp. 78 and 173; Lai, 1970, p. 136). See also Domenach, 1992, p. 208; Williams and Wu, 2004, pp. 87–90 and 104–105.

38. Zhang Xianliang, 1994, p. 11, and for the preceding sentence, Domenach, 1992, pp. 174 and 587; Wu Hongda (Harry), 1992, pp. 37, 65, and 103.

39. Guinzbourg, 1980, p. 170. According to a witness, after the death of the poet Osip Mandelstam, his camp neighbors managed to obtain two days of his rations by doing the same thing and raising his arms like a puppet during roll call (Werth, 2012, p. 105).

40. Wu Hongda (Harry), 1995, pp. 150 and 159. For the remainder of the paragraph, see ibid., pp. 155, 157, 162–163, and 187–191.

41. Yang Xianhui, 2010, pp. 53, 56, 77, 107, 109, 150, 291, 295, and 351. See also Pu, 1994, pp. 185–186; Pasqualini, 1975, pp. 226–228, 236, and 252.

42. Applebaum, 2005, pp. 552–558; Solzhenitsyn, 1974, vol. 2, p. 160; Guinzbourg, 1980, p. 171.

43. Tchistiakov, 2012, p. 70. For the beginning of the paragraph, see Applebaum, 2005, pp. 337–338, 348, and 385.

44. See, in order, Pu, 1994, pp. 65–67; Lai, 1970, p. 157; Solzhenitsyn, [1976] 2010.

45. Zhang Xianliang, 1994, pp. 227–242. The examples in the rest of the paragraph can be found in Williams and Wu, 2004, pp. 88, 92, and 167; Lai, 1970, p. 137; Pu, 1994, p. 186.

46. Zhang Xianliang, 1996, p. 101; Domenach, 1992, p. 491; Seymour and Anderson, 1998, pp. 109 and 165; Williams and Wu, 2004, pp. 141–142 and 163.

47. While pretty much silent for the 1920s, the official mortality rates for the period between the Great Turn and Stalin's death were from 3 to 4 percent in 1930–1931. They rose after 1932 because of the famine, which killed more than 15 percent of the *zeks* in 1933. Then after a year of transition (4.3 percent in 1934), the rates fell to between 2 and 2.75 percent in 1935–1937, followed by a sharp but brief rise in 1938 (6.7 percent) due to the Great Terror (many executions and a deterioration in hygienic conditions following the inflow of new prisoners). There was then a short-lived return to normal figures (around 3 percent in 1939–1940), before the war broke the record rates of 1933 (one *zek* in four died in 1942, more than one in five [22.4 percent] in 1943, and one in eleven [9.2 percent] in 1944). After the transition in 1945, there was a return to normal rates in 1946 and 1948 (but with a higher rate during the 1947 famine) and, as we have seen, a sharp fall in mortality at the end of the period. Full statistics may be found in Applebaum, 2005, p. 929, to which I have sometimes preferred the reports on the gulag published in Khlevniuk, 2004, among others, Document 63, p. 211. These are the two best studies on the subject that I consulted. See Applebaum, 2005, pp. 560 and 930, and especially Khlevniuk, 2004, pp. 68, 77, 105–106, 172, 178, 185, 211, 253, and 322–327.

48. Hence the joke made by Zhang Xianliang, 1994, p. 152: "Between 1958 and 1976, I gave up capitalist practices, like washing my face."

49. On the sanitary conditions and overcrowding, see especially the many public archive documents published in Khlevniuk, 2004, and, among others, pp. 173–177, 209–212, 253–255, and 276–279. But the numerous other sources and accounts are equally eloquent, for instance Applebaum, 2005, pp. 344, 353–354, and

610–613; Solzhenitsyn, 1974, vol. 2, pp. 42 and 162–166; Chalamov, 2003, p. 1395; Guinzbourg, 1980, pp. 18, 59, and passim; Razgon, 1991, p. 129. For *laogai*, refer to Williams and Wu, 2004, pp. 93–98; Domenach, 1992, pp. 214–216; Seymour and Anderson, 1998, p. 99; Pu, 1994, pp. 83 and 97; Lai, 1970, p. 139; Wu Hongda (Harry), 1992, p. 67; Yang Xianhui, 2010, pp. 263, 271, and 354.

50. Applebaum, 2005, p. 599; Solzhenitsyn, [1976] 2010, pp. 94–96, 176, and passim; Razgon, 1991, pp. 236–238; Chalamov, 2003, pp. 59–62, quoted in Werth, 2012, pp. 95–96.

51. Lai, 1970, pp. 147–150, 152, and 155–157. For what precedes that, see Pu, 1994, pp. 107 and 184; Zhang Xianliang, 1994, pp. 42, 48, 52, and 72; Zhang Xianliang, 1986a, pp. 4, 5, 12, 18, and passim; Wu Hongda (Harry), 1995, pp. 105–106, 127, and 130.

52. Werth, 2012, pp. 65–67. For the rest of the paragraph, see Luba Jurgenson in the preface to Tchistiakov, 2012, p. 25; Margolin, 2010, p. 177.

53. Solzhenitsyn, [1976] 2010. For the remainder of the paragraph, see Applebaum, 2005, pp. 583 and 585–587.

54. I have deliberately quoted Bu (or Pu) Ning, alias Bu Naifu, alias Wu Mingshi (1917–2002), because he provides an antithesis to Zhang Xianliang (1936–). Wu, Yenna, 2006, p. 149, considers Pu Ning far more reliable than Zhang Xianliang, who was cautious because he was published in the People's Republic, whereas the uncompromising Pu took refuge in Taiwan before publishing his memoirs, and then those of Han Weitian. I don't agree, for I found Zhang's irony and distance, interspaced with sarcasm, more convincing than Pu's litany of denunciations and, on occasion, pathos. Many people do not share my preference for Zhang (expressed above)! I admit that he tends to exaggerate in his emotional recollections of many guards and communist cadres, even their paternalistic kindness, and the reader may chomp at the bit when reading some of his complacent tirades. Furthermore, a large part of a book such as *Half of Man Is Woman* and all of *Mimosa* cover a period in which the hero has become a "freed prisoner" after serving his sentence. We should be wary therefore of imagining that the convict's life resembled the one seen through the prism of the far more supple regime in which the leading characters in these two books were living. I nevertheless maintain that Zhang and not Pu Ning might have said, like Primo Levi: "… I have deliberately used the sober and level-headed language of a witness rather than the pathos of the victim or vehemence of the avenger" (Levi, [1987] 1993, p. 191). For the references in this paragraph, see Solzhenitsyn, [1976] 2010, p. 132; Zhang Xianliang, 1986b, pp. 231–235; Zhang Xianliang, 1996, p. 33; Pu, 1985, p. 60; Pu, 1994, pp. 136–140; Lai, 1970, p. 170.

55. This contrast is clear in Domenach, 1992, who distinguishes the "first archipelago" (book 2) from the period after the GLF (books 3 and 4).

56. Solzhenitsyn, 1974, vol. 2, p. 412; Razgon, 1991, pp. 118–121.

57. Razgon, 1991, pp. 109–114. For what precedes this, see Tchistiakov, 2012, p. 51; Applebaum, 2005, p. 87; Domenach, 1992, p. 86; Lai, 1970, p. 157; Chalamov, 2003, pp. 599–602. Hooper, 2013, pp. 125, 131, quotes other "examples" of rape and torture.

58. Khlevniuk, 2004, p. 41. For the remainder of the paragraph, see, in order, Applebaum, 2005, pp. 365, 382, 425, 435, 450–458, and 460; Seymour and Anderson, 1998, pp. 97, 101, and 176; Wu Hongda (Harry), 1995, p. 269; Yang Xianhui, 2010, pp. 250 and 354–368; Domenach, 1992, p. 395; Lai, 1970, p. 154; Razgon, 1991, pp. 12–13 and 124–125; Guinzbourg, 1980, pp. 313–314; Werth, 2012, pp. 61–62.

59. Werth, 2012, pp. 61 and 67. For what precedes that paragraph, see Domenach, 1992, p. 207; Lai, 1970, pp. 147–153; Applebaum, 2005, pp. 90 and 401; Razgon, 1991, pp. 124–126.

60. See, in order, forty-eighth Kvadrat camp: Margolin, 2010, p. 236; 285 out of 800: Khlevniuk, 2004, p. 233; punishment cell like a coffin: Wu Hongda (Harry), 1995, pp. 247–254; hut without a stool: Lai, 1970, p. 130; at the bottom of a well: Pu, 1994, pp. 3–18.

61. Another prisoner, still in *laogai*, spent two years in a punishment cell. When he left it, he broke his coccyx simply by trying to walk (Liao, 2013, p. 551). In the gulag—under Khrushchev!—one *zek* was locked up in a punishment cell of four by eight meters for a whole year. There were altogether forty people in that cell, "standing, squashed up one against another"; ten did not survive (Werth, 2012, p. 54). For the remainder of the paragraph, see Margolin, 2010, p. 236; Khlevniuk, 2004, p. 233; Wu, Hongda (Harry), 1995, pp. 247–254; Lai, 1970, p. 130; Pu, 1994, pp. 3–18; end of the paragraph, the round hole in which prisoners froze and died: Razgon, 1991, p. 108.

62. "Mosquito torture" was already a classic forty years earlier in the swampy Solovetsky Islands (Duguet, [1927] 2004, pp. 199–202). See also Applebaum, 2005, pp. 413–420; Solzhenitsyn, 1974, vol. 2, p. 312; Guinzbourg, [1967] 1997, pp. 92 and 241–244; Domenach, 1992, pp. 181–182; Khlevniuk, 2004, p. 233 and passim; Williams and Wu, 2004, pp. 122–125. For the rest of the paragraph, see ibid., pp. 108, 115–116, and 128–135; Zhang Xianliang, 1994, pp. 92–95 and 205; Wu Hongda (Harry), 1992, pp. 37–38 and 69–72; Wu Hongda (Harry), 1995, pp. 222, 326, and 329.

63. Applebaum, 2005, pp. 776–808; Craveri, 2003.

64. On "Kenguir's forty days," see also, Solzhenitsyn, 1974, vol. 3, pp. 234–269 and Barnes, Steven A., 2011, chap. 6. On resistance in the gulag in general, Applebaum, 2005, and Craveri, 2003, may be supplemented by Khlevniuk, 2004, pp. 47–51, 213, and 280–281; Graziosi, 1992; Werth, 2012, pp. 50–51; Margolin, 2010, pp. 413–417. From the point of view of the guards, Tchistiakov, 2012, pp. 239–249, devotes ten pages to the *refusniks,* female in this case, who first refused, finally accepted, and then balked again at the idea of building a bridge over the Baikal-Amur railway, working without boots or gloves in the icy river water.

65. Domenach, 1992, pp. 98–99, 194–196, 218, 294, and 522; Wu Hongda (Harry), 1992, pp. 73 and 116–117; Wei, 1997.

66. The best introduction to thought reform in China is Domenach, 1992, chaps. 5 and 14.

67. Bell 2013, p. 126.

68. Applebaum, 2005, p. 127.

69. L. Averbach, quoted in Solzhenitsyn, 1974, vol. 2, p. 81. For what precedes, see Seymour and Anderson, 1998, p. 17; Applebaum, 2005, pp. 116–119, 126–127, and 152–155. Baron, 2001, p. 646. The camp Julius Margolin was transferred to in the spring of 1941 was labeled, like the previous one, "corrective labor," "but those who knew it took away with them a lasting horror at the very idea of labor and an incomparable mastery in ridding themselves of its conscientious accomplishment" (Margolin, 2010, pp. 373–374, and also pp. 182 and 193). See also Luba Jurgenson's preface to Tchistiakov, 2012, pp. 20–22 and 29.

70. Wu Hongda (Harry), 1995, p. 102 and passim. For what precedes, see Williams and Wu, 2004, p. 13 and 113; Applebaum, 2005, p. 129.

71. Guinzbourg, [1967] 1997, pp. 63–303. For the remainder of the paragraph and the following one, see Rickett and Rickett, [1957] 1973, pp. 94 and 128–130; Wu Hongda (Harry), 1995, pp. 95–96, 211, and 315–316; Wu Hongda (Harry), 1992, pp. 27–33.

72. Domenach, 1992, p. 170.

73. Ibid., p. 187. For the remainder, see Pasqualini, 1975, p. 83.

74. Rissov, 1986, p. 27, quoted in Domenach, 1992, p. 197. For the beginning of the paragraph, see Lai, 1970, pp. 187–188, 190, and 204–208; Wu Hongda (Harry), 1995, p. 211 and passim. Liu Binyan is quoted in Wu Yenna, 2006, p. 44.

75. I will restrict myself to a few references from the first explicit work (the memoir rather than the novels) by Zhang Xianliang, 1994, pp. 116, 121, 141, 183, 210, 212, 216, and 222, but we could add examples taken from any one of his works.

76. Memoirs: Zhang Xianliang, 1994, 1996; novels: Zhang Xianliang, 1986a and 1986b.

77. Wu Yenna, 2006, p. 51; Todorov, 1994, p. 182.

78. Rickett and Rickett, [1957] 1973, p. 333.

79. Ibid., p. 344.

80. Ibid., p. 255.

81. Examples: other imprisoned couples could see each other every day although not to talk, but the two Americans never saw each other. And the wife interpreted that prohibition with her habitual benevolence: "I am certain that the authorities deliberately kept us apart to relieve, particularly me, of the emotional strain of seeing each other" (ibid., p. 299); in the epilogue, which they wrote together, "Our experience in living in and reading the press of both countries has led us to the conclusion that the Chinese today are still receiving a clearer picture of what is

happening here than the American people are of what is taking place in China" (ibid., p. 331).

82. Bianco, 1973, p. 866. I have already quoted that passage: I should have gone to a Chinese prison. It would have instilled some modesty in me! For the remainder of the paragraph, see Bianco, "La révolution fourvoyée," *Le Monde*, 10 September 1976.

83. See the moving description by Robert Lifton of an "apparent convert," the daughter of a Canadian missionary, who was also traumatized by the thought reform she was subjected to during her years of captivity, but was later able to challenge not only her lifestyle and ideals, but also the values drummed into her in her Chinese prison. It goes without saying that other prisoners interviewed by the author also resisted the brain-washing experience—though some in appearance only (Lifton, 1961, pp. 144–160 and passim).

84. Guinzbourg, [1967] 1997, pp. 319–320 and passim; Solzhenitsyn, 1974, vol. 2, pp. 255 and 257. For the rest of the paragraph, see Domenach, 1992, p. 517; Wu Hongda (Harry), 1995, p. 201.

85. Simon Leys, quoted in Domenach, 1992, p. 164. See also ibid., p. 163. For the following sentence, ibid., pp. 227–327 and 490. That was observed by the painter, art critic, and former convict Gao Ertai, taken out of the camp in order to paint a vast propaganda mural in a hotel, where he was well fed for the duration: "As my body came back to life, so my soul advanced towards death. I had lost my being, I had become a docile tool in another's hand; I had become something else" (Gao Ertai, 2009, p. 103).

86. See, in order after Chalamov: Guinzbourg, 1980, p. 404; Jin Hua: Liao, 2013, pp. 464–465; morals my ass: Zhang Yihe, 2013, p. 35; Margolin, 2010, p. 373; the guard: Tchistiakov, 2012, p. 164; Dostoyevsky ("who has ever been corrected by hard labor?") quoted in Solzhenitsyn, 1974, vol. 2, p. 467; Levi, [1987] 1993, p. 111. Reading Werth, 2012, p. 177, reminded me of that passage in *The Drowned and the Saved*.

87. Solzhenitsyn, 1974, vol. 2, in order, pp. 466, 463, 462, 452, 463, 468 (quotation of Pisarev), then 466 ("steadfast personality"), 469 ("rich inner life"), 454 ("good place to think" and "total freedom"), 456 ("dried-up former soul" and "you have gauged your weakness"), 451 ("prison regenerates a man"), and 452 ("enriches one's being" and the quotation from Kouznetsov, 1974).

88. Werth, 2012, pp. 24 and 177; Solzhenitsyn, 1974, vol. 2, pp. 459–460; Levi, [1987] 1993, p. 214. I will refrain from adding a page to second (and repeat) Solzhenitsyn's point of view, expressed this time by a *laogai* "graduate." I would have chosen Zhang Xianliang, always ready to beat his breast as a privileged intellectual who, thanks to the camp, learned what it was to be hungry, how much humanity and goodness were concealed in simple and poor people, how to act as an aware and complete human being, and so forth. And yet at the same time he was more eloquent than anyone else in suggesting just how much the camp had damaged him.

89. "One usually entered the German *Lager* never to leave again. Death was the only planned exit" (Levi, [1987] 1993, p. 202).

90. Hooper, 2013, p. 120.

91. Alexander Etkind, 2009, p. 628. The sentence before that: Wheatcroft, 1996, quoted in ibid.

92. Bell, 2013, for the two last paragraphs. Precise references or quotations pp. 119, 121, 140.

93. Getty and Naumov, 2008, p. 272, n. 39, quoted in Bell, 2013, p. 140. On the relationships between guards and prisoners being less inhuman than in the Nazi camp, see again Levi, [1987] 1993, p. 202.

Chapter 9   Dictators

1. Roux, 2009, pp. 585–586. I refer to this solid (and detailed) biography in French.

2. It nearly cost eleven-year-old Sosso (Stalin's childhood name) his life and exempted the future generalissimo from military service during World War I.

3. Li Zhisui, 1994. On Mao working at night and sleeping in the day, see, among others, Pantsov, 2012, p. 364.

4. We saw in chapter 5 how the local authorities prepared a visit from Mao. The impressions that he got from his "surveys," even in full famine, prevented him from believing that someone like Liu Shaoqi or Peng Dehuai could possibly have been distressed after a visit to the same region.

5. Service, 2005, pp. 272–273.

6. Trotsky. Nikolai Sukhanov, Stalin's future victim, remembered, "Although the Bolshevik party had some great leaders, Stalin at the time [March 1917], gave the impression, and not only on me, of a gray blot, that sometimes lit up with a rather poor light, but left no trace" (Sukhanov, 1965, p. 115).

7. See, among others, Roux, 2009, chap. 2; Schram, 1986, pp. 800–802; Pantsov, 2012, pp. 90–91; Short, [1999] 2005, p. 97.

8. "Stalin's mind was an accumulator and regurgitator" (Service, 2005, p. 570).

9. This episode is described in Graziosi, 2010, pp. 76–77: Those who were concerned with equilibrium tried to plead for a more "genealogical" view of the plan that took existing conditions into account, but Stalin decided in favor of the "teleological" view, which first set the objectives to be achieved and depended on development occurring as rapidly as possible. The specialists in charge of working out the details were therefore obliged to concoct a plan they did not believe in. Those who refused were pushed aside until more appropriate sanctions could be taken against them.

10. Lewin, 1987, p. 393.

11. Service, 2005, p. 345. For the preceding sentence, see Smedley, 1944, pp. 121–122, quoted in Dittmer, [1974] 1998, p. 210, as well as in Leys, 1976, p. 173.

12. Service, 2005, p. 345.

13. Ibid., pp. 544, 548, and 592; Barbusse, quoted in Gauchet, 2010, p. 347.

14. Barmé, 1996. On Dai Qing, see the sources in the Appendix. There is an excellent analysis of the Mao cult in Meisner, 1982, chap. 6.

15. The poet Anna Akhmatova, quoted in Tchoukovskaïa, 1980, p. 273.

16. Zhou, 2012, p. 105.

17. Mao's retort has been quoted countless times. See Yang Jisheng, [2008] 2012, p. 61, to draw attention once again to this important book. English edition, 2012, (*Tombstone*), p. 105.

18. On the Futian incident, see Chen Yung-fa, 1994; Averill, 1995; Roux, 2009, pp. 277–286; Short, [1999] 2005, pp. 235–251; Pantsov, 2012, pp. 239–245.

19. MacFarquhar and Schoenhals, 2006, pp. 280–281.

20. See Pye, 1996, p. 108; Pye, 2000, p. 152; and more generally, Pye, 1976. For Stalin, see, among others, Bullock, 1992, pp. 348–351. For the end of the paragraph, see Service, 2005, p. 345.

21. Which does not exclude a contradictory trait of character, as emphasized by Bukharin. Stalin "is unhappy at not being able to convince everyone, himself included, that he is greater than everyone; and this unhappiness of his may be his most human trait, perhaps the only human trait in him. But what is not human, but rather something devilish, is that because of this unhappiness he cannot help taking revenge on people, on all people but especially those who are in any way higher or better than he" (quoted in Tucker, 1973, pp. 424–425).

22. Souyri, 1970, p. 95; Griesse, 2010, pp. 98–99.

23. Su Yang, 2011.

24. See, among others, Blum and Werth, 2010, pp. 12–13; Khlevniouk, 1996; for the remainder, see Kotkin, 1995.

25. I would like to thank Jean-Luc Domenach for having suggested the Helmsman's stance.

26. An inspector of "special populations," called Shpek, was put in charge of setting up a concentration camp in 1933 on the banks of the Nazina, a tributary of the Ob some nine hundred kilometers north of Tomsk. When he started searching for clothing and shoes for the "socially dangerous elements" he had to settle and who had nothing, he obtained the following reply from the head of the district Party Committee: "Comrade Shpek, you know nothing about the policies of our state, do you really think that those elements were sent here to be re-educated? No comrade, we must act in such a way that next spring they will all be dead even if we have to do this skillfully: give them sufficient clothing so that they can cut at least some wood before snuffing it. You can see for yourself the state they're in when they send them here, all ragged or naked when we pick them up

on the banks of the river. If the state really wanted to re-educate them, it would clothe them without our help!" (Werth, 2006, pp. 78 and 81). For the quotations by the same author at the beginning of the paragraph, see Werth, 2010b, pp. 132, 134, and 136.

27. Fourteen thousand inhabitants from underpopulated Karelia were arrested (and more than 12,500 were executed) in case a Finish spy might be lurking among them (Werth, 1997, p. 254; Werth, 2009, p. 236).

28. They never succeeded and cost more for the state than they earned because of the improvisation, incompetence, and lack of coordination between the center in Moscow and the rest of the country, the climatic, as well as social and political conditions in the Soviet Far East. However, that is no reason to refrain from extolling the "broken records": "in 65, 70 days," boasted the person in charge of special populations in western Siberia, "we have succeeded in colonizing the Narym region, something the Czarist regime failed to do in 350 years." That colonization included the "deportation-abandonment" of more than 6,000 colonists on a deserted island on the Ob, which was known as "cannibal island" by the neighboring Ostyak people because of the cannibalism practiced there by the "socially dangerous" deportees. After three months, only one third survived, an exploit that Czarism also failed to achieve (Werth, 2006, p. 163, passim).

29. On Martemyan Ryutin, see above, chapter 3, note 2.

30. Roux, 2009, p. 607.

31. I'm using the official vocabulary; those "masses" were in fact not very numerous, whether in the 1976 demonstrations in Beijing or, still less, the students' one in 1957.

32. A saying often quoted by Stalin (see, among others, Graziosi, 2005, p. 464).

33. Lewin, 2003a, pp. 130–131 and 150; Razgon, 1991, pp. 9–15.

34. Service, 2005, pp. 374 and 523–524.

35. Vogel, 2011, does him justice.

36. See Li Zhisui, 1994, Thurston's intelligent commentary, 1996, pp. 98–99 and 104–105, on her collaboration with the author. See also Pye, 1996, pp. 108–109; Leys, 1976, pp. 170 and 173–175; Teiwes and Sun, 1999, pp. 218–222 and 228.

37. Slogans endlessly repeated by all and sundry, paraphrasing the leader; see, among other authors, Stephen Cohen, [1971] 1980, pp. 260, 263, and 314; Schapiro, 1967, p. 412.

38. Service, 2005, pp. 412 and 416.

39. Dunham, [1976] 1990, p. 245; see also pp. 130 and 190.

40. "Clean up the mess," according to the eloquent expression used by Teiwes, 2010, p. 138. For the rest of the paragraph, see especially Huang Jing, 2000; as well as Schram, 1991, p. 53.

41. Bukharin. Stalin told him that they were the two Himalayas in a political leadership peopled by nonentities, which shows what little esteem he had for the Stalinists he was placing in the Politburo.

42. Khlevniouk, 1996, pp. 31–32, 108–109, and passim.

43. See Andrieu, 2002, who dissects a multitude of quotations of that kind.

44. Bianco, 1970 (reprinted in Bianco, 2010, pp. 17–51). I'm also basing this on Bianco, [1994] 1997, pp. 93–95; Bianco, 2007, p. 324. Referring, as I have done here, to my earlier reasoning should not conceal the relevance and value of Maurice Meisner's work on the subject. He establishes a parallel between Maoist aspirations and those shared by both the reputed (by Marx) utopian socialists and the Russian populists. In countries such as France during the Restoration, or Russia under Alexander II, where capitalism was underdeveloped, Fourier, Herzen, and others were (like Mao) attached to the virtues of the rural world, and hardly inclined (like Marx) to confer a privileged revolutionary vocation on the urban proletariat, particularly since they (Fourier, Herzen, etc.) were skeptical of bureaucratic organizations and the centralizing state. They trusted historical determinism less than they trusted disinterested voluntarism and the power of example to promote socialism. The Russian populists, like Mao, even counted on backwardness being an advantage for triggering revolutionary vocations (Meisner, 1982, chaps. 2 and 3, and passim).

45. Meisner, 1982, p. 121.

46. Lewin, 2003a, p. 190. See also Lewin, 1987, pp. 390–400 and 407; Dobrenko, 2011, p. 107.

47. Pomian, 1995, p. 20.

48. What follows uses and develops the analyses sketched out in Bianco, [1994] 1997, pp. 95–97.

49. They are detailed in three excellent accounts available in French: MacFarquhar and Schoenhals, 2006; Roux, 2009, chap. 16; Short, [1999] 2005, chap. 15.

50. Meisner, 1982, preface, p. xii.

51. Stalin's letter of 14 October 1937, quoted in Werth, 2009, p. 140. See also Blum and Werth, 2010, pp. 7–11.

52. Werth, 2009, pp. 7–11.

53. Very well analyzed in Kotkin, 1995, chap. 7, who describes the people's participation in the denunciations and the endless accusations during the purges of 1937–1938.

54. In principle only: from early 1967, Mao has to order a vacillating army to "support the left," in other words to support its own partisans in the street fighting that was raging. Six months later, he was almost trapped by a serious munity in Wuhan. On these episodes, see, among others, MacFarquhar and Schoenhals, 2006, chap. 12; Roux, 2009, pp. 789–792; Short, [1999] 2005, pp. 489 and 493–494.

55. Even if the violence and fighting between Red Guards was less deadly than the repression by the army and the militia, their fanaticism made a minority of the Chinese population (part of the urban youth) accomplices in their leader's crimes. Nevertheless, that shared responsibility of the "masses" did not prevent the Chinese, like the Russians, North Koreans, etc., from being guinea pigs first and foremost.

56. According to Andrew Walder's estimates for the years 1966–1971: Walder, 2015, p. 334.

57. Werth, 2009, pp. 16, and, further on, pp. 48, 67, 18, and 33.

58. 1968 was the bloodiest year. Three-quarters of the deaths were perpetrated by the army and the authorities: Walder, 2015, p. 334.

59. Meisner, 1982, pp. 193–194.

60. Why on earth would Stalin attack accomplices who were as obedient and zealous as Molotov and Kaganovich? The fact that, much later, he ended up wanting to get rid of Molotov says far more about Stalin than about his old accomplice.

61. The *troika* comprised three judges (in principle from among the regional Party leaders, the NKVD, and the courts) who often expedited the ruling and the sentence within a few minutes. Apart from a few (exceptional) acquittals, the *troika* issued only two sentences: ten years in the camps and death.

62. "That's when I understood that what matters above all for the Soviet government, is the plan. ... The state is like the figure 1, and men are the zero that increases it ten-fold" (Anna [Sergeyevna] on her memories of collectivization and the famine in Grossman, 1972, p. 192).

63. Werth, 2009, pp. 161–162, and, further on, 141 and 146.

64. Su Yang, 2006, p. 108.

65. Arendt, 1972, pp. 218 and 221. The previous quotation may be found in Tucker, [1977] 2008, p. 108.

Conclusion

1. That was not the opinion of Jung Chang and Jon Halliday, who describe Mao as a monster from birth to death. Far from containing only lies, this biography is like the imagination according to Montaigne, "all the more deceitful in that it does not always deceive" (Chang and Halliday, 2006).

2. Remember what Trotsky wrote in 1904 about "political substitutism": "In the internal politics of the Party these methods lead to the Party organization 'substituting' itself for the Party, the Central Committee substituting itself for the Party organization, and finally the dictator substituting himself for the Central Committee." Trotsky dedicated his book *Our Political Tasks,* from which this quotation is taken, to the Menshevik leader, Pavel Axelrod, who had denounced

the bureaucratic Bonapartist regime imposed by Lenin "and his accomplices." See also Rosa Luxembourg in 1904 and Alexander Parvus in 1905, in Lenin (Lénine) [1902], 1966, pp. 259–267 and 289–295 (quotation from Trotsky on p. 295). See also Papaioannou, 1965, p. 298 and Meisner, 1982, pp. 91–92.

3. Service, 2012, pp. 434–435.

4. Lewin, 1978, p. 151.

5. For a rather different (and more scholarly) interpretation of the "testament," see Colas, 1998, pp. 244–256.

6. Lewin, 1978, chap. 9 (quotation p. 127); Carrère d'Encausse, 1972, pp. 151–155; Carrère d'Encausse, 1998, pp. 586–594.

7. Lenin called Stalin the "marvelous Georgian" in a letter to Gorky dated 1913, almost a decade before he became disillusioned with him in 1922 (Service, 2005, p. 85).

8. Colas, 1983, p. 181.

9. Papaioannou, 1983, p. 296.

10. Ibid., p. 347. For this paragraph and more, see also ibid., pp. 298, 308, 313, 353, and 365–375, as well as Colas, 1998, chap. 4, who, in addition to the army, sees the orchestra, the machine, and the factory as Party models.

11. Hegel, 1965, p. 129. Hegel adds that the honor of great men "is precisely due to their having turned their backs on accepted values" (ibid., p. 128). See also Hegel, [1953] 1986, p. 43.

12. All these character traits were shown by Raymond Aron (Aron, 2002, p. 98). Has a Stalinist or a Maoist ever shown such generosity—or simply honesty—as that self-confessed opponent?

13. "As soon as there is no longer a social class to be held in subjection, … nothing remains to be repressed and it is no longer necessary to have a special repressive force, a state. The first act by virtue of which the state really constitutes itself as the representative of the whole of society—by taking possession of the means of production in the name of society—is at the same time its last independent act as a state. … The government of persons is replaced by the administration of things. … The state is not 'abolished.' *It dies out.*" The italics were in the original text, the English translation here is by Emile Burns from the 1894 edition. With the exception of the last chapter, written by Marx, Engels wrote *Anti-Dühring* (in 1877), but Marx agreed with the content of the book (https://www.marxists.org/archive/marx/works/1877/anti-duhring/index.htm).

14. Papaioannou, 1972, pp. 491–492, provides an abridged version of that famous article written in 1957 by the author of *Main Currents of Marxism*. My judgmental remarks about Marxism are based on, among other works, Papaioannou, 1965, pp. 123 and 221; Id., 1983, pp. 16–19, 189, 195, 197, 227, and 302–304; Aron, 1983, pp. 93–94, 283, 286, 287, 293–96, 606, 631, and 660; Berlin, 1962 and 2011.

15. Kolakowski, [1977] 2008, p. 297. See also pp. 291, 294, and passim.

16. Badie, 1984, pp. 107–110.

17. Ciliga, [1938] 1977, p. 120. For the early days of the NEP, see Brovkin, 1998, p. 15 and passim; Doudintsev, 1957 for the French translation, p. 32; Neumann is quoted in Bruneteau, 2010, p. 483.

18. Viola, 2007, p. 192; Schram, 1991, p. 18; Harding, 1981, p. 1. When interviewed in Jean-Michel Carré's documentary, the literary critic Qian Liqun, who was Maoist under Mao, liberal under Deng Xiaoping, and nationalist always, merely deplored that Mao had not improved the Chinese people's living standards.

19. Besançon, 1977, pp. 290–291. See also Furet, 2012, pp. 36–37.

20. Guinzbourg, 1980, p. 144, 216. "Looking back at my life with disgust": Eugenia Ginzburg quoted Pushkin's *Recollections at Tskarskoye Selo*." Her eighteen years of hell comprised ten in the Gulag and eight in exile in Eastern Siberia.

21. After Pushkin, Racine; here Joad in *Athaliah* (English translation from Donkersley's adaptation, 1873). To go from the intellectual (the future *zek*), to the people at large, let's take as an example Ginzburg's mother-in-law, who admonishes her, "Yevgenia my child! There is a font of intelligence in you, but you are also incredibly naïve" (Guinzbourg, [1967] 1997, p. 31). The pure gold could be the enthusiasm of millions of Russian and Chinese readers for Pavel Korchagin, the model hero—and a semiautobiographic one at that—in *How the Steel Was Tempered*. In the best of cases, the gold was transmuted into a demand for truth, once disillusionment set in. In 1979–1980, Chinese readers greeted even mediocre or superficial works with the same relief and jubilation as Soviet readers had in 1954–1956, simply because they expressed truths that had been silenced until then.

22. In 1921, Lenin, who had just declared that the Russian working class had "ceased to exist as a class," was ironically congratulated by Shliapnikov, one of the rare "old Bolsheviks" from a working-class background, "for exercising dictatorship in the name of a class that does not exist" (Baynac, 1975, p. 17).

23. Not to forget those who justified it: "The crowd absolutely requires a salutary lie, a golden dream" (Gorky); "Yes, Soviet literature is tendentious, ... and we're proud of that" (Zhdanov).

24. Pilniak, quoted in Heller, Michel, 1990, p. 149.

25. Details of all these examples may be found in Brovkin, 1998, pp. 173, 186, 220–223. For the OGPU's secret reports, see, among others, Werth and Berelowitch, 2011. In 1920, the head of the Ukrainian Cheka defined the assignment of the secret police as follows: "We should not only be the military wing of the Revolution, but also the eyes and ears of the regime" (ibid., p. 17).

26. Soljenitsyne, 1974, vol. 2, p. 480. The teenage Morozov denounced his father as a kulak, but was later killed by his uncle and then celebrated as a hero.

27. Quoted in Applebaum, [2005] 2008, p. 841.

28. Graziosi, 2010, pp. 295, 312; Havel, quoted in Rupnik, 1984, p. 55; Gorbachev, in Popper, 1993, p. 59.

29. They referred to the Soviet sputnik, launched the preceding year, and which proved the superiority of the socialist camp. All the events mentioned in this paragraph and the following one are drawn from the most detailed study of the great Chinese famine: Yang, Jisheng, [2008] 2012. They may be found, along with others in the same vein, on pp. 127, 202–203, 217, 222, 231, 257, 372, 400, 406–407, 443–444, and 469.

30. Ibid., p. 231. English edition, *Tombstone*, p. 60.

31. Solzhenitsyn, "Not living in lies," quoted in Besançon, 1977, p. 298; see also Saraskina, 2010, pp. 710–711; Liu, Xiaobo, 2011, "Subverting the system of lies with truth," pp. 139 and 141.

32. Trifonov is quoted in Etkind et al., 1990, p. 724; Grossman, 1972, p. 112. Regarding the fear of the fateful knocks on the door at night in 1937–1938, two future *zeks* got into the habit of calling each other nearly every evening to check if the other was still there (Razgon, 1991, pp. 84–85).

33. Dombrovski, 1979, p. 387.

34. For Marx, who deplored the "total loss" of man's humanity under capitalism, socialism was to inaugurate "the total re-conquest of man." As for Trotsky, he placed himself on the intellectual, rather than the moral, ground and confidently announced that "the average man will reach the stature of an Aristotle, a Goethe or a Marx" (Bruneteau, 2011, p. 117). Dombrovsky (the following sentence) is quoted in Etkind et al., 1990, p. 833.

35. Loh, 1963, pp. 60, 137, 140, 251.

36. Vogel, 1965. This paper was written prior to the Cultural Revolution, during which personal relationships deteriorated further still.

37. Domenach, 2012, pp. 74–75, 380; Bianco and Chevrier, 1985, p. 169.

38. Dunham, [1976] 1990, p. 70; Iachine, quoted in Link, 2000, p. 273.

39. Li Shu in 1986, ten years after Mao's death (a remark mentioned in Barmé, 1999, p. 58). In Mao's lifetime, Li Shu was the editor of *Lishi yanjiu* (Historical Research) (Goldman, 1981, p. 53). The following sentence: Berdiaev [1938], 1951, p. 255.

Appendix

1. According to Mao, three "mistaken tendencies" were undermining the work of the Party: subjectivism, sectarianism, and formalism. The first of these, which was also the most serious, was subdivided into dogmatism and empiricism.

2. Wang Fanxi, 1985, pp. 87–88, quoted in Dai, 1994, p. 76. To anyone who might doubt the sincerity of that testimony (a Trotskyite wanting to clear the name of

another—since in the Soviet Union, and therefore in China, being a Trotskyite was a major crime—I'll back it with my own memory of that witness, now deceased. After working for a year with my friends Cheng Yingxiang and Claude Cadart interviewing the Chinese Trotskyite, Peng Shuzhi, who had nothing good to say about Wang Fanxi (they had serious disagreements that led to a split in 1941), I determined to find out for myself, and in 1985 I went to Leeds to meet Wang. He welcomed me warmly and offered to share his very modest lodgings with me. He talked late into the night, going over his memories with a sincerity that warmed my heart every bit as much as his kind welcome. Wang's *Memoirs of a Chinese Revolutionary 1919–1949* relates his disagreements and arguments with Peng (Wang Fan-hsi, 1980, pp. 234–239).

3. Pasternak was the only member of the Union of Writers to refuse to sign a letter praising the execution of Bukharin and Rykov.

4. However, in 1956 and 1957 Mao had to be far more insistent in encouraging the writers and intellectuals to express themselves publicly, distressed as they were by the recent persecution of Hu Feng. His two speeches of February 1942 had been far more discrete. That Wang Shiwei, Ding Ling, and others dared to be so bold may have been due to the fact that they were the forerunners. Unlike their successors in 1957, they had not yet relinquished the climate of free speech that had prevailed in Shanghai. In other words, they were insufficiently reeducated (Mao was right on that score); they had not reformed their thinking (Teiwes, 1993, pp. 59–60).

5. Lefort, 1999, pp. 60–61.

Works Cited

Alitto, Guy S. 1979. *The Last Confucian. Liang Shu-ming and the Chinese Dilemma of Modernity.* Berkeley: University of California Press.

Andreas, Joel. 2009. *Rise of the Red Engineers. The Cultural Revolution and the Origins of China's New Class.* Stanford, Calif.: Stanford University Press.

Andrieu, Jacques. 2002. *Psychologie de Mao Tsé-toung.* Brussels: Complexe.

Applebaum, Anne. 2005/2008. *Goulag, une histoire.* Translated by P.-E. Dauzat. Paris: Gallimard, "Folio Histoire."

Arendt, Hannah. 1972. *Le Système totalitaire.* Translated by J.-L. Bourget, R. Davreu, and P. Lévy. Paris: Seuil.

Aron, Raymond. 1962. *Dix-huit leçons sur la société industrielle.* Paris: Gallimard, "Idées."

——. 1965. *Démocratie et totalitarisme.* Paris: Gallimard.

——. 2002. *Le marxisme de Marx, texte établi, préfacé et annoté par J-C. Casanova et C. Bachelier.* Paris: Editions de Fallois.

Ash, Robert B. 2006. "Squeezing the Peasants. Grain Extraction, Food Consumption and Rural Living Standards in Mao's China." *The China Quarterly,* no. 188: pp. 959–998.

Aubert, Claude. 1990. "Économie et société rurales." In M.-C. Bergère, L. Bianco, and J. Domes (eds.), *La Chine au xxe siècle,* vol. 2, *de 1949 à aujourd'hui,* pp. 149–180. Paris: Fayard.

Aucouturier, Michel. 1998. *Le réalisme socialiste.* Paris: PUF, "Que sais-je ?"

Averill, Stephen C. 1995. "The Origins of the Futian Incident." In T. Saich and H. van de Ven (eds.), *New Perspectives on the Chinese Communist Revolution,* pp. 79–115. Armonk, N.Y.: Sharpe.

Badie, Bertrand. 1984. "Les ressorts culturels du totalitarisme." In Hermet, Hassner, and Rupnik (eds.), *Totalitarismes*, pp. 103–118. Banister, Judith. 1987. *China's Changing Population*. Stanford, Calif.: Stanford University Press.

Banister, Judith. 1987. *China's Changing Population*. Stanford, Calif.: Stanford University Press.

Barmé, Geremie R. and John Minford, eds. 1988. *Seeds of Fire. Chinese Voices of Conscience*. New York: Hill & Wang.

———. 1991, "Using the Past to Save the Present: Dai Qing's Historical Dissent." *East Asian History*, 1, June: pp. 141–181.

———. 1996. *Shades of Mao. The Posthumous Cult of the Great Leader*. Armonk, N.Y.: Sharpe.

———. 1999. *In the Red. On Contemporary Chinese Culture*. New York: Columbia University Press.

Barnes, Julian. 2016. *The Noise of Time*. London: Jonathan Cape.

Barnes, Steven A. 2011. *Death and Redemption: The Gulag and the Shaping of Soviet Society*. Princeton, N.J.: Princeton University Press.

Barnett, A. Doak. 1967. *Cadres, Bureaucracy and Political Power in Communist China*. With a contribution by Ezra Vogel. New York: Columbia University Press.

Baron, Nick. 2001. "Conflict and Complicity: The Expansion of the Karelian Gulag, 1923–1933." *Cahiers du Monde russe*, 42, nos. 2–4: pp. 615–647.

Bastid-Bruguière, Marianne. 2006. "Education." In T. Sanjuan (ed.), *Dictionnaire de la Chine contemporaine*, pp. 84–85. Paris: Armand Colin.

Baynac, Jacques, with Alexandre Skirda and Charles Urjewicz. 1975. *La Terreur sous Lénine (1917–1924)*. Paris: Le Sagittaire.

Becker, Jasper. 1996/1998. *Hungry Ghosts. China's Secret Famine*. London: John Murray. Quotations from the French edition, *La grande Famine de Mao*. Translated by M. Pencréac'h, Dagorno.

Béja, Jean-Philippe, and Wojtek Zafanolli. 1981. *La face cachée de la Chine. Trois nouvelles traduites du chinois*. Paris: Editions Pierre-Emile.

Bell, Wilson T. 2013. "Was the Gulag an Archipelago? De-convoyed Prisoners and Porous Borders in the Camps of Western Siberia." *The Russian Review*, 72: pp. 116–141.

Bensidoun, Sylvain. 1975. *L'agitation paysanne en Russie de 1881 à 1902*. Paris: Presses de la Fondation nationale des sciences politiques.

Benton, Gregor (ed.). 1982. *Wild Lilies, Poisonous Weeds. Dissident Voices from People's China*. London: Pluto.

———. 1999. *New Fourth Army. Communist Resistance along the Yangtze and the Huai, 1938–1941*. Richmond: Curzon Press.

Benton, Gregor, and Alan Hunter (eds.). 1995. *Wild Lily, Prairie Fire. China's Road to Democracy, Yan'an to Tian'anmen, 1942–1989*. Princeton, N.J.: Princeton University Press.

Berdiaev, Nicolas. 1938/1951. *Les sources et le sens du communisme russe.* Translated by L. Daniel-Mayer Cain. Paris: Gallimard.

Berelowitch, Wladimir. 2005. *Le grand Siècle russe d'Alexandre Ier à Nicolas II.* Paris: Gallimard.

Bergère, Marie-Claire. 1987/2000. *La Chine de 1949 à nos jours.* 3rd ed. Paris: Armand Colin.

———. 1994. *Sun Yat-sen.* Paris: Fayard.

———. 2002. *Histoire de Shanghai.* Paris: Fayard.

———. 2013. *Chine. Le nouveau capitalisme d'État.* Paris: Fayard.

Berlin, Isaiah. 1962. *Karl Marx, sa vie, son œuvre.* Translated by A. Guérin and P. Tilche. Paris: Gallimard.

———. 2011. *Le Sens des réalités.* Preface by G. Delannoi. Paris: Les Belles Lettres.

Bernstein, Thomas P. 1967. "Leadership and Mass Mobilisation in the Soviet and Chinese Collectivisation Campaigns of 1929–30 and 1955–56: A Comparison." *The China Quarterly*, no. 31: pp. 1–47.

———. 1970. "Keeping the revolution going. Problems of Village Leadership after Land Reform." In J. W. Lewis (ed.), *Party Leadership and Revolutionary Power in China*, pp. 239–267. Cambridge: Cambridge University Press.

———. 1977. *Up to the Mountains and Down to the Villages. The Transfer of Youth from Urban to Rural China.* New Haven, Conn.: Yale University Press.

———. 1984. "Stalinism, Famine, and Chinese Peasants. Grain Procurements during the Great Leap Forward." *Theory and Society*, 13, no. 3: pp. 339–377.

———. 2006. "Mao Zedong and the Famine of 1959–1960: A Study in Wilfulness." *The China Quarterly,* no. 186: pp. 421–445.

———. 2010. "Introduction." In Bernstein and Li (eds.), *China Learns,* pp. 1–23.

Bernstein, Thomas P., and Hua-Yu Li (eds.). 2010. *China Learns from the Soviet Union, 1949–Present.* Lanham, Md.: Lexington Books.

Bernstein, Thomas P., and Lü Xiaobo. 2003. *Taxation without Representation in Contemporary Rural China.* Cambridge: Cambridge University Press.

Bertaux, Daniel, and Véronique Garros. 1998. *Lioudmilla, une Russe dans le siècle.* Saint-Étienne: Impressions Dumas.

Besançon, Alain. 1977. *Les Origines intellectuelles du Léninisme.* Paris: Calmann-Lévy.

———. 1980. *Présent soviétique et passé russe.* Paris: Le Livre de poche.

———. 1998/2005. *Le malheur du siècle. Communisme–Nazisme–Shoah.* Paris: Perrin.

Bianco, Lucien. 1967/2007. *Les origines de la révolution chinoise.* 4th augmented ed. Paris: Gallimard, "Folio Histoire."

———. 1970. "La page blanche." *Politique aujourd'hui*, nos. 5–6, May: pp. 96–112; June: pp. 59–72. Republished in Bianco 2010: pp. 18–51.

———. 1973. "Le monde chinois et la Corée." In M. Crouzet (ed.), *Le monde depuis 1945*, vol. 2, *Les pays pauvres et la naissance de nouveaux mondes*, pp. 853–930. Paris: PUF.

———. 1981. "Birth Control in China: Local Data and Their Reliability." *The China Quarterly*, no. 85: pp. 119–137.

———. 1985. "Family Planning Program and Fertility Decline in Taïwan and Mainland China: A Comparison." *Issues and Studies*, 21, no. 11: pp. 53–95.

———. 1986. "Peasant Movements." In Fairbank and Feuerwerker (eds.), *The Cambridge History of China* (hereafter *CHOC*), vol. 13, pp. 270–328.

———. 1994/1997. *La Chine*. 2nd ed. Paris: Flammarion.

———. 2001. *Peasants without the Party. Grass-roots Movements in Twentieth-Century China*. Armonk, N.Y.: Sharpe.

———. 2005. *Jacqueries et révolution dans la Chine du xxe siècle*. Paris: La Martinière.

———. 2010. *La révolution fourvoyée. Parcours dans la Chine du xxe siècle*. La Tour-d'Aigues: Éd. de L'Aube.

Bianco, Lucien, and Yves Chevrier (eds.). 1985. *Dictionnaire biographique du mouvement ouvrier international. La Chine*. Paris: Les Éditions ouvrières, Presses de la FNSP.

Birch, Cyril. 1991. "Literature under Communism." In MacFarquhar and Fairbank (eds.), *CHOC*, vol. 15: pp. 743–812.

Blum, Alain. 1994/2004. *Naître, vivre et mourir en URSS*. Paris: Payot-Rivages.

Blum, Alain, Marta Craveri, and Valérie Nivelon (eds.). 2012. *Déportés en URSS, Récits d'Européens au goulag*. Paris: Éditions Autrement.

Blum, Alain, and Martine Mespoulet. 2003. *L'anarchie bureaucratique. Statistique et pouvoir sous Staline*. Paris: La Découverte.

Blum, Alain, and Nicolas Werth (eds.). 2010. "La grande terreur en URSS." *Vingtième siècle*, Revue d'histoire, no. 107: pp. 3–113.

Bonnin, Michel. 2004/2013. *Génération perdue. Le mouvement d'envoi des jeunes instruits à la campagne en Chine, 1968–1980*. Paris: Éd. de l'EHESS. English edition. Translated by Krystyna Horko: *The Lost Generation. The Rustication of China's Educated Youth (1968–1980)*. Hong Kong: The Chinese University Press.

Boorman, Howard L. (ed.). 1968. *Biographical Dictionary of Republican China*. Vol. 2. New York: Columbia University Press.

Boulgakov, Mikhaïl. 1968. *Le maître et Marguerite*. Translated by C. Ligny, introduction by S. Ermolinski. Paris: Robert Laffont.

———. 1970. *La garde blanche*. Paris: Robert Laffont.

Bounine, Ivan. 2011. *Le village*. Translated by M. Parijnanine. Paris: Bartillat.

Bramall, Chris. 2011. "Agency and Famine in China's Sichuan Province, 1958–1962." *The China Quarterly*, no. 208: pp. 990–1008.

Brovkin, Vladimir. 1995. *Behind the Front Lines of the Civil War. Political Parties and Social Movements in Russia, 1918–1922*. Princeton, N.J.: Princeton University Press.

———. 1998. *Russia after Lenin. Politics, Culture & Society*. New York: Routledge.

Brown, Edward J. 1969. *Russian Literature since the Revolution*. Corners.

Brown, Jeremy. 2011. "Great Leap City: Surviving the Famine in Tianjin." In Manning and Wemheuer (eds.), *Eating Bitterness*, pp. 226–250.

Bruneteau, Bernard. 2010. *Le totalitarisme. Origines d'un concept, genèse d'un débat, 1930–1942*. Paris: Éd. du Cerf.

———. 2011. *L'âge totalitaire. Idées reçues sur le totalitarisme*. Paris: Le cavalier bleu.

Bu Ning, Pu Ning's Pinyin Transcription; see Wu Mingshi/Ming-shih; real name Bu/Pu Naifu.

Buber-Neumann, Margarete. 1986/1988. *Déportée en Sibérie. Prisonnière de Staline et d'Hitler*. 2 vols. Paris: Éd. du Seuil, "Points."

Bullock, Alan. 1992. *Hitler and Stalin. Parallel Lives*. New York: Knopf.

Bullock, Philip Ross. 2011. "Utopia and the Novel after the Revolution." In Dobrenko and Balina (eds.), *Cambridge Companion*, pp. 79–96.

Bunin: see Bounine.

Cabestan, Jean-Pierre. 1994. *Le système politique de la Chine populaire*. Paris: PUF.

Carrère d'Encausse, Hélène. 1972. *Une révolution, une victoire. L'Union soviétique de Lénine à Staline, 1917–1953*. Paris: Ed. Richelieu.

———. 1998. *Lénine*. Paris: Fayard.

Castoriadis, Cornélius. 1973. *La Société bureaucratique*. 2 vols. Paris: UGE.

Chalamov, Varlam. 2003. *Récits de la Kolyma*. Translated by Sophie Benech, Catherine Fournier, and Luba Jurgenson. Paris: Verdier.

Chang, Jung, and Jon Halliday. 2006. *Mao. L'histoire inconnue*. Paris: Gallimard, "NRF Biographies."

Cheek, Timothy (ed.). 2010. *A Critical Introduction to Mao*. New York: Cambridge University Press.

Chen, Jian. 1994. *China's Road to the Korean War. The Making of the Sino-American Confrontation*. New York: Columbia University Press.

———. 2001. *Mao's China and the Cold War*. Chapel Hill: University of North Carolina Press.

Chen, Yixin. 2011. "Under the Same Maoist sky. Accounting for Death Rate Discrepancies in Anhui and Jiangxi." In Manning and Wemheuer (eds.), *Eating Bitterness*, pp. 197–225.

Chen, Yung-fa. 1986. *Making Revolution. The Communist Movement in Eastern and Central China, 1937–1945*. Berkeley: University of California Press.

————. 1994. "The Futian Incident and the Anti-Bolshevik League: The 'Terror' in the CCP Revolution." *Republican China*, 19, no. 2: pp. 1–51.

Chi, Pang-yuan, and David Der-wei Wang (eds.). 2000. *Chinese Literature in the Second Half of a Modern Century. A Critical Survey.* Bloomington: Indiana University Press.

Cholokhov, Mikhaïl. 1959/1971. *Le Don paisible.* Translated by A. Vitez. 4 vols. Paris: Le Livre de poche.

Ciliga, Anton. 1938/1977. *Au pays du mensonge déconcertant. Dix ans derrière le rideau de fer.* Paris: 10/18.

Clark, Katerina. 2011. "Russian Epic Novels of the Soviet Period." In Dobrenko and Balina (eds.), *Cambridge Companion,* pp. 135–152.

Cœuré, Sophie. 1999. *La grande lueur à l'Est. Les Français et l'Union soviétique 1917–1939.* Paris: Éd. du Seuil.

Cohen, Stephen F. 1971/1980. *Bukharin and the Bolshevik Revolution. A Political Biography, 1888–1938.* Oxford: Oxford University Press.

Cohen, Yves. 1997. "Des lettres comme action. Staline au début des années 1930 vu depuis le fond Kaganovic." *Cahiers du monde russe,* 37, no. 3: pp. 307–346.

Colas, Dominique. 1982/1998. *Le Léninisme.* Paris: PUF.

————. 1983. "Auto-interprétations du stalinisme et interprétations de la révolution russe." In Évelyne Pisier-Kouchner (ed.), *Les Interprétations du stalinisme,* pp. 175–195. Paris: PUF.

Conquest, Robert. 1970. *The Great Terror. Stalin's Purge of the Thirties.* New York: Macmillan.

Coquin, François Xavier. 1965. *La révolution russe.* Paris: PUF, "Que sais-je?"

Courtois, Stéphane (ed.). 2007. *Dictionnaire du communisme.* Paris: Larousse.

Courtois, Stéphane, Nicolas Werth, Jean-Louis Panné, Andrzej Paczkowski, Karel Bartosek, and Jean-Louis Margolin (eds.). 1997. *Le livre noir du communisme. Crimes, terreur, repression.* Paris: Robert Laffont.

Craveri, Marta. 2003. *Resistenza nel Gulag. Un capitolo inedito della destalinizzazione in Unione Sovietica.* Soveria Mannelli: Rubbettino.

Dai, Qing. 1994. *Wang Shiwei and "Wild Lilies." Rectification and Purges in the Chinese Communist Party, 1942–1944.* Armonk, N.Y.: Sharpe.

Danilov, Viktor, and Alexis Berelowitch. 1994. "Les documents des VCK-OGPU-NKVD sur la campagne soviétique, 1918–1937: documents de l'OGPU, 1923–1930." *Cahiers du monde russe,* 35, no. 3: pp. 633–682.

Davies, Robert W. 1980. *The Socialist Offensive. The Collectivisation of Soviet Agriculture, 1929–1930.* London: Macmillan.

————. 1993. "Economic Aspects of Stalinism." In Alec Nove (ed.), *The Stalin Phenomenon,* pp. 39–74. London: Weidenfeld & Nicolson.

Davies, Robert W., and Stephen G. Wheatcroft. 2004. *The Years of Hunger. Soviet Agriculture, 1931–1933*. New York: Palgrave Macmillan.

Denis, Juliette. 2012. "Les images de l'enfance." In Blum, Craveri, and Nivelon (eds.), *Déportés en URSS*, pp. 109–131.

Depretto, Jean-Paul. 1997. *Les Ouvriers en URSS, 1928–1941*. Paris: Publications de la Sorbonne, Institut d'études slaves.

Dikötter, Frank. 2010. *Mao's Great Famine. The History of China's Most Devastating Catastrophe, 1958–1962*. London: Bloomsbury.

———. 2013. *The Tragedy of Liberation: A History of the Chinese Revolution, 1945–1957*. London: Bloomsbury.

Dittmer, Lowell. 1974/1998. *Liu Shaoqi and the Chinese Cultural Revolution*. Rev. ed. Armonk, N.Y.: Sharpe.

———. 1981. "Death and Transfiguration: Liu Shaoqi's Rehabilitation and Contemporary Chinese Politics." *Journal of Asian Studies*, 40, no. 3: pp. 455–479.

Djilas, Milovan. 1957/1962. *The New Class. An Analysis of the Communist System*. New York: Praeger.

Dobrenko, Evgeny. 2011. "Socialist Realism." In Dobrenko and Balina (eds.). *Cambridge Companion*, pp. 97–114.

Dobrenko, Evgeny, and Marina Balina (eds.). 2011. *The Cambridge Companion to Twentieth-Century Russian Literature*. Cambridge: Cambridge University Press.

Dolot, Miron. 1985. *Execution by Hunger: The Hidden Holocaust*. New York: Norton.

Dombrovski, Iouri (Yuri). 1979. *La Faculté de l'inutile*. Translated by D. Seseman. Paris: Albin Michel.

———. 2005. *Le conservateur des antiquités*. Translated by J. Cathala. Paris: La Découverte.

Domenach, Jean-Luc. 1992. *Chine. l'archipel oublié*. Paris: Fayard.

———. 2012. *Mao, sa cour et ses complots. Derrière les murs rouges*. Paris: Fayard.

Doolin, Dennis J. 1964. *Communist China. The Politics of Student Opposition*. Stanford, Calif.: Hoover Institution on War, Revolution, and Peace.

Dossier. 2010. "Quel rôle pour la littérature chinoise aujourd'hui ? L'exemple de Gao Xingjian." *Perspectives chinoises*, no. 2: pp. 2–57.

Doudintsev, Vladimir. 1957. *l'homme ne vit pas seulement de pain*. Paris: Julliard.

Dubois, Vincent, Valérie Lozac'h, and Jay Rowell. 2005. "Jeux bureaucratiques en régime communiste." *Sociétés contemporaines*, 1, no. 57: pp. 5–19.

Duguet, Raymond. 1927/2004. *Un bagne en Russie rouge. Solovki, l'île de la faim, des supplices, de la mort*. Edited with a preface by N. Werth. Paris: Balland.

Dumont, Louis. 1966. *Homo hierarchicus. Essai sur le système des castes*. Paris: Gallimard, "Bibliothèque des sciences humaines."

————. 1977. *Homo aequalis. Genèse et épanouissement de l'idéologie économique.* Paris: Gallimard, "Bibliothèque des sciences humaines."

Dunham, Vera S. 1976/1990. *In Stalin's Time. Middleclass Values in Soviet Fiction.* Durham, N.C.: Duke University Press.

Dutrait, Noël. 2006. *Petit précis à l'usage de l'amateur de littérature chinoise contemporaine.* Paris: Éd. Philippe Picquier.

————. 2010. "Ne pas avoir de -isme, un -isme pour un homme seul." *Perspectives chinoises,* no. 2: pp. 8–14.

Economist. 2012, 26 May.

Edele, Mark. 2012. "Stalinism as a Totalitarian Society. Geoffrey Hosking's Socio-cultural History." *Kritika,* 13, no. 2: pp. 441–452.

Edgerton-Tarpley, Kathryn. 2008. *Tears from Iron. Cultural Responses to Famine in Nineteenth-Century China.* Berkeley: University of California Press.

Ellman, Michael. 2007. "Discussion Article: Stalin and the Soviet Famine of 1932–1933 Revisited." *Europe-Asia Studies,* 59, no. 4: pp. 663–693.

Ermolaev, Herman. 1990. "Mikhaïl Cholokhov (1905–1984)." In Etkind et al., *Histoire de la littérature russe,* vol. 3: pp. 82–96.

Etkind, Alexander. 2009. "A Parable of Misrecognition: *Anagnorisis* and the Return of the Repressed from the Gulag." *Russian Review,* 68: pp. 623–640.

Etkind, Efim, Georges Nivat, Ilya Serman, and Vittorio Strada (eds.). 1987/1988/1990. *Histoire de la littérature russe. Le xxe siècle.* Vol. 1, *L'âge d'argent;* vol. 2, *La révolution et les années vingt;* vol. 3, *Gels et dégels.* Paris: Fayard.

Evans, Grant. 1988. "The Accursed Problem: Communists and Peasants." *Peasant Studies,* 15, no. 2: pp. 73–102.

Fabre, Guilhem, 1990. *Génèse du pouvoir et de l'oppoition en Chine. Le printemps de Yan'an: 1942.* Paris, Edition L'Harmattan.

Fainsod, Merle. 1958/1963. *Smolensk Under Soviet Rule.* New York: Vintage.

Fairbank, John K. (ed.). 1983. *The Cambridge History of China,* vol. 12, *Republican China, 1912–1949,* pt. 1. Cambridge: Cambridge University Press.

Fairbank, John K., and Albert Feuerwerker (eds.). 1986. Vol. 13, *Republican China 1912–1949,* pt. 2. Cambridge: Cambridge University Press.

Faligot, Roger, and Rémi Kauffer. 1987. *Kang Sheng et les services secrets chinois (1927–1987).* Paris: Robert Laffont.

Far Eastern Economic Review. 1999. Hong Kong: 10 October.

Ferro, Marc. 1980. *Des soviets au communisme bureaucratique. Les mécanismes d'une subversion.* Paris: Gallimard/Julliard, "Archives."

Feuerwerker, Mei Yi-tsi. 1998. *Ideology, Power, Text. Self-Representation and the Peasant "Other" in Modern Chinese Literature.* Stanford, Calif.: Stanford University Press.

Figes, Orlando. 2003. *Natasha's Dance: A Cultural History of Russia*. London: Penguin.

———. 2007a. *La révolution russe, 1891–1924. la tragédie d'un peuple*. Translated by P.-E. Dauzat. Paris: Denoël.

———. 2007b. *The Whisperers. Private Life in Stalin's Russia*. New York: Metropolitan Books.

Filtzer, Donald. 2010. *The Hazards of Urban Life in Late Stalinist Russia. Health, Hygiene, and Living Standards, 1943–1953*. New York: Cambridge University Press.

———. 2014. "Privilege and Inequality in Communist Society." In Stephen A. Smith (ed.), *The Oxford Handbook of the History of Communism*, pp. 505–521. Oxford: Oxford University Press.

Fitzpatrick, Sheila (ed.). 1978. *Cultural Revolution in Russia, 1928–1931*. Bloomington: Indiana University Press.

———. 1979. *Education and Social Mobility in the Soviet Union, 1921–1934*. Cambridge: Cambridge University Press.

———. 1992. *The Cultural Front. Power and Culture in Revolutionary Russia*, Ithaca, N.Y.: Cornell University Press.

———. 1994. *Stalin's Peasants. Resistance and Survival in the Russian Village after Collectivization*. New York: Oxford University Press.

———. 1999/2002. *Le stalinisme au quotidien. La Russie soviétique dans les années 30*. Translated by J.-P. Ricard and F.-X. Nérard. Paris: Flammarion.

Friedman, Edward, Paul G. Pickowicz, and Mark Selden. 2005. *Revolution, Resistance, and Reform in Village China*. New Haven, Conn.: Yale University Press.

Frolic, Michael B. 1982. *Le people de Mao. Scènes de la vie en Chine révolutionnaire*. Translated by J. Reclus. Paris: Gallimard, "Témoins."

Fu, Hualing. 2005. "Re-education through Labour in Historical Perspective." *The China Quarterly*, no. 184: pp. 811–830.

Furet, François. 1995. *Le passé d'une illusion. Essai sur l'idée communiste au xxe siècle*. Paris: Robert Laffont/Calmann-Lévy.

———. 2012. *Inventaires du communisme*, C. Prochasson (ed.). Paris: Éd. de l'EHESS.

Gao, Ertai. 2009. *In Search of My Homeland. A Memoir of a Chinese Labor Camp*. Translated by Robert Dorsett and David Pollard. New York: HarperCollins.

Gao, Hua. 2011. "Food Augmentation Methods and Food Substitutes during the Great Famine." In Manning and Wemheuer (eds.), *Eating Bitterness*, pp. 171–196.

Gao, Wangling. 2006. *Renmin gongshe shiqi Zhongguo nongmin "fanxingwei" diaocha* [Investigations on the "Counter-Actions" by Chinese Peasants in the Era of the People's Communes]. Beijing: Zhonggongdangshi chubanshe.

———. 2011. "A Study of Chinese Peasant 'Counter-Action.'" In Manning and Wemheuer (eds.), *Eating Bitterness*, pp. 272–294.

Gao, Xingjian. 2000. *Le Livre d'un homme seul*. Translated by N. and L. Dutrait. La Tour-d'Aigues: Éd. de l'Aube.

———. 2004. *Le Témoignage de la littérature*. Translated by N. and L. Dutrait. Paris: Éd. du Seuil.

———. 2010. "Limitée et illimitée: l'esthétique de la création." Translated by N. and L. Dutrait. *Perspectives chinoises*, no. 2: pp. 51–57.

Garnaut, Anthony. 2014. "The Geography of the Great Leap Famine." *Modern China*, 40, no. 3: pp. 315–348.

Gatrell, Peter. 2006. "Economic and Demographic Change. Russia's Age of Economic Extremes." In Suny, *Cambridge History of Russia*, pp. 383–410.

Gauchet, Marcel. 2010. *L'Avènement de la démocratie, III. À l'épreuve des totalitarismes, 1914–1974*. Paris: Gallimard, "Bibliothèque des sciences humaines."

Getty, J. Arch. 1993. "The Politics of Stalinism." In Alec Nove (ed.), *The Stalin Phenomenon*, pp. 100–151. London: Weidenfeld & Nicolson.

Getty, J. Arch, and Oleg V. Naumov. 1999. *The Road to Terror. Stalin and the Self-Destruction of the Bolsheviks, 1932–1939*. New Haven, Conn.: Yale University Press.

———. 2008. *Yezhov: The Rise of Stalin's "Iron Fist."* New Haven, Conn.: Yale University Press.

Giafferri-Huang, Xiaomin. 1991. *Le roman chinois depuis 1949*. Paris: PUF, "Écriture."

Goldman, Merle. 1966. "The Fall of Chou Yang." *The China Quarterly*, no. 27: pp. 132–148.

———. 1967. *Literary Dissent in Communist China*. Cambridge, Mass.: Harvard University Press.

——— (ed.). 1977. *Modern Chinese Literature in the May Fourth Era*. Cambridge, Mass.: Harvard University Press.

———. 1981. *China's Intellectuals Advise and Dissent*. Cambridge, Mass.: Harvard University Press.

———. 1987a. "The Party and the Intellectuals." In MacFarquhar and Fairbank (eds.), *CHOC*, vol. 14: pp. 218–258.

———. 1987b. "The Party and the Intellectuals. Phase Two." In MacFarquhar and Fairbank (eds.), *CHOC*, vol. 14: pp. 432–477.

Graziosi, Andrea. 1989/2013. "'Lettres de Kharkov.' La famine en Ukraine et dans le Caucase du Nord à travers les rapports des diplomates italiens, 1932–1934." *Cahiers du monde russe et soviétique*, 30, nos. 1–2: pp. 5–106. New, updated, and enlarged edition: Graziosi, Andrea, with the collaboration of Iryna Dmytrychyn (eds.), *Lettres de Kharkov, La famine en Ukraine*. Lausanne: Les Éditions Noir sur Blanc.

———. 1992. "The Great Strikes of 1953 in Soviet Labor Camps in the Accounts of Their Participants. A Review." *Cahiers du Monde russe et soviétique, 33*, no. 4: pp. 419–446.

———. 1994. "Collectivisation, révoltes paysannes et politiques gouvernementales à travers les rapports du GPU d'Ukraine de février-mars 1930." *Cahiers du monde russe, 35*, no. 3: pp. 437–472.

———. 1996. *The Great Soviet Peasant War. Bolsheviks and Peasants, 1917–1933.* Cambridge, Mass.: Harvard University Press.

———. 2005. "Les famines soviétiques de 1931–1933 et le Holodomor ukrainien: une nouvelle interprétation est-elle possible et quelles en seraient les conséquences?" *Cahiers du monde russe, 46*, no. 3: pp. 453–472.

———. 2010. *Histoire de l'URSS.* Paris: PUF.

———. 2015. "The Uses of Hunger: Stalin's Solution of the Peasant and National Question in Ukraine, 1932–1933." In Declan Curran, Lubomyr Luciuk, and Andrew G. Newby (eds.), *Famines in European Economic History: The Last Great European Famines Reconsidered*, pp. 223–260. London: Routledge.

Gregor, A. James. 2009. *Marxism, Fascism, and Totalitarianism: Chapters in the Intellectual History of Radicalism.* Stanford, Calif.: Stanford University Press.

Griesse, Malte. 2010. "Journal intime, identité et espaces communicationnels pendant la Grande Terreur." In Blum and Werth (eds.), "La grande terreur en URSS": pp. 83–100.

Grossman, Vasily. 1972. *Tout passe.* Translated by J. Lafond. Paris: Stock.

———. 1980. *Vie et destin.* Translated by A. Berelowitch. Lausanne: l'Âge d'homme.

———. 2008. *Pour une juste cause.* Translated by L. Jurgenson. Lausanne: l'Âge d'homme.

Guinzbourg, Evguénia S. 1967/1997. *Le vertige, I. Chronique des temps du culte de la personnalité.* Paris: Éd. du Seuil.

———. 1980. *Le vertige, II. Le ciel de la Kolyma.* Paris: Éd. du Seuil.

Han, Xiaorong. 2005. *Chinese Discourses on the Peasant, 1900–1949.* Albany: State University of New York Press.

Harding, Harry. 1981. *Organizing China. The Problem of Bureaucracy, 1949–1976.* Stanford, Calif.: Stanford University Press.

Hartford, Kathleen J. 1980. "Step by Step: Reform, Resistance, and Revolution in Chin-Ch'a-Chi Border Region, 1937–1945." Ph.D. diss. Stanford University.

Hartford, Kathleen J., and Steven M. Goldstein (eds.). 1989. *Single Sparks. China's Rural Revolutions.* Armonk, N.Y.: Sharpe.

Haupt, Georges. 1972. Preface to Roy Medvedev. *Le Stalinisme. Origines, histoire, conséquences.* Paris: Éd. du Seuil.

Hayford, Charles W. 1990. *To the People. James Yen and Village China*. New York: Columbia University Press.

Hayhoe, Ruth, ed. 1984. *Contemporary Chinese Education*. London: Croom Helm.

He, Donghui. 2010. "Coming of Age in the Brave New World. The Changing Reception of the Soviet Novel *How the Steel Was Tempered* in the People's Republic of China." In Bernstein and Li (eds.), *China Learns*, pp. 393–420.

Hegel, Georg W. F. 1953/1986. *Reason in History. A General Introduction to the Philosophy of History*. Translated and introduced by R. S. Hartman. New York: Macmillan.

———. 1965. *La Raison dans l'Histoire. Introduction aux leçons sur la philosophie de l'Histoire*. Translated, introduced, and annotated by K. Papaioannou. Paris: Plon.

Heller, Leonid. 1988. "Evguéni Zamiatine, 1884–1937." In Etkind et al., *Histoire de la littérature russe*, vol. 2: pp. 457–474.

Heller, Michel. 1990. "Les années trente." In Etkind et al., *Histoire de la littérature russe*, vol. 3, pp. 140–167.

Heller, Michel, and Aleksandr Nekrich. 1982. *L'utopie au pouvoir. Histoire de l'URSS de 1917 à nos jours*. Translated by W. Berelowitch. Paris: Calmann-Lévy.

Hermet, Guy, Pierre Hassner, and Jacques Rupnik (eds.). 1984. *Totalitarismes*. Paris: Economica, "Politique comparée."

Hinton, William. 1971. *Fanshen. La révolution communiste dans un village chinois*. Translated by J.-R. Major. Paris: Plon.

———. 1983. *Shenfan. The Continuing Revolution in a Chinese Village*. New York: Random House.

Hippius, Zinaïda. 2006. *Journal sous la Terreur*. Translated by M. Gourg, O. Melnik-Ardin, and I. Sokologorsky. Monaco: Éd. du Rocher.

Holloway, David. 2006. "Science, Technology and Modernity." In Suny (ed.), *Cambridge History of Russia*, pp. 549–578.

Holquist, Peter. 2002. *Making War, Forging Revolution. Russia's Continuum of Crisis, 1914–1921*. Cambridge, Mass.: Harvard University Press.

Hong, Zicheng. 2007. *A History of Contemporary Chinese Literature*. Translated by M. M. Day. Boston: Brill.

Hooper, Cynthia V. 2013. "Bosses in Captivity? On the Limitations of Gulag Memoir." *Kritika*, 14, no. 1: pp. 117–142.

Hsia, Chih-tsing. 1961. *A History of Modern Chinese Fiction, 1917–1957*. New Haven, Conn.: Yale University Press.

Huang, Jing. 2000. *Factionalism in Chinese Communist Politics*. Cambridge: Cambridge University Press.

Jiang, Yihua. 2010. "Perspective I. On Mao Zedong." In Cheek (ed.), *A Critical Introduction to Mao*, pp. 332–343.

Jin, Qiu. 1999. *The Culture of Power. The Lin Biao Incident in the Cultural Revolution.* Stanford, Calif.: Stanford University Press.

Johnson, Chalmers A. 1962/1969. *Peasant Nationalism and Communist Power. The Emergence of Revolutionary China 1937–1945.* Stanford, Calif.: Stanford University Press. French translation by L. Jospin, *Nationalisme paysan et pouvoir communiste. Les débuts de la révolution chinoise (1937–1945).* Paris: Payot.

Joseph, William A., Christine P. W. Wong, and David Zweig (eds.). 1991. *New Perspectives on the Cultural Revolution.* Cambridge, Mass.: Harvard University Press.

Kau, Ying-Mao. 1971. "Patterns of Recruitment and Mobility of Urban Cadres." In John Lewis (ed.), *The City in Communist China,* pp. 97–122. Stanford, Calif.: Stanford University Press.

Kempton, Nicole, and Nan Richardson (eds.). 2009. *Laogai. The Machinery of Repression in China. Preface by A. Nathan.* New York: Umbrage/London: Turnaround.

Ken, Ling. 1972. *The Revenge of Heaven: Journal of a Young Chinese.* English Text prepared by Miriam London and Ta-Ling Lee. New York: Ballantine Books.

Kerblay, Basile. 1964. "A.V. Cajanov, un carrefour dans l'évolution de la pensée agraire en Russie de 1908 à 1930." *Cahiers du monde russe et soviétique,* 5, no. 4: pp. 411–460.

Khlevniouk, Oleg. 1996. *Le cercle du Kremlin. Staline et le Bureau politique dans les années 30: les jeux du pouvoir.* P. Forgues and N. Werth (trans.). Paris: Éd. du Seuil.

———(Khlevniuk). 2004. *The History of the Gulag. From Collectivization to the Great Terror.* New Haven, Conn.: Yale University Press.

King, Richard. 2010. *Heroes of China's Great Leap Forward. Two Stories.* Honolulu: University of Hawaii Press.

———. 2011. "Romancing the Leap: Euphoria in the Moment before Disaster." In Manning and Wemheuer (eds.), *Eating Bitterness,* pp. 51–71.

Kinkley, Jeffrey C. 1987. *The Odyssey of Shen Congwen.* Stanford, Calif.: Stanford University Press.

———. 2014. *Visions of Dystopia in China's New Historical Novels.* New York: Columbia University Press.

Klid, Bohdan, and Alexander J. Motyl (eds.). 2012. *The Holodomor Reader: A Sourcebook on the Famine of 1932–1933 in Ukraine.* Edmonton: Canadian Institute of Ukrainian Studies Press.

Ko, Kilkon, and Cuifen Weng. 2012. "Structural Changes in Chinese Corruption." *The China Quarterly,* no. 211: pp. 718–740.

Kolakowski, Leszek. [1977] 2008. "Stalinism Versus Marxism? Marxist Roots of Stalinim." In Robert Tucker (ed.), *Stalinism, Essays in Historical Interpretation,* pp. 283–298. New Brunswick, N. J.: Transaction Publishers.

Kotkin, Stephen. 1995. *Magnetic Mountain. Stalinism as a Civilization.* Berkeley: University of California Press.

Kouo, Mo-jo. 1970. *Autobiographie. Mes années d'enfance.* Translated by P. Ryckmans. Paris: Gallimard.

Kouznetsov, Edouard. 1974. *Journal d'un condamné à mort.* Translated and prefaced by J. Cathala. Paris: Gallimard, "Témoins."

Kraus, Richard Curt. 1981. *Class Conflict in Chinese Socialism.* New York: Columbia University Press.

Kriegel, Annie. 1972 *Les grands procès dans les systèmes communistes. La pédagogie infernale.* Paris: Gallimard, "Idées."

Kung, James Kai-sing, and Shih Chen. 2011. "The Tragedy of the Nomenklatura. Career Incentives and Political Radicalism during the Great Leap Famine." *American Political Science Review*, 105, no. 1: pp. 27–45.

Kuo, Warren. 1971. *Analytical History of the Chinese Communist Party,* Book 4. Taipei: Institute of International Relations.

Kupferman, Fred. 1979/2007. *Au pays des Soviets. Le voyage français en Union soviétique, 1913–1939.* Paris: Tallandier.

Lai, Ying. 1970. *Les prisons de Mao. Une femme dans l'enfer rouge.* Translated and presented by Edward Behr and Sidney Liu. Paris: Raoul Solar.

Laran, Michel. 1973. *Russie-URSS. 1870–1970.* Paris: Masson.

Laran, Michel, and Jean-Louis Van Regemorter. 1996. *La Russie et l'ex-URSS de 1914 à nos jours.* Paris: Armand Colin.

Lardy, Nicholas R. 1987. "The Chinese Economy under Stress, 1958–1965." In MacFarquhar and Fairbank (eds.), *CHOC*, vol. 14: pp. 360–397.

Lee, Leo Ou-Fan. 1986. "Literary Trends. The Road to Revolution, 1927–1949." In Fairbank and Feuerwerker (eds.), *CHOC*, vol. 13: pp. 421–491.

Lefort, Claude. 1971. *Éléments d'une critique de la bureaucratie.* Geneva: Droz.

———. 1999. *La Complication. Retour sur le communisme.* Paris: Fayard.

Lénine. 1902/1966. *Que faire?* Introduced and annotated by J.-J. Marie. Paris: Éd. du Seuil, "Points Politique."

Levi, Primo. 1987/1993. *Si c'est un homme.* Paris: Presses Pocket.

———. 1989. *Les naufragés et les rescapés. Quarante ans après Auschwitz.* Paris: Gallimard.

Lew, Roland. 1986. "Etat et bureaucratie dans la Chine contemporaine." In R. Lew and F. Thierry (eds.), *Bureaucraties chinoises,* pp. 43–65. Paris: L'Harmattan.

Lewin, Moshe. 1966/1976. *La paysannerie et le pouvoir soviétique, 1928–1930.* 2nd ed. Paris/La Haye: Mouton.

———. 1978. *Le dernier combat de Lénine.* Paris: Éd. de minuit, "Arguments."

———. 1987. *La formation du système soviétique. Essais sur l'histoire sociale de la Russie dans l'entre-deux-guerres.* Translated by P.-E. Dauzat. Paris: Gallimard.

————. 2003a. *Le siècle soviétique*. Translated by D. Paillard and F. Prudhomme. Paris: Fayard/Le Monde diplomatique.

————. 2003b. "Rebuilding the Soviet Nomenklatura, 1945–1948." *Cahiers du monde russe*, 44, nos. 2–3: pp. 219–252.

Lewis, John Wilson (ed.). 1971. *The City in Communist China*. Stanford, Calif.: Stanford University Press.

Leys, Simon. 1974. *Ombres chinoises*. 10–18. UGE.

————. 1976. *Images brisées. Confucius, Lin Piao, Chou En-lai, Mao Tse-tung & Li Yi-che*. Paris: Robert Laffont.

————. 1998. *Essais sur la Chine*. Paris: Robert Laffont.

Li, Che. 2012. "Dajihuang niandai fei zhengchang siwang de ling yizhong jisuan" [A New Estimate of the Number of Abnormal Deaths at the Time of the Great Famine]. *Yanhuang chunqiu*, no. 7: pp. 46–52.

Li, Cheng, and Lynn White. 1990. "Elite Transformation and Modern Change in Mainland China and Taiwan: Empirical Data and the Theory of Technocracy." *The China Quarterly*, no. 121: pp. 1–35.

Li, Choh-ming. 1962. *The Statistical System of Communist China*. Berkeley: University of California Press.

Li, Huaiyin. 2006. "The First Encounter. Peasant Resistance to State Control of Grain in East China in the mid-1950s." *The China Quarterly*, no. 185: pp. 145–162.

Li, Hua-yu. 2006. *Mao and the Economic Stalinization of China, 1948–1953*. Lanham, Md.: Rowman & Littlefield.

————. 2010. "Instilling Stalinism in Chinese Party Members. Absorbing Stalin's Short Course in the 1950s." In Bernstein and Li, *China Learns*, pp. 107–130.

Li, Lillian. 2007. *Fighting famine in North China*. Stanford, Calif.: Stanford University Press.

Li, Zhisui. 1994. *The Private Life of Chairman Mao*. New York: Random House. Quoted from the French edition *La vie privée du président Mao*. Translated by H. Marcel, F. Straschitz, and M. Leroi-Batistelli. Paris: Plon.

Liao, Yiwu. 2013. *Dans l'Empire des ténèbres. Un écrivain dans les geôles chinoises*. Preface by Marie Holzman and Jean-François Bouthors, postface by Herta Müller. Paris: François Bourin.

Lifton, Robert Jay. 1961. *Thought Reform and the Psychology of Totalism. A Study of "Brainwashing" in China*. London: Penguin.

Lih, Lars T., Oleg V. Naumov, and Oleg Khlevniouk (eds.). 1995. *Stalin's Letters to Molotov, 1925–1936*. New Haven, Conn.: Yale University Press.

Link, Perry (ed.). 1983. *Stubborn Weeds. Popular and Controversial Chinese Literature after the Cultural Revolution*. Bloomington: Indiana University Press.

————. 2000. *The Uses of Literature. Life in the Socialist Chinese Literary System*. Princeton, N.J.: Princeton University Press.

Linz, Juan, J. 2006. *Régimes totalitaires et autoritaires*. Translated by M. S. Darviche and W. Genieys. Paris: Armand Colin.

Liu, Qing. 1982. *J'accuse devant le tribunal de la société*. Translated by Collectif pour l'étude du mouvement démocratique en Chine. Paris: Robert Laffont.

Liu, Xiaobo. 2011. *La philosophie du porc et autres essais*, translated and introduced by J.-Ph. Béja. Paris: Gallimard, "Bleu de Chine."

———. 2012a. *Vivre dans la vérité*, textes choisis. Translated by J.-Ph. Béja, J. Bonnin, H. Denès, G. Fabre, M. Holzman, G. Imbot-Bichet, C. Lévi, and J. Lévi, edited by Geneviève Imbot-Bichet. Paris: Gallimard.

———. 2012b. *No Enemies, No Hatred. Selected Essays and Poems*. P. Link, T. Martin-Liao, and Liu Xia (eds.). Cambridge, Mass.: Harvard University Press.

Liu, Zaifu. 2000. "Farewell to the Gods. Contemporary Chinese Literary Theory's Fin-de-siècle Struggle." In Chi and Wang (eds.), *Chinese Literature*, pp. 1–13.

Loh, Robert, with H. Evans. 1963. *Je suis un évadé de la Chine rouge*. Paris: Plon.

Lozac'h, Valérie. 2005. "Jeux de miroir dans l'administration est-allemande: les usages croisés du stéréotype bureaucratique après l'unification." *Sociétés contemporaines*, 1, no. 57: pp. 83–104.

Lü, Xiaobo. 2000. *Cadres and Corruption. The Organizational Involution of the Chinese Communist Party*. Stanford, Calif.: Stanford University Press.

Lüthi, Lorenz M. 2010. "Sino-Soviet Relations during the Mao Years, 1949–1969." In Bernstein and Li (eds.), *China Learns*, pp. 27–59.

MacFarquhar, Roderick. 1960/1974. *The Hundred Flowers Campaign and the Chinese Intellectuals*. New York: Octagon Books.

———. 1983. *The Origins of the Cultural Revolution, II. The Great Leap Forward, 1958–1960*. New York: Columbia University Press.

MacFarquhar, Roderick, and John K. Fairbank (eds.). 1987. *The Cambridge History of China (or CHOC)*, vol. 14, *The People's Republic, Part I, The Emergence of Revolutionary China 1949–1965*. Cambridge: Cambridge University Press.

———. 1991. *CHOC*, vol. 15, *The People's Republic, Part II, Revolutions within the Chinese Revolution, 1966–1982*. Cambridge: Cambridge University Press.

MacFarquhar, Roderick, and Michael Schoenhals. 2006. *Mao's Last Revolution*. Cambridge, Mass.: Belknap.

Malia, Martin. 1995. *La tragédie soviétique. Histoire du socialisme en Russie 1917–1991*. Paris: Éd. du Seuil.

Mallory, Walter H. 1926. *China, Land of Famine*. New York: American Geographical Society.

Malsagov, Sozerko (Serge). 1926. *An Island Hell: A Soviet Prison in the Far North*. London: A.-M. Philpot.

Mandelstam, Nadejda. 1972–1975. *Contre tout espoir. Souvenirs.* Translated by M. Minoustchine. 3 vols. Paris: Gallimard.

Manning, Kimberley Ens, and Felix Wemheuer (eds.). 2011. *Eating Bitterness. New Perspectives on China's Great Leap Forward and Famine.* Vancouver: University of British Columbia Press.

Mao, Tsé-toung. 1959. *Oeuvres choisies,* T. 4 (1941–1945). Paris: Editions sociales.

Margolin, Julius. 2010. *Voyage au pays des Ze-Ka.* Paris: Le bruit du temps.

Martin, Terry. 2001. *The Affirmative Action Empire.* Ithaca, N.Y.: Cornell University Press.

Marx, Karl. 1948. *Les luttes de classes en France (1848–1850). Le 18 brumaire de Louis Bonaparte.* Paris: Éditions sociales.

Mayer, Françoise. 2012. "L'URSS, terre de promesses?" In Blum, Craveri, and Nivelon (eds.), *Déportés en URSS:* pp. 29–47.

Mazuy, Rachel. 2002. *Croire plutôt que voir? Voyages en Russie soviétique (1919–1939).* Paris: Odile Jacob.

McDougall, Bonnie S. 1977. "The Impact of Western Literary Trends." In Goldman (ed.), *Modern Chinese Literature,* pp. 37–61.

McGregor, Richard. 2010. *The Party. The Secret World of China's Communist Rulers.* New York: HarperCollins.

Medvedev, Roy. 1975. *Qui a écrit le "Don paisible"?* Paris: Christian Bourgois.

Meisner, Maurice. 1982. *Marxism, Maoism and Utopianism. Eight Essays.* Madison: University of Wisconsin Press.

Michael, Franz. 1962. "The Role of Law in Traditional, Nationalist and Communist China." *The China Quarterly,* 9, January–March: pp. 124–148.

Milosz, Czeslaw. 1953. *La pensée captive. Essai sur les logocraties populaires.* Paris: Gallimard, "Folio essais."

Moine, Nathalie. 2005. "'Mesurer le niveau de vie': administration statistique et politique des données en URSS, de la reconstruction au dégel." *Sociétes contemporaines,* 57, no. 1: pp. 41–62.

Montefiore, Simon Sebag. 2005. *Staline, la cour du Tsar rouge.* Translated by A. Roubichou-Stretz and F. Labruyère. Geneva: Éd. des Syrtes.

Moussa, Pierre. 1959. *Les nations prolétaires.* Paris: Presses Universitaires de France.

Mu, Fu-sheng. 1962. *The Wilting of the Hundred Flowers. The Chinese Intelligentsia under Mao.* New York: Praeger.

Mühlhahn, Klaus. 2009. *Criminal Justice in China. A History.* Cambridge, Mass.: Harvard University Press.

Naimark, Norman M. 2010. *Stalin's Genocides.* Princeton, N.J.: Princeton University Press.

Nien, Cheng. 1987. *Vie et mort à Shanghai.* Paris: Albin Michel.

Nove, Alec. 1992. *An Economic History of the USSR 1917–1991.* London: Penguin.

———. 1993. "Stalin and Stalinism—Some Introductory Thoughts." In Alec Nove (ed.), *The Stalin Phenomenon*, pp. 1–38. London: Weidenfeld & Nicolson.

O'Brien, Kevin. 2002. "Collective Action in the Chinese Countryside." *The China Journal*, no. 48: pp. 139–154.

Ohayon, Isabelle. 2006. *La sédentarisation des Kazakhs dans l'URSS de Staline. Collectivisation et changement social (1928–1945)*. Preface by N. Werth. Paris: Maisonneuve et Larose.

Oi, Jean C. 1989. *State and Peasant in Contemporary China. The Political Economy of Village Government*. Berkeley: University of California Press.

Oksenberg, Michel. 1968. "The Institutionalisation of the Chinese Communist Revolution. The Ladder of Success on the Eve of the Cultural Revolution." *The China Quarterly*, no. 36: pp. 61–92.

"'Opérations de masse' de la 'Grande Terreur' en URSS, 1937–1938 (Les)." 2006–2007. *Bulletin de l'IHTP*, no. 86.

Osburg, John. 2013. *Anxious Wealth: Money and Morality among China's New Rich*. Stanford, Calif.: Stanford University Press.

Ostrovski, Nicolas. 2012. *Et l'acier fut trempé*. Translated by V. Feldman and P. Kolodkine. Pantin: Le Temps des cerises.

Pan, Philip P. 2008. *Out of Mao's Shadow: The Struggle for the Soul of a New China*. New York: Simon & Schuster.

Pantsov, Alexander V., with Steven Levine. 2007/2012. *Mao: The Real Story*. New York: Simon & Schuster.

Papaioannou, Kostas. 1965. *Les Marxistes*. Paris: J'ai lu.

———. 1972. *Marx et les marxistes*. Paris: Flammarion.

———. 1983. *De Marx et du marxisme*. Preface by R. Aron. Paris: Gallimard.

Pasqualini, Jean. 1975. *Prisonnier de Mao. Sept ans dans un camp de travail en Chine*. Translated by A. Delahaye. Paris: Gallimard.

Pasternak, Boris. 1958/2009. *Le docteur Jivago*. Paris: Editions Gallimard, Folio.

Penner, D'Ann R. 1998. "Stalin and the *Ital'ianka* of 1932–1933 in the Don Region." *Cahiers du monde russe*, 39, nos. 1–2: pp. 27–68.

Pepper, Suzanne. 1987. "Education for the New Order." In MacFarquhar and Fairbank (eds.), *CHOC*, vol. 14: pp. 185–217.

———. 1991. "Education." In MacFarquhar and Fairbank (eds.), *CHOC*, vol. 15: pp. 540–593.

Pianciola, Niccolo. 2004. "Famine in the Steppe: The Collectivisation of Agriculture and the Kazakh Herdsmen, 1928–1934." *Cahiers du monde russe*, 45, nos. 1–2: pp. 137–191.

Pipes, Richard. 1990. *The Russian Revolution*. New York: Vintage.

Pisier-Kouchner, Évelyne (ed.). 1983. *Les interprétations du stalinisme*. Paris: PUF, "recherches politiques."

Pollock, Ethan. 2009. "From Partiinost' to Nauchnost' and Not Quite Back Again. Revisiting the Lessons of the Lysenko Affair." *Slavic Review*, 68, no. 1: pp. 95–115.

Pomian, Krzysztof. 1995. "Totalitarisme." *Vingtième Siècle*, no. 47: pp. 4–25.

Popper, Karl. 1993. *La leçon de ce siècle. Entretien avec Giancarlo Bosetti*. Translated by J. Henry and Cl. Orsoni, Anatolia. Paris: "Bibliothèques 10/18."

Pu, Ning [see also Wu, Ming-shih]. 1985. *The Scourge of the Sea. A True Account of My Experiences in the Hsia-sa Village Concentration Camp*. Taipei: Compilation Department, Kuang Lu Publishing Service.

———. 1994. *Red in Tooth and Claw. Twenty-Six Years in Communist Chinese Prisons*. New York: Grove Press.

Pye, Lucian W. 1976. *Mao Tse-tung. The Man in the Leader*. New York: Basic Books. Quoted from French edition, *Mao Tse-toung. Un portrait*. Translated by C. Yelnick. Paris: Hachette.

———. 1996. "Rethinking the Man in the Leader." *The China Journal*, no. 35: pp. 107–112.

———. 2000. "The Thin Line between Loyalty and Treachery in Mao's China." *The China Journal*, no. 44: pp. 145–152.

Qian, Zhongshu. 1987a. *Cinq essais de poétique*, translated and introduced by N. Chapuis. Paris: Christian Bourgois.

———. 1987b. *La forteresse assiégée*. Translated by S. Servan-Screiber and Wang L. Paris: Christian Bourgois.

Qiu, Shipian. 2013. "Dang'an zhong de Wang Shiwei si yin" (What caused Wang Shiwei's death: The evidence from the archives)." *Yanhuang chunqiu*, no. 6: pp. 8–10.

Razgon, Lev. 1991. *La vie sans lendemain*. Translated by Anne Coldefy-Faucard and Luba Jurgenson. Paris: Horay.

Rickett, Allyn, and Adele Rickett. 1957/1973. *Prisoners of Liberation. Four Years in a Chinese Communist Prison*. New York: Anchor Press.

Rissov, Constantin. 1986. *Le dragon enchaîné, de Chiang Kai-shek à Mao Zedong, trente-cinq ans d'intimité avec la Chine*. Paris: Robert Laffont.

Rittenberg, Sidney, and Amanda Bennett. 1993. *The Man Who Stayed Behind*. New York: Simon & Schuster.

Rittersporn, Gabor Tamas. 1980–1981. "Du Goulag de la littérature à l'histoire de la politique pénale en Union soviétique, 1933–1953." *Critique politique*, nos. 7–8: pp. 3–68.

Rocca, Jean-Louis. 1991. *L'Empire et son milieu. La criminalité en Chine populaire.* Paris: Plon.

Rohlf, Gregory. 2010. "The Soviet Model and China's State Farms." In Bernstein and Li (eds.), *China Learns*, pp. 197–228.

Rossi, Jacques. 1997. *Le manuel du Goulag.* Paris: Le Cherche Midi.

Roux, Alain. 2009. *Le singe et le tigre. Mao, un destin chinois.* Paris: Larousse.

Roziner, Félix. 1990. "La musique russe sous Staline (1930–début des années 1950)." In Etkind et al., *Histoire de la littérature russe*, vol. 3: pp. 267–289.

Rozman, Gilbert. 2010. "Concluding Assessment. The Soviet Impact on Chinese Society." In Bernstein and Li (eds.), *China Learns*, pp. 517–525.

Rubin, Kyna. 1981. "Interview with Mr. Wang Ruowang." *The China Quarterly*, no. 87, September: pp. 501–517.

Rupnik, Jacques. 1984. "Le totalitarisme vu de l'Est." In Hermet, Hassner, and Rupnik (eds.), *Totalitarismes*, pp. 43–71.

Saich, Tony. 1996. *The Rise to Power of the Chinese Communist Party.* Armonk, N.Y.: M.E. Sharpe.

———, and Hans van de Ven eds. 1995. *New Perspectives on the Chinese Communist Revolution.* Armonk, N.Y.: M.E. Sharpe.

Saraskina, Lioudmila. 2010. *Alexandre Soljenitsyne.* Paris: Fayard.

Scalapino, Robert A. (ed.). 1972. *Elites in the People's Republic of China.* Seattle: University of Washington Press.

Schapiro, Leonard. 1967. *De Lénine à Staline. Histoire du Parti communiste de l'Union soviétique.* Translated by Aanda Golem. Paris: Gallimard, "La suite des temps."

Schneider, Laurence. 2003. *Biology and Revolution in Twentieth Century China.* Lanham, Md.: Rowman & Littlefield.

———. 2010. "Lysenkoism and the Suppression of Genetics in the PRC, 1949–1956." In Bernstein and Li (eds.), *China Learns,* pp. 327–358.

Schram, Stuart R. (ed.). 1974. *Mao Tse-tung Unrehearsed. Talks and Letters: 1956–71.* London: Penguin.

———. 1986. "Mao Tse-tung's Thought to 1949." In Fairbank and Feuerwerker (eds.), *CHOC*, vol. 13: pp. 789–870.

———. 1991. "Mao Tse-tung's Thought from 1949 to 1976." In MacFarquhar and Fairbank (eds.), *CHOC*, vol. 15: pp. 1–104.

Schurmann, Franz. 1968. *Ideology and Organization in Communist China.* 2nd ed. Berkeley: University of California Press.

Schwartz, Benjamin. 1964. *In Search of Wealth and Power: Yen Fu and the West.* Cambridge, Mass.: Belknap.

————. 1968/1970. *Communism and China. Ideology in Flux.* Cambridge, Mass.: Harvard University Press.

Scott, James C. 1985. *Weapons of the Weak. Everyday Forms of Peasant Resistance.* New Haven, Conn.: Yale University Press.

————. 1989. "Everyday Forms of Resistance." In F. D. Colburn (ed.), *Everyday Forms of Resistance*, pp. 3–32. Armonk, N.Y.: Sharpe.

Service, Robert. 2005. *Stalin. A Biography.* Cambridge, Mass.: Belknap.

————. 2012. *Lénine.* Translated by M. Devillers-Argouarc'h. Paris: Perrin.

Seybolt, Peter J. 1986. "Terror and Conformity. Counterespionage Campaigns, Rectification, and Mass Movements, 1942–1943." *Modern China*, 12, no. 1: pp. 39–74.

Seymour, James D., and Richard Anderson. 1998. *New Ghosts, Old Ghosts. Prisons and Labor Reform Camps in China.* Armonk, N.Y.: Sharpe.

Shanin, Teodor (ed.). 1971. *Peasants and Peasant Societies.* London: Penguin.

Short, Philip. 1999/2005. *Mao Tsé-toung.* Translated by C. Lahary-Gautié. Paris: Fayard.

Smedley, Agnes. 1944. *Battle Hymn of China.* London: Victor Gollancz.

Smith, Mark B. 2010. *Property of Communists. The Urban Housing Program from Stalin to Khrushchev.* DeKalb: Northern Illinois University Press.

Smith, S. A. 1983. *Red Petrograd. Revolution in the Factories, 1917–1918.* Cambridge: Cambridge University Press.

————. 2000. *A Road Is Made. Communism in Shanghai, 1920–1927.* Honolulu: University of Hawaii Press.

————. 2002. *Like Cattle and Horses. Nationalism and Labor in Shanghai, 1895–1927.* Durham, N.C.: Duke University Press.

————. 2008. *Revolution and the People in Russia and China. A Comparative History.* Cambridge: Cambridge University Press.

Snyder, Timothy. 2010/2012. *Bloodlands. Europe between Hitler and Stalin.* New York: Basic Books. French edition *Terres de sang. L'Europe entre Hitler et Staline.* Translated by P.-E. Dauzat. Paris: Gallimard.

Sokoloff, Georges. 2000. *1933, l'année noire. Témoignages sur la famine en Ukraine.* Paris: Albin Michel.

Soljenitsyne, Alexandre. 1968. *Le pavillon des cancéreux.* Paris: Julliard, Le Livre de poche.

————. 1974. *L'archipel du Goulag.* 3 vols. Paris: Éd. du Seuil.

————. 1975. *Le chêne et le veau. Esquisses de la vie littéraire.* Translated by R. Marichal. Paris: Éd. du Seuil.

————. 1976/2010. *Une journée d'Ivan Denissovitch.* Translated by J. and L. Cathala. Paris: Robert Laffont.

Souyri, Pierre. 1970. *Le marxisme après Marx*. Paris: Flammarion, "Questions d'histoire."

Strada, Vittorio. 1990. "Le réalisme socialiste." In Etkind et al., *Histoire de la littérature russe*, vol. 3: pp. 11–35.

Su, Wei. 2000. "The School and the Hospital. On the Logics of Socialist Realism." In Chi and Wang (eds.), *Chinese Literature*, pp. 65–75.

Su, Yang. 2006. "Mass Killings in the Cultural Revolution: A Study of Three Provinces." In J. W. Esherick, P. G. Pickowicz, and A. G. Walder (eds.), *The Chinese Cultural Revolution as History*, pp. 96–123. Stanford, Calif.: Stanford University Press.

———. 2011. *Collective Killings in Rural China during the Cultural Revolution*. Cambridge: Cambridge University Press.

Sukhanov, Nicolas N. 1965. *La Révolution russe de 1917*. Paris: Stock.

Sumpf, Alexandre. 2013. *De Lénine à Gagarine*. Paris: Gallimard, Folio Histoire.

Sun, Yat-sen. 1927. *San Min Chu I: The Three Principles of People*. Translated by Frank W. Price, edited by L. T. Chen. Shanghai: China Committee, Institute of Pacific Relations.

Suny, Ronald Gregory. 2006. *The Cambridge History of Russia*, vol. 3, *The Twentieth Century*. Cambridge: Cambridge University Press.

Svirski, Grigori. 1981. *Écrivains de la liberté. La résistance littéraire en Union soviétique depuis la guerre*. Translated by D. Olivier. Paris: Gallimard, "bibliothèque des idées."

———. 1990. "La littérature pendant la Seconde Guerre mondiale." In Etkind et al., *Histoire de la littérature russe*: pp. 328–354.

Swedberg, Richard. 2005. *The Max Weber Dictionary. Key Words and Central Concepts*. Stanford, Calif.: Stanford University Press.

Taubman, William. 2003. *Khrushchev, the Man and His Era*. New York: Norton.

Tchistiakov, Ivan. 2012. *Journal d'un gardien du goulag*, translated, prefaced, and annotated by L. Jurgenson, introduction by Irina Shcherbakova. Paris: Denoël.

Tchoukovskaïa, Lydia. 1980. *Entretiens avec Anna Akhmatova*. Paris: Albin Michel.

Teiwes, Frederick C. 1993. *Politics and Purges in China. Rectification and the Decline of Party Norms, 1950–1965*. 2nd ed. Armonk, N.Y.: Sharpe.

———. 1995. "From a Leninist to a Charismatic Party: The CCP's Changing Leadership, 1937–1945." In Tony Saich and Hans van de Ven (eds.), *New Perspectives on the Chinese Communist Revolution*, pp. 339–387. Armonk, N.Y.: M.E. Sharpe.

———. 2010. "Mao and His Followers." In Cheek (ed.), *Critical Introduction to Mao*, pp. 129–157.

Teiwes, Frederick C., and Warren Sun. 1993. *The Politics of Agricultural Cooperativization in China. Mao, Deng Zihui, and the "High Tide" of 1955*. Armonk, N.Y.: Sharpe.

————. 1996. *The Tragedy of Lin Biao. Riding the Tiger during the Cultural Revolution.* Honolulu: University of Hawaii Press.

————. 1999. *China's Road to Disaster: Mao, Central Politicians, and Provincial Leaders in the Unfolding of the Great Leap Forward, 1955–1959.* Armonk, N.Y.: Sharpe.

Thaxton, Ralph A. 2008. *Catastrophe and Contention in Rural China. Mao's Great Leap Forward Famine and the Origins of Righteous Resistance in Da Fo Village.* New York: Cambridge University Press.

————. 2011. "How the Great Leap Forward Famine Ended in Rural China. Administrative Intervention versus Peasant Resistance." In Manning and Wemheuer (eds.), *Eating Bitterness*, pp. 251–271.

Thurston, Anne, F. 1996. "The Politics of Survival. Li Zhisui and the Inner Court." *The China Journal*, no. 35: pp. 97–105.

Todorov, Tzvetan. 1994. *Face à l'extrême.* Paris: Éd. du Seuil, "Points Seuils."

Townsend, James R. 1969. *Political Participation in Communist China.* Berkeley: University of California Press.

Tucker, Robert C. 1963. *The Soviet Political Mind. Studies in Stalinism and Post-Stalin Change.* New York: Praeger.

————. 1973. *Stalin as Revolutionary, 1879–1929: A Study in History and Personality.* New York: Norton.

————. [1977] 2008, "Stalinism as Revolution from Above." In Robert Tucker (ed.), *Stalinism, Essays in Historical Interpretation*, pp. 77–108. New Brunswick (U.S.A.) and London: Transaction Publishers.

Tung, Chi-ping, and Humphrey Evans. 1967. *The Thought Revolution.* London: Leslie Frewin.

Union Research Institute. 1968. *The Case of Peng Teh-Huai, 1959–1968.* Hong Kong: Union Press.

Vaissié, Cécile. 2008. *Les Ingénieurs des âmes en chef. Littérature et politique en URSS (1944–1986).* Preface by C. Lefort. Paris: Belin.

Veg, Sebastian. 2014. "La création d'un espace littéraire pour débattre de l'ère maoïste, La fictionalisation du Grand Bond en avant dans Les Quatre Livres de Yan Lianke." *Perspectives chinoises*: pp. 7–16.

Vichnevski, Anatoli. 2000. *La faucille et le rouble. La modernisation conservatrice en URSS.* Translated by M. Vichnevskaïa. Paris: Gallimard.

Vidal, Christine. 2006. "À l'épreuve du politique. Les intellectuels non-communistes chinois et l'émergence du pouvoir maoïste dans la première moitié du xxe siècle." 2 vols. Ph.D. diss. Paris: EHESS.

Viola, Lynne. 1996. *Peasant Rebels under Stalin. Collectivization and the Culture of Peasant Resistance.* Oxford: Oxford University Press.

————. 2005. "La famine de 1932–1933 en Union soviétique." *Vingtième Siècle*, no. 88: pp. 5–22.

————. 2007. *The Unknown Gulag. The Lost World of Stalin's Special Settlements*. Oxford: Oxford University Press.

Viola, Lynne, Viktor Petrovich Danilov, N. A. Ivnitskii, and Denis Kozlov (eds.). 2005. *The War Against the Peasantry, 1927–1930. The Tragedy of the Soviet Countryside*. New Haven, Conn.: Yale University Press.

Vogel, Ezra F. 1965. "From Friendship to Comradeship. The Change in Personal Relations in Communist China." *The China Quarterly*, no. 21: pp. 46–60.

————. 1967a. "From Revolutionary to Semi-bureaucrat. The 'Regularisation' of Cadres." *The China Quarterly*, no. 29: pp. 36–60.

————. 1967b. "Voluntarism and Social Control." In D. W. Treadgold (ed.), *Soviet and Chinese Communism. Similarities and Differences*, pp. 168–184. Seattle: University of Washington Press.

————. 1969. *Canton under Communism. Programs and Politics in a Provincial Capital, 1940–1968*. Cambridge, Mass.: Harvard University Press.

————. 2011. *Deng Xiaoping and the Transformation of China*. Cambridge, Mass.: Belknap.

Voslensky, Michael. 1980. *La nomenklatura. Les privilégiés en URSS*. Paris: Belfond.

Wakeman, Frederic, Jr. 2003. *Spymaster. Dai Li and the Chinese Secret Service*. Berkeley: University of California Press.

Walder, Andrew G. 1991. "Cultural Revolution radicalism. Variations on a Stalinist Theme." In Joseph, Wong, and Zweig (eds.), *New Perspectives on the Cultural Revolution*, pp. 41–61.

————. 2015. *China under Mao: A Revolution Derailed*. Cambridge, Mass.: Harvard University Press.

Wang, David Der-wei. 1992. *Fictional Realism in Twentieth-Century China. Mao Dun, Lao She, Shen Congwen*. New York: Columbia University Press.

————. 2000. "Reinventing National History: Communist and Anti-Communist Fiction of the Mid-Twentieth Century." In Chi and Wang (eds.), *Chinese Literature*, pp. 39–64.

————. 2004. *The Monster That Is History. History, Violence, and Fictional Writing in Twentieth-Century China*. Berkeley: University of California Press.

Wang, Fan-hsi (Fanxi). 1980. *Chinese Revolutionary: Memoirs (1919–1949)*. Translated and introduced by Gregor Benton. Oxford: Oxford University Press.

Wang, Feng, Yong Cai, and Baochang Gu. 2013. "Population, Policy, and Politics: How Will History Judge China's One-Child Policy?" *Population and Development Review* 38, suppl. 1: pp. 115–129.

Wang, Xiaojue. 2011. "From Asylum to Museum. The Discourse of Insanity and Schizophrenia in Shen Congwen's 1949 Transition." *Modern Chinese Literature and Culture*, 23, no. 1: pp. 133–168.

Wang, Youqin. 2007. "Trouver une place pour les victimes: la difficile écriture de l'histoire de la Révolution culturelle." *Perspectives chinoises,* no. 4: pp. 67–77.

Wedeman, Andrew. 2012. *Double Paradox: Rapid Growth and Rising Corruption in China.* Ithaca, N.Y.: Cornell University Press.

Wei, Jingsheng. 1997. *Lettres de prison, 1981–1993.* Translated by M. Holzman. Paris: Plon.

Wemheuer, Felix. 2011. "'The Grain Problem Is an Ideological Problem': Discourses of Hunger in the 1957 Socialist Education Campaign." In Manning and Wemheuer (eds.), *Eating Bitterness,* pp. 107–129.

———. 2014. *Famine Politics in Maoist China and the Soviet Union.* New Haven, Conn.: Yale University Press.

Werth, Nicolas. 1984. *La vie quotidienne des paysans russes de la révolution à la collectivisation (1917–1939).* Paris: Hachette Littérature.

———. 1990/2004. *Histoire de l'Union soviétique.* 5th ed. Paris: PUF.

———. 1995/1998. *Histoire de l'Union soviétique de Lénine à Staline, 1917–1953.* Paris: PUF, "Que sais-je?"

———. 1997. "Un État contre son peuple." In Courtois et al. (eds.), *Le livre noir du communisme,* pp. 43–295.

———. 2003. "Le pouvoir soviétique et la paysannerie dans les rapports de la police politique (1930–1934)." *Bulletin de L'IHTP,* nos. 81–82.

———. 2006. *L'île aux cannibales. 1933, une déportation-abandon en Sibérie.* Paris: Perrin.

———. 2007. *La terreur et le désarroi. Staline et son système.* Paris: Perrin.

———. 2009. *L'ivrogne et la marchande de fleurs. Autopsie d'un meurtre de masse, 1937–1938.* Paris: Tallandier.

———. 2010a. "Famines soviétiques, famine ukrainienne." *Le débat,* no. 162: pp. 142–151.

———. 2010b. "Retour sur la violence du stalinisme." *Le débat,* no. 162: pp. 132–141.

———. 2011a. "The Great Ukrainian Famine of 1932–33." In *Online Encyclopedia of Mass Violence,* 26 September. http://www.massviolence.org/The-1932-1933-great-famine-in-ukraine.

———. 2011b. "Dekulakisation as Mass Violence." In *Online Encyclopedia of Mass Violence,* 2 October. www.massviolence.org/Dekulakisation-as-mass-violence-nicolas-werth.

———. 2012. *La route de la Kolyma. Voyage sur les traces du goulag.* Paris: Belin.

Werth, Nicolas, and Alexis Berelowitch. 2011. *L'État soviétique contre les paysans. Rapports secrets de la police politique (Tcheka, GPU, NKVD), 1918–1939.* Paris: Tallandier.

Werth, Nicolas, and Gaël Moullec. 1994. *Rapports secrets soviétiques. La société russe dans les documents confidentiels, 1921–1991.* Paris: Gallimard, "La Suite des temps."

Westad, Odd Arne. 2003. *The Chinese Civil War, 1946–1950. Decisive Encounters.* Stanford, Calif.: Stanford University Press.

Wheatcroft, Stephen G. 1996. "The Scale and Nature of German and Soviet Repression and Mass Killings." *Europe-Asia Studies* 48, no. 8: pp. 1319–1353.

———. 2008. "Famines in Russia and China in Historical Perspective." Report to the Hunger, Nutrition, and Systems of Rationing under State Socialism (1917–2006) seminar, Wien University.

Whyte, Martin King. 1973. "Corrective Labor Camps in China." *Asian Survey*, 13, no. 3: pp. 253–269.

———. 1975. *Small Groups and Political Rituals in China*. Berkeley: University of California Press.

Williams, Philip F., and Yenna Wu. 2004. *The Great Wall of Confinement. The Chinese Prison Camp through Contemporary Fiction and Reportage*. Berkeley: University of California Press.

——— (eds.). 2006. *Remolding and Resistance among Writers of the Chinese prison camp*. London: Routledge.

Wood, Tony. 2012 / 2013. "Russia Vanishes." *London Review of Books*, 34, no. 23: 6 December. Translated by A. Boutang: "Le laboratoire russe." *Books*, no. 49: pp. 32–38.

Wou, King-tseu. 1976. *Chronique indiscrète des mandarins*. Translated by Tchang Fou-jouei. Paris: Gallimard, "Connaissance de l'orient."

Wu, Hongda (Harry). 1992. *Laogai. The Chinese Gulag. Boulder*, Colo.: Westview.

———. 1995. *Vents amers*. Translated by B. Laroche. Paris: Bleu de Chine.

Wu, Jingzi: see Wou, King-tseu.

Wu, Ming-shih (Anonymous), for Bu Naifu, alias Bu Ning (see Pu, Ning). 1985. *The Scourge of the Sea. A True Account of My Experiences in the Hsia-sa Village Concentration Camp*. Taipei: Kuang Lu.

Wu, Yenna. 2006. "Expressing the 'Inexpressible.' Pain and Suffering in Wumingshi's Hongsha (Red Sharks)." In Williams and Wu (eds.), *Remolding and Resistance*, pp. 123–156.

Wylie, Raymond F. 1980. *The Emergence of Maoism. Mao Tse-tung, Ch'en Po-ta and the Search for Chinese Theory, 1935–1945*. Stanford, Calif.: Stanford University Press.

Xian, Yanzhong. 2010. "Recent Mao Zedong Scholarship in China." In Cheek (ed.), *Critical Introduction to Mao*, pp. 273–287.

Xiao-Planès, Xiaohong. 2013a. "Famine et commune populaire: Deng Zihui en 1958–1962." Communication to the study session INALCO-EHESS (Paris: 18 October): "Famines soviétique et chinoise."

———. 2013b. "Les descendants des cadres supérieurs et les premiers gardes rouges pendant la révolution culturelle." Communication to the study session INALCO (Paris: 8 July): "Les formes de politisation dans la Chine des xxe et xxie siècles."

Xin, Yi. 2011. "On the Distribution System of Large-Scale People's Communes." In Manning and Wemheuer (eds.), *Eating Bitterness*, pp. 130–147.

Yan, Lianke. 2010. *Les quatre livres*. Translated by Sylvie Gentil. Paris: Editions Philippe Picquier. 2012; first edition: Sishu. Hong Kong: Mingpao.

Yang, Dali L. 1996. *Calamity and Reform in China. State, Rural Society, and Institutional Change since the Great Leap Famine*. Stanford, Calif.: Stanford University Press.

Yang, Jiang. 1983. *Six récits de l'école des cadres*, I. Landry and Zhi S. (trans.). Paris: Christian Bourgois.

Yang, Jisheng. 2008/2012. *Mubei. Zhongguo liushi niandai dajihuang jishi*. Hong Kong: Tiandi tushu youxian gongsi. French edition: *Stèles. La grande famine en Chine, 1958–1961*. Translated by L. Vincenolles and S. Gentil. Paris: Éd. du Seuil. English Edition: *Tombstone. The Great Chinese Famine, 1958–1962*. Translated by Stacy Mosher and Guo Jian. Edited by Edward Friedman, Guo Jian, and Stacy Mosher. Introduction by Edward Friedman and Rodrick MacFarquhar. New York: Farrar, Straus and Giroux.

Yang, Xianhui. 2010. *Le chant des martyrs dans les camps de la mort de la Chine de Mao*. Translated by P. Barbe-Girault. Paris: Balland.

Yang, Xiaobin. 2000. "Answering the Question: What Is Chinese Postmodernism/Post-Mao-Dengism?" In Chi and Wang (eds.), *Chinese Literature*, pp. 193–215.

Zamiatine, Eugène. 1971. *Nous autres*. Translated by B. Cauvet-Duhamel. Paris: Gallimard.

Zhang, Xianliang. 1986a. *Half of Man Is Woman*. Translated by M. Avery. New York: Ballantine.

———. 1986b. *Mimosa et Xor Bulak, l'histoire d'un routier*. Translated by Pan A. and A. Curien. Beijing: Littérature chinoise, "Panda."

———. 1994. *Grass Soup*. Translated by M. Avery. London: Minerva.

———. 1996. *My Bodhi Tree*. Translated by M. Avery. London: Secker & Warburg.

Zhang, Yihe. 2013. *Madame Liu*. Translated by F. Sastourné. Paris: Hachette Livre, "Ming Books."

Zhang, Yinde. 2003. *Le Monde romanesque chinois au xxe siècle. Modernités et identités*. Paris: Honoré Champion.

Zhou, Xun (ed.). 2012. *The Great Famine in China, 1958–1962. A Documentary History*. New Haven, Conn.: Yale University Press.

Zweig, David. 1989. *Agrarian Radicalism in China, 1968–1981*. Cambridge, Mass.: Harvard University Press.

Index

Politburo (Political Bureau), 45, 56, 58, 86, 114–115, 141, 145, 147, 157, 160, 162, 173, 194, 197, 221–222, 281, 295, 314, 319, 338–339, 356, 380n89, 405n41

Pomeshchik (noble landowner or squire), 77, 94

Preobrazhensky, Yevgeni, 25, 81, 319, 322

primitive accumulation, xi, 30, 83, 109, 119, 131, 343

private plot, 86, 95, 111–113, 115–116, 119, 122, 141, 166

Prokofiev, Sergei, 214–215

Proletariat (small number of workers at an early stage in both countries), xix, 66, 76, 101, 321

Pushkin, Alexander, 9, 10, 213

Q

Qian Zhongshu, 240–242

Qin Shihuangdi, 58, 73, 313, 368n49

Qing dynasty, 5–6, 69

Quotas:
of arrestment, 61, 333–334; of executions, 303, 310–311, 315, 333; of production and procurement, 61–62, 79, 95, 105, 110, 114–115, 119, 131–132, 136, 141, 144–145, 149, 153, 165, 252, 265, 271, 273, 275,347, 392n11, 396n34

R

Red Guards, 12, 169, 179, 303, 327, 329–330, 379n85, 383n28, 387n32, 393n14, 406n55

revisionism (imputed to Khrushchev by Mao), 31, 71, 75, 179, 210, 302

Rickett, Adele and Allyn, 285–286

Ryutin, Martemyan, 52, 313, 332, 364n2

S

Saint Petersburg, 3, 6–8

sanfan (Three Antis Campaign), 186, 366n26

science, 9, 194, 224–228

seredniak (middle peasant), 82–83, 85, 87, 111–112, 119, 131–132, 138, 253, 367n36

Sha Yexin, 184

Shakhty Trial, 173, 227, 253

Shalamov, Varlam, 255, 271, 275, 279, 288, 391n4, 396n34

Shanghai, 3, 6–8, 20, 151, 155, 188, 206, 242, 258–259, 263, 267, 304, 326, 349, 378n74, 384n46, 393n15, 410n4

Shen Congwen, 240–241, 246, 315

Sholokhov, Mikhail, 233–239

Short Course, 54, 63, 69, 70,368n42

Shostakovich, Dmitri, 212, 214, 222, 243

Sichuan, 125–127, 142, 144, 150–151, 158, 303, 373n3, 378n74, n80, 379n84, n86

siliang (death rations, especially during famines). See famine

Simonov, Konstantin, 205, 214–215, 232

Sinyavsky, Andrei, 217, 232, 234

smychka (collaboration, union of workers and peasants), 81–82, 85, 86, 102

socialism in one country, 323

socialist construction, 30, 52, 65, 72, 110, 113, 280, 368n48

socialist education campaign (1957), 113; socialist education movement (1962–1965), 64

socialist realism, xii, 201, 205–206, 219, 221, 237–238, 353

Socialist Revolutionaries, 12–13, 118, 172, 253, 327, 338, 365n16, 366n26

Solovetski, or Solovski, 87, 274, 280

Solzhenitsyn, Alexandr, 207, 209, 213, 217, 228, 232, 234–236, 242, 244, 249, 255, 258, 271, 274, 287–290, 337, 348, 384n51, 387n30, 389n51, 392n10, 398n28

Soviet help (to China), 54, 301

Soviet model, xvii, 32–33, 51, 55, 63, 75, 108, 120, 221, 225, 251, 280, 286–287, 296

stages in politics, 51–53; in cultural policies, 201–204

Stalin, Joseph:
against bureaucracy, 60, 332–333; against formalism in art,

212–214; as a modern Ivan, or
Peter the Great, 30, 50, 324; as
intellectual, 294–296, 402n6; Big
Deal (Dunham), 71, 174; creates
a proletarian intelligentsia, 173;
criticized by Lenin, 339; cruel,
160–162, 258–260, 297, 309, 310–
314, 395n23; Cult, 298; depicted
by Bukharin, 403n21; "Dizzy
with success," 91, 133; efficient,
30, 318; exalts Russian past, 73;
favors economic progress over
equality, 71, 323–324; led astray
by ideology, yet realist, xiii, 60,
318; Mandelstam's poem, 244,
389n54; nationalist, state-builder,
hard-worker, 317–318; Himalayas
(one of two), 405n41; night owl,
294; relationships with Mao,
299–302; Sosso, 293, 402n2; war
on peasants, 83, 86, 114, 132
Standing Committee (of Political
Bureau), 58
steel (production targets), 26, 29, 32–33,
61, 113, 141, 145
Stolypin, Pyotr, 5, 82, 84, 118
Sun Yat-sen, 4, 15–16, 41, 344, 351,
360n11; Sun Yat-sen University, 351
superstructure vs infrastructure, 68, 72, 120

T

Taiwan, xx, 16, 33–34, 165, 242, 243,
372n50, 398n54
Tan Sitong, 14
teleological targets, 26, 107, 402n9
thaw, 45, 172, 184, 203–204, 217, 234,
242, 245, 246, 385n6, 390n64
thought reform (in camps), xii, 279–287
Tibet (Tibetans in *laogai*), 256–257,
394n17
Tolstoy, Aleksey, 205, 210, 232
Tolstoy, Leo, 9–10, 46, 213–214, 244, 246
Totalitarianism, xiv, 57, 59, 63–64, 159,
246, 248, 276, 286, 309, 340, 364n6,
367–368n39

troika(s). *See* Camps
Trotsky, Leon, 1, 13, 25, 31, 45, 54, 57,
67, 70, 72, 80, 177, 186, 295–297,
338, 354–355, 366n26, 402n6, 406n2,
409n34, 409–410n2; Trotskyism, 210,
354, 357; Trotskyite, 62, 253, 262,
280, 319, 325, 334, 353, 365n16
Trudoden, 96
Tsarism (compared toGuomindang),
17–19
tufta (within and outside camps), 273
Tukhachevsky, Mikhail, 205
Tvardovsky, Aleksandr, 211, 242–243
two fronts, 70, 318–320

U

Ukraine famine, 125, 127–128, 130, 132,
134–140, 154, 155–158, 160–164,
373n2, 375n28, n34, 376n35, 377n67,
378n74
urban population, 36–37, 40, 84, 129
urbanization, 36–37, 40, 46, 77, 129–131,
153
Uspensky, Gleb, 118, 372n51

V

Vavilov, Nikolai, 191, 224, 361n2
vožd, 57, 175, 181, 190, 333
Voroshilov, Kliment, 182, 222
Vydvizhentsy, 173
Vyshinsky, Andrey, 311

W

Wang Fanxi, 409–410n2
Wang Guangmei, 158, 305
Wang Meng, 204, 387n23
Wang Ming (Chen Shaoyu), 354
Wang Shiwei, 183, 352–357, 410n4
Wang Shouxin, 187–192
Wei Jingsheng, 279, 395n23
Witte, Sergei, 6, 18, 24–25, 344, 360n5
women:
    detained in camps, 257, 394n20;